HIRATSUKA RAICHŌ AND EARLY JAPANESE FEMINISM

BRILL'S JAPANESE STUDIES LIBRARY

EDITED BY

H. BOLITHO AND K.W. RADTKE

VOLUME 19

HIRATSUKA RAICHŌ
AND EARLY JAPANESE
FEMINISM

BY

HIROKO TOMIDA

BRILL
LEIDEN · BOSTON
2004

This book is printed on acid-free paper.

Library of Congress Cataloging-in-Publication Data

Tomida, Hiroko.
    Hiratsuka Raichō and early Japanese feminism / by Hiroko Tomida.
        p. cm. — (Brill's Japanese studies library ; v. 19)
    Includes bibliographical references and index.
    ISBN 90-04-13298-8
    1. Hiratsuka, Raichō, 1886-1971. 2. Feminists—Japan—Biography.
    3. Feminism—Japan. 4. Women—Japan—Social conditions. I. Title. II. Series.

    HQ1762.5.H57T66 2003
    305.42'092—dc22
    [B]   2003055919

ISSN   0925-6512
ISBN   90 04 13298 8

PRINTED IN THE NETHERLANDS

This book is dedicated to my parents,
Tomida Seiji and Tomida Yōko,
in return for their love, intellectual and cultural support.
My mother did not see its completion due to her premature death.

CONTENTS

PREFACE AND ACKNOWLEDGEMENTS

The project of this book started in 1990, as part of my Ph.D. thesis. The necessary material collecting, reading, translation and related work, during my full-time teaching career, meant that this book has been a long time coming to fulfilment. Japanese women's history is still an under-researched area despite its importance and popularity among university students. At many points I had to justify the significance of my work. Furthermore, while I was conducting this research, I was based in Britain, and had to return to Japan many times to collect material.

I have many acknowledgements. I am particularly grateful to Gordon Daniels for his supervision of my early research and careful comments on successive drafts, and for his advice and continued support. I also wish to express my gratitude to Hiratsuka's daughter, the late Tsukizoe Akemi, for providing me with stimulating interviews on her parents, which considerably extended my original interest in Hiratsuka. I am also grateful to the late Usui Takeshi for providing me with much information about Okumura Hiroshi. I extend my warmest gratitude to the leading women's historian Yoneda Sayoko for her constant encouragement and advice on my research, and for her inspiring discussions with me on Hiratsuka. My debt to her research is obvious in the frequent citation of her works on Hiratsuka. Helen Parker and Keith Snell too have been sources of enthusiasm and stimulating conversation. I have also benefitted from the rigorous comments of Delia Davin and Janet Hunter. My M.Phil. supervisor, W. H. Brock, nurtured my passion for women's history. Many works on British feminism and women's movements by Olive Banks, who also taught me, helped my understanding and led me to compare Japanese women's movements with their western counterparts.

Kurt Radtke encouraged the publication of this book and gave valuable advice. I have gained much from the support of my publisher, Brill, especially from Albert Hoffstädt (the Oriental editor of Brill), Maartje van Bruggen and Patricia Radder. The staff of the Ōtsuki Publishing Company, notably Shutō Kunio, have my gratitude for allowing me to reproduce photographs of Hiratsuka. I extend my thanks to Yukari Hitchcock, Jenny Leech, Nagai Miyuki and Lisa

Knowles for typing assistance, and to the librarians and staff of the Ichikawa Fusae Memorial Centre, the Japan Women's University, Tsuda Juku University, Seijō Gakuen, the Women's Research Centre at Ochanomizu Women's University, the National Diet Library, the National Women's Education Centre, Kanagawa Prefectural Women's Centre and many other libraries and women's centres where I worked. I am also grateful to the students and staff of universities where parts of the book were given as lectures, and especially to the students who attended my Japanese women's modules and modern Japanese history classes at Sheffield and Edinburgh Universities for their lively interest in Hiratsuka and her contemporary feminists.

I would never have completed the work but for the encouragement of my family (Tomida Seiji, Tomida Yuji and Tomida Harumi) and support from my friends in Japan and Britain, including Rosemary Chiba, Maria Collins, Phyllis Collins, Eric Dennis, Sheila Lenten, Morita Yaeko, Gill Pemberton, Irena Powell, Sue Preston, Jennifer Reynolds, Roderick Smith, Yoyoi Smith, Takada Yasuko, Audry Tristram, Ken Tristram, Sonia Walker and Shirley Wild. I am most indebted to my late mother, Tomida Yōko (a graduate from the Japan Women's University), for collecting valuable material on the Japan Women's University and its founder, Naruse Jinzō, and for her strong faith in me and my research. Takada Yasuko has been invaluable in providing research assistance, helping me to locate relevant material on Hiratsuka.

There are many others to whom I am indebted in various ways, and I have space only to list their names and express my gratitude. They have included Terry Burnham, the late Kate Cole, the late Margaret Daniels, Ian Gow, Gill Goddard, Malcolm Goyns, Fiona Harrison, Harukiyo Hasegawa, Ichikawa Misao, Colin Holmes, Ikegami Keiko, Kubo Kimiko, Kinpara Fuyuko, Kobayashi Tomie, the late Stanley Mills, Nakamura Michiko, Nishibori Wakako, Nuita Hanako, Gaye Rowley, Margaret Taylor, the late Gerry Wiseman and the late Yamauchi Akino.

TECHNICAL PREFACE

I have used Japanese words sparingly, and they are italicized. English translations have been given in brackets after the Japanese. Titles of Japanese books, articles, newspapers and magazines have sometimes been given in English, in brackets after the Japanese, to help show their substance; but unless clearly indicated this does not mean that the works themselves have been translated into English. Quotations from Japanese texts are largely my own translations unless otherwise indicated.

Many Japanese historical, literary and political figures appear in this book. In Japanese convention, surnames come before first (or given) names, so in my text and its Japanese references normal Japanese practice has been followed for Japanese names (i.e. Tomida Hiroko). However, in the citations of English language references, the normal English practice (authors' given names followed by surnames) has been followed, even for the names of Japanese authors (i.e. Hiroko Tomida).

Hiratsuka Haru was Hiratsuka Raichō's real maiden name. In 1941 her name was entered in the family register of her lifelong partner Okumura Hiroshi, and she used her married name Okumura Haru only for private correspondence. However, she was widely known by her pen name Hiratsuka Raichō. Raichō is a snow grouse (ptarmigan) which lives in the Japan Alps. It is believed to have existed since the ice age. It lives on alpine plants, but it is a stout and strong-looking bird, whose feathers turn snow-white in winter. Hiratsuka often heard about the bird and saw its chicks when she lived near the Japan Alps three months before she founded the Seitō Society. She became so fond of the bird that she used it as part of her pen name. She first used this pen name in the initial issue of *Seitō* (1911), and she then used it for the rest of her life. All her published writing after 1911 was as Hiratsuka Raichō. In order to avoid confusion I have consistently used Hiratsuka Raichō. Her contemporary feminists and female writers changed their surnames upon marriage, divorce, remarriage, or adoption. Some of them also used pen names. I have constantly used one surname for each woman to avoid confusion. Detailed biographical sketches of twelve of Hiratsuka

Raichō's contemporary feminists have been given in Appendix 1. Short biographical sketches of other feminists, politicians, education-alists and literary figures have been given where necessary in footnotes.

For footnotes, after the initial full reference to a publication sub-sequent references are abbreviated. Place of publication is Tokyo unless otherwise stated.

This book also contains appendices including a chronology of Hiratsuka's life, and her family tree. A bilingual glossary of characters, organisations, magazines and newspapers is included. A bilingual bib-liography is also given. These are intended to assist English language readers.

As far as stylistic conventions are concerned, Japanese words have been romanised in accordance with the Hepburn system. Under this system, a long vowel (such as oo, ee) has been designated by a macron, apart from some cases of well-known place names such as Kyoto, Osaka and Tokyo.

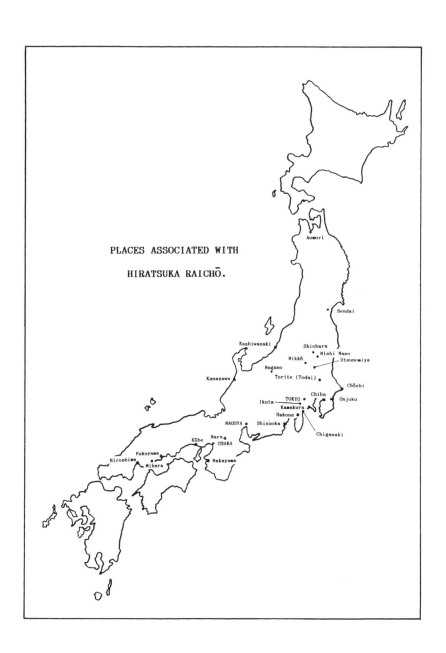

PLACES ASSOCIATED WITH

HIRATSUKA RAICHŌ.

INTRODUCTION

After the end of the Meiji era, particularly during the Taishō period, female organisations were established to support women's education, wider female employment, legal reform affecting marriage, divorce and child custody, women's health, birth control, suffrage and the like. Ichikawa Fusae, Katō Shidzue, Oku Mumeo, Yamakawa Kikue, Hiratsuka Raichō and others devoted themselves to such causes.[1] Like other Japanese feminists, Hiratsuka Raichō applied her convictions to such varied problems. However, she made a unique contribution through her involvement with the Seitōsha (the Seitō Society) and the inauguration of its magazine, *Seitō*, in September 1911.[2] 'Genshi josei wa taiyō de atta' ('In the beginning woman was the sun'), a statement of editorial intent by Hiratsuka in the inaugural issue of *Seitō*, is considered to be the first declaration of 'feminism' in Japan.[3] The Society's objectives were extensive, and *Seitō* later became famous for some of its statements on women's causes.[4]

After the dissolution of the Seitō Society, Hiratsuka continued her involvement with problems of concern to women. In particular she developed her interest in *bosei hogo* (the protection of motherhood). She engaged in the so-called '*bosei hogo ronsō*' (controversy over the protection of motherhood) with Yosano Akiko, Yamada Waka and Yamakawa Kikue.[5] After Hiratsuka visited textile factories in Aichi Prefecture in the summer of 1919, she showed much interest in female factory workers, and wrote articles on them.[6] In autumn 1919 Hiratsuka established the Shin Fujin Kyōkai (the Association of New Women) with Ichikawa Fusae and Oku Mumeo, and she launched

---

[1] See Appendix 1 (Biographical sketches of Hiratsuka Raichō's contemporary feminists and feminist writers).

[2] Hiratsuka Raichō, *Hiratsuka Raichō Jiden: Genshi Josei wa Taiyō de Atta*, 4 vols (1971–3, 1992 edn), vol. 1, pp. 315–76; Hiratsuka Raichō, *Watakushi no Aruita Michi* (1955, 1994 edn), pp. 73–91.

[3] Higuchi Kiyoyuki, *Nippon Joseishi Hakkutsu* (1979), p. 11.

[4] Ide Fumiko, 'Kaisetsu', in Fuji Shuppan (ed.), *Seitō Kaisetsu, Sōmokuji, Sakuin* (1983), p. 13.

[5] Hiratsuka, *Genshi*, vol. 3, pp. 32–47.

[6] *Ibid.*, pp. 57–65; Hiratsuka, *Watakushi*, pp. 170–1.

a magazine called *Josei Dōmei* (the *Women's League*) in October 1920.[7] The immediate goal of the Association was the amendment of Article Five of the Peace Police Law, and the Association contributed to amending that law.[8] After the dissolution of the Association, Hiratsuka withdrew from the forefront of the women's movement.[9] She joined the Musan Fujin Geijutsu Renmei (the Proletarian Women's Arts League) organised by Takamure Itsue in 1930.[10] In the same year Hiratsuka established a consumers' association, *Warera no ie* (Our house) in Seijō, Tokyo, and became its leader.[11] She devoted herself to it until it came to an end in 1938. When Japan declared war against Britain and the United States on 8 December 1941, Hiratsuka, who was opposed to the war and had no intention of cooperating with it, left Tokyo for Todai Village in Ibaraki Prefecture. She spent six years there, engaged in farming and leading a self-sufficient life. After 1945 her main concern was the peace movement, and she founded the Nihon Fujin Dantai Rengōkai (the Federation of Japanese Women's Groups) in April 1953 and became its chairwoman.[12] Although she resigned from that position in 1955, she devoted the rest of her life to the peace movement.[13] She died of cancer on 24 May 1971.[14]

Because of Hiratsuka's contribution to many women's causes before 1945, she is usually considered to be one of the most influential feminists in Japan.[15] One cannot talk about Japanese feminist movements

---

[7] Hiratsuka, *Genshi*, vol. 3, pp. 49–237; Hiratsuka, *Watakushi*, pp. 171–233; Ichikawa Fusae, *Ichikawa Fusae Jiden: Senzen Hen* (1974), pp. 50–101; Oku Mumeo, *Nobi Akaaka to: Oku Mumeo Jiden* (1988), pp. 45–72.

[8] Hiratsuka, *Genshi*, vol. 3, pp. 88–9, 202; Hiratsuka, *Watakushi*, pp. 176, 215; Ichikawa, *Jiden: Senzen Hen*, pp. 52–98; Oku, *Nobi*, pp. 47–72.

[9] Hiratsuka, *Genshi*, vol. 3, p. 262; Hiratsuka, *Watakushi*, p. 234.

[10] Hiratsuka, *Genshi*, vol. 3, pp. 303–10.

[11] *Ibid.*, pp. 289–98.

[12] Hiratsuka, *Genshi*, vol. 4, pp. 130–40; Hiratsuka, *Watakushi*, pp. 244–65; Kushida Fuki, *Sutekini Nagaiki* (1991), pp. 161–9; Kobayashi Tomie, *Hiratsuka Raichō: Hito to Shisō* (1983, 1988 edn); Kushida Fuki, 'Josei Kaihō e no jōnetsu' in Maruoka Hideko et al., *Hiratsuka Raichō to Nihon no Kindai* (1986), pp. 39–41.

[13] Hiratsuka, *Genshi*, vol. 4, pp. 86–288; Hiratsuka, *Watakushi*, pp. 244–65; Kushida, 'Josei Kaihō e no jōnetsu', pp. 39–41; Kobayashi, *Hito to Shisō*, pp. 208–9.

[14] 'Wūman libu no senkusha Hiratsuka Raichō-san shikyo', *Mainichi Shinbun* (24 May, 1971); 'Nihon fujin undō no senkusha Hiratsuka Raichō-san shikyo', *Akahata* (25 May, 1971); 'Hiratsuka Raichō-san shikyo de kakukai no hitobito ga chōmon', *Akahata* (25 May, 1971); 'Libu no tōshi mo kenka, sayonara Raichō-san', *Asahi Shinbun* (31 May, 1971); 'Hiratsuka Raichō-san shikyo', *Asahi Shinbun* (25 May, 1971).

[15] Kobayashi, *Hito to Shisō*, p. 4; Maruoka Hideko, 'Seitō kara Kokusai Fujin Nen e', in Maruoka Hideko et al., *Hiratsuka Raichō to Nihon no Kindai* (1986), pp. 2–25;

between 1910 and 1945 without great attention to her. She was also notorious for her love affairs, and she caused great consternation in society by attempting double-suicide in the so-called Shiobara Incident, and by living with Okumura Hiroshi (an artist younger than herself) without marrying him, and having two illegitimate children. Her views at the beginning of the Taishō period appear radical and new, and in Japan such cohabitation is considered controversial even now. Such feminist activities and personal codes of behaviour contributed to make Hiratsuka the most influential and best-known feminist in Japanese history.[16]

More than thirty years have passed since Hiratsuka Raichō died in 1971, but her fame has grown. Her four-volume autobiography has been widely read not only by academics but by numerous house-wives, students and career women, and it has become one of the best selling autobiographies in Japan.[17] According to its publisher, the thirtieth edition appeared in 1990, and more than 200,000 copies (in four volumes) were sold between 1971 and 1991.[18] Further, in March 1992 a four-volume pocket paperback edition was published due to demand, and this is still selling very well.[19] Even her more expensive eight-volume collected writings sold well, contrary to the publisher's expectations: more than 30,000 copies of the full-volume work were sold between 1983 and 1991.[20] Setouchi Harumi added to Raichō's public fame when she wrote a novel entitled *Seitō*.[21] Even a short biography of Hiratsuka designed for children has been writ-ten by Hino Takako entitled *Josei ga Kagayaku Jidai o Hiraku Hiratsuka Raichō* (*Hiratsuka Raichō, Pioneer of the Time When Women Flourish*).[22]

Ōoka Shōhei, 'Raichō sensei to watashi', in Maruoka *et al.*, *Hiratsuka Raichō to Nihon no Kindai*, pp. 35–6; Kushida, 'Josei Kaihō e no jōnetsu', p. 39.

[16] Ueno Chizuko, 'Jiko chōetsu isshō no kadai ni', *Asahi Shinbun* (5 December, 1997); 'Hiratsuka Raichō botsugo 20-shūnen, josei kaihō no genten kangaenaosu', *Nihon Keizai Shinbun* (24 April, 1991).

[17] Personal interview with Shutō Kumio, 1 April, 1992, Tokyo.

[18] *Ibid.*

[19] *Ibid.*

[20] *Ibid.*

[21] Setouchi Harumi, *Seitō* (1984, 1987 edn). Setouchi Harumi (1922–), one of the most popular and productive modern female novelists, is well-known for her bio-graphical novels of female writers such as Tamura Toshiko, Itō Noe and Okamoto Kanoko. Her *Tamura Toshiko* won the first Tamura Toshiko Prize in 1960. In 1973 she became a Buddhist nun and began to publish under the name of Setouchi Jakuchō. On Setouchi, see Muramatsu Sadataka & Watanabe Sumiko (eds), *Gendai Josei Bungaku Jiten* (1990), pp. 181–3.

[22] Hino Takako, *Josei ga Kagayaku Jidai o Hiraku: Hiratsuka Raichō* (1989).

Hiratsuka has now over-shadowed many of her contemporaries, such as Ichikawa Fusae, Katō Shidzue, Kamichika Ichiko, Yamada Waka, Itō Noe, Yamanouchi Mina, Oku Mumeo and Yamakawa Kikue. 'The Raichō boom', as it has been called, seems to grow annually.[23] Many seminars and public lectures on her have been organised. Some small-scale Hiratsuka study groups were also founded in the 1980s and 1990s by enthusiasts. One of the best-known of these is Raichō o Yomu Kai (the Society for the Reading of Raichō), established in April 1985.[24] Two public lectures hosted by Nihon Fujin Dantai Rengōkai (the Federation of Japanese Women's Groups), in 1986 and 1991, underlined her popularity.[25] The public lecture to commemorate the 100th anniversary of her birth, entitled *Kinen Shinpojiumu* (memorial symposium), in February 1986, had an extraordinarily large attendance, beyond the organisers' expectations.[26] Another lecture, on a much larger scale even than that, was held on 11 May, 1991 to celebrate both the 20th anniversary of Hiratsuka's death and the 80th anniversary of the first publication of *Seitō*.[27] It had more than three thousand in the audience.[28] Again, a very spacious hall, the Chiyoda Kōkaidō (Chiyoda Public Hall) in Tokyo, was absolutely packed with so-called 'Raichō fans'.[29] Takarai Kinō, a leading female story teller, recounted the life of Hiratsuka on stage in July 1991.[30] When a special ceremony to commemorate the 23rd anniversary of Hiratsuka's death was held on 24 May, 1994, about 500 enthusiastic devotees attended it.[31]

Hiratsuka Raichō's monument was erected in Takasago Park in Chigasaki, Kanagawa Prefecture on 23 May, 1998.[32] A public lecture

[23] Personal interview with Yoneda Sayoko, 10 April, 1993, Tokyo.
[24] Yoneda Sayoko, 'Hiratsuka Raichō o Yomu Kai no ayumi', in Hiratsuka Raichō o Yomu Kai (ed.), *Raichō Soshite Watashi, Part 3* (1991), pp. 110–1.
[25] *Ibid.*, p. 110.
[26] *Ibid.*, p. 110.
[27] 'Seitō sōkan 80-nen kinen: 1991 Raichō saihakken', *Mainichi Shinbun* (3 February, 1991); 'Kotoshi wa Raichō botsugo 20-nen: kakukai no josei ga kinen no tsudoi', *Mainichi Shinbun* (27 April, 1991); 'Hiratsuka Raichō botsugo 20-shūnen: josei kaihō no genten o kangaenaosu', *Nihon Keizai Shinbun* (24 April, 1991).
[28] 'Seitō sōkan 80-nen o kinenshite', *Asahi Shinbun* (15 October, 1991).
[29] *Ibid.*
[30] 'Hiratsuka Raichō no shōgai kōza ni', *Asahi Shinbun* (15 July, 1991).
[31] 'Hatsu no Raichō-ki ni 500-nin', *Asahi Shinbun* (25 May, 1994); 'Hatsu no Raichō-ki de Setouchi Jakuchō-san ga kōen', *Asahi Shinbun* (30 May, 1994); 'Sono ikikata minaoshitai: Hiratsuka Raichō-ki, nijū yokka ni kaisai', *Asahi Shinbun* (25 May, 1994).
[32] Kobayashi Tomie, '21-seki e Raichō kara no messēji', *Josei to Undō* (November, 1998), p. 12.

entitled 'Kikoemasuka Raichō kara no messēji' ('Can you hear the message from Raichō?') to commemorate both the 90th anniversary of the first publication of *Seitō* and the 30th anniversary of Hiratsuka's death was held at Hitotsubashi Hall in Tokyo on 19 May, 2001.[33] Hiratsuka Raichō no Eiga o Tsukuru Kai (The Association to Make a Hiratsuka Raichō Film) was formed by Setouchi Jakuchō and others. It organised fund-raising campaigns and collected money from 28,000 people.[34] Using this money, Haneda Sumiko, a well-known female film director, made a documentary film about her entitled 'Genshi josei wa taiyō de atta: Hiratsuka Raichō no shōgai' ('In the beginning woman was the Sun: Hiratsuka Raichō's life').[35] It was shown at the Iwanami Hall in Tokyo between 23 March and 28 June and drew 45,000 people.[36] Many reviews, almost all favourable, appeared in leading newspapers.[37]

The foundation of a Hiratsuka Raichō Kinenkan (a Hiratsuka Raichō Memorial Hall) has also been under serious consideration.[38] On 23 May, 1992 Hiratsuka Raichō o Kinensuru Kai (the Association for the Commemoration of Hiratsuka Raichō) was established by Hiratsuka's children, Kushida Fuki and others.[39] It served as a preparatory committee working towards the foundation of a Hiratsuka Raichō Memorial Hall. There was debate about building it on her son's land in Nagano Prefecture.[40]

Apart from the recently produced film on her, public interest in Hiratsuka owed most to the posthumous publication of her writings. While she was alive, many people had heard her name, but they had little opportunity to discover more about her life, her work and

---

[33] Ichibangase Yasuko, 'Raichō to watashi', *Josei to Undō* (May, 2001), p. 38.

[34] 'Hiratsuka Raichō no eiga, Osaka de kōkai, 31-nichi kara', *Asahi Shinbun* (27 August, 2002), p. 21.

[35] Haneda Sumiko had worked for the Iwanami Film Company between 1950 and 1981. She directed more than 90 films and won many prizes even though female film directors are rare in Japan. She is famous as a documentary film director. In recent years she dealt with the problems of an ageing society and produced a film on senile dementia. For more information about Haneda, see 'Intabyū Haneda Sumiko', *Josei to Undō* (April, 2000), pp. 4–6.

[36] The information was obtained from the Iwanami Hall on 20 September, 2002.

[37] See 'Haneda Sumiko-san eiga Hiratsuka Raichō no shōgai o totta hito', *Asahi Shinbun* (26 March, 2002), p. 2; 'Hiratsuka Raichō no koe: shijin Inoue Yōko-shi', *Nihon Keizai Shinbun* (30 April, 2002, evening edn), p. 13; 'Shinnen ni chūjitsuna jinsei tsuranuku, dokyumentarii eiga Hiratsuka Raichō no shōgai', *Osaka Yomiuri Shinbun* (29 August, 2002, evening edn), p. 9.

[38] 'Hiratsuka Raichō Kinenkan o Tokyo ni', *Mainichi Shinbun* (20 June, 1992).

[39] 'Hiratsuka Raichō o Kinensuru Kai', *Mainichi Shinbun* (9 May, 1992).

[40] Personal interview with Yoneda Sayoko, 23 September, 2002.

writing. There was as yet no published edition of collected writing by her, except for her short autobiography *Watakushi no Aruita Michi* (*The Road I Walked*) published in 1955. Only a very limited number of historians and literary critics, who had shown interest in her work, had access to her writing, which appeared in early women's magazines or literary journals available in well stocked libraries. However, the publication of her four-volume autobiography, *Genshi Josei wa Taiyō de Atta* (*In the Beginning Woman was the Sun*), between 1971 and 1973, the subsequent publication of her eight-volume collected writings between June 1983 and November 1984, and the re-publication of women's magazines such as *Seitō* and *Josei Dōmei*, which Hiratsuka launched and contributed to, in the 1980s made her life and work familiar to many.[41] Her writing is now more widely available.

These publications, and in particular her autobiographies, have had considerable influence upon contemporary Japanese women. Hiratsuka's *Watakushi no Aruita Michi* (*The Road I Walked*) was written by her. However, Kobayashi Tomie (a journalist and an active member of the Fudanren, which was founded by Hiratsuka) helped to collect material for it.[42] This work covered her early life up to her involvement in the peace movement. However, it hardly discussed the Shiobara Incident, or her life between 1922 and 1945. Hiratsuka's four-volume autobiography *Genshi Josei wa Taiyō de Atta* (*In the Beginning Woman was the Sun*) was an extended version of her first autobiography and covered her life from her birth until 1962 without any notable gaps. According to Kobayashi, one-third of her four-volume 'autobiography' was taken from her first autobiography.[43] The rest of it was partially written by Hiratsuka and mainly written by Kobayashi.[44] Kobayashi's section was written on the basis of frequent interviews with Hiratsuka.[45] She transcribed the interviews and assembled information. Kobayashi's writing was then carefully read and corrected

---

[41] Hiratsuka Raichō, *Hiratsuka Raichō Jiden: Genshi Josei wa Taiyō de Atta*, 4 vols (1971–3, 1992 edn), Hiratsuka Raichō (ed. by Hiratsuka Raichō Chosakushū Henshū Iinkai), *Hiratsuka Raichō Chosakushū*, 8 vols (1983–4); Hiratsuka Raichō & Itō Noe (eds), *Seitō*, 52 vols (September 1911 – February 1916, 1983 edn); Shin Fujin Kyōkai (ed.), *Josei Dōmei*, 16 vols (October 1920 – December 1922, 1985 edn).

[42] Kobayashi Tomie, 'Raichō sensei to watashi', in Hiratsuka, *Genshi*, vol. 2, p. 296.

[43] Kobayashi Tomie, 'Genpon atogaki', in Hiratsuka, *Genshi*, vol. 3, p. 333.

[44] Kobayashi Tomie, 'Genpon atogaki', in Hiratsuka, *Genshi*, vol. 4, p. 353.

[45] Kobayashi, 'Raichō sensei to watashi', p. 305.

by Hiratsuka. Some parts, which Hiratsuka was dissatisfied with, were entirely rewritten by Hiratsuka. The first two and a half volumes were closely monitored and proof-read by Hiratsuka and were completed before her death.[46] However, the rest was completed by Kobayashi after Hiratsuka's death.[47] Although Hiratsuka had read parts of the last one and a half volumes, these were heavily dependent on her first autobiography, Kobayashi's interviews with Hiratsuka, and help from Hiratsuka's children.[48]

Her four-volume autobiography and the film on her life appeal particularly to young people. Women today are struck by her fearless behaviour in living with her lover, and giving birth to two illegitimate children. Such conduct is still disapproved of in modern Japanese society. They are also impressed by her challenge to the *ie* system and her way of translating her novel ideas into action.

Despite Hiratsuka's popularity in Japan, she has been less widely known at the international level. Unlike Ichikawa Fusae, Hiratsuka's name hardly ever appears in international women's dictionaries and encyclopaedias. This was partly because unlike Ichikawa Fusae and Katō Shidzue, Hiratsuka never went abroad, and had few close connections with western feminists.[49] Consequently, female socialists and left-wing feminists such as Yamakawa Kikue and Kaneko Fumiko have been much more studied in English by western Japanologists.[50] For example, *Reflections on the Way to the Gallows: Rebel Women in Prewar Japan* gave biographical accounts of a handful of leading socialist women in Japan, and presented excerpts from their writing.[51] Vera Mackie's *Creating Socialist Women in Japan: Gender, Labour and Activism, 1900–1937* is a study in English of the main activities and achievements of leading socialist women, socialist women's organisations such as Sekirankai (the Red Wave Society) and socialist women's

---

[46] *Ibid.*, pp. 302–3.
[47] Kobayashi, 'Genpon atogaki', in Hiratsuka, *Genshi*, vol. 3, pp. 332–3.
[48] Kobayashi, 'Genpon atogaki', in Hiratsuka, *Genshi*, vol. 4, p. 353.
[49] Ichikawa, *Jiden: Senzen*, pp. 104–23; Maruoka, '*Seitō* kara Kokusai Fujin Nen e', pp. 16–7; Shidzue Ishimoto, *Facing Two Ways: The Story of My Life* (1935, Stanford, 1984 edn), pp. 145–202.
[50] Kaneko Fumiko (1903–26) was an associate of the Korean anarchist, Pak Yeol, and was charged with conspiracy to assassinate the Crown Prince in the aftermath of the Great Earthquake. She was sentenced to life imprisonment and hanged herself in prison.
[51] Mikiso Hane (ed. & trans.), *Reflections on the Way to the Gallows: Rebel Women in Prewar Japan* (Berkeley, 1988).

journals.[52] However, research on Japanese feminists generally has been until recently little pursued by English-speaking scholars. Helen Hopper's political biography of Katō Shidzue, *A New Woman of Japan*, Helene Bowen Raddeker's *Treacherous Women of Imperial Japan: Patriarchal Fictions, Patricidal Fantasies* (which provides life stories and writings of two socialist women, Kanno Suga and Kaneko Fumiko), and Akiko Tokuza's *The Rise of the Feminist Movement in Japan* (which is a biography of Oku Mumeo), have been the only major publications on this subject in English.[53] There is no comprehensive book on Hiratsuka Raichō in English. There are also hardly any original book chapters or articles on this topic in English. Dorothy Robins-Mowry's *The Hidden Sun* (which gives a brief outline of the history of Japanese women) briefly refers to Hiratsuka's involvement with the Seitō Society and the Association of New Women.[54] Sharon Sievers' *Flowers in Salt* (a study of the development of feminist consciousness in the Meiji period) examines Hiratsuka's commitment to the Seitō Society and *Seitō*.[55] *Recreating Japanese Women, 1600–1945*, edited by Gail Lee Bernstein, examines how women's roles changed and what women's issues were discussed from the Edo period to 1945, and *Japanese Women Working*, edited by Janet Hunter, gives extensive perspectives on working women in Japan over the last century.[56] These last two books each have a chapter on Hiratsuka's participation in the debate over *bosei hogo ronsō* (the controversy over the protection of motherhood) by Laurel Rasplica Rodd and Barbara Molony.[57] They are virtually the only books on the subject in English. Akiko Tokuza's *The Rise of the Feminist Movement in Japan* and Barbara Molony's article 'Women and the state in modern Japan' are the only published works in

---

[52] Vera Mackie, *Creating Socialist Women in Japan: Gender, Labour and Activism, 1900–1937* (Cambridge, 1997).

[53] Helen M. Hopper, *A New Woman of Japan: A Political Biography of Katō Shidzue* (Boulder, Colorado, 1996); Helene Bowen Raddeker, *Treacherous Women of Imperial Japan: Patriarchal Fictions, Patricidal Fantasies* (London, 1997); Akiko Tokuza, *The Rise of the Feminist Movement in Japan* (1999).

[54] Dorothy Robins-Mowry, *The Hidden Sun: Women of Modern Japan* (Boulder, Colorado, 1983).

[55] Sharon L. Sievers, *Flowers in Salt: The Beginnings of Feminist Consciousness in Modern Japan* (Stanford, 1983), pp. 163–88.

[56] Gail Lee Bernstein (ed.), *Recreating Japanese Women, 1600–1945* (Berkeley, 1991); Janet Hunter (ed.), *Japanese Women Working* (London, 1993).

[57] Laurel Rasplica Rodd, 'Yosano Akiko and the Taishō debate over the "New Woman"', in Bernstein (ed.), *Recreating Japanese Women*, pp. 175–98; Barbara Molony, 'Equality versus difference: the Japanese debate over 'motherhood protection', 1915–50', in Hunter (ed.), *Japanese Women Working*, pp. 122–48.

English on Hiratsuka's involvement in the Shin Fujin Kyōkai (the Association of New Women), although the Association was one of the most significant feminist ventures Hiratsuka was engaged in, and it had a great impact on the development of the women's suffrage movement in Japan.[58] Almost all the other publications on Hiratsuka in English only examine the Seitō Society.[59] Moreover, the writings on Hiratsuka in English are generally derivative and heavily dependent on Japanese secondary sources. Apart from the chapters in Sievers, Tokuza, Bernstein and Hunter's books, they do not examine her original works, as found in her autobiographies, her collected writings, and the two magazines she launched. They contain basic factual mistakes, and errors in people's names and place names. None of them fully outline Hiratsuka's life or her full career as perhaps Japan's leading feminist, for they omit her involvement in a wide range of feminist activities.

There have been few publications mentioning Hiratsuka in English, but more have been published on her in Japanese. This occurred after 1945. It was difficult for women's history to be written between 1930 and 1945, since freedom of learning was not safeguarded legally and the government censored historical writing.[60] One of the first historians to discuss Hiratsuka after 1945 was Inoue Kiyoshi. In his book *Nihon Joseishi*, one of the first 'long views' of women's history which dramatically rewrote Japanese history by emphasising women, he discussed Hiratsuka's activities in the Seitō Society and the Association of New Women.[61] However Inoue, a Marxist historian, rather

---

[58] Barbara Molony, 'Women and the state in modern Japan', in Janet Hunter (ed.), *Japan: State and People in the Twentieth Century* (London, 1999), pp. 23–67; Tokuza, *The Rise of the Feminist Movement in Japan*, pp. 107–91.

[59] Pauline Reich, 'Japan's literary feminists: the Seitō group', *Signs*, 2:1 (Autumn 1976), pp. 280–91; Livia Monnet, '"In the beginning woman was the sun": autobiographies of modern Japanese women writers, 1', *Japan Forum*, 1:1 (1989), pp. 55–81; Nancy Andrew, 'The Seitōsha: an early Japanese women's organisation, 1911–1916', *Harvard University East Asian Research Centre Papers on Japan*, 6 (1972), pp. 45–69.

[60] Even leading academic members of Tokyo and Kyoto Universities, who expressed radical or liberal views in public, were forced to resign from academic posts in the 1930s. Both the Takikawa and Yanaihara Incidents are examples of this. Similarly, Marxist historians were suppressed, and many books with radical or left-wing views were banned. Japanese women's historiography before 1945 is discussed in Hiroko Tomida, 'The evolution of Japanese women's historiography', *Japan Forum*, 8:2 (1996), pp. 189–93.

[61] Inoue Kiyoshi, *Nihon Joseishi* (1948, 1954 edn), pp. 241–3, 255. Inoue Kiyoshi's contributions to the development of women's historiography is discussed in Noriyo Hayakawa, 'The development of women's history in Japan', in Karen Offen *et al.*

curtly described Hiratsuka's organisations as bourgeois, and down-
played their roles.[62] He expressed much more sympathy with women's
socialist societies such as the Sekirankai (the Red Wave Society), and
he evaluated socialist feminists such as Fukuda Hideko and Yamakawa
Kikue more highly than Hiratsuka.[63]

Takamure Itsue was probably the first female historian in Japan
to challenge traditional male-centred history and to undertake serious research on Japanese women's history. She produced some well-
researched and original work including *Bokeisei no Kenkyū* (*Research on
the Matrilineal System*), *Shōseikon no Kenkyū* (*Research on Matrilocal Marriage*),
Josei no Rekishi (*Women's History*), and *Nihon Koninshi* (*The History of Japanese
Marriage*), and was one of the first historians to discuss Hiratsuka
after 1945.[64] In *Josei no Rekishi* Takamure assessed Hiratsuka with special attention to the Seitō Society, the controversy over the protection of motherhood and the Association of New Women.[65]

(eds), *Writing Women's History: International Perspectives* (London, 1991), pp. 171–2;
Koshō Yukiko, 'Kaidai', in Koshō Yukiko (ed.), *Shiryō, Joseishi Ronsō* (1987), pp.
283–4; Ishizuki Shizue, 'Josei undōshi to joseishi', in Rekishi Kagaku Kyōgikai (ed.),
Joseishi Kenkyū Nyūmon (1991), p. 264; Itō Yasuko, 'Saikin no Nihon joseishi kenkyū',
Rekishigaku Kenkyū, 376 (September, 1971), reprinted in Koshō (ed.), *Joseishi Ronsō*,
p. 103; Itō Yasuko, *Joseishi Nyūmon* (1992), p. 29; Murakami Nobuhiko, 'Joseishi
kenkyū no kadai to tenbō', *Shisō*, 549 (March, 1970), reprinted in Koshō (ed.),
Joseishi Ronsō, p. 64; Hiroko Tomida, *Japanese Writing on Women's History* (Nissan
Occasional Paper Series 26, Oxford, 1996), pp. 5–7.

[62] Inoue, *Nihon Joseishi*, pp. 243, 255.

[63] *Ibid.*, pp. 229–31, 256–7.

[64] Takamure Itsue, *Bokeisei no Kenkyū* (1938); Takamure Itsue, *Shōseikon no Kenkyū*
(1953); Takamure Itsue, *Josei no Rekishi*, 2 vols (1954–8, 1972 edn); Takamure Itsue,
Nihon Koninshi (1963). Takamure Itsue (1894–1964) was well-known as a poet, anarchist, feminist and women's historian. She first worked in a cotton spinning factory
and then as a primary school teacher. At twenty-six she went to Tokyo to pursue
a literary career. Her first volume of poetry *Taiyō Tsuki no Ue ni* (*Above the Sun and
the Moon*) was an immediate success, and was followed by another volume of poetry,
Hōrōsha no Shi (*A Wanderer's Poems*). After she established her name as a poet, she
founded the Musan Fujin Geijutsu Renmei (the Proletarian Women's Arts League)
in 1930, and also contributed to its magazine, *Fujin Sensen* (*Women's Front*). From
1931 to her death she devoted herself to pioneering research on Japanese women's
history, especially tracing the development of Japanese marriage patterns. On
Takamure, see Ito, *Joseishi Nyūmon*, p. 27; Ishizuki, 'Josei undōshi to joseishi', pp.
268–9; Kano Masanao, *Fujin, Josei, Onna* (1989), pp. 62–3; Kōno Nobuko, 'Joseishi
no hōhō oboegaki', *Takamure Itsue Zasshi*, 21 & 31 (November, 1973 & April, 1976),
reprinted in Koshō (ed.), *Joseishi Ronsō*, p. 10; Kōno Nobuko, *Takamure Itsue* (1990);
Jeanette Chabot, 'Takamure Itsue: the first historian of Japanese women', *Women's
Studies International Forum*, 8:4 (1985), pp. 287–90; Masanao Kano, 'Takamure Itsue:
pioneer in the study of women's history', *Feminist International*, 2 (1980), pp. 67–9.

[65] Takamure, *Josei no Rekishi*, vol. 2, pp. 268–305.

The Fujin Mondai Kenkyūkai (the Research Society for Women's Issues), which was founded by Mitsui Reiko in 1948 and whose founding members included Mitsui, Nagahara Kazuko, Murata Shizuko and Ide Fumiko, was the first female research team to undertake research on Japanese women's emancipation and suffrage movements after the Meiji Restoration. It produced biographical sketches of leading feminists such as Hiratsuka, Ichikawa Fusae and Oku Mumeo.[66] Ide Fumiko, who was one of the most active members of this study group, became a leading researcher on Hiratsuka, publishing books on her and the Seitō Society.[67] Tatewaki Sadayo, another active member, published *Nihon no Fujin (Japanese Women)*.[68] Although Tatewaki was more interested in the overall history of the women's movement than individual feminists, she discussed Hiratsuka's contributions to the women's movement through her involvement in the Seitō Society and the Association of New Women.[69] The Fujin Mondai Kenkyūkai made a contribution to the development of Japanese women's historiography, helping to educate female researchers such as Ide and Tatewaki, who later became historians of the women's movements.

In the 1960s Murakami Nobuhiko, an amateur women's historian who was critical of existing work on women's history, wrote *Meiji Joseishi (The History of Women in the Meiji Period)*.[70] In it he presented a more critical analysis of Hiratsuka, although his main concern was to present a fuller picture of social life and a general account of the roles of ordinary women in the Meiji period.[71]

In spite of such significant post-war works, publications on Hiratsuka were very limited until the 1980s and 1990s. In these decades the

---

[66] Hayakawa, 'The development of women's history in Japan', p. 172. On the Fujin Mondai Kenkyūkai, see Ishizuki, 'Josei undōshi to joseishi', pp. 264–6; Nishimura Ryōko, 'Joseishi o manabu tameni: joseishi kenkyū no susume', in Rekishi Kagaku Kyōgikai (ed.), *Joseishi Kenkyū Nyūmon*, pp. 12–3; Nagahara Kazuko & Yoneda Sayoko, *Onna no Shōwashi* (1986), p. 160; Tomida, *Japanese Writing on Women's History*, pp. 7–8; Hiroko Tomida, *Women's History in Japan: Its Origins and Development* (Sheffield University East Asia Research Centre Papers, 1996), pp. 11–2.

[67] Ide Fumiko, *Seitō no Onnatachi* (1975); Ide Fumiko, *Hiratsuka Raichō: Kindai to Shinpi* (1987); Ide Fumiko, 'Kaisetsu', in Fuji Shuppan (ed.), *Seitō Kaisetsu, Sōmokuji, Sakuin* (1983), pp. 5–26. Murata Shizuko, another active member, produced a comprehensive biographical study of Fukuda Hideko and her feminist and socialist contributions. See Murata Shizuko, *Fukuda Hideko: Fujin Kaihō Undō no Senkusha* (1959).

[68] Tatewaki Sadayo, *Nihon no Fujin* (1957, 1976 edn).

[69] *Ibid.*, pp. 10–36, 47–56.

[70] Murakami Nobuhiko, *Meiji Joseishi*, 4 vols (1969–72).

[71] *Ibid.*, vol. 4, pp. 392–431.

Japanese government made legal changes sympathetic to women's aspirations.[72] These legislative changes helped to encourage the foundation of women's studies and academic societies, which were significant in promoting further research into women's history.[73] Among women's academic societies, the Joseishi Sōgō Kenkyūkai (the Society for the Comprehensive Study of Women's History) produced significant historical writing.[74] One of its publications, *Nihon Joseishi* (*Women's History in Japan*), provided readers with a much fuller picture of women from different class backgrounds, from elite women including Hiratsuka Raichō to female miners, prostitutes, female textile workers and female social outcasts. Yoneda Sayoko's article 'Bosei shugi no rekishiteki igi' ('Historical significance of the principles of motherhood'), which appeared in *Nihon Joseishi*, examines Hiratsuka's participation in the consumer movement and Takamure Itsue's *Fujin Sensen* (*Women's Front*).[75] *Bosei o Tou: Rekishiteki Hensen* (*The Investigation of Motherhood: Its Historical Transition*), an outcome from the Joseishi Sōgō Kenkyūkai's thematic research led by Wakita Haruko, provided readers with an interpretation of the significance of motherhood in different periods.

[72] The United Nations launched its U.N. Decade for Women at an international conference held in Mexico in June 1975. It aimed to achieve the abolition of all forms of sexual discrimination at an international level. Japan duly signed the Joshi Sabetsu Teppai Jōyaku (the Convention on the Elimination of All Forms of Discrimination Against Women). Accordingly, it had to amend internal discriminatory laws under very mandatory circumstances in order to ratify this convention, in time for the world conference in Nairobi in 1985. The Japanese government accordingly revised some key areas of legislation affecting women. Yoneda Sayoko, 'Nihon no fujin undō to kokusai rentai', *Fujin Tsūshin* (February, 1976), reprinted in Yoneda Sayoko, *Fujinron Nōto* (1986), pp. 230–2; Yoneda Sayoko, 'Sabetsu teppai jōyaku to watakushitachi no tachiba', *Fujin Tsūshin* (March, 1981), reprinted in Yoneda, *Fujinron Nōto*, pp. 233–40; Kano, *Fujin, Josei, Onna*, pp. 37–9; Kinjō Kiyoko, *Hō Joseigaku no Susume* (1983, 1989 edn), pp. 54–6; Nagahara & Yoneda, *Onna no Shōwashi*, pp. 280–1; Inoue Teruko, *Joseigaku e no Shōtai* (1992), pp. 196–201; Gotō Yasuko & Ōkubo Kazunori, *Josei to Hō* (1990), pp. 151–5.
[73] Inoue, *Joseigaku e no Shōtai*, pp. 10–1; Kano, *Fujin, Josei, Onna*, pp. 64–5.
[74] Ito, *Joseishi Nyūmon*, pp. 53–61. The Joseishi Sōgō Kenkyūkai published *Nihon Joseishi* (*Women's History in Japan*), *Nihon Josei Seikatsushi* (*The History of Women's Lives in Japan*), *Bosei o Tou: Rekishiteki Hensen* (*The Investigation of Motherhood: Its Historical Transition*) and *Nihon Joseishi Kenkyū Bunken Mokuroku* (*Research Material for Japanese Women's History*). Joseishi Sōgō Kenkyūkai (ed.), *Nihon Joseishi*, 5 vols (1982, 1985 edn); Joseishi Sōgō Kenkyūkai (ed.), *Nihon Joseishi Kenkyū Bunken Mokuroku*, 3 vols (1983–94); Joseishi Sōgō Kenkyūkai (ed.), *Nihon Josei Seikatsushi*, 5 vols (1990); Wakita Haruko (ed.), *Bosei o Tou: Rekishiteki Hensen*, 2 vols (1985).
[75] Yoneda Sayoko, 'Bosei shugi no rekishiteki igi: *Fujin Sensen* jidai no Hiratsuka Raichō o chūshin ni', in Joseishi Sōgō Kenkyūkai (ed.), *Nihon Joseishi*, vol. 5 (1982, 1985 edn), pp. 115–48.

It included Hiratsuka and other Seitō members' discussions about motherhood and her contributions to the controversy over the protection of motherhood.[76] Among members of the Joseishi Sōgō Kenkyūkai, Yoneda Sayoko produced many scholarly publications on the Seitō Society and Hiratsuka.[77]

Responding to political and legal changes to upgrade women's status, the publishing industry also began to show more interest in original historical texts, autobiographies, and other documents written by or on women. By the end of the 1980s, most eminent feminists' autobiographies and the collected writings of Hiratsuka Raichō, Yamakawa Kikue and Kishida Toshiko had been published.[78] Many important women's magazines closely related to pre-war feminist movements, including *Seitō* and *Josei Dōmei* (*Women's League*), had been reprinted.[79] Moreover, the publication of the ten-volume *Nihon Fujin Mondai Shiryō Shūsei* (*Compilation of Reference Material on Women's Issues in Japan*), a collection of official documents and periodicals closely related to the women's movement and legal reforms, provided historians with still more primary resources.[80] These, especially many writings by Hiratsuka, became available in the 1970s and 1980s, and gave historians, literary critics and journalists more incentive to

---

[76] Araki Tomiyo, 'Bosei ishiki no mezame: *Seitō* no hitobito', in Wakita (ed.), *Bosei o Tou*, vol. 2, pp. 130–57; Nishikawa Yūko, 'Hitotsu no keifu: Hiratsuka Raichō, Takamure Itsue, Ishimure Michiko', in Wakita (ed.), *Bosei o Tou*, vol. 2, pp. 158–91.

[77] Personal interview with Yoneda Sayoko, 28 April, 1994, Tokyo. Yoneda Sayoko is an emeritus professor of the Yamanashi Prefectural Women's Junior College. Her best known publications are Yoneda Sayoko, *Kindai Nihon Joseishi*, 2 vols (1972, 1990 edn), Yoneda Sayoko (ed.), *Kāsan ni Hana o* (1981); Nagahara Kazuko & Yoneda Sayoko, *Onna no Shōwashi* (1986). Her publications on Hiratsuka are Yoneda Sayoko, 'Hasen no suifu: Hiratsuka Raichō no kindai', in Hiratsuka Raichō o Yomu Kai (ed.), *Raichō Soshite Watashi* (1988), pp. 1–7; Yoneda, 'Bosei shugi no rekishiteki igi', pp. 115–48; Yoneda Sayoko, '*Seitō* to shakai no setten: Raichō to Chōkō o chūshin ni', *Yamanashi Kenritsu Joshi Tanki Daigaku Kiyō*, 24 (March, 1991), pp. 69–82; Yoneda Sayoko, 'Hiratsuka Raichō ni okeru shizen to shakai', *Sōgō Joseishi Kenkyūkai Kaihō*, 4 (August, 1987), pp. 1–26; Yoneda Sayoko, 'Jidai o ikinuku', in Maruoka *et al.*, *Hiratsuka Raichō to Nihon no Kindai*, pp. 60–3; Yoneda Sayoko, '*Seitō* no ryakudatsu', in Hiratsuka Raichō o Yomu Kai (ed.), *Raichō Soshite Watashi, Part 3* (1991), pp. 100–9; Yoneda Sayoko, '*Seitō* o ikita onnatachi kara no messēji', in Hiratsuka Raichō Kenkyūkai (ed.), *Seitō no 50-nin* (1996, 1997 edn), pp. 106–7. Her most recent book is entitled *Hiratsuka Raichō: Kindai Nihon no Demokurashii to Jendā* (*Hiratsuka Raichō: Democracy and Gender in Modern Japan.*)

[78] Ishizuki, 'Josei undōshi to joseishi', pp. 268–71.

[79] *Ibid.*, p. 275; Itō, *Joseishi Nyūmon*, pp. 183–9; Josei no Jōhō o Hirogeru Kai (ed.), *Onnatachi no Benrichō* (1991), p. 175.

[80] Ichikawa Fusae *et al.* (eds), *Nihon Fujin Mondai Shiryō Shūsei*, 10 vols (1976–1981).

research on her. Apart from Ide Fumiko and Yoneda Sayoko, Horiba
Kiyoko and Kobayashi Tomie brought out publications on her.[81]
Hiratsuka's writings allowed enthusiastic amateur historians to study
her. The most representative non-professional Hiratsuka study group,
Raichō o Yomu Kai (the Society for the Reading of Raichō), was
founded by Yoneda Sayoko to meet a demand for serious study of
her thought.[82] Its members' research reports were published in an
occasional magazine called *Raichō Soshite Watashi* (*Raichō and Myself*).[83]

Although there are many more publications in Japanese than in
English, these Japanese publications are not necessarily high in quality.
The Japanese publications are more informative and factually accurate. However, works on Hiratsuka in Japanese by journalists and
amateur historians generally lack analytical and critical approaches.[84]
They accept the picture given by Hiratsuka in her autobiographies
and do not examine it critically.

Publications on Hiratsuka produced by Japanese academics may
be divided into two academic disciplines—literature and history. They
tend to be narrowly circumscribed in a disciplinary sense. For example, academics specialising on Japanese literature tend to focus on
the Seitō Society and its impact upon female literature, and to overlook its social and historical dimensions. On the other hand, academic historians draw much attention to the historical significance of

---

[81] Horiba Kiyoko, *Seitō no Jidai* (1988); Kobayashi Tomie, *Hiratsuka Raichō: Ai to
Hangyaku no Seishun* (1977, 1986 edn); Kobayashi Tomie, *Hiratsuka Raichō: Hito to
Shisō* (1983, 1988 edn); Kobayashi Tomie & Kozai Yoshishige, *Ai to Jiritsu: Shikon,
Raichō, Yuriko o Kataru* (1983), pp. 100–64. Horiba Kiyoko edits the literary magazine *Ishutaru*. Her research on Takamure Itsue is well known. Kobayashi Tomie
worked for the Mainichi Newspaper Company as a reporter. She is a member of
the Nihon Fujin Dantai Rengōkai (Federation of Japanese Women's Groups) and
helped to compile Hiratsuka Raichō's four-volume autobiography.

[82] 'Hiratsuka Raichō o Yomu Kai no tsudoi', *Asahi Shinbun* (3 February, 1989);
Yoneda Sayoko, 'Hiratsuka Raichō o Yomu Kai no ayumi', in Hiratsuka Raichō
o Yomu Kai (ed.), *Raichō Soshite Watashi, Part 3*, pp. 110–1. The membership of the
Raichō o Yomu Kai comprised housewives, working mothers and women's historians. They regularly met, read Hiratsuka Raichō's writing under Yoneda Sayoko's
guidance and considered modern Japanese women in the light of her work. Some
of this activity has led to insights of equal value to any deriving from academics.
Although the Raichō o Yomu Kai was dissolved in March 1995, ten years after its
foundation, a revived Raichō study group *Raichō Kenkyūkai* (Raichō Research Circle)
was established in April 1995.

[83] Hiratsuka Raichō o Yumu Kai (ed.), *Raichō Soshite Watashi*, 3 vols (1987–91).

[84] Yatayama, Kobayashi and Hino's books on Hiratsuka are good examples. See
Yatayama Seiko, *Hi no Onna, Raichō: Hiratsuka Raichō no Shōgai* (1991); Hino Takako,
Josei ga Kagayaku Jidai o Hiraku Hiratsuka Raichō (1989); Kobayashi, *Ai to Hangyaku no
Seishun*; Kobayashi, *Hito to Shisō*.

Hiratsuka's activities, but fail to discuss the cultural or literary aspects which were so important to her. Unlike in western countries, in Japan there is considerable reservation about inter-disciplinary research on women, stemming from a respect for subject divisions and their official embodiments, and a courteous desire not to encroach upon other academic territory. This appears to be a corollary of wider deferential attitudes, social formalism and enclosed notions of professionalism.

Moreover, unlike western academics, Japanese academics make few international comparisons, and concentrate on Hiratsuka with little effort to introduce a cross-cultural perspective. This is mainly because Japanese academics who have done research on Hiratsuka tend to be experts on Japanese history or Japanese literature, and lack the linguistic skill to appreciate western feminists' works produced in English, and to compare them to Hiratsuka's. As a result, many academic publications on Hiratsuka lack depth, subtlety and originality, and without an international perspective none of them is analytically complete, with the possible exception of the work of Yoneda Sayoko. Yoneda developed a particular interest in Hiratsuka, and attempted to provide readers with background historical information, so as to place Hiratsuka into her historical context. Her analysis of Hiratsuka's revolt against the male-dominated family system, and her close observation of the relationship between Hiratsuka and Ikuta Chōkō, are new and welcome developments.[85] However, even her book on Hiratsuka, which is a collection of her previously published short articles, still does not provide a comprehensive contextual picture of Hiratsuka.

There are many other significant subjects missing in both English and Japanese publications on Hiratsuka. Many do not examine her childhood, upbringing, family and education, which were the roots of her radical feminism. Almost all of them also fail to give an account of the Shiobara Incident, which had a great impact on Hiratsuka's later life. Virtually no English work covers Hiratsuka's life after she left the Association of New Women in 1921, and only a limited number of publications in Japanese cover her work after 1945, especially her involvement in the peace movement and her role as chairwoman of Nihon Fujin Dantai Rengōkai (the Federation of Japanese Women's Groups).[86]

---

[85] Yoneda, 'Seitō to shakai no setten', pp. 62–82.
[86] Kobayashi, Ide and Tachi are the only major Raichō researchers who discussed her post-war work. See Kobayashi, *Hito to Shisō*, pp. 187–209; Ide, *Kindai to*

Virtually no work in any language considers Hiratsuka's life-long partner, Okumura Hiroshi, or discusses the role he played in her life. He has always been treated as an inconspicuous man living in her shadow. He was criticised and described by her co-workers as a worthless, pleasure-loving and feeble character, who failed to per-form the duties of a responsible partner to Hiratsuka and her chil-dren, failing to find regular employment and being financially dependent upon Hiratsuka.[87] Many have formed the impression that her relationship with Okumura was far from beneficial, and did noth-ing to assist her feminism. Hardly anybody has challenged such a view, and almost no work evaluates the relationship between Hiratsuka and Okumura, or considers how he may have contributed to her feminist life. This book explores this relationship.

Hiratsuka worked closely with Ichikawa Fusae, Yamada Waka, Oku Mumeo, Itō Noe, Kamichika Ichiko and other feminists when she established the Seitō Society and the Association of New Women.[88] It is obvious, however, that their motivations, objectives and expec-tations were diverse, but no work in any language has adequately compared their respective views. Similarly, most publications do not compare Hiratsuka with her contemporary leading feminists in Japan, notably Yamakawa Kikue and Katō Shidzue, or consider in what ways Hiratsuka was different from them. No work has challenged the view that 'Hiratsuka was the most celebrated, almighty, influential and popular feminist leader Japan has ever produced.'[89] Hiratsuka has been idolised in such language and put on a pedestal in the his-tory of the Japanese feminist movement, both by the public and by almost all Japanese publications. A critical evaluation of this view is long overdue.

On another level, there is no doubt that Hiratsuka was influenced by the ideas and theories of some western feminists such as Ellen Key. However, hardly any work assesses the impact which these

---

Shinpi, pp. 231–71; Tachi Kaoru, 'Hiratsuka Raichō to *Ofudesaki*', *Ochanomizu Joshi Daigaku Josei Bunka Shiryō Kanpō*, 7 (1986), pp. 103–12.

[87] Yamanouchi Mina, *Yamanouchi Mina Jiden: 12–sai no Bōseki Jokō kara no Shōgai* (1975), p. 84; Hiratsuka Raichō, 'Shin Fujin Kyōkai no kaiko', *Fujin Kōron* (March-July 1923), reprinted in Hiratsuka, *Hiratsuka Raichō Chosakushū*, vol. 3, pp. 303–4.

[88] Hiratsuka, *Genshi*, vol. 2, pp. 63–68, 165–75, 223–8; Hiratsuka, *Genshi*, vol. 3, pp. 49–237; Ichikawa, *Jiden: Senzen Hen*, pp. 50–101; Oku, *Nobi*, pp. 45–72.

[89] Personal interview with Kobayashi Tomie, 30 May, 1991, Tokyo.

western feminists had on her and how she absorbed their ideas and adopted them in her Japanese feminist activities.

This book is a study of the life and work of Hiratsuka Raichō in the light of contexts and changes affecting women in Japan, focusing on her pre-war activities with a comparative eye to similar historical changes and movements in western countries, notably Britain and the United States. This study attempts to produce a less heroic, fuller and more contextual analysis of this major Japanese figure.

This book also aims to cover four further areas. First, it examines Hiratsuka's special qualities as a feminist, writer, and a founder, regular contributor and editor of *Seitō* and the *Women's League*. It is necessary to piece together when and how her radicalism and feminism emerged, how much her educational and family background contributed to the formation of her feminism, and what actions she took, even in her early years, to challenge a society largely bound by the *ie* system and by legislation that was highly detrimental to women. In order to appreciate Hiratsuka's courage, the social, political and legal situation of women at that time needs to be understood. Her participation in the Keishū Bungakukai (the Keishū Literary Society) and her attempted double suicide at Shiobara will be investigated. We can observe how her feminist attitudes, which were formed before the Seitō Society, were transformed through the Seitō Society and the Association of New Women. Her writings in *Seitō*, the *Women's League* and other contemporary magazines will be considered. This will lead to assessment of the extent to which her activities upgraded women's status, evaluating them within Japanese women's history. Although she withdrew from the forefront of the women's movement after the dissolution of the Association of New Women, it is instructive to examine the other work in which she engaged.

Although the main focus in this work will be on Hiratsuka, the activities and achievements of contemporary Japanese feminists and women's organisations will also be examined. In particular, comparison will be made between Hiratsuka and other Japanese feminists at the level of personal biography and associated ideas. The views contemporary feminists had of Hiratsuka, and the criticism of her made by socialist women such as Yamakawa Kikue will be outlined.[90]

---

[90] Yamakawa Kikue, 'Hiratsuka Haruko-shi e: Shin Fujin Kyōkai ni kansuru shokan', *Fujin Kōron* (April, 1921), reprinted in Yamakawa Kikue (ed. by Suzuki

I will also analyse how Hiratsuka, who did not share socialist perspectives and advocated distinctly separate feminist views, responded
to such criticism. Her writing will be compared with that of other
feminists. The aim is to form a clearer understanding of Hiratsuka's
qualities as a leading feminist, and to challenge the public perception of her as a feminist icon, in order to locate her accurately within
the history of the Japanese women's movement.

I will try to define the relationship between European and Japanese
women's 'feminist' ideologies and views of women in history, especially at the level of defining vocabularies and terminology. International
comparisons at the level of personal biography and associated ideas
will be made in this book. For example, some socialist women contemporary to Hiratsuka, especially Yamakawa Kikue, were much
influenced by the ideas of western socialists and feminists to whom
they compared themselves.[91] Did such western influence affect Hiratsuka
as well? At this level it is useful to discuss to what extent Hiratsuka
was familiar with western feminists' theories and movements, and
how much she learned from and was influenced by them. Such discussion is needed partly because British and American women's movements had a great impact on women's movements in many other
countries including Japan. In addition, the time between 1910 and
1920, when Hiratsuka founded the Seitō Society and the Association
of New Women, coincided with the period when British and American
suffrage campaigns were at their peak and were receiving the utmost
international publicity, not least in Japan.[92]

In attempting to realize these objectives, different sources will be
used. Hiratsuka's published writings will be closely examined. These
included her first autobiography *Watakushi no Aruita Michi* (*The Road
I Walked*), her four-volume autobiography *Genshi Josei wa Taiyō de
Atta* (*In the Beginning Woman was the Sun*), her eight-volume collected
writings *Hiratsuka Raichō Chosakushū* (*Collected Writings of Hiratsuka Raichō*),
Hiratsuka Raichō Hyōronshū (*The Collected Essays of Hiratsuka Raichō*) and

---

Yūko), *Yamakawa Kikue Josei Kaihō Ronshū*, 3 vols (1984), vol. 2, pp. 1–7; Yamakawa
Kikue, 'Shin Fujin Kyōkai to Sekirankai', *Taiyō* (July, 1921), reprinted in Yamakawa,
Yamakawa Kikue Josei Kaihō Ronshū, vol. 2, pp. 10–17.

[91] Hane, *Reflections on the Way to the Gallows*, p. 162.

[92] Ichikawa, *Jiden: Senzen*, pp. 108, 116–22; Christine Bolt, *The Women's Movements
in the United States and Britain from the 1790s to the 1920s* (Hemel Hempstead, 1993),
pp. 3–4; Barbara Ryan, *Feminism and the Women's Movement* (London, 1992), pp.
28–34.

Seitō Josei Kaihō Ronshū (The Collected Essays on Women's Emancipation from Seitō).[93] *Seitō* and the *Women's League*, which she founded and frequently contributed to, will be assessed. This book has also involved extensive research with other primary sources. These include Yamakawa Kikue's recollections and Morita Sōhei's autobiographical novel *Baien*, which was based on the Shiobara Incident.[94] My sources include other feminists' autobiographies, memoirs and collected works, such as those by Ichikawa Fusae, Oku Mumeo, Yamanouchi Mina, Yamakawa Kikue and Katō Shidzue.[95] Other primary materials will include newspaper articles, to discover more about the public or media views of her activities, and the official record of the proceedings of the Imperial Diet, to judge the accuracy of information provided in the *Women's League*. Publications on the Japan Women's College from which Hiratsuka graduated, and on its founder Naruse Jinzō, will also be examined.

I also use oral history sources. Having much interest in the development of oral history in Britain, I believed that using this method would illuminate Hiratsuka's life and work in a number of ways. In order to assess her life and career accurately, I interviewed Hiratsuka's daughter Akemi on a number of occasions. I also interviewed her old acquaintances such as Professor Usui Takeshi, who was taught painting and drama by her husband Okumura Hiroshi when Usui was a student at Seijō High School. He was also a frequent visitor at Hiratsuka's house in his youth, and kept in close contact with Hiratsuka's family.[96] I also interviewed Yoneda Sayoko, Kobayashi Tomie, and Shutō Kunio of the Ōtsuki Publishing Company, which published Hiratsuka's autobiography and collected writings.[97] Shutō

---

[93] Horiba Kiyoko (ed.), *Seitō Josei Kaihō Ronshū* (1991); Hiratsuka Raichō (ed. by Kobayashi Tomie & Yoneda Sayoko), *Hiratsuka Raichō Hyōronshū* (1987, 1991 edn).

[94] Yamakawa Kikue, *Onna Nidai no Ki* (1972, 1987 edn), pp. 127–31; Yamakawa Kikue, *20-seiki o Ayumu: Aru Onna no Ashiato* (1978); Morita Sōhei, *Baien* (1909), in Chikuma Shobo (ed.), *Gendai Nihon Bungaku Taikei*, vol. 29 (1971).

[95] For example, Ichikawa, *Jiden: Senzen*; Oku, *Nobi*; Yamanouchi, *Jiden*; Yamakawa, *Onna Nidai no Ki*; Ishimoto, *Facing Two Ways*.

[96] Personal interview with Usui Takeshi, 15 April, 1992, Tokyo. Usui Takeshi was an emeritus professor of Seijō University.

[97] Yoneda Sayoko was most helpful, discussed her research and publications on Hiratsuka, and provided me with valuable information. Kobayashi Tomie, who was initially a journalist with the Mainichi Newspaper Company, who helped Hiratsuka to complete her four-volume autobiography and to edit her collected writings, and who also wrote several biographies of her, was reluctant to discuss her work on Hiratsuka with me.

was in charge of these publications and had close contacts with Hiratsuka and her family.[98] I also interviewed women who graduated from the Japan Women's College in the Taishō and Shōwa periods, to investigate its educational policy and their student lives there. I met with Ichikawa Misao (Ichikawa Fusae's adopted daughter), and Nuita Hanako (chairwoman of the Ichikawa Memorial Hall) to obtain information about Ichikawa, her private life, her attitude towards her feminist and political activities, and her relationship with Hiratsuka.

It is virtually impossible to obtain unpublished material on Hiratsuka before 1945.[99] According to Kobayashi Tomie, who assisted in completing Hiratsuka's four-volume autobiography, Hiratsuka hardly made any effort to keep personal records such as correspondence.[100] She left very few diaries or memoranda. She did not even keep copies of books she had written. Kobayashi was convinced that Hiratsuka's indifference to her own personal records was because she looked ahead rather than backwards.[101] Moreover, hardly any letters written by Hiratsuka before 1945 can be traced.[102] The great majority of them were lost or burned during the Great Kantō Earthquake and the American bombing of Japan during World War II. Most of her published letters were personal ones to her relatives and friends, which were largely irrelevant to her feminist activities.[103] Very little unpublished material on the Seitō Society has survived.[104] Hiratsuka gave everything relating to the Seitō Society to Itō Noe when she handed over *Seitō*.[105] Itō was later assassinated, with her lover Ōsugi Sakae, and her belongings went missing.[106] Through my interviews with Tsukizoe Akemi and Yoneda Sayoko I discovered that some

---

[98] Personal interview with Shutō Kunio, 1 April, 1992, Tokyo.

[99] Personal interview with Yoneda Sayoko, 23 December, 1993, Tokyo.

[100] Kobayashi, 'Raichō sensei to watashi', p. 296.

[101] *Ibid.*, p. 296.

[102] Kobayashi Tomie, 'Shokanshū chūkai', in Hiratsuka, *Hiratsuka Raichō Chosakushū*, vol. 8, p. 158.

[103] Hiratsuka's surviving letters, the great majority of which were written after 1945, were published by the Ōtsuki Publishing Company. See Hiratsuka, *Hiratsuka Raichō Chosakushū*, vol. 8, pp. 9–157.

[104] The only unpublished material left on the Seitō Society is a daily record for some days of the Seitō Society (*Seitōsha Jimu Nisshi*).

[105] Hiratsuka, *Genshi*, vol. 2, p. 227.

[106] Personal interview with Yoneda Sayoko, 15 April, 1995, Tokyo.

unpublished sources on Hiratsuka after 1945 exist.[107] However, they belong either to the headquarters of the Nihon Fujin Dantai Rengōkai (the Federation of Japanese Women's Groups), of which Hiratsuka was the chairwoman, or to Kobayashi Tomie.[108] Kobayashi used these in her work on Hiratsuka. Over the past fifteen years she has established herself as an authority on Hiratsuka and gained much publicity in this role. Kobayashi was also an active member of the Federation of Japanese Women's Groups, and gained privileged access to some unpublished post-war sources on Hiratsuka kept in the Federation's headquarters. As a result, access to these materials by other researchers has been restricted. Given such difficulties, conducting original research on Hiratsuka has been particularly hard even for Japanese researchers. That said, large numbers of her articles and publications have been reprinted or are still readily accessible, and there are also all the books, articles and writings by others who knew her, and by members of the Raichō o Yomu Kai (The Society for the Reading of Raichō). My own work therefore makes full use of such publications, as well as information I have gathered by interviews, and other primary material which is available.

---

[107] Personal interview with Yoneda Sayoko, 10 April, 1993, Tokyo; personal interview with Tsukizoe Akemi, 7 April, 1992, Tokyo.

[108] Personal interview with Yoneda Sayoko, 10 April, 1993, Tokyo; personal interview with Tsukizoe Akemi, 7 April, 1992. According to Hiratsuka's daughter, Akemi, Kobayashi now possesses most of Hiratsuka's post-war private correspondence, documents, books and other private items. Because Hiratsuka's daughter and her son, who initially inherited them by her will, thought that Kobayashi (who was still completing Hiratsuka's four-volume autobiography at that time) would make best use of them, they gave most of the material to her.

CHAPTER ONE

WOMEN'S STATUS IN THE EDO AND MEIJI PERIODS

Introduction

The main objective of this book is an assessment of the life and work of Hiratsuka Raichō, a leading feminist, who greatly contributed to raise women's status. However, one cannot evaluate her challenge to society without discussing women's status, especially in the Meiji period. What rights were women at that time deprived of? What laws existed detrimental to women? One also needs to go back to the Edo period. Many customs, conventions and aspects of the family system dated from that period, when women's social status was at a low ebb. Even after the Meiji Restoration many 'feudal' ideas remained to keep women's status low. Moreover, one needs to discuss women's campaigns and movements that predated Hiratsuka's activities, to gain a better estimate of her achievements.

Women in the Edo Period

In the periods of warrior rule, from as early as 1192 or before, the value of people was dependent upon military structures.[1] Accordingly, the social status of women fell, or at least remained very low. In the 14th century virilocal marriage and patrilineal systems were reinforced.[2] Freedom of marriage was very restricted. Women had minimal inheritance rights. Women were considered as child-rearing means, to produce male heirs.[3] Many women were forced to marry for political reasons, and even in the Edo period women's status probably continued to fall.[4]

---

[1] Miyagi Eishō *et al.* (eds), *Shinkō Nihon Joseishi* (1974), p. 128.
[2] Hayashi Reiko *et al.* (eds), *Nihon Joseishi* (1987).
[3] Miyagi *et al.* (eds), *Shinkō Nihon Joseishi*, p. 129.
[4] *Ibid.*, pp. 134–7; Hayashi *et al.* (eds), *Nihon Joseishi*, pp. 105–7, 114.

The Edo period has been described as 'the worst time in the history of Japanese women'.[5] There were two main factors which degraded women's status. The first was the strict hierarchical class system, termed the *shi-nō-kō-shō* system, in which all people in Japan were divided into four classes: warriors, farmers, artisans and merchant traders.[6] This was introduced by Tokugawa Ieyasu, the first shōgun of the Tokugawa regime to reinforce his authority. High-class warriors, who occupied the top rank, became rulers and exercised great power.[7] A large gulf developed between those from the warrior class and people from other classes.[8] Each class was assigned different duties and people could not change social status. Marriage across class boundaries was restricted (most notably between warriors and the rest). This system of strict differentiation affected not only men but also women.

Tokugawa Ieyasu employed the Confucian scholar Hayashi Razan as his main advisor, and officially adopted a modified form of Confucianism as the basis of the *shi-nō-kō-shō* system, as well as to construct a stable central government.[9] Confucian teaching, which valued the paternalistic relationship between master and servant, and emphasised the latter's unquestioning loyalty and obedience to the former, perfectly suited the Tokugawa regime. As Confucianism also imposed the teaching of *danson johi* (predominance of men over women), women had to carry their gendered burden from an early age. Boys and girls were brought up together until seven years of age, but they had to lead entirely separate lives thereafter.[10] This

---

[5] Higuchi Kiyoyuki, *Nippon Joseishi Hakkutsu* (1979), p. 208.

[6] Fukuchi Shigetaka, *Kindai Nihon Joseishi* (1977), p. 10; Eiko Ikegami, *The Taming of the Samurai: Honorific Individualism and the Making of Modern Japan* (Cambridge, Mass., 1995), pp. 164–6; Conrad Totman, *Japan before Perry: A Short History* (Berkeley, 1981), pp. 151–2.

[7] Miyagi *et al.* (eds), *Shinkō Nihon Joseishi*, pp. 140–2. Warriors accounted for about ten per cent of the population.

[8] Sōgō Joseishi Kenkyūkai (ed.), *Nihon Josei no Rekishi: Sei, Ai, Kazoku* (1992), pp. 129–31.

[9] Morosawa Yōko, *Onna no Rekishi* (1970), vol. 1, p. 214; Robert J. Smith, 'The Japanese (Confucian) family: the tradition from the bottom up', in Tu Wei-Ming (ed.), *Confucian Traditions in East Asian Modernity: Moral Education and Economic Culture in Japan and the Four Mini-Dragons* (Cambridge, Mass., 1996), pp. 157–9; Peter Nosco, 'Introduction: Neo-Confucianism and Tokugawa discourse', in Peter Nosco (ed.), *Confucianism and Tokugawa Culture* (1984, Princeton, 1989 edn), pp. 11–2; Herman Ooms, 'Neo-Confucianism and the formation of early Tokugawa ideology: contours of a problem', in Nosco (ed.), *Confucianism and Tokugawa Culture*, pp. 29–47.

[10] Miyagi *et al.* (eds), *Shinkō Nihon Joseishi*, p. 144.

was portrayed in the saying, *Danjo nana-sai ni shite seki o onajū sezu* (when a boy and a girl become seven years old, they must not sit together).[11] Boys began to enjoy certain privileges from that age, while girls faced discrimination, and had to lead more confined lives. Women were also expected to abide by Confucian ideas, including the teaching of 'three obediences' (*sanjū no oshie*): before their marriage, women obey their fathers; when they are married, they obey their husbands; when they are widowed, they obey their eldest sons.[12] The teaching of these three obediences imposed tight restrictions upon women's lives, not only as an everyday ideology, but also as an ideal model. Many *jokunsho* (books on women's lessons, books of prohibitions for women), which expounded how women could become obedient and how they should be subservient to husbands and parents-in-law, appeared in the Edo period.[13] These books clearly delineated contemporary male expectations of women.

Among them, *Onna Daigaku* (1716) (*The Greater Learning for Women*) was most influential in defining the roles of women according to Confucian teaching.[14] It provided readers with an absolute set of rules for female conduct and training. According to it, all women were expected to marry and abide by Confucian rules.[15] The author advocated the following relationship of husband and wife:

> A woman has no particular lord. She must look to her husband as her lord, and must serve him with all worship and reverence, not despising or thinking lightly of him. The great lifelong duty of a woman is obedience. In her dealings with her husband, both the expression of her countenance and style of her address should be courteous, humble and conciliatory, never peevish and intractable, never rude and

[11] Fukuchi, *Kindai Nihon Joseishi*, p. 11.

[12] Itoya Toshio, *Meiji Ishin to Josei no Yoake* (1976), pp. 16–7; Miyagi *et al.* (eds), *Shinkō Nihon Joseishi*, p. 148; Kaibara Ekken, *Wazoku Dōshi Kun* (1710), in Matsuda Michio (ed.), *Kaibara Ekken* (1969), pp. 233–4; R. P. Dore, *Education in Tokugawa Japan* (1965, London, 1992 edn), p. 65; Matsuda Michio, 'Kaibara Ekken no jugaku', in Matsuda Michio (ed.), *Kaibara Ekken*, pp. 7–54.

[13] Fukuchi, *Kindai Nihon Joseishi*, p. 11; Morosawa, *Onna no Rekishi*, vol. 1, pp. 215–7; Sōgō Joseishi Kenkyūkai (ed.), *Bunka to Shisō*, pp. 118–9; Jennifer Robertson, 'The Shingaku woman: straight from the heart', in Bernstein (ed.), *Recreating Japanese Women*, pp. 91–3.

[14] Although the authorship of *Onna Daigaku* is usually believed to be Kaibara Ekken, some Japanese historians think that his wife Tōken was its author. Shingorō Takaishi, *Women and Wisdom of Japan* (London, 1905), pp. 11–29; Robertson, 'The Shingaku woman', p. 91. A detailed account of *Onna Daigaku* is given in L. I. Okazaki-Ward, 'Women and their education in the Tokugawa period of Japan' (unpublished M.Phil. thesis, University of Sheffield, 1993), pp. 76–85.

[15] Itoya, *Meiji Ishin*, p. 17.

arrogant—that should be a woman's first and chief care. When the husband issues his instructions the wife must never disobey. If in doubt she should inquire of her husband, and obediently follow his commands. If ever her husband should question her, she should answer to the point—to answer in a careless fashion is a mark of rudeness. Should her husband be roused at any time to anger, she must obey him with fear and trembling, and not set herself up against him in anger and forwardness. A woman should look on her husband as if he were Heaven itself, and never be weary of thinking how she may yield to him and thus escape celestial castigation.[16]

This teaching advocated wives' absolute submission. The author also stated that women suffered from five weaknesses: disobedience, anger, slanderousness, jealousy, and lack of intelligence.[17] As a result women, thought to have so many faults, had to obey without question their fathers or husbands or eldest sons, who must dominate them. Moreover, its author reiterated the seven reasons for divorce, which were disobedience, sterility, lewdness, jealousy, leprosy, talking too much and stealing.[18] These were called *shichikyo* (seven reasons for leaving). *Onna Daigaku* was considered to be the Bible of Japanese women's moral training, and in particular it was valued by warriors.[19] As it was widely used at *terakoya* (temple schools) and at home, this teaching gradually infiltrated into even merchant and peasant classes as well.[20] Its spread was helped by the growth of literacy in society. Consequently, women from all classes came to be restricted by such teaching, which became strongly entrenched in people's minds, and it died hard even after the Meiji Restoration.[21]

Another major reason for some downgrading of female status during the Edo period was the *ie* (family) system, which was reinforced over this time.[22] Under this system the head of a family had absolute authority over his blood relatives and their spouses and exercised numerous other rights.[23] His family members formed links in the

---

[16] Quotation taken from Takaishi, *Women and Wisdom of Japan*, pp. 38–9.
[17] *Ibid.*, pp. 38–46.
[18] *Ibid.*, pp. 35–8.
[19] Morosawa, *Onna no Rekishi*, vol. 1, pp. 214–8.
[20] Sōgō Joseishi Kenkyūkai (ed.), *Nihon Josei no Rekishi, Bunka to Shisō* (1993), pp. 128–30.
[21] Itoya, *Meiji Ishin*, p. 19; Kasahara Kazuo, 'Nyonin shoki', in Tokyo Daigaku (ed.), *Tokyo Daigaku Kōkai Kōza: Otoko to Onna*, vol. 18 (1974), p. 65.
[22] Miyagi *et al.* (eds), *Shinkō Nihon Joseishi*, pp. 144–5.
[23] An account of the *ie* system is given in Takamure Itsue, *Josei no Rekishi*, vol. 1

chain of a vertically-structured family system. The prosperity of a family and its continuity were of the highest priority under the *ie* system, and so individual family members' freedom and personalities were prone to be disregarded.[24] Individual desires and feelings were considered harmful within this system, because they weakened family bonding and supposedly lessened the appropriate sentiments of family life. The rest of the family were forced to obey its head, and family rules and his dictum dominated, even if some family members were financially independent.[25] All family members had to obtain his consent to change their abode, to marry, to divorce and to adopt. If any of these occurred against his will or without his agreement, he had the power to punish those responsible.[26] No family members could challenge his power. During the Edo period a woman was not entitled to become a family head.[27] The main function of the *ie* was to preserve the family from generation to generation. The headship almost invariably passed to a male, usually the eldest son, because women were considered incapable of conducting ancestral rites or playing a public role in society.[28] If there were only daughters, a male heir who could succeed as head had to be found. Since a male successor did not have to be a real son, the head of a family with no children or no sons could either adopt a son or adopt the eldest daughter's husband as his son. These adoptions were very common in the Edo period.[29] The family head was responsible for arranging marriages for his daughters. Marriage was usually arranged in the warrior class, and the social standing of families was an important consideration in this.[30]

The *ie* system was a key pillar of Tokugawa society, initially only practised among the warrior class, but it gradually spread to other

---

(1972), pp. 380–1; Kathleen S. Uno, 'Women and changes in the household division of labor', in Bernstein (ed.), *Recreating Japanese Women*, pp. 23–6.

[24] Miyagi *et al.* (eds), *Shinkō Nihon Joseishi*, pp. 145–7; Fukuo Takeichirō, *Nihon Kazoku Seidoshi Gaisetsu* (1972), p. 151.

[25] *Ibid.*, pp. 158–9.

[26] Inoue Kiyoshi, *Nihon Joseishi* (1948, 1954 edn), p. 116.

[27] Fukuo, *Nihon Kazoku Seidoshi*, p. 188.

[28] Inoue, *Nihon Joseishi*, pp. 115–6; Fukuo, *Nihon Kazoku Seidoshi*, pp. 158–62.

[29] *Ibid.*, pp. 169–76. Both an adopted son (*yōshi*) and an adopted son-in-law (*muko yōshi*) had exactly the same rights as a real son in terms of succession and inheritance. Another important rule of the *ie* system was that if the head of a family had more than two sons, only one of them (almost always the eldest) could succeed.

[30] Itoya, *Meiji Ishin*, p. 12; Fukuchi, *Kindai Nihon Joseishi*, p. 14.

classes.[31] Under it women had very few legal, economic, political
and marital rights. Women from the warrior class were most heavily
affected. Married women's social freedom within marriage was almost
non-existent. Although *Shūmon Aratamechō* (Religious Inquiry Census),
which served as a family register in the Edo period, gave lists of
names and ages of almost all family members, in many cases the
names and ages of wives were omitted, and their status in families
was simply stated as 'wives' because wives were not then considered
to be independent individuals.[32] Married women were unable to
inherit or own property.[33] Producing male heirs was a vital task especially for wives from the warrior class. This was because the *chigyō
seido* (the annual stipend system), by which lords provided retainers
with feudal tenure of land in their domains, operated in the warrior class.[34] This system was hereditary and only a son had the right
to inherit land. Absence of a male heir led to the extinction of the
family line, and the confiscation of family land. Therefore the chief
purpose of marriage for the warrior class was the continuation of a
family, and a wife's main role was to bear a boy.[35] An infertile wife
was despised and called *umazume* (barren woman), in many cases
being divorced by her husband.[36] In some cases, marriage was not
registered until the birth of a son; this was termed '*ashiirekon*' (ten-
tative marriage) and was commonly practised.[37] The head of a family
was also legally allowed to have a mistress. There were many cases
in which his legal wife and his mistress lived under the same roof.
This dual system of wife and mistress was particularly useful for the
head of a family whose legal wife failed to produce a male heir, but
whose mistress was successful in this, as it maintained his lineage
and family name.[38]

[31] Miyagi *et al.* (eds), *Shinkō Nihon Joseishi*, pp. 144–6.
[32] *Ibid.*, p. 147.
[33] Inoue, *Nihon Joseishi*, p. 117.
[34] Itoya, *Meiji Ishin*, p. 8; Fukuchi, *Kindai Nihon Joseishi*, p. 12; Inoue, *Nihon Joseishi*, p. 116; Ikegami, *The Taming of the Samurai*, pp. 160–1. The size of a vassal's land was decided mainly according to his social standing and meritorious deeds.
[35] Fukuchi, *Kindai Nihon Joseishi*, p. 12; Inoue, *Nihon Joseishi*, p. 117; Itoya, *Meiji Ishin*, p. 8.
[36] Kittredge Cherry, *Womansword: What Japanese Words Say about Women* (1987, New York, 1991 edn), pp. 90–2.
[37] Inoue, *Nihon Joseishi*, p. 117.
[38] Fukuchi, *Kindai Nihon Joseishi*, p. 15; Inoue, *Nihon Joseishi*, pp. 117–8.

As far as divorce was concerned, in the Edo period only husbands could decide upon it, and wives had no rights to divorce husbands.[39] A popular saying in the Edo period, 'Nyōbo to tatami wa atarashikereba atarashii hodo yoi' (the newer both wives and tatami mats are, the better they are), suggested how easy divorce was for husbands.[40] Husbands were free to change their wives as many times as they liked, much as they renewed tatami mats. Moreover, an expression such as *hima o dasu* (which has two implications, to dismiss one's employee and to divorce one's wife) was widely used by husbands to discard their wives.[41] The phrase highlighted husbands' privilege and wives' low status: like that of their husbands' employees. Husbands from the warrior class simply submitted their reason for divorce to the shōgunate and the head of their fiefs, and obtained their approval.[42] Among people from the other classes, a very short note called a *mikudarihan* (three-and-a-half lines), which normally included the reason for divorce, had to be sent to wives or their guardians, to obtain that divorce.[43] On the other side, even battered or abused wives had no grounds for divorce, and the only way for such wives to escape from an unbearable marriage was to take refuge in one of the Buddhist convents, known as *enkiri dera* (temples which cut the ties between husbands and wives) or *kakekomi dera* (refuge temples).[44] *Mantokuji* (Mantoku Temple in Ueno, Yamanashi Prefecture) and *Tōkeiji* (Tōkei Temple in Kamakura) were the best known divorce temples. These two nunneries sometimes granted run-away women who had stayed there for more than two years rights of divorce, being able to do this because these nunneries had close links with

[39] Fukuchi, *Kindai Nihon Joseishi*, p. 15.
[40] Miyagi *et al.* (eds). *Shinkō Nihon Joseishi*, p. 3.
[41] Fukuchi, *Kindai Nihon Joseishi*, p. 16.
[42] Sōgō Joseishi Kenkyūkai (ed.), *Nihon Josei no Rekishi: Sei, Ai, Kazoku* (1992), pp. 133–4.
[43] Fukuo, *Nihon Kazoku Seidoshi*, pp. 184–6; Takagi Tadashi, *Mikudari Han to Enkiri Dera* (1992), pp. 43–110; Takagi Tadashi, *Mikudari Han: Edo no Rikon no Joseitachi* (1987), pp. 178–204; Morishita Misako, *Edo no Hanayome* (1992), pp. 124–30.
[44] Fukuo, *Nihon Kazoku Seidoshi*, pp. 186–7; Takagi, *Mikudari Han to Enkiri Dera*, pp. 111–86; Hozumi Shigetō, *Rienjō to Enkiri Dera* (1942); Charles J. Dunn, *Everyday Life in Traditional Japan* (1969, London, 1989 edn), p. 174; Anne Walthall, 'The life cycle of farm women in Tokugawa Japan', in Bernstein (ed.), *Recreating Japanese Women*, pp. 60–1. On enkiri dera, see also Inoue Zenjō, *Kakekomi Dera, Tōkeiji-shi* (1980); Igarashi Tomio, *Enkiri Dera* (1972); Ishii Ryōsuke, *Edo no Rikon: Mikudari Han to Enkiri Dera* (1965).

the Tokugawa Shōgunate.[45] In many cases wives were one-sidedly divorced without any convincing reason. Divorced women were forced to leave the family residence without any maintenance or 'consolation' money.[46] Wives had no child custody, and were strongly discouraged from remarrying. According to the criminal law *Kujigata Osadamegaki Hyakkajō* (1742) enacted by the 8th shōgun, Tokugawa Yoshimune, adultery committed by wives was punishable by death, while husbands could keep concubines.[47] Husbands were not punished if they killed wives who committed adultery and/or their partners.

Marriage, divorce, remarriage and child custody were far less regulated among the more numerous peasant class, which was least affected by the *ie* system.[48] In many cases marriage for them was not registered in the first place. Both peasant men and women initiated divorce.[49] Peasant women could simply leave their husbands' home as a means of divorce. Remarriage had less of a stigma attached to it than in samurai society. Some peasant women even remarried three or four times.[50] Child custody was also less influenced by samurai norms, and peasant women often took their children with them when they left their husbands.

Confucian teaching favoured separate and limited education for women, which led to ruling prejudices against such education. A popular saying in the Edo period—'Onna wa sainaki o motte tokuto suru' (women without ability are virtuous)—highlighted this.[51] Matsudaira Sadanobu, the Shōgun's Chancellor from 1786 to 1793, disapproved of raising the level of women's education:

> It is well that women should be unlettered. To cultivate women's skills would be harmful. They have no need of learning. It is enough if they can read books in *kana* [the Japanese syllabary alphabet]. Let it be that way.[52]

---

[45] Fukuo, *Nihon Kazoku Seidoshi*, pp. 186–7; Takagi, *Mikudari Han to Enkiri Dera*, p. 138.

[46] Takagi, *Mikudari Han: Edo no Rikon*, pp. 104–22; Fukuchi, *Kindai Nihon Joseishi*, p. 16.

[47] Miyagi *et al.* (eds), *Shinkō Nihon Joseishi*, p. 151; Takamure, *Josei no Rekishi*, vol. 1, p. 417; Takamure Itsue, *Nihon Koninshi* (1963, 1990 edn), pp. 234–6; Sōgō Joseishi Kenkyūkai (ed.), *Sei, Ai, Kazoku*, pp. 120–1.

[48] Higuchi, *Nippon Joseishi Hakkutsu*, pp. 220–3.

[49] Walthall, 'The life cycle of farm women', pp. 60–1.

[50] *Ibid.*, p. 62.

[51] Miyagi *et al.* (eds), *Shinkō Nihon Joseishi*, p. 171.

[52] Herbert Passin, *Society and Education in Japan* (New York, 1965), p. 46.

Intelligent or educated women were often considered impertinent, crafty, and likely to interfere in family affairs to an extent that might ruin their family.[53] Such beliefs about women's education had wide public acquiescence. Women's education did differ to some degree between the classes, but generally speaking women had far less educational opportunities than their male equivalents.[54]

Daughters from the warrior class were normally educated at home by their mothers, grandmothers and other female relatives. Textbooks used at home were usually *jokunsho* (books on women's lessons, books on 'things not to do' for women).[55] Among them *Onna Daigaku* was widely used.[56] Confucian concepts were at the heart of the education of women from the warrior class. Apart from such Confucian education, women were encouraged to receive more practical training such as housekeeping, sewing, weaving, embroidery, cookery and washing.[57] They were expected to learn good manners, and were encouraged to master traditional rituals such as the tea ceremony, flower arrangement, dance, song and the playing of some musical instruments. They were also allowed to learn some rather aristocratic

---

[53] Matsudaida Sadanobu's view of women's education is discussed in Miyagi *et al.* (eds), *Shinkō Nihon Joseishi*, p. 171; R. P. Dore, *Education in Tokugawa Japan* (1965, London, 1992 edn), p. 66; Robert L. Backus, 'Matsudaira Sadanobu and samurai education', in Andrew Gerstle (ed.), *18th Century Japan: Culture and Society* (North Sydney, 1989), pp. 132–48; Okazaki-Ward, 'Women and their education in the Tokugawa period of Japan', pp. 86–7.

[54] Shibukawa Hisako, *Kindai Nihon Joseishi: Kyōiku* (1970), p. 2; Karasawa Tomitarō, *Joshi Kagusei no Rekishi* (1979), p. 3; Sōgō Joseishi Kenkyūkai (ed.), *Bunka to Shisō*, p. 129; Dunn, *Everyday Life*, p. 170. At the beginning of the Edo period education was considered to be a privilege for men of the warrior class. Men from other classes hardly received formal education outside their homes—officials were mainly interested in education for men of the warrior class, and commoners were left to their own devices. Even so, as the Edo period progressed officials came to expect male commoners to be sufficiently literate to read public notices. On education in the Edo period, see Tetsuya Kobayashi, *Society, Schools and Progress in Japan* (Oxford, 1976), pp. 11–22; Nobuo K. Shimahara, *Adaptation and Education in Japan* (New York, 1979), pp. 45–6; Tokiomi Kaigo, *Japanese Education: Its Past and Present* (1965), pp. 31–48.

[55] Shibukawa, *Kyōiku*, p. 2; Okazaki-Ward, 'Women and their education in the Tokugawa period of Japan' pp. 120–2; Miyagi *et al.* (eds), *Shinkō Nihon Joseishi*, pp. 170–1. *Jokunsho* advocated Confucian ideals, including the teachings of *sanjū* (three obediences) and *shigyō* (four virtues), comprising *futoku* (women's virtues), *fugen* (women's terms or expressions), *fukō* (women's conduct, service) and *fuyō* (women's attentiveness to their personal appearance).

[56] Fukuchi, *Kindai Nihon Joseishi*, pp. 11–2; Uno, 'Women and changes in the household devision of labor', p. 30.

[57] Shibukawa, *Kyōiku*, pp. 2–3; Dore, *Education in Tokugawa Japan*, p. 67.

accomplishments such as calligraphy, the composing of poems, and the reading of classical Japanese literature.[58] Their education was limited to a basic level of learning and the refinement of their art, which enabled them to be literate and cultivated. Unlike their brothers, they were not entitled to pursue academic interests or to acquire deep knowledge of anything.[59] Their education outside their homes was retarded. Domain schools, private academies and shōgunal schools (where their brothers were taught), were shut to them.[60] Nevertheless, educational standards even among women probably rose in the late eighteenth century and early nineteenth century.

The great majority of women of the peasant class were illiterate, because they had neither time nor money to acquire basic reading and writing.[61] They devoted themselves to hard labour and domestic work. The only form of education available to them was *musume yado* (maiden's inn) and *ohariya* (needle shops), which taught them certain practical skills, and this occurred only during the agricultural off-seasons.[62]

The daughters of the craftsmen and merchants had the best opportunity to receive education outside their homes, as they were expected to play a significant role in helping to run their fathers' and husbands' shops.[63] In order to fulfil their obligations, they were required to receive vocational training, such as the use of the abacus, and to master basic skills including the three Rs and letter writing, which

---

[58] Shibukawa, *Kyōiku*, p. 2.

[59] Dunn, *Everyday Life*, pp. 46–8. Tokugawa Ieyasu emphasized the need for education of warrior-class men. In 1615 he issued *Buke Shohatto* (a set of instructions for the regulation of military houses). Article 1 of this called upon the samurai to devote themselves to learning and the military arts, and stated that learning should be accorded highest priority. His policy was taken over by later shōguns. They felt that even higher education was required by the samurai to sustain their position and efficiency as the governing class. This appreciation of learning created a more educated male warrior class.

[60] Shibukawa, *Kyōiku*, pp. 2–3; Passin, *Society and Education in Japan*, pp. 46–7. Passin stated that practically all boys of the warrior class attended a school. They were educated at *hanjuku* (domain schools), *shijuku* (private academies) and *shōgunal schools*.

[61] Miyagi *et al.* (eds), *Shinkō Nihon Joseishi*, p. 170; Itoya, *Meiji Ishin*, pp. 20–8.

[62] Fukuchi, *Kindai Nihon Joseishi*, p. 13; Shiga Tadashi, *Nihon Joshi Kyōikushi* (1977), pp. 276–81; Walthall, 'The life cycle of farm women', pp. 45–6; Okazaki-Ward, 'Women and their education in the Tokugawa period of Japan', p. 126.

[63] Hayashi *et al.* (eds), *Nihon Joseishi*, pp. 155–8; Itoya, *Meiji Ishin*, pp. 29–35; Okazaki, 'Women and their education in the Tokugawa period of Japan', pp. 122–4; Dunn, *Everyday Life*, p. 172.

were taught at *terakoya* (temple schools).[64] They also gained knowledge of the tea ceremony, flower arrangement, composition, calligraphy, sewing and Japanese painting.[65] However, no academic subjects
were taught to them. Women's academic education was characterised
by an utter lack of opportunity and encouragement from parents and
officials of the Tokugawa Shōgunate.[66] Such a state of affairs largely
continued in the Edo period.

To a greater or lesser degree, women from all classes in the Edo
period were bound by Confucian codes, the hierarchical laws of the
Tokugawa regime, and the *ie* system. Restrictions fell most on women
from the warrior class, who were completely tied by the *ie* system.
Physical movement of married women from the warrior class had
also been heavily circumscribed in the Edo period. They were discouraged from being seen in public and were largely confined to
home. Wives of *daimyō* (feudal lords) were permanently detained in
their husbands' residences. Women from merchant and peasant classes,
who worked alongside men in their family and contributed more
directly to production, while still being subject in many ways, enjoyed
more freedom and independence than warrior women.[67]

The view of the sexual functions of women was reinforced during the Edo period when prostitution became legal. The Tokugawa
Shōgunate granted a licence to Yoshiwara (in Edo) in 1617.[68] Twenty-
five large-scale licensed prostitute quarters, with official permission,
existed in Japan.[69] These were places of hardship and privation,
where prostitutes were sex slaves of the feudal system. The majority

---

[64] Hayashi *et al.* (eds), *Nihon Joseishi*, pp. 150–4; Dore, *Education in Tokugawa Japan*,
p. 254; Dunn, *Everyday Life*, pp. 170–1. The only educational institution intended
for children of commoners was called *terakoya*. *Terakoya*, in which samurai taught
alongside Buddhist priests, medical doctors, Shintō priests and learned commoners,
provided children with only basic education. With the rapid increase of the number of *terakoya* since the beginning of the eighteenth century, it had become quite
common for the sons of merchants, rich artisans and wealthy farmers to be educated in them.
[65] Sōgō Joseishi Kenkyūkai (ed.), *Bunka to Shisō*, pp. 126–7.
[66] Miyagi *et al.* (eds), *Shinkō Nihon Joseishi*, p. 171.
[67] *Ibid.*, pp. 145–6.
[68] Hayashi *et al.* (eds), *Nihon Joseishi*, p. 129; Higuchi, *Nippon Joseishi Hakkutsu*, pp.
228–9; Sōgō Joseishi Kenkyūkai (ed.), *Sei, Ai, Kazoku*, p. 155; Yasutaka Teruoka,
'The pleasure quarters and Tokugawa culture', in Gerstle (ed.), *18th Century Japan:
Culture and Society*, pp. 5–6; Cecilia Segawa Seigle, *Yoshiwara: The Glittering World of
the Japanese Courtesan* (Honolulu, 1993), pp. 23–8.
[69] Morosawa, *Onna no Rekishi*, vol. 1, p. 220.

of such prostitutes were daughters or wives of poor peasants who could not pay the land tax.[70] Treating daughters or wives as commodities and selling them to brothels to rebuild family finances was considered acceptable, since continuation of the family was greatly valued. Women did as they were told by fathers or husbands. Indeed the Yoshiwara survived after the Meiji Restoration and lasted until the Anti-Prostitution Act of 1956.[71]

Women's Status in the Meiji Period

After the collapse of the Tokugawa regime, responsibility for state administration returned to the Emperor in January, 1868. Various measures were taken to lift many 'feudalistic' restrictions. *Han* (domains) were abolished, and the new administrative unit called the *ken* (prefecture) was established throughout Japan in 1871.[72] The *shi-nō-kō-shō* system was abolished, and the four classes became equal before the law, which removed occupational restrictions.[73] The *sekisho* (barrier stations, which had imposed restrictions on travel) were also abolished, and accordingly freedom of movement was granted.[74] These measures were taken to transform Japan into a modern nation. The Japanese were also encouraged to adopt western culture. The Meiji Government sent officials and many students to universities in advanced western countries, where they studied subjects like law, medicine, education, engineering and shipbuilding.[75]

---

[70] Miyagi *et al.* (eds), *Shinkō Nihon Joseishi*, p. 165; Sōgō Joseishi Kenkyūkai (ed.), *Sei, Ai, Kazoku*, p. 158.

[71] Mitsui Reiko (ed.), *Gendai Fujin Undōshi Nenpyō* (1974), p. 229; Dunn, *Everyday Life*, pp. 183–4.

[72] This was called the *haihan chiken* (the abolition of the domains and establishment of prefectures). See Janet E. Hunter, *The Emergence of Modern Japan: An Introductory History since 1853* (London, 1989), p. 166; R. H. P. Mason and J. G. Caiger, *A History of Japan* (1973, 1997 edn), p. 282.

[73] In the Edo period only people from the warrior class were privileged to use surnames and to wear swords, but in 1870 people from all classes were permitted surnames. In 1871 the status of social outcasts, who were known as *eta* and *hinin* (pariahs), and previously deprived of all rights, was upgraded, and they gained occupational freedom.

[74] Miyagi *et al.* (eds), *Shinkō Nihon Joseishi*, p. 203.

[75] Mason & Caiger, *A History of Japan*, p. 271; W. G. Beasley, *The Rise of Modern Japan* (1990, London, 1995 edn).

With the abolition of 'feudalistic' customs and the introduction of new rules to modernise society, some restrictions on women were altered. Strict limitations which prevented people from marrying and adopting across class boundaries were removed in 1871.[76] From 1873 women became able to marry foreigners, if they received government approval.[77] Under the *Dajōkan Fukoku* (the early Meiji Cabinet's Ordinance No. 162, in May 1873), wives became able to claim divorce.[78] These changes for women affected not only their legal position but also their daily lives. Women's sphere of activity was considerably extended, and customs affecting them earlier began to die out.[79]

Women's Educational Reform in the Meiji Period

Among these changes, the most significant for women was educational reform. In 1871 the government took the first experiment to improve women's education. It sent five girls, aged between 7 and 14, to America to study as government-funded scholars, with male pupils, as a part of the Iwakura Mission.[80] This was hardly a significant number, and the move would have amounted to nothing more than a modernising gesture were it not for the fact that Tsuda Umeko, who later founded Joshi Eigaku Juku (Women's Institute of English Studies) and became one of the leading female educationalists in Japan, was the youngest of these five girls.[81] The government acted

---

[76] Fukuchi, *Kindai Nihon Joseishi*, pp. 30–1.

[77] Sōgō Joseishi Kenkyūkai (ed.), *Sei, Ai, Kazoku*, p. 171.

[78] Fukuchi, *Kindai Nihon Joseishi*, p. 30; Mitsui (ed.), *Gendai Fujin Undōshi Nenpyō*, p. 9.

[79] Miyagi *et al.* (eds), *Shinkō Nihon Joseishi*, pp. 211–2. Women in the Edo period had been expected to shave off their eyebrows and blacken their teeth when they married. The Empress Meiji was the first to discontinue this, and the general public followed her example. The custom went out of use in the early Meiji period. See also Appendix 2.

[80] Itoya, *Meiji Ishin*, pp. 74–8; Karasawa Tomitarō, *Joshi Gakusei no Rekishi* (1979), pp. 8–11; Hunter, *The Emergence of Modern Japan*, p. 140; Letter from Kaitakushi to Tsuda Umeko entitled 'Monjo Kaitakushi reisho' (November, 1872), Archives of Tsuda Juku Daigaku, no reference number; Imperial message from Empress Meiji to Tsuda Umeko entitled 'Osata gaki' (November, 1872), Archives of Tsuda Juku Daigaku, no reference number.

[81] Itoya, *Meiji Ishin*, pp. 77–8; Yamazaki Takako, *Tsuda Umeko* (1962, 1988 edn), pp. 27–35; Barbara Rose, *Tsuda Umeko and Women's Education in Japan* (New Haven,

according to the advice of Kuroda Kiyotaka, who appreciated the
close links between women's education and national development,
and believed that the girls might set an example to others by thinking progressively about female education, and by the contribution
that they might later make to their own generations.[82]

A year later, in 1872, the Gakusei (Fundamental Education Law),
which followed the French educational system, was promulgated.[83]
It laid stress upon the ways in which education would influence people's later lives. Its purpose was described as follows:

> Learning is the key to success in life, and no man can afford to neglect
> it. It is ignorance that leads man astray, makes him destitute, disrupts
> his family, and in the end destroys his life . . . Every man should there-
> fore pursue learning; and in so doing he should not misconstrue its
> purpose. Accordingly, the Department of Education will soon estab-
> lish an educational system and will revise the regulations relating thereto
> from time to time; wherefore there shall, in the future, be no com-
> munity with an illiterate family, nor a family with an illiterate person.
> Every guardian, acting in accordance with this, shall bring up his chil-
> dren with tender care, never failing to have them attend school. While
> advanced education is left to the ability and means of the individual,
> a guardian who fails to send a young child, whether a boy or a girl,
> to primary school shall be deemed negligent of his duty.[84]

The Fundamental Education Law introduced compulsory elementary education regardless of sex and class for the first time in Japan.
It greatly extended female educational opportunities, and guaranteed
a girl full educational equality at elementary school. This was a radical departure from women's education in the Edo period, which
had placed stress upon obedience and self-abnegation.

1992), pp. 8–10; Yoshiko Furuki, *The White Plum: A Biography of Ume Tsuda* (New
York, 1991), pp. 3–18; Yoshiko Furuki, 'Introduction', in Yoshiko Furuki *et al.* (eds),
The Attic Letters: Ume Tsuda's Correspondence to her American Mother (New York, 1991),
p. ix.
    [82] Fujii Chie & Kanamori Toshie, *Onna no Kyōiku 100-nen* (1977), pp. 18–9.
    [83] Shibukawa, *Kyōiku*, p. 13; Karasawa, *Joshi Gakusei*, p. 11; Itoya, *Meiji Ishin*,
p. 80; Katayama Kiyoichi, *Kindai Nihon no Joshi Kyōiku* (1984), p. 2; Monbushō,
'Gakusei', *Monbushō Futatsu*, 13 Bessatsu (2 August, 1872), reprinted in Mitsui (ed.),
Nihon Fujin Mondai Shiryō Shūsei, vol. 4, pp. 147–8; Hunter, *The Emergence of Modern
Japan*, p. 192; Monbushō (comp.), *Gakusei 120-nen-shi* (1992), pp. 15–8; Michael
D. Stephens, *Education and the Future of Japan* (Folkestone, 1991), p. 72; Cyril Simmons,
Growing up and Going to School in Japan: Tradition and Trends (Buckingham, 1990), pp.
24–9.
    [84] Quotation from Passin, *Society and Education in Japan*, pp. 210–11.

It is worth considering why such a revolutionary educational law
was introduced by the government. Some of the new leaders, like
Mori Arinori and Iwakura Tomomi, had been to western countries,
and they came back convinced that the key to modernise Japan was
the education of both men and women, as was occurring in the
west. They believed that the development of such education would
recruit a wider pool of talented people, and thus accelerate Japan's
advancement and industrialisation.[85] Through their experience abroad,
they had also become aware of American and British women's relatively high social status, and the responsibilities accorded them.[86]
They felt that the education of western women made them good
companions to their husbands, and that this was crucial vis-à-vis children's education at home—the latter being an essential element in
the formation of a modern nation.[87] They were convinced also that
much would depend upon the education of the next generation of
mothers. How to proceed in public policy was not however an easy
matter for them. Because of their strong recommendations, the
Japanese government, coming to realise the importance of education,
especially for girls, introduced the Gakusei in 1872.[88] This gave girls
the right to receive a compulsory elementary education equal to that
for boys.

The government also introduced a policy of increasing the number of publicly funded elementary schools, and by 1875 their number
throughout Japan exceeded 24,200.[89] These educational changes carried elements of western liberal ideas. They were supposed to improve
women's educational standards and status, but in practice the results
were unrewarding. Female elementary school attendance rates remained
very low, especially by comparison with western countries such as
America and England, being only 36.5 percent even in 1892.[90] The
female attendance rate was much lower than that for boys, which
was 71.7 percent in the same year.[91] Moreover, girls' elementary

---

[85] Fujii, *Onna no Kyōiku*, p. 18.
[86] Yamazaki, *Tsuda Umeko*, pp. 27–8; Furui, *The White Plum*, p. 9; Rose, *Tsuda Umeko and Women's Education*, pp. 9–10.
[87] Fujii & Kanamori, *Onna no Kyōiku*, p. 18; Fukuchi, *Kindai Nihon Joseishi*, pp. 31–2.
[88] Sōgō Joseishi Kenkyūkai (ed.), *Bunka to Shisō*, pp. 193–4; Itoya, *Meiji Ishin*, p. 79.
[89] Shibukawa, *Kyōiku*, p. 16.
[90] Karasawa, *Joshi Gakusei*, p. 11; Shibukawa, *Kyōiku*, pp. 16–9.
[91] *Ibid.*, p. 17.

school attendance rates did not rise much during the first twenty-
five years of the Gakusei.

There are many reasons for this. The great majority of Japanese
people had been so accustomed to the conventional idea of female
education, as represented by Matsudaira Sadanobu, that they were
very reluctant to send their daughters even to elementary schools.[92]
The Gakusei, which was based on American and later French educational systems, could not easily fit Japanese society. It was highly
idealistic, and had little to do with Japanese reality for many reasons.[93]
The curricula of elementary school education focused on a wide
range of academic learning, failing to meet parents' requirements for
their daughters' education, which they felt ought to include elements
of practical training, such as sewing.[94] As most parents felt that highly
academic subjects would be of no use to girls, they strongly supported the conventional view that female education should be carried out at home.[95] Moreover, even elementary school education was
not free at that time, and parents had to pay their children's tuition
fees.[96] Poor parents could not afford to send daughters to school.
Parents also did not like the idea of co-education.[97] For reasons like
these, girls' elementary school attendance rates did not rise easily.

By 1890 the Japanese government had become concerned that
westernizing trends had become too powerful and it promulgated
the *Kyōiku Chokugo* (the Imperial Rescript on Education) on 30 October
1890.[98] The contents of this rescript were largely based upon Confucianism.[99] Its ultimate goal of school education was to recruit a
nation which would obey the emperor unconditionally and regard

---

[92] *Ibid.*, pp. 17–9.
[93] Fujii & Kanamori, *Onna no Kyōiku*, p. 27.
[94] Karasawa, *Joshi Gakusei*, p. 12.
[95] Shibukawa, *Kyōiku*, p. 19.
[96] Katayama, *Kindai Nihon no Joshi Kyōiku*, p. 9; Fujii & Kanamori, *Onna no Kyōiku*,
p. 27; William K. Cummings, *Education and Equality in Japan* (Princeton, 1980), p. 24.
[97] Katayama, *Kindai Nihon no Joshi Kyōiku*, p. 9.
[98] Monbushō (comp.), *Gakusei 120-nen-shi*, pp. 22–3; Itoya, *Meiji Ishin*, pp. 222–6;
Shibukawa, *Kyōiku*, pp. 41–4; 'Kyōiku ni kansuru chokugo' (30 October, 1890), in
Mitsui (ed.), *Nihon Fujin Mondai Shiryō Shūsei*, vol. 4, p. 197. The translation of the
Kyōiku Chokugo is given in Ian Reader *et al.*, *Japanese Religions: Past and Present*
(Folkestone, 1993), p. 171.
[99] Katayama, *Kindai Nihon no Joshi Kyōiku*, pp. 59–60; Itoya, *Meiji Ishin*, pp. 222–3;
Takashima Nobuyoshi, *Kyōiku Chokugo to Gakkō Kyōiku* (1990), pp. 11–24.

obedience to him as the highest virtue. Until 1890, female education had been positive and expansive in many ways, enhancing the level of female culture. However, this new policy based on patriotic teaching changed thereafter, into the *ryōsai kenbo shugi kyōiku* (education for making good wives and wise mothers).[100] The first person believed to have used the term 'ryōsai kenbo' was Mori Arinori.[101] When he was Education Minister, he stated that the key to transforming Japan into a rich and strong nation was education, in particular women's education. His ideal of female education was to train girls to become good wives, who can manage household affairs, and wise mothers who can educate children to be adults of service to the country.[102]

Kikuchi Dairoku, another Education Minister, established this educational policy.[103] In a speech delivered at a girls' high school conference in March 1902, he officially introduced this policy:

> In Japan we take it for granted that girls should get married and become wives and mothers. Getting married and becoming good wives and wise mothers is the great majority of girls' primary task. The main objective of girls' education ought to be to help them accomplish this.[104]

Under this educational policy, manners, discipline, home-making and domestic training were seen as far more important in female education than academic training. To meet the main objectives of the Kyōiku Chokugo, the Ministry of Education redesigned the elementary school curriculum, in which subjects such as sewing, cooking, singing and music lessons were given greater emphasis.[105] After the introduction of the Kyōiku Chokugo, girls' elementary school attendance rates gradually began to rise, and in 1897 they exceeded 50

---

[100] The works on *ryōsai kenbo*, see Katano Misako, 'Ryōsai kenbo shugi no genryū', in Kindai Joseishi Kenkyūkai (ed.), *Onnatachi no Kindai* (1978), pp. 32–57; Nagahara Kazuko, 'Ryōsai kenbo shugi kyōiku ni okeru ie to shokugyō', in Joseishi Sōgō Kenkyūkai (ed.), *Nihon Joseishi*, vol. 4 (1982, 1985 edn), pp. 149–84; Kathleen S. Uno, 'The death of "good wife, wise mother"?', in Andrew Gordon (ed.), *Postwar Japan as History* (Berkeley, 1993), pp. 293–303; Sievers, *Flowers in Salt*, pp. 22–4.

[101] Haga Noboru, *Ryōsai Kenboron* (1990), p. 8.

[102] *Ibid.*, p. 8.

[103] *Ibid.*, p. 8. On Kikuchi Dairoku's views of women's education, see Kikuchi Dairoku, *Japanese Education: Lectures Delivered in the University of London* (London, 1909), pp. 268–81.

[104] Kikuchi Dairoku, 'Fujin no shimei', cited in Haga, *Ryōsai Kenboron*, pp. 20–1.

[105] Shibukawa, *Kyōiku*, p. 19; Katayama, *Kindai Nihon no Joshi Kyōiku*, pp. 26–7.

percent.[106] They finally exceeded 90 percent in 1904 when the Russo-Japanese War broke out.[107]

As far as secondary education was concerned, it was still considered as very much a boy's privilege in the Meiji period, and girls were discouraged from proceeding to high school by their parents. In addition, the number of girls' high schools in Japan was very limited.[108] There were two kinds of girls' high schools, private and public. The former was dominated by *misshon sukūru* (missionary girls' high schools) founded by missionaries.[109] Beginning with Ferris Jogakkō (Ferris Women's Seminary) founded by the American missionary Mary Kidder (1834–1910) in 1875 in Yokohama, about thirty missionary girls' high schools had been established by the end of the nineteenth century, which greatly enhanced the standard of women's secondary education.[110] Compared to the rapid expansion of the missionary girls' high schools, the development of female public high schooling was very slow in the early and mid Meiji era.[111] Although Tokyo Jogakkō (Tokyo Girls' High School), the first national girls' high school to be subsidised by the Ministry of Education, was founded in 1872, only eight more national and prefectural girls' high schools had been established in Japan by 1885, when the Kazoku Jogakkō (Peeresses' High School) was founded.[112] However, the num-

---

[106] Monbushō, 'Joshi kyōiku ni kansuru kunrei', *Monbushō Kunrei* (22 July, 1893), reprinted in Mitsui (ed.), *Nihon Fujin Mondai Shiryō Shūsei*, vol. 4, p. 206. The government did its best to meet parents' expectations for their daughters' education, and made efforts to raise girls' elementary school attendance. For example, the Ministry of Education issued instructions entitled '*joshi kyōiku ni kansuru ken*' ('matters relating to women's education') in July 1893, which allowed separate education for boys and girls. For this purpose, different classes were adopted for boys and girls even at the lower grade of elementary school, and separate male and female elementary schools were set up.

[107] Monbushō (comp.), *Gakusei 80-nen-shi*, (1954), pp. 1036–7.

[108] Katayama, *Kindai Nihon no Joshi Kyōiku*, p. 82.

[109] Shibukawa, *Kyōiku*, pp. 31–5. Many missionary girls' high schools were situated in or near open ports such as Yokohama, Kobe and Nagasaki.

[110] Fujii & Kanamori, *Onna no Kyōiku*, pp. 2–17; Suzuki Minako *et al.* (eds), *Ferris Jogakuin 110-nen Shōshi* (Yokohama, 1982), pp. 3–17; Ferris Jogakuin (ed.), *Kidder Shokanshū: Nihon Saisho no Joshi Kyōikusha no Kiroku* (Yokohama, 1975), pp. 43–79; Ferris Jogakuin 100-nen-shi Henshū Iinkai (ed.), *Ferris Jogakuin 100-nen-shi* (Yokohama, 1970), pp. 3–81; Monbushō (comp.), *Gakusei 120-nen-shi*, p. 35.

[111] Katayama, *Kindai Nihon no Joshi Kyōiku*, pp. 81–3.

[112] Alice Bacon (trans. by Kuno Akiko), *Kazoku Jogakkō Kyōshi no Mita Meiji Nihon no Uchigawa* (1994), pp. 21–8; Shibukawa, *Kyōiku*, pp. 25–31; Yamazaki, *Tsuda Umeko*, p. 172; 'Jogakkō setsuritsu no hitsuyō ni kansuru jōsō no kei nado' (15 October, 1871), reprinted in Mitsu (ed.), *Nihon Fujin Mondai Shiryō Shūsei*, vol. 4, pp. 141–2;

ber of girls' public high schools increased after 1899, up to 52 in 1900 and 70 in 1901.[113] This was due to the promulgation of the Kōtō Jogakkō Rei (Girls' High Education Act) in 1899.[114] Under that Act, the Ministry of Education stipulated that each prefecture must set up more than one girls' high school subsidised by the prefectural government.

As far as women's higher education was concerned, it was extremely rare for women in the Meiji period to study at this level. The number of educational institutions which could offer women higher education was extremely limited.[115] No national and private universities admitted women as degree students. They did not even allow women to sit in some classes as non-degree occasional students. Yamakawa Kikue recalled her bitter feelings when her request to sit in psychology classes at Tokyo Imperial University (now Tokyo University) was rejected by the Faculty Board.[116] It was not until the beginning of the Taishō period that a few universities began to open their doors to women.[117] Before 1900 there had been no women's higher education institutions in Japan, apart from Tokyo Joshi Kōtō Shihan Gakkō (Tokyo Girls' Higher School).[118] In 1900 three more women's higher educational institutions were established: Tsuda Umeko's Joshi

'Kanritsu jogakkō secchi ni kansuru Monbushō Futatsu', *Monbushō Futatsu* (December, 1871), reprinted in Mitsui (ed.), *Nihon Fujin Mondai Shiryō Shūsei*, vol. 4, pp. 142–4; Michael D. Stephens, *Japan and Education* (Basingstoke, 1991), p. 38. In 1890 Tokyo Jogakkō became a high school attached to Tokyo Joshi Kōtō Shihan Gakkō (Tokyo Girls' Higher School), and its official name was changed to Tokyo Joshi Kōtō Shihan Gakkō Fuzoku Kōtō Jogakkō (Girls' High School Attached to Tokyo Girls' Higher School). However, partly because of the long official name, and also partly because of its location (the school was situated in Ochanomizu, Tokyo), it was widely known to the public as Ochanomizu Girls' High School.

[113] Katayama, *Kindai Nihon no Joshi Kyōiku*, pp. 89–90; Yamazaki, *Tsuda Umeko*, p. 173.

[114] 'Kōtō jogakkō rei', *Chokurei*, 31 (8 February, 1899), reprinted in Mitsui (ed.), *Nihon Fujin Mondai Shiryō Shūsei*, vol. 4, pp. 262–3; Shibukawa, *Kyōiku*, pp. 45–7.

[115] Rose, *Tsuda Umeko and Women's Education*, p. 129; Yamazaki, *Tsuda Umeko*, p. 174.

[116] Yamakawa, *Onna Nidai no Ki*, pp. 136–7.

[117] Mitsui (ed.), *Gendai Fujin Undōshi Nenpyō*, p. 77. Tōhoku Imperial University (now Tōhoku University) first opened its door to women in September 1913, which was followed slightly later by Hokkaidō Imperial University (now Hokkaidō University) and Kyūshū Imperial University (now Kyūshū University).

[118] Yamazaki, *Tsuda Umeko*, p. 174; Fujii & Kanamori, *Onna no Kyōiku*, p. 35. Tokyo Girls' Higher School, the predecessor of the present Ochanomizu Women's University, was a women's higher teachers' training college founded in 1890, and was also the first women's higher educational institution in Japan.

Eigaku Juku (Women's Institute of English Studies), Yoshioka Yayoi's
Tokyo Joi Gakkō (Tokyo Women's Medical College), and Yokoi
Tomoko and Satō Shizu's Joshi Bijutsu Gakkō (Women's Art College).[119] Naruse Jinzō's Nihon Joshi Daigakkō (Japan Women's College)
was founded in 1901.[120] However, none of these was given university
status, mainly because the government continued to adopt a negative
attitude towards women's higher education.[121] After the promulgation of the Senmon Gakkō Rei (Vocational Colleges Act) in March
1903, only Joshi Eigaku Juku and Nihon Joshi Daigakkō were promoted to the higher status of *senmon gakkō* (vocational colleges or special women's higher educational institutions) in 1904, and Tokyo Joi
Gakkō in 1912.[122] Although vocational colleges were still well below
university status, they were approved by the government and were
also the highest rank women's education institutions supported by
the Japanese state. Some more women's vocational colleges and
teachers' training colleges were founded towards the end of the Meiji
period.[123]

Women and Employment Opportunities in the Meiji Period

Even before the Meiji Restoration, women rendered service as a
valuable workforce in the fields of farming and business.[124] Merchants'
daughters and wives usually helped to run their family trade, and
some of them could give full play to their business talent.[125] Similarly,
daughters and wives of peasant women worked in their tenant or

---

[119] Yamazaki, *Tsuda Umeko*, p. 179; Shibukawa, *Kyōiku*, p. 47; Rose, *Tsuda Umeko and Women's Education*, pp. 126–7; Furuki, *The White Plum*, pp. 98–100.

[120] Fujii & Kanamori, *Onna no Kyōiku*, pp. 34–5; Nakamura Masao (ed.), *Nihon Joshi Daigakkō 40-nen-shi* (1942), p. 58.

[121] Yamazaki, *Tsuda Umeko*, pp. 211–2.

[122] Shibukawa, *Kyōiku*, p. 49; Rose, *Tsuda Umeko and Women's Education in Japan*, pp. 138–9.

[123] Shibukawa, *Kyōiku*, p. 49. These were Nara Joshi Kōtō Shihan Gakkō (Nara Women's Higher School) in 1909, Kobe Jogakuin Senmon Gakkō (Kobe Women's Vocational College) in 1909, and Dōshisha Joshi Senmon Gakkō (Dōshisha Women's Vocational College) in 1912.

[124] Fukuchi, *Kindai Nihon Joseishi*, pp. 17–8; Hayashi *et al.* (eds), *Nihon Joseishi*, pp. 155–8; Miyagi *et al.*, *Shinkō Nihon Joseishi*, p. 225.

[125] Sōgō Joseishi Kenkyūkai (ed.), *Bunka to Shisō*, p. 120; Dunn, *Everyday Life*, p. 172.

family farms with their fathers, brothers and husbands.[126] Peasant
women were sometimes hired out as day labourers on neighbouring
farms.[127] The daughters and wives of poor lower-class samurai did
weaving and piecework at home to help their family finances.[128] In
spite of their contributions, the sphere of work for women in the
Edo period was mainly restricted to the family's trade. Such work
was defined by the family unit and was unpaid. It was not common
for them to work away from home.[129] The daughters of high and
middle-rank samurai worked for the households of the Tokugawa
Shōgunate and *daimyō* (feudal lords) as servants, governesses and wet-
nurses.[130] Women from other classes who left home to work usually
became professional entertainers, courtesans and housemaids in the
Edo period.[131]

Even in the early Meiji period opportunities for women's paid
work outside the home remained scarce. Professional entertainers,
teachers of traditional Japanese music, hairdressers and midwives
belonged to this minority working group.[132] However, opportunities
for female paid work gradually widened after the Meiji government
adopted an active policy to promote both heavy and light industries.
The government began to run mines and model factories, and invested
in imported industrial technology, adopting manufacturing techniques
from industrially advanced countries to increase production.[133] It was
particularly eager to develop spinning and silk-reeling industries, and
it opened the Tomioka Silk Reeling Mill in Gunma Prefecture in
1872.[134] The mill was equipped with the most up-to-date machinery
imported from France, and also employed French engineers and silk-
reeling women.[135] Four hundred women were recruited from all over
Japan to work in the mill, and this was perhaps the inauguration

---

[126] Hayashi *et al.* (eds), *Nihon Joseishi*, pp. 140–50.
[127] Sōgō Joseishi Kenkyūkai (ed.), *Bunka to Shisō*, p. 120; Sievers, *Flowers in Salt*,
p. 57.
[128] *Ibid.*, p. 57.
[129] *Ibid.*, p. 58; Miyagi *et al.* (eds), *Shinkō Nihon Joseishi*, p. 162.
[130] Morosawa, *Onna no Rekishi*, vol. 1, p. 235.
[131] Miyagi *et al.* (eds), *Shinkō Nihon Joseishi*, p. 225.
[132] *Ibid.*, p. 225.
[133] Fukuchi, *Kindai Nihon Joseishi*, p. 67; Hayashi *et al.* (eds), *Nihon Joseishi*, p. 211.
[134] Mitsui, *Gendai Fujin Undōshi Nenpyō*, pp. 6–9; Yoneda, *Kindai Nihon Joseishi*,
vol. 1, pp. 30–1.
[135] Sievers, *Flowers in Salt*, p. 59; Miyagi *et al.* (eds), *Shinkō Nihon Joseishi*, pp. 213–4.

of female paid workers in a modern factory in Japan. Many were daughters of the ex-warrior class.[136] Experienced French women taught Japanese female trainees mechanised silk-reeling techniques. After they finished their training, many were transferred to other newly opened government-run or private silk mills to work as instructors. As the government hoped, their newly acquired skills were passed on to many female workers throughout Japan, laying the foundation for Japan's successful silk industry.[137] By the 1880s privately owned silk mills had been developed throughout Japan.[138] The spinning industry also advanced and from about 1887 it became extremely dependent on its female workforce.[139] With the rapid advance of the silk-reeling and spinning industries, which became core industries in Japan, a substantial number of female workers were required in the mechanised manufacturing processes. These industries recruited a huge number of women.[140] Although many of the first workers at the Tomioka Silk Reeling Mill were women of ex-samurai origin, the great majority of female workers at textile mills were daughters of impoverished tenant farmers, who were struggling to pay their rent.[141] These farmers sent their daughters, who had often not completed even compulsory education, to factories to assist the family budget. Their fathers received payment in advance from mills, in exchange for contracts, and the daughters' wages were

---

[136] In spite of a nationwide recruitment campaign, at first the government found it extremely difficult to recruit female workers for mills, because of wild rumours that, given the 'barbarian' habits of foreigners, going to work in them was a form of human sacrifice. Therefore the government asked local governments to supply a total of up to 15 girls in a compulsory manner. Daughters of civil servants working for local governments first went to such work to prove that mills were safe for young women. An account of the Tomioka Silk Reeling Mill is given in Janet Hunter, 'Labour in the Japanese silk industry in the 1870s: *The Tomioka Nikki* of Wada Ei', in Gordon Daniels (ed.), *Europe Interprets Japan* (Tenterden, Kent, 1984), pp. 20–1; Sievers, *Flowers in Salt*, p. 59; Yoneda, *Kindai Nihon Joseishi*, vol. 1, p. 30; Morosawa, *Onna no Rekishi*, vol. 2, pp. 47–52.

[137] Hunter, 'Labour in the Japanese silk industry in the 1870s', p. 21.

[138] Siever, *Flowers in Salt*, p. 61.

[139] In 1887 many spinning mills were opened, such as Tokyo Bōseki Gaisha (Tokyo Spinning Factory), Kyoto Orimono Gaisha (Kyoto Textile Factory), Kurashiki Bōsekijo (Kurashiki Spinning Mill), Nihon Orimono Gaisha (Japan Textile Factory) and Wakayama Bōseki Gaisha (Wakayama Spinning Factory). Mitsui, *Gendai Fujin Undōshi Nenpyō*, pp. 28–30; Takamure, *Josei no Rekishi*, vol. 2, p. 386.

[140] Sakurai, *Bosei Hogo Undōshi*, p. 35.

[141] *Ibid.*, p. 35; Sievers, *Flowers in Salt*, p. 61.

used to pay rents and debts.[142] Apart from textile mills, working-class women also left home to work in coal mines and other factories.[143]

As far as middle-class women were concerned, their work opportunities also began to broaden gradually after the enactment of the Gakusei (the Fundamental Education Law) in 1872.[144] After the foundation in 1874 of the Tokyo Joshi Shihan Gakkō (Tokyo Girls' Higher School), a teachers' training institution, other similar schools were established.[145] Many female school teachers were recruited and taught at elementary schools and girls' high schools.[146] Apart from teaching, nursing became another middle-class women's occupation. Nurses' schools such as the Training School for Nurses attached to the Yūshi Kyōritsu Tokyo Byōin (Voluntary Public Tokyo Hospital, now Jikeikai Hospital), the Dōshisha Byōin Fuzoku Kangofu Gakkō (Nurses' School Attached to the Dōshisha Hospital in Kyoto), and that run by the Red Cross Society of Japan, were founded in 1885-7.[147] Ogino Ginko became the first formally qualified female doctor in Japan, and set up her own medical practice in 1885.[148] This opened a new occupational path for a minority of middle-class women.

Along with the development of transport and communications, the government also began to employ middle-class women in its new enterprises. For example, at the government-funded telephone exchange, which was opened in 1890, women were employed as telephone operators.[149] From 1900 the government-funded railway department recruited female ticket inspectors.[150] In 1906 the Ministry of Communications, having employed women from 1891, also began to recruit female junior officials.[151] Local government offices also began to hire women. However, such female positions were still low in status, no higher than the lower-level non-clerical male workers.

---

[142] Sōgō Joseishi Kenkyūkai (ed.), *Sei, Ai, Kazoku*, p. 188; Fuse, *Kekkon to Kazoku*, p. 78; Morosawa, *Onna no Rekishi*, vol. 2, pp. 143–5.

[143] Sievers, *Flowers in Salt*, p. 58; Hayashi *et al.* (eds), *Nihon Joseishi*, pp. 215–6.

[144] Yoneda, *Kindai Nihon Joseishi*, vol. 1, p. 63.

[145] Fukuchi, *Kindai Nihon Joseishi*, p. 72.

[146] By 1882 about 2,500 female elementary school teachers had been recruited. Miyagi *et al.* (eds), *Shinkō Nihon Joseishi*, p. 225.

[147] Fukuchi, *Kindai Nihon Joseishi*, pp. 73–5; Mitsui, *Fujin Undōshi Nenpyō*, pp. 24–31.

[148] Yoneda, *Kindai Nihon Joseishi*, vol. 1, p. 64; Takamure, *Josei no Rekishi*, vol. 2, p. 423; Mitsui, *Fujin Undōshi Nenpyō*, pp. 22–3.

[149] Yoneda, *Kindai Nihon Joseishi*, vol. 1, p. 63; Miyagi *et al.* (eds), *Shinkō Nihon Joseishi*, p. 226.

[150] Fukuchi, *Kindai Nihon Joseishi*, p. 71.

[151] *Ibid.*, p. 71.

The Bank of Japan first employed a woman in 1890, and thereafter the number of banks, companies and hospitals hiring women increased. Similarly, the number of shop assistants rose from 1900.[152] Partly due to the spread of women's higher education, and the expansion of a modern economy, various new occupations such as typists, photographers, pharmacists, dentists, stenographers and journalists became available to middle-class women.[153] The scope of middle-class women's work had expanded remarkably by the end of the Meiji period. Such recruitment of female workers was welcomed by employers because they were hard-working, earned lower wages than males, and were more obedient. However in Japan, as elsewhere, both female employees and their employers often regarded such work as temporary before marriage.[154] It gave unmarried middle-class women more of an opportunity to see the world and experience paid work. But employers did not even consider providing them with child-care facilities, such was the presumption that they would quit such work when married.

Other Legal Changes

Apart from educational and occupational changes, further legislation of relevance to this book was introduced between 1889 and 1900. In particular there was the Dai Nihon Teikoku Kenpō (the Imperial Japanese Constitution), based upon the Imperial German model and promulgated in February 1889.[155] Under chapter two of the Constitution, fundamental human rights were guaranteed. These included freedom to change residence, entitlement to legal protection, inviolability of one's home, privacy of correspondence, inviolability of

---

[152] Miyagi *et al.* (eds), *Shinkō Nihon Joseishi*, p. 226.
[153] Hayashi *et al.* (eds), *Nihon Joseishi*, p. 232; Takamure, *Josei no Rekishi*, vol. 2, p. 425.
[154] Miyagi *et al.* (eds), *Shinkō Nihon Joseishi*, p. 226.
[155] Gotō Yasuko & Ōkubo Kazunori, *Josei to Hō* (1990), p. 10; Itoya, *Meiji Ishin*, pp. 215–21; Beasley, *The Rise of Modern Japan*, pp. 76–80; Mason & Caiger, *A History of Japan*, p. 289; Hunter, *The Emergence of Modern Japan*, pp. 168–70; Mackie, *Creating Socialist Women in Japan*, pp. 30–1; Sharon H. Nolte and Sally Ann Hastings, 'The Meiji state's policy toward women, 1890–1910', in Bernstein (ed.), *Recreating Japanese Women*. This constitution was widely known as the Meiji Kenpō (The Meiji Constitution). Its promulgation was a direct response to the demand for a constitution made by the Freedom and People's Rights Movement in the 1870s.

ownership, freedoms of religion, speech, the press, assembly and association, and the right to petition the government.[156] In return for these rights people had two obligations: a legal obligation to pay one's taxes, and military service for men. The Constitution also established the Imperial Diet which consisted of two Houses—the House of Representatives and the House of Peers—and the Diet became a legislative body.[157]

Apart from the Meiji Constitution, the Shūgiin Giin Senkyo Hō (Electoral Law to choose members of the House of Representatives), the Kizokuin Hō (House of Peers' Act), and other laws such as the Giin Hō (Diet Law), the Kaikei Hō (Public Accounts Act), were all promulgated in 1889, but none of them aimed to significantly upgrade women's status.[158] Although a constitutional draft prepared by one of the leading activists of the Freedom and People's Rights Movement, Ueki Emori, included provisions for female suffrage, the Meiji Constitution conferred no national political rights or voice to women.[159] Under the Shūgiin Giin Senkyo Hō, the right to vote for members of the House of Representatives was given only to men of 25 years or over, who were imperial Japanese subjects, and paid more than

[156] The historian Emura Eiichi stated that the provisions to ensure people's rights in the Constitution were minimal, and could be limited by law. This was because the basic principle of the Meiji Constitution was the inviolable sovereignty of the Emperor, who had extensive prerogatives, and he had authority to withdraw or impose restrictions on the human rights guaranteed by the Constitution. See Emura Eiichi, *Meiji no Kenpō* (1992), pp. 37–8.

[157] *Ibid.*, p. 39; Hunter, *The Emergence of Modern Japan*, p. 216. Activists of the Freedom and People's Rights submitted the *minsen giin setsuritsu kenpakusho* (a written petition requesting the foundation of the Diet, elected by the people) in January 1874. In it they urged that it was absolutely essential to rebuild government on the basis of an elected assembly which would value and reflect public opinion, since the people had natural human rights and shouldered the burden of taxation. Responding to this, the Imperial Diet was established.

[158] Emura, *Meiji no Kenpō*, p. 34; Hopper, *A New Woman of Japan*, p. 36. The Kizokuin Hō defined the structure of the House of Peers, a body which was entirely independent from the people and the House of Representatives. The major roles of the House of Peers were to protect the Imperial Household and to govern the House of Representatives, which was chosen by the electorate. Its members comprised people from the Imperial family, titled persons, learned scholars or men of merits, appointed by the Emperor, and high taxpayers elected by vote.

[159] Tanaka (ed.), *Josei Kaihō Shisō*, pp. 50–1; Sotozaki Mitsuhiro, *Nihon Fujin Ronshi: Jokenron Hen*, vol. 1 (1986), p. 72; Sotozaki Mitsuhiro, *Kōchiken Fujin Kaihō Undōshi* (1975), pp. 40–1. Ueki Emori (1857–1892) helped Itagaki Taisuke to found the Jiyūtō (Japan's first political party) and was editor of *Jiyū Shinbun*, the organ of the Jiyūtō.

15 yen direct national tax.[160] Eligibility for election was only given
to enfranchised men of 30 years or over.[161] Women lacked civil rights,
and could not hold office in government or take up any other public office.[162]

The promulgation of the Shūkai Oyobi Seisha Hō (Assembly and
Political Organisation Law) on 25 July 1890 also deprived women
of their existing freedom to participate in political activities.[163] Article
4 stipulated that all women were banned from attending political
speech meetings and political assemblies (along with servicemen,
policemen, teachers, students and minors). Article 25 stipulated that
all women were forbidden from joining political organisations. These
articles closed the door on further female participation in politics.
The enactment of this law enabled the government to suppress
women's involvement in all political matters, as we shall see.[164] Articles
4 and 25 of the Shūkai Oyobi Seisha Hō were incorporated into
Article 5 of the Chian Keisatsu Hō (the Peace Police Law), enacted
in March 1900.[165]

The legislation which had most effect on women's status was the
Meiji Minpō (the Meiji Civil Code), which was promulgated in
1898.[166] Its main objectives were to prioritise family lineage and a

---

[160] 'Shūgiin Senkyo Hō', *Hōritsu*, 3 (11 February, 1889), reprinted in Ichikawa
(ed.), *Nihon Fujin Mondai Shiryō Shūsei*, vol. 2, pp. 105–25; 'Daiikkai Shūgiin giin
sōsenkyo no kekka', *Gikai Seido 70–nen-shi, Teikoku Gikaishi*, vol. 1 (1904), reprinted
in Ichikawa (ed.), *Nihon Fujin Mondai Shiryō Shūsei*, vol. 2, p. 125; Itoya, *Meiji Ishin*,
p. 217. According to the poll-books, the whole electoral roll amounted to only
450,000 in the first general election in 1890. This was only 1.24 percent of the
entire population. As election was by open ballot, it was easy for government to
interfere.

[161] Miyagi *et al.* (eds), *Shinkō Nihon Joseishi*, p. 222. Although fuller male suffrage
was achieved in 1925, when any man of twenty-five years or more became enfranchised, women did not gain this until the end of World War II.

[162] Emura, *Meiji no Kenpō*, p. 39; Fukuchi, *Kindai Nihon Joseishi*, p. 53.

[163] Itoya, *Meiji Ishin*, pp. 221–2; Yoneda, *Kindai Nihon Joseishi*, vol. 1, p. 58, Mackie,
Creating Socialist Women, p. 35; Sotozaki, *Nihon Fujin Ronshi*, vol. 1, pp. 205–6.

[164] *Ibid.*, pp. 192–3.

[165] Suzuki Yūko, *Joseishi o Hiraku*, vol. 1 (1989), pp. 80–1; Itoya Toshio, *Josei
Kaihō no Senkusha: Nakajima Toshiko to Fukuda Hideko* (1984), p. 169. In 1922, a partial amendment of Article 5 of the Peace Police Law was made, and women were
allowed to attend political meetings. However, they remained banned from joining
political organisations until the end of the Second World War.

[166] 'Meiji 31–nen Minpō, Shinzokuhen, Sōzokuhen' (June, 1898), in Yuzawa (ed.),
Nihon Fujin Mondai Shiryō Shūsei, vol. 5, pp. 239–76; Takamure, *Josei no Rekishi*,
vol. 2, p. 124; Igeta Ryōji, 'Meiji Minpō to josei no kenri', in Joseishi Sōgō Kenkyūkai
(ed.), *Nihon Joseishi*, vol. 4 (1982, 1985 edn), pp. 58–76; Fuse Akiko, *Kekkon to Kazoku*

patriarchal family system. It retained strong elements of the *ie* system.[167] The *ie* system, which now became legally prescribed in the Meiji Civil Code, was established in all households regardless of social status, while in the Edo period it had been largely limited to the warrior class. Unlike the *ie* system in the Edo period, the Meiji Civil Code allowed a woman to become a family head.[168] However, this was to be a temporary measure taken in extraordinary circumstances. As soon as she married or adopted a child (preferably a son), she was expected to retire from such a position.

Under the Meiji Civil Code, women's inheritance rights compared extremely unfavourably with men's.[169] For example, in a family with a legitimate elder daughter and a younger son, the son's inheritance took precedence. In a family with legitimate sons and daughters, only the eldest son was able to succeed to the headship of a house; this was modelled on the inheritance system practised among the warrior class in the Edo period. In the case of a family with a legitimate elder daughter and a younger brother born out of wedlock, but acknowledged by his father, the younger brother took precedence over the legitimate elder daughter. The adoptive marriage (in which a husband was adopted into his wife's family) very often took place in a family with only daughters, for the sake of the continuation of the family.

Under the Meiji Civil Code a man over 17 years and a woman over 15 years could marry, but marriage between minors required consent from both heads of their families and their parents.[170] A man over 30 years and a woman over 25 years could marry without parental consent.[171] The Meiji Civil Code stipulated that the marital

---

(1993), pp. 67–72; Mackie, *Creating Socialist Women*, pp. 32–7; Yoshiko Miyake, 'Doubling expectations: motherhood and women's factory work under state management in Japan in the 1930s and 1940s', in Bernstein (ed.), *Recreating Japanese Women*, pp. 270–1.

[167] Fukuchi, *Kindai Nihon Joseishi*, p. 57; Fuse, *Kekkon to Kazoku*, p. 71; Sievers, *Flowers in Salt*, pp. 111–2.

[168] Miyagi *et al.* (eds), *Shinkō Nihon Joseishi*, p. 223; Fukuo, *Nihon Kazoku Seidoshi*, p. 203.

[169] The details of inheritance prescribed in the Meiji Civil Code are given in 'Meiji 31-nen Minpō, Shinzokuhen, Sōzokuhen', pp. 259–76; Takamure, *Josei no Rekishi*, vol. 2, p. 126; Itoya, *Meiji Ishin*, p. 232.

[170] The details of marriage prescribed in the Meiji Civil Code are given in 'Meiji 31-nen Minpō, Shinzokuhen, Sōzokuhen', pp. 243–5; Fukuchi, *Kindai Nihon Joseishi*, p. 59; Miyagi *et al.* (eds), *Shinkō Nihon Joseishi*, p. 223; Itoya, *Meiji Ishin*, p. 232.

[171] Women were expected to marry young. Women over 25 years old who

wishes of the person concerned formed the prerequisite for marriage.[172] This was a significant change from marriage for a female
family member among the warrior class in the Edo period, which
was decided by her family head at his own discretion, and her consent or refusal was often not taken into consideration. However, in
spite of the Meiji Civil Code, the wishes for marriage of the person
concerned were often not valued in practice. The Meiji Civil Code
stated that the consents of the family head, parents or guardians
were required prior to marriage.[173] As a result, marriage remained
very much a union between two families rather than a union between
two individuals. Under the Meiji Civil Code bigamy was banned.[174]
However, this provision was not fully enforced in the sense that
many husbands continued to have mistresses.

As far as a woman's economic and financial rights were concerned,
when an unmarried woman reached 20 years of age, she was regarded
as an adult and gained control over her own money and property
under the Meiji Civil Code.[175] However, upon marriage she lost that
control; her husband took charge of her property, unless she had
made a prior financial agreement with him that she would continue
to handle it.[176] In the event of her husband's death, she did not have
a right to inherit her husband's property. If she had children, normally her eldest son inherited from her husband. If she had no children, his parents inherited his property. In some cases, even the
property she inherited or the money she earned were taken away
from her. If she decided to remarry, she either left her children by
her late husband at his or her parents' house or took them to her
new husband's house.[177] It was quite common for a woman who had
lost her husband to remain a widow for the rest of her life, for the
sake of keeping her children.

---

remained single were considered abnormal and despised. Some women married for
love, but marriage for love was not publicly welcomed.

[172] Itoya, *Meiji Ishin*, p. 232.
[173] Fukuchi, *Kindai Nihon Joseishi*, pp. 57–8.
[174] Hayashi *et al.* (eds), *Nihon Joseishi*, p. 201.
[175] Fukuchi, *Kindai Nihon Joseishi*, pp. 60–1.
[176] The details of a wife's financial rights are given in 'Meiji 31-nen Minpō,
Shinzokuhen, Sōzokuhen', pp. 245–6; Gotō & Ōkubo, *Josei to Hō*, p. 12; Takamure,
Josei no Rekishi, vol. 2, pp. 128–9.
[177] Miyagi *et al.* (eds), *Shinkō Nihon Joseishi*, p. 224.

In 1873 wives became able to claim divorce.[178] Under the Meiji Civil Code two divorce methods were available to both husbands and wives: *kyōgi rikon* (divorce by mutual consent) and *saiban rikon* (divorce by court proceedings).[179] Court proceedings gave wives minimal rights to initiate divorce. Husbands had many advantages over wives.[180] For example, if a wife committed adultery, her husband could divorce her by establishing that fact, without regard to the marital status of the man she committed adultery with. Her husband could also have her sentenced to prison for up to two years. On the other hand, when a husband committed adultery with an unmarried woman, he escaped any blame or punishment. When he committed adultery with a married woman, his wife could divorce him only when the woman's husband brought a suit against him, and if he was then sentenced. Even when wives brought suits for divorce, the results were in most cases favourable to husbands. Wives often ended up meekly accepting the most unfavourable decisions, thereafter paying the further penalty of recriminatory ill-treatment within the marriage.[181]

In the event of divorce, under the Meiji Civil Code child custody went to fathers.[182] A mother gained custody only when her husband died or went missing, or if her child was born out of wedlock and

---

[178] Mitsui (ed.), *Gendai Fujin Undōshi Nenpyō*, pp. 8–9.

[179] The details of divorce prescribed in the Meiji Civil Code are given in 'Meiji 31-nen Minpō, Shinzokuhen, Sōzokuhen', pp. 246–7; Sotozaki, *Nihon Fujin Ronshi*, vol. 1, pp. 210–3; Igeta, 'Meiji Minpō to josei no kenri', pp. 73–4. In the event of divorce by court proceedings, divorce could be authorised for one of the following reasons:
A spouse had committed bigamy.
A wife had committed adultery.
A spouse was legally sentenced to prison.
Cruel treatment or insult, such that it became impossible to live with the perpetrator.
A spouse harboured malice towards the other, and abandoned him/her.
Cruel treatment or insult by a spouse's parents.
Cruel treatment of one's spouse's parents or grievous insult to one's spouse's parents.
One's spouse went missing and his/her location was unknown for more than three years.
A husband, marrying into the family of his bride (and being adopted as her parents' son), had this adoption cancelled by her family.

[180] Fukuchi, *Kindai Nihon Joseishi*, p. 63; Takamure, *Josei no Rekishi*, vol. 2, pp. 130–1; Itoya, *Meiji Ishin*, p. 234.

[181] Tanaka (ed.), *Josei Kaihō no Shisō*, p. 113.

[182] 'Meiji 31-nen Minpō, Shinzokuhen, Sōzokuhen', p. 252.

was not acknowledged by the father. Women who gave birth to illegitimate children were regarded as social outcasts and were generally abused. The fundamental welfare of mothers and children was
not guaranteed under the Meiji Civil Code.

Many of that Code's provisions demonstrated male-dominated,
Confucian features common to the earlier warrior family system.
The Code preserved and systematically legalised many principles of
the *ie* system, having a pervasive effect upon people's private lives.[183]
It also corresponded to the Emperor-based notion of the perfect
woman: one who had strong loyalty and patriotism, womanly virtues
based on Confucian teaching, who conformed to the *ie* system, and
served as a faithful servant to husband or head of family.[184] Such
views pervaded Japanese women's lives, taking other identities and
options from them. The Meiji Constitution and the Imperial Rescript
on Education were also used to reinforce the ideology and authority of the *ie* system.[185] Through educational policies whose main
objectives were to encourage men to offer their services to the state,
and encourage women to become 'good wives and wise mothers',
the government imparted ideas of patriotic nationalism, and tied its
educational policies to the *ie* system.[186] No doubt some women gained
respect by living by the ideals expected of them. However, the women
who became the worst victims of the Meiji Civil Code were those
from poor family backgrounds, whose abject subservience to family
heads led to large numbers of them being sold to brothels or to factories. The Meiji Civil Code allowed such women to be treated as
usable commodities, and gave no redress against ill-treatment.

Although Japan was long behind the leading western European
countries in establishing capitalism, it was successful in developing
light industry such as spinning and silk-reeling against fierce com-
petition from other countries, and in accumulating capital after the
Meiji Restoration.[187] As in early nineteenth-century England, Japan

---

[183] Hopper, *A New Woman of Japan*, pp. 187–8. It was extraordinary that the Meiji
Civil Code survived for half a century, until the new civil code came into effect
on 1 January, 1948. That finally abolished the *ie* system, and deprived the head of
a family of his authority and rights.

[184] Tanaka (ed.), *Josei Kaihō no Shisō*, pp. 115–6.

[185] Mackie, *Creating Socialist Women*, pp. 30–1; Miyake, 'Doubling expectations',
p. 270.

[186] Itoya, *Meiji Ishin*, p. 235.

[187] Hayashi *et al.* (eds), *Nihon Joseishi*, p. 214; Yoneda, *Kindai Nihon Joseishi*, vol. 1,
p. 74.

achieved this partly through the extremely cheap labour provided by female textile workers.[188] Many of these women were daughters of poor farmers, who were sent into factories to take pressure off family sizes.[189] Their fathers received their daughters' wages. No doubt societal structures based on the *ie* system were an advantage to capitalist employers in Japan, fostering a habit of unquestioning deference and obedience.[190] Capitalist employers imposed many strict restrictions on female textile workers, who endured extraordinarily long working hours, unhygienic working conditions, and often lived in unsanitary dormitories.[191] The food provided was coarse and lacked nutritional value. Many female workers became ill, suffering occupationally related disease such as tuberculosis, which was widespread in factories.[192]

There were no laws to protect such workers until 1916 when the Kōjō Hō (Factory Law) came into force.[193] Although the Meiji Government had intended to draw up factory legislation more than thirty years earlier, and factory bills were submitted to the Diet many times, they all fell through.[194] These bills met strong opposition from employers who disapproved of any ban on late-night work, which would reduce their profit margins. However, the Rōdō Kumiai Kiseikai (Society for the Promotion of Labour), which was founded in 1897, showed much interest in the enactment of factory legislation.[195] It

---

[188] Miyagi *et al.* (eds), *Shinkō Nihon Joseishi*, pp. 214–5; Sakurai, *Bosei Hogo Undōshi*, pp. 36–7; Sievers, *Flowers in Salt*, p. 76.

[189] Hayashi *et al.* (eds), *Nihon Joseishi*, p. 217; Tanaka (ed.), *Josei Kaihō no Shisō*, pp. 150–3; Yamamoto Shigemi, *Aa Nomugi Tōge* (1968, 1994 edn), pp. 14–5; Barbara Molony, 'Activism among women in the Taisho cotton textile industry', in Bernstein (ed.), *Recreating Japanese Women*, p. 223.

[190] Itoya, *Meiji Ishin*, p. 235; Sakurai, *Bosei Hogo Undōshi*, p. 36.

[191] Yoneda, *Kindai Nihon Joseishi*, vol. 1, pp. 75–6; Hosoi Wakizō, *Jokō Aishi* (1925, 1988 edn), pp. 194–6; Molony, 'Activism among women', p. 232; Sievers, *Flowers in Salt*, pp. 66–76; Janet Hunter, 'Textile factories, tuberculosis and the quality of life in industrializing Japan', in Janet Hunter (ed.), *Japanese Women Working* (London, 1993), pp. 87–8; Patricia Tsurumi, *Factory Girls* (Princeton, 1990), pp. 67–8; Kawai Yōko, 'Dokusen shihon no keisei to jokō no kekkaku' in Joseishi Sōgō Kenkyūkai (ed.), *Nihon Joseishi*, vol. 5 (1982, 1985 edn), pp. 44–5.

[192] Yamamoto, *Aa Nomugi Tōge*, pp. 152–4; Ōshima Eiko, 'Ryōtaisenkan no joshi rōdō: bōseki, seishi jokō o chūshin ni', in Joseishi Sōgō Kenkyūkai (ed.), *Nihon Joseishi*, vol. 5 (1982, 1985 edn), pp. 7–8; Sievers, *Flowers in Salt*, p. 77; Hunter, 'Textile factories', pp. 74–83; Tsurumi, *Factory Girls*, pp. 169–72.

[193] Sakurai, *Bosei Hogo Undōshi*, p. 40; Mackie, *Creating Socialist Women in Japan*, p. 76.

[194] Sakurai, *Bosei Hogo Undōshi*, p. 40; Yoneda, *Kindai Nihon Joseishi*, vol. 1, p. 205.

[195] Sakurai, *Bosei Hogo Undōshi*, pp. 39–40.

organised many public meetings, submitted draft bills to the Diet,
and pressurised the Government. As a result, a factory law was finally
enacted in 1911, coming into effect in 1916. Even so, the Government
greatly compromised with employers, and the law was of little utility.
For example, it stipulated that female operatives should work twelve
hours a day, but they could work for fourteen hours for the first
fifteen years after its enactment.[196] The Law 'banned' women's later-
night work (between 10 p.m. and 4 a.m.), but this ban did not apply
to female shift workers for the first fifteen years after its enactment.
Only five weeks maternity leave was given, and this did not cover
the period before childbirth. This factory legislation therefore was
largely ineffectual in protecting female workers, being little more than
a token gesture by the government.

The Women's Reform Movement before the Seitō Society

Some historians have argued that the Seitō Society launched the first
women's movement in Japan.[197] However, prior to it there were
other movements and societies advocating an improvement in women's
status. At the beginning of the Meiji period, steps to upgrade women's
position began to be taken by male intellectuals like Fukuzawa Yukichi,
Mori Arinori and Nakamura Masanao, who had been to the west
to study.[198] These men founded the Meirokusha (the Meiji Six Society)

---

[196] *Ibid.*, p. 41; Yoneda, *Kindai Nihon Joseishi*, vol. 1, p. 205; Mackie, *Creating Socialist Women*, p. 76; Molony, 'The Japanese debate over motherhood protection, 1915–50', pp. 124.

[197] Tatewaki, *Nihon no Fujin*, p. 1; Higuchi, *Nihon Joseishi Hakkutsu*, p. 157.

[198] Itoya, *Meiji Ishin*, p. 99. Fukuzawa Yukichi (1835–1901), a prominent educator, studied Dutch, and went to America and Europe on Bakufu service. He studied western civilization and introduced aspects of western thought to Japan in the Meiji period. He founded Keiō Gijuku (now Keiō University) and launched a newspaper *Jiji Shinpō* in 1882. On Fukuzawa Yukichi, see Fukuzawa Yukichi (trans. by Eiichi Kiyooka), *The Autobiography of Fukuzawa Yukichi* (1960, 1981 edn); Carmen Blacker, *The Japanese Enlightenment: A Study of the Writings of Fukuzawa Yukichi* (1964, Cambridge, 1969 edn). Mori Arinori (1847–1889) went to Britain to study in 1865. On his return, he joined the new Meiji government and was sent to America, China and England as Japan's envoy. He served in Itō Hirobumi's cabinet as Education Minister from 1885. Mori was assassinated by a Shintoist extremist on 11 February 1889. On Mori Arinori, see Ivan Parker Hall, *Mori Arinori* (Cambridge, Mass., 1973); Ōkubo Toshiaki, *Mori Arinori Zenshū*, 3 vols (1971).

in January 1873, and published its journal *Meiroku Zasshi* (*The Meiji Six Journal*) from March 1874.[199] They advocated the positive adoption of western education, life-styles and ideas.[200] Although all members of the Society had belonged to the warrior class, they were critical of the male-dominated Confucian social order. They even stated that the long-lived convention of *danson johi* (males respected, females despised) and unequal position of women characterised an uncivilized country, and prevented Japan from making progress.[201] They disdained 'feudal' ideas about marriage and discrimination against women, and advocated the need to abolish such concepts and mores, and to encourage women to have independence and self-respect. They were influenced by English utilitarianism, especially the social theories of John Stuart Mill and Herbert Spencer, and they supported western advanced teaching on human rights and equal opportunities between the sexes.[202]

Fukuzawa Yukichi, who was particularly influenced by J. S. Mill, strongly criticised older ideas and advocated equality regardless of class and sex.[203] His book *Gakumon no Susume* (*An Encouragement of Learning*) (1872–76), gave his perspective on human rights.[204] The famous starting passage, '*Ten wa hito no ue ni hito o tsukurazu hito no shita ni hito o tsukurazu*' ('It is said that heaven does not create a man above or below another.'), highlighted a more western approach to equality.[205]

---

[199] On the Meirokusha, see Tanaka (ed.), *Josei Kaihō no Shisō*, pp. 22–41; Itoya, *Meiji Ishin*, pp. 99–105; Morosawa, *Onna no Rekishi*, vol. 2, pp. 23–36; Sōgō Joseishi Kenkyūkai (ed.), *Bunka to Shisō*, pp. 183–5; Takamure, *Josei no Rekishi*, vol. 2, pp. 206–24; Inoue, *Nihon Joseishi*, pp. 210–2; Sotozaki, *Nihon Fujin Ronshi*, vol. 1, pp. 10–30; Yoneda, *Kindai Nihon Joseishi*, vol. 1, pp. 25–8; Sievers, *Flowers in Salt*, pp. 16–7; Mackie, *Creating Socialist Women*, pp. 24–5. On *Meiroku Zasshi*, see William Reynolds Braisted, *Meiroku Zasshi: Journal of the Japanese Enlightenment* (Cambridge, Mass., 1976).

[200] Yamashita Etsuko, *Nihon Josei Kaihō Shisō no Kigen* (1988), pp. 34–5; Nozaki Kinue, 'Mori Arinori, Fukuzawa Yukichi, Ueki Emori no joseiron', in Ichibangase Yasuko (ed.), *Nyūmon Josei Kaihōron* (1975), pp. 193–222.

[201] Tanaka (ed.), *Josei Kaihō no Shisō*, p. 26; Watanabe Tokusaburō, *Fukuzawa Yukichi: Katei Kyōiku no Susume* (1985), pp. 158–72; Hane, *Reflections on the Way to the Gallows*, pp. 7–8.

[202] Takamure, *Josei no Rekishi*, vol. 2, p. 206; Sōgō Joseishi Kenkyūkai (ed.), *Bunka to Shisō*, p. 184.

[203] Morosawa, *Onna no Rekishi*, vol. 2, pp. 23–5; Takamure, *Josei no Rekishi*, vol. 2, p. 206; Watanabe, *Fukuzawa Yukichi*, pp. 158–72; Sievers, *Flowers in Salt*, pp. 18–25.

[204] Fukuzawa Yukichi, *Gakumon no Susume* (1872–76, 1998 edn).

[205] Quotation taken from Fukuzawa Yukichi (trans. by D. A. Dilworth), *An Encouragement of Learning* (1969).

He held all people equal by nature, and openly disapproved of *Onna Daigaku*:

> *Onna Daigaku* preaches the teaching of three obediences for women . . . It is understandable for girls to obey their parents when young, but it is unreasonable for them to obey their husbands. According to the teaching of *Onna Daigaku*, wives should obey their husbands, honour and respect them even though their husbands lead dissipated lives, indulging themselves in drinking and visiting brothels, abusing their wives and scolding their children severely . . . In other words, once women marry they have no choice but to endure even lewd husbands, or husbands who commit adultery, no matter how wives are insulted or humiliated by husbands . . . *Shichikyo* [seven reasons for husbands to divorce wives], as also preached in *Onna Daigaku*, one-sidedly blames women . . . The teaching of *Onna Daigaku* suits husbands' convenience, and is extremely biased.[206]

Fukuzawa stated that '*Otoko mo hito nari onna mo hito nari*' (A man is a human being and a woman is also a human being).[207] He wrote that men's tyrannical misconduct towards women ought to be banned, and that women should receive freedom as well as the right to equal education, since they are no less human than men.[208] In *Gakumon no Susume* he also raised objections to polygamy:

> The practice of a husband keeping not only a legal wife but also a few mistresses violates the laws of nature. Such conduct is no better than a beast's . . . In my opinion, the household in which both a legal wife and a mistress are kept by a husband cannot be classed as a decent human being's house, but is a '*chikurui no koya*' [beast's pen]. I have never heard of a legal wife, living under the same roof as her husband's mistress, getting on well with the mistress. One must not forget that mistresses are human beings. A husband who takes a mistress because of a temporary obsession, treats her like a beast, corrupts morals in his family, and causes damage to his descendants. He ought to be called a criminal.[209]

Fukuzawa spoke for women who could not easily speak for themselves, and he denounced scathingly the idea of *danson johi*. His book

---

[206] Fukuzawa, *Gakumon no Susume*, pp. 77–8. This is my translation, partly using Dilworth's translation. See, Fukuzawa, *An Encouragement of Learning*, p. 52.

[207] Fukuzawa, *Gakumon no Susume*, p. 77.

[208] *Ibid.*, p. 77.

[209] *Ibid.*, pp. 78–9.

Gakumon no Susume was regarded by many Japanese as an ideal guide book, providing readers with advice as to how to live in the new era.[210] It was widely read by educated men and women of all ages, and became a best-seller in the early Meiji period.[211] After this he wrote and spoke on other women's issues. He published two critiques of the *Onna Daigaku* (*The Greater Learning for Women*).[212] In '*Onna Daigaku* hyōron' Fukuzawa criticised *Onna Daigaku* for teaching the domination of men over women, and for lacking humanity.[213] He stated that since the feudal period was over, 'feudalistic' morals from the Edo period were no longer valid. In 'Shin *Onna Daigaku*' Fukuzawa expressed a view about how women's education in a civilized society ought to replace *Onna Daigaku*.[214] In 1885 he wrote a series of articles entitled 'On Japanese women' for the *Meiroku Zasshi*, of which he was an editor, which included discussion of women's problems and issues of educational reform affecting women.[215] His writing and articles on women in the *Meiroku Zasshi* had a considerable impact on women, raising awareness of discrimination.[216]

Mori Arinori, another leading member of the Meirokusha, showed much interest in women's education, and also believed in equality of the sexes.[217] He wrote an article entitled 'Saishōron' ('Discussion of wives and concubines'), which was serialised in the *Meiroku Zasshi*.[218]

---

[210] Morosawa, *Onna no Rekishi*, vol. 2, p. 24.

[211] Aida Kurakichi, *Fukuzawa Yukichi* (1974), p. 181; Sōgō Joseishi Kenkyūkai (ed.), *Bunka to Shisō*, p. 184; Fukuzawa, *The Autobiography of Fukuzawa Yukichi*, p. 54.

[212] These were 'Shin *Onna Daigaku*' ('The new *Greater Learning for Women*'), which was written in the manner of J. S. Mill's *The Subjection of Women*, and '*Onna Daigaku* hyōron' ('The critique of *The Greater Learning for Women*'). See Fukuzawa Yukichi, *Onna Daigaku Hyōron, Shin Onna Daigaku* (1899); Fukuzawa Yukichi (trans. and ed. by Eiichi Kiyooka), *Fukuzawa Yukichi on Japanese Women* (1988), pp. 170–244.

[213] Nozaki, 'Mori Arinori, Fukuzawa Yukichi, Ueki Emori no joseiron', p. 210–1.

[214] Fukuzawa Yukichi, 'Shin *Onna Daigaku*', *Jiji Shinpo* (14 April – 23 July, 1899), reprinted in Mitsui (ed.), *Nihon Fujin Mondai Shiryō Shūsei*, vol. 4, pp. 336–48.

[215] Nozaki, 'Mori Arinori, Fukuzawa Yukichi, Ueki Emori no joseiron', pp. 207–8; Fukuzawa, *Fukuzawa Yukichi on Japanese Women*, pp. 6–69.

[216] Sotozaki, *Nihon Fujin Ronshi*, vol. 2, p. 28.

[217] Itoya, *Meiji Ishin*, pp. 100–1; Yoneda, *Kindai Nihon Joseishi*, vol. 1, p. 26; Sievers, *Flowers in Salt*, pp. 20–2; Hall, *Mori Arinori*, pp. 233–45.

[218] Mori Arinori, 'Saishōron', *Meiroku Zasshi*, 8, 11, 15, 22 & 27 (1874–1875), reprinted in Yuzawa (ed.), *Nihon Fujin Mondai Shiryō Shūsei*, vol. 5, pp. 341–6. Braisted translated Mori's 'Saishōron'. William Reynolds Braisted, *Meiroku Zasshi* (Cambridge, Mass., 1976), pp. 104–5, 143–5, 189–91, 252–3.

In it he criticised traditional marriage, which allowed a husband to keep concubines:

> In our country it is still customary and is considered perfectly accept-able that a husband treats his wife as his servant, has one or more mistresses, and in many cases keeps both wife and mistress under the same roof. This highlights the fact that marriage in our country is merely nominal, and that there is no substance in it.[219]

In part 5 of 'Saishōron' Mori blamed the legal system for damaging relationships between many husbands and wives. He tentatively drafted his ideal marriage law on the basis of such law in western countries.[220] His draft stipulated that it was absolutely vital for both persons to consent to marriage, and that it was necessary to abolish forced marriage. Any man over twenty-five and any woman over twenty should be free to marry without approval from parents or family heads. Any marriage arranged by deception or the exercise of parents' or others' power over the parties concerned was not valid, and ought to be cancelled. Husband and wife should not commit bigamy. Wives could claim divorce if they were ill-treated by their husbands or they found out that their husbands had committed adultery. In the event of divorce under these circumstances, wives could obtain 'consolation' money. Wedding ceremonies had to have a witness and official approval. This proposed marriage law was radically new, and was modelled on monogamy as supposedly practised in western societies. Considering that the great majority of marriages in Japan at that time were arranged by parents, Mori's proposal was far ahead of his time.

He also put his ideal of marriage into practice. When he married Hirose Atsune in 1875, he had the Governor of Tokyo Prefecture and Fukuzawa Yukichi as his main witnesses, and he signed a written agreement in which equality between husband and wife was mentioned.[221] He invited many other guests to his wedding to witness this. Ironically his new and advanced form of marriage, based on an equal union between husband and wife rather than a union

---

[219] Mori, 'Saishōron', p. 342.
[220] The outline of Mori's ideal marriage law is given in Mori, 'Saishōron', pp. 345–6.
[221] Itoya, *Meiji Ishin*, p. 103; Hall, *Mori Arinori*, pp. 251–3; Ōkubo Toshiaki (ed.), *Mori Arinori Zenshū*, vol. 1 (1972), p. 251.

between two families, came to a rather unfortunate end. His marriage was dissolved because his wife committed adultery.[222] No doubt
many Japanese men nodded sagely at this news. Even so, his ideas
and example probably influenced some of the more westernised
families.

Members of the Meirokusha such as Tsuda Mamichi and Nakamura
Masanao were also active.[223] Nakamura, who was a translator of
Mill's *On Liberty* and Samuel Smiles's *Self-Help*, spread ideas of self-
help and popular rights. He also wrote an article entitled 'Zenryō
naru haha o tsukuru setsu' ('The doctrine of creating good-natured
and honest mothers').[224] In it he discussed providing women and
men with equal education, which he felt was the prerequisite for
sexual equality. Tsuda Mamichi, an eminent legal scholar, submitted a petition on banning the slavery of women, and wrote an article entitled 'Haishōron' ('Discussion of the abolition of licensed
prostitution').[225]

The Meirokusha's concepts were based upon what they believed
to be a universal standard of 'civilization': to educate and develop
'reason', which they thought was immanent in any individual by
nature. There is little doubt that the Meirokusha not only had a
major influence in the proliferation of western views, especially
Enlightenment concepts, but also were significant in advocating
improved women's status. This was the first group to raise the issue
of women's emancipation in Japan. It broke new ground in setting
out two new theories to the public: one was the establishment of a
monogamous system, and the idea of gender equality. The Meirokusha
attempted to reform general views of women.

---

[222] Itoya, *Meiji Ishin*, p. 103.
[223] Sievers, *Flowers in Salt*, pp. 22–3; Tsuda Mamichi (1829–1903) was a legal
scholar and government official. He published the first book on western law written in Japanese entitled *Taisei Kokuhōron* (*On Western Law*) in 1868. He served in the
Genrōin (Chamber of Elders) and acted as vice-president of the Diet. Nakamura
Masanao (1832–1891) studied English and Dutch, and studied in England between
1866 and 1868 under the sponsorship of the Bakufu. He founded the Dōjinsha
School and later became principal of the Tokyo Girls' Higher School. He also
taught at Tokyo University. On Nakamura Masanao, see Braisted, *Meiroku Zasshi*,
pp. xxx–xxxi; Masaaki Kōsaka (ed.), *Japanese Thought in the Meiji Era* (1958), pp.
113–21.
[224] Nakamura Masanao, 'Zenryō naru haha o tsukuru setsu', *Meiroku Zasshi*, 33
(March, 1875), reprinted in Yuzawa (ed.), *Nihon Fujin Mondai Shiryō Shūsei*, vol. 5,
pp. 348–50.
[225] Sotozaki, *Nihon Fujin Ronshi*, p. 18; Braisted, *Meiroku Zasshi*, pp. 517–8.

However, the 'equality of the sexes' which the Meirokusha advocated was not the same as most late twentieth-century interpretations of that phrase. What was meant was extremely limited, and
applied to equality between husband and wife and to equitable property distribution. The idea of allowing women full equal political and
social rights never occurred to the Meirokusha. Even Fukuzawa
Yukichi stated that while men and women should be equal, this did
not mean that women should have equal rights to men.[226] His explanation was that men were physically different from women, so male
roles and rights ought to be different from women's. He believed
that women's roles were home-based. His womanly ideal was an
intellectual housewife in a modern family: a westernised version of
ryōsai kenbo (good wives and wise mothers). He believed that doing
away with Confucian customs, and improving women's status, health
and education, would produce more capable mothers who would
promote national strength. Mori Arinori and Nakamura Masanao
shared the view that a wife's most significant role was as a housewife and mother.[227] They emphasised women's education because
they believed that it would enable women to perform their assigned
duties more effectively. Tsuda Mamichi was opposed to equal rights
for the sexes, and stated that married couples' equal rights had never
existed in any civil code.[228] He referred favourably to the French
civil code, on which some features of Japanese government were
modelled. Ono Azusa, who had studied law in America and England,
introduced the term 'women's suffrage' to the public, but he was
utterly opposed to the idea:

> One must not even consider giving suffrage to women, mainly because
> women are completely dependent on men. Women are supported
> by their parents until their marriage. After marriage they belong
> to their husbands. Therefore it is natural for women not to have the
> franchise.[229]

These members had views on married women's rights and female
suffrage which were thus compatible with the policy of the Japanese
government, and its conception of Japan as a modern nation. They

---

[226] Tanaka (ed.), *Josei Kaihō no Shisō*, pp. 27–8.
[227] Itoya, *Meiji Ishin*, pp. 104–5; Nozaki, 'Mori Arinori, Fukuzawa Yukichi, Ueki
Emori no joseiron', pp. 203–4.
[228] Cited in Sotozaki Mitsuhiro, *Kōchiken Fujin Kaihō Undōshi* (1975), pp. 16–7.
[229] Cited in *ibid.*, p. 23.

had strong affiliations with such nationalism and regarded women as a useful tool of the state.[230] They were extremely keen on improving women's strength and intelligence to make them fitter mothers, to produce better-educated and stronger men who would become future leaders and enhance Japan's national strength.[231] Western eugenics showed its influence here. The Meirokusha never went beyond the limits of government policy in its thinking along these lines. It was entirely male-dominated, had no female members, and never made any effort to recruit them. Considering these points, and the small contribution its activities made for women, the Meirokusha cannot be classified as a 'women's emancipation movement' in any more modern sense.

Shortly after dissolution of the Meirokusha, the Jiyū Minken Undō (Freedom and People's Rights Movement) appeared.[232] This was originally based on conceptions of freedom and equality most associated with the French philosopher Jean Jacques Rousseau.[233] Like the Meirokusha, the Freedom and People's Rights Movement was affected by western ideas of gender equality. Its supporters were initially discontented *shizoku* (descendants of a samurai), but over the years it obtained support from more people, including poor farmers and even women.[234] The number of supporters was said to have risen to 200,000 by 1881, while the backers of the Meirokusha were a handful of intellectuals and government officials.[235] Compared to the Meirokusha, the Freedom and People's Rights Movement had much broader purposes. In 1874 it called for a Diet and a Constitution. It then changed political direction, demanding land-tax reduction and revision of the unequal Treaties. Over the years it further extended itself, calling for freedom of speech, equal opportunities for both sexes, and male suffrage. It helped to introduce ideas of women's equality and social and political rights in a more modern sense. It

---

[230] Morosawa, *Onna no Rekishi*, vol. 2, p. 31.

[231] Tanaka (ed.), *Josei Kaihō no Shisō*, pp. 39–41; Itoya, *Meiji Ishin*, pp. 104–7; Sotazaki, *Nihon Fujin Ronshi*, pp. 17–8.

[232] On the Jiyū Minken Undō, see Kōsaka (ed.), *Japanese Thought in the Meiji Era*, pp. 134–59; Mackie, *Creating Socialist Women*, pp. 26–7.

[233] Tanaka (ed.), *Josei Kaihō no Shisō*, p. 48; Miyagi *et al.* (eds), *Shinkō Nihon Joseishi*, p. 220.

[234] Itoya, *Meiji Ishin*, pp. 114–5.

[235] Tanaka (ed.), *Josei Kaihō no Shisō*, p. 43; Yoneda, *Kindai Nihon Joseishi*, vol. 1, p. 39.

also raised the issue of women's suffrage for the first time in Japan, through Itagaki Taisuke's petition in 1874.[236]

In these regards the Freedom and People's Rights Movement was more radical than the Meirokusha, which did not advocate female suffrage. Ueki Emori, one of the leading activists of the Freedom and People's Rights Movement, was much influenced by Herbert Spencer's view of women.[237] Spencer's *Social Statistics* and Mill's *The Subjection of Women*, with their analysis of female emancipation, were widely read by many others in the Freedom and People's Rights Movement. Spencer's *Social Statistics* became the Bible of the Freedom and People's Rights Movement.[238] Its male activists began to deliver speeches on these subjects, and helped to spread notions of women's equal rights. They also expressed such views on women through their writing. Doi Kōka wrote *Bunmeiron Onna Daigaku* (*Civilized Ideas of the Greater Learning for Women*) in 1876, in which he argued against the *ie* system and 'feudal' conventions.[239] In 1876 Hirayama Yasuhiko advocated women's suffrage in the second local governors' conference.[240] Ueki Emori wrote 'Tōyō no fujo' ('Oriental women') in 1887, urging women to seek freedom and equality.[241] He was considered the most radical activist working to upgrade women's status. When he campaigned for the establishment of the Diet, he submitted his own draft constitution, suggesting giving women the vote as well as eligibility for election.[242] He delivered speeches on the need for married couples' equal rights, stated the importance of domestic harmony, and advocated the abolition of licensed prostitution.

---

[236] Sotozaki, *Nihon Fujin Ronshi*, vol. 1, pp. 67–9; Itoya, *Meiji Ishin*, pp. 117–9. Itagaki Taisuke was an eminent politician in the Meiji period. He entered the new government in 1869, but resigned in 1873. He founded the Tosa Risshisha (Tosa Self-Help Society) in 1874 and the Aikokusha (Society of Patriots) in 1875. He then became a leader of the Freedom and People's Rights Movement. He also founded the Jiyūtō (Liberal Party) which was the first major political party in Japan. He entered Itō Hirobumi's cabinet as Home Minister in April 1896.

[237] Sotozaki, *Kōchiken Fujin Kaihō*, p. 28; Mackie, *Creating Socialist Women*, p. 27.

[238] Itoya, *Meiji Ishin*, p. 170; Tanaka (ed.), *Josei Kaihō no Shisō*, pp. 50–1.

[239] Miyagi *et al.* (eds), *Shinkō Nihon Joseishi*, p. 220; Morosawa, *Onna no Rekishi*, vol. 2, p. 36; Sotozaki, *Kōchiken Fujin Kaihō*, p. 16; Hirota Masaki, 'Bunmei kaika to josei kaihōron', in Joseishi Sōgō Kenkyūkai (ed.), *Nihon Joseishi*, vol. 4, p. 21.

[240] Tanaka (ed.), *Josei Kaihō no Shisō*, pp. 51–2.

[241] Nozaki, 'Mori Arinori, Fukuzawa Yukichi, Ueki Emori no joseiron', pp. 220–1.

[242] Tanaka (ed.), *Josei Kaihō no Shisō*, pp. 56–7; Yoneda, *Kindai Nihon Joseishi*, vol. 1, p. 42; Sotozaki, *Nihon Fujin Ronshi*, vol. 1, pp. 71–2; Sotozaki, *Kōchiken Fujin Kaihō*, pp. 40–1; Mackie, *Creating Socialist Women*, p. 27.

In many regards the contribution of the Freedom and People's Rights Movement to women's causes was far more significant than that of the Meirokusha, and it also encouraged women's participation. Responding to such radical male encouragement, many women from different classes and age groups began to take part in the Freedom and People's Rights Movement.[243] They attended its speech meetings, and became more aware of sexual discrimination and inequality. Kusunose Kita, who lived in Tōjin-machi, Kōchi City, Tosa, was an example.[244] Tosa became the centre of the Freedom and People's Rights Movement after the Risshisha (a local political organisation) was founded there in April 1874 by Itagaki Taisuke.[245] Speech meetings to promote the Freedom and People's Rights Movement were held, and many people living locally, including women, attended them. Kusunose became a regular attender. It was through her close associations with the Freedom and People's Rights Movement that she became familiar with ideas of people's rights and gained the confidence to speak out.[246] She became the first woman to demand female suffrage in Japan. The event which gave her the opportunity to do this was the first local election for members of a ward assembly in Tosa in 1878.[247] As she had heard that all heads of families were entitled to vote, Kusunose—who had been the (female) head of a family as well as a tax-payer since her husband's death in 1872—went to the ward office, expecting to vote for the election. However, she was told that she was debarred from voting because of her sex. She was so disillusioned with this that she refused to pay her tax.[248] She received letters demanding it from the local office. Responding to them, she wrote the following letter 'Nōzei no gi ni tsuki goshirei negai no koto' ('I ask for your instructions with regard to payment of taxes') to her prefectural office:

---

[243] Hayashi et al. (eds), Nihon Joseishi, pp. 196–7.

[244] An account of women in the Jiyū Minken Undō is given in Sotozaki, Kōchiken Fujin Kaihō, pp. 26–7; Hane, Reflections on the Way to the Gallows, p. 17; Sievers, Flowers in Salt, pp. 26–53; Mackie, Creating Socialist Women, p. 28.

[245] Itoya, Meiji Ishin, pp. 126–7; Sotozaki, Kōchiken Fujin Kaihō, p. 25.

[246] An account of Kusunose Kita is given in Itoya, Meiji Ishin, pp. 127–9; Yoneda, Kindai Nihon Joseishi, vol. 1, pp. 41–2; Sievers, Flowers in Salt, pp. 29–31; Sotozaki, Kōchiken Fujin Kaihō, pp. 26–7.

[247] Itoya, Meiji Ishin, p. 128; Hayashi et al. (eds), Nihon Joseishi, p. 196; Sotozaki, Kōchiken Fujin Kaihō, pp. 26–7.

[248] An account of Kusunose's complaint is given in Sotozaki, Kōchiken Fujin Kaihō, pp. 26–7.

Although I am a common woman, I have been the head of a family for some time, and have fulfilled various duties required as head of a family. Therefore I automatically assumed that the government gave all heads of families equal rights regardless of sex. However, I recently found that this is not the case. I was told that I have no right to vote even for members of the ward assembly as I am a woman. I was also told that for the same reason I am unable to stand surety as a guarantor for somebody's legal documents, although I have my registered legal seal. There is a world of difference between male and female heads of families in terms of rights. Since rights and duties are coextensive, it should logically be the case that if the head of a family has the right to vote, she has an obligation to pay tax; but if there is no vote, there should be no tax obligation. However, I have to pay tax although I have no right to vote. Considering this, I feel that my rights have been slighted. I am very dissatisfied with the current system and its arrangements. If the female family head's rights became exactly the same as the male head's, I would be happy to incur the same tax obligation as the male head ... I feel that the whole system is utterly illogical, so I cannot see why I ought to pay tax.[249]

This letter was very significant as a statement about the lack of votes for women tax-payers, being the first complaint of its kind by any woman in Japan.[250] She introduced the notion of enfranchising women on the grounds that tax-payers must not be deprived of representation. Replying to her, her prefectural office demanded that she should immediately pay her unpaid tax, because national law stipulated that the public had duties to pay taxes, and there was no provision that people's taxes might be varied depending upon the relative rights they had.[251] However, the prefectural office stated that the female head of a family could now stand surety for somebody.[252] As the prefectural office's reply did not satisfy Kusunose, she took the further step of sending a complaint to the Ministry of the Interior.[253] *The Tokyo Nichi Nichi Shinbun* reported Kusunose's case and suggested reasons for her conduct:

---

[249] Kusunose Kita's letter entitled 'Nōzei ni tsuki goshirei negai no koto', which was addressed to the Kōchi Prefectural Office, 16 September, 1878, cited in Sotozaki Mitsuhiro, *Meiji Zenki Fujin Kaihōronshi* (Kōchi, 1963), p. 77.

[250] Itoya, *Meiji Ishin*, p. 128; Sotozaki, *Nihon Fujin Ronshi*, vol. 1, p. 69.

[251] Yoneda, *Kindai Nihon Joseishi*, vol. 1, pp. 41–2.

[252] Sotozaki, *Meiji Zenki Fujin Kaihōronshi*, p. 78; Sotozaki, *Nihon Fujin Ronshi*, vol. 1, p. 71.

[253] Itoya, *Meiji Ishin*, p. 129; Sotozaki, *Kōchiken Fujin Kaihō*, p. 27.

Kusunose's efforts to attend virtually all the speech meetings organised by the Risshisha since 1877, regardless of the weather, has enabled her to become aware of her own rights and duties as a human being.[254]

Her argument confirmed that ideas of women's rights had finally penetrated some women's minds. Kusunose now began to share platforms advocating such rights with members of the Risshisha, and to campaign in Shikoku. As a result, she was nicknamed '*Minken Bāsan*' (the people's rights' Grandma).[255]

Her conduct and support from a few male members of the Risshisha proved effective, and helped to promote the suffrage campaign in Tosa. In 1880 one town (Kami Machi) and one village (Odakazaka Mura) in Kōchi took the initiative in enacting regulations endowing women with eligibility for election, as well as the right to vote for members of an assembly.[256] This was the first occurrence of such practice in Japan. It exerted an immeasurable influence on women in Kōchi. Unfortunately it was promptly suppressed by the intervention of a Kōchi Prefectural ordinance.[257]

Apart from Kusunose Kita, the Freedom and People's Rights Movement also recruited better known female orators such as Kishida Toshiko and Fukuda Hideko, who delivered speeches on women's equal rights.[258] Kishida delivered the first speech 'Fujo no michi' ('Women's way') at a political meeting organised by the Rikken Seitō

---

[254] *The Tokyo Nichi Nichi Shinbun* (31 January, 1879).

[255] Hayashi *et al.* (eds), *Nihon Joseishi*, p. 221; Yoneda, *Kindai Nihon Joseishi*, vol. 1, pp. 41–2; Miyagi *et al.* (eds), *Shinkō Nihon Joseishi*, p. 221. Kusunose continued to have close contacts with some of the active participants in the Jiyū Minken Undō such as Kōno Hironaka after it came to an end. See letter from Kusunose Kita to Kōno Hironaka, 6 December, 1903 (Kōno Hironaka Documents, the National Diet Library Archive).

[256] Sotozaki, *Nihon Fujin Ronshi*, vol. 1, p. 71; Sotozaki, *Kōchiken Fujin Kaihō*, pp. 27–8; Hane, *Reflections on the Way to the Gallows*, p. 17.

[257] Itoya, *Meiji Ishin*, p. 131.

[258] Hane, *Reflections on the Way to the Gallows*, pp. 17–8; Mackie, *Creating Socialist Women*, p. 28. Kishida Toshiko (1863–1901) worked in the imperial court and served Empress Shōken (Emperor Meiji's wife), teaching her Chinese and Japanese classics. After she left the court, she was involved in the Freedom and People's Rights Movement. On Kishida Toshiko, see Sharon L. Sievers, 'Feminist criticism in Japanese politics in the 1880s: the experience of Kishida Toshiko', *Signs*, 6:4 (Summer 1981), pp. 602–16; Sievers, *Flowers in Salt*, pp. 33–48; Suzuki Yūko, 'Kaisetsu', in Kishida Toshiko (ed. by Suzuki Yūko), *Kishida Toshiko Hyōronshū* (1985), pp. 9–28; Itoya Toshio, *Josei Kaihō no Senkushua: Nakajima Toshiko to Fukuda Hideko* (1984), pp. 16–98; Tanaka Ariko, 'Kishida Toshiko', in Setouchi Harumi (ed.), *Shin Jidai no Paioniatachi* (1989), pp. 164–96.

(the Rikken Political Party), held at the Asahiza (Asahi Theatre) in Dōtonbori, Osaka on 1 April, 1882.[259] The *Hōchi Shinbun* (Hōchi Newspaper) reported the event:

> After many well-known male speakers finished their speeches, the next speaker who entered the stage was Kishida Toshiko ... As she came on stage, the audience immediately cheered. She is a woman who had never made any political speeches before, and so people in her party had no idea how competent she would be as a public speaker. They began to fear for the quality of her speech, but their doubts soon cleared away. Although her voice was high-pitched, it was very clear and it rang like a bell through the theatre. Moreover, her speech was so well-constructed, convincing, persuasive and fluent that it made a great impression on the audience. As women's speeches are very rare, the audience, who had never heard a woman's speech before, were overwhelmed with such amazement that they couldn't stop clapping in applause.[260]

Kishida was the first woman to raise issues such as sexual equality and anti-female discrimination in public and before a mixed audience.[261] She set out on a campaigning tour of the Kansai, Kinki, Shikoku, Chūgoku and Kyūshū regions, speaking on women's issues.[262] Many women heard her speeches, and some joined the Freedom and People's Rights Movement as a result. Fukuda Hideko reported on Kishida's speeches in Okayama, and discussed the impact they had on local women.

> Well-known Kishida Toshiko came to my area to give speeches. I went to hear them for three days. Every day the hall was packed. Her speeches were extremely fluent, and she advocated noble causes such as the extension of women's rights. Her speeches roused me to action. During her visit, I consulted interested local women who had heard her speeches and were also inspired by them, and we organised a women's social meeting, which helped to promote women's coopera-

---

[259] *Nihon Rikken Seitō Shinbun* (15 March, 1882). The *Rikken Seitō* was founded in Osaka by Nakajima Nobuyuki (who later became Kishida's husband) as a branch of the Jiyūtō (the Liberal Party).

[260] Cited in Morosawa, *Onna no Rekishi*, vol. 2, pp. 70–1.

[261] Suzuki, 'Kaisetsu', pp. 10–2.

[262] Itoya, *Meiji Ishin*, pp. 138–40; *Nihon Rikken Seitō Shinbun*, 47 (9 May, 1882); *Sanyō Shinpō*, 960 (13 May, 1882); *Futsu Shinbun*, 1809 (27 June, 1882); *Asano Shinbun*, 2616 (2 July, 1882); *Jiyū Shinbun*, 4 (4 July, 1882); *Asano Shinbun*, 2636 (26 July, 1882), *Kumanoto Shinbun*, 1386 (31 October, 1882), *Kumamoto Shinbun*, 1387 (1 November, 1882); *Asano Shinbun*, 2724 (15 November, 1882), *Jiyū Shinbun*, 120 (26 November, 1882).

tion. Even after her visit, we continued to invite guest speakers who lectured on women's issues.[263]

Kishida's most memorable speech was 'Hakoiri musume' ('Daughters-in-a-box'), which she gave on 12 October 1883 in Ōtsu.[264] She criticised parents' over-protective education of daughters, and encouraged them to release sheltered daughters from confined boxes (i.e. restrictions set by parents), and to give them greater freedom:

> *Hakoiri musume*, in my definition, are girls who cannot act, cannot talk, cannot even move their hands and feet, as if they were trapped in a box... Their parents may say, "Well, we're not doing this to limit her freedom, but to give her a good moral education, and because we love her." However, they don't realize that their actions do end up limiting girls' freedom and causing them pain.[265]

Kishida stressed that the speech she gave was purely academic, intended to upgrade women's education.[266] However, the police insisted that her talk violated article ten of Shūkai Jōrei (the Assembly Regulation), which had been amended in July 1882.[267] The police accused her of pretending to deliver an academic address, but of actually making a political speech. They were sure that this violated the Shūkai Jōrei, which laid down that 'in an academic meeting a speaker must not discuss or give a lecture on political issues'. The police were convinced that her term 'box' meant the Shūkai Jōrei, which had been instituted to control freedom of speech and attendance at political meetings. It was also felt that her terms 'parents' meant the government, 'daughters' the people, and 'a manservant and a maidservant' the police. The police interpreted her speech as direct criticism of government policy to keep freedom of speech under control. Immediately after the meeting she was arrested, sent to prison and fined five yen.[268] After release, she gave up speaking in public, but contributed to a small newspaper *Jiyū no Tomoshibi* (*A Light of Freedom*) edited by Hoshi Tōru, which supported the Jiyūtō

---

[263] Fukuda Hideko, *Warawa no Hanseigai* (1904, 1970 edn), pp. 15–6.

[264] Kishida's speech entitled 'Hakoiri musume' was printed in Kishida, *Kishida Toshiko Hyōronshū*, pp. 213–9.

[265] *Ibid.*, p. 214.

[266] *Jiyū Shinbun*, 385 (19 October, 1883).

[267] The full account of the police is given in Kishida, *Kishida Toshiko Hyōronshū*, pp. 207–28.

[268] *Jiyū Shinbun*, 391 (26 October, 1883); *Nihon Rikken Seitō Shinbun* (15–22 November, 1883).

(the Liberal Party).[269] Kishida's article 'Dōhō shimai ni tsugu' ('Appealing to my fellow countrywomen') was serialised in this newspaper in 1883.[270] In it she wrote:

> There are various wicked manners and customs which have existed from ancient times. Of these, the worst that I can think of is the way in which men are valued and women devalued, which is completely nonsensical. Human society consists of men and women, and it is impossible for men alone to construct the world. If women disappear, it will be the end of the world . . . In the beginning women had equal rights to men. However, men resorted to violence, a barbarous method, and always oppressed women, which was a big mistake.[271]

She gave much evidence showing that women were not inferior to men in intelligence and financial acumen. She continued to write articles on women's rights for *Jogaku Zasshi* (*Women's Educational Magazine*), but after she married Nakajima Nobuyuki in 1884, she retired from the Movement.[272] However, she had influenced many young Japanese women, including Tomii Oto, Shimizu Shikon and Fukuda Hideko.[273]

Of these, Fukuda Hideko became a prominent activist in the People's Freedom and Rights Movement.[274] She realised that the only way to release women from an enslaved condition was financial independence for them.[275] She believed that female education would help to achieve that, and she worked as a school teacher for the betterment of female education. Her encounter with Kishida Toshiko in 1882 raised her awareness of women's rights. She founded a small women's liberal group called the Okayama Joshi Kondankai (the

---

[269] Itoya, *Meiji Ishin*, p. 142.
[270] Kishida Toshiko, 'Dōhō shimai ni tsugu', *Jiyū no Tomoshibi*, 2–32 (18 May, 1884 – 22 June, 1884), reprinted in Kishida, *Kishida Toshiko Hyōronshū*, pp. 54–78.
[271] *Ibid.*, p. 55.
[272] Itoya, *Josei Kaihō no Senkusha*, pp. 83–9; Suzuki, 'Kaisetsu', pp. 24–6.
[273] Sōgō Joseishi Kenkyūkai (ed.), *Bunka to Shisō*, p. 187.
[274] An account of Fukuda Hideko's involvement in the Freedom and People's Rights Movement is given in Fukuda Hideko, 'Jiyū Minken jidai no fujin seiji undō', *Fusen*, 1: 2–4 (February-April 1927), reprinted in Ichikawa (ed.), *Nihon Fujin Mondai Shiryō Shūsei*, vol. 2, pp. 95–101; Hane, *Reflections on the Way to the Gallows*, pp. 29–33; Sievers, *Flowers in Salt*, pp. 48–51. A biographical sketch of Fukuda is given in Appendix 1. On Fukuda, see Murata Shizuko, *Fukuda Hideko: Fujin Kaihō Undō no Senkusha* (1959); Fukuda, *Warawa no Hanseigai*; Itoya, *Josei Kaihō no Senkusha*, pp. 100–187; Marukawa Kayoko, 'Fukuda Hideko', in Setouchi Harumi (ed.), *Hangyaku no Roman* (1989), pp. 54–93.
[275] Inoue, *Nihon Joseishi*, p. 222.

Informal Discussion Gathering for Women in Okayama).[276] In 1883 Fukuda set up a private girls' school called Jōkō Gakusha, with an ideology of freedom and people's rights, adopting ideas of advanced education. Her school was ordered to close by a prefectural ordinance. It was accused of violating the Shūkai Jōrei (the Assembly Regulation), and the law to suppress freedom of speech, which prohibited students and teachers from attending meetings to discuss political issues.[277] After the closure, she went to Tokyo and participated in the anti-government campaign.[278] She mixed with many leading members of the Freedom and People's Rights Movement, including Itagaki Taisuke and Ōi Kentarō. She became involved in the Osaka Jiken (the Osaka Incident), which was led by Ōi Kentarō, was found guilty in November 1885 of a political crime, and imprisoned.[279] Among the sixty-three defendants involved in the incident, she was the only woman. As a result she received much publicity, and gained the nickname '*Tōyō no Jannu Daruku*' ('The Joan of Arc of the Orient'), a rather curious historical comparison.[280] By then Kishida had retired from the Movement, and Fukuda took over her position, becoming an idol to her young female supporters.[281]

Unlike most of their male counterparts, these female activists were highly committed, lost no opportunity to put views of women's equal rights into practice, and were extremely successful in propagating their ideas and gaining support from other women. While the female activists lived up to their principles, the male activists showed many contradictions between what they said in public and what they did in their private lives. The men supported monogamy in theory, but

---

[276] Itoya, *Josei Kaihō no Senkusha*, pp. 107–8; Murata, *Fukuda Hideko*, pp. 19–24; *Sanyō Shinpo*, 960 (13 May, 1882); *Asahi Shinbun*, 981 (31 May, 1882); *Nihon Rikken Seitō Shinbun*, 64 (1 July, 1882).

[277] Itoya, *Josei Kaihō no Senkusha*, pp. 108–11; Murata, *Fukuda Hideko*, pp. 24–6; *Jiyū Shinbun* (13 August, 1884).

[278] Itoya, *Josei Kaihō no Senkusha*, pp. 111–5; Murata, *Fukuda Hideko*, pp. 28–48.

[279] Fukuda Hideko, 'Gokuchū jukkai', in Suzuki Yūko (ed.), *Josei: Hangyaku to Kakumei to Teikō to* (1990), pp. 16–22. The Osaka Incident was an anti-government plot to create a disturbance in Korea large enough to agitate the Meiji government. However, the plan failed and about 130 people mostly in Osaka, including Fukuda Hideko and Ōi Kentarō, were arrested. An account of the Osaka Incident is in Hane, *Reflections on the Way to the Gallows*, pp. 39–50; Itoya, *Josei Kaihō no Senkusha*, pp. 121–45.

[280] *Kaishin Shinbun* (11 December, 1885).

[281] Inoue, *Nihon Joseishi*, pp. 223–4.

many of them had mistresses and concubines.[282] Ueki Emori was an extreme case of hypocrisy. Though he was considered the most progressive activist working to upgrade women's status, his progressive ideas on women's emancipation and his private life were poles apart: he was highly dissipated, frequenting brothels and completely neglecting his wife.[283]

Fukuda was very disappointed with her male counterparts' loose morals and poor discipline. Many of them retained and practised very patriarchal ideas. She concluded that her male fellow thinkers were most unreliable and no better than men opposed to women's emancipation.[284] The female activists were more consistent, and they showed that Japanese women could make political speeches and conduct political campaigns. This boded well for the future amelioration of women's position. Equal rights between the sexes and women's suffrage became more widely discussed. The old view of *danson johi* seemed to be fading. However, the promulgation of the Shūkai Oyobi Seisha Hō (Assembly and Political Organisation Law) in July 1890 made it illegal for any woman to join a political party, organise a political association, or attend a political movement.[285] Female activists of the Freedom and People's Rights Movement were forced to give up their campaigns in 1890. This effectively terminated the first Japanese women's movement launched by women.[286] Early hopes were thwarted in the 1890s, as the Assembly and Political Organisation Law, the Meiji Civil Code, the Meiji Constitution, the Imperial Rescript on Education and the Peace Police Law reinforced Confucian ideas and the *ie* system, and depressed Japanese women's status.[287]

This raises the question of whether a women's movement existed between 1890 and 1911. Before 1890 women's issues were first discussed by the Meirokusha and the Freedom and People's Rights Movement. In both cases well-educated men, influenced by western

---

[282] Morosawa, *Onna no Rekishi*, vol. 2, pp. 93–5.

[283] Tanaka (ed.), *Josei Kaihō no Shisō*, p. 61; Itoya, *Meiji Ishin*, p. 178.

[284] Yoneda, *Kindai Nihon Joseishi*, vol. 1, p. 46; Morosawa, *Onna no Rekishi*, vol. 2, pp. 94–5.

[285] Takamure, *Josei no Rekishi*, vol. 2, p. 233. See also 'Shūkai oyobi Seisha Hō', *Hōritsu*, 53 (25 July, 1890), reprinted in Ichikawa (ed.), *Nihon Fujin Mondai Shiryō Shūsei*, vol. 2, pp. 131–4.

[286] Miyagi *et al.* (eds), *Shinkō Nihon Joseishi*, p. 222.

[287] Samuel Hideo Yamashita, 'Confucianism and the Japanese state, 1904–1945', in Tu Wei-Mung (ed.), *Confucian Traditions in East Asian Modernity* (Cambridge, Mass., 1996), p. 132.

thinkers, took the initiative in advocating sexual equality, and the promotion of women's education and political rights. No women's participation occurred in the Meirokusha, and women made minor contributions to the Freedom and People's Rights Movement. This contrasted with the emergence of women's movements in countries like Britain and America, where women took the initiative.[288] However, the women's movement in Japan took a new direction after 1890. From then women began to take positive action to found women's associations, which finally launched campaigns demanding female political rights. The first women's group which took political action was the Tokyo Kirisutokyō Fujin Kyōfūkai (Tokyo Women's Christian Temperance Union) founded in 1886.[289] Its members submitted the first petition to the Prime Minister requesting amendment of the Shūkai Oyobi Seisha Hō (Assembly and Political Organisation Law) to allow women to attend political meetings.[290] The amendment of this law was also discussed in *Jogaku Zasshi* (*Women's Educational Magazine*).[291]

The Nihon Kirisutokyō Fujin Kyōfūkai (Japan Women's Christian Temperance Union) founded in 1893, an offshoot from the Tokyo Women's Christian Temperance Union), campaigned for two issues— to establish monogamy, and to control the practice of sending Japanese prostitutes abroad.[292] It submitted petitions on these matters to the Diet.[293] It also organised many public meetings for women and

[288] Barbara Ryan, *Feminism and the Women's Movement* (New York, 1992), pp. 9–16; Olive Banks, *Faces of Feminism* (Oxford, 1981), pp. 28–47.

[289] 'Fujin Kyōfūkai setsuritsu, yakuin oyobi kiyaku', *Jogaku Zasshi*, 44 (15 December, 1886), reprinted in Ichikawa (ed.), *Nihon Fujin Mondai Shiryō Shūsei*, vol. 1 (1978), pp. 206–7; Asai Saku, 'Kyōfūkai no mokuteki', *Tokyo Fujin Kyōfū Zasshi*, 1 (April, 1888), reprinted in Ichikawa (ed.), *Nihon Fujin Mondai Shiryō Shūsei*, vol. 1, pp. 211–3.

[290] 'Fujin kenpaku', *Kokumin Shinbun* (3 August, 1890).

[291] 'Joshi no seidan bōchō', *Jogaku Zasshi*, 225 (9 August, 1890), reprinted in Ichikawa (ed.), *Nihon Fujin Mondai Shiryō Shūsei*, vol. 2, pp. 135–6; Shimizu Toyoko, 'Naze ni joshi wa seidan shūkai ni sanchōsuru koto o yurusarezaruka', *Jogaku Zasshi*, 228 (30 August, 1890), reprinted in Ichikawa (ed.), *Nihon Fujin Mondai Shiryō*, pp. 137–9.

[292] Itoya, *Meiji Ishin*, p. 202; Tanaka (ed.), *Josei Kaihō no Shisō*, pp. 90–1; Hayashi et al. (eds), *Nihon Joseishi*, pp. 204–5; Fukuchi, *Kindai Nihon Joseishi*, p. 84; Morosawa, *Onna no Rekishi*, vol. 2, pp. 98–108; Etsuko Kaji and Jean Inglis, 'Sisters against slavery: a look at anti-prostitution movements in Japan', *Ampo: Japan-Asia Quarterly Review*, 6:2 (Spring 1974), pp. 19–23. The Nihon Kirisutokyō Fujin Kyōfūkai, which was a nation-wide women's Christian organisation, later became the largest and most powerful women's organisation in Japan.

[293] Morosawa, *Onna no Rekishi*, vol. 2, p. 108; Mitsui, *Gendai Fujin Undōshi Nenpyō*, pp. 44–5.

founded a home in 1893 where ex-prostitutes could be accommo-
dated and rehabilitated.

After the enactment of the Peace Police Law, another women's
political campaign was launched by socialist women such as Imai
Utako and Nishikawa Fumiko from the Heiminsha (Commoners'
Society).[294] Their campaign focused on the amendment of Article 5
of the Peace Police Law, which remained a persistent obstacle to
women's political involvement.[295] They first submitted a petition of
459 signatures demanding amendment of the law to the House of
Representatives in 1905.[296] That petition was considered in the *seigan
iinkai* (Petition Committee) of the House, and their request for amendment of Clause 2, Article 5, of the Peace Police Law passed the
House of Representatives on 19 February 1906, only to be defeated

---

[294] Itoya, *Josei Kaihō no Senkusha*, pp. 169–71; Ōki Motoko, 'Meiji shakai shugi
undō to josei', in Joseishi Sōgō Kenkyūkai (ed.), *Nihon Joseishi*, vol. 4, pp. 122–4;
Mackie, *Creating Socialist Women in Japan*, pp. 62–4. On the women of the Commoners'
Society, see Nishikawa Fumiko (ed. by Amano Shigeru), *Heiminsha no Onna: Nishikawa
Fumiko Jiden* (1984).

[295] The Chian Keisatsu Hō (Peace Police Law) had been passed on 10 March
1900. Clause 1 of Article 5 stipulated that people belonging to any of the following categories were forbidden to join political organisations:
   1. Army and navy officers on active service, or those who are called up for
      service in the armed forces, or those who are reserve troops.
   2. Policemen.
   3. Shinto priests, Buddhist monks and the teachers of other religious sects.
   4. Teachers and students of state, prefectural and private schools.
   5. Women.
   6. Minors.
   7. People who were deprived of their civil rights or suspended from them.
      Clause 2, Article 5, provided that women and minors were forbidden to
      organise or attend political assemblies. Under this women were deprived of
      political rights, and were excluded from almost all overt political activities.
See 'Chian Kensatsu Hō', *Hōritsu*, 36, (10 March, 1900), p. 139, reprinted in Ichikawa
(ed.), *Nihon Fujin Mondai Shiryō Shūsei*, vol. 2, pp. 139–40.

[296] Kodama Katsuko, *Fujin Sanseiken Undō Shōshi* (1981), pp. 29–30; 'Heiminsha
no joseitachi ni yoru Chian Keisatsu Hō kaisei undō', *Dai Nijū Ikkai Teikoku Gikai
Shūgiin Giji Sokkiroku*, 22 (28 February, 1905), reprinted in Ichikawa (ed.), *Nihon Fujin
Mondai Shiryō Shūsei*, vol. 2, pp. 140–4; 'Fujin no yōkyū', *Heimin Shinbun*, 62 (15
January, 1905), reprinted in Ichikawa (ed.), *Nihon Fujin Mondai Shiryō Shūsei*, vol. 2,
p. 140; 'Fujin no seiji undō ni kansuru seigan', *Heimin Shinbun*, 64 (29 January,
1905), reprinted in Ichikawa (ed.), *Nihon Fujin Mondai Shiryō Shūsei*, vol. 2, p. 141;
'Chian Keisatsu Hō Daigojō kaisei seigansho teishutsu', *Seigan Iinkai Tokubetsu Hōkoku*,
12 (25 January, 1905), reprinted in Ichikawa (ed.), *Nihon Fujin Mondai Shiryō Shūsei*,
vol. 2, pp. 141–2; 'Chian Keisatsu Hō seigan saitaku ni kansuru Shūgiin giji
sokkiroku', *Dai Nijū Ikkai Teikoku Gikai Shūgiin Giji Sokkiroku*, 22 (28 February, 1905),
reprinted in Ichikawa (ed.), *Nihon Fujin Mondai Shiryō Shūsei*, vol. 2, pp. 142–4.

in the House of Peers. After that they continued to submit petitions until 1907. Their campaign was followed (up to 1910) by that of Iwano Kiyoko, which was also blocked in the House of Peers.[297]

Sekai Fujin (*Women of the World*), launched by Fukuda Hideko, also played a significant part in this period of the women's movement in Japan. Fukuda, who had been active in the Freedom and People's Rights Movement, became closely associated with socialists such as Kōtoku Shūsui and Sakai Toshihiko, and she inaugurated *Sekai Fujin* in January, 1907.[298] It was the first women's socialist newspaper, and Fukuda clarified its main objective in the inaugural issue:

> My aim in launching *Sekai Fujin* is to free women from the existing laws, customs, morals and all the other circumstances which entangle them, and then to explore women's innate characters and appointed tasks . . . I hope to infuse the reform movement into the hearts of women. However, if one looks at the state of contemporary society, almost all circumstances persecute and oppress women's innate character. Therefore I feel that a socialist movement for women ought to be launched. As this looks likely to be a long-term commitment, I may not achieve this target in *Sekai Fujin*. However, I would like to try to implant the idea of women's innate character into women's minds through *Sekai Fujin*.[299]

Fukuda was influenced by the socialist thought of Kōtoku Shūsui and Sakai Toshihiko, and *Sekai Fujin* held to such views.[300] Fukuda wished to gain the attention of women from different social backgrounds, and to do this she covered an extensive range of topics.

---

[297] Kodama, *Fujin Sanseiken Undō Shōshi*, p. 34; Mitsui, *Gendai Fujin Undōshi Nenpyō*, p. 66. Iwano (maiden name was Endō) Kiyoko (1882–1920) worked as an elementary school teacher, and then at the Telegram News Agency. Between 1905 and 1909 she joined the campaign for the revision of the Peace Police Law. She married the critic and writer Iwano Hōmei in 1913.

[298] *Sekai Fujin* came out twice a month initially, and thirty-eight issues were published. Its circulation was said to be between one thousand and two thousand copies. It ended on 5 July 1909. An account of *Sekai Fujin* is given in Murata, *Fukuda Hideko*, pp. 122–3; Itoya, *Josei Kaihō no Senkusha*, pp. 174–5; Ōki, 'Meiji shakai shugi undō to josei', pp. 138–47; Miyakawa Torao, '*Sekai Fujin* kaisetsu', in Rōdō Undōshi Kenkyūkai (ed.), *Meiji Shakai Shugi Shiryōshū*, Bessatsu 1 (1961), pp. 3–9; Sievers, *Flowers in Salt*, pp. 126–30; Mackie, *Creating Socialist Women*, pp. 60–2; Raddeker, *Treacherous Women of Imperial Japan*, p. 163; Hane, *Reflections on the Way to the Gallows*, pp. 31–2.

[299] Fukuda Hideko, 'Hakkan no ji,' *Sekai Fujin*, 1 (1 January, 1907), p. 1.

[300] Itoya, *Josei Kaihō no Senkusha*, pp. 174–5; Murata, *Fukuda Hideko*, pp. 127–8; Miyagawa, '*Sekai Fujin* kaisetsu', p. 5; Inoue, *Nihon Joseishi*, p. 230; Yamazaki Tomoko, *Ajia Josei Kōryūshi: Meiji Taishō-ki Hen* (1995), p. 56.

These included household management (for example, how to cook traditional Japanese dishes, and how to sew working women's clothing), discussion of many literary works and some short biographical sketches of eminent western women like Florence Nightingale and Harriet Beecher Stowe.[301]

Sekai Fujin had very strong political affiliations. As its title indicated, it aimed to achieve female emancipation at an international level. It reported on women's international political, social, religious and educational issues. It also carried news on the women's movement in western countries.[302] *Sekai Fujin* was also one of the earliest newspapers to deal with women's issues and women's political movements in other Asian countries such as China and Korea.[303]

Sekai Fujin of course drew great attention to Japanese women's political movements, regularly reporting domestic progress, especially the campaigns against the Peace Police Law as conducted by the Heiminsha.[304] *Sekai Fujin*'s concern with politics extended to issues unrelated to women, like Tanaka Shōzō's appeals to the government over the Ashio copper mine pollution.[305]

In contrast with the post-1900 campaigns against the Peace Police Law, it took a while for campaigns against the *ie* system to emerge. Women had begun to be described as victims of the *ie* system in some novels of the Meiji period.[306] Some women who were conscious of their own lack of freedom also began to challenge arranged

---

[301] 'Harriet Beecher Stowe ryakuden', *Sekai Fujin*, 4 (15 February, 1907), p. 1; 'Nightingale joshi to senkyo mondai', *Sekai Fujin*, 5 (11 March, 1907), p. 3.

[302] See 'Eikoku fujin no senkyo undō', *Sekai Fujin*, 1 (1 January, 1907), p. 3; 'Dokuritsu Rōdōtō to fujin undō', *Sekai Fujin*, 3 (1 February, 1907), p. 3; 'Eikoku fujin senkyoken undō', *Sekai Fujin*, 7 (1 April, 1907), p. 3; 'Sekai ni okeru fujin senkyo undō', *Sekai Fujin*, 21 (1 January, 1908), p. 3; 'Eikoku fujin senkyoken nariyuki', *Sekai Fujin*, 25 (5 June, 1908), p. 10.

[303] See 'Kankoku fujin no raichō', *Sekai Fujin*, 1 (1 January, 1907), p. 2; 'Manshū no onna bazoku', *Sekai Fujin*, 4 (15 February, 1907), p. 3; 'Kōma fujin no kōzoku', *Sekai Fujin*, 6 (15 March), p. 7.

[304] See 'Seijijō ni okeru fujin no yōkyū', *Sekai Fujin*, 1 (1 January, 1907), p. 2; 'Fujin no seigan undō', *Sekai Fujin*, 2 (15 January, 1907), p. 2; 'Seigan undō no keika', *Sekai Fujin*, 4 (15 February, 1907), p. 4; 'Seigan undō no yūbō', *Sekai Fujin*, 6 (15 March, 1907), p. 2; 'Warera no seigan Shūgiin o tsūkasu', *Sekai Fujin*, 7 (1 April, 1907), p. 2.

[305] See 'Ashio kōfu no daikatsuyaku', *Sekai Fujin*, 4 (15 February, 1907), p. 2; 'Tanaka-ō shōsoku', *Sekai Fujin*, 4 (15 February, 1907), p. 4; 'Ashio Jiken no yoshin kettei', *Sekai Fujin*, 12 (15 June, 1907), p. 2; 'Tanaka Shōzō-ō yori', *Sekai Fujin*, 12 (15 June, 1907), p. 7.

[306] Yamashita Etsuko, *Nihon Josei Kaihō Shisō no Kigen* (1988), pp. 72–8.

marriage, and to claim freedom of love and marriage. However, even members of the Nihon Kirisutokyō Fujin Kyōfūkai, the socialist women in the Heiminsha and Fukuda Hideko never actually confronted the *ie* system. Hiratsuka Raichō's Seitō Society was the first women's group which openly spoke against it. Having sketched in this chapter the context and status of women in the Meiji period, and the early movements on their behalf, we can now move in subsequent chapters to focus on Hiratsuka, who founded the Seitō Society and the Association of New Women.

CHAPTER TWO

HIRATSUKA RAICHŌ'S EARLY LIFE AND THE FORMATION OF HER RADICALISM AND FEMINISM

Family Background

Hiratsuka Haru, subsequently known by her pen name Hiratsuka Raichō, was born on 10 February 1886, in a middle-class residential area, Sanbanchō near Kudanshita, Chiyoda Ward, Tokyo, as the third daughter of Hiratsuka Sadajirō and his wife, Tsuya.[1] The Hiratsuka family had been samurai, tracing their ancestry back to the Genpei Wars in the eleventh century.[2] In the Edo period they worked for the Kishū family in Wakayama Prefecture (formerly called Kii).[3] In 1871 feudal domains were abolished and a centralised prefectural system was established by the Meiji Government. Due to this change, ordinary samurai people, who had lived on *shōroku* (a small stipend in the Edo period), lost their financial entitlements and many came to feel more insecure. Hiratsuka Raichō's grandfather Tametada concerned about his future, left his home region and came to Tokyo with his second wife Yae and their children Ai and Sadajirō.[4] Sadajirō was educated at a German language school called Gaikokugo Gakkō (Foreign Language School) in Surugadai, Tokyo.[5] As the German

[1] Hiratsuka Raichō, *Watakushi no Aruita Michi* (1955, 1994 edn), p. 9; Hiratsuka Raichō, 'Omoide no naka no toritachi', in Hiratsuka, *Chosakushū*, vol. 5, pp. 362–5; Hiratsuka Raichō, 'Saisho no kioku', *Josei Nihon* (December, 1936), reprinted in Hiratsuka, *Chosakushū*, vol. 6, pp. 159–60. See also the Chronology for Hiratsuka Raichō, Appendix 4.
[2] Hiratsuka Raichō, *Hiratsuka Raichō Jiden: Genshi Josei wa Taiyo de Atta*, vol. 1 (1971, 1992 edn), pp. 33–4; Hiratsuka, *Watakushi*, p. 12.
[3] Hiratsuka Raichō, 'Ryochū zakki', in Hiratsuka, *Chosakushū*, vol. 6, pp. 324–5; Hiratsuka Raichō, 'Watakushi no kyōri', *Josei Bunka* (July, 1935), reprinted in Hiratsuka, *Chosakushū*, vol. 6, p. 50.
[4] Hiratsuka, *Watakushi*, p. 16; Hiratsuka Raichō, 'Sosen o kataru', in Hiratsuka, *Chosakushū*, vol. 5, pp. 316–23.
[5] Hiratsuka, *Genshi*, vol. 1, p. 39; Kobayashi Tomie, 'Hiratsuka Raichō shōden', in Hiratsuka Raichō (ed. by Kobayashi Tomie & Yoneda Sayoko), *Hiratsuka Raichō Hyōronshū* (1987), p. 327.

language was in great vogue in the new Meiji government, his ability in it helped him to enter government service. After having worked for the Ministries of Agriculture and Foreign Affairs, in 1887 Sadajirō transferred to the Ministry of Finance, where he worked for forty years until his retirement.[6] In 1888 (when Hiratsuka Raichō was one year old) he went to Europe and the United States as an aide to Viscount Watanabe Noboru, to research accountancy law.[7] With the enactment of the Meiji Constitution, the government needed to enact similar legislation. Upon returning to Japan, he contributed to this area of Japanese law. He also helped to found German language schools, set up financial studies courses, taught at the Military Accounting School, taught German at Ikkō (the First High School), wrote German textbooks, and translated German economics books.[8]

His wife Tsuya was the third daughter of Iijima Hōan, a samurai who had worked for the Tayasu Family. She received an old-fashioned and very basic education. She married Sadajirō at the age of seventeen by arranged marriage.[9] After marriage, she attended classes at Sakurai Jojuku (Sakurai Women's Academy), a missionary school whose principal was Yajima Kajiko, and which employed many western teachers. She studied English as a part-time student while her husband was away in Europe. Sadajirō felt that as a government official's wife Tsuya had to learn English to entertain his foreign guests.[10]

Hiratsuka Raichō was raised in a very close extended family, comprising father, mother, paternal grandmother Yae, father's younger sister Ai, and her elder sister Taka.[11] Its structure aside, her family was typical of the westernised upper-middle class, employing two resident housemaids and a nanny when Hiratsuka Raichō was born.[12] The early pages of her autobiography recount many happy childhood memories. She recalled frequent family outings:

---

[6] Hiratsuka, 'Naki chichi o shinobite', *Fujin Kōron* (May, 1941), reprinted in Hiratsuka, *Chosakushū*, vol. 6, p. 343; Furubayashi Kamejirō (ed.), *Gendai Jinmei Jiten*, vol. 2 (1912), p. 9. Sadajirō did many translations and interpreting jobs with the German Hermann Roesler, who had been a legal adviser to the Japanese government since 1881 and had been closely involved in drafting the Meiji Constitution.

[7] Hiratsuka, *Genshi*, vol. 1, pp. 40–1.

[8] Kobayashi, 'Hiratsuka Raichō shōden', p. 327.

[9] Hiratsuka, *Genshi*, vol. 1, pp. 42–3; Hiratsuka, *Watakushi*, pp. 19–20.

[10] Kobayashi Tomie, *Hiratsuka Raichō: Ai to Hangyaku no Seishun* (1977), p. 19.

[11] Hiratsuka, *Genshi*, vol. 1, p. 22. Raichō's eldest sister Ine died in infant. See Hiratsuka Raichō's family tree, Appendix 3.

[12] Hiratsuka, *Watakushi*, pp. 17–19.

> On Sundays my parents, my elder sister and myself often went out together . . . We went to Ueno Zoo, Koishikawa Botanical Garden and other interesting places.[13]

As she admitted, family outings were rare in the Japan of that time. It was common for a husband to go out on his own to enjoy himself, and for a wife to go out with her children and mother-in-law.[14] Raichō's father was a very rare and unusual man in being so family-orientated in the Meiji period. It may be that her father's familiarity and associations with western culture lay behind this. His experience of western cultures had a great impact on him, broadened his horizons, and was also reflected in his life-style.[15] He was a liberal and relatively open-minded man, willing to accept some western ideas and manners, and he had progressive views on family values.[16]

Hiratsuka Raichō lived in comfort and received her family's attention and love, especially her father's. In her autobiography she tells of her father's affection for her:

> He was very fond of me because I was the youngest child in our family . . . He taught me different kinds of card games and the game of *go* [the national board game of Japan] . . . Especially during the New Year holiday, when he had time off, he spent ages playing simple card games with me without showing any signs of boredom. Moreover, in winter sitting around a charcoal brazier, he used to tell me children's stories, all of them western ones such as Grimms' and Aesop's Tales . . . I wonder how he managed to find much time for me, considering that he was always incredibly busy doing responsible and highly demanding work for the Ministry of Finance.[17]

Hiratsuka Raichō also shared some of her father's hobbies, and he often took her fishing with him until she entered girls' high school.[18] He even knitted a pair of gloves for her when she suffered from

---

[13] Hiratsuka, *Genshi*, vol. 1, p. 55.

[14] Kobayashi, *Ai to Hangyaku no Seishun*, pp. 36–7; Kobayashi Shigeyoshi, *Meiji no Tokyo Seikatsu: Josei no Kaita Meiji no Nikki* (1991), pp. 93–4, 210; Kobayashi Tomie, *Hiratsuka Raichō: Hito to Shisō* (1983), p. 17.

[15] Hiratsuka, *Genshi*, vol. 1, pp. 38–42; Kobayashi, *Ai to Hangyaku no Seishun*, pp. 77–8; Kobayashi Tomie & Kozai Yoshishige, *Ai to Jiritsu: Shikon, Raichō, Yuriko o Kataru* (1983), p. 111.

[16] Kobayashi, *Hito to Shisō*, pp. 14–5.

[17] Hiratsuka, *Genshi*, vol. 1, pp. 49–50.

[18] *Ibid.*, pp. 49, 87, 130–1; Kobayashi, *Ai to Hangyaku no Seishun*, p. 58; Hiratsuka Raichō, 'Waga shōjo no hi', in Ikuta Hanayo *et al.*, *Waga Shōjo no Hi* (Kyoto, 1941), reprinted in Hiratsuka, *Chosakushū*, vol. 6, pp. 355–8.

chapped hands in winter.[19] At that time a husband exercised enormous power over his wife and children under the Meiji Civil Code
and Constitution, and there was a clear distinction between men's
and women's work in the home. Childcare and domestic work, like
knitting, were left entirely to wives, perhaps assisted by servants.
Although he was liberal enough to knit for her, he did not want
this known, and told her not to tell anybody at school that her gloves
were knitted by him rather than her mother.[20] Hiratsuka Raichō had
a very positive view of her father in her childhood, describing him
as an affectionate, approachable family man who she could easily
relate to.[21] Such positive images bear a surprising resemblance to
more modern ideals of fatherhood. They have little in common with
the negative descriptions of many fathers at the time, so often seen
as oppressive, stubborn, domineering and unapproachable.

Hiratsuka Raichō stated that her daily life at home was very peaceful, without angry words in the house.[22] She seemed to have been
fully contented with her childhood, and this contrasts sharply with
the childhoods of some of her contemporaries who became feminists,
such as Ichikawa Fusae and Oku Mumeo.[23] Ichikawa, for example,
repeatedly witnessed terrible scenes of her father beating her mother.[24]
These memories became deeply etched upon her mind, and left her
with considerable feelings of bitterness, and a sense that women like
her mother needed legal protection.[25] Oku's early life included many
similar events. Unlike Ichikawa, Oku never witnessed wife beating,
but was convinced that her mother suffered mental torture. Oku
described her mother as a victim, a person plagued to death by her
husband's tyrannical behaviour as well as by frequent and unwanted
childbearing.[26]

[19] Hiratsuka, *Genshi*, vol. 1, p. 51.
[20] *Ibid.*, pp. 51–2.
[21] *Ibid.*, p. 42; Hiratsuka, 'Naki chichi o shinobite', pp. 342–3.
[22] Hiratsuka, *Genshi*, vol. 1, p. 47.
[23] Ichikawa Fusae, *Ichikawa Fusae Jiden: Senzen Hen* (1974), pp. 2–6; Oku Mumeo, *Nobi Akaaka to: Oku Mumeo Jiden* (1988), pp. 14–16.
[24] Ichikawa, *Jiden: Senzen*, p. 2; Ichikawa Fusae, *87-sai no Seishun: Ichikawa Fusae Shōgai o Kataru* (video, produced by the Sakura Eigasha, Tokyo, 1981).
[25] Ichikawa, *Jiden: Senzen*, pp. 2–3; Ichikawa, *87-sai no Seishun*.
[26] Oku, *Nobi*, pp. 14–7; Akiko Tokuza, *The Rise of the Feminist Movement in Japan* (1999), p. 93.

Ichikawa and Oku's experiences in this regard clearly contributed to their later feminism and radicalism.[27] Surprisingly, very few women's historians have examined Hiratsuka Raichō's childhood, family and educational backgrounds, and have attempted to trace aspects of her radicalism to her early life.[28] The great majority of women's historians drew the hasty and dubious conclusion that Hiratsuka's privileged childhood could not possibly relate to the formation of her feminism.[29] The usual view is that her ideas date from her later involvement with the Seitō Society.[30] A very small number of writers take the view that it was not until the Shiobara Incident that her radical attitudes emerged.[31] The great majority of sources available on Hiratsuka fail to discuss her early life and also overlook the point that Hiratsuka was one of the first generation of women in Japan who received a higher education, not assessing how she benefitted from that education, and how it may have laid the groundwork for her feminist activity.

Educational Background

In the spring of 1890 Hiratsuka began school at the age of four, in Fujimi Yōchien (Fujimi Kindergarten), which was attached to Fujimi Shōgakkō (Fujimi Elementary School) near her house.[32] At that time it was by no means universal for children to go to kindergarten.[33]

---

[27] The similar point about Ichikawa's case was made by K. S. Molony, 'One woman who dared: Ichikawa Fusae and the Japanese Women's Suffrage Movement' (unpublished Ph.D. thesis, University of Michigan, 1980), chapter 1.

[28] Ide, Kobayashi and Horiba were the only women's historians who drew attention to Hiratsuka Raichō's childhood and family and educational backgrounds. See Horiba Kiyoko, Seitō no Jidai (1988), pp. 12–22; Kobayashi, Ai to Hangyaku no Seishun, pp. 12–106; Kobayashi, Hito to Shisō, pp. 12–44; Ide Fumiko, Hiratsuka Raichō: Kindai to Shinpi (1987), p. 9–38.

[29] Nakayama Kazuko, 'Onna de aru koto no imi: Seitō-ha o megutte', Kokubungaku, 25:15 (December, 1980), p. 71.

[30] Morosawa, Onna no Rekishi, vol. 2, pp. 161–4; Tachi Kaoru, 'Hiratsuka Raichō to ofudesaki', Ochanomizu Joshi Daigaku Josei Bunka Shiryō Kanpō, 7 (1986), pp. 104–6; Yoneda, 'Jidai o ikinuku', p. 62; Maruoka, 'Seitō kara Kokusai Fujin Nen e', pp. 4–14; Suzuki, Joseishi o Hiraku, vol. 1, pp. 26–48; Hayashi et al. (eds), Nihon Joseishi, p. 231.

[31] Yatayama Seiko, Hi no Onna, Raichō (1991), pp. 30–81; Sasaki Hideaki, Atarashii Onna no Tōrai (Nagoya, 1994), pp. 3–6.

[32] Hiratsuka, Genshi, vol. 1, pp. 59–83; Hiratsuka, Watakushi, pp. 23–28.

[33] The first kindergarten in Japan was founded in Tokyo in 1876. It was attached

Among all the early feminist leaders in Japan, Katō Shidzue and
Hiratsuka Raichō were the only ones who received a full kindergarten education.[34] Hiratsuka recalled that in her kindergarten children learned *oyūgi* (playing and dancing to music), *shōka* (singing) and
various kinds of *shukō* (minor skills and crafts) such as *tsumiki* (playing with building blocks), *origami* (the art of folding paper into various figures), *mamezaiku* (bean handiwork) and *mugiwara zaiku* (straw
work).[35] At that time kindergartens did not teach even basic reading, writing and arithmetic.[36] She did not benefit academically there,
but did gain socially. The fact that both Hiratsuka Raichō and her
sister were sent to kindergarten demonstrated their parents' appreciation of western-style education and their keenness for it.

Hiratsuka Raichō's two-year kindergarten education was followed
by elementary school. She entered Fujimi Shōgakkō (Fujimi Elementary
School) in 1892 and later changed to another publicly run elementary school called Seino Shōgakkō (Seino Elementary School) in
Hongō Ward, Tokyo, in 1894, when she was in the third year of
elementary school.[37] Although she did not give detailed descriptions

to *Tokyo Joshi Shihan Gakkō* (Tokyo Girls' Higher School). Its full quota was 150
children and its monthly tuition fee was 15 *sen* (1 sen was 1/100 yen). This was a
model institution founded by the new government, and with this as a start, more
government-run, public kindergartens and some private ones were founded. By 1897
their number had increased to 222 and their pupils to 19,727. See Yamakawa
Kikue, *Onna Nidai no Ki*, (1972), pp. 34–5; Ochanomizu Joshi Daigaku Bunkyōiku
Gakubu Fuzoku Yōchien (ed.), *Nenpyō: Yōchien 100-nen-shi* (1976), pp. 21–9.

[34] Katō Shidzue, *Ai wa Jidai o Koete* (1988, 1990 edn), p. 17; Shidzue Ishimoto,
Facing Two Ways: The Story of My Life (1935, Stanford, 1984 edn), pp. 41–3; Hiratsuka,
Genshi, vol. 1, pp. 59–64; Hiratsuka, *Watakushi*, pp. 23–5.

[35] The subjects taught at Hiratsuka's kindergarten were more or less the same
as those at Katō's kindergarten (which was the Kindergarten of the Peeresses' School,
where entry was very restricted and to which boys and girls of aristocratic birth
were brought). See Hiratsuka, *Genshi*, vol. 1, p. 61; Hiratsuka, *Watakushi*, pp. 23–5;
Ishimoto, *Facing Two Ways*, pp. 42–3.

[36] Ishimoto, *Facing Two Ways*, pp. 41–3; Yamakawa, *Onna Nidai no Ki*, p. 34;
Ochanomizu Joshi Daigaku Bunkyōiku Gakubu Fuzoku Yōchien (ed.), *Yōchien 100-
nen-shi*, pp. 23–4.

[37] Hiratsuka, *Genshi*, vol. 1, pp. 65–9; Hiratsuka, *Watakushi*, p. 26. The elementary school attendance rate in 1890 was 31.1 per cent for girls and 65.1 per cent
for boys, and these tended to be children from more privileged families. The elementary school system at that time was very different from now. There were two
types of elementary schools. One adopted a six year system, attached to *shihan gakkō*
(higher schools, whose main objective was to recruit teachers, and which were similar to teachers' training colleges now). The other type was the ordinary elementary school, which accounted for the great majority of elementary schools. Ordinary

of her elementary school in her autobiography, the subjects which were taught at elementary schools at that time were geography, history, arithmetic, singing, sewing, calligraphy and *shūshin* (morals).[38] She recalled that all the subjects which she studied at elementary school were extremely easy and she was always top of her year.[39] Almost all the feminists who were her contemporaries such as Oku, Ichikawa and Yamakawa had outstandingly good records in their elementary studies, and the great majority of them including Hiratsuka proceeded to *jogakkō* (girls' high schools).[40]

Having completed her elementary school education, which was compulsory for both boys and girls, Hiratsuka entered Ochanomizu Kōtō Jogakkō (Ochanomizu Girls' High School) in April 1898, when she was twelve years old. She wrote about the numbers of female students who progressed to the next stage of education in her class at elementary school:

> The great majority of my female classmates who completed elementary school education did not proceed to a school of higher grade. I was the only person who went on to Ochanomizu Girls' High School. A couple of students who vied with me for the top position in my class entered the Metropolitan Girls' High School in Tokyo. Some girls also went to Watanabe Saihō Jogakkō (Watanabe Girls' Sewing High School) in Yushima, Hongō Ward in Tokyo. This private sewing school gave students intensive lessons in *wasai* (the art of cutting and sewing kimono). The graduates from this school were awarded a certificate to be qualified to teach sewing at elementary school.[41]

As this quotation indicates, few girls from elementary school went on to secondary school. The widespread view was that secondary

---

elementary schools were divided into two levels: *jinjō shōgakkō* (normal elementary schools) and *kōtōka* (advanced level elementary schools). The former were lower level schools, which provided students between 6 and 10 years old with a four-year compulsory education. For the first two years all the classes were mixed, and during the last two years boys and girls were educated separately. The *kōtōka* were higher level elementary schools, which provided students between 10 and 12 years old with a two-year education. Any girl at that time who wished to proceed to *jogakkō* (girls' high school) had to graduate from either *kōtōka* or *shihan gakkō*.

[38] 'Kyōiku rei', *Dajōkan Fukoku*, 45 (29 September, 1879), reprinted in Mitsui (ed.), *Nihon Fujin Mondai Shiryō Shūsei*, vol. 4, p. 176.

[39] Hiratsuka, *Watakushi*, p. 26; Hiratsuka Raichō, 'Shōgakkō jidai no omoide hitotsu', in Hiratsuka, *Chosakushū*, vol. 5, pp. 168–71.

[40] Hiratsuka, *Genshi*, vol. 1, p. 90; Ichikawa, *Jiden: Senzen*, p. 12; Oku, *Nobi*, p. 19; Yamakawa, *Onna Nidai no Ki*, p. 121.

[41] Hiratsuka, *Genshi*, vol. 1, p. 90.

education was very much a boy's privilege. As Hiratsuka's entrance
into Ochanomizu Girls' High School pre-dated the introduction of
the *Kōtō Jogakkō Rei* (Girls' High School Act) in 1899, the number
of girls' high schools situated within commuting distance which she
could apply to was very restricted, and she did not have many
options.[42] She listed seven girls' high schools in her area. Among
them four were private, mainly missionary schools, and the remaining three were Ochanomizu Girls' High School funded by the Ministry
of Education, Furitsu Kōjō (the Metropolitan Girls' High School in
Tokyo) funded by the Tokyo Municipal Government, and Kazoku
Jogakkō (Peeresses' High School), which was a national school, mainly
designed for daughters of the Imperial family and the new nobility.[43]

Proceeding to Ochanomizu Girls' High School was not her choice,
but her father's. As he was a government official, sending a daughter
to private missionary school never crossed his mind, and he naturally
preferred to send her to the government-funded girls' high school,
Ochanomizu Girls' High School.[44] As other elite government officials
and eminent people also wanted to send their daughters there, entry
was quite competitive, but she easily passed the entrance exam.[45]

This school was attached to Tokyo Joshi Kōtō Shihan Gakkō
(Tokyo Girls' Higher School) which was founded in 1890 as an institution to train female secondary school teachers.[46] These schools were
funded by the government and under the control of the Ministry of
Education. They adopted government-approved education to produce
'good wives and wise mothers'.[47] When Hiratsuka entered Ochanomizu

---

[42] *Ibid.*, pp. 90–1; Katayama Kiyoichi, *Kindai Nihon no Joshi Kyōiku* (1984) p. 83;
Yamazaki Takako, *Tsuda Umeko* (1962, 1988 edn), pp. 171–3; Tamie Kamiyama,
'Ideology and patterns in women's education in Japan (unpublished Ph.D. thesis,
Saint Louis University, 1977), pp. 84–92; 'Kōtō Jogakkō Rei', pp. 262–3; Shibuya,
Kyōiku, pp. 45–7. Under the Kōtō Jogakkō Rei, the Ministry of Education stipu-
lated that each prefecture must set up more than one girls' high school subsidised
by the prefectural government.

[43] Hiratsuka, *Genshi*, vol. 1, pp. 90–1; Katō, *Ai wa Jidai o Koete*, pp. 17–9; Ishimoto,
Facing Two Ways, pp. 53–74; Yamazaki, *Tsuda Umeko*, p. 172; Alice Bacon (trans.
by Kuno Akiko), *Kazoku Jogakkō Kyōshi no Mita Meiji Nihon no Uchigawa* (1994);
Kobayashi, *Ai to Hangyaku no Seishun*, p. 59.

[44] Hiratsuka, *Genshi*, vol. 1, p. 91; Hiratsuka, *Watakushi*, p. 28.

[45] Hiratsuka, *Genshi*, vol. 1, p. 93.

[46] Nakamura Hidekatsu, 'Ochanomizu Joshi Daigaku no seiritsu', *Ochanomizu Joshi
Daigaku Josei Bunka Shiryō Kanpō*, 2 (1980), p. 61.

[47] Katayama, *Kindai Nihon no Joshi Kyōiku*, p. 157; Kobayashi, *Ai to Hangyaku no
Seishun*, pp. 60–2; Hiratsuka Raichō, 'Mukashi no jogakusei to ima no jogakusei',
Josei Kaizō (January, 1950), reprinted in Hiratsuka, *Chosakushū*, vol. 7, pp. 76–7.

School, this policy was in full operation.[48] The rules were very strict. As in boys' schools, students' freedom was suppressed, and the school hindered the growth of spontaneous expression. Its curriculum followed educational guidelines in the *Kōtō Jogakkō Rei* (The Girls' High School Act).[49] The subject regarded as most important was *shūshin* (morals), which was the core of this kind of education.[50] Other practical subjects such as housekeeping, sewing handicrafts and etiquette, thought to be extremely useful for domestic life, were given higher priority than academic subjects like mathematics, Japanese, Chinese literature and English, although these were also taught.[51]

Hiratsuka recalled that the great majority of students came from upper or upper-middle class families, and their fathers were peers of *daimyō* (feudal lords in the Edo period) descent, powerful military figures, government officials, businessmen with political affiliations, famous academics and educationalists.[52] She described her school as comprising daughters of the influential men who ran Japan and planned its future. As the daughter of a minor government official, she was surrounded by girls from such well-to-do and influential families, and felt uncomfortably inferior there. The atmosphere of the school was aristocratic, authoritarian, and pervaded by a sense of catering for elite students.[53]

Moreover, many teachers were graduates from the Tokyo Joshi Kōtō Shihan Gakkō (Tokyo Girls' Higher School), and were trained to give a formalistic education based on Confucian and 'feudal' principles. The great majority of them followed formal and inflexible teaching methods, as taught at the Tokyo Girls' Higher School.[54] Hiratsuka gave vivid descriptions of the typical teaching by one of the teachers, Mrs Yahagi Tetsu, a characteristic product of the Tokyo Girls' Higher School:

---

[48] Hiratsuka, *Watakushi*, p. 29; Hiratsuka, *Genshi*, vol. 1, p. 101; Kobayashi, *Hito to Shisō*, p. 30; Aoki Takako, *Kindaishi o Hiraita Joseitachi: Nihon Joshi Daigaku ni Mananda Hitotachi* (1990), p. 49.

[49] Katayama, *Kindai Nihon no Joshi Kyōiku*, p. 157; Haga Noboru, *Ryōsai Kenboron* (1990), p. 18; 'Kōtō Jogakkō Rei', pp. 262–3.

[50] Haga, *Ryōsai Kenboron*, p. 18; Karasawa Tomitaro, *Joshi Gakusei no Rekishi* (1979), pp. 86–7.

[51] Hiratsuka, *Watakushi*, p. 29.

[52] Hiratsuka, *Genshi*, vol. 1, p. 93.

[53] *Ibid.*, pp. 93–106.

[54] Katayama, *Kindai Nihon no Joshi Kyōiku*, p. 157; Kobayashi, *Hito to Shisō*, pp. 31–4.

Yahagi taught us all the subjects of study perfunctorily, following the
textbooks provided. She made us learn all the information in the textbooks off by heart. She never gave us extra reading lists. She did not
even bother to encourage students to read books other than the textbooks. Her teaching method neither made us think for ourselves, nor
gave us an opportunity to think carefully. What was worse, it never
roused our interest in study. Yahagi taught us Japanese, mathematics,
history, geography, science and a couple of other subjects.[55]

Hiratsuka criticised Yahagi's classes for being dull and unimagina-
tive, and lacking a good rapport between teacher and pupils. She
concluded that her studies had been monotonous and lacking in
intellectual stimulation, as Yahagi had taken charge of her class for
five years.[56] However, she noticed that her dissatisfaction was not
shared by the great majority of pupils, and recalled how impressed
she was with their patience.[57] Most pupils were brought up not to
doubt teachers, who had absolute authority over them.

Although this school was a big disappointment to Hiratsuka, she
contained her dissatisfaction and did not rebel for the first two years.[58]
She had outstandingly good records, apart from *shōka* (singing), and
was top of her year. She did badly in singing because she had problems with her voice from an early age. In her third year she formed
a discussion group called *Kaizoku Gumi* (the Pirate Gang) with four
friends, who were also dissatisfied.[59] This idea came from the *Wakō*
(Japanese pirates) whom they studied in their history class.[60] The
Wakō's lives appealed to pupils hedged in by school regulations and
education to make good wives and wise mothers.[61] Hiratsuka stated
that she felt like a little bird in a small cage, about to suffocate.[62]

---

[55] Hiratsuka, *Genshi*, vol. 1, p. 102.

[56] *Ibid.*, p. 92.

[57] *Ibid.*, p. 117.

[58] Hiratsuka, *Watakushi*, p. 30.

[59] Hiratsuka, *Genshi*, vol. 1, pp. 95–6; Kobayashi, *Ai to Hangyaku no Seishun*, pp.
67–8; Hiratsuka Raichō, '30-nen mae no watashi', *Fujo Shinbun* (10 May, 1930),
reprinted in Hiratsuka, *Chosakushū*, vol. 5, p. 187.

[60] Hiratsuka, *Genshi*, vol. 1, pp. 113–4. The *Wakō* raided the coasts of East Asia
(mainly the southern coast of Korea and China's Shandong Peninsula), pillaged
rice, cloth, coins and other items, and wielded much power in the 13th and 14th
centuries. See Kōdansha (comp.), *Japan: An Illustrated Encyclopaedia* (1993, 1996 edn),
p. 1683; Kokushi Daijiten Henshū Iinkai (ed.), *Kokushi Daijiten*, vol. 14 (1993), pp.
886–7.

[61] Hiratsuka, *Genshi*, vol. 1, p. 114; Hiratsuka Raichō, 'Sei ni mezameru koro no
omoide', *Oku no Oku* (May, 1936), reprinted in Hiratsuka, *Chosakushū*, vol. 6, p. 121.

[62] Hiratsuka, *Watakushi*, p. 31.

The women in her group expressed frustration with school objectives and conventions. They were particularly interested in discussing marriage and careers, planning to escape from traditional arranged marriages and find suitable jobs which would allow them to stay single.[63]

Hiratsuka boycotted classes for the compulsory *shūshin* (morals) course.[64] This course for girls was the core education to create good wives and wise mothers.[65] Female students were required to read aloud textbooks written in classical Japanese, and to listen to teachers' translations. The contents of the textbooks were edifying stories about two types of women: one being eminent female figures such as Empress Shōken, Kasuga no Tsubone and Empress Kōmyō; the other being wives and mothers of male historical figures whose success was owed to these women, like Toyotomi Hideyoshi's wife or Yamanouchi Kazutoyo's wife.[66] The textbooks sang the praises of women who were diligent, thrifty and virtuous, who supported their husbands and sons. The classes did not give students any opportunity to ask questions, or comment on the women they studied.[67]

---

[63] Hiratsuka, *Genshi*, vol. 1, pp. 110-1.

[64] *Ibid.*, p. 116; Kobayashi, *Ai to Hangyaku no Seishun*, p. 72. The *shūshin* class was devoted to moral training, which entered the school curriculum when the *Gakusei* (the Fundamental Education Law) was enforced. Both males and females had to study it at primary and secondary schools, apart from private schools, between 1872 and 1945. Textbooks for this course were written and supplied by the government. At secondary-school level, where a co-educational system was not in effect, girls' high schools used textbooks designed for girls only, entirely different from their male equivalents. On the *shūshin* class, see Katayama, *Kindai Nihon no Joshi Kyōiku*, pp. 228-67; Shibukawa, *Kyōiku*, pp. 53-4.

[65] Katayama, *Kindai Nihon no Joshi Kyōiku*, pp. 132-8; Karasawa, *Joshi Gakusei no Rekishi*, pp. 86-7; Uno, 'The death of "good wife, wise mother"?', pp. 293-303; Kamiyama, 'Ideology and patterns', pp. 134-51; Nolte & Hastings, 'The Meiji state's policy toward women, 1890-1910', pp. 158-9; Sievers, *Flowers in Salt*, pp. 109-13.

[66] Hiratsuka, *Genshi*, vol. 1, p. 116; Hiratsuka Raichō, '*Seitō* undō no haikei: Meiji no onna', *Zuihitsu* (January, 1957), reprinted in Hiratsuka, *Chosakushū*, vol. 7, pp. 352-3; Haga, *Ryōsai Kenboron*, pp. 19-20; Karasawa, *Joshi Gakusei no Rekishi*, p. 86. Yamanouchi Kazutoyo (1545-1605) was born as the son of a petty baron of Owari Province and entered the service of Toyotomi Hideyoshi in 1573. He distinguished himself in two battles and obtained the status of *daimyō* in 1585. Kazutoyo's wife (1557-1617) devoted herself to her husband, and apparently did much to sort out his problems. As a result, she was portrayed as the provident and perspicacious model of a samurai wife.

[67] Hiratsuka, *Genshi*, vol. 1, pp. 116-7; Yamakawa, *Onna Nidai no Ki*, p. 120; Karasawa, *Joshi Gakusei no Rekishi*, pp. 90-3; Kobayashi, *Ai to Hangyaku no Seishun*, p. 72.

Hiratsuka recalled that the textbook for her *shūshin* course was full of stories written in *Onna Daigaku* style: dull and uninspiring.[68] She avoided the remaining classes of her *shūshin* course. She was the only student who boycotted the course, an action requiring courage.[69] Absence from *shūshin* classes appeared to challenge school policy, but she was not reprimanded, mainly because of her outstanding marks on other courses.[70] All aspects of her behaviour here demonstrated an independent mind and a potential that later became more publicly evident. Her reaction against this education later developed into her feminism and opposition to the *ie* system. Hiratsuka believed that if she had been educated at a missionary school, where an education for making good wives and wise mothers was not practised, and where equality of the sexes existed, allowing girls more independence of mind, she might never have come to agitate against sexual discrimination.[71]

After she graduated at the age of seventeen, in March 1903, she entered Nihon Joshi Daigakkō (the Japan Women's College). At that time, there were few graduates from girls' high schools who proceeded to the next stage of education. Hiratsuka recalled that less than 10 students out of 40 in her school year went on to higher education.[72]

All women's higher educational institutions, apart from the Japan Women's College, had a specific objective and provided students with a narrow specialised education. For example, the main purpose of Tokyo Joshi Kōtō Shihan Gakkō (Tokyo Girls' Higher School) was to train women as school teachers, and Tokyo Joi Gakkō (Tokyo Women's Medical College) was designed to train female medical doctors.[73] Joshi Bijutsu Gakkō (Women's Art College) provided students with artistic training, and Joshi Eigaku Juku (Women's Institute of English Studies) gave high priority to English language teaching.[74]

---

[68] Hiratsuka, *Genshi*, vol. 1, p. 116.

[69] Hiratsuka, *Watakushi*, p. 31; Hiratsuka, *Genshi*, vol. 1, p. 117; Kobayashi, *Ai to Hangyaku no Seishun*, pp. 60–2; Fujii Chie & Kanamori Toshie, *Onna no Kyōiku 100-nen* (1977), p. 28; Shibukawa, *Kyōiku*, p. 54; Karasawa, *Joshi Gakusei no Rekishi*, p. 89.

[70] Hiratsuka, *Watakushi*, p. 31.

[71] Ferris Jogakuin 100-nen-shi Henshū Iinkai (ed.), *Ferris Jogakuin 100-nen-shi* (Yokohama, 1970), p. 85; Kobayashi, *Hito to Shisō*, pp. 29–30.

[72] Hiratsuka, *Watakushi*, p. 36; Hiratsuka, *Genshi*, vol. 1, p. 157. I translated Nihon Joshi Daigakkō as the Japan Women's College and Nihon Joshi Daigaku (renamed as such in 1948) as the Japan Women's University.

[73] Yamazaki, *Tsuda Umeko*, p. 174; Shibukawa, *Kyōiku*, pp. 194–220; Yamazaki Takako (ed.), *Tsuda Juku 60-nen-shi* (1960), p. 57; Barbara Rose, *Tsuda Umeko and Women's Education in Japan* (New Haven, 1992), pp. 126–7.

[74] Yamakawa, *Onna Nidai no Ki*, pp. 132–3; Kamichika Ichiko, *Kamichika Ichiko*

Unlike these four, the Japan Women's College hoped to provide students with a wide ranging general education. It had three departments: English, Japanese literature and domestic science.[75] Although it was much smaller than the imperial universities and leading private universities, which only men could attend, the Japan Women's College was private, and much larger than any of the above four institutions in terms of campus size, facilities, student numbers and the range of subjects available.[76]

According to *Nihon Joshi Daigaku no 80-nen* (*the Eighty-Year History of the Japan Women's University*), there was a large attendance at the opening ceremony of the Japan Women's College on 20 April 1901.[77] More than 1,300 people comprising students, their parents, the staff, school trustees and celebrities attended as guests. The number of students who newly registered with the Japan Women's College that day was 222. More than 54 experienced teachers who sympathised with Naruse Jinzō's educational policy were employed.[78] Naruse, who had many useful contacts, was successful in recruiting many trustees, the great majority of whom were prominent figures in politics or the business world, including Iwakura Tomomi, Ōkuma Shigenobu,

---

Jiden: Waga Ai Waga Tatakai (1972), pp. 91–2; Yamazaki, *Tsuda Umeko*, p. 179; Yamazaki (ed.), *Tsuda Juku 60-nen-shi*, p. 57.

[75] Nihon Joshi Daigaku (ed.), *Nihon Joshi Daigaku no 80-nen* (1981), pp. 24–5; Hiratsuka, *Genshi*, vol. 1, p. 153.

[76] Fujii & Kanamori, *Onna no Kyōiku 100-nen*, pp. 34–5.

[77] Nihon Joshi Daigaku (ed.), *Nihon Joshi Daigaku no 80-nen*, p. 22; Nakamura Masao (ed.), *Nihon Joshi Daigakkō 40-nen-shi* (1942), pp. 26, 81–2.

[78] Nihon Joshi Daigaku (ed.), *Nihon Joshi Daigaku no 80-nen*, p. 26; Nakamura (ed.), *Nihon Joshi Daigakkō 40-nen-shi*, pp. 80–1. Naruse Jinzō (1858–1919) was a leading educationalist who played a pioneering part in the promotion of women's higher education in Japan. After a period in missionary work, he went to America in 1890 to research women's education. He returned to Japan in 1894 and became principal of Baika Jogakkō (Baika Girls' High School) in Osaka. He founded Nihon Joshi Daigakkō in 1901. In 1948 it was given university status and became Nihon Joshi Daigaku. On Naruse, see Watanabe Eiichi (ed.), *Nihon Joshi Daigaku Sōritsusha: Naruse Sensei* (1928); Nishina Setsuko, 'Naruse sensei no koto', in Nihon Joshi Daigaku (ed.), *Joshidai Tsūshin*, 15 (March, 1950), p. 1; 'Ko Naruse Jinzō sensei rireki', *Katei Shūhō*, 507, (14 March, 1919), p. 1; 'Naruse-shi ryakureki', *Fujo Shinbun*, 982 (14 March, 1919), p. 1; 'Naruse Jinzō-kun o itamu', *Fujin Mondai*, 2:4 (April, 1919), pp. 86–9; 'Yukeru hito: Naruse Jinzō-shi to sono jigyō', *Fujin Gahō*, 159 (May, 1919), pp. 38–42; Kabashi Miyoko, 'Joshi Kyōiku kai no senkakusha, Naruse sensei o oshimu', *Fujin Shūhō*, 5:9 (March, 1919), pp. 1–3; Nishina Setsu (ed.), *Naruse Sensei Den* (1928); Nishina Setsu (ed.), *Naruse Sensei Kinenchō* (1936); Nishina Setsu & Ōhashi Hiro (eds), *Naruse Sensei no Oshie* (1951); Nihon Joshi Daigaku Joshi Kyōiku Kenkyūjo Naruse Kinenkan (ed.), *Naruse Kenkyū Bunken Mokuroku* (1984); Nihon Joshi Daigaku Joshi Kyōiku Kenkyūjo Naruse Kinenkan (ed.), *Naruse Jinzō, Sono Shōgai* (1990); Nihon Joshi Daigaku Toshokan (ed.), *Nihon Joshi Daigaku Naruse Bunko Mokuroku* (1979).

Shibusawa Eiichi, and leaders of the three major *zaibatsu* (financial combines): Mitsui, Mitsubishi and Sumitomo.[79] The grand opening of the Japan Women's College contrasted sharply with the humble opening ceremonies of Tokyo Women's Medical College and the Women's Institute of English Studies.[80]

Moreover Tsuda (the founder of the Women's Institute of English Studies) and Yoshioka (the founder of Tokyo Women's Medical College) had to endure financial worries and were constantly forced to engage in fund-raising.[81] On the other hand, as Barbara Rose stated, Naruse used his connections to raise substantial sums from his many prominent friends, and his college also received much government financial support despite its status as a private institution.[82]

Going to the Japan Women's College was Hiratsuka's own decision. She was inspired by her reading of its founder Naruse Jinzō's *Joshi Kyōiku* (*Women's Education*), which was published in February 1896, five years prior to its foundation.[83] The book was written following his viewing of many American higher educational institutions, including women's colleges, universities and schools for the deaf and dumb,

---

[79] Nakamura (ed.), *Nihon Joshi Daigakkō 40-nen-shi*, pp. 30–5, 46; Yoshiko Furuki, *The White Plum: A Biography of Ume Tsuda* (New York, 1991), pp. 98–9; Rose, *Tsuda Umeko and Women's Education*, pp. 87–9. The Japan Women's College's campus was built on spacious land donated by the Mitsui family, which headed the Mitsui Combine.

[80] Shibukawa, *Kyōiku*, p. 47, 208; Yamazaki, *Tsuda Umeko*, p. 185; Nihon Joshi Daigaku (ed.), *Nihon Joshi Daigaku no 80-nen*, p. 26; Yamazaki, *Tsuda Juku 60-nen-shi*, pp. 57, 62; Fujii & Kanamori, *Onna no Kyōiku*, p. 34; Tsuda Umeko, 'Kaikōshiki shikiji' in Yamazaki Takako (ed.), *Kaiteiban, Tsuda Umeko Monjo* (1980, 1984 edn), pp. 1–4; Furuki Yoshiko, *Tsuda Umeko* (1992), p. 151; Ōba Minako, *Tsuda Umeko* (1990), p. 218; Yoshikawa Toshikazu (ed.), *Tsuda Umeko Den* (1956), p. 242; Yamazaki (ed.), *Tsuda Juku 60-nen-shi*, p. 62; Rose, *Tsuda Umeko and Women's Education in Japan*, p. 129; Furuki, *The White Plum*, p. 103. Yoshioka Yayoi opened the former with only four students and two teaching staff in one small room which was a part of her hospital. Tsuda Umeko opened the latter with only 10 students in a rented house in Kōjimachi Ward, Tokyo; and only 17 people, comprising 10 students, 5 staff and a couple of guests were present at the opening ceremony.

[81] Shibukawa, *Kyōiku*, pp. 211–2; Yoshiko Furuki *et al.* (eds), *The Attic Letters: Ume Tsuda's Correspondence to her American Mother* (New York, 1991), p. 362. Tsuda looked to the United States for most of the financial support for her college, and the Philadelphia Committee, founded by her American friends, regularly sent donations to her. Her American friends, Alice Bacon and Anna Hartshorne, offered to teach at her school without pay.

[82] Rose, *Tsuda Umeko and Women's Education*, p. 153.

[83] Hiratsuka, *Genshi*, vol. 1, pp. 152–3; Fujii & Kanamori, *Onna no Kyōiku*, p. 40; Katayama, *Kindai Nihon no Joshi Kyōiku*, p. 157; Nishina (ed.), *Naruse Sensei Den*, pp. 223–34; Aoki, *Kindaishi o Hiraita Joseitachi*, p. 50.

and it was influenced also by his reading on American education. Naruse discussed many western examples of women's education, advancing his own ideas of women's higher education in Japan.[84] The fundamental principles for women's higher education in his book were very similar to the stated purposes of his college:

> The main educational policy our college will pursue will be to edu-cate students firstly as human beings, secondly as women, and thirdly as Japanese citizens. When one evaluates older but still existing edu-cation available to women, one will notice that such education has focused on providing them with practical information and performing art skills. It completely failed to educate women as human beings. This was mainly because most people treated women as machinery. Educating women as human beings is not the only purpose of general education. Another purpose is professional and technical education. Educating women as human beings will enable them to develop their faculties mentally and physically. It will also enable them to become well-inte-grated, refined and cultivated women. Such education will enable them to improve qualities essential for all humanity.[85]

Hiratsuka was impressed by Naruse's aim to educate female students in this way.[86] This was very different from the educational policy adopted at Ochanomizu Girls' High School, which she abhorred. She was very excited by the prospect of the Japan Women's College. She had no difficulty in securing a place there. It did not have an entrance examination, and allowed entry to any motivated woman who graduated from a girls' high school with a good school record.[87] Hiratsuka easily met such criteria. However, she had much difficulty in obtaining permission from her father to enter the College. He strongly opposed her aim to study English, and she did not antici-pate this, for he had hitherto shown much interest in his daughters' education, at least up to high school level.[88] He had studied German

[84] Hiratsuka, *Genshi*, vol. 1, p. 153; Nishina (ed.), *Naruse Sensei Den*, pp. 163–6.

[85] Naruse Jinzō, 'Nihon Joshi Daigakkō setsuritsu no shushi', in Nihon Joshi Daigaku Joshi Kyōiku Kenkyūjo (ed.), *Kongo no Joshi Kyōiku: Naruse Jinzō Joshi Daigaku Ronsenshū* (1984), pp. 65–6.

[86] Hiratsuka, *Genshi*, vol. 1, pp. 152–8; Hiratsuka, *Watakushi*, pp. 37–9.

[87] Hiratsuka, *Genshi*, vol. 1, p. 156; Nakamura (ed.), *Nihon Joshi Daigakkō 40-nen-shi*, p. 80; Hiratsuka Raichō, 'Mejiro no omoide', *Tokyo Asahi Shinbun* (1–3 December, 1939), reprinted in Hiratsuka, *Chosakushū*, vol. 6, p. 309.

[88] Hiratsuka, *Genshi*, vol. 1, p. 155; Hiratsuka, *Watakushi*, pp. 36–7; Hiratsuka Raichō, 'Musume ni haha no musume jidai o kataru', *Fujin Kōron* (May, 1935), reprinted in Hiratsuka, *Chosakushū*, vol. 6, p. 19. This article was also reprinted in Hiratsuka Raichō, *Haha no Kotoba* (1937) and Hiratsuka Raichō, *Boshi Zuihitsu* (1948).

and visited western countries as a government official in the early
Meiji period.[89] Hiratsuka Raichō therefore expected him to be more
sympathetic to women's higher education. He felt that he had already
fulfilled his duty towards his daughters' education by sending them
to Ochanomizu Girls' High School.[90] And he believed that giving a
daughter extra academic training would do her more harm than
good. These views were widely shared among the upper and upper-
middle classes.[91] There were a number of common prejudices against
female higher education, which have been summarised as follows:
Women's higher education makes women impertinent, conceited,
insolent or big-headed; that it makes women cold-hearted; it detracts
from female worldly wisdom, and renders them ignorant of the world;
it harms female health; and it has a bad influence on their children's education.[92]

Such reactions were probably more strongly expressed in Japan
than in northern areas of Europe, but there are echoes here of feelings against female further education found in many other countries.[93] Some similar arguments were used against the education of
women in Girton and Newnham Colleges, Cambridge, and they
were expressed more widely in parts of America and the Mediterranean
countries. Hiratsuka's father expected her to master traditional 'accomplishments' such as flower arrangement, tea ceremony, calligraphy
and *koto* (playing a Japanese zither), which were basic requirements
for a woman hoping to marry into a respectable family, rather than
enter the Japan Women's College.[94] However, her mother persuaded
her husband to give way, with the provision that she should enrol
to study domestic science instead of English. She duly entered the
department of domestic science in April 1903, two years after its
foundation.[95] She recalled that she lost her bearings at first, as it was

[89] Kobayashi, *Hito to Shisō*, pp. 13–4.
[90] Hiratsuka, *Genshi*, vol. 1, p. 154; Hiratsuka, *Watakushi*, pp. 36–7.
[91] Ishimoto, *Facing Two Ways*, p. 80.
[92] Katayama, *Kindai Nihon no Joshi Kyōiku*, pp. 107–8.
[93] Perry Williams, 'Pioneer women students at Cambridge, 1869–81', in Felicity
Hunt (ed.), *Lessons for Life: The Schoolings of Girls and Women, 1850–1950* (Oxford,
1987), pp. 171–89.
[94] Hiratsuka, *Watakushi*, p. 36.
[95] Hiratsuka, *Genshi*, vol. 1, pp. 156–8; Hiratsuka, *Watakushi*, p. 37, Hiratsuka,
'Mejiro no omoide', pp. 310–1; Hiratsuka Raichō, '25-nen mae no watakushi', *Fujin
no Tomo* (April, 1928), reprinted in Hiratsuka, *Chosakushū*, vol. 5, p. 29.

an entirely different world for her. In particular, she was surprised
by a new type of student she met on campus:

> I was stunned by the big difference between the atmosphere of stu-
> dents at this women's college and Ochanomizu Girls' High School. I
> felt as if I had stepped into an adult world all at once. I was much
> bewildered and embarrassed by this. The range of students which the
> college had then was very extensive. Some had already taught at ele-
> mentary schools for several years, and others were widows or married
> women with husbands and children. There was also a large age gap
> among students, and some of them were middle-aged women. I also
> noticed that there were many students from provincial areas. The lan-
> guage they used sounded very rough to me, after the extremely polite
> language used at Ochanomizu Girls' High School. I remember that
> many of them had different dialects . . . their manners were rough and
> far from the polite and refined manners I had become accustomed to
> at Ochanomizu. I felt as if I were left behind on my own in a circle
> of foreigners.[96]

Hiratsuka's account contrasted with Oku Mumeo's descriptions there
about ten years later. Oku stated that her classmates were daughters
from wealthy families, including daughters of the Mitsui family.[97] She
recalled that she felt most uncomfortable surrounded by sly and pre-
tentious women with incredibly polite manners, and could not mix
with them because she was a straightforward rural girl. According
to *Nihon Joshidai 80-nen* (*The Eighty-Year History of the Japan Women's
University*), the College did not have any age limits, so there was a
large disparity in students' ages when it was founded.[98] The students
ranged from 18 to 35 years old. The great majority of students were
daughters from educated classes, and those from provincial areas
tended to be daughters of business magnates or landowners.[99]

Hiratsuka's initial doubts among other students quickly faded and
she began to feel satisfied.[100] The Japan Women's College's curriculum was totally different from the Women's Institute of English
Studies'.[101] The latter offered a very narrow range of subjects, and

---

[96] Hiratsuka, *Genshi*, vol. 1, p. 157. The similar comments about Hiratsuka's fellow students were made in her article, 'Mejiro no omoide', pp. 310–1.

[97] Oku, *Nobi*, p. 27.

[98] Nihon Joshi Daigaku (ed.), *Nihon Joshi Daigaku no 80-nen*, p. 25.

[99] Karasawa, *Joshi Gakusei no Rekishi*, p. 102.

[100] Hiratsuka, *Genshi*, vol. 1, p. 158; Hiratsuka, 'Mejiro no omoide', p. 311.

[101] Nakamura (ed.), *Nihon Joshi Daigakkō 40-nen-shi*, pp. 75–9; Yamazaki (ed.), *Tsuda
Juku 60-nen-shi*, pp. 82–3.

gave high priority to English language teaching, which was the aim
of Tsuda Umeko, its founder.[102] The Japan Women's College offered
a much wider range of subjects, in accordance with Naruse's wish
to provide a general education.[103] Hiratsuka's recollection of the subjects she studied underscored this:

> At the Japan Women's College I attended all the compulsory subjects
> for my home economics course, which comprised practical ethics, moral
> philosophy, pedagogy, experimental psychology, child psychology, biol-
> ogy, applied chemistry, hygiene, physiology, economics and practical
> training in cookery.[104]

The College also allowed students, who were registered with one
department, to attend as many courses at different departments as
they wished.[105] This was very convenient for Hiratsuka, who had
been persuaded to register with the department of home economics
by her parents, although she wanted to study English. Hiratsuka
attended many optional classes for students specialising in English
and Japanese literature, including ones on Japanese and western history, art history and literature.[106] All these would benefit her future
activities.

She also gained from excellent teaching at the Japan Women's
College, which contrasted with the Women's Institute of English
Studies where there were few teaching staff.[107] The Japan Women's
College employed many well-qualified academics, some of them doctors of literature, medicine and pharmacy, including some professors
of Tokyo Imperial University.[108] All of them approved of the educational policy introduced by Naruse, and wanted to advance the
cause of women's higher education.

---

[102] Yamazaki, *Tsuda Umeko*, pp. 180–1; Yamazaki (ed.), *Tsuda Juku 60-nen-shi*,
p. 61.
[103] Nakamura (ed.), *Nihon Joshi Daigakkō 40-nen-shi*, pp. 75–9. Naruse's view of
women's education is given in his article, 'The education of Japanese women', in
Ōkuma Shigenobu (ed.), *Fifty Years of New Japan*, vol. 2 (London, 1910), pp. 192–225.
[104] Hiratsuka, *Genshi*, vol. 1, p. 164.
[105] Nihon Joshi Daigaku (ed.), *Nihon Joshi Daigaku no 80-nen*, p. 30; Hiratsuka,
'25-nen mae no watakushi', p. 29.
[106] Hiratsuka, *Genshi*, vol. 1, pp. 165–6.
[107] Nakamura (ed.), *Nihon Joshi Daigakkō 40-nen-shi*, pp. 80–1; Yamazaki (ed.), *Tsuda
Juku 60-nen-shi*, p. 73.
[108] Nakamura (ed.), *Nihon Joshi Daigakkō 40-nen-shi*, pp. 80–1; Nihon Joshi Daigaku
(ed.), *Nihon Joshi Daigaku no 80-nen*, p. 26.

The traditional teaching method of cramming knowledge into students was not used at the Japan Women's College.[109] Naruse particularly disliked students' passive memorising attitudes to learning, and he wrote about his more effective method in his book *Shin Jidai no Kyōiku* (*Education in the New Era*):

> All human beings have inborn within them precious self-motivation. The fundamental method, which produces the highest possible educational result, is to develop and cultivate students' voluntary motivation.[110]

Naruse encouraged students to acquire the habit of *jigaku jishū* (studying for themselves), and he also put emphasis on *sōzōsei no sonchō* (respect for creativity).[111] In order to put his ideas into practice, the curriculum of the Japan Women's College was carefully constructed. To increase time for students' study, it restricted teaching to a maximum of 25 hours a week. Students were encouraged to experiment and observe.[112] Regular staff-student seminars were organised and guest speakers were also invited. These arrangements were made to develop students' intellectual faculties, to broaden their horizons and promote character building.[113]

Students were not under any severe pressure. They had no examinations to take, and were never asked to write essays. The only requirement each student had to fulfil to graduate was to submit a dissertation, on any topic.[114] This contrasted with the very strict regime which the Women's Institute of English Studies offered, where students had to take regular examinations, do much homework, and those who did not meet academic standards had to repeat the year.[115]

Hiratsuka was tired of inflexible education which forced teachers' opinions onto students, using rote memorising as practised at Ochanomizu Girls' High School. In contrast she was attracted by

---

[109] Hiratsuka, *Genshi*, vol. 1, p. 158.

[110] Cited in Fujii & Kanamori, *Onna no Kyōiku*, p. 42.

[111] Naruse Jinzō, 'Jigaku jidō shugi', in Nihon Joshi Daigaku Joshi Kyōiku Kenkyujo (ed.), *Kongo no Joshi Kyōiku*, pp. 183–6.

[112] Fujii & Kanamori, *Onna no Kyōiku*, p. 43.

[113] Nihon Joshi Daigaku (ed.), *Nihon Joshi Daigaku no 80-nen*, pp. 26–30; Nakamura (ed.), *Nihon Joshi Daigakkō 40-nen-shi*, pp. 94–5.

[114] Hiratsuka, *Watakushi*, p. 49; Hiratsuka, *Genshi*, vol. 1, pp. 158, 199–201; Oku, *Nobi*, p. 32.

[115] Hiratsuka, *Genshi*, vol.1, pp. 204–7; Yamakawa, *Onna Nidai no Ki*, pp. 133–9; Kamichika, *Jiden*, pp. 91–2; Yamazaki, *Tsuda Umeko*, p. 184.

the educational policy of the Japan Women's College.[116] The College met her wish to study a wide range of academic subjects. Of those subjects, she particularly benefitted from *jissen rinri* (practical ethics), taught by Naruse.[117] This was a compulsory general course, which provided a basic moral and academic training.[118] Naruse covered a wide range of topics, such as the basic principles of women's higher education, the main objectives of the Japan Women's College and introductory sessions on academic subjects such as religion, philosophy and ethics.[119] Hiratsuka wrote that

> I attended Naruse's lectures without missing a single one. I took detailed notes, and asked him many questions in the class. Even after the class I grabbed him to throw many questions at him until I was completely satisfied with his answers.[120]

Naruse's teaching, based on his learning in religion, philosophy and ethics, and his experience as a clergyman and educationalist, opened a new world for Hiratsuka, and she became his ardent admirer.[121] She decided to live in a dormitory, to promote better understanding of Naruse's educational principles among her fellow students. Dormitories at the Japan Women's College were considered to be the best places to impart such views, being used not only for boarding but also as a venue in which to spread ideas of women's education.[122]

---

[116] Hiratsuka, *Genshi*, vol. 1, p. 158. On further details on Naruse's educational policy of the Japan Women's College, see Ōhashi Hiro, 'Naruse Jinzō sensei to hongaku no kyōiku rinen', in Nihon Joshi Daigaku (ed.), *Joshidai Tsūshin*, 1 (January, 1949), p. 1; 'Naruse-shi no risō to sesshi: joshi sōgō daigaku no naiyō', *Fujo Shinbun*, 982 (14 March, 1919), p. 2.

[117] Hiratsuka, *Genshi*, vol. 1, pp. 158–60; Hiratsuka, *Watakushi*, p. 39; Hiratsuka Raichō, 'Gakkō o deta koro no watakushi: jiga o tōshite kami ni hairu', *Joseisen* (March, 1948), reprinted in Hiratsuka, *Chosakushū*, vol. 7, pp. 23–4; Hiratsuka, 'Mejiro no omoide', p. 313; Hiratsuka, '25–nen mae no watakushi', p. 31.

[118] Nishina (ed.), *Naruse Sensei Den*, pp. 304–17; Katayama, *Kindai Nihon no Joshi Kyōiku*, p. 158; Nihon Joshi Daigaku (ed.), *Nihon Joshi Dai no 80-nen*, pp. 30–2; Nakamura (ed.), *Nihon Joshi Daigakkō 40-nen-shi*, pp. 142–4; Aoki, *Kindaishi o Hiraita Joseitachi*, pp. 51–2; Nihon Joshi Daigakkō (ed.), *Joshi Daigaku Kōgiroku, Jissen Rinri* (n.d.).

[119] Nihon Joshi Daigaku (ed.), *Nihon Joshi Daigaku no 80-nen*, pp. 30–2; Nishina (ed.), *Naruse Sensei Den*, pp. 304–17; Naruse Jinzō, 'Jissen rinri kōwa' (September 1906–December 1907), reprinted in Nihon Joshi Daigaku Joshi Kyōiku Kenkyūjo (ed.), *Kongo no Joshi Kyōiku*, pp. 132–82; Nihon Joshi Daigakkō (ed.), *Joshi Daigaku Kōgiroku, Jissen Rinri* (n.d.).

[120] Hiratsuka, *Genshi*, vol. 1, p. 160.

[121] Hiratsuka, *Watakushi*, p. 39; Hiratsuka, 'Mejiro no omoide', p. 313; Hiratsuka, *Genshi*, vol. 1, pp. 158–160.

[122] Nihon Joshi Daigaku (ed.), *Nihon Joshi Dai no 80-nen*, pp. 51–3; Katayama,

However, dormitory life did not fulfil her expectations, and she rapidly became disillusioned. Sharing an eight mat *tatami* room with four other students, she lacked privacy. As the dormitory's purpose involved self-sacrifice and cooperative service, she had to attend many social activities in the evenings there.[123] She recalled that most of the students in dormitories hardly studied, and simply proclaimed themselves to be great admirers of Naruse, repeating his words mechanically.[124] For all their pretence at understanding his lectures, they had little idea of their meaning. They were not interested in acquiring knowledge, but prided themselves upon being under the influence of a great educationalist. Disappointed with her fellow students' lack of enthusiasm for study, she was even more disturbed at the way in which they treated her own enthusiasm as freakish and odd. She was constantly told to socialise with other students rather than study.[125] She was also criticised by senior students for being selfish and lacking a sense of cooperative service, which annoyed her. Under such circumstances, she began to isolate herself from students in the dormitories, and found consolation in reading:

> I was driven by an utterly uncontrollable desire for reading. I devoured books as if I was a real book worm . . . Most of the books I read in the college library were on religion, philosophy and ethics. I read them randomly, without any plan.[126]

At night she tiptoed out of the dormitory and read by candlelight in a dining room, despite being told to return to bed. She never settled down, and alienated herself from other students.[127] Using illness as an excuse, she left and returned home, commuting to college until her graduation. This left her isolated, treated as an eccentric,

Kindai Nihon no Joshi Kyōiku, p. 108; Isomura Haruko, *Ima no Onna: Shiryō Meiji Joseishi* (1913, 1986 edn), pp. 222–6; Hiratsuka, *Watakushi*, p. 39.

[123] Hiratsuka, 'Mejiro no omoide', p. 312; Hiratsuka, *Watakushi*, p. 39. Similar points were made by Kinpara Fuyuko and Yamauchi Akino, who were graduates from the Japan Women's College and stayed in its dormitories. Kinpara graduated in 1928 and Yamauchi in 1932. Personal interview with Kinpara Fuyuko, 19 January, 1996, Hamamatsu, Shizuoka Prefecture; personal interview with Yamauchi Akino, 25 April, 1994, Tokyo.

[124] The account of her fellow students who had lived in dormitories at the Japan Women's College is given in Hiratsuka, *Genshi*, vol. 1, pp. 169–71.

[125] *Ibid.*, pp. 163–4, 175–6; Kobayashi, *Hito to Shisō*, pp. 42–3.

[126] Hiratsuka, *Genshi*, vol. 1, pp. 176–7.

[127] Hiratsuka, 'Mejiro no omoide', p. 315; Hiratsuka, *Genshi*, vol. 1, p. 176; Aoki, *Kindaishi o Hiraita Joseitachi*, p. 52.

and lacking close friends. Although she continued to attend the optional classes which interested her, she avoided compulsory classes on her special subject, especially practical training in cooking.[128] Three years after she entered the Japan Women's College, she graduated from the department of domestic science, aged twenty, in March 1906 on the basis of her dissertation.[129] This was very short (about twenty pages), on an aspect of the history of religion.[130] It had no connection with the domestic science which she was supposed to have specialised in, which she neither studied nor cared for. As the deadline approached, she had simply opted to write on a familiar topic, and to her surprise it met the graduation requirement.[131]

She was not an exceptional case. Oku Mumeo, who also registered with the department of domestic science, did no work for her special subject for three years while a student there.[132] She submitted a dissertation on a French poet, Romain Rolland (1866–1944), which was completely irrelevant to her special subject.[133] Just like Hiratsuka, Oku graduated from the college without difficulty.

Hiratsuka and Oku gave the impression that the Japan Women's College did not have very strict degree requirements. One might think that the degrees awarded there did not compare with those from other universities open to men only. The ease with which students graduated from the Japan Women's College contrasted with the difficulty students had to complete their degree at the Women's Institute of English Studies, which adopted a far more systematic and strict assessment, one that frequently failed students. Moreover, the Women's Institute of English Studies assigned students regular

---

[128] Hiratsuka, *Genshi*, vol. 1, pp. 165–6, 183–4; Hiratsuka, *Watakushi*, p. 42.

[129] Hiratsuka, *Genshi*, vol. 1, p. 201; Hiratsuka, *Watakushi*, p. 49; Nihon Joshi Daigakkō (comp.), *Nihon Joshi Daigakkō Sotsugyōsei Meibo*, 1906; Ōfūkai (comp.), *Ōfūkai Kaiin Meibo* (1992); Hiratsuka, 'Musume ni haha no musume jidai o kataru', p. 18. Unfortunately, as her dissertation was not kept in the library at the Japan Women's College, I could not locate it.

[130] Hiratsuka, *Genshi*, vol. 1, p. 201.

[131] Hiratsuka, *Watakushi*, p. 49.

[132] Oku, *Nobi*, pp. 27–32. Like Hiratsuka, Oku missed many classes, and spent most of her time in the college library, devoting herself to a wide range of reading.

[133] *Ibid.*, p. 32. Oku graduated from the Japan Women's College in 1916. See Nihon Joshi Daigakkō (comp.), *Nihon Joshi Daigakkō Sotsugyōsei Meibo* (1916); Ōfūkai (comp.), *Ōfūkai Kaiin Meibo* (1992); Hoshi Ruriko *et al.* (eds), *Ōfūkai no 100-nin: Nihon Joshidai Monogatari* (1996), p. 364; Tokuza, *The Rise of the Feminist Movement in Japan*, pp. 96–7.

examinations and essays apart from dissertations for graduation purposes.[134]

Neither Hiratsuka nor Oku praised the education they received at Japan Women's College. They criticised its education for being basic and irrelevant to their future careers.[135] However, the College gave them much freedom and reading time, the range of academic subjects was wide, taught in many cases by eminent lecturers like Asō Shōzō, Miyake Shū and Togawa Antaku, and it included the reading of western books.[136] The College created opportunities to meet other women, who would later become supporters of their feminist activities. Although Hiratsuka did not have a high opinion of the other students while she was there, the great majority of early members and supporters of the Seitō Society were graduates from the College.[137] Oku thought that the main benefit it provided her with was the chance to meet interesting graduates, who went on to establish themselves as successful career women.[138]

Conclusion

At this point it is useful to compare Hiratsuka's early life up to college graduation with those of her other feminists such as Ichikawa, Oku, Yamakawa, Kamichika and Katō.[139] It is also interesting to set their lives into an international comparative frame, to see what they shared with their counterparts among feminists in England, not least because these Japanese women were very aware of the feminism being developed in the West, and associated themselves with it in many ways.

These Japanese feminists were exceptionally well-educated compared with the great majority of Japanese women who completed

---

[134] Yamakawa, *Onna Nidai no Ki*, pp. 132–8; Kamichika, *Jiden*, pp. 91–2; Furuki, *Tsuda Umeko*, p. 162; Yamazaki, *Tsuda Umeko*, pp. 202–3.

[135] Oku, *Nobi*, p. 28.

[136] Nihon Joshi Daigaku (ed.), *Nihon Joshi Daigaku no 80-nen*, p. 39; Nakamura (ed.), *Nihon Joshi Daigakkō 40-nen-shi*, pp. 80–1; Oku, *Nobi*, pp. 27–8; Hiratsuka, *Genshi*, pp. 176–8.

[137] Horiba, *Seitō no Jidai*, p. 20; Aoki, *Kindaishi o Hiraita Joseitachi*, pp. 38–95, 134–68.

[138] Oku, *Nobi*, pp. 29–30.

[139] See Appendix 1, which contains biographical sketches of Hiratsuka's contemporary feminists.

their education at elementary school. These feminists were products
of new women's higher education institutions. Oku and Hiratsuka
were graduates from the Japan Women's College, and Yamakawa
and Kamichika graduated from the Women's Institute of English
Studies. Ichikawa went to Aichi Kenritsu Joshi Shihan Gakkō (Aichi
Prefectural Girls' Higher School), a female teachers' training college.[140]
Katō was the only leading feminist who did not receive higher education in Japan. However, she graduated from the Peeresses' High
School, and after her marriage to Baron Ishimoto went to America
and received further education at the Ballard School in New York,
as recommended by her husband.[141] Although they may have expressed
some dissatisfaction with their higher education, all these feminists
benefitted considerably from the opening of higher education to them.
It gave them confidence to articulate their views, and to engage in
public feminist campaigns in a society where the penalties for doing
this were more severe than in any other industrial country.

Yamakawa and Kamichika made themselves proficient in English
as a result of the very intensive English language training they received
at the Women's Institute of English Studies.[142] Their English skills
later allowed them to translate western feminists' works into Japanese,
and to write books and articles in Japanese introducing and analysing
western feminists' theories and the history of European and American
feminist movements.[143] Such linguistic aptitude was crucial when they
were serving as intermediaries between the several cultures, relaying
developments from another into their own, and deriving confidence
from western examples. Yamakawa and Kamichika certainly contributed to promoting a better understanding of western feminist
causes and activities, using skills acquired in higher education.

These Japanese feminists all took education seriously from an early
age, were well-motivated and hard-working, and achieved excellent
results in their studies.[144] Despite their academic attainments, their

---

[140] Ichikawa, *Jiden: Senzen*, pp. 15–21; Ichikawa, *87-sai no Seishun*.
[141] Ishimoto, *Facing Two Ways*, pp. 177–85; Katō, *Ai wa Jidi o Koete*, pp. 28–52;
Hopper, *A New Woman of Japan*, pp. 9–11.
[142] Yamakawa, *Onna Nidai no Ki*, pp. 133–5; Kamichika, *Jiden*, pp. 92–4; Hane,
Reflections on the Way to the Gallows, p. 166.
[143] Kamichika Ichiko, *Josei Shisōshi* (1974), pp. 15–140; Yamakawa, *Onna Nidai no
Ki*, pp. 223–4; Tanaka Sumiko, 'Gendai ni ikiru riron', in Yamakawa Kikue Seitan
100-nen o Kinen Suru Kai (ed.), *Gendai Feminizumu to Yamakawa Kikue* (1990), p. 154.
[144] Yamakawa, *Onna Nidai no Ki*, pp. 126–7; Oku, *Nobi*, pp. 25–7; Hiratsuka,
Genshi, vol. 1., p. 156.

educational institutions never satisfied their intellectual expectations, and left them feeling starved of a higher education equal to that of men. They felt themselves to be victims of a discriminatory educational system in the Meiji and early Taishō periods. Despite this, they persevered and improved themselves educationally, via Japanese and western literature on many subjects.[145] Hiratsuka and Yamakawa took private tuition from leading literary critics and social commentators such as Baba Kochō and Ikuta Chōkō. Ichikawa, Hiratsuka and Kamichika all studied the Swedish feminist Ellen Key's works under Yamada Kakichi's guidance, and they paid particular attention to works by European and American female authors.[146] Hiratsuka, Oku and Ichikawa's editorial skills, as later displayed in their edited magazines like *Seitō* and *Josei Dōmei (Women's League)*, and their careers as female literary and social critics, bore testimony to their academic ability, and to their determination to rise above the prevailing cultural presumptions that they were inherently inferior to men.

Such a fondness for learning and the experience of suffering from educational discrimination against girls—resulting in strong pleas for better female education—were characteristics common among many British Victorian feminists and their Japanese counterparts.[147] In both countries, feminists were acutely aware of how crucial education was to achieving their long-term aims.

Through higher education these Japanese feminists acquired the skills to become financially independent. Many of them used such skills to become in effect 'career women' before they committed themselves to feminist causes. In many cases the same skills were also useful for their later feminist activities. Ichikawa worked as an elementary school teacher and then became the first female journalist working for the Nagoya Newspaper Company.[148] Oku assisted the editorial work of *Fujin Shūhō (Women's Weekly)*.[149] Kamichika worked

---

[145] Yamakawa, *Onna Nidai no Ki*, pp. 127–37; Oku, *Nobi*, pp. 23–8; Hiratsuka, *Genshi*, vol. 1, pp. 155–78.

[146] Ichikawa, *Jiden: Senzen*, pp. 37–9; Hiratsuka, *Genshi*, vol. 2, pp. 169–72.

[147] Nakajima Kuni, 'Joshi Kyōiku o shakai kara tou: Ryōsai kenbo kyōiku hihan', in Yomakawa Kikue Seitan 100-nen o Kinen Suru Kai (ed.), *Gendai Feminizumu to Yamakawa Kikue* (1990), p. 159; Carol Dyhouse, *No Distinction of Sex? Women in British Universities, 1870–1939* (London, 1995), chapter 2 & chapter 5; Williams, 'Pioneer women students at Cambridge', pp. 171–90.

[148] Ichikawa, *Jiden: Senzen*, pp. 24–36; Nagoya Joseishi Kenkyūkai (ed.), *Haha no Jidai* (Nagoya, 1969), pp. 312–5; Ichikawa, *87-sai no Seishun*.

[149] Oku, *Nobi*, pp. 29–30. *Fujin Shūhō (Women's Weekly)* was run by Kobashi Miyoko, who was Oku's senior at the Japan Women's College. Under Kobayashi's guidance

as a school teacher, a journalist and a translator.[150] Yamakawa worked as a translator.[151] Hiratsuka never took up full-time work, but she worked as a part-time stenographer for distinguished academics.[152] In that regard she differed from some of feminists, for this work did not follow logically from her higher education; but while her education may not have related closely to her feminist activities, it was later of obvious value to someone in journalism.

A further characteristic common to Yamakawa, Ichikawa, Oku and Hiratsuka was that all of them, reacting against *ryōsai kenbo kyōiku* (education to create good wives and wise mothers), became rebellious in their high school days, and manifested the first signs of their feminism in defiant attitudes towards that education. Hiratsuka set up the *Kaizoku Gumi* (Pirate Gang) and boycotted *shūshin* (morals) classes. Yamakawa, who was utterly demoralised by an education designed to transform her into 'a good wife and wise mother', nearly abandoned her high school education when she was in its fourth year. She was persuaded not to do so by a friend and her teacher.[153] Oku, who was also irritated by such education, rebelled against high school teachers who advised her father to arrange her marriage.[154] Among these feminists, Ichikawa took the boldest action against this extremely conservative education. When in the fourth year of Aichi Prefectural Girls' Higher School, together with her 28 classmates, she compiled a list of 28 complaints against her school's education and submitted it to the principal. She and her classmates conducted a strike for some days, protesting against the education for making good wives and wise mothers.[155] Ichikawa's outlook revealed itself at the age of fourteen, when she was bold enough to apply to study in America. Her application was rejected by the police, who felt that sending a fourteen-year old Japanese girl to America on her own would not be safe.[156]

Oku mastered the editorial work, which Oku found extremely useful when editing the *Women's League* with Ichikawa and Hiratsuka.

[150] Kamichika, *Jiden*, pp. 109–33.

[151] Yamakawa, *Onna Nidai no Ki*, pp. 223–4; Tanaka, 'Gendai ni ikiru riron', p. 154.

[152] Hiratsuka, *Genshi*, vol. 1, pp. 203–4.

[153] Yamakawa, *Onna Nidai no Ki*, p. 120; Nakajima, 'Joshi kyōiku o shakai kara tou', pp. 164–5.

[154] Oku, *Nobi*, pp. 23–5.

[155] Ichikawa, *Jiden: Senzen*, pp. 19–21; Ichikawa, *87-sai no Seishun*.

[156] Ichikawa, *Jiden: Senzen*, pp. 10–11; Ichikawa, *87-sai no Seishun*.

These feminists came from very different family backgrounds. Using class terms loosely, Katō was from the upper class, Hiratsuka and Yamakawa were from the upper-middle class, Oku was from the middle class, and Ichikawa was from the working class. Katō, Hiratsuka and Yamakawa's fathers were all from the *samurai* class; they were well-educated, proficient in western languages, and had visited western countries.[157] On the other hand, Oku and Ichikawa's fathers were uneducated. Oku's father was a blacksmith, and Ichikawa's father was a farmer.[158] The only feature seemingly common to all these fathers was that they appreciated or were sympathetic to women's education, more so than most other men of their time. Those who were educated, especially Katō and Hiratsuka's fathers, were keen to give their daughters the best education available, from kindergarten to high school.[159] However, both of them felt that they had completed their obligation towards their daughters' education when they had graduated from high school, and they were equally opposed to women's higher education, believing that it caused harm.[160] By comparison, Ichikawa and Oku's uneducated fathers greatly valued education, and allowed their daughters to receive even higher education.[161] Ichikawa's father, who was a farmer, had hardly any education himself, and he bitterly regretted this. He sent even his daughters to higher educational institutions although he could hardly afford to do so, and had to borrow a considerable sum of money for this purpose.[162]

Similarly, Oku's father, who had been persuaded to abandon his own higher education in order to follow his father in the family business, was obsessed with his children's education. Oku remembered that her father never discouraged her from studying because she was a girl, and in her household neglecting one's study was considered a major sin.[163] Oku and her elder brother satisfied their father's

---

[157] Hiratsuka, *Genshi*, vol. 1, pp. 38–42; Yamakawa, *Onna Nidai no Ki*, pp. 58–63, Ishimoto, *Facing Two Ways*, pp. 6–7; Katō, *Ai wa Jidai o Koete*, p. 15.

[158] Oku, *Nobi*, pp. 12–4; Ichikawa, *Jiden: Senzen*, p. 3; Ichikawa Fusae, *Nonaka no Ippon Sugi* (1981), p. 15.

[159] Hiratsuka, *Genshi*, vol. 1, p. 91; Ishimoto, *Facing Two Ways*, p. 78.

[160] Hiratsuka, *Genshi*, vol. 1, p. 154; Ishimoto, *Facing Two Ways*, p. 80.

[161] Oku, *Nobi*, pp. 12–4; Ichikawa, *Jiden: Senzen*, pp. 5–6; Ichikawa, *Nonaka no Ippon Sugi*, p. 11.

[162] Ichikawa, *Jiden: Senzen*, pp. 5–6; Ichikawa, *87-sai no Seishun*; Ichikawa, *Nonaka no Ippon Sugi*, p. 11.

[163] Oku, *Nobi*, p. 13. Oku vividly recalled that he never tired of saying: 'I will

educational expectations, and she proceeded to the Japan Women's College with her father's blessing, while her brother went to Tokyo Imperial University.[164]

Both Oku and Ichikawa's fathers treated their daughters and sons equally, which was most unusual and progressive at that time.[165] This unorthodox background was undoubtedly an important factor in Ichikawa's and Oku's later feminism. Such gendered even-handedness, and similarly unorthodox treatment, were experienced by some British feminists such as Mary Carpenter and Barbara Bodichon.[166] Their superior education gave them the confidence to try to bring social conditions into line with those of their own family. Something similar seems to be evident in the case of several Japanese feminists.

Hiratsuka's family background and upbringing differed from some other feminists insofar as her father lacked a son, and he probably compensated for this by treating Hiratsuka as his companion and friend in her childhood. However, as a government official, he was expected to set an example in paternalistic domination. Hiratsuka recalled that as her father rose higher in the Ministry of Finance, she noticed that he displayed more predictable signs of being a civil servant.[167] He began to exert his authority more firmly over his wife and his elder daughter Taka. Although Taka received an almost identical education to her sister Hiratsuka Raichō, she was completely different from Raichō in temperament and personality.[168] Taka was modest and obeyed her parents. Her father arranged a marriage for Taka without consulting her. Taka did not complain and married Yamanaka Yonejirō, who met her father's social expectations, and

---

send both of you [Oku Mumeo and her brother] to even higher educational institutions if you wish. Therefore you must study extremely hard.'

[164] *Ibid.*, p. 26.

[165] Ichikawa, *Jiden: Senzen*, pp. 5–6; Oku, *Nobi*, pp. 13–4.

[166] In Carpenter and Bodichon's biographies one also sees how unusual family conditioning and presumptions could play a major role in shaping their expectations and reforming hopes for the wider society that they consequently found themselves mismatched to. On Mary Carpenter, see Jo Manton, *Mary Carpenter and the Children of the Streets* (London, 1976), pp. 17–28. On Barbara Bodichon, see Sheila R. Herstein, *Mid-Victorian Feminist, Barbara Leigh Smith Bodichon* (New Haven, 1985), pp. 1–23.

[167] Hiratsuka, *Genshi*, vol. 1, p. 139.

[168] Taka attended the same kindergarten, elementary school and girls' high school as her sister. Both of them entered the Japan Women's College, but Taka specialised in Japanese literature and Raichō in domestic science.

Taka's husband later succeeded her father as head of the family.[169] As she got older, Hiratsuka Raichō felt less comfortable with her father. After she entered Ochanomizu Girls' High School she became increasingly critical of and distant from him.[170] However, her father hardly exerted his authority over her, and never forced her to act against her will. He accepted her strong personality, showed much patience towards her and hardly ever criticised her or interfered.[171] His broad-minded and lenient attitudes may have helped Raichō to develop her radicalism and feminism.

It seems that the mothers of these feminists were less influential in the formation of their ideas than their fathers. The exception was Yamakawa Kikue's mother, who was exceptionally well-educated for a woman of her generation (she was one of the very early graduates from Ochanomizu Girls' High School).[172] She exercised considerable authority over her children, and was the most important influence on Yamakawa's early life. Yamakawa, Katō and Hiratsuka's mothers were from the samurai class.[173] Although Katō and Hiratsuka's mothers were educated at girls' missionary schools, they were obvious examples of 'good wives and wise mothers'.[174] Both Oku and Ichikawa's mothers were uneducated, and Ichikawa's mother was illiterate.[175] They were all very affectionate towards their daughters, and prepared to assist them in any way. Hiratsuka wrote that

> My mother had faith in my sister and myself. For example, even when I became the target of public criticism or took a defiant attitude towards her, she never deserted me and never stopped loving me. She always observed my activities with affection and patience, and continued to trust and support me. After I became a mother of two children, I became more appreciative of my mother's strong love for me.[176]

---

[169] *Ibid.*, pp. 147–8, 217–8; Tsunesaburō Kamesaka (ed.), *Who's Who in Japan* (1937), p. 127.

[170] Hiratsuka, *Genshi*, vol. 1, pp. 139–40.

[171] *Ibid.*, p. 268.

[172] Yamakawa, *Onna Nidai no Ki*, pp. 36–48; Nakajima, 'Joshi kyōiku o shakai kara tou', p. 165; Hane, *Reflections on the Way to the Gallows*, p. 162.

[173] Hiratsuka, *Genshi*, vol. 1, pp. 42–3; Ishimoto, *Facing Two Ways*, pp. 9–10; Yamakawa, *Onna Nidai no Ki*, pp. 9–10; Hopper, *A New Woman of Japan*, p. 3

[174] Hiratsuka, *Genshi*, vol. 42–6; Katō, *Ai wa Jidai o Koete*, pp. 16–7, Ishimoto, *Facing Two Ways*, pp. 11–2; Hopper, *A New Woman of Japan*, p. 3.

[175] Ichikawa, *Jiden: Senzen*, p. 5; Ichikawa, *Nonaka no Ippon Sugi*, p. 10, Ichikawa, *87-sai no Seishun*; Oku, *Nobi*, p. 14.

[176] Hiratsuka Raichō, 'Haha de aru yorokobi', *Shiro Bato* (February, 1937), reprinted

To be 'a good wife and wise mother' could in some ways under-
mine its own conservative purpose. These mothers' supportive devotion even to their daughters' socially wayward desires can only be
understood if we appreciate that such mothers felt that they must
support and endorse their offspring. To have tried to suppress their
daughters would have conflicted with their own maternal purpose,
inculcated by their own upbringing. There is no evidence whatever
that the daughters clashed with their humble and supportive mothers,
with the small exception of Oku's mother who worried that her
daughter's education might spoil her marital prospects.[177] This contrasts markedly with the daughter-mother relations experienced by
some British feminists, who seem to have been more affected by
strong-minded maternal restrictions.[178] Any tensions in the Japanese
cases tended to be between daughters and fathers, and we have seen
that these were relatively slight. As far as the Japanese daughters
were concerned, their mothers appeared to them as victims: women
who had sacrificed their lives to domineering husbands. The daughters were often acutely aware of their mothers' unhappiness, and this
perception played a crucial part in their own decisions to involve
themselves in feminist activities. Ichikawa and Oku were outstanding examples of this phenomenon.[179] Compared with Ichikawa's and
Oku's mothers, Hiratsuka's mother had a much better marriage and
never suffered from physical abuse and financial difficulty. Nevertheless,
Hiratsuka still felt that her mother had been a victim of the *ie* system.[180] This was because her mother had suppressed her emotions,
given up hobbies and compromised her personality in serving her
husband. Japanese society was to discover that wisely humble mothers were not effective instruments to control disillusioned daughters,
and that those daughters would often form their own judgements on
their mothers' predicaments, and focus their own lives in deliberately contrary ways.

---

in Hiratsuka, *Chosakushū*, vol. 6, p. 214. This article was also reprinted in Hiratsuka,
Haha no Kotoba (1937) and Hiratsuka, *Boshi Zuihitsu* (1948).

[177] Oku, *Nobi*, p. 18.

[178] C. D. Firth, *Constance Louisa Maynard* (London, 1969), pp. 93, 102.

[179] Oku, *Nobi*, pp. 14–6; Ichikawa, *Jiden: Senzen*, pp. 2–6; Ichikawa, *Nonaka no
Ippon Sugi*, pp. 11–2; Ichikawa, *87-sai no Seishun*.

[180] Hiratsuka, *Watakushi*, p. 20.

CHAPTER THREE

THE SHIOBARA INCIDENT (1908) AND ITS INFLUENCE ON HIRATSUKA RAICHŌ

The Keishū Literary Society

After Hiratsuka graduated from the Nihon Joshi Daigakkō (Japan Women's College), she continued her studies by improving her English at Tsuda Umeko's Joshi Eigaku Juku (Women's Institute of English Studies) in Kōjimachi, Tokyo. She also attended lectures on Chinese classics at a private school, the Nishō Gakusha in Tokyo.[1] Tsuda's school did not meet Hiratsuka's expectations of an informal and highly personal form of teaching, so she transferred to the Seibi Joshi Eigo Gakkō (Seibi Women's English School) in January 1907.[2] This was a private women's language school in Kudanshita, Tokyo, established by Christians. The school was known for providing students with excellent English language translation skills. It employed highly qualified staff, most of them graduates of Tokyo Imperial University.[3] The students there were mainly graduates from *jogakkō* (girls' high schools). Hiratsuka recalled that she read European novels and poetry.[4] By contrast with the teaching methods used by the Women's Institute of English Studies, the Seibi Women's English School offered a more relaxed atmosphere, and the lectures there were better suited to improve her reading and translation skills.[5] The translation skills she acquired became essential when she launched *Seitō* and did translation work for it.

She also became a member of the Keishū Bungakukai (Keishū Literary Society). This was founded in the Seibi Women's English

[1] Hiratsuka, *Genshi*, vol. 1, p. 202; Hiratsuka, *Watakushi*, p. 52.

[2] Hiratsuka, *Genshi*, vol. 1, p. 223; Yamakawa Kikue, *20-seiki o Ayumu* (1979), p. 65.

[3] Hiratsuka, *Genshi*, vol. 1, pp. 223–4.

[4] These included Dickens' *Cricket*, Tennyson's *Enoch Arden*, Hans Andersen's fairy tales, Charles Lamb's *Tales from Shakespeare* and Goethe's *The Sorrows of Young Werther* in English. See Hiratsuka, *Watakushi*, p. 52.

[5] Kobayashi, *Hito to Shisō*, p. 55; Kobayashi, *Ai to Hangyaku no Seishun*, pp. 128–9.

School in June 1907 by Ikuta Chōkō, a graduate from the highly
prestigious Tokyo Imperial University.[6] Hiratsuka's involvement with
the Keishū Literary Society had a great impact on her own literary
development. Ikuta, who read western literature extensively, was particularly impressed with the writing produced by women.[7] His teaching post enabled him to establish a women's literary society. He
named this the Keishū Bungakukai, while some of the participants
in the society called it Kinyōkai (the Golden Leaf Society).[8] The
term, 'keishū' literally means 'women who surpass others in literary
accomplishments', and as this name indicates, one of the aims of
this society was to produce outstanding female writers.[9] Ikuta's initial enthusiasm is clearly demonstrated in a newspaper notice which
appeared at the time of its founding:

> The main objective of this literary society will be to lecture on both
> Japanese and western literature in plain language, to encourage ordi-
> nary women to take an interest in literature and thereby to produce
> literary women. The society will organise lectures by Yosano Akiko,
> Baba Kochō, Morita Sōhei, Ikuta Chōkō and others. Lectures will be
> given from 8 to 9 o'clock every morning excluding Saturdays and
> Sundays in the Seibi Women's English School in Kudanshita, Tokyo.[10]

---

[6] Hiratsuka, *Genshi*, vol. 1, pp. 225–6; Yamakawa, *20-seiki o Ayumu*, pp. 65–6;
Kobayashi, *Hito to Shisō*, p. 58; Kobayashi, *Ai to Hangyaku no Seishun*, p. 131. Ikuta
Chōkō (1882–1936) studied philosophy at Tokyo Imperial University. While there,
he became a member of the literary coterie *Geien*. In 1911 he translated Nietzsche's
Also Sprach Zarathustra. He was greatly influenced by Nietzsche, whose thought became
the foundation for Ikuta's critical comments on literature. In 1914 he launched
Hankyō (Echo). Around that time he began to show a deep interest in social prob-
lems, and became associated with socialists such as Sakai Toshihiko and Ōsugi
Sakae. Ikuta was best known as a literary and social critic. On Ikuta Chōkō, see
Hisamatsu Senichi *et al.* (eds), *Gendai Nihon Bungaku Daijiten* (1965), pp. 52–3; Odagiri
Susumu (ed.), *Nihon Kindai Bungaku Daijiten* (1984), pp. 77–9; Satō Haruo, 'Senshi o
omou: fuyoi senmanna Ikuta Chōkō shōron', in Abe Jirō *et al.*, *Kindai Nihon Bungaku
Taikei*, vol. 40 (1973), pp. 446–50; Senichi Hisamatsu, *Biographical Dictionary of Japanese
Literature* (New York, 1976), pp. 269–70.
[7] Hiratsuka, *Genshi*, vol. 1, p. 226; Kobayashi, *Hito to Shisō*, p. 58.
[8] Yamakawa, *Onna Nidai no Ki*, p. 127; Horiba, *Seitō no Jidai*, p. 50; Sasaki Hideaki,
Atarashii Onna no Tōrai (Nagoya, 1994), p. 22; Morita Sōhei, *Baien, Tokyo Asahi Shinbun*
(1 January, 1909 – 16 May, 1909), reprinted in Chikuma Shobō (ed.), *Gendai Nihon
Bungaku Taikei*, vol. 29 (1971), p. 106; Okamoto Kanoko, *Okamoto Kanoko Zenshū*,
vol. 12 (1994), pp. 453–4; Hiratsuka Raichō, *Tōge*, in *Jiji Shinpō* (1–21 April, 1915),
reprinted in Hiratsuka, *Chosakushū*, vol. 2, p. 61.
[9] Nihon Daijiten Kankōkai (ed.), *Nihon Kokugo Daijiten*, vol. 7 (1976), p. 113.
[10] *Yomiuri Shinbun* (25 May, 1907).

Unlike other literary societies, which were entirely dominated by men, the Keishū Literary Society was designed to give intensive lessons in creative writing to young women. The initial number of students in the society was about sixteen, consisting of some from the Seibi Women's English School, including Hiratsuka, and some external students such as Yamakawa Kikue and Okamoto Kanoko.[11] Almost all the student members were literary novices while the lecturers (apart from Yosano Akiko) were young literary men, many of them members of the Shinshisha (New Poetry Society).[12] Yosano Akiko (the female lecturer) was the only one who had already fully established a literary career, through her contributions to *Myōjō* (*Morning Star*), her collected *tanka* entitled *Midaregami* (*The Tangled Hair*), and her anti-war poetry during the Russo-Japanese war.[13] The lecturers included Sōma Gyofū and other writers like Togawa Shūkotsu and Hirata Tokuboku.[14]

The society provided lecture-based classes on Japanese and western literature. Hiratsuka described some lectures:

---

[11] Okamoto, *Okamoto Kanoko Zenshū*, vol. 12, pp. 453–4; Yamakawa, *Onna Nidai no Ki*, pp. 127–8; Hiratsuka, *Genshi*, p. 226; Hiratsuka Raichō, 'Yamakawa Kikue-san', *Fujin Kōron* (November, 1925), reprinted in Hiratsuka, *Chosakushū*, vol. 4, pp. 141–4. Okamoto (maiden name was Ōnuki) Kanoko (1889–1939) studied under Yosano Akiko. Kanoko contributed tanka poems to literary magazines like *Myōjō* (*Morning Star*) and *Subaru* (*The Pleiades*). In 1910 she married the cartoonist Okamoto Ippei, and had a son Tarō (who became a leader in the Japanese avant-garde art movement). On Okamoto Kanoko, see Hisamatsu *et al.* (eds), *Gendai Nihon Bungaku Daijiten*, pp. 173–6; John Lewell, *Modern Japanese Novelists: A Biographical Dictionary* (New York, 1993), pp. 336–9; Sachiko Schierbeck, *Japanese Women Novelists in the 20th Century* (Copenhagen, 1994), pp. 95–9.

[12] Hiratsuka, *Genshi*, vol. 1, p. 226; Yamakawa, *Onna Nidai no Ki*, pp. 127–8.

[13] On Yosano, see Akiko Yosano (trans. by Sanford Goldstein & Seishi Shinoda), *Tangled Hair: Selected Tanka from Midaregami* (1987); Irie Shunkō, *Yosano Akiko* (1985), pp. 20–32; Yamamoto Chie, *Yama no Ugoku Hi Kitaru: Hyōden, Yosano Akiko* (1986), pp. 54–6; Motobayashi Katsuo, 'Onna no Roman to jojō: Yosano Akiko to Yamakawa Tomiko', *Kokubungaku*, 25:15 (December, 1980), pp. 62–6; Sakamoto Masanori, 'Myōjō no joryū sakka', *Kokubungaku*, 9:15 (December, 1964), pp. 31–7; Bettina L. Knapp, *Images of Japanese Women: A Westerner's View* (New York, 1992), pp. 166–72; Hisamatsu, *Biographical Dictionary of Japanese Literature*, pp. 350–2.

[14] Hiratsuka, *Genshi*, vol. 1, p. 226; Yamakawa, *Onna Nidai no Ki*, pp. 127–8; Yamakawa, *20-seiki o Ayumu*, p. 66; Kobayashi, *Hito to Shisō*, p. 58. Sōma Gyofū (1883–1950) studied English literature at Waseda University. After his graduation, he became engaged in editing *Waseda Bungaku*. He taught English literature at Waseda University. In 1916 he left the academic world and became a full-time essayist. On Sōma Gyofū, see Odagiri (ed.), *Nihon Kindai Bungaku Daijiten*, pp. 813–4; Hisamatsu *et al.* (eds), *Gendai Nihon Bungaku Daijiten*, pp. 622–3.

We had lectures on *Genji Monogatari* (*The Tale of Genji*) from Yosano Akiko. We also had our composition of *tanka* corrected by her. Baba Kochō gave an outline of modern European and American novels. Morita Sōhei gave some talks on Greek tragedies, and Ikuta Chōkō lectured on the novel.[15]

Ikuta also gave lectures on German literature, and Morita taught Ibsen's *A Doll's House* and D'Annunzio's plays. Shakespeare's works were also analysed.[16] Hiratsuka recalled that the textbooks used at the Keishū Literary Society were English translations of Ibsen's plays, Turgenev's works, Edgar Allan Poe's prose poems, and Maupassant's works, which were chosen by Ikuta.[17]

Of these staff, Hirata Tokuboku later became a noted scholar of English literature, and highly respected in academic circles for his translations of Dickens and Lamb.[18] Baba Kochō also became well-known as a critic and translator of western literature.[19] Togawa Shūkotsu later became an eminent scholar of English literature and professor at Keiō University.[20] He had devoted his life to translating English literature into Japanese, and to publishing on English history, literature and culture. The Keishū Literary Society was small, but it gave students a good introduction to western literature and

---

[15] Hiratsuka, *Genshi*, vol. 1, p. 226. *The Tale of Genji* was Yosano's speciality and she later translated it into modern Japanese. Yosano also received acclaim for her sensual *tanka* poems.

[16] Yamakawa, *Onna Nidai no Ki*, pp. 127–8.

[17] Hiratsuka, *Genshi*, vol. 1, p. 228.

[18] Hirata Tokuboku (1873–1943) studied English literature at Tokyo Higher School (now Tsukuba University). While he was a student there, he joined the influential literary magazine *Bungakukai*. After his graduation, he went to England to study at Oxford University for three years between 1903 and 1906. After he returned to Japan, he held teaching posts at Tokyo Higher School, Gakushūin and Sankō. In his later years he taught at Hōsei and Rikkyō Universities. On Hirata Tokuboku, see Odagiri (ed.), *Nihon Kindai Bungaku Daijiten*, pp. 1238–9; Hisamatsu *et al.* (eds), *Gendai Nihon Bungaku Daijiten*, p. 939.

[19] While Baba Kochō (1869–1940) was a student of Meiji Gakuin University, he became acquainted with the novelist Shimazaki Tōson and became a member of the Bungakukai (The Literary World). Although his own novels and poems lacked originality, he was distinguished as a translator of western literature. He became a professor of Keiō University, and taught European languages. See Odagiri (ed.), *Nihon Kindai Bungaku Daijiten*, pp. 1192–3; Hisamatsu *et al.* (eds), *Gendai Nihon Bungaku Daijiten*, p. 896.

[20] Togawa Shūkotsu (1870–1939) studied English literature at Tokyo Imperial University. He was a member of Bungakukai (The Literary World). He translated many English and American novels into Japanese, and wrote scholarly essays marked by humour and satire. On Togawa Shūkotsu, see Odagiri (ed.), *Nihon Kindai Bungaku Daijiten*, pp. 987–8; Hisamatsu *et al.* (eds), *Gendai Nihon Bungaku Daijiten*, p. 745.

translation. It would be difficult to think of a better choice of teaching staff at that time.

This successful recruitment of staff owed much to Ikuta's efforts and literary contacts. By this time he had been recognised as a young literary critic and translator of great potential. His critical essay on the novelist Oguri Fuyō, in the April 1906 issue of *Geien*, had brought him acclaim in literary circles.[21] He knew many eminent writers like Yosano Akiko.[22] He was therefore well placed to ask his literary friends to contribute to the female literary society he had founded.

Such lessons helped students to develop their literary talents. Hiratsuka's membership of this society much influenced her intellectual life. Despite the elite education she had previously received, she was now reading a new type of literature, beyond Japanese philosophy and religion.

The Society also taught her more about Japanese literature. Later Hiratsuka recalled that she read almost all the Japanese classics, such as *Manyōshū* (the 8th century collection of Japanese verse), *Kokinshū* (a collection of Japanese poems which was completed about 905), *Genji Monogatari* (*The Tale of Genji*), *Makura no Sōshi* (*The Pillow Book*) and *Tsurezuregusa* (*Essays in Idleness*) at the Ueno Imperial Library in Tokyo.[23] Such reading and her resulting familiarity with Japanese literature helped her later in her editorial work for *Seitō*.

Hiratsuka recalled that soon after she joined the Society she composed about 10 *tanka*, the first she had attempted. One of them was published in *Myōjō* (*Morning Star*), an innovative literary magazine founded by Yosano Tekkan in 1900.[24] This was Hiratsuka's first publication. This success helped to strengthen her literary confidence.[25]

---

[21] Hisamatsu *et al.* (eds), *Gendai Nihon Bungaku Daijiten*, pp. 52–3; Odagiri (ed.), *Nihon Kindai Bungaku Daijiten*, pp. 77–9.

[22] Hiratsuka, *Genshi*, vol. 1, pp. 226–7.

[23] *Ibid.*, p. 228.

[24] *Myōjō* was a journal of the literary society Shinshisha (New Poetry Society) which Yosano Tekkan founded in 1899. *Myōjō* was best known for its sensual romanticism. Yosano Tekkan discontinued its publication with the one hundredth issue in November 1908. On *Myōjō*, see Shioda Ryōhei, '*Myōjō-ha* no bungakushiteki igi', *Kokubungaku*, 9:15 (December, 1964), p. 8; Sasabuchi Tomoichi, '*Myōjō-ha* no bungaku undō', *Kokubungaku*, 9:15 (December, 1964), p. 19; Hiraoka Toshio *et al.* (eds), *Meiji no Bungaku: Kindai Bungakushi*, vol. 1 (1972), pp. 118–20; Hisamatsu *et al.* (eds), *Gendai Nihon Bungaku Daijiten*, pp. 1196–1200.

[25] More of Hiratsuka's *tanka* appeared in the final issue of *Myōjō*. Hiratsuka Raichō, 'Yūshū', *Myōjō* (November, 1908), reprinted in Hiratsuka, *Chosakushū*, vol. 1, pp. 9–13.

The foundation of a magazine for circulation among members of the Society then gave Hiratsuka an opportunity to write her first novel, *Ai no Matsujitsu* (*The Last Day of Love*), which appeared in the magazine.[26] The Keishū Literary Society opened a new world to her, and gave her the opportunity to become personally acquainted with other young writers. She relished the free atmosphere which the literary circle provided, which helped to liberate her from her restricted upbringing, contributing to the development of her later radicalism and feminism. Furthermore, the literary contacts she made were extremely useful to her later, to obtain advice from eminent literary figures. Teachers of the Keishū Literary Society such as Yosano Akiko, Baba Kochō and Ikuta Chōkō gave much encouragement and support to the Seitō Society.[27]

In such ways, the Keishū Literary Society had a great impact on Hiratsuka, being a valuable apprenticeship in literature, writing and translation skills. The Keishū Literary Society played a significant role in providing background experience which was to prove valuable for the Seitō Society and *Seitō*, although it has been neglected by most scholars assessing her.[28]

Even at this stage, Hiratsuka's feminism and radicalism had begun to develop. Her first short novel *Ai no Matsujitsu* (*The Last Day of Love*) was said to have demonstrated her feminism.[29] Hiratsuka gave the following brief outline of this work:

---

[26] Hiratsuka, *Genshi*, vol. 1, p. 236; Hiratsuka, *Watakushi*, p. 59; Yamakawa, *Onna Nidai no Ki*, pp. 130–1.

[27] Both Baba and Ikuta gave talks at meetings organised by the Seitō Society. Yosano Akiko contributed some essays, *tanka* poems and articles for *Seitō*, including 'Sozorogoto', 'Wagaya', 'Utsuriyuku kokoro', 'Kaze', 'Yume' and others. See Hiratsuka Raichō, 'Baba Kochō sensei o shinobite', in Hiratsuka, *Chosakushū*, vol. 6, p. 328; Kobayashi, *Hito to Shisō*, pp. 97–100; Hiratsuka, *Genshi*, vol. 1, pp. 325–7, 339–41; Hiratsuka, *Genshi*, vol. 2, pp. 98–9; Hiratsuka Raichō, 'Akiko sensei to watakushi', *Tanka Kenkyū* (May, 1951), reprinted in Hiratsuka, *Chosakushū*, vol. 7, pp. 149–50.

[28] The only researchers who drew attention to the Keishū Literary Society were Ide Fumiko, Kobayashi Tomie and Horiba Kiyoko. See Ide, *Hiratsuka Raichō: Kindai to Shinpi*, pp. 23–4; Kobayashi, *Ai to Hangyaku no Seishun*, pp. 130–50; Kobayashi, *Hito to Shisō*, pp. 58–9; Horiba, *Seitō no Jidai*, pp. 28–9.

[29] No copy of the novel has survived, so it is impossible to evaluate it. However, Yamakawa and Hiratsuka's autobiographies, Hiratsuka's novel *Tōge* (*The Mountain Pass*) and Morita Sōhei's *Baien* (*Smoke*) are significant sources which refer to it. Hiratsuka, *Genshi*, vol. 1, pp. 235–7; Hiratsuka, *Watakushi*, p. 59; Hiratsuka, *Tōge*, pp. 125–6; Yamakawa, *Onna Nidai no Ki*, pp. 130–1; Morita, *Baien*, pp. 119–20.

My novel *Ai no Matsujitsu* was not based on my experience. I created it out of my imagination . . . The heroine, a young well-educated intellectual woman who was a graduate from a women's college, was disgusted with her lover's weak character and his agreement with everything. Although he begged her to marry him, she deserted him. She buried the past and started a new life, leaving Tokyo and taking up a teaching post at a girls' high school in a provincial area. The creation of this novel was not based on careful reflection. I just wrote it naturally without much thought.[30]

Yamakawa Kikue gave a more detailed account of Hiratsuka's novel:

Hiratsuka's maiden work *Matsujitsukō* appeared in the Keishū Literary Society's magazine. The story was about a young woman, a student at a women's college. I vividly remember one scene, in which the heroine got out of her lover's bed and began to point out their different views one after another. She bitterly criticised him and then decided to leave him, tore herself out of his grasp and left for a new teaching post at a provincial girls' high school.[31]

Hiratsuka's own account of her first novel resembled Yamakawa's except for minor details. Yamakawa shrewdly identified some resemblances between the heroine of this novel and its author.[32] Hiratsuka's own strong, positive personality was reflected in her modern, optimistic and dynamic heroine. The heroine contrasted sharply with contemporary models of correct female behaviour. This novel left a strong impression on Yamakawa.[33] This was mainly because Hiratsuka had produced a completely new type of modern heroine with a full personality, of a sort that male novelists at that time had never created. Indeed many of Hiratsuka's contemporaries could not even imagine the existence of such a woman. Yamakawa was probably correct in suggesting that Hiratsuka's creation of this new type of heroine was an early sign of her feminism. Her heroine's behaviour was certainly unusual for her time. Although this kind of narrative, featuring a strong-minded heroine, can often be found in later Japanese novels, it was unknown in 1907.[34] Hiratsuka created such a heroine,

---

[30] Hiratsuka, *Genshi*, vol. 1, p. 236.
[31] Yamakawa, *Onna Nidai no Ki*, p. 130. Yamakawa called Hiratsuka's short novel *Matsujitsukō* instead of *Ai no Matsujitsu*.
[32] *Ibid.*, pp. 130–1.
[33] *Ibid.*, p. 130.
[34] Kobayashi, *Ai to Hangyaku no Seishun*, pp. 136–7; Sasaki, *Atarashii Onna no Tōrai*, pp. 27–8.

who prided herself on her own economic independence, at a time when almost all Japanese women were still deprived of modern rights. Hiratsuka's heroine provided a striking contrast both to ordinary women and to female characters in literary works up to then. Such women were dominated by men and were passive and subservient. The heroine's action in unilaterally deserting her lover was considered radical, irrational and unwomanly.[35] It was generally considered that only men had the right to choose their lovers and partners, and to terminate their relationships. Moreover, the heroine's decision to give her career priority over marriage was highly unconventional, since most middle-class Japanese women then shared the view that marriage was the only 'career' open to women.

Hiratsuka's heroine questioned society's low expectations of women, and attempted to demonstrate women's further capabilities. Her heroine bears marked similarities with the heroines who appeared in Ibsen and the so-called 'New Woman Fiction' in Britain in the 1890s, as in works by Shaw, Gissing, Hardy and others.[36] In particular, Hiratsuka's heroine resembled Rhoda Nunn, the heroine of George Gissing's *The Odd Women* (1893), who was considered an exemplar of the 'new woman' appearing in Victorian novels.[37] There is no evidence that Hiratsuka had read Gissing's work, but Rhoda's positive attitude in finding a role to prepare women for some destiny

---

[35] Horiba, *Seitō no Jidai*, p. 29.

[36] On New Woman Fiction, see John Goode, *George Gissing: Ideology and Fiction* (London, 1978), chapter 5; Sally Ledger, *The New Woman: Fiction and Feminism at the Fin de Siecle* (London, 1997); Gail Cunningham, *The New Woman and the Victorian Novel* (London, 1978), chapters 3 & 4; Viv Gardner, 'Introduction', in Viv Gardner & Susan Rutherford (eds), *The New Woman and Her Sisters* (Hemel Hempstead, 1992), pp. 1–13; Jill Davis, 'The New Woman and the new life', in Gardner & Rutherford (eds), *The New Woman and Her Sisters*, pp. 17–33; Lesley Ferris, 'The golden girl', in Gardner & Rutherford (eds), *The New Woman and Her Sisters*, pp. 37–53.

[37] George Gissing, *The Odd Women* (1893, London, 1984 edn). *The Odd Women* is set in London in the 1890s and gives the story of five women (Rhoda Nunn, Mary Barfoot and the three Madden sisters, Virginia, Alice and Monica). Although the Madden sisters are a respectable doctor's daughters, they are left with very little money and no training after their father's death, and are reduced to poverty. Monica, the youngest and prettiest sister, chooses a loveless marriage to escape from her situation. Virginia finds secret consolation in drinking. Rhoda Nunn and Mary Barfoot devote their lives to helping young women find independence. In particular, Rhoda is a spirited woman who contrasts sharply with the helpless Madden sisters. Although she was attracted to Mary Barfoot's cousin Everard, she turns down his proposal of marriage and prepares for a life other than marriage. She devotes herself to running a school for girls.

other than marriage resembled Hiratsuka's heroine. For this reason Hiratsuka's heroine can be classified as a Japanese version of 'the new woman'. Already Hiratsuka's own radical ideas on marriage and career, and her criticism of contemporary male-dominated society, had begun to emerge.

Another example of Hiratsuka's challenge to traditional society can be found in the language she used in *The Last Day of Love*. As Yamakawa pointed out, Hiratsuka used the male expression *yo* (which literally means I), to refer to herself.[38] *Yo* had been used only by men since the Heian period, and even after the Meiji Restoration it was considered a very formal, pompous word, mainly used by distinguished men.[39] Yamakawa recalled that she was amazed to see such a masculine term used by a woman, which was still unheard of in 1907.[40] As Yamakawa later wrote, even such a small act, which highlighted Hiratsuka's early radicalism, hinted that she might in due course develop this even further.

The Shiobara Incident

Yamakawa's predictions were realised when the Shiobara Jiken (Shiobara Incident) occurred. This was an attempted double suicide involving two members of the Keishū Literary Society: a lecturer, Morita Sōhei, who was already married with a child, and Hiratsuka.[41] The Shiobara Incident had a great impact on Hiratsuka's feminism. Its significance has often been underestimated. Most English articles on Hiratsuka completely fail to evaluate the incident and even Japanese writers have neglected it.[42]

---

[38] Yamakawa, *Onna Nidai no Ki*, p. 131.
[39] Nihon Daijiten Kankōkai (ed.), *Nihon Kokugo Daijiten*, vol. 20, p. 48.
[40] Yamakawa, *Onna Nidai no Ki*, p. 131.
[41] Hiratsuka, *Genshi*, vol. 1, pp. 252–63; Hiratsuka, *Watakushi*, pp. 59–65. Horiba, *Seitō no Jidai*, pp. 29–35; Kobayashi, *Hito to Shisō*, pp. 64–72; Kobayashi, *Ai to Hangyaku no Seishun*, pp. 185–77.
[42] See Sasaki, *Atarashii Onna no Tōrai*, pp. 8–100; Kobayashi, *Hito to Shisō*, pp. 58–80; Kobayashi, *Ai to Hangyaku no Seishun*, pp. 133–205. Sasaki's book is a scholarly and erudite work based on primary sources. However Sasaki, whose specialism is modern Japanese literature, focused on the literary value of the incident rather than its historical significance. He was particularly interested in analysing how it affected Natsume Sōseki's later writing, especially the creation of his heroines, who had in them elements of 'new women', reminiscent of Hiratsuka.

The seeds of the incident had originated in an unexpected letter Hiratsuka received from Morita towards the end of January 1908. Morita, who had read her novel *The Last Day of Love*, wrote to her and they began a regular correspondence. From early February they began to go out together.[43] In a short time they became close friends and ran away together.

According to the account given by the press, Hiratsuka ran away from home in everyday clothes at about nine o'clock on the evening of 21 March, 1908.[44] Her family, worried about her safety, immediately sent people to look for her in Tokyo, Kamakura, Hakone and Chōshi. They also asked the police for help. Her father searched as far as Shizuoka, but no trace of her was found. In the evening of 22 March, a short letter from Hiratsuka was delivered to a friend's house. There were signs that she had boarded a train from Ueno for Utsunomiya or the Nikkō region. Her family asked the police in Utsunomiya, Sendai and Aomori to search for her, and her mother went to Utsunomiya with Ikuta Chōkō to look for her. On the morning of 24 March they learnt that Morita and Hiratsuka had been found by a policeman walking hand in hand at the Obana Pass, which was in the mountains of Shiobara and covered in deep snow. The press stated that Morita and Hiratsuka had become inseparable, and had decided to commit double suicide. This was clear from their letters to friends after they left Tokyo. The *Yorozuhō* and the *Tokyo Asahi Shinbun* reported that they had left Tokyo to find a place to commit double suicide, but had been detained by the police before they could do so.[45] The press treated the Shiobara Incident as an attempted double suicide, and gave it full coverage.[46] The first coverage was a short notice in the *Jiji Shinpō*:

> A student, Hiratsuka Haru [Raichō] (age 23), who has been lodging at Ōuchi Ushinosuke's house in Komagome, Hongō, Tokyo, has gone missing. Ōuchi Ushinosuke would be extremely grateful if anybody who sees Hiratsuka Haru (the girl concerned) could apprehend her and contact the Nikkō Police.[47]

---

[43] Hiratsuka, *Genshi*, vol. 1, pp. 237–52; Morita, *Baien*, pp. 119–81.

[44] My summary here is from 'Morita Sōhei to Shiobara e shinjūkō, sekichū de hakken', *Tokyo Asahi Shinbun* (25 March, 1908).

[45] *Yorozuhō* (27 March, 1908); *Tokyo Asahi Shinbun* (25 March, 1908).

[46] Horiba, *Seitō no Jidai*, p. 30.

[47] 'Mudan iede de sōsaku negai', *Jiji Shinpō* (23 March, 1908).

This notice was inserted by her parents.[48] Her uncle's name and address were given in the newspaper instead of her father's. This was to avoid scandal and to protect the reputation of her father, who was a civil servant.

Following the appearance of this short notice, various newspapers competed with each other in taking up the story.[49] Surprisingly, even one of the leading serious newspapers of the day, *the Tokyo Asahi Shinbun*, devoted considerable space to it.[50] Although double suicides are little known in western countries, they were frequent occurrences in Japan in the Edo period, when many strict social codes and customs controlled marriage across class barriers.[51] 'Double suicide' is the English translation of *shinjū* or *jōshi* (love suicide). Many lovers who could not be united because of differences in class or family backgrounds, or because the woman was already married, committed double suicide to avoid punishment, hoping to be united in Heaven, a notion derived from Buddhist teaching.[52] Chikamatsu Monzaemon, the distinguished seventeenth-century playwright, may have contributed to the increase in double suicide in the Edo period.[53] His play *Sonezaki Shinjū* (*The Love Suicide at Sonezaki*) (1703) was based on a real double suicide in Osaka, and this began a 'fashion' for love suicide.[54] In succeeding years love suicides, both in real life and on the stage, multiplied and became so frequent that in 1722 officials for a time prohibited the performance of plays on this theme.[55]

---

[48] Kobayashi, *Ai to Hangyaku no Seishun*, p. 173.

[49] 'Reijō no funshitsu', *Tokyo Niroku Shinbun* (23 March, 1908); 'Mudan iede de Sōsaki negai', *Jiji Shinpō* (23 March, 1908); 'Jōshi misui', *Tokyo Asahi Shinbun* (25 March, 1908); 'Iede wa jibun no seishin o tsuranuku tame to kokuhaku', *Yorozuhō* (27 March, 1908); 'Rokumenkan', *Tokyo Asahi Shinbun* (28 March, 1908); 'Dōjō shōsan no fuchō manen o ureeru', *Jiji Shinpō* (29 March, 1908).

[50] 'Jōshi misui', *Tokyo Asahi Shinbun* (25 March, 1908); 'Rokumenkan', *Tokyo Asahi Shinbun* (28 March, 1908).

[51] Sōgō Joseishi Kenkyūkai (ed.), *Sei, Ai, Kazoku*, pp. 115–20; Donald H. Shively, *The Love Suicide at Amijima* (1953, Ann Arbor, Michigan, 1991 edn), pp. 24–5.

[52] Sōgō Joseishi Kenkyūkai (ed.), *Sei, Ai, Kazoku*, pp. 118–9; Shūichi Katō (trans. & ed. by Don Sanderson), *A History of Japanese Literature from the Manyōshū to Modern Times* (Richmond, 1997), pp. 144–5; Shively, *The Love Suicide*, pp. 24–6; Donald Keene, *World Within Walls: Japanese Literature of the Pre-Modern Era, 1600–1867* (London, 1976), p. 256; Katō Shūichi, *Nihon Bungakushi Josetsu*, vol. 2 (1980), p. 88.

[53] Sōgō Joseishi Kenkyūkai, *Sei, Ai, Kazoku*, p. 120; Keene, *World Within Walls*, pp. 255–6; Hisamatsu, *Biographical Dictionary of Japanese Literature*, pp. 166–7.

[54] Cecilia Segawa Seigle, *Yoshiwara: The Glittering World of the Japanese Courtesan* (Honolulu, 1993), pp. 196–7.

[55] Shively, *The Love Suicide*, p. 25.

Although Japanese society changed considerably after the Meiji Restoration, double suicides remained a final resort of lovers who could not be united in life.

Double suicides were therefore not rare when the Shiobara Incident occurred. Such incidents were frequently reported, and were usually treated as very minor news items.[56] It is surprising that Morita and Hiratsuka's attempt received so much media and public attention since they were both virtually unknown at that time, and it is worth considering why the press became so excited by the Incident. As the *Tokyo Asahi Shinbun* stated, the main reason related to the participants' educational background:

> Although double suicide has been fairly common for a long time, the Shiobara Incident is a most unusual case. It is well-known that double suicide itself is an absurd and foolish action, in many cases committed by commoners who do not have much education or common sense. However, the man and the woman who were involved in this attempted double suicide belong to an entirely different class. In spite of their high standard of education, they surprisingly imitated commoners' folly and attempted double suicide, and this is unheard of.[57]

There were very few university graduates at that time, as only the most gifted or privileged people from wealthy backgrounds could enter university.[58] Japanese society normally treated graduates with great respect, investing high hopes in them, and expecting them to act as responsible leaders.[59] Morita and Hiratsuka, both of whom were from respectable families and had received the best possible higher education, had failed to fulfil social expectations. It was the rarity of such an incident, involving as it did two elite figures, that attracted interest, and Hiratsuka's father's position as a senior government official probably contributed to the wave of publicity.

In spite of this press coverage, very few journalists attempted fully to investigate the incident and its real causes. They drew a quick conclusion that Hiratsuka and Morita had decided to kill themselves mainly because of his marital status and that, like other couples, they wished to be united in Heaven.[60] However, the Shiobara Incident

---

[56] Ide, *Seitō no Onnatachi*, pp. 21–2.
[57] 'Morita Sōhei to Shiobara e shinjūkō, sekichū de hakken', *Tokyo Asahi Shinbun* (25 March, 1908).
[58] Kobayashi, *Ai to Hangyaku no Seishun*, p. 179.
[59] Ide, *Seitō no Onnatachi*, p. 22.
[60] *Ibid.*, p. 23.

was different from most other double suicides, such as the later double suicide of the eminent novelist Arishima Takeo in 1923.[61] Arishima, a widower, had had an affair with a married journalist, Hatano Akiko.[62] Her husband discovered her adultery and Arishima was confronted with it. Arishima and Hatano decided upon a double suicide.[63] Under Article 183 of the criminal law, which remained effective until 1947, if a married woman had an affair both she and her lover could be sent to prison for adultery if her husband brought charges against them.[64] Arishima and Hatano took their lives to avoid this outcome. However, Morita failed in his attempt at double suicide and was quite different from Arishima in his objectives. Under the law a married man such as Morita was free to divorce his wife and marry somebody else.[65] Yosano Tekkan and Yosano Akiko provided a good example of this occurring. Tekkan was married, Akiko was not. So when they fell in love Tekkan simply divorced his wife and married Akiko. There were no legal problems apart from Akiko's family's opposition to the marriage. After marriage, Akiko was ostracised by her family and was not allowed to attend her father's funeral. Morita and Hiratsuka's circumstances were similar to those of Yosano Tekkan and Akiko. Morita could easily have divorced his wife and married Hiratsuka, who was single, and this was indeed suggested to him by Natsume Sōseki after the incident. It is unlikely therefore that Morita's marital status was a central feature in the Shiobara Incident.

One can approach the real cause via Morita's novel *Baien* (*Smoke*), and Hiratsuka's autobiographies and her novel *Tōge* (*The Mountain Pass*). *Baien* appeared less than a year after the incident in serial form in the *Tokyo Asahi Shinbun*.[66] It was an autobiographical novel based

---

[61] On Arishima's double suicide, see Sawano Hisao, 'Arishima Takeo, Karuizawa jōshi jiken', *Rekishi to Jinbutsu* (April, 1980), pp. 86–91; Matsumoto Seichō (ed.), *Meiji Hyakunen Hyakudaijiken*, vol. 2 (1968, 1984 edn), pp. 32–7; Fuse Akiko, *Kekkon to Kazoku* (1993), pp. 70–1; Katō, *Nihon Bungakushi Josetsu*, vol. 2, p. 407. Arishima Takeo (1878–1923) was a novelist and essayist. When Mushanokōji Saneatsu founded the magazine *Shirakaba* in 1910, he became a member and embarked on his literary career, becoming well known through his novel *Aru Onna* (*A Certain Woman*).

[62] Hatano Akiko worked for the *Fujin Kōron*. Matsumoto, *Meiji Hyakunen Hyakudaijiken*, p. 33; Sawano, 'Arishima Takeo', pp. 86–91.

[63] Matsumoto, *Meiji Hyakunen Hyakudaijiken*, p. 36; Fuse, *Kekkon*, pp. 70–1.

[64] Sawano, 'Arishima Takeo', pp. 86–91.

[65] Fuse, *Kekkon*, pp. 70–1.

[66] Morita Sōhei, *Baien*, *Tokyo Asahi Shinbun* (1 January, 1909 – 16 May, 1909),

on his experience of the incident.[67] The hero, Kobayashi Yōkichi, was modelled on himself, and the heroine Manabe Tomoko on Hiratsuka.[68] In addition, Hiratsuka began to give her own view in the spring of 1915 (seven years after the incident) when part of her serialised novel *Tōge* was published in the *Jiji Shinpō*.[69] This followed a request from a journalist from the *Jiji Shinpō* to present her side of the story. However, her serialisation did not continue through many issues and in its coverage did not reach the events at Shiobara, because she became pregnant and was unable to continue writing.[70] Her view of the whole incident thus remained unexpressed for many years. She gave her full view much later. Her short autobiography *Watakushi no Aruita Michi* (*The Road I Walked*) (1955), referred to the incident, but did not go into details.[71] These had to wait until her four-volume autobiography *Genshi Josei wa Taiyō de Atta* (*In the Beginning Woman was the Sun*) (1971–3), in which she addressed the incident more frankly and in greater depth.[72]

Hiratsuka's account of the incident in the four-volume autobiography, which matched Morita's in *Baien*, was as follows. From early February Morita and Hiratsuka regularly went out together, and spent much time discussing literature, especially the western literature with which Morita was familiar.[73] D'Annunzio's *The Triumph of Death* repeatedly appeared in Morita's conversation. Morita, who had had many affairs before, was clearly interested in having a sexual affair with Hiratsuka. He took her to *machiai* (a low-class love hotel) with this intent. On the other hand, Hiratsuka, who was still a virgin, refused to have a physical relationship with him and made an evasive statement that she was neither a man nor a woman. She was a new type of woman, one he had never met before, and he

---

reprinted in Chikuma Shobō (ed.), *Gendai Nihon Bungaku Taikei*, vol. 29 (1971), pp. 83–196. *Baien* was also published in book form by two publishing companies (Kinyōdō and Shinchōsha) between February 1910 and November 1913.

[67] 'Morita Sōhei no *Baien* yokoku', *Tokyo Asahi Shinbun* (4 December, 1908).

[68] Kataoka Ryōhei, 'Morita Sōhei no ichi to sakufū', in Chikuma Shobō (ed.), *Gendai Nihon Bungaku Zenshū*, vol. 22 (1955), p. 404; Sasaki, *Atarashii Onna no Tōrai*, p. 8.

[69] Hiratsuka Raichō, *Tōge*, *Jiji Shinpō* (1–21 April, 1915), reprinted in Hiratsuka, *Chosakushū*, vol. 2, pp. 61–105.

[70] Hiratsuka, *Genshi*, vol. 2, pp. 229–30.

[71] Hiratsuka, *Watakushi*, pp. 59–65.

[72] Hiratsuka, *Genshi*, vol. 1, pp. 235–78.

[73] *Ibid.*, pp. 237–52; Morita, *Baien*, pp. 119–81.

could neither read her mind nor know how to treat her. As he felt that his love would not be returned by her, he conceived the idea of killing her, an idea probably derived from *The Triumph of Death*. He sent her the following letter outlining his plan to kill her.

> The moment that any woman dies is the most beautiful moment in her life. I will kill you. I am an artist. I am a poet. I am an envoy of beauty. I must observe your last dying moment, which will be the most beautiful moment in your life.[74]

This was followed by the following letter three or four days later:

> I love you dearly. Every day I think about you and adore you. No matter how much I love you, I know that my love will never be returned by you . . . When I am on my own and thinking about you, I cannot help thinking that you should die soon. You are a person who dies young.[75]

After these letters, Hiratsuka continued to see him. She then received another letter, in which he expressed a strong inclination to kill her. As quoted in *Baien*, the wording was as follows:

> I think that I will be able to kill you. I have no choice but to kill you so as to become your sole possessor.[76]

Several days after this, on 21 March 1908, Morita told her that the time had come for him to put his scheme of killing her into practice. She agreed to run away with him and be killed by him. They promised to meet near Tabata Station after dark on the same day.[77] Hiratsuka returned home and wrote Kimura Masako a short note hinting at her death, asking her to dispose of the diaries and letters which she sent her.[78] After dark she ran away from home, taking an old dagger belonging to her mother and her letters from Morita, leaving a short suicide note for her family. She met Morita at Tabata Station in Tokyo, and they boarded the last train to Ōmiya. They stayed a night at an inn in Ōmiya and the following morning took a train to Nishi Nasu, from where they travelled by rickshaw to Shiobara (a town in northern Tochigi Prefecture noted for its

---

[74] *Ibid.*, pp. 179–80. Also in Hiratsuka, *Genshi*, vol. 1, p. 246.
[75] Morita, *Baien*, p. 147. Also in Hiratsuka, *Genshi*, vol. 1, pp. 246–7.
[76] Morita, *Baien*, p. 178.
[77] *Ibid.*, pp. 181–2; Hiratsuka, *Genshi*, vol. 1, pp. 253–5.
[78] *Ibid.*, pp. 254–5; Morita, *Baien*, p. 186.

dramatic scenic gorges). They stayed a night at Shiobara, which was then covered with deep snow. The following morning they climbed a mountain road, which was largely concealed by snow.[79]

When they reached a precipitous cliff, which overlooked a steep gorge, they burned their letters with whisky on the snow. After that Morita attempted to kill Hiratsuka with her mother's dagger. However, he failed to do so through lack of determination. He suddenly raised the dagger overhead and threw it down into the valley. Although the sun had already set and it was dark, they decided to go down the mountain. They spent the night in the open air, covered with snow.[80] The following morning they were walking hand in hand at the Obana Pass when they were found by policemen sent from Utsunomiya Police Station to search for them.

Although Hiratsuka's account of this matched Morita's story in most respects, there were some discrepancies. The most significant was that Morita stated that it was an attempted double suicide, while Hiratsuka wrote that Morita tried to kill her but never mentioned that he would die with her.[81] Morita did not discuss his motives, but many clues can be found in *Baien*, his letters to Natsume Sōseki, and his biography of Natsume Sōseki. When Morita first met Hiratsuka, he claimed to have lost interest in life.[82] He was disillusioned with a 'dull-witted' wife with whom he claimed he was mentally incompatible. He also hated his teaching position, which he continued merely for the pay.[83] Although well-educated and with literary talent, he had lost his literary aspirations and confidence. In contrast he saw Hiratsuka as intelligent, beautiful and as having qualities similar to those of modern heroines in western writing like Ibsen's *A Doll's House*.[84] Modelling Tomoko (the heroine) on her, he gave the following account:

> I was extremely thrilled to meet Tomoko. Tomoko is a very self-willed, egotistical and proud woman who is not satisfied unless she has her

---

[79] This account is from Hiratsuka, *Genshi*, vol. 1, pp. 255–60; Morita, *Baien*, pp. 184–94.

[80] Hiratsuka, *Genshi*, vol. 1, pp. 260–3; Morita, *Baien*, pp. 195–6.

[81] Hiratsuka, *Genshi*, vol. 1, p. 251.

[82] Cited in Kobayashi, *Ai to Hangyaku*, pp. 138–9.

[83] Natsume Shinroku, 'Chichi no tegai to Morita-san', in Chikuma Shobō (ed.), *Gendai Nihon Bungaku Taikei*, vol. 29 (1971), p. 417.

[84] Morita, *Natsume Sōseki* (1967), pp. 99–100.

own way. I always felt that such a woman existed only in fantasy, and not in the real world. However, I am mistaken. I haven't the faintest idea what she is thinking.[85]

Tomoko was described as a strong-minded, confident, intelligent woman of advanced views, advocating the independence of her sex and defying convention. She was completely different from any previous female character in Japanese novels. And her steadfast refusal to surrender physically to the hero was a striking contrast to the usual heroines, who readily submitted to men.[86] Morita's heroine shared many characteristics with the 'new women' of western novels. Like those 'new women', and like Morita's heroine, Hiratsuka was very different from other Japanese women, and Morita gave this reason for being attracted to her. He placed his hopes in her, as an escape from his limited life.[87] In *Baien* he described his heroine as an extraordinary woman who idealized ugly and common things.[88] He also portrayed her as akin to a Saviour sent from Heaven to rescue him from a chaotic life.[89] However, before long he realised that his affection would not be returned. He became obsessed with the idea of not losing her to another man, and he was convinced that he had to kill her to become her sole possessor.[90] As described in *Baien*, he planned a double suicide, murdering her before stabbing himself.

In contrast Hiratsuka claimed that he had no intention of dying.[91] She was not sure whether he really intended to kill her, and in her later years she became convinced that he had wanted to enact an incident as material for a novel.[92] Morita had been watching for an opportunity to make a debut in the world of letters. According to Hiratsuka, he knew that the best way to succeed was to write a new and original work based on his experience.[93] Hiratsuka felt that she had been used to this selfish end. Morita denied this.[94]

---

[85] Morita, *Baien*, p. 135.
[86] *Ibid.*, p. 179.
[87] Morita, *Natsume Sōseki*, pp. 99–100.
[88] Morita, *Baien*, p. 135.
[89] *Ibid.*, p. 135.
[90] *Ibid.*, p. 178.
[91] Hiratsuka, *Genshi*, vol. 1, p. 251.
[92] Cited in Kobayashi, *Hito to Shisō*, p. 64.
[93] *Ibid.*, pp. 64–5.
[94] Morita, *Natsume Sōseki*, pp. 99–100.

Another point where Hiratsuka's interpretation was very different from Morita's was that she was convinced that Morita used the main storyline of D'Annunzio's *The Triumph of Death*, by which he was greatly influenced, to plan the 'double suicide' and later write *Baien*.[95] Morita strongly denied this and persistently claimed that *Baien* was based on the facts of the Shiobara Incident, and had nothing to do with *The Triumph of Death*.[96] However, some readers of *Baien* like Natsume Sōseki shared Hiratsuka's view. Natsume wrote:

> *Baien* is believed to be an autobiographical novel, based on the Shiobara Incident. I find the whole story very unrealistic, especially the passion shown by the heroine and the hero, which seems to be highly theatrical, and has nothing in common with real passion exhibited by normal couples. The behaviour of the heroine and hero bears no relation to real life.[97]

Like Hiratsuka, Natsume Sōseki claimed that *Baien* was in essence derived from foreign literature, by which Morita was over-influenced.[98] He also agreed that *Baien*'s main plot bore a close resemblance to D'Annunzio's *The Triumph of Death*.[99] According to Natsume, Aurispa, the hero of *The Triumph of Death*, was akin to the hero of *Baien*, Kobayashi Yōkichi. Like Aurispa, Yōkichi decided to destroy the heroine because of intense love, becoming obsessed by death and his wish to kill her. The storyline of *Baien* is more or less identical with this except that its heroine was willing to die with the hero, while D'Annunzio's heroine refused this.[100] Baba Kochō also agreed with Natsume Sōseki, stating that *Baien* was a complete fabrication as an account of the events at Shiobara, being thoroughly interwoven with such literary influences.[101] It would appear, nevertheless, that fact and fiction in this case had become thoroughly intertwined— both in the plan for the 'double suicide' itself, and in the later rendition of the event in *Baien*. In the actions of both actors, one sees

---

[95] Hiratsuka, *Genshi*, vol. 1, p. 261.
[96] Morita, *Natsume Sōseki*, pp. 99–100.
[97] Cited in Natsume, 'Chichi no tegami', p. 419.
[98] *Ibid.*, p. 419.
[99] Cited in Sasaki, *Atarashii Onna*, p. 9. A statement similar to Natsume's was made by Mori Ōgai. See Hiraoka *et al.* (eds), *Meiji no Bungaku*, p. 210.
[100] See Gabriele D'Annunzio (trans. by Georgina Harding), *The Triumph of Death* (1894, New York, 1975 edn).
[101] Cited in Yamakawa Kikue, 'Morita Sōhei-shi no yokogao' in Shūeisha (ed.), *Gōkaban Nihon Bungaku Zenshū 18-kan Geppō* (July, 1975), p. 41.

how certain western literary influences had appealed to and affected in a complex way their own Japanese lives and attitudes.

The question remains—why Hiratsuka was attracted to Morita and seemingly had agreed to be killed by him? When she first met him, she formed a rather low opinion of her teacher, well demonstrated in her autobiography:

> Morita lectured on ancient Greek plays, but I did not have a chance to talk to him properly outside classes. He did not strike me as an experienced teacher. I felt that he was forced to teach by Ikuta, who was a close friend of his. Morita always seemed to grab the two ends of his desk and cast his eyes downwards while he was teaching. He talked with frequent pauses, with some embarrassment, as if he was talking to himself. I can never forget the odd way he taught us. Compared to Ikuta, who appeared to be sociable, quick-witted, perfect in many ways and as sharp as a razor, Morita was the opposite in appearance, mannerism and temperament. Morita, with his big head and body, was naturally slow in his movements. He struck me as a dull, clumsy character with many faults.[102]

Her comments suggest that she found him a rather unimpressive character, and there was no sign of her showing an interest in him. However, Morita's long letter commenting on *The Last Day of Love*, full of excessive praise, probably affected her.[103] Hiratsuka described it as 'the strangest letter I've received in my life', and it appealed to her literary and intellectual appetite. Hiratsuka was absorbed in literature and eager to expand her knowledge, especially of western literature, and Morita seemed well suited to help her, being knowledgeable on this subject.[104] She wrote:

> Morita had such a deep attachment to literature that I felt that he was almost possessed by it . . . He had a pleasant personality. His movement was slow and his manners were clumsy, but as I got accustomed to them, they became his personal charms and could not help stimulating the irresponsible playfulness concealed within myself.[105]

When the women's historian Kobayashi Tomie interviewed Hiratsuka in her later years, Hiratsuka admitted that she had been attracted to Morita.[106] However, despite Morita's expectations, she asserted

---

[102] Hiratsuka, *Genshi*, vol. 1, pp. 236–7.
[103] *Ibid.*, p. 237.
[104] *Ibid.*, pp. 248–52.
[105] *Ibid.*, p. 252.
[106] Kobayashi, *Hito to Shisō*, p. 243.

that their relationship was purely intellectual on her side, and that she had no intention of becoming physically involved with him. In Kobayashi's interview Hiratsuka also made the following remarks:

> When I first met Morita, I was not badly off. I had too much spare time. I was full of energy. However, I did not know what to do and I did not have any aim in my life. My running away with Morita was an adventure of my youth.[107]

She had little 'fear' at this young age, and she had virtually no knowledge of sex even though she was twenty-three years old.[108] It was normal for a girl from a background like Hiratsuka's to be largely innocent of sexual matters. Innocence and inexperience were considered important conditions for marriage. One still wonders whether she seriously wished to die. Her suicide note reproduced in her autobiography said:

> I will accomplish my lifelong intention. I will die for my own sound reasons. Nobody should be blamed for my death.[109]

This quotation suggests that she did not have a strong attachment to life, and she wrote that family ties and commitment weighed heavily on her mind, as if they were invisible monsters.[110] With an independent mind, she wanted to have her own way, but she felt that she could not because of restricted decision making for women caused by the *ie* system. Kobayashi Tomie stated that death was the solution chosen by Hiratsuka to escape these problems.[111] As long as the decision to end her life was her own, she was content with it. As elaborated in the autobiography, she chose death as the only way to free herself from the male regulation of women under the *ie* system, even if it was to be death at the hands of a man.[112]

Her ambivalence to contemporary society is perhaps also illustrated by the symbolism of her theft of her mother's dagger, with which to perform the suicide. This and the accompanying details are open to a number of interpretations of an anthropological kind, none of them 'provable', but worth outlining as interpretative pos-

---

[107] Cited in Kobayashi, *Hito to Shisō*, p. 243.
[108] Hiratsuka, *Genshi*, vol. 1, pp. 244, 259.
[109] *Ibid.*, p. 256.
[110] *Ibid.*, p. 258.
[111] Kobayashi, *Hito to Shisō*, pp. 67–8.
[112] Hiratsuka, *Genshi*, vol. 1, p. 258.

sibilities nevertheless, particularly for a culture like that of Japan that places such weight on symbolic meanings. What follows is offered as one interpretation of the implicit meanings of these details, not as a statement of fact. When her mother married her father, an old dagger with a long family history was presented to her as one of the wedding presents from the head of her family.[113] Her mother, Tsuya, had treasured it since then, and Hiratsuka had always been fascinated by it. When she left home to die, she took this dagger instead of, for example, stealing her father's gun. Her mother's dagger represented a long family tradition, by which she as daughter was also bound. She challenged conventional family ties and wanted to escape from them. As an heirloom the dagger may have represented such family tradition. She handed over the dagger to Morita who was planning to kill her with it.[114] Morita did not succeed in killing her, and he dealt with his failure by throwing her time-honoured dagger over the cliff into the valley. Such action might symbolise a weakening of any obligation to her family lineage. It may also have opened up a prospect of freedom for her future life, one less tied by traditional family bonds. Perhaps she was testing the man, or perhaps she had no intention of dying from the beginning—this is suggested by her bringing an old blunt dagger, which might not easily kill anyone. This is supported by her choice of the dagger in preference to her father's pistol kept in his study, which would certainly have been a more effective means of death.

Whatever her thinking, possible symbolic connotations of these actions would not have been missed by some of those interested in and reading about the case. What kind of association does a dagger have? A dagger, normally used for thrusting and stabbing, unquestionably represents a means of death. In its connotations also, it might appear as predominantly a male weapon. Nevertheless, in Japan, especially during the Edo period, all men and women belonging to the *samurai* class carried daggers with them. This was partly through a desire to protect themselves, and partly because they used daggers when committing suicide. Of course suicide was by no means an everyday occurrence; but the dagger symbolised the sense of

---

[113] *Ibid.*, p. 255.
[114] *Ibid.*, pp. 260–1. In Japanese double suicide, the man usually kills the woman, then himself.

honour behind such a possible recourse for this particular rank of
society. In Hiratsuka's time the carrying of daggers had become less
universal and women seldom carried them. In other words, daggers
were usually associated with men. Across many cultures the dagger
is often regarded as a phallic symbol.[115] This reminds one even more
of its male connections.

The Shiobara Incident becomes even more intriguing when one
thinks of such possible symbolism and its social and sexual features.
Morita never had sexual intercourse with Hiratsuka. She refused to
sleep with him and in any case he told her he was impotent.[116] In
fact, he went on later to have children with other women, but that
does not bear on his understanding at that stage with Hiratsuka.[117]
That relationship, for whatever reason, was celibate. One might speculate that the dagger, as an aggressive phallic symbol, was seen to
be redundant in his case, whether by choice or weakness of Japanese
masculinity. In fact, one might speculate that to Hiratsuka the dagger was redundant in all regards. It was not much valued by her as
a symbol of a rusty family tradition, and she was not to be obedient to such a tradition's dictates. It was ineffective as a symbol of
violent male superiority. It was perhaps redundant to her as a symbol of the superiority of the samurai class—her family dagger (dat-
ing from the Edo period) was after all blunt, ineffective and historically
dated. She gave it to Morita to kill her with, but nothing much happened.[118] Whether her gesture may have been in anticipation of such
an ineffectual outcome or not is debatable. If it was, then she was
intending herself to be killed by a man wielding her own family heirloom, a symbol of all that she later rebelled against. That man failed
to 'perform', as indeed by mutual consent and his admission was his
custom sexually. This was hardly a sign of male adequacy, in the
male and samurai traditions of Japan. He failed to kill her. He then
threw the dagger away far down into the valley, so that it became

---

[115] As for example witnessed in many western painters, for example Titian,
Raphael, Delacroix, Mucha and others, or as shown in some of the worst sexual
atrocities committed by Japanese troops at Nanking and elsewhere. Edward Lucie-
Smith, *Eroticism in Western Art* (London, 1972), pp. 117, 238–41.
[116] Hiratsuka, *Genshi*, vol. 1, pp. 259, 312–3.
[117] Hisamatsu *et al.* (eds), *Gendai Nihon Bungaku Daijiten*, p. 1149; Odagiri (ed.),
Nihon Kindai Bungaku Daijiten, pp. 1481–2.
[118] Hiratsuka, *Genshi*, vol. 1, p. 260.

impossible to find.[119] It was no longer any threat to her, and its presence as a symbol of her family was gone. By the hand of a man, even if an ineffectual one, she thus became free of all that that dagger may have symbolised. This is a speculative reading of the details, one deliberately pitched at an interpretative level, going beyond what the evidence will prove. Nevertheless, the complex symbolic aspects of this event invite thoughts at this level, and may be one reason for the heightened public concern that ensued.

The Aftermath of the Shiobara Incident

Symbolism aside, the outcome of the incident, especially the dignified way in which Hiratsuka confronted the strong public criticism of her, and the influence the incident exerted upon contemporary young women, came to be far more important than the cause and details of the incident. Until Shiobara Hiratsuka had led a relatively uneventful life, and was considered an innocent, attractive, well-brought-up daughter from a respectable family, with good marital prospects. But Shiobara transformed her life and reputation. In one night these events reduced her social status from that of 'hakoiri musume' ('a girl brought up in a box'), to that of a notorious young woman who had disgraced her family. The event left the twenty-three year Hiratsuka in an embarrassing position, and certainly changed the course of her life.

The press now made concentrated attacks on Hiratsuka.[120] She was depicted as an immoral, selfish, possessive woman, who had tried to destroy Morita's marriage and take him from his wife and child. By contrast, the press were sympathetic to Morita, who was portrayed as Hiratsuka's victim. The Tokyo Asahi Shinbun went to extremes in its condemnation, stating that such an immoral woman as Hiratsuka ought to be sent into the slums to be embraced by a beggar, to teach her a lesson.[121] Despite its vulgar sexual prescription, calculated to reduce her to the lowest form of female life, it

---

[119] Ibid., p. 261.
[120] Yorozuhō (27 March, 1908); Tokyo Asahi Shinbun (28 March, 1908); Jiji Shinpō (29 March, 1908).
[121] Tokyo Asahi Shinbun (28 March, 1908).

conveyed a message that many people shared—that such a woman
should be punished.

Her name was removed from the list of the alumni association of
the Japan Women's College, on the grounds that she had brought
disgrace to the institution, which had a reputation as an ideal educational establishment producing elite women who could become fine
examples to others.[122] Her name was not restored to that list until
1992.[123] She was harassed for several months.[124] Many newspaper
reporters were extremely forceful and visited her house, demanding
interviews. She received many obscene letters, including half-joking
marriage proposals. On one occasion she received a parcel of porno-
graphic prints. The Shiobara Incident brought disgrace on her family who had to endure humiliation, especially her father at work. He
was put under extreme pressure and advised to resign his post by
some colleagues.[125] Although he did not do so, there is no doubt
that the Shiobara Incident damaged his reputation.

There are many reasons why the press and public criticised her.
Many saw her conduct in running away from home with a married
man and attempting double suicide as a challenge to the established
family system. Under this system virginity was valued as the second
most important thing next to her life for an unmarried woman,
although an unmarried man enjoyed considerable sexual freedom
before marriage.[126] Hiratsuka did not lose her virginity to Morita,
but at the time people naturally assumed that she had, having spent
three nights with him.[127] In fact she lost her virginity to a young
Buddhist priest in charge of Kairyū Temple, who was supervising
her Zen meditation in the summer of 1910, two years after the incident. But even at that time she felt that there was nothing immoral
about an unmarried woman losing her virginity before marriage.[128]

---

[122] Hiratsuka, *Genshi*, vol. 1, pp. 272–3; Horiba, *Seitō no Jidai*, p. 30; Kobayashi, *Hito to Shisō*, p. 73; Aoki, *Kindaishi o Hiraita Joseitachi*, pp. 57, 64; Ōfūkai (comp.), *Ōfūkai Kaiin Meibo* (1908–1991).

[123] '84-nen burini fukken: Hiratsuka Raichō no fujin undō o minaosō', *Mainichi Shinbun* (26 April, 1992); Aoki, *Kindaishi o Hiraita Joseitachi*, p. 64; 'Hiratsuka Raichō fukken: dōsōkai meibo ni 84-nen buri ni kisai', *Nihon Keizai Shinbun* (4 May, 1992); Ōfūkai (comp.), *Ōfūkai Kaiin Meibo* (1992).

[124] This account is from Hiratsuka, *Genshi*, vol. 1, p. 273.

[125] Hiratsuka, *Genshi*, vol. 1, p. 274; Kobayashi, *Hito to Shisō*, p. 73.

[126] Horiba, *Seitō no Jidai*, p. 32.

[127] Hiratsuka, *Genshi*, vol. 1, pp. 264–5, 312–3.

[128] *Ibid.*, pp. 312–3; Hiratsuka Raichō, 'Shojo no shinka', *Shin Kōron* (March,

Many people took the view that Hiratsuka, who had broken society's codes, should be used as a warning to other women.[129] They also hoped that attacking her would make her reflect on her outrageous conduct and dissuade her from any further such actions, which could have a harmful influence on other women and might damage the family system. In this sense she was a victim of a hypocritical male-dominated society, and as a result of its double standards she endured great harassment and criticism.

What was most remarkable was the way in which she dealt with the criticism. She never surrendered to it, and faced up to it in a dignified way.[130] When Yamakawa Kikue visited her, being worried about the state to which Hiratsuka may have been reduced, she was surprised that Hiratsuka was unperturbed.[131] Yamakawa recalled vividly that Hiratsuka remained extremely calm, as usual, and talked about Zen meditation in an assured manner.[132]

Hiratsuka asserted her views independently. For example, immediately after the incident, Morita's mentor, Natsume Sōseki, sent Ikuta Chōkō to suggest that Hiratsuka and Morita should marry. She was disgusted with the idea and rejected it immediately.[133] The press and many in the middle classes expected Hiratsuka to apologise for having caused anxiety to her family and those who knew her. Instead, immediately after returning to her father's house, she gave journalists from the *Yorozuhō* and *Tokyo Asahi Shinbun* her version of the incident in a bold and unashamed manner, expressing no regret or self-criticism.[134] Public criticism of Hiratsuka was aggravated by the resulting newspaper articles. Responding to her fearless conduct, an unnamed 'educationalist', who knew her family well, made the following statement to the *Jiji Shinpō*:

> I do not understand Hiratsuka Haru's [Raichō's] behaviour at all. She cannot be in her right mind. However, she does not strike me as a madwoman . . . After having so seriously troubled her family, her friends

1915), reprinted in Hiratsuka, *Chosakushū*, vol. 2, pp. 53–60; Kobayashi, *Hito to Shisō*, pp. 78–80.

[129] 'Dōjō shōsan no fuchō manen o ureeru', *Jiji Shinpō* (29 March, 1908).

[130] Horiba, *Seitō no Jidai*, p. 3.

[131] Yamakawa, *20-seiki o Ayumu*, pp. 67–8.

[132] *Ibid.*, p. 68.

[133] Hiratsuka, *Genshi*, vol. 1, p. 268.

[134] Her interviews were published in *Yorozuhō* (27 March, 1908) and the *Tokyo Asahi Shinbun* (28 March, 1908).

and teachers, she should have been very ashamed even to show her face to them. To my surprise, she unashamedly went straight back to her parents' house soon after the incident. She should have fully appreciated her family's generous gesture in taking her back. She should have confined herself to her room and thrown herself down in tears. She should not have had the nerve to show her face in public. On the contrary apparently she couldn't care less about what she has done. She shamelessly gave interviews to journalists who visited her house, giving them a detailed account of her activities after she ran away from home, including how she spent the first night with Morita, and how they tried to commit double suicide. Her way of talking was almost as if she had rendered distinguished service to society. It did not show any sign of her having a sense of shame. I find her conduct outrageous and extremely hard to understand. To sum up, she has a very high opinion of herself and prides herself on being the cleverest person in the world.[135]

Throughout this controversy, Hiratsuka held to her own views, and demonstrated courage and intelligence. She was clearly seeking to break away from Japanese middle-class conventions. Many felt that her life was now ruined, but there is little doubt that the events of 1908 helped her development as a feminist.

She received constant support from her family after Shiobara. Her father was criticised because he had failed to act as an effective head of his family, and keep his daughter under control.[136] However, her parents always respected her and never coerced her, continuing to support her financially.[137] Most Japanese parents in the same situation would probably have punished their daughter severely and tried to destroy her developing personality, but Hiratsuka's parents' broad-mindedness was important in developing her independent spirit.

Apparently Hiratsuka's behaviour exerted much influence on young women. It was reported that many female students showed sympathy for her and praised her conduct.[138] Journalists and educationalists interpreted the incident as a negative influence on young women, and showed strong concern about it. One commentator saw Hiratsuka's conduct as a social threat, poisoning the minds of innocent young

---

[135] *Jiji Shinpō* (29 March, 1908).
[136] Hiratsuka, *Genshi*, vol. 1, pp. 264–74.
[137] *Ibid.*, p. 278.
[138] *Jiji Shinpō* (19 March, 1908).

women.[139] He said that he had to stop the spread of her dangerous ideas, and ended by warning parents with daughters:

> In the future even ordinary people must pay close attention to their daughters and must take great care that their daughters do not turn into peculiar women like Hiratsuka Haru [Raichō]. If the worst comes to the worst, and you find that your daughter starts to develop signs of becoming a mad-woman like Hiratsuka, you must send her to a juvenile reformatory immediately. If you think she has no hope of recovering, you must send her to a nunnery and force her to become a nun.[140]

Such comments illustrate contemporary expectations. Daughters from the upper and upper-middle classes were prevented from having social relationships with men outside their family. They were expected to obey their fathers. Hiratsuka was by no means the only girl from a respectable family who was unhappy with familial expectations.[141] Two other parallel events occurred in 1908 involving daughters from upper-middle class backgrounds. One featured the daughter of the Lord Mayor of Ogura, Suehiro Naokata, who was then a student at Peeress's High School.[142] She won the first prize in a beauty contest sponsored by a newspaper, a trivial piece of news by modern standards, but it occupied the front pages of many newspapers.[143] Women who had entered beauty contests in the past were professional entertainers and it was unheard of for a woman from a respectable family to enter.[144] She was expelled from school because her behaviour did not meet the requirements for young ladies from 'decent' family backgrounds.[145]

Another case concerned Mori Ritsuko, the daughter of a lawyer, Mori Hajime, who was from Atomi Girls' High School in Tokyo.[146] She enrolled at a training school for actresses, which also made the

---

[139] *Jiji Shinpō* (29 March, 1908).
[140] *Ibid.*
[141] Horiba, *Seitō no Jidai*, p. 32.
[142] 'Chōsen ni ōji', *Tokyo Nichi Nichi Shinbun* (22 March, 1908); Katō, *Ai wa Jidai o Koete*, pp. 18–9.
[143] Horiba, *Seitō no Jidai*, p. 37.
[144] *Ibid.*, pp. 37–8.
[145] 'Chōsen ni ōji', *Tokyo Nichi Nichi Shinbun* (22 March, 1908); Katō, *Ai wa Jidai o Koete*, pp. 18–9.
[146] This account is from Horiba, *Seitō no Jidai*, p. 38.

headlines. Acting was a profession reserved for women from humble backgrounds. The outcome was that Mori Ritsuko's name was
removed from the graduates' association list of her school.

Just like Hiratsuka, these two young women showed independent
behaviour, and were punished for it, although their actions were not
as serious as Hiratsuka's. These three incidents taken together startled
the public, made many parents question women's higher education,
and attempt to further restrict their daughters.[147]

Criticism of Hiratsuka turned into an attack on the whole system
of women's higher education, from which she had benefitted. Many
people articulated the view that such education was to blame for having created a threatening woman like Hiratsuka, and they concluded
that this education was a sinful thing, implanting damaging liberal
ideas.[148] Many became reluctant even to send their daughters to girls'
high schools. Admissions to such schools dropped dramatically the
year after the Shiobara Incident.[149] Leading educationalists like Tsuda
Umeko, Miwata Gendō and Tanabashi Ayako urged a return to the
teaching of *Onna Daigaku*. They produced 'Seinen jōshi no danshi ni
taisuru kokoroe' ('Rules stating how young women ought to behave
towards men'), entitled 'Shin *Onna Daigaku* an' ('New *Onna Daigaku*
plan').[150] The incident gave educationalists cause to rethink women's
higher education, and they had to justify it against criticism which
held it responsible for Hiratsuka's attitude and behaviour.[151]

However, some men with more advanced views welcomed the
emergence of the Japanese 'new woman', seeing an example of her
in Hiratsuka.[152] Miyata Shū, headmaster of Seijo Girls' High School,
who wanted to abandon the ideal of 'a good wife and wise mother'
in women's education and who felt the need to create a stronger
personality for women, thought highly of Hiratsuka and praised her
as the finest example of a female college graduate.[153] Similarly, many

---

[147] *Ibid.*, p. 39.
[148] *Ibid.*, p. 39.
[149] *Ibid.*, p. 39.
[150] This plan was first introduced in the 15 May, 1909 issue of *Kyōiku Jiron*
(*Comments upon Current Educational Events*). It stated that when a young woman meets
a man, somebody should sit with them to keep an eye on them. If she unavoid-
ably meets a man by herself, she should do so in a public place. See 'Shin *Onna
Daigaku* an', *Kyōiku Jiron* (15 May, 1909).
[151] 'Bekarazu kun', *Tokyo Asahi Shinbun* (30 September, 1908).
[152] Horiba, *Seitō no Jidai*, p. 40.
[153] Cited in Horiba, *Seitō no Jidai*, pp. 41–2.

young female students, who were becoming more conscious of their own value and importance and wanted to express their own views, were deeply moved by Hiratsuka's behaviour.[154] Hiratsuka became an idol for some teenage girls. Her actions showed them that women were capable of making their own decisions like men, and that women also had the right to choose or reject men. Hiratsuka's example gave encouragement to these young women. Although she stated that she saw no likeness between herself and the heroine of *Baien*, this heroine appealed to many young women, who consciously or unconsciously gained inspiration from her.[155] The novel's heroine, like Hiratsuka, refused to surrender herself physically to the hero, and attempted to accomplish her own purpose in life, a theme that fascinated young girls. In this respect, *Baien* had a significant effect. A number of women who became active members of the Seitō Society, such as Otake Kōkichi, Araki Ikuko or Ikuta Hanayo, had read *Baien* and were much taken by its heroine.[156] Otake Kōkichi recalled that she was seized by a strange urge to meet Hiratsuka after reading the novel.[157]

At the same time the new type of heroine which Morita had introduced made a great impact in Japanese literary circles.[158] Before *Baien*, such a 'new woman' had never appeared in Japanese literature.[159] Morita's heroine opened up a new range of characterisation in Japanese novels.

The Shiobara Incident was therefore highly influential. What if anything did Hiratsuka and Morita achieve through it? Morita lost his English teaching post, but he gained in other ways.[160] Many copies of *Baien* were sold. Although he denied that he had planned such an autobiographical novel before the incident, he took full advantage of the public curiosity and wide newspaper coverage. His involvement in the Shiobara Incident became a significant stepping stone in his literary career. After *Baien* his creative writing developed, and he produced many works including *Hatsukoi* (*First Love*).[161] In

---

[154] *Ibid.*, pp. 41–2.
[155] Hiratsuka, *Genshi*, vol. 1, pp. 298–9.
[156] Horiba, *Seitō no Jidai*, pp. 41–4.
[157] *Ibid.*, p. 44.
[158] Kumasaka Atsuko, 'Morita Sōhei *Baien* no Tomoko', *Kokubungaku*, 25:4 (March, 1980), p. 53.
[159] Sasaki, *Atarashii Onna no Tōrai*, pp. 1–4.
[160] Natsume, 'Chichi no tegami', p. 417.
[161] Hisamatsu *et al.* (eds), *Gendai Nihon Bungaku Daijiten*, pp. 1148–51.

November 1909 he joined the literary section of the *Tokyo Asahi Shinbun*. In 1920 he was appointed a professor of Hōsei University, Tokyo where he taught until 1930.[162]

The incident had much influence on Hiratsuka's development. She learnt much about the press through being its victim, making her wary of it, but also helping her to handle it later. Having faced press criticism and public pillory, she developed a broader empathy with other women's difficulties and began to understand some of the problems of less privileged women. This was to help her when she dealt with women voicing their views in the 'Letters to the Editor' column of *Seitō*. When some young *Seitō* readers with family problems ran away from home and turned to the Seitō Society for help, Hiratsuka listened to their problems and gave them financial support and accommodation, showing a sympathetic attitude that may have derived from the incident.

The criticism from the press probably strengthened her capacity to resist traditional forces in Japanese society. The support she received from other young women made her realise that she was not the only woman unhappy with the *ie* system and its conventions, who wanted to be released from them. After the incident, she became more determined to fight against those conventions and to improve women's status. The fact that she survived such harsh criticism gave her confidence to handle women's social issues. Her notoriety and fame resulting from newspaper coverage and from *Baien* was an advantage when she launched *Seitō*. Young women who had become her admirers took an almost permanent interest in her.[163] They purchased many early copies of *Seitō* out of curiosity, much as they had bought *Baien*.[164] Hiratsuka did not need to spend money on publicity, for *Seitō* immediately obtained enthusiastic support from young women, many of them becoming members of the Seitō Society.

The Shiobara Incident had at least one seemingly destructive consequence. The Keishū Literary Society, which appeared to have real potential to develop into a successful women's literary society, was forced to dissolve following the adverse publicity surrounding the

---

[162] Odagiri (ed.), *Nihon Kindai Bungaku Daijiten*, pp. 1481–2.
[163] Horiba, *Seitō no Jidai*, pp. 41–4.
[164] *Ibid.*, pp. 46–7.

incident. Hiratsuka admitted that the magazine of this Society, which was published once but then discontinued, might have developed into an influential women's literary magazine, and might have contributed to raise the quality of women's writing, as *Seitō* later did. This never occurred, although *Seitō* was to step in and take over this role.

PLATES

All photographs are courtesy of Ōtsuki Shoten, reprinted with permission. They are from the four-volume Hiratsuka Raichō autobiography, *Hiratsuka Raichō Jiden: Genshi Josei wa Taiyō de Atta* (published by Ōtsuki Shoten).

Plate 1. Hiratsuka Raichō (right) with her mother (middle)
and her elder sister Taka (left), *circa* 1888.

Plate 2. Hiratsuka Raichō in the first year of
Ochanomizu Girls'High School, *circa* 1898.

Plate 3. Hiratsuka Raichō in her second year at the Japan Women's College (1904) and members of the Kaizoku Gumi (her friends from Ochanomizu Girls' High School). Right to left: Nagata, Kobayashi, Hiratsuka Raichō and Ichihara.

Plate 4. A meeting of the Seitō Society at Iwano Kiyoko's house in Sugamo, Tokyo, in spring, 1916. Right to left: Hiratsuka Raichō, Yasumochi Yoshiko, Araki Ikuko, Nakano Hatsuko, Iwano Kiyoko and Kobayashi Katsuko.

Plate 5. Hiratsuka Raichō with her daughter Akemi and her partner Okumura Hiroshi, at Chigasaki in 1916.

Plate 6. Members of the Association of New Women. Front row, right to left: Tsukamoto Nakako, Oku Mumeo, Yorita and Kikuchi Mitsu. Second row, right to left: Yabe Hatsuko, Tajima Hide, Tanaka Yoshiko, Hiratsuka Raichō, Sasaki Itoko and Sakamoto Makoto.

Plate 7. Hiratsuka Raichō at home in Sendagaya, Tokyo, with her daughter Akemi, her son Atsubumi and her partner Okumura Hiroshi, *circa* 1923.

Plate 8. Hiratsuka Raichō at home in Sendagaya, Tokyo. This photograph was taken by her partner Okumura Hiroshi, *circa* 1923.

Plate 9. Hiratsuka Raichō in old age.

CHAPTER FOUR

THE SEITŌ SOCIETY AND NEW WOMEN

Introduction

After the Shiobara Incident, Hiratsuka turned her attention to her further education. She went to Shinshū (present-day Nagano Prefecture) in September 1908, and used this interlude to recover from stress, and to develop her literary skills.[1] Her time was divided between Zen meditation, walking, reading and writing. Through the Keishū Literary Society, she had accumulated a knowledge of literature, but she had not had sufficient opportunity to improve her own literary style. She read in particular Edgar Allan Poe's verse and Henrik Ibsen's *Hedda Gabler* in English.[2] During this time she translated some of Poe's prose poems into Japanese, and wrote essays based on her life in Shinshū.[3]

After she returned to Tokyo, most of her time was spent reading Japanese and western literature in public libraries, studying English grammar, translating at the Seisoku English Language School and sitting in Zen meditation.[4] She began to subscribe to haiku magazines, attended literary meetings at Baba Kochō's house, and visited Ikuta Chōkō for private tuition.[5] Three years after the Shiobara Incident Hiratsuka founded the *Seitōsha* (the Seitō Society), in spring 1911, and inaugurated its magazine *Seitō* in September 1911.

---

[1] Hiratsuka, *Genshi*, vol. 1, pp. 278–9.

[2] *Ibid.*, pp. 280–1.

[3] Her work at this time—translations and two essays entitled 'Kōgen no aki' ('Autumn in the highlands') and 'Waga manako' ('My eyes')—were later published in *Seitō*. Hiratsuka Raichō, 'Kōgen no aki', *Seitō*, 1:3 (November, 1911), pp. 88–103 & 1:4 (December, 1911), pp. 49–64. Her reading of *Hedda Gabler* was also profitable as she later edited a special issue on Ibsen's *A Doll's House* and wrote some reviews of Ibsen's works.

[4] Hiratsuka, *Genshi*, vol. 1, pp. 301–3.

[5] *Ibid.*, pp. 304–9. Hiratsuka studied haiku composed by haiku masters such as Bashō, Issa, Buson and others and began to compose haiku. She published her haiku in *Seitō*. See Hiratsuka Raichō, 'Hana fuyō', *Seitō*, 1:2 (October, 1911), p. 64.

The Seitō Society was little studied before 1945, but most Japanese women's history books published after that date have seen it as a pioneering organisation.[6] More publications on it have appeared than on other activities that Hiratsuka was involved with.[7] Some of these focus on Seitō women like Itō Noe and Yamada Waka. There are few on Hiratsuka based on primary sources.[8] Existing publications rarely discuss the background from which the Seitō Society emerged; they omit Hiratsuka's motivations and expectations, and they do not discuss how the Seitō Society differed from its rival women's organisation, the Shin Shin Fujinkai (the Real New Women's Association).

---

[6] Inoue, *Nihon Joseishi*, pp. 241–3; Yoneda, *Kindai Nihon Joseishi*, vol. 1, pp. 104–10; Hayashi *et al.* (eds), *Nihon Joseishi*, pp. 228–32; Morosawa, *Onna no Rekishi*, vol. 2, pp. 164–8; Higuchi, *Nippon Joseishi Hakkutsu*, pp. 285–6; Miyagi *et al.* (eds), *Shinkō Nihon Joseishi*, pp. 229–32; Sōgō Joseishi Kenkyūkai (ed.), *Sei, Ai, Kazoku*, pp. 202–3; Sōgō Joseishi Kenkyūkai (ed.), *Bunka to Shisō*, pp. 206–12; Yamashita, *Nihon Josei Kaihō Shisō no Kigen*, pp. 81–103; Tatewaki, *Nihon no Fujin*, pp. 10–28; Kamichika, *Josei Shisōshi*, pp. 188–197.

[7] For works on the Seitō Society in Japanese, see Yamazaki Tomoko, *Ameyuki-san no Uta: Yamada Waka no Sūki Naru Shōgai* (1978, 1991 edn), pp. 184–207; Ide Fumiko, *Seitō no Onnatachi* (1975), pp. 7–260; Horiba, *Seitō no Jidai*, pp. 2–250; Araki Tomiyo, 'Bosei ishiki no mezame: *Seitō* no hitobito', in Wakita Haruko (ed.), *Bosei o Tou*, vol. 2 (1985), pp. 130–57; Ide Fumiko, 'Kaisetsu', in Fuji Shuppan (ed.), *Seitō Kaisetsu, Sōmokuji, Sakuin* (1983), pp. 5–26; Hiratsuka Raichō o Yomu Kai (ed.), *Seitō no 50-nin* (1996), pp. 6–117; Yoneda Sayoko, '*Seitō* to shakai no setten: Raichō to Chōkō o chūshin ni', *Yamanashi Kenritsu Joshi Tanki Daigaku Kīyō*, 24 (March, 1991), pp. 69–82; Nakayama Kazuko, 'Onna de aru koto no imi: *Seitō*-ha o megutte', *Kokubungaku*, 25:15 (December, 1980), pp. 67–71; Yoneda Sayoko, '*Seitō* no ryaku-datsu', in Hiratsuka Raichō o Yomu Kai (ed.), *Raichō Soshite Watashi: Part III* (1991), pp. 100–9. In English, see Nancy Andrew, 'The Seitōsha: an early Japanese women's organization, 1911–1916', *Papers on Japan*, 6 (1972), pp. 45–69; Sievers, *Flowers in Salt*, pp. 163–88; Toshihiko Satō, 'Ibsen's drama and the Japanese Bluestockings', *Edda: Scandinavian Journal of Literary Research*, 5 (1981), pp. 265–93; Livia Monnet, 'In the beginning woman was the sun: autobiographies of modern Japanese women writers, 1', *Japan Forum*, 1:1 (April, 1989), pp. 55–81; Pauline Reich, 'Japan's literary feminists: the Seitō group', *Signs*, 2:1 (Autumn 1976), pp. 280–91; Yamazaki, *The Story of Yamada Waka*, pp. 116–26; Ken Miyamoto, 'Itō Noe and the Bluestockings', *Japan Interpreter*, 10:2 (Autumn 1975), pp. 190–204; Anon., 'Feminist Kamichika Ichiko', *East*, 25:2 (July/August, 1989), pp. 17–23; Harumi Setouchi (trans. by Sanford Goldstein & Kazuji Ninomiya), *Beauty in Disarray* (1993).

[8] Horiba Kiyoko and Ide Fumiko published on the Seitō Society. Ide's *Seitō no Onnatachi* (*Women in the Seitō Society*) gives a chronological account from a literary angle of how the society developed and was dissolved. Horiba's *Seitō no Jidai* (*The Age of the Seitō*) makes use of some original documents from the Japan Women's College.

The Foundation of the Seitō Society

The charismatic opening sentence of Hiratsuka's manifesto for the initial issue of *Seitō*—'Genshi josei wa taiyō de atta' ('In the beginning woman was the sun')—which highlighted her feminist ideas, has had a continuous fascination for Japanese women.[9] The line has always been connected with Hiratsuka, and it has long been believed by the public that the idea of founding the society came from her.[10] This, however, is incorrect. It has also been a mistake to believe that *Seitō* was a feminist magazine from the beginning. It was in fact Hiratsuka's mentor, Ikuta Chōkō, who first broached the idea of a literary society and magazine which only women contributed to, edited and ran.[11] His aim was to establish a women's literary society along the lines of his Keishū Literary Society.[12] Within the latter, Ikuta had been successful in encouraging young women with potential literary talent, who might improve the quality of women's writing. But the society had come to an abrupt end, failing to fulfil its potential because of the public scandal caused by the Shiobara Incident.[13]

Ikuta wanted to recruit and educate young women of literary talent. He was convinced of the need for a women's literary magazine, as the mouthpiece of a women's literary society, feeling that this would unite female writers. Such a literary magazine written solely by women would provide women writers with opportunities to publish their work, exchange ideas and appraise each other's writing. Ikuta, who appreciated Hiratsuka's literary talent, strongly recommended her to found such a society and to inaugurate its magazine. However, she initially turned a deaf ear to this proposal, because her immediate goal at that time was to pursue her identity and potential, and to accomplish herself in rather different terms.[14] She also felt that she was unsuited to the task because she had no intention of making a career as a writer. But for Ikuta, the Seitō Society and *Seitō* would have never existed.

---

[9] Fukuchi, *Kindai Nihon Joseishi*, p. 91; Momose Meiji *et al.*, *Mei Serifu Nihonshi* (1987), pp. 214–5.

[10] Higuchi, *Nippon Joseishi*, pp. 10–11; Tatewaki, *Nihon no Fujin*, p. 12.

[11] Hiratsuka, *Genshi*, vol. 1, pp. 317–8.

[12] Yoneda, '*Seitō* to shakai no setten', p. 69.

[13] Hiratsuka, *Genshi*, vol. 1, p. 318. Ikuta never blamed Hiratsuka for having ruined his Keishū Literary Society.

[14] *Ibid.*, pp. 316–8.

The birth of the Seitō Society was also closely connected with the social and political conditions of the time.[15] After the Russo-Japanese War, the Japanese government promoted economic development, and Japan increasingly became a country which could compare with the world powers.[16] However, its government adopted a ruthless attitude towards socialists and anarchists; the *Taigyaku Jiken* (High Treason Incident) being an early example of this.[17] Having sentenced twelve socialists and anarchists to death for plotting to assassinate the emperor, the government, wanting to place the nation under stricter control, set up the Special Higher Police in the Metropolitan Police Headquarters, to suppress socialist and labour movements.[18] In its educational policy, its objectives were to create strong armed forces and a more efficient workforce.[19] With regard to women's education, it emphasised the aim of producing *ryōsai kenbo*, rather than to develop women's ability to think more independently, as did the missionary schools.[20] Japanese historians have referred to government policy during this period as '*fuyu no jidai*' (the winter period).[21] From this repressive social and political climate there emerged reforming initiatives led by white-collar workers and the intelligentsia (such as teachers, academics and journalists), whose numbers were increasing with the development of a more advanced economy.[22] They objected to the government's exercise of absolute power and wished to advance democracy and destroy *hanbatsu seiji* (clan government).[23] A number of *kensei yōgo undō* (campaigns to defend constitutionalism) and related demonstrations took place throughout Japan from late December

---

[15] Tanaka, *Josei Kaihō no Shisō*, pp. 188–90.

[16] Hayashi *et al.* (eds), *Nihon Joseishi*, p. 229.

[17] Yoneda, *Kindai Nihon Joseishi*, vol. 1, pp. 97–100. Kanno Suga was one of the people executed in January 1911. On the High Treason Incident, see Sakamoto Taketo, *Kōtoku Shūsui: Meiji Shakaishugi no Ittōsei* (1984), pp. 207–17; Kondō Tomie, 'Kanno Suga', in Setouchi Harumi (ed.), *Hangyaku no Onna no Roman* (1989), pp. 20–48; Itoya Toshio, *Kōtoku Shūsui* (1973), pp. 183–203; Hane, *Reflections on the Way to the Gallows*, pp. 51–74; Raddeker, *Treacherous Women of Imperial Japan*, pp. 6–7, 40–62.

[18] Yoneda, *Kindai Nihon Joseishi*, pp. 100–1.

[19] *Ibid.*, pp. 101–2.

[20] Morosawa, *Onna no Rekishi*, vol. 2, p. 169.

[21] For example, Imai Seiichi, *Taishō Demokurashii* (1984, 1991 edn), p. 123.

[22] Yoneda, *Kindai Nihon Joseishi*, vol. 1, pp. 105–6.

[23] The monopoly of political power by men belonging to Satsuma and Chōshū was referred to as *hanbatsu seiji* by their opponents, and it reached its peak between 1890 and 1918. See Tanaka, *Josei Kaihō no Shisō*, p. 189.

1912 to early January 1913, and these were to be major factors in bringing down the Katsura Cabinet.[24]

Comparable developments emerged in literature, thought and theatre from the end of the Meiji period to the beginning of the Taishō period. In the field of literature, *shizen-shugi bungaku* (the literature of naturalism) reached its peak during this time.[25] From 1909 the most naturalistic literary works were produced by Shimazaki Tōson, Tayama Katai, Iwano Hōmei and Tokuda Shūsei. Among them, Shimazaki's *Ie* (*House*) and Tayama's *Inaka Kyōshi* (*A Country Teacher*) were considered to be the most important works of Japanese Naturalism. As the historian Tanaka Sumiko suggested, the main theme of these novels was how to pursue and make best use of self-development, and in this they reflected the mood of the times, which aimed to break down conventionalism, escape from old family and social ties, and pursue ideas of freedom.[26] Such male writers' advocacy of emancipation applied only to men. Their key characters were always male. Nevertheless, literary naturalism exerted a considerable influence on the creation of *Seitō*.[27] Seitō women, most of them middle-class, learned ideas of self-awakening and self-development from the literature of naturalism.[28] They applied these ideas to women.

Seitō women were also inspired by the literary journal *Shirakaba* (*White Birch*), launched on April 1910 by eminent novelists such as Mushanokōji Saneatsu and Shiga Naoya.[29] Members of *Shirakaba*

---

[24] Yoneda, *Kindai Nihon Joseishi*, vol. 1, p. 105. Katsura Tarō (1847–1913) held key positions in the army and was also a politician. He first became prime minister in 1901 and served as in that role with three cabinets until February 1913.

[25] Yamashita Etsuko, *Nihon Josei Kaihō Shisō no Kigen* (1988), pp. 106–7. Shizen-shugi (Naturalism) was a significant literary movement in Japan, which started around 1906 and came to an end in the late 1920s. It was highly influenced by the late nineteenth-century European model of Naturalism. On Japanese Naturalism, see Kano Masanao, *Taishō Demokurashii* (1976), pp. 32–3; Odagiri Hideo (ed.), *Kōza, Nihon Kindai Bungakushi*, vol. 2 (1956), pp. 141–86; Usui Yoshimi, *Taishō Bungakushi* (1963), pp. 19–28; Katō Shūichi, *Nihon Bungakushi Josetsu*, vol. 2 (1980), pp. 378–91.

[26] Tanaka, *Josei Kaihō no Shisō*, pp. 188–9. Shimazaki's *Ie* is a good example. It portrays its hero's struggle against the fetters of his family's conventions, and his desire to lead a free life.

[27] *Ibid.*, p. 189.

[28] Yamashita, *Nihon Josei Kaihō Shisō*, p. 106.

[29] Mushanokōji Saneatsu (1885–1976) was a novelist, poet and playwright. He played a central part in *Shirakaba* (*White Birch*). In 1918 he founded a utopian commune called *Atarashiki Mura* (New Village) in Hyūga in Kyūshū. Shiga Naoya (1883–1971) was considered as perfecting the Watakushi Shōsetsu (I-novel or personal novel). On *Shirakaba*, see Usui, *Taishō Bungakushi*, pp. 47–74; Odagiri (ed.), *Nihon Kindai Bungakushi*, vol. 3, pp. 20–8.

believed that developing one's potential was of service to mankind. They admired Tolstoy, Rodin, Whitman and Romain Rolland, and introduced these authors to Japan.[30] They also openly criticised established authority. *Shirakaba* created a sensation in the world of literature. Its humanitarianism captured the imagination of well-read young people, including Seitō women, who were searching for new meaning in their lives. It also gave them courage to live more freely. Another contribution to the launching of *Seitō* was the development of women's higher education.[31] It was from this social, political and educational background that the Seitō Society and *Seitō* emerged.

Although the precise date of the foundation of the Seitō Society cannot be traced, Hiratsuka founded it some time in spring 1911 with Yasumochi Yoshiko, a friend and classmate of Hiratsuka's elder sister, Taka, at the Japan Women's College, who was then a lodger in Hiratsuka's household and agreed to help her.[32] They first drew up the following *shuisho* (main objectives of the Society):

> As things are now, women are no longer in a position to live perpetually in idleness. They must come to their senses as soon as possible, and must fully cultivate their abilities, which Heaven has equally bestowed even on them. Hereby, with only women's joint efforts, we establish the Seitō Society as an organ designed for women to promote their ideas, to improve their knowledge of literature, and to cultivate their minds. At the same time we hereby launch our society's magazine, *Seitō*, which will be open to unknown women who share literary interests with us or who are willing to work for the same cause with us. We hope and also trust that *Seitō* will produce eminent *joryū tensai* (female geniuses) some time in the future.[33]

Such key aims were very similar to Article 1 of the general regulations of the Seitō Society, which stated that the main objectives of the Society were to promote the standard of women's literature, to allow women to display their innate talents, and to produce female

---

[30] Imai, *Taishō Demokurashii*, pp. 118–22.

[31] Horiba, *Seitō no Jidai*, pp. 19–21.

[32] As Hiratsuka did not keep a diary or retain old documents, the only reliable source of information about the starting date and major activities she engaged in before the inauguration of *Seitō* was Yasumochi Yoshiko's *Seitōsha Jimu Nisshi* (the daily record of business matters of the Seitō Society). See Horiba, *Seitō no Jidai*, pp. 58–9. On Yasumochi, see Hiratsuka Raichō o Yomu Kai (ed.), *Seitō no 50-nin*, pp. 98–9; Ichibangase Yasuko *et al.* (eds), *Nihon Josei Jinmei Jiten* (1993), p. 1052.

[33] Hiratsuka, *Genshi*, vol. 1, p. 323.

literary geniuses at some time in the future.[34] The objectives and regulations had high hopes for women. Both Hiratsuka and Yasumochi were highly intellectual, strong-minded, dissatisfied with women's status, and the ways in which women were treated and discriminated against. At the same time they were irritated by most women who accepted low status without objection and question. Seitō aimed to correct the distorted picture of incompetent, untalented women. Hiratsuka and Yasumochi had a sense of mission, and wanted to stimulate other women to demonstrate their talents.

By the end of May 1911, preparations for *Seitō* had made steady progress. Its founders proved themselves quite capable of making decisions on their own, but Hiratsuka was also indebted to Ikuta for his assistance.[35] He played a leading part in the inauguration of *Seitō*. His international knowledge led to the naming of the Seitō Society after the eighteenth-century British women's literary circle, the Bluestocking Society. 'Bluestocking' was the nickname for literary meetings held at eminent ladies' houses in London after about 1750.[36] In the 1790s the expression 'Bluestocking' had positive connotations, referring to women who were intellectual, literary and learned. However, attitudes changed and by the early nineteenth century in England it had come to be used in a rather negative and sometimes cynical sense, indicating women who did new, unconventional or 'unwomanly' things.[37]

Ikuta adopted this term 'bluestocking', thus making a comparison between Japanese women writers in the early twentieth century and earlier English ones. He indicated that the Japanese writers should openly proclaim themselves in this way, facing up to the criticism that was inevitable when a literary society was controlled by women.[38] Ikuta believed that this new venture, excluding men completely, would be path-breaking and certainly raise the standards of women's writing. As such it would inevitably be seen as a threat or challenge to existing literary circles. There seemed little point in trying to avoid

---

[34] Seitōsha, 'Seitōsha no gaisoku', *Seitō*, 1:1 (September, 1911), p. 132.

[35] Hiratsuka, *Genshi*, vol. 1, pp. 325–6.

[36] Lisa Tuttle, *Encyclopedia of Feminism* (1986, London, 1987 edn), p. 46; Dale Spender, *Women of Ideas and What Men Have Done to Them: From Aphra Behn to Adrienne Rich* (1982, London, 1983 edn), pp. 101–2; Kobayashi, *Hito to Shisō*, pp. 91–2.

[37] C. T. Onions (ed.), *The Shorter Oxford English Dictionary*, 2 vols (London, 1983), vol. 1, p. 208.

[38] Hiratsuka, *Genshi*, vol. 1, p. 327; Horiba, *Seitō no Jidai*, pp. 59–60.

criticism stemming from this—hence Ikuta's advocacy of this bold initiative, with its members announcing themselves as 'Bluestocking Ladies'. By definition, they would openly adopt radical and challenging 'unfeminine' ideas against the male-dominated literary elite.[39] Contrary to the erudite Ikuta, Hiratsuka later confessed that she had never come across the term 'Bluestocking', and did not know the meaning of the word.[40] However, after listening to Ikuta's explanation she accepted the name, eventually thinking it ideal for her society. Ikuta also helped Hiratsuka find the most suitable Japanese translation for the 'Bluestocking Society'. They agreed on the original, updated term '*Seitōsha*', and used *Seitō* as the name of their literary magazine.[41]

Ikuta also recommended Hiratsuka to have female authorities on literature as *sanjoin* (supporting members). He gave her a comprehensive list of female writers, and advised her to include wives of eminent authors.[42] Ikuta's view about the need for supporting members was based on his argument that *Seitō* would end up being nothing but a *joryū dōjin zasshi* (a women's literary coterie magazine) if only unknown young female writers were involved. Hiratsuka had no idea how much her magazine would benefit from his suggestion at that time. However, the proposal to have supporting members became one key to success and helped to establish literary networks.[43] In addition, Ikuta looked through the draft objectives and regulations

---

[39] Kobayashi, *Hito to Shisō*, p. 90.

[40] Hiratsuka, *Genshi*, vol. 1, p. 326.

[41] *Ibid.*, p. 327; Kobayashi, *Hito to Shisō*, p. 90. Apparently, the term 'Bluestocking Society' was first translated as *Kontabitō* ('*kon*' literally means dark blue, '*tabi*' means Japanese-style socks, worn with sandals or Japanese wooden clogs when people dressed up in a traditional Japanese costume with *kimonos*, and '*tō*' means society). This translation appeared some time in the 1890s and certainly went with the current of the time, for the majority of Japanese people then still wore *kimonos*. By the time Hiratsuka founded her society in 1911, more people had begun to dress in western clothes, although most Seitō members still wore *kimonos* and did not bother to wear the blue stockings that symbolised the name of the society. This was unlike the members of the eighteenth-century British Bluestocking Society, with their frame-work-knitted blue stockings. As Hiratsuka felt that the expression '*Kontabitō*' sounded a little old-fashioned, she wanted to update the translation. With the assistance of Ikuta, she spent some time trying to find the most suitable translation for 'the Bluestocking Society'. They took their hint from a new translation that Mori Ōgai produced for 'stockings', and eventually came up with the updated term '*Seitōsha*'.

[42] Hiratsuka, *Genshi*, vol. 1, pp. 325–6.

[43] *Ibid.*, p. 326.

of the Seitō Society, amending them in various ways. He was also closely involved in assessing manuscripts for the initial issue of *Seitō*.[44]

After the names of the society and its magazine were decided, Hiratsuka and Yasumochi recruited three more *hokkinin* (founding members): Nakano Hatsuko, Kiuchi Teiko and Mozume Kazuko.[45] Both Nakano and Kiuchi were Yasumochi's friends from the Japan Women's College, and Mozume's elder sister and Hiratsuka were classmates at Ochanomizu Girls' High School.[46] These founders were all unmarried, well-educated women in their early twenties. All except for Mozume Kazuko were graduates of the Japan Women's College. Their family backgrounds were predominantly upper-middle class. Their fathers were professionals who valued female education and were wealthy enough to invest money in their daughters' higher education.[47] They were bound together by a common interest in literature, and they had some literary ability. All of them had received a literary training, had enough knowledge of Japanese and western literature to evaluate work and to write review articles, and had already embarked on literary activities.[48] They produced short novels, *haiku* and *tanka*. Some of them published in literary magazines before

---

[44] *Ibid.*, p. 342.

[45] Hiratsuka Raichō, 'Fujin undō 50-nen o kaerimite: *Seitō* sōkan no koro', *Fujin Kōron* (November, 1961), reprinted in Hiratsuka, *Chosakushū*, vol. 7, p. 393; Hiratsuka Raichō, 'Joryū sakka ga yo ni deru made: Seitōsha no koto nado', *Bungaku Kurabu* (April, 1950), reprinted in Hiratsuka, *Chosakushū*, vol. 7, pp. 92–3. On Nakano, see Hiratsuka Raichō o Yomu Kai (ed.), *Seitō no 50-nin*, pp. 64–5; Ichibangase *et al.* (eds), *Nihon Josei Jinmei Jiten*, pp. 770–1. On Kiuchi, see Hiratsuka Raichō o Yomu Kai (ed.), *Seitō no 50-nin*, pp. 44–5; Ichibangase *et al.* (eds), *Nihon Josei Jinmei Jiten*, pp. 347–8. On Mozume, see Hiratsuka Raichō o Yomu Kai (ed.), *Seitō no 50-nin*, pp. 92–3; Ichibangase *et al.* (eds), *Nihon Josei Jinmei Jiten*, p. 1033; *Asahi Shinbun* (30 July, 1997).

[46] Horiba, *Seitō no Jidai*, p. 20; Ōfūkai (comp.), *Ōfūkai Kaiin Meibo* (1992).

[47] Hiratsuka's father was a government official. Kiuchi's father, who was then retired, used to work as a civil servant. Nakano's father was a publisher, and Mozume's father, Mozume Takami, was an eminent scholar of Japanese philology and a professor of Tokyo University.

[48] Nakano, Kiuchi and Yasumochi, all of whom were graduates from the Department of Japanese Literature at the Japan Women's College, had read Japanese literature widely, and had studied subjects like literary theory. The first two women had had literary apprenticeships under the writer Kōda Rohan's guidance, which was more practical than academic and improved their writing skills. Hiratsuka was an active member of the Keishū Literary Society, and had close associations with literary critics and writers such as Ikuta Chōkō, Morita Sōhei and Baba Kochō. Mozume Kazuko was a disciple of the eminent novelist, Natsume Sōseki.

Seitō.[49] They also had close associations with some contemporary writers of eminence. Although these founding members were not well-known in literary circles and did not compare with authors like the female poet Yosano Akiko in terms of literary flair and reputation, they were not complete novices in writing articles and editing a women's literary magazine.[50] All of them apart from Hiratsuka wanted to establish themselves as successful writers and develop their literary careers through close associations with *Seitō.* They were united by a desire to bring women writers together in *Seitō,* to create a close literary network, and to upgrade the standard of women's literature. At its launch therefore, *Seitō* certainly had potential.

Hiratsuka and Yasumochi organised the first meeting for founding members on 1 June, 1911.[51] They recruited seven supporting members: Hasegawa Shigure, Okada Yachiyo, Katō Kazuko, Yosano Akiko, Kunikida Haruko, Koganei Kimiko and Mori Shigeko.[52] According

---

[49] Hiratsuka Raichō's maiden short story entitled *Ai no Matsujitsu* (*The Last Day of Love*) came out in the first issue of the Keishū Literary Society's circulating magazine. Yasumochi Yoshiko's *haiku* appeared in *Fujin Sekai* (*Women's World*), and Mozume Kazuko's short story '*Kanzashi*' ('An ornamental hairpin') was published in the July issue of an eminent literary magazine, *Hototogisu* (*A Little Cuckoo*), in 1910. Kiuchi had natural literary flair, as demonstrated in some of her short stories which appeared before *Seitō.* Among them her novel *Onna* (*A Woman*) published in *Hototogisu* (*A Little Cuckoo*) in September 1910, in which she challenged the *ie* system, is considered to be the best. Nakano wrote a couple of children's stories, which appeared in *Shōjo no Tomo* (*Young Girls' Companion*) before her *Seitō* involvement.

[50] Compared to the other three founding members, Kiuchi and Nakano were more experienced, and their literary skill was acknowledged by contemporaries before their involvement with *Seitō.* Both of them had already commenced a career as journalists, and were regular contributors to well-known magazines. Kiuchi was asked to take charge of one of the columns of *Fujin Sekai* (*Women's World*), and to write regular articles. Nakano took on the editorship of a children's magazine *Shōgakusei* (*Elementary School Students*). This first employment was followed by a journalistic career as a female reporter of the Tokyo Niroku Newspaper Company, which she took up in February 1908. By the time she joined Seitō, she had plenty of editorial experience, and had established useful contacts with publishers. See 'Tōsei Fujin Kisha', *Tokyo Asahi Shinbun* (25 October, 1909); 'Atarashii onna', *Yomiuri Shinbun* (11 June, 1912).

[51] Yasumochi Yoshiko, *Seitōsha Jimu Nisshi* (*The Daily Record of Business Matters of the Seitō Society*), 1 June, 1911 (unpublished material belonging to the Hiratsuka Raichō o Kinensuru Kai Archive).

[52] Yasumochi, *Seitōsha Jimu Nisshi*, 3 & 6 June, 1911. On Okada Yachiyo, see Hiratsuka Raichō o Yomu Kai (ed.), *Seitō no 50-nin*, pp. 28–9; Ichibangase *et al.* (eds), *Nihon Josei Jinmei Jiten*, p. 221; Muramatsu Sadataka & Watanabe Sumiko (eds), *Gendai Josei Bungaku Jiten* (1990), pp. 85–6. On Hasegawa Shigure, see Hiratsuka Raichō o Yomu Kai (ed.), *Seitō no 50-nin*, pp. 74–5; Ichibangase *et al.* (eds), *Nihon Josei Jinmei Jiten*, p. 822; Muramatsu & Watanabe (eds), *Gendai Josei Bungaku Jiten*,

to the general regulations of the Seitō Society, female literary scholars, who approved of the objectives of the Seitō Society, were qualified to become supporting members.[53] However, Yosano and Hasegawa were the only ones who were established as literary figures. The rest were either the wives or sisters of eminent contemporary writers. Even so, as they had extensive and useful literary connections, their participation was beneficial.[54]

The founding members sent the objectives and regulations of the Society to their friends, families, old classmates at Japan Women's College and other acquaintances.[55] According to Article 5 of the regulations of the Seitō Society, any woman regardless of race, who approved of the Society's objectives, who was a literary figure or wished to establish herself in literature, or was a devotee of literature, was qualified to become a *shain* (ordinary member).[56] Eighteen

---

pp. 268–9; Hasegawa Hitoshi & Kōno Toshirō (eds), *Hasegawa Shigure: Hito to Shōgai* (1982); Ogata Akiko, *Nyonin Geijutsu no Sekai: Hasegawa Shigure to Sono Shūhen* (1980); Jō Natsuko, 'Hasegawa Shigure', in Setouchi Harumi (ed.), *Koi to Geijutsu e no Jōnetsu* (1989). On Katō Kazuko, see Hiratsuka Raichō o Yomu Kai (ed.), *Seitō no 50-nin*, pp. 36–7; Ichibangase *et al.* (eds), *Nihon Josei Jinmei Jiten*, p. 310. On Kunikida Haruko, see Hiratsuka Raichō o Yomu Kai (ed.), *Seitō no 50-nin*, pp. 46–7; Ichibangase *et al.* (eds), *Nihon Josei Jinmei Jiten*, p. 395; Muramatsu & Watanabe (eds), *Gendai Josei Bungaku Jiten*, pp. 117–8. On Koganei Kimiko, see Hiratsuka Raichō o Yomu Kai (ed.), *Seitō no 50-nin*, pp. 48–9; Ichibangase *et al.* (eds), *Nihon Josei Jinmei Jiten*, p. 438; Muramatsu & Watanabe (eds), *Gendai Josei Bungaku Jiten*, pp. 130. On Mori Shigeko, see Hiratsuka Raichō o Yomu Kai (ed.), *Seitō no 50-nin*, pp. 94–5; Ichibangase *et al* (eds), *Nihon Josei Jinmei Jiten*, pp. 1037–8; Muramatsu & Watanabe (eds), *Gendai Josei Bungaku Jiten*, pp. 348; Kobori Annu, 'Chichi e no tegami', in Mori Ōgai (ed. by Kobori Annu), *Tsuma e no Tegami* (1938, 1996 edn), pp. 191–227; Mori Mayumi, 'Kaisetsu: yofuke, kaze no naka no ashioto', in Mori, *Tsuma e no Tegami*, pp. 229–38; Hiratsuka Raichō, 'Ōgai fusai to *Seitō*', *Bungei* (August, 1962), reprinted in Hiratsuka, *Chosakushū*, vol. 7, pp. 406–8; Hiratsuka Raichō, 'Ōgai sensei ni tsuite', *Bungaku Sanpo*, 15 (1 October, 1962), reprinted in Hiratsuka, *Chosakushū*, vol. 7, p. 412.

[53] Seitōsha, 'Seitōsha gaisoku', p. 132.

[54] Okada (maiden name Osanai) Yachiyo (1883–1962) was a sister of Osanai Kaoru (a theatrical impresario, playwright and creator of the movement for a modern theatre). She wrote theatre reviews for *Kabuki* (a monthly drama journal). Katō Kazuko (1883–1956) was the wife of Oguri Fuyō (a novelist best known as an early Japanese exponent of Naturalism). She published in *Shinchō*, *Chūō Kōron* and *Joshi Bundan*. Kunikida Haruko (1879–1962) was the wife of the Naturalist novelist Kunikida Doppo. She published her maiden work 'Teichan' in the January 1903 issue of *Fujinkai*. Koganei Kimiko (1870–1956) was the sister of the eminent novelist Mori Ōgai. She received much attention as a translator. Mori Shigeko (1880–1936) was the second wife of Mori Ōgai. Her maiden work 'Shashin' ('Photograph') appeared in *Subaru* in 1909. Hasegawa Shigure (1879–1941) was a novelist and playwright, who published *Uzumibi* (*An Ash Fire*) and *Kaichōon* (*The Sound of the Tide*).

[55] Yasumochi, *Seitōsha Jimu Nisshi*, 1 June, 1911.

[56] Seitōsha, 'Seitōsha gaisoku', p. 132.

such members were initially recruited, the majority of them from the Japan Women's College.[57] Hiratsuka also persuaded Naganuma Chieko, another graduate from the Japan Women's College to do a front-page illustration for *Seitō*.[58] It is clear that the Seitō Society was a product of the growth of women's higher education.

In June and July the founding members found a publisher and printer for *Seitō*, and made necessary financial arrangements. They solicited advertisements, since advertising would become an important source of income. They arranged to exchange advertisements with other literary magazines. In order to secure regular subscribers they sent a thousand postcards to wives of celebrities, informing them about *Seitō* and inviting them to become readers or members.[59] Hiratsuka's mother provided her with 100 yen, for the initial cost of paper and printing.[60]

Hiratsuka felt that the venture was not taken seriously by many commentators, to whom it seemed to be a creation of spoiled women with time on their hands. Tamura Toshiko, one of the initial members of *Seitō*, who had written a novel entitled *Akirame (Resignation)*, remarked that the founders were unsuited to such a serious task.[61] When Hiratsuka visited Yosano to persuade her to become a supporting member, Yosano agreed to become one, but made negative comments about women's ability:

> Yosano repeatedly stated that women are incompetent and inferior to men. She has been reading many *tanka* manuscripts sent from all over Japan. She stated that among them the outstanding ones were always composed by men. Hearing Yosano's negative remarks about women, I felt as if I was being rebuked by her for having a high opinion of myself and having the impertinence to launch a magazine contributed

---

[57] Horiba, *Seitō no Jidai*, pp. 19–20, 66; *Ōfūkai* (comp.), *Ōfūkai Kaiin Meibo* (a list of graduates from the Japan Women's College between 1904 and 1911).

[58] Yasumochi, *Seitōsha Jimu Nisshi*, 1 June, 1911.

[59] Yasumochi, *Seitōsha Jimu Nisshi*, 23 August, 1911.

[60] Hiratsuka speculated that this money was a part of the sum her parents had set aside for her wedding, an interesting thought suggesting that the venture was in some ways an alternative to marriage. 100 yen was not a small sum then, and was as much as Hiratsuka's father's year-end bonus. In addition, her mother regularly provided her with small sums which were spent on miscellaneous expenses for *Seitō*. Her mother also paid the deficit whenever a monthly issue of *Seitō* ran at a loss, until Hiratsuka left her house. Hiratsuka, *Genshi*, pp. 321–3; Kobayashi, *Hito to Shisō*, pp. 86–7.

[61] Hiratsuka, *Genshi*, vol. 1, pp. 372–3.

to and edited by women, which aimed to encourage female writers. At the same time, I felt as if Yosano was encouraging me to do my best in this new venture. I could not make out what she was driving at.[62]

Hiratsuka realised that Yosano approved of Seitō when she read Yosano's manuscript 'Sozorogoto' ('A rambling talk'). But Hiratsuka did not have much confidence in *Seitō* to begin with, and none of the founding members predicted that the first issue would create a public sensation.

The Publication of the Inaugural Issue of Seitō

One thousand copies were published on 1 September 1911. A small advertisement appeared in the *Tokyo Asahi Shinbun*, *Yomiuri Shinbun* and *Kokumin Shinbun*. Each copy of *Seitō* sold for 25 sen, which was slightly more expensive than other magazines.[63] The *Tokyo Asahi Shinbun*'s advertisement, which began with 'Yuiitsu no joryū bungaku zasshi, *Seitō*' ('the only women's literary magazine available, *Seitō*') attracted public attention, although this information was not strictly accurate.[64] However, such catch-phrases helped to secure a market for *Seitō*. The unfamiliar and attractive word '*Seitō*' also aroused interest.[65] It had a charismatic effect, reworking a British term into Japanese, another example of British influence upon Japan and one that attracted readers.

The initial issue was composed entirely of articles and translations by women.[66] The front cover was drawn by Naganuma Chieko The main text was 131 pages long, followed by notice of the second issue; the general regulations of the Seitō Society; a list of its members; a

---

[62] *Ibid.*, p. 339.
[63] Hiratsuka, *Genshi*, vol. 1, p. 354.
[64] *Tokyo Asahi Shinbun* (3 September, 1911).
[65] Tatewaki, *Nihon no Fujin*, pp. 12–3; Ide, *Seitō no Onnatachi*, p. 10.
[66] Yosano Akiko, 'Sozorogoto', *Seitō*, 1:1 (September, 1911), pp. 1–9; Mori Shigeko, 'Shi no Ie', *Seitō*, 1:1, pp. 10–19; Yasumochi Yoshiko, 'Sarusuberi', *Seitō*, 1:1, pp. 20–1; Tamura Toshiko, 'Namachi', *Seitō*, 1:1, pp. 22–36; Hiratsuka Raichō, 'Genshi josei wa taiyō de atta', *Seitō*, 1:1, pp. 37–52; Kunikida Haruko, 'Neko no nomi', *Seitō*, 1:1, pp. 53–6; Araki Ikuko, 'Yōshin no tawamure', *Seitō*, 1:1, pp. 62–89; Yasumochi Yoshiko, 'Iso no hiru', *Seitō*, 1:1, pp. 90–1; Mozume Kazuko, 'Tanabata no yoru', *Seitō*, 1:1, pp. 92–109; Edgar Allan Poe (translated by Hiratsuka Raichō), 'Kage', *Seitō*, 1:1, pp. 62–89; Merezhkovski (translated by Hiratsuka Raichō), '*Hedda Gabler* ron', *Seitō*, 1:1, pp. 110–31. See Appendix 5 for translations.

column entitled *henshūshitsu yori* (from the editorial room); the rules for potential contributors, subscribers and people wishing to insert advertisements; and many advertisements covering 15 pages.[67]

The women's historian Miki Hiroko claimed that the publication of *Seitō* was revolutionary.[68] Indeed, *Seitō* was epoch-making in the history of Japanese women's magazines, but it was not unique. Her survey has identified about 160 women's magazines in the Meiji period.[69] *Seitō* was launched in 1911, and her survey shows an unexpectedly large number of 150 women's magazines published before this. The first publication of a women's magazine in Japan was in February 1877, when *Kosodate no Sōshi* (*Guidebook for Child Rearing*) appeared.[70] The great majority of women's magazines before 1897 were morally improving or religious—their most striking feature was a strong religious tone.[71] *Jogaku Zasshi* is a good example. It was written from a Christian point of view. It aimed to improve women's status, especially the availability of female education, and it favoured western concepts of women's rights. Unlike *Jogaku Zasshi*, *Seitō* lacked a religious theme.

What most distinguished *Seitō* from earlier women's magazines was that almost all its contributors were women. Only a limited number of men who approved of the Society and were respected by Seitō women were allowed to become *kyakuin* (visiting members).[72] However, in practice men's participation as members was virtually non-existent.

---

[67] Seitōsha, 'Seitōsha gaisoku', *Seitō*, 1:1 (September, 1911), pp. 132–3; Nakano Hatsu, 'Henshūshitsu yori', *Seitō*, 1:1, p. 134. These advertisements included ones for cosmetics, fountain pens, recently published books and other literary magazines such as *Subaru*, *Joshi Bundan*, and *Shin Fujin*.

[68] Miki Hiroko, 'Meiji fujin zasshi no kiseki', in Kindai Josei Bunkashi Kenkyūkai (ed.), *Fujin Zasshi no Yoake* (1989), p. 3.

[69] *Ibid.*, p. 4.

[70] *Ibid.*, p. 9. The main objective of *Kosodate no Sōshi* (*Guidebook for Child Rearing*) was to help women become better mothers. It was followed by *Jogaku Shinshi* (*New Magazine for Women's Study*) in 1884, which became *Jogaku Zasshi* in 1885. However, the women's magazines which appeared in the first half of the Meiji period were few. The majority of them came subsequently. They can be roughly divided into four categories. There were *keimō zasshi* (enlightenment magazines), *shōgyō zasshi* (commercial magazines), *fujin dantai no kikanshi* (organs of women's associations) and magazines advocating equal rights or women's emancipation. Commercial magazines might be further sub-divided into three types: *bungaku zasshi* (literary magazines), *kyōiku zasshi* (educational magazines) and *jitsuyō zasshi* (magazines for use in daily domestic life).

[71] *Ibid.*, pp. 11–2.

[72] Seitōsha, 'Seitōsha gaisoku', p. 132.

Although *Seitō* differed greatly from earlier women's magazines, it bore a closer resemblance to contemporary literary magazines such as *Subaru, Shin Shichō* and *Shirakaba*—in format, content, literary topics and translated work from western publications.[73] This was not a coincidence. It is certain that *Seitō* imitated the literary format of these successful magazines, aiming to achieve a similar literary reputation. However, *Seitō* differed in some important respects. It was designed as a women's literary magazine. Unlike most other literary magazines, whose contributors were mainly prominent writers, the contributors to the initial issue of *Seitō* (except for Yosano Akiko and Tamura Toshiko) were hardly known to the reading public.[74] For this reason Hiratsuka lacked confidence in it and under-estimated its commercial potential. In her autobiography she criticised the amateurishness of many of its contributors.[75]

Contrary to her rather pessimistic expectations, the initial issue was greeted enthusiastically by many young women with an interest

---

[73] Ide, *Seitō no Onnatachi*, p. 11; Horiba, *Seitō no Jidai*, p. 79. *Shin Shichō (New Currents of Thought)* was a literary magazine, first launched by Osanai Kaoru in 1907, aiming to introduce modern drama and new literary trends to Japan. It published short stories, poems and essays, and was opposed to Japanese Naturalism. On *Shin Shichō*, see Usui, *Taishō Bungakushi*, pp. 196–8. *Subaru (The Pleiades)* was a monthly literary magazine between 1909 and 1913. It published poems, stories, plays and critical essays, and was considered to be a successor to *Myōjō*. It opposed Japanese Naturalism, and was one of the most influential literary magazines of its period. On *Subaru*, see Usui, *Taishō Bungakushi*, pp. 30–46. *Shirakaba (White Birch)* was a monthly publication on literature and art, lasting between 1910 and 1923. It played a major part in introducing modern western art. Its contributors included Mushanokōji Saneatsu, Satomi Ton, Arishima Takeo and Shiga Naoya. On *Shirakaba*, Usui, *Taishō Bungakushi*, pp. 47–74; Odagiri, *Nihon Kindai Bungakushi*, vol. 3, pp. 20–8.

[74] Tamura Toshiko (1884–1945) briefly studied at the Japan Women's College. In 1909 she married the writer Tamura Shōgyo. In 1910 she published her novel *Akirame (Resignation)*, and became a best-selling author. She joined the Seitō Society from its start. In 1917 she had an affair with Suzuki Etsu, a married journalist, and followed Suzuki to Vancouver. After Suzuki's death in 1936, Toshiko returned to Japan, but failed to make a comeback as a novelist. Her works include *Miira no Kuchibeni (Lip Rouge on a Mummy)*, *Onna Sakusha (Woman Writer)* and *Yamamichi (Mountain Road)*. On Tamura Toshiko, see Hiratsuka Raichō o Yomu Kai (ed.), *Seitō no 50-nin*, pp. 60–1; Muramatsu & Watanabe, *Gendai Josei Bungaku Jiden*, pp. 211–5; Maruoka Hideko, *Tamura Toshiko to Watashi* (1977); Setouchi Harumi, *Tamura Toshiko* (1964, 1976 edn); Setouchi Harumi, 'Tamura Toshiko', in Setouchi Harumi (ed.), *Hi to Moeta Joryū Bungaku* (1989); Sachiko Schierbeck, *Japanese Women Novelists in the 20th Century* (Copenhagen, 1994), pp. 34–9; Hiratsuka Raichō, 'Tamura Toshiko-san', *Chūō Kōron* (August, 1914), reprinted in Hiratsuka, *Chosakushū*, vol. 1, p. 397; Yukiko Tanaka, *To Live and to Write: Selections by Japanese Women Writers, 1913–1938* (Seattle, 1987), pp. 5–10.

[75] Hiratsuka, *Genshi*, vol. 1, pp. 361, 373.

in literature. Hiratsuka wrote that the reception was far more favourable than she had expected.[76] *Seitō* was also saluted favourably by the press. One of the earliest comments on the inaugural issue, a review in a liberal newspaper in Akita Prefecture called *Akita Sakigake Shinpō*, was most complimentary:

> The first issue of *Seitō*, of which we have heard so much, has been published at last . . . It looks like a serious literary magazine published in the manner of *Subaru*. If it has truly been produced in all regards (including the drawing of its front cover and its editing) only by women, as it claims, it deserves much praise. We look forward to its promising future, which may give new scope to the promotion of women's literature.[77]

A newspaper article in the *Yorozuhō* also praised *Seitō* highly and claimed that its publication was one of the major literary events of 1911, which would earn a place in history.[78] Even many eminent male writers such as Mori Ōgai and Arishima Takeo respected *Seitō* and the integrity underpinning it, praising the Seitō women's vitality and determination to provide women with more literary openings.[79]

The contributors demonstrated enthusiasm and talent. Among them Yosano's opening poem 'Sozorogoto' and Hiratsuka's 'Genshi josei wa taiyō de atta' had a particular impact.[80] In 'Sozorogoto' Yosano praised Seitō women's determination to express their views and to claim their own identities. She waited impatiently for other women to follow this lead. Yosano had become a literary authority despite the fetters upon women, breaking new ground in the field of *tanka*.[81] She advocated women's emancipation and expected other women to follow her. Her poem in praise of Seitō women was well-suited for the inaugural issue.[82] This began as follows:

---

[76] *Ibid.*, p. 355.
[77] *Akita Sakigake Shinpō* (13 September, 1911).
[78] *Yorozuhō* (1 January, 1912).
[79] Hiratsuka, *Genshi*, vol. 2, p. 236.
[80] Hiratsuka, *Genshi*, vol. 1, p. 355.
[81] Yamashita, *Nihon Josei Kaihō Shisō no Kigen*, pp. 79–81; Motobayashi Katsuo, 'Onna no roman to jojō: Yosano Akiko to Yamakawa Tomiko', *Kokubungaku*, 25:15 (December, 1980), pp. 62–6; Irie Shunkō (ed.), *Yosano Akiko* (1985), pp. 32–44; Yamamoto Chie, *Yama no Ugoku hi Kitaru: Hyōden, Yosano Akiko* (1986), pp. 78–83.
[82] Nakayama, 'Onna de arukoto no imi', p. 67.

The day has arrived when the mountains are about to become active.
People do not believe me when I say this.
The mountains have simply been dormant for a while.
In those times long ago
the mountains all erupted with fire, and were alive.
Even so, you need not hold such views.
O people, believe only this,
now all the women who lay dormant are rousing themselves.[83]

The poem suggested that, after a long period of submission, women were finally awakening, about to speak their minds and take action. Hiratsuka believed that Yosano's ideas derived from the objectives and rules of the Seitō Society.[84]

The mountains were of course a metaphor for women seeking emancipation. The metaphor applies in different ways. Yosano tells readers that long ago the mountains were active and volcanic. Most contemporary readers perceived women as destined to remain in long-established, subservient roles. Yosano believed this to be false. Just like active mountains, women were once full of vitality. Yosano believed that Japan had once been a matrilineal society in which women exercised much power.[85]

Yosano appealed for that earlier power to be recognised. The second verse of her poem starts:

If only one could write things in the first person.
I am a woman!
If only one could write things in the first person.
I, I . . .[86]

Yosano uses the pronoun 'ware' to express 'I'. Her statement is not exclusively about language, but has deeper implications. Even in 1911 when Yosano composed this, it was unusual for women to use the pronoun 'I' and write in the first person.[87] Using 'I' was very much a male privilege, and men could express their own views and feelings while women could not. Yosano ventured to use 'I' to abandon this convention, speaking for herself and expressing her own feelings.

---

[83] Yosano, 'Sozorogoto', pp. 1–2.
[84] Hiratsuka, Genshi, vol. 1, pp. 340–1.
[85] Yamamoto, Yama no Ugoku Hi Kitaru, p. 82.
[86] Yosano, 'Sozorogoto', p. 2.
[87] Sōgō Joseishi Kenkyūkai (ed.), Bunka to Shisō, p. 209.

Hiratsuka was inspired by Yosano's manuscript and wrote her famous manifesto 'Genshi josei wa taiyō de atta.'[88] It begins as follows:

> In the beginning, woman was truly the sun.
> An authentic person.
> Now, woman is the moon.
> Living dependent on others,
> Reflecting their brilliance,
> She has the moon's face,
> And its unhealthy pallor.
> And now, *Seitō* cries, newly born.
> Created by the brains and hands
> Of today's Japanese women,
> *Seitō* cries, newly born,
> Women's undertaking is only sneered at, but I [Hiratsuka] am convinced that there is hidden potential there.
> And I am not in the least frightened . . .
> I wonder whether women deserve such disgust as this.
> Well, who is an authentic person?
> We did as much work as we could, like modern Japanese women.
> *Seitō* is the baby we wholeheartedly gave birth to . . .
> In the beginning, woman was truly the sun.
> An authentic person.
> Now, woman is the moon.
> Living dependent on others,
> Reflecting their brilliance,
> She has the moon's face,
> And its unhealthy pallor.
> Now she must restore her hidden sun.
> Reveal her own hidden sun and her hidden potential.
> This is our ceaseless cry to ourselves, our uncontrollable and immovable yearning, and the only instinct of our final personification, into which all our mixed and partial instincts are gathered.
> This cry, this yearning and this final instinct will lead to spiritual concentration among us.
> When spiritual concentration reaches its extreme level, noble and foremost talent will shine.
> Article 1 of the regulations of the Seitō Society states that the Society aims to produce female geniuses. All women are suppressed geniuses, without exception. They have potential to become outstanding. This will become real. I bitterly regret that women, with such potential, will end their lives with it still dormant, never bringing it to full play because of their inadequate powers of concentration.

---

[88] Hiratsuka, *Genshi*, vol. 1, p. 353; Hiratsuka Raichō, 'Akiko sensei to watakushi', *Tanka Kenkyū* (May, 1951), reprinted in Hiratsuka, *Chosakushū*, vol. 7, pp. 149–50.

Make us continue ceaselessly with our ardent prayer and spiritual
concentration.
Make us do these to the best of our ability
until the day when we will bring hidden female talent into the open,
until the day when the hidden sun begins to shine again.
On that day we will rule everything, the entire world will fall into our
hands.
On that day woman will no longer be the moon.
On that day she will become the sun, as in the beginning.
She will become an authentic person . . .
We are trying to build a golden palace on a crystal mountain, in the
eastern provinces where the sun rises.
Women, choose a gilded ceiling on which to paint your own portraits.
Even if I die before I realize my ambition,
Even if I sink to the bottom of the sea, like a sailor on a forsaken
ship,
I will still cry at the last, 'Women, go forward! Forward!', raising both
my hands, benumbed by the cold.[89]

This rallying cry harmonised with Yosano's poem. Hiratsuka's sum-
mons to women revealed her anger and frustration, but also her
enthusiasm to upgrade women's status via *Seitō*.

The keynote of Hiratsuka's message and advocacy of *Seitō* was her
call for female self-awakening. Under the patriarchal system, women
had to aim to be obedient and virtuous. Society assumed female
abnegation. However, Hiratsuka believed in women's potential power,
and aimed to show through *Seitō* that all women had inherent talent.[90] She tried to encourage women to awaken to themselves and
their abilities. However, even she stated that to achieve this would
not be simple, given women's suppression over a long period, their
low social status and expectations.[91] According to her, women must
abandon preconceived ideas, escape from current social reality, seek
a spiritual revolution to free themselves from suppression and social
pressures, and then enter a world of abstract ideas.[92] In order to
enter that realm, women had to rid themselves of all worldly thoughts
and attain perfect serenity of mind, which would be achieved by

---

[89] Hiratsuka, 'Genshi josei wa taiyō de atta', pp. 37–51. This is my translation,
but I consulted Sharon Siever's accomplished translation of the first two sections.
Sievers, *Flowers in Salt*, p. 163.
[90] Hiratsuka, *Genshi*, vol. 1, p. 362.
[91] Hiratsuka, 'Genshi josei wa taiyō de atta', p. 41.
[92] *Ibid.*, p. 46.

powers of concentration. She stated that such power of spiritual concentration would be reached by mental discipline, via meditation.[93]
She believed that with due effort, women would eventually reach an
extreme point, where the possibility of self-liberation and fulfilment
would become more readily obtainable. She believed that the power
of meditation and determined prayer would be a key element, and
here she brought Japanese religious traditions to bear upon 'feminism', creating a cultural conjunction of much originality.

Although her manifesto brims over with vitality, it is hard to com-
prehend fully what Hiratsuka meant in places. Perhaps this is partly
because of her frequent use of uncommon terms: *nessei* (devotion),
seishin shūchū (power of spiritual concentration), *munen musō* (rid one-
self of all worldly thoughts), *shinkū* (vacuum) and *kyomu* (nothingness).
Her message was neither logical nor pragmatic, but it was inspira-
tional, and gave the impression of spontaneous composition. Hiratsuka,
who was a strong and rare personality much preoccupied with her
ideological inner world, presented her own ideas about liberation
with scant regard to the ideas of others. Her message drew upon
the processes she herself had gone through to realize her own identity and potential. Her dependency upon prayer and concentration
to elevate herself was spiritual, and certainly one has the impression
that this approach was much influenced by Zen and her training in
religious meditation. She had been absorbed in Zen meditation for
several years.[94] Several writers believe that it is likely that in meditation she had seen the sun as a God, and had identified herself in
unity with it.[95] This assumption is tied to the fact that Amaterasu
Ōmikami, the principal female deity of Japanese mythology, who
was considered to be the originator of the imperial line, was identified
with the sun. Hiratsuka's manifesto also highlighted the will-power
of *miko* (a virgin consecrated to a deity, who chanted spells and had
magical powers of a shamanistic kind in ancient history), saying that
she had a particular admiration for *miko*.[96] She was well-read in
ancient Japanese history, like Yosano, and admired the lively independent women who appeared in Japanese classics such as *Manyōshū*

---

[93] *Ibid.*, pp. 50–1.
[94] Hiratsuka, *Genshi*, vol. 1, pp. 207–12.
[95] Ide, 'Kaisetsu', p. 9; Yamashita, *Nihon Josei Kaihō no Kigen*, p. 92; Sasaki, *Atarashii Onna no Tōrai*, p. 131.
[96] Hiratsuka, *Genshi*, vol. 1, p. 365.

and *Kojiki*. It is clear that she drew upon historical interpretations of such women in her rallying call and other writing.[97]

Hiratsuka's use of metaphors of the sun and moon can be considered further. Instead of volcanic mountains, which are the metaphor Yosano used for women in her poem, Hiratsuka took the sun and the moon as metaphors for the female sex. She described contemporary women as being deprived of their humanity, made slaves to male autocracy, treated as incompetent and worthless under the patriarchal system—like the moon. She portrayed women in ancient times as akin to the sun. She also relayed an image of future womankind full of promise and hope, with her sun symbolism. In this way she expressed a contrast between contemporary women, and the luminaries they might become.

These metaphors of sun and moon have many anthropological precedents, but they may have been influenced in this case by Nietzsche.[98] Hiratsuka had shown much interest in Nietzsche's writings since her student days, and had read many works by him including *Also Sprach Zarathustra*.[99] A rhetoric of sun and moon often appears in Nietzsche. According to him, the sun represents the idea of perfection coupled with freedom and hope, while the moon represents troubled selfish desire and egoism.[100] In spite of its vivid symbolism, this manifesto had limitations. Later critics and historians such as Inoue Kiyoshi criticised Hiratsuka for disconnected thinking.[101]

In spite of any limitations, her defiant call was an excellent beginning for *Seitō*. It produced very successful results, and has been commended by most Japanese women's historians. Takamure Itsue called it '*Nihon ni okeru joken no sengen no dai issei*' ('the first public address declaring women's rights in Japan'), and her view has been widely shared by others.[102] One wonders whether Hiratsuka deliberately wrote it as the declaration of women's rights, although in her autobiography she later claimed that she did not intend it as such.[103] If

---

[97] *Ibid.*, p. 363.
[98] Sasaki, *Atarashii Onna no Tōrai*, pp. 169–70; Yamashita, *Nihon Josei Kaihō Shisō no Kigen*, pp. 92–3; Nakayama, 'Onna de aru koto no imi', p. 69.
[99] Hiratsuka, *Genshi*, pp. 363–4.
[100] Friedrich Nietzsche (translated by Tezuka Tomio), *Zarathustra* (1883, 1973), p. 528.
[101] Inoue, *Nihon Joseishi*, p. 243.
[102] Takamure, *Josei no Rekishi*, vol. 2, p. 277.
[103] Hiratsuka, *Genshi*, vol. 1, p. 362.

one considers the climate of the times, often characterised as 'the winter period' and certainly a very repressive one for women, it would have been impossible for her to make an open declaration of women's rights and call loudly for political reform in the manner of contemporary British and American feminists.[104] According to Hiratsuka, she did not intend her manifesto to go beyond a fearless confirmation of women's selfhood, and she little dreamt that it would exert a powerful influence on the women's emancipation movement in Japan in the 1920s.[105] Against her expectations, her readers interpreted it as a declaration of women's rights.[106] Like Yosano's poem, Hiratsuka's manifesto contained prophetic elements, like the possibility of overturning certain social foundations. It stirred deep emotions in many women, who were distressed by the disparity between rapid socioeconomic change after the Russo-Japanese War and the unchanged low status of women. Many emotional and enthusiastic letters praising this manifesto came in to the head office of the Seitō Society.[107] Her opening sentence 'Genshi josei wa taiyō de atta' produced among women a strong affinity with her, and became a symbol of women's freedom; in time it gained mythical status.[108]

This theme of women's self-awakening was well reiterated by Naganuma Chieko's front cover illustration for the inaugural issue of *Seitō*.[109] That cover captured many people's imagination: a full-length women's figure painted in dark brown, which stood out against a pale cream background. It was completely different from the covers of any other women's magazines before *Seitō*, which were usually

---

[104] On the 'winter period', see Yoneda, *Kindai Nihon Joseishi*, vol. 1, p. 104.

[105] *Ibid.*, p. 362.

[106] Horiba Kiyoko, 'Sōkan sengen nado', in Horiba Kiyoko (ed.), *Seitō Josei Kaihō Ronshū* (1991), p. 10.

[107] Hiratsuka, *Genshi*, vol. 1, pp. 369–70.

[108] Horiba, 'Sōkan sengen', p. 1.

[109] See Appendix 6. After Naganuma Chieko (1886–1938) graduated from the Japan Women's College, she attended the Taiheiyō Gakai Kenkyūjo (Pacific Ocean Painting Research Institute) to learn oil painting. In 1914 she married Takamura Kōtarō (a sculptor and poet). In 1931 she developed schizophrenia, and died in a mental hospital at the age of 52. Kōtarō's love poems were compiled in *Chiekoshō* (*Chieko's Sky*). On Naganuma Chieko, Hiratsuka Raichō o Yomu Kai (ed.), *Seitō no 50-nin*, pp. 66–7; Kurumi Akiko, 'Takamura Chieko', in Setouchi Harumi (ed.), *Koi to Geijutsu e no Jōnen* (1989), pp. 170–98; Takamura Kōtarō, *Chiekoshō Sonogo* (1950); Hiratsuka Raichō, 'Takamura Chieko-san no inshō', in Hiratsuka, *Chosakushū*, vol. 7, pp. 372–5; Hiratsuka Raichō, 'Takamura Kōtarō to Chieko fusai', *Fujin Kōron* (August, 1951), reprinted in Hiratsuka, *Chosakushū*, vol. 7, pp. 182–3.

conventional and boring, showing women in traditional Japanese *kimono*. Unlike these, the *Seitō* cover seemed more like a classical or Egyptian goddess, sent Cleopatra-like to release vulnerable Japanese women. She also symbolised the 'New Woman': advanced in thinking and frames of reference, one set upon questioning convention and the *ie* system by which women were tied down. There was a further resemblance to some of the drawings used in the contemporary British suffrage campaigns. These symbolic connotations of the image seemed highly appropriate to herald the fresh departure of *Seitō*, calling for women's active participation in literary activity, and the artistic presentation of their unique sensibilities in Japan.

The response to the inaugural issue of *Seitō* exceeded Hiratsuka's anticipations. She recalled that the head office of the Seitō Society was for some days flooded with enthusiastic letters, expressing delight, sympathy and encouragement, enquiring about membership and subscriptions.[110] The office also began to receive many visitors, requesting membership or asking to meet Hiratsuka. Other founders were equally overwhelmed by the stir *Seitō* caused.[111] They found themselves extremely busy dealing with these unexpected guests, sending out information, and writing letters to supporters. The great majority of new members were predominantly young women with literary interests and a good educational background. Among them were some working women, including school teachers and journalists.[112]

Seitō developed smoothly in its first year, not receiving any very damaging criticism.[113] Its copies stocked at bookshops in Tokyo and provinces such as Nagoya and Osaka sold out quickly, and its circulation soon went up to 2,000.[114] It seems to have been popular among young women in particular, who led restricted lives. The only field open to them was literature, and they could express their frustration only in writing.[115] The literary emphases of *Seitō* need to be understood in this light. *Seitō* provided women with an ideal opportunity to publish literary works.

---

[110] Hiratsuka, *Genshi*, vol. 1, pp. 369–70 & vol. 2, p. 24.
[111] Ide, 'Kaisetsu', p. 9; Horiba, *Seitō no Jidai*, p. 9.
[112] *Ibid.*, pp. 66–7; Ide, *Seitō no Onnatachi*, pp. 51–2.
[113] Horiba, *Seitō no Jidai*, pp. 78–9.
[114] Ide, *Seitō no Onnatachi*, p. 45.
[115] Something similar is sometimes argued for the novel (as a female form) in eighteenth- and early nineteenth-century Britain.

What distinctive characteristics did *Seitō* have? The works appearing in the early stage of *Seitō* were predominantly short stories, review articles, western-style poems and *tanka* poems. They manifested women's feelings of unhappiness resulting from rigid social convention, and this became the essential characteristic of *Seitō*. The worlds these literary works dealt with were narrow. Many of the short stories were concerned with the problems in everyday lives of middle or upper-middle class women.[116] These included marriage for women who had passed 'marriageable' age, quarrels between husband and wife, childbirth, childcare, married women's difficulty in finding employment, unrequited love, unfaithful husbands, mistresses, conflicts between wife and mother-in-law, and divorce. *Seitō* authors had experienced the issues they took up in writing, and their works seem often to have been autobiographical. Based on real lives, female fictional characters in *Seitō* appeared more realistic than male descriptions of women, their characterization coming from female authors.[117] They appealed to many female readers, even though they sometimes lacked dramatic effect, or imagination, and even though such writing was generally unpolished and of a low standard compared with the works of several established writers such as Tamura Toshiko and Yosano Akiko. These literary characteristics seen in the early stage of *Seitō* stayed as its characteristic throughout.

The Special Issues on Nora and Magda

It is worth noting that initially the number of works analysing women's issues in *Seitō* was extremely limited. Among them, Hiratsuka's article 'Marumado yori—onna toshite no Higuchi Ichiyō' and special issues on Ibsen's *A Doll's House* and *Magda* deserve careful attention.[118]

---

[116] For example, see Tamura Toshiko, 'Namachi', *Seitō*, 1:1 (September, 1911), pp. 22–36; Ojima Kikuko, 'Aru yo', *Seitō*, 1:2 (October, 1911), pp. 32–49; Koganei Kimiko, 'Taiko no oto', *Seitō*, 1:2, pp. 1–6; Chino Masa, 'Onna no uta', *Seitō*, 1:2, pp. 21–4; Iwano Kiyo, 'Kare kusa', *Seitō*, 2:2 (February, 1912), 2:2, pp. 43–51; Iwata Yumi, 'Haha no shi', *Seitō*, 2:3 (March, 1912), pp. 21–34; Ueda Kimi, 'Tabi', *Seitō*, 2:4 (April, 1912), pp. 67–81; Katō Midori, 'Shūchaku', *Seitō*, 2:4, pp. 9–26.

[117] Ide, *Seitō no Onnatachi*, p. 64. Male writers' contact with women was then very limited, except for their mothers, wives and sisters. They had little understanding of women's minds, and in many cases failed to recognise women's everyday difficulties. They created unrealistic and superficial female characters.

[118] Hiratsuka Raichō, 'Marumado yori—onna toshite no Higuchi Ichiyō', *Seitō*, 2:10 (October, 1912), pp. 102–128.

The special issue on *A Doll's House* (the Japanese translation is *Ningyō no Ie*) appeared in January 1912. This play was chosen as the subject of the first special issue because the inaugural issue of *Seitō*, in September 1911, coincided with the first performance of *A Doll's House* in Japan, by the Bungei Kyōkai (the Literary Association).[119] Although it was performed at a small theatre in Tokyo built for Tsubouchi Shōyō (the founder and then leader of the Bungei Kyōkai), it was well received and reviewed.[120] The Bungei Kyōkai, pleased with its favourable reception, had a repeat performance in November 1911 at the newly-opened and spacious Teikoku Gekijō (Imperial Theatre).[121] This performance drew a large audience and provoked considerable literary and public response. As Hiratsuka wanted *Seitō* to deal with the most up-to-date literary topics, it was natural for Seitō women to discuss the play.

This special issue provided them with the first real opportunity to discuss women's causes. *A Doll's House* was a perfect choice, as the main theme of the play is the predicament of women and the necessity for their self-liberation.[122] The play was performed in many western

---

[119] Ide, *Seitō no Onnatachi*, p. 67; Ōmura Hiroyoshi, *Tsubouchi Shōyō* (1958), pp. 194–5.

[120] Horiba, *Seitō no Jidai*, p. 82. Tsubouchi Shōyō (1859–1935) was acclaimed as a novelist, playwright, translator and literary critic. He was also a professor of Waseda University and lectured on western history and literature. In 1891 he founded the university's literary journal *Waseda Bungaku* (*Waseda Literature*) to recruit talented young writers. In 1905 he founded a literary association called the Bungei Kyōkai, which helped reform Japanese theatre and contributed to a new theatre movement. On Tsubouchi Shōyō, see Ōmura, *Tsubouchi Shōyō*; John Lewell, *Modern Japanese Novelists: A Biographical Dictionary* (New York, 1993), pp. 439–47; Odagiri, *Nihon Kindai Bungakushi*, vol. 2, pp. 244–6.

[121] Ōmura, *Tsubouchi Shōyō*, pp. 194–7; Ide, 'Kaisetsu', p. 10.

[122] Ibsen disapproved of laws enacted by men for men, which treated women as men's dolls, and he had particular sympathy for women trapped in conventional marriage, revealed in the hypocrisy analysed in the play. Nora, the heroine, an inexperienced, youthful middle-class wife with three children, was protected from hardships of the world outside the family. She was expected to suppress her desires in deference to the wishes of her father, and then her husband. She lacked a life of her own, had no personal opinions and ideas, and her duties were simply to obey and please her husband, and to bring up their children. She had had no chance to discover a personal identity and develop her potential. She was a victim of the conventional feminine role, and her destiny lay in men's hands. The play portrays her transformation from her husband's doll-wife to a woman awakened to self-liberation, who refuses to play her role any longer. In the famous ending, Nora, who no longer believes in family, duty, law and associated values, leaves her husband and children, slamming the door behind her, hoping to become a real person, to learn about herself in the real world, and to educate herself into independence. See Henrik Ibsen, *A Doll's House* (1879, London, 1985).

countries, and had a great impact on women.[123] Nora has been considered by western literary critics to be an exemplar of the so-called 'new woman', as found in so much literature of that period, in works by Thomas Hardy, George Gissing and others, and this phenomenon was widely commented on at that time.[124] The play stimulated and caught the mood of the growing spirit of feminism. It helped many educated women to become aware of their own identities and potential.

Its relevance for Seitō women was obvious. The subject was ideal for a magazine that appealed to young literary women and which aimed to deal with women's issues. Hiratsuka (who had first come across and been very taken by the play while at the Japan Women's College) was keen to discuss it.[125] Her enthusiasm was clear in the editorial of the November 1911 issue, where she invited other members to contribute reviews on the play.[126] The advertisement provided a select reading list by Hiratsuka, comprising 12 Japanese and 26 non-Japanese sources on Ibsen.[127] It manifested her high expectations of potential contributors, encouraging among them an understanding of the women's questions raised by Ibsen. It also illustrated her desire to maintain high literary standards, matching other contemporary literary journals, such as *Subaru* (*The Pleiades*), which were edited by eminent literary men.[128]

---

[123] *A Doll's House* was first published in December 1879, and soon after performed at the Theatre Royal in Copenhagen. In Britain it was first performed professionally at the Novelty Theatre, Kingsway in London, in 1889. The London production was taken on a world tour and played in Australia, New Zealand, the United States and India. See Michael Meyer, *Ibsen on File* (London, 1985), pp. 33–5; J.L. Styan, *Modern Drama in Theory and Practice*, vol. 1 (1981, Cambridge, 1991 edn), pp. 20–5.

[124] Meyer, *Ibsen on File*, p. 35.

[125] Hiratsuka, *Genshi*, vol. 2, p. 12. Even before this special issue, *Seitō* produced a couple of articles on Ibsen. These were Hiratsuka's translation of Dmitri Sergeyevich Merezhkovski's critical essay on Ibsen's *Hedda Gabler* and a joint review on *Hedda Gabler* by Seitō members. See Merezhkovski (trans, by Hiratsuka Raichō), '*Hedda Gabler* ron', *Seitō*, 1:1 (September, 1911), pp. 110–131. See also Hiratsuka Raichō & Yasumochi Yoshiko, '*Hedda Gabler* gappyō', *Seitō*, 1:2 (October, 1911), pp. 91–108.

[126] Seitōsha, '*Seitō* daiyongō yokoku', *Seitō*, 1:3 (November, 1911), p. 109.

[127] Yasumochi Yoshiko & Hiratsuka Raichō, 'Shain shoshi e: henshūshitsu yori', pp. 106–108.

[128] Hiratsuka, *Genshi*, vol. 2, p. 12. The advertisement provoked an enthusiastic response from subscribers to *Seitō*, and many articles were sent. Only a select number of these were published in the special issue because of limited space.

The special issue on *A Doll's House* appeared as a supplement to the January 1912 issue. It was surprisingly long (more than 110 pages, nearly two-thirds of the issue). There were review articles on Nora by Ueno Yōko, Katō Midori, Ueda Kimiko, Yasumochi Yoshiko and Hiratsuka Raichō; two translations of English reviews of *A Doll's House* by Janet Lee and G.B. Shaw; an article by an unnamed author entitled 'A play which is similar to *A Doll's House*'; and an article entitled 'The hardest problem which Matsui Sumako experienced when acting as Nora', based on an interview with her.[129] The special issue was an informative assessment of the play. All contributors apart from Hiratsuka gave assessments, and their responses to Nora's leaving her husband and children were like those of western female readers and audiences. They understood Nora's speech when she left her husband's house:

> I must educate myself. And you can't help me with that. It's some-thing I must do by myself . . . I must stand on my own feet if I am to find out the truth about myself and about life . . . I believe that I am first and foremost a human being, like you—or anyway, that I must try to become one.[130]

They saw Nora's action as inevitable and respected her for it. Katō Midori argued that Nora's self-awakening was a women's problem common to contemporary Japanese women, and she appears to have envied the stance that Nora eventually took.[131] Ueno Yōko thought

---

[129] Ueno Yōko, '*Ningyō no Ie* yori josei mondai e', *Seitō*, 2:1 (January, 1912), pp. 62–114; Katō Midori, '*Ningyō no Ie*', *Seitō*, 2:1, pp. 115–25; Ueda Kimiko, '*Ningyō no Ie* o yomu', *Seitō*, 2:1, pp. 126–32; Hiratsuka Raichō, 'Nora-san ni', *Seitō*, 2:1, pp. 133–41; Yasumochi Yoshiko, '*Ningyō no Ie* ni tsuite', *Seitō*, 2:1, pp. 143–54; Janet Lee (trans. by Takeichi Aya), '*Ningyō no Ie*', *Seitō*, 2:1, pp. 156–61; Matsui Sumako, 'Butai no ue de ichiban komatta koto', *Seitō*, 2:1, pp. 162–3; G.B. Shaw (trans. by Hiratsuka Raichō), '*Ningyō no Ie*', *Seitō*, 2:1, pp. 167–70; anon, '*Ningyō no Ie* ni nita gikyoku', *Seitō*, 2:1, pp. 164–6. Five photographs, all borrowed from the theatrical research institute at Waseda University, were inserted. Three photographs of three actresses, Paula Somary, Agnes Sorma and Matsui Sumako, who played the part of Nora, and two stage photographs from scenes in acts 1 and 2. Matsui Sumako (1886–1919) was the first actress to complete theatrical training at the Bungei Kyōkai. She came into the limelight with her performance as Nora, which helped to estab-lish her career as Japan's first western-style actress. On Matsui, see Tonegawa Yutaka, 'Hōgetsu ni junjita joyū, Sumako', *Rekishi to Jinbutsu Tokushū: Kindai Renai Jiken Hiwa* (April, 1980), pp. 104–9.

[130] Ibsen, *A Doll's House*, pp. 99–100.

[131] Katō, '*Ningyō no Ie*', pp. 115–25. Katō Midori (1888–1922) studied literature under Tokuda Shūsei (a writer associated with Japanese Naturalism). In 1909 she

that Nora's self-awakening should be an example to women every-where.[132] The *Seitō* review articles demonstrated great sympathy and self-association with Nora. In contrast, Hiratsuka heaped criticism on Nora:

> We Japanese women would be able to understand if such an instinc-tive and thoughtless woman like you [Nora] were only a 14 or 15 year-old girl, but we find it extremely hard to believe that you are a married woman with three children.[133]

Hiratsuka criticised Nora for two main reasons. She felt that Nora was naive and inexperienced, and that she overestimated men.[134] She expected too much from her husband in return for her love and devotion. Hiratsuka argued that Nora should have known that men are always selfish and calculating, and never risk their lives for women except when their honour and aspirations are at stake. Hiratsuka claimed that any sensible woman knows this to be common sense.[135] She also criticised Nora for not having a more complex view of life, as other people had. She thought that Nora should have played the part of a faithful wife, while having another role which would have enabled her to evaluate life objectively as an onlooker.[136] She was convinced that Nora's failure to have a more complex outlook had caused conflict with her husband, and the resulting family tragedy.

As with most western audiences, other Seitō reviewers of the play thought that Nora's leaving her husband boded well for her future. They thought that she would now find her identity and become

---

married Katō Chōchō. She joined Seitō in 1911. From 1914 she began to work for Tokyo Nichi Nichi Newspaper Company. She died of cancer aged 33. On Katō Midori, see Hiratsuka Raichō o Yomu Kai (ed.), *Seitō no 50-nin*, pp. 38–9.

[132] Ueno Yōko, '*Ningyō no Ie* yori josei mondai e', *Seitō*, 2:1 (January, 1912), reprinted in Horiba Kiyoko (ed.), *Seitō Josei Kaihō Ronshū* (1991), pp. 44–5. After Ueno (maiden name Inaba) Yōko (1886–1928) graduated from Tokyo Girls' Higher School, she became a teacher of Fukui Girls' High School. In 1910 she married Ueno Nanao. In November 1911 she joined Seitō. Her husband was an elite naval officer, but she continued to teach until an illness killed her at 42. On Ueno Yōko, see Hiratsuka Raichō o Yomu Kai (ed.), *Seitō no 50-nin*, pp. 22–3; Hiratsuka Raichō, '*Seitō* jidai', *Asuka* (January-July, 1937), reprinted in Hiratsuka, *Chosakushū*, vol. 6, pp. 186–93.

[133] Hiratsuka, 'Nora-san ni', *Seitō*, 2:1 (January, 1912), reprinted in Horiba (ed.), *Seitō Josei Kaihō Ronshū*, p. 62.

[134] *Ibid.*, p. 64.

[135] *Ibid.*, p. 64.

[136] *Ibid.*, p. 62.

independent.[137] They did not think that this would be difficult. However, Hiratsuka was pessimistic about Nora's future, not convinced that her conduct would enable her to find a distinct and new identity:

> Nora, the noise you made when you slammed the door of your husband's house was high-spirited. However, you set foot outside and into the pitch-dark. You could not even distinguish west from east. You walked with most unsteady steps . . . You deserted your 'doll's house' stating that you believed that above everything else you are a human being, or at any rate you will try to become one. But to me, you did not become a human being. You had finally come to realise that you ought to be a human being, but you had not the faintest idea of what a human being really is . . . I cannot easily believe that you became this and obtained your real identity simply by walking out on your family. You are completely mistaken if you think that you will achieve a real identity through such a trifling gesture. One cannot possibly find one's own identity like this . . . From now on you will be able to move in this direction, but you must know that there are many difficulties awaiting you . . . When you . . . kill off all traces of Nora, you will then be able to find your own identity, and become an individual as well as 'a new woman' in a real sense.[138]

Hiratsuka was not convinced that Nora's action would lead to self-awakening.[139] In her recent work the historian Horiba Kiyoko claimed that Hiratsuka's assessment of the play was scathing, and neither precise nor to the point, because the play was a western one and Hiratsuka did not fully understand it.[140] She had misread Nora, and made illogical statements against Nora's conduct. In my view, Horiba's interpretation underestimates Hiratsuka's assessment of the play. Hiratsuka was a woman who had developed a distinct identity and potential. She did not achieve this by accident or good luck. She had to make great efforts, as stated in her 'Genshi josei wa taiyō de atta'. It was therefore understandable for her to disapprove of any easy view about Nora's self-awakening. According to Hiratsuka, Nora's action was only the first step in a long journey, which would require much determination.[141]

---

[137] Ueda, 'Ningyō no Ie o yomu', pp. 60–1; Katō, 'Ningyō no Ie', pp. 52–4; Ueno, 'Ningyō no Ie yori josei mondai e', p. 46; Yasumochi, 'Ningyō no Ie ni tsuite', p. 79.
[138] Hiratsuka, 'Nora-san ni', pp. 64–6.
[139] Ibid., p. 66.
[140] Horiba, Seitō no Jidai, pp. 89–90.
[141] Hiratsuka, 'Nora-san ni', p. 66.

This special issue on Nora, an exemplar of the 'new woman' ('*atarashii onna*'), led to Seitō women being identified as '*atarashii onna-tachi*' ('new women'), and the Seitō Society started to be called '*wasei Nora yōseijo*' ('a training school designed to recruit Japanese versions of Nora).[142] According to Horiba Kiyoko, the term '*atarashii onna*' became common following Tsubouchi Shōyō's 1910 extra-mural lectures on 'Kinsei geki ni mietaru atarashii onna' ('New women in modern plays').[143] He discussed Ibsen's Nora and Hedda, Sudermann's Magda, and Shaw's Vivie, all of whom were regarded as exemplars of 'new women'.[144] When the *Seitō* special issue on Nora was published, the term 'new women' was not used in any negative sense. This special issue gave *Seitō* a distinctive profile, and differentiated it from other women's literary magazines (edited by men). It was also the first significant step towards *Seitō*'s later change of direction, from a women's literary magazine to a feminist magazine dealing with women's issues.

Three months after this special issue on Nora, the sale of *Seitō* was forbidden in April 1912.[145] Araki Ikuko's short story 'Tegami' ('A letter'), which appeared in that issue, was responsible for the prohibition.[146] This story took the form of a letter from a married woman to her young lover.[147] Under the *ie* system of the Meiji Civil Code, an adultery committed by a married woman was an offence, and both an adulterous wife and her lover could be imprisoned if her husband took legal action against them. In spite of this, Araki vividly depicted her heroine's joy in having a secret meeting with the lover, expressing her strong disapproval of conventional marriage. In the early days of the Seitō Society Araki was unique in that most members were well educated women from good families who knew little about wider life. By contrast, Araki was very liberal and ran a family

---

[142] Hiratsuka, *Genshi*, vol. 2, pp. 33–4.

[143] Horiba, *Seitō no Jidai*, p. 51.

[144] His lectures on 'new women' were later published. See Tsubouchi Shōyō, *Iwayuru Atarashii Onna* (1912).

[145] Tokkō Keisatsu Kokusho Henshū Iinkai (ed.), *Tokkō Keisatsu Kokusho* (1977), pp. 78–9.

[146] Araki Ikuko (1890–1943) ran a hotel in Kanda, Tokyo. She joined Seitō from its start, and published nine pieces in *Seitō*. Her life style was free and fearless, and she had several lovers, but remained single throughout her life. She later became an alcoholic. On Araki Ikuko, see Hiratsuka Raichō o Yomu Kai (ed.), *Seitō no 50-nin*, pp. 10–1.

[147] Araki Ikuko, 'Tegami', *Seitō*, 2:4 (April, 1912), pp. 102–6.

business as well as looking after her family. Because of Araki's short story, the police visited Mozume Kazuko's house, where the Seitō office was located. They confiscated the remaining copies of the April 1912 issue on the grounds that it violated Article 19 of the Shuppan Hō (Publication Law).[148]

In spite of this prohibition, Seitō women published another special issue on the German playwright Hermann Sudermann's *Magda* in June 1912.[149] Like *A Doll's House*, *Magda* was presented by the Bungei Kyōkai in May 1912, and Matsui Sumako (who played Nora in *A Doll's House*) played Magda (the heroine of the play).[150] The plot of the play was that Magda's father, who was a strict, stubborn and domineering man, tried to force her to marry a clergyman living in a provincial area.[151] Magda, who did not agree to this, was consequently driven out of the house. She was then deceived by an insincere man, named Keller, and gave birth to his illegitimate child. Subsequently deserted by him, she had to work as an opera singer to support herself and her child. After she became successful in this, she returned home and saw her father. He reproached her again, causing a heated argument in which he died in a fit of anger. The Japanese government, which disapproved of Magda's rebellious conduct, was concerned about the bad influence this play might have on Japanese women, and the Interior Ministry forbade its performance.[152] Shimamura Hōgetsu, one of the leading members of the Bungei Kyōkai, visited the Interior Minister to plead for a withdrawal of the prohibition, which he obtained on the condition that Shimamura would insert an apology from Magda at the end of the play.[153]

---

[148] Tokkō Keisatsu Kokusho Henshū Iinkai (ed.), *Tokkō Keisatsu Kokusho*, pp. 78–9.

[149] They were Hasegawa Shigure's 'Bungei Kyōkai no *Magda*', *Seitō*, 2:6 (June, 1912), furoku pp. 1–5; Otake Kōkichi *et al.*, '*Magda* ni tsuite', *Seitō*, 2:6, furoku, pp. 14–7; Hiratsuka Raichō, 'Yonda *Magda*', *Seitō*, 2:6, reprinted in Hiratsuka, *Chosakushū*, vol. 1, pp. 103–9.

[150] Ōmura, *Tsubouchi Shōyō*, pp. 199–200; Imai, *Taishō Demokurashii*, pp. 110–1.

[151] The outline of the play is given in Tsubouchi, *Iwayuru Atarashii Onna*, pp. 270–85.

[152] Imai, *Taishō Demokurashii*, pp. 110–1; Ōmura, *Tsubouchi Shōyō*, pp. 200–1; Yoneda, *Kindai Nihon Joseishi*, vol. 1, p. 107; Tokkō Keisatsu Kokusho Henshū Iinkai (ed.), *Tokkō Keisatsu Kokusho*, pp. 51, 78–9.

[153] Ōmura, *Tsubouchi Shōyō*, pp. 200–3. Shimamura Hōgetsu (1871–1918) was a novelist, playwright and literary critic. He was taught by Tsubouchi Shōyō at Waseda University before further study at Oxford and Berlin Universities. He became a lecturer at Waseda University. He was a founding member of the Bungei Kyōkai, and introduced many European plays. On Shimamura Hōgetsu, see, Odagiri (ed.),

Hiratsuka wrote an article 'Yonda *Magda*' ('My reading of *Magda*'), in which she assessed Magda. Much like Nora, Magda was regarded as an example of 'a new woman' by audiences, but Hiratsuka disapproved of her:

> Magda might be termed a so-called 'new woman', but she is not a 'new woman' in any real sense. This is because she does not have enough ability and vitality to become a representative of new ideas.[154]

Hiratsuka evidently had very high expectations of 'new women' and expected more from Magda. However, she agreed that Magda was one step ahead of Nora, because Magda became aware of her own identity after she gave birth to an illegitimate child, endured public criticism, and became financially independent.[155] It is surprising that Hiratsuka never mentioned nor protested against the prohibition affecting the play. Nor did she compare the social and family problems depicted in the play with the *ie* system.

Hiratsuka's Views on Higuchi Ichiyō

Another significant work which dealt with women's issues in the early phase of *Seitō* was Hiratsuka's 1912 article 'Onna toshite no Higuchi Ichiyō' ('Higuchi Ichiyō as a woman').[156] In it she analysed and criticised Higuchi, a talented female novelist who described the limits which social conventions placed on women. Hiratsuka claimed that Higuchi was 'furui onna' ('a woman with old-fashioned ideas'), and criticised her for not having a critical mind, and for cherishing old morals and customs.[157] Higuchi's life was based on self-sacrifice for her family, and in her works she depicted women who led suppressed lives and endured their lot.[158] Her realistic portrayal of such women

---

Nihon Kindai Bungakushi, vol. 2, pp. 244–6; Kōno Taeko, 'Matsui Sumako', in Setouchi Harumi (ed.), *Koi to Geijutsu e no Jōnetsu* (1989), pp. 36–46.

[154] Hiratsuka, 'Yonda *Magda*', p. 104.

[155] *Ibid.*, pp. 105–6.

[156] Hiratsuka Raichō, 'Onna toshite no Higuchi Ichiyō', *Seitō*, 2:10 (October, 1912), reprinted in Hiratsuka, *Chosakushū*, vol. 1, pp. 152–72.

[157] *Ibid.*, p. 154.

[158] Wada Yoshie, *Higuchi Ichiyō* (1972), pp. 120–68; Miyoshi Yukio, 'Ichiyō to Nihon kindai no teihen', *Kokubungaku*, 25:15 (December, 1980), pp. 52–5; Shigematsu Yasuo, 'Shokugyō toshite no joryū sakka: Meiji 28-nen to 29-nen no Ichiyō no shushi ni furete', *Kokubungaku*, 25:15 (December, 1980), pp. 56–60; Sōgō Joseishi

aroused many female readers' sympathy and made her works popular. Hiratsuka did not admire Higuchi's qualities and criticised her work for lacking originality and an independent ideology.[159] To Hiratsuka, the world Higuchi described was gloomy and negative, which contrasted with Hiratsuka's own more hopeful outlook. Her attack on Higuchi was scathing and one-sided. It also revealed Hiratsuka's limitations, for she had little idea of the lives women from a poorer background (such as Higuchi) had experienced, and she made no effort to find out. Nevertheless, Hiratsuka certainly differentiated herself from Higuchi, claiming that Higuchi lived in the past, while she represented the future of Japanese women.[160]

Although these two special issues and Hiratsuka's article on Higuchi discussed women's problems, the mainstay of *Seitō* in its early stage remained literary articles. It was only from January 1913 that *Seitō* began to take on the character of a women's magazine with stronger feminist implications.[161]

Scandals Linked to Seitō Women

Although *Seitō* sold well in its first year, the literary reputation and favourable responses it received were damaged by two seemingly trivial 'scandals', which involved a handful of Seitō members. The first scandal, known as the *Goshiki no Sake Jiken* (the five coloured liquor incident), was caused by Otake Kōkichi, a new Seitō member.[162] She went to a fashionable restaurant-cum-bar called *Mezon Kōnosu* ('Maison Swans' Nest') in Nihonbashi, Tokyo, which was then a popular gathering place for artists and writers. This place frequently put

---

Kenkyūkai (ed.), *Bunga to Shisō*, p. 206; Yamashita Etsuko, *Nihon Josei Kaihō Shisō no Kigen*, pp. 75–7.

[159] Hiratsuka, 'Onna toshite no Higuchi Ichiyō', p. 171; Hiratsuka Raichō, 'Seitō undō no haikei', *Zuihitsu* January, 1957), reprinted in Hiratsuka, *Chosakushū*, vol. 7, pp. 350–1.

[160] *Ibid.*, p. 172.

[161] Ide, 'Kaisetsu', p. 13; Horiba, *Seitō no Jidai*, p. 145.

[162] Orii Miyako & Takai Yō, *Azami no Hana: Tomimoto Kazue Shōden* (1985), pp. 67–8. Otake Kōkichi (1893–1966) was a daughter of Otake Etsudō (an eminent Japanese-style painter). She joined Seitō for a short period in 1912. She received much attention as a rising painter. In 1914 she launched *Safuran* (*Saffron*) and married Tomimoto Kenkichi (an eminent modern potter). On Otake Kōkichi, see Hiratsuka Raichō o Yomu Kai (ed.), *Seitō no 50-nin*, pp. 34–5; Muramatsu & Watanabe, *Gendai Josei Bungaku Jiten*, pp. 94–5.

advertisements in other literary magazines, and Otake went there to canvass for advertisements for *Seitō*.[163] The landlord gave her a demonstration of how to make an exotic cocktail with five colours, then in fashion in France. Otake, an artist with a good sense of colour, was fascinated by the drink, and wrote about it as if she had drunk it (although she never tasted it) in the column *henshūshitsu yori* (from the editorial room) in *Seitō*.[164] On another occasion she wrote about a Seitō member's drinking party.[165] Although only a handful of Seitō women (including Hiratsuka) drank, most Japanese people gained the impression that all Seitō members were heavy drinkers. Drinking was still considered to be very much a male privilege at that time, so most Japanese people disapproved of Seitō women drinking, especially as they were well-educated and from 'good' family backgrounds.[166]

This incident was shortly followed by another known as the *Yoshiwara Hōmon Jiken*, the consequence of some Seitō members' visit to the Yoshiwara (the large-scale licensed red-light district near Tokyo). Otake Kōkichi's uncle, Otake Chikuha (a distinguished Japanese-style painter), invited some Seitō members to visit the Yoshiwara.[167] Chikuha, who was a supporter of the Seitō Society, strongly recommended the visit because he felt that Seitō women could not fully discuss women's issues, and achieve women's emancipation in a real sense, without understanding the plight of the most unfortunate women who were sold to brothels to work as prostitutes. He made all the arrangements for the visit and paid for it. Hiratsuka accepted his invitation, and three Seitō members (Otake Kōkichi, Nakano Hatsuko and Hiratsuka), went to a high-class brothel called *Daimonjirō* in the Yoshiwara.[168] They spent an evening with a courtesan called Eizan,

---

[163] Hiratsuka, *Genshi*, vol. 2, p. 37. *Mezon Kōnosu*'s advertisement appeared in the July 1912 issue of *Seitō*.

[164] *Ibid.*, p. 37.

[165] 'Henshūshitsu yori', *Seitō*, 2:6 (June, 1912), pp. 121–5.

[166] Orii & Takai, *Azami no Hana*, p. 65.

[167] The account of this incident is given in Hiratsuka, *Genshi*, vol. 2, pp. 37–8; Orii & Takai, *Azami no Hana*, pp. 68–9.

[168] The Yoshiwara (in Edo) was the most notorious government-regulated headquarters of prostitution for almost three hundred and fifty years. It was founded in 1617 when the Tokugawa Shōgunate granted a licence. It survived until 1957 when the Prostitution Prevention Law was promulgated, which abolished the licensed quarters. On the Yoshiwara, see Cecilia Segawa Seigle, *Yoshiwara: The Glittering World of the Japanese Courtesan* (Honolulu, 1993); Lisa Dalby, *Geisha* (Berkeley, 1983), pp. 54–5.

talking to her and finding out about the lives of women in the Yoshiwara, and they stayed overnight there.[169] As the Yoshiwara was normally open only to male customers, it should have been a good opportunity for these rather inexperienced Seitō women to broaden their social perspectives. Against Otake Chikuha's expectations, their visit to the Yoshiwara did not lead to many insights into this environment. Even after the visit, Hiratsuka made no further attempt to investigate and discuss prostitution. She showed little interest in active campaigns for the abolition of prostitution, as then conducted by the Kyōfūkai (Women's Christian Temperance Union).[170] She was only concerned with women's issues when they pertained to her own class, paying little attention to women such as prostitutes who were at the bottom of society. Her attitude did not change easily, and became one of her biggest limitations when she was more fully involved in the women's movement.

The three Seitō women's visit might have best been kept secret. However, Otake Kōkichi talked openly about it, and so provided journalists, who had been keeping a close eye on Seitō women, with ideal material.[171] The first newspaper article on it appeared in the Tokyo daily *Yorozuhō*, with the headline '*Onna bunshi no Yoshiwara asobi*' ('Literary women having fun at the Yoshiwara').[172] The article was followed by a series of others entitled '*Iwayuru atarashii onna*' ('The so-called new women') in *Kokumin Shinbun*.[173] The first article published reported that:

> Some key members of the Seitō Society, which is now considered to be a group of so-called 'new women', have absurdly and outrageously been to the Yoshiwara. They have gone so much on the loose that even men would have been put to shame. They also write about iconoclastic and unconventional things.[174]

Leading newspapers competed in reporting this, giving it prominent coverage.[175] The Yoshiwara was a male pleasure domain and was

---

[169] Hiratsuka, *Genshi*, vol. 2, pp. 38–9.

[170] *Ibid.*, p. 39. On the Kyōfūkai's anti-prostitution campaigns, see Sōgō Joseishi Kenkyūkai (ed.), *Sei, Ai, Kazoku*, pp. 197–200; Yoshimi Kaneko, *Fujin Sanseiken* (1971), pp. 218–20.

[171] Hiratsuka, *Genshi*, vol. 2, pp. 39–40.

[172] *Yorozuhō* (10 July, 1912).

[173] *Kokumin Shinbun* (12–14 July, 1912).

[174] *Kokumin Shinbun*, (12 July, 1912).

[175] Ide, *Seitō no Onnatachi*, p. 74; Ide, 'Kaisetsu', p. 14.

not thought suitable for such women to visit. Young Seitō women from respectable families going to stay overnight in a brothel was unheard of. Hiratsuka explained that they only talked to a courtesan; but the story was distorted, written in an interesting manner (as with the Shiobara Incident), and gave readers the impression that Seitō women indulged in the Yoshiwara entertainments just like men.[176] After this, many articles on Seitō women were written, and the great majority of them misrepresented Seitō women as disreputable sluts with depraved thoughts, without shame or morals, who led dissipated lives.[177] The public, misled by such press coverage, began to believe that all Seitō women were dangerous, and to regard them with contempt, and the term 'new women', came to be used in a derogatory sense.[178] Only a handful of Seitō women had been involved in these two incidents, but the criticism came to apply to all Seitō women, causing great damage to the reputation of the Seitō Society and its magazine.

In particular, as in the aftermath of the Shiobara Incident, educational leaders became wary of Seitō women.[179] They felt that Seitō women's conduct threatened their educational policy of recruiting *ryōsai kenbo*, and became convinced that they would implant corrupt and immoral ideas in young women's minds and exert a harmful influence on them.[180] Even Tsuda Umeko, who fundamentally disapproved of *ryōsai kenbo* education, criticised the Seitō Society on religious and moral grounds.[181] Tsuda, who was an ardent Christian, saw Seitō women's conduct as immoral, and told her students that the Seitō Society was devil-like. She banned them from joining and contributing to its magazine.

After the newspaper coverage of the Yoshiwara Incident, public criticism of Seitō women intensified and they came under blistering attack. Hiratsuka was the major target. According to her, some people did distasteful and spiteful things to torment and harass her.[182] Many stones were thrown at her house. Suspicious looking men came

---

[176] Hiratsuka, *Genshi*, vol. 2, pp. 38–9.
[177] Ide, *Seitō no Onnatachi*, pp. 76–7.
[178] Hiratsuka, *Genshi*, vol. 2, p. 42.
[179] Yamashita, *Nihon Josei Kaihō Shisō no Kigen*, p. 102.
[180] Horiba, *Seitō no Jidai*, pp. 144–5.
[181] Yamakawa, *Onna Nidai no Ki*, p. 155; Rose, *Tsuda Umeko and Women's Education*, pp. 142–3; Kamichika, *Jiden*, p. 105.
[182] Hiratsuka, *Genshi*, vol. 2, p. 40.

to her house, demanding to see her. She also received many threatening letters. All this was very similar to what she had faced after the Shiobara Incident. In spite of ruthless public criticism, her family continued to be supportive and never criticised her or interfered with her involvement in the Seitō Society.[183]

These two incidents created disunity inside the Seitō Society.[184] Yasumochi Yoshiko, who was one of its founding members, sent Hiratsuka a strongly worded letter to express her indignation:

> I hear that three of you went to the Yoshiwara. How dare you do such a disgraceful thing to destroy our good reputation! I felt very humiliated and badly let down by you. I was extremely disappointed and sad to hear of your outrageous behaviour.[185]

Yasumochi's criticism of their visit to the Yoshiwara as unladylike and immoral was identical to much public criticism. Moreover, in her letter Yasumochi expressed dissatisfaction with the way *Seitō* had been run:

> In recent issues of *Seitō* pedantry and a lack of seriousness have become conspicuous. In the earlier stage *Seitō* was indeed a heartfelt, trustworthy and distinguished magazine, but it has lost these good qualities. I can no longer honour it. Because of your thoughtless conduct, all Seitō women have gained a bad reputation for doing away with past conventions and attempting things women have never done before . . . I lament the ways in which the Seitō Society has turned into a society with no grace and dignity.[186]

This criticism was endorsed by many other strictly brought up members of the Seitō Society, who had joined the Society simply because of their interest in literature. Hiratsuka noticed conspicuous changes in such women's attitudes.[187] Many became agitated and worried about severe public criticism. Others who had taken pride in being members and in being called 'new women' began to back away, rejecting the label 'new women'. Although the Seitō Society did not suffer from serious internal discord, it lost many members.[188] Some

---

[183] *Ibid.*, pp. 40–1.
[184] Hiratsuka, *Watakushi*, p. 118.
[185] Cited in Hiratsuka, *Genshi*, vol. 2, p. 41.
[186] Cited in *ibid.*, p. 41.
[187] Hiratsuka, *Watakushi*, pp. 117–8.
[188] Kobayashi, *Hito to Shisō*, p. 119; Nagoya Joseishi Kenkyūkai (ed.), *Haha no Jidai* (Nagoya, 1969), pp. 142–5.

left of their own accord; others were forced to leave by their families. Mozume Kazuko's father feared that his daughter's association
with such an infamous Society would destroy any chance of her marrying into a respectable family, and he forced her to resign.[189] In
provincial areas *Seitō* lost many members and subscribers, the great
majority of them being school teachers. They cancelled their mem-
berships for fear that their school authorities might discover their
connections with the society, and then dismiss them. Other Seitō
members requested the Seitō office not to place their names on the
membership list, because they were afraid of detrimental consequences. The number of contributors to *Seitō* writing under pseudo-
nyms to hide their identity increased. Mozume Kazuko for example
was forced to resign from the Society by her father, but continued
to contribute articles under her pseudonym Fujioka Kazue, which
she kept secret from her family.[190] Kamichika Ichiko, then a student
at Joshi Eigaku Juku, contributed articles under her pseudonym
'Sakaki Ō', because the headmistress of Joshi Eigaku Juku, Tsuda
Umeko, prohibited students from becoming members of the Society.[191]
Although Kamichika kept her membership of the Seitō Society secret,
it was discovered and she was expelled by her college.[192] As punishment, she was sent by Tsuda Umeko to a girls' high school in the
remote Tōhoku area to teach English for a year. However, at the
end of her first term there the headmaster of her school discovered
that she was a member of the Seitō Society, and she was immediately dismissed. Kamichika's unfortunate experience demonstrated
how Seitō women had become the target of criticism, especially in
educational circles.

Otake Kōkichi, who had instigated these incidents and thought-
lessly released news of them, was much criticised within the Society.[193]
Remaining Seitō members insisted that she resign, but Hiratsuka,

---

[189] Hiratsuka, *Genshi*, vol. 2, p. 42; Hiratsuka Raichō o Yomu Kai (ed.), *Seitō no 50-nin*, p. 92.
[190] *Ibid.*, p. 92; Hiratsuka, *Watakushi*, p. 118.
[191] Yamakawa, *Onna Nidai no Ki*, p. 155; Kamichika, *Jiden*, pp. 105–6; Horiba, *Seitō no Jidai*, pp. 124–5.
[192] Kamichika, *Jiden*, pp. 105–7, 114–5; Rose, *Tsuda Umeko and Women's Education*, pp. 142–3; Orii & Takai, *Azami no Hana*, p. 96; Hiratsuka Raichō, 'Watakushi no shitteiru Kamichika Ichiko-san', *Onna no Sekai* (January, 1917), reprinted in Hiratsuka, *Chosakushū*, vol. 2, pp. 248–51.
[193] Hiratsuka, *Genshi*, vol. 2, pp. 40–2; Ide, *Seitō no Onnatachi*, pp. 94–6; Horiba, *Seitō no Jidai*, p. 114.

who valued Otake's vitality and artistic talent, supported her. Other members found Hiratsuka's protective attitude towards Otake too generous.

Hiratsuka as 'A New Woman'

For a while Hiratsuka kept silent and did nothing to remove mis-understanding about these incidents. As a victim of the press after the Shiobara Incident, she may have felt that the best way to deal with distorted newspaper coverage and public criticism was to avoid contact with journalists and allow the issue to die away. She advised other Seitō members to stay calm. However, there were no indications that journalistic interest in Seitō women would decline. In October 1912 a series of articles on Seitō women was published under the title of 'Atarashigaru onna' ('Women who always want to be new'), in the *Tokyo Nichi Nichi Shinbun*.[194] They were written by Ono Kentarō, Otake's family friend who had worked for Tokyo Nichi Nichi Newspaper Company as a journalist.[195] His accounts were written on the basis of information provided by Otake Kōkichi herself. They were most damaging and intrusive, even prying into Hiratsuka's private affairs.[196] Hiratsuka now reached the limit of her patience, and realised that drastic action should be taken to protect her privacy and to overcome the crisis facing the Seitō Society.[197] In these circumstances she wrote her declaration 'Atarashii onna' ('A new woman') for the prestigious magazine *Chūō Kōron*.[198] The statement went as follows:

I.
I am a new woman.
Day by day I seek and make every effort to be the true new woman I want to be.

---

[194] *Tokyo Nichi Nichi Shinbun* (25–31 October, 1912).
[195] Hiratsuka, *Genshi*, vol. 2, pp. 74–5; Hiratsuka, 'Seitō jidai', p. 177.
[196] Orii & Takai, *Azami no Hana*, pp. 83–4.
[197] Hiratsuka, *Genshi*, vol. 2, p. 94.
[198] Hiratsuka Raichō, 'Atarashii onna', *Chūō Kōron* (January, 1913), reprinted in Hiratsuka, *Chosakushū*, vol. 1, pp. 257–9. *Chūō Kōron* (*The Central Review*) dealt with topics like literature, education, economics and politics. Towards the end of World War II, it was suppressed by the Japanese military authorities, but in 1946 it resumed. It still exists as an influential magazine.

The only thing which is truly and eternally renewed is the Sun.
I am the Sun.
Day by day I seek and make every effort to be the Sun I want to be.

II.
An old Chinese proverb says, the virtue of the Sun is renewed day by day.
A new woman places a curse on 'yesterday'.
She can no longer endure silently and obediently to walk the path which an oppressed old-fashioned woman walked.
A new woman is not satisfied with the life of an oppressed old woman, who was made ignorant, made a man's slave and was treated as nothing but a lump of meat by male selfishness.
A new woman wishes to destroy old morals and laws, which were created for men's convenience.

III.
However, various ghosts which occupied an old-fashioned woman's mind persistently pursue a new woman.
When 'today' becomes purposeless for a new woman, 'yesterday', which awaited its chance, enters forcibly into her.
Day by day a new woman fights against various kinds of ghosts.
The moment a new woman is off her guard, she will turn into an old woman.

IV.
I am the new woman.
I am the Sun.
I am the only one.
Day by day I seek and make every effort to be the true one.

V.
A new woman not only attempts to destroy old morals and laws which were built out of male selfishness, but day by day she attempts to create a new kingdom where a new religion, new morals and new laws, based on the spiritual values and virtues of the Sun, will be enforced.
Truly, the mission of a new woman is the creation of a new kingdom.
What then is a new kingdom?
What is a new religion?
What are new morals?
What are new laws?
A new woman does not yet know. A new woman studies, pursues knowledge, makes efforts and struggles over these still unknown things, to fulfil her own mission.

VI.
The new woman now single-mindedly aims to gain power.
She desperately seeks power to fulfil her mission. She seeks sufficient power to enable her to study, pursue knowledge, making efforts and struggling for the sake of still unknown things.

She seeks neither beauty nor virtue.
She cries out for the power which will enable her to create this still
unknown kingdom, and to fulfil her sacred mission.[199]

This remarkable statement is worth quoting in full. There is probably
nothing to compare with it in international feminist literature. Equating
herself with Amaterasu, the Sun goddess, Hiratsuka announced herself as a 'new woman' for the first time.[200] She attempted in this
very personal way to defend Seitō women from public criticism, to
justify their activities, and to recover their names and the reputation
of the Seitō Society.[201] One might see it as her declaration of war
against public criticism. She also hoped that her strong words would
inspire the Seitō Society's members who were hesitating.[202] The essay's
vivid advocacy, expressed as poetic individualism but on behalf of
other women, reveals Hiratsuka's vitality and brave determination to
fight against male-dominated Japanese society, and to transform it
into a better place for women.[203]

In writing these sentences, she provided a Japanese feminist expo-
sition of problems faced by 'revolutionaries' in different contexts in
countless historical situations. They wished to overturn or reform a
previous form of society, but felt themselves inadequate or unskilled
to do so, and so strove for self-improvement to accomplish the task.
They were aiming for an outcome which was still impressionistic
and unfocused. The situation that Hiratsuka hoped for, like her counterparts elsewhere, had still to be clarified, and she showed herself
alive to the impossibility of defining its precise form. She was aware
however of the need to strive for a reformed world, even though
she knew she could not be definite about the precise form it might
take. To modern western feminists, the outline of a future society
that meets a feminist agenda can be readily perceived. However, in
early twentieth-century Japan, within the context of such an utterly
male-dominated society, religion and culture, it was much more

---

[199] Hiratsuka, 'Atarashii onna', pp. 257–9. This is my translation, but I consulted
Goldstein and Ninomiya's translation. Setouchi, *Beauty in Disarray*, pp. 163–4.
[200] Ide, 'Kaisetsu', p. 14; Horiba, *Seitō no Jidai*, pp. 149–50; Suzuki, *Joseishi o
Hiraku*, vol. 1, p. 27.
[201] Horiba, *Seitō no Jidai*, p. 149; Maruoka, 'Seitō kara Kokusai Fujin Nen e', pp.
4–5.
[202] Ide, *Seitō no Onnatachi*, p. 132; Iwata Yasuko, 'Atarashii onna', in Raichō o
Yomu Kai (ed.), *Raichō soshite Watashi, Part III* (1991), p. 63.
[203] Horiba, *Seitō no Jidai*, p. 151.

difficult for women like Hiratsuka (growing within and out of that male-dominated culture) to envisage the future society that she desired for herself and women. In western terms, one might read lines like these by Hiratsuka and recognise in them aspirations of a revolutionary utopianism, of a forward-looking hope for a new moral kingdom upon earth. To Hiratsuka, the overwhelming moral change she looked for was one in the self-confidence and status of women.[204] In a passage like that cited above, there was less sense of an ideological aspiration for wider socio-political reform, going beyond reform in the self-evaluation and power of women. In this sense Hiratsuka was ideologically distant from some western feminists. Nor is there much sign in statements like this that she had a socialist or class awareness, for she apparently spoke for women as a whole. As one can see, however, she certainly had a charismatic and powerful sense of mission—using words that many men would have thought insane or extraordinarily egotistical—and she was vividly aware of major hurdles to be surmounted and of a new female consciousness to be arrived at.

Special Issues on New Women

The second measure Hiratsuka took to overcome the crisis of the Seitō Society was the publication of two special issues on 'new women'.[205] The first, 'Atarashii onna sonota fujin mondai ni tsuite' ('New women and other women's issues'), appeared as a supplement to the January 1913 issue.[206] It was the first gesture Seitō women

---

[204] Suzuki, *Joseishi o Hiraku*, vol. 1, p. 27.

[205] Ide, *Seitō no Onnatachi*, pp. 132–4; Ide, 'Kaisetsu', pp. 14–5; Tanaka (ed.), *Josei Kaihō no Shisō*, p. 191; Horiba, *Seitō no Jidai*, p. 150; Hiratsuka Raichō, 'Yahina kōgeki o mikanete: *Chūō Kōron* sōkan 900-gō kinen sairokushū yori', *Chūō Kōron* (October, 1962), reprinted in Hiratsuka, *Chosakushū*, vol. 7, pp. 414–5.

[206] The first special issue of 'new woman' comprised 8 articles (two of them written by non-Seitō members, Miyazaki Mitsuko and Hori Yasuko, and the rest by Seitō members). They were Hiratsuka's *'Renai to Kekkon'* (*'Love and Marriage'*), Itō Noe's 'Atarashiki onna no michi' ('New women's path'), Iwano Kiyoko's 'Jinrui toshite no dansei to josei wa byōdō de aru' ('Women and men are equal'), Katō Midori's 'Atarashii onna ni tsuite' ("With regard to 'new women'"), Ikuta Hanayo's 'Atarashii onna no kaisetsu' ('Commentary on "new women"'), Ueno Yōko's 'Chōdatsu-zokukan' ('Ultra-unworldly view'), Miyazaki Mitsuko's 'Shoshi ni nozomu' (My hope for many women') and Hori Yasuko's 'Watashi wa furui onna desu' ('I am an old-fashioned woman').

took in self-defence. Hiratsuka placed high hopes in the issue. She wanted Seitō women to express their own views freely, and discuss 'What is a "new woman"?' and 'How a true "new woman" ought to behave'.[207] She expected them to justify their conduct and correct distorted images of Seitō women. However, the issue hardly matched her expectations. In her article Iwano Kiyoko stated that men and women were initially equal and so sexual discrimination was caused by the social system.[208] She advocated the need for women to obtain not only an ideological independence but also their economic independence.[209] Both Iwano Kiyoko and Ueno Yōko interpreted women's equality and freedom as inborn, and they advocated the need for women to regain these.[210] Although their articles were encouraging, they never used the term 'new women', and their views were out of line with the main theme of the issue. Katō Midori discussed the dilemma a 'new woman' experienced when she married and had a child.[211] Ikuta Hanayo too, discussed 'new women' in her article, but neither Ikuta nor Katō, still lacking knowledge of western 'new women', had much of a grasp of women's issues, and ended by making unsophisticated and vague comments on the subject.[212] Only Hiratsuka and Itō matched the subject they had set themselves, though even Hiratsuka's article lacked strength.[213] She had already written a most effective essay 'A new woman' for *Chūō Kōron* in which

---

[207] Hiratsuka, *Genshi*, vol. 2, pp. 90–1.

[208] Iwano Kiyoko, 'Jinrui to shite dansei to josei wa byōdō de aru', *Seitō*, 3:1 (January, 1913), reprinted in Horiba (ed.), *Seitō Josei Kaihō Ronshū*, p. 96. Iwano Kiyoko joined Seitō from its start and began to write novels. On Iwano Kiyoko, see Hiratsuka Raichō o Yomu Kai (ed.), *Seitō no 50-nin*, pp. 18–9; Muramatsu & Watanabe, *Gendai Josei Bungaku Jiten*, p. 70.

[209] Iwano, 'Jinrui to shite dansei to josei wa byōdō de aru', p. 98.

[210] *Ibid.*, p. 96; Ueno Yōko, 'Chōdatsuzokukan', *Seitō*, 3:1 (January, 1913), furoku, pp. 46–56.

[211] Katō Midori, 'Atarashii onna ni tsuite', *Seitō*, 3:1 (January, 1913), furoku pp. 29–35.

[212] Ikuta Hanayo, 'Atarashii onna no kaisetsu', *Seitō*, 3:1 (January, 1913), furoku, pp. 36–45. Ikuta Hanayo (1888–1970) was an elementary school teacher. In 1912 she joined the Seitō Society, and in 1914 she married the poet Ikuta Shungetsu. She became a reporter for *Yomiuri Shinbun*. She was troubled by her husband's adulteries. He killed himself in 1930. She was a member of *Nyonin Geijutsu* (*Women's Arts*) and *Kagayaku* (*Shine*). On Ikuta Hanayo, Hiratsuka Raichō o Yomu Kai (ed.), *Seitō no 50-nin*, pp. 12–3; Muramatsu & Watanabe, *Gendai Josei Bungaku Jiten*, pp. 38–40; Hiratsuka, 'Seitō jidai', pp. 194–203.

[213] Hiratsuka Raichō, '*Renai to Kekkon*', *Seitō*, 3:1 (January, 1913), furoku, pp. 1–19; Itō Noe, 'Atarashiki onna no michi', *Seitō*, 3:1, furoku, pp. 20–2.

she expressed her views, and she seems to have exhausted her ideas at this stage. She ended by writing about why she had overlooked women's issues up to then, and what had changed her mind. The article introduced Ellen Key and Hiratsuka's translation of sections of Key's *Love and Marriage*.[214] It was an intellectually weak piece.

The next issue was also a special one on new women.[215] It was on a smaller scale, and three out of four contributors were non-Seitō members. Hiratsuka wanted to air male views as well as socialist women's opinions on new women, and this issue had two male contributors and one socialist, Fukuda Hideko.[216] Fukuda's article demonstrated her socialism, and she stated that women's emancipation in a real sense would only be achieved in socialist society, and so this issue was promptly banned by the Ministry of the Interior on the grounds that it disturbed public security and order.[217]

These issues failed to measure up to Hiratsuka's expectations; they were unsuccessful in correcting the distorted images of Seitō women, and the derogatory understanding of 'new women'. However, they marked a significant change in direction for *Seitō*, from a women's literary magazine to a women's magazine with a feminist direction, dealing with serious women's causes and problems. They drew even more journalistic attention to Seitō women. Many national and even local newspapers competed with each other in publishing articles on

[214] Ellen Key (1849–1926) was a Swedish writer, social reformer and feminist. She was born in Sundsholm, Sweden as a daughter of a wealthy landowner. She was educated at home and became a teacher. While working as a school teacher in Stockholm, she began lecturing on social issues especially women's sexual emancipation, and wrote more than thirty books including *The Century of the Child* and *Love and Marriage*. Her views on motherhood had an international influence. On Ellen Key, see *The Penguin Biographical Dictionary of Women* (London, 1998), pp. 353–4; Sheila Rowbotham, *A Century of Women: The History of Women in Britain and the United States* (1997, London, 1999 edn), pp. 621–2.

[215] The second special issue on new women comprised Hiratsuka Raichō's translation of Ellen Key's *Renai to Kekkon* (*Love and Marriage*), Fukuda Hideko's 'Fujin mondai no kaiketsu' ('Solving women's problems'), Iwano Hōmei's 'Reikoku naru aijōkan no fujin mondai' ('A view of insensitive love and women's problems' and Abe Jirō's 'Danwa no kawari ni' ('Instead of my informal talk').

[216] Abe Jirō, 'Danwa no kawari ni', *Seitō*, 3:2 (February, 1913), furoku, pp. 16–22; Fukuda Hideko, 'Fujin mondai no kaiketsu', *Seitō*, 3:2, furoku pp. 1–7; Hiratsuka Raichō, *'Renai to Kekkon' Seitō*, 3:2, furoku, pp. 23–27; Iwano Hōmei, 'Reikoku naru aijōkan no fujin mondai', *Seitō*, 3:2, furoku, pp. 8–15.

[217] Hiratsuka, *Genshi*, vol. 2, p. 102; Murata, *Fukuda Hideko*, pp. 177–81; Hiratsuka Raichō, 'Fukuda Hideko-san no omoide', *Tosho* (May, 1959), reprinted in Hiratsuka, *Chosakushū*, vol. 7, pp. 381–2.

Seitō women.[218] Typical examples were entitled 'Atarashii onna no kinkyō—Raichō to Kōkichi' ('The Recent situation of new women— Raichō and Kōkichi'), 'Kōkichi no e ga ureru—300 yen de oiran miuke no uwasa' ('Kōkichi sold her painting—the rumour going around that she redeemed a courtesan by paying the 300 yen ransom for her.'), and a series of articles published under the title of 'Onna eshi' ('A female painter'), referring to Otake Kōkichi.[219]

These issues on 'new women' provoked much controversy among authors and educationalists.[220] They also triggered a journalistic boom on 'new women' in 1913.[221] Journalists showed even greater interest in the subject.[222] Active discussion of a wider range of women's issues began to develop, not only in women's magazines but also in more general magazines, such as *Chūō Kōron* and *Taiyō*.[223] Women's issues had finally become a major public concern.

Hiratsuka also began to receive many letters from female readers, which displayed the doubts they felt about their lives.[224] They asked Hiratsuka's advice. Some readers, notably those who suffered from serious home problems, appeared on the Seitō Society's doorstep, imploring Hiratsuka for help. She would often provide them with accommodation, food and financial assistance.[225] In these regards these two special issues of *Seitō* contributed a great deal to promote awareness of women's problems.

---

[218] Orii & Takai, *Azami no Hana*, p. 93.

[219] 'Atarashii onna no kinkyō—Raichō to Kōkichi', *Sanyō Shinpō* (31 January, 1913); 'Kōkichi no e ga ureru—300 yen de oiran miuke no uwasa', *Yomiuri Shinbun* (8 April, 1913); 'Onna eshi', *Kokumin Shinbun* (5 September, 1913); 'Gendai joryū iro wake', *Niroku Shinpō* (25 January, 1913); 'Hiratsuka Haruko to Otake Kōkichi', *Asahi Shinbun* (25 July, 1913).

[220] Ide, *Seitō no Onnatachi*, pp. 149–52, 155–8.

[221] Hiratsuka, *Genshi*, vol. 2, pp. 132–6; Ide, *Seitō no Onnatachi*, pp. 147–9; Ide, 'Kaisetsu', p. 15.

[222] Hatoyama Haruko's article 'Atarashiki onna' ('New women'), in the April 1913 issue of *Fujin Sekai* (*Women's World*), was a good example.

[223] For example, the January 1913 issue of *Chūō Kōron* had a special issue featuring articles on women's issues by 15 eminent women. The July 1913 issue of *Chūō Kōron* also had an extra special issue featuring women's issues. In this issue assessments of Hiratsuka Raichō were given by seven people who knew her, Otake Kōkichi, Satō Haruo, Tamura Toshiko, Baba Kochō, Yosano Akiko, Iwano Hōmei, and the owner of the publishing company Tōundō. The June 1913 issue of *Taiyō* (which was a leading monthly magazine published on pragmatic and intellectual topics) also published 'Kinji no fujin mondai' ('The current women's problems'). See Horiba, *Seitō no Jidai*, pp. 173–4; Ide, *Seitō no Onnatachi*, pp. 150–1.

[224] Hiratsuka, *Genshi*, vol. 2, p. 225.

[225] *Ibid.*, p. 225.

Hiratsuka also organised the first lecture meeting on 'new women' at the YMCA Hall in Kanda, Tokyo on 15 February 1913.[226] She recalled that the hall was packed with about a thousand people, but she was disappointed that about two-thirds of the audience were men.[227] She was relieved that the male audience were for the most part serious and did not jeer or interrupt the speakers. She had hoped that many women would attend, as that would give Seitō women an ideal opportunity to justify themselves against criticism, defend their names and discuss women's issues directly with a female audience.[228] She disliked involving men. She also noticed that the great majority of Seitō members did not seem willing to become involved. For such reasons this first lecture meeting organised by the Seitō Society was also the last.[229] However, it contributed much to the foundation of the Seitō Society's rival women's society, the Shin Shin Fujinkai (the Real New Women's Association).[230] Hiratsuka later wrote about this:

> The Seitō Society's first lecture meeting produced an unexpected result, which was the Real New Women's Association. Its founders introduced themselves as 'real new women', in rivalry with Seitō women who were said to be simply 'new women', and they launched it under the slogan of the anti-Seitō Society.[231]

---

[226] The meeting began with Yosumochi Yoshiko's opening address: 'Honsha no seishin to sono jigyō oyobi shōrai no mokuteki' ('The motive spirit of the Seitō Society, its activities and its future aims'). This was followed by Itō Noe and Iwano Kiyoko, and three male supporters, Ikuta Chōkō, Iwano Hōmei and Baba Kochō, whose talks were entitled, respectively, 'Saikin no kansō' ('My recent thoughts'), 'Atarashii onna o ronzu' ('Discussing "new women"'), 'Otoko no yōkyū' ('Men's demands') and 'Fujin no tame ni' ('For the sake of women'), and 'Shisōjō no dokuritsu to keizaijō no dokuritsu' ('Women's ideological and economical independence'). The meeting concluded with an address by Hiratsuka. See *Asahi Shinbun* (16 February, 1913); *Yomiuri Shinbun* (16 February, 1913); Yamakawa, *Onna Nidai no Ki*, p. 153; Hiratsuka, 'Baba Kochō sensei o shinobite', p. 328; Hiratsuka, 'Seitō jidai', pp. 177–9; Hiratsuka Raichō, 'Meiji kara Taishō e, joryū yūbenkai no ugoki', in Hiratsuka, *Chosakushū*, vol. 5, pp. 192–3; Setouchi, *Beauty in Disarray*, pp. 177–8. Iwano Hōmei (1873–1920) was a novelist, critic, playwright and poet. Hōmei contributed to *Bundan* (*Literary World*), and he is regarded as one of the major representatives of Japanese Naturalism.

[227] Hiratsuka, *Watakushi*, p. 125. A similar account is given in *Miyako Shinbun* (16 February, 1913); *Yomiuri Shinbun* (16 February, 1913).

[228] Hiratsuka, *Genshi*, vol. 2, pp. 91, 114–5.

[229] Hiratsuka, *Watakushi*, pp. 128–9.

[230] Hiratsuka, 'Seitō jidai', pp. 179–82.

[231] Hiratsuka, *Genshi*, vol. 2, p. 115.

The Foundation of the Shin Shin Fujinkai

The Shin Shin Fujinkai was founded by Nishikawa Fumiko, Miyazaki Mitsuko and Kimura Komako soon after the Seitō Society's first meeting.[232] It was officially launched by its first women's speech meeting held at the Wakyōgakudō Hall (a Noh auditorium) in Kanda, Tokyo on 16 March, 1913.[233] The leaders of the Shin Shin Fujinkai disapproved of the Seitō women's reputations and behaviour as reported in the press.[234] In particular, Miyazaki Mitsuko criticised the Seitō Society in public and accused it of being a group of dissolute women.[235] The members of the Shin Shin Fujinkai wanted to maintain the positive implications of the term 'new women', widely used in western countries, and inaugurated their magazine *Shin Shin Fujin* (*Real New Women*) in May 1913.[236] Journalists paid great attention to these contemporary women's societies, calling them two societies of new women, treating them as rivals, and inflaming their contrary purposes.[237]

In her autobiography Hiratsuka also gave an account of the establishment of the Shin Shin Fujinkai:

> I have the impression that the members of the Real New Women's Association were brought together in order to attack the Seitō Society. They did not have any particular serious objectives. They intended to take advantage of public criticism and antipathy against our society, in order to draw more public attention to their own association. They were hoping to gain a reputation simply on the basis of attacking our society.[238]

Hiratsuka's one-sided criticisms of the Real New Women's Association in May 1914 were made in a mood of retaliation after it had

---

[232] On Nishikawa Fumiko, see Muramatsu & Watanabe, *Gendai Josei Bungaku Jiten*, pp. 253–4.

[233] *Miyako Shinbun* (17 March, 1913); *Yomiuri Shinbun* (17 March, 1913); Yamakawa, *Onna Nidai no Kī*, p. 155; Ide, *Seitō no Onnatachi*, p. 137; Amano Shigeru, 'Fujin Kaihōron kaisetsu', in Nishikawa Fumiko, *Fujin Kaihōron* (1914, 1986 edn), pp. 10–1; Nishikawa Fumiko (ed. by Amano Shigeru), *Heiminsha no Onna: Nishikawa Fumiko Jiden* (1984), p. 357; Hiratsuka, 'Meiji kara Taishō e, joryū yūbenkai no ugoki', pp. 193–4.

[234] Horiba, *Seitō no Jidai*, pp. 160–1.

[235] Hiratsuka, *Genshi*, vol. 2, p. 116.

[236] Nishikawa, *Heiminsha no Onna*, p. 361; Amano, 'Fujin Kaihōron kaisetsu', p. 16; Okano Yukie, 'Kaisetsu', in Fuji Shuppan (ed.), *Shin Shin Fujin Kaisetsu, Sōmokuji, Sakuin* (1994), p. 5.

[237] Nishikawa, *Heiminsha no Onna*, p. 357.

[238] Hiratsuka, *Genshi*, vol. 2, p. 116.

criticised the Seitō Society.[239] Her gesture was understandable, one
of self-defence, to preserve the reputation of her society. However,
many people have readily accepted her judgement on the Association,
contributing to the Real New Women's Association remaining obscure
in the history of the Japanese women's movement.

Hiratsuka's Views on the Family

In April 1913 Hiratsuka wrote 'Yo no fujintachi e' ('Addressed to
women in the world'): one of her most important works.[240] It was
written in opposition to the mounting press and public criticism of
the Seitō Society. She began by saying that she was irritated by
many women who asked her whether Seitō women were *dokushin
shugisha* (women who had a policy to remain single).[241] She then criticised the great majority of contemporary women for assuming that
women should marry, and for not having their own principles about
marriage, nor any critical views of the *ie* system and existing marriage law.[242] She suggested that they should open their eyes to the
limitations of the current system:

> The so-called women's virtues exist only for men's convenience. The
> lives of many wives are no more than being their husbands' slaves
> during the daytime and their prostitutes at night . . . If love arises from
> such marriage, it must be only a pretence, and no more than the
> result of calculating interests and convenience in many cases. Therefore,
> I cannot subscribe to the codes of the existing marriage system. Under
> the current social system, marriage is the relationship between the ruler
> [husband] and his subordinate [wife], which lasts their entire lives. I
> know that wives are treated as no more than minorities or disabled
> people. Wives have no rights to own property and no legal rights over
> their children. Although their adulteries are punished, their husbands'
> are forgiven. I have no inclination to get married or to become a legal
> wife, going to the extent of obeying such an unethical, unlawful and
> unreasonable marriage system, one which I do not approve of.[243]

---

[239] Hiratsuka Raichō, 'Nishikawa Fumiko-shi no *Fujin Kaihōron* o hyōsu', *Seitō*, 4:5,
(May, 1914), reprinted in Hiratsuka, *Chosakushū*, vol. 1, p. 307.
[240] Hiratsuka Raichō, 'Yo no fujintachi e', *Seitō*, 3:4 (April, 1913), reprinted in
Kobayashi Tomie & Yoneda Sayoko (eds), *Hiratsuka Raichō Hyōronshū* (1987), pp.
25–32.
[241] *Ibid.*, p. 25.
[242] *Ibid.*, p. 26.
[243] *Ibid.*, pp. 30–1.

Hiratsuka raised strong doubts about the *ryōsai kenbo kyōiku* (the educational policy to train good wives and wise mothers), disapproved of ordinary female forms of living dominated by marriage, and summed up the unreasonable nature of the existing marriage system, in particular the provisions of the Meiji Civil Code, which were inequitable to married women in many regards. She encouraged women to alter their lifestyles. This was also her first declaration that she had no intention of marrying.

It was not surprising that the government, annoyed and offended by the article, did not overlook it. After its publication, a Special Higher Police Section at the Metropolitan Police Department issued an order requiring a representative of the Seitō Society to report personally to the police.[244] Two founding members of the Seitō Society, Nakano and Yasumochi, went and received the following warning:

> When we read the recent issues of *Seitō*, we found many statements which disturb the conventional virtues of Japanese women. In ordinary circumstances we would prohibit the sale of this issue of *Seitō* straight away, but we will overlook it this time and simply give you a warning. Hereafter we will keep much stricter control, so we would like you to be more careful about what you write and to avoid expressions which will corrupt public morals and order.[245]

The warning shows that the government was more moderate and flexible towards middle-class feminists than to working-class socialist women. Hiratsuka ignored the warning and included 'Yo no fujintachi e' in her first book, *Marumado yori* (*From the Round Window*), which was a collection of fifteen of her essays from *Seitō* and other magazines.[246] This time, as predicted, the sale of *Marumado yori* was banned immediately upon publication (on 1 May, 1913) on the grounds that it attacked the *ie* system and would corrupt public morals.[247] Hiratsuka knew that 'Yo no fujintachi e' was the main cause of this ban, so she removed it, changed the cover and managed to publish a new edition under the title of *Tozashi aru Mado*

---

[244] Hiratsuka, *Genshi*, vol. 2, p. 128; Hiratsuka, *Watakushi*, p. 123.
[245] 'Gogatsu-gō no henshūshitsu yori', *Seitō*, 3:5 (May, 1913), pp. 155–6.
[246] Hiratsuka Raichō, *Marumado yori* (1913).
[247] Hiratsuka, *Genshi*, vol. 2, p. 128; Fukushima Shirō, '*Marumado yori* no hatsubai kinshi', *Fujo Shinbun* (13 June, 1913); Hiratsuka, 'Fujin undō 50-nen o kaerimite', pp. 396–7; Tokkō Keisatsu Kokusho Henshū Iinkai (ed.), *Tokkō Keisatsu Kokusho*, p. 79.

nite (*At a Locked Window*) on 10 June, 1913.[248] The Ministry of Education and the Ministry of the Interior imposed stricter control on women's magazines from then on, and the sales of many other women's magazines such as *Jogaku Sekai* and *Joshi Bundan* were prohibited, something frequently reported in the press.[249]

Hiratsuka and Yasumochi had planned to establish a Seitō Society study group to run culture courses in the spring of 1913.[250] However, this failed because owners of halls had become wary of Seitō women, and refused to let their venues for Seitō courses. The cancellation of this venture compounded a sense of frustration among Seitō members.[251] Coupled with the pressures coming from the government, it contributed to a period of strain within the society. Now only a small number of people supported *Seitō*, and it was generally disapproved of by the public. Hiratsuka, impatient with the situation facing her, wrote 'Tozashi aru mado nite' ('At a locked window').[252] She commented that:

> The public and the government always stand opposite to each other. However, the emergence of anything new in society makes them join forces. Even if such cooperation is temporary, it does considerable harm to any innovation and its development. This has been proved by history.[253]

She took the emergence of Seitō women or 'new women' as her example of this:

> With regard to the pressures put upon us, the public was the first to criticise us. The press no doubt assisted, and so public criticism intensified . . . When the voice of public criticism became extremely loud, the government intervened. As the government was very struck by the public criticism of us 'new women', it felt that the issue was too serious to be left unattended to, even though it was not sure what the problem was . . . The government, with neither fixed nor definite policies had no choice but to respond to public criticism. It joined forces to suppress 'new women'. The public, who had now gained the

---

[248] Hiratsuka Raichō, *Tozashi aru Mado nite* (1913).
[249] 'Atarashii onna no torishimari, Naimushō', *Osaka Jiji Shinpō* (21 April, 1913); 'Fujin zasshi no torishimari', *Yomiuri Shinbun* (27 April, 1913).
[250] Hiratsuka, *Watakushi*, p. 128.
[251] Hiratsuka, *Genshi*, pp. 126–8.
[252] Hiratsuka Raichō, 'Tozashi aru mado nite', *Seitō*, 3:6 (June, 1913), reprinted in Kobayashi & Yoneda (eds), *Hiratsuka Raichō Hyōronshū*, pp. 33–40.
[253] *Ibid.*, p. 33.

support of the government, increased its voice, and criticism of us was aggravated ... The government then stated that it would control women's thought and speech, and restrict their freedom of expression. I felt as if the government was saying "Close your eyes, new women. Go to sleep. Or if not, keep your mouths shut." Soon the government began to take action to control us, and frequently gave orders to ban the sale of our *Seitō* on grounds of having corrupted public morality and order ... People with old-fashioned or conservative ideas regard those with progressive views as dangerous, and treat them as devils who disturb public morals and order. This is inexcusable ... The people with old-fashioned ideas are those who hold fossils in their arms and make useless efforts to give them heat, hoping to bring them back to life. They are possessed with the wrong idea that women's virtues are invariable and will stay the same for ever ... Nothing is logical about what they say.[254]

Hiratsuka here developed her attack on the public, press and government. She was particularly disappointed by critical letters from many members of the public. Her criticism also extended to leaders of women's higher education, such as Shimoda Utako, Hatoyama Haruko, Kaetsu Takako and Tsuda Umeko.[255] Hiratsuka accused them of having fallen into line with the press's criticism. She challenged them as narrow-minded, wrong-headed and inflexible.[256] Because of the contents of this article, the sale of the June 1913 issue of *Seitō* was soon interrupted by the government.[257]

The Encounter and Cohabitation with Okumura Hiroshi

In spite of the increasingly frequent prohibition of *Seitō*, Hiratsuka continued to write articles to defend her position. 1913 was also a memorable year in her private life, as she started a relationship with a young painter, Okumura Hiroshi. Hiratsuka first met Okumura,

---

[254] *Ibid.*, pp. 36–8.
[255] *Ibid.*, pp. 38–9; Hiratsuka, *Genshi*, vol. 2, pp. 132–3. Hatoyama Haruko helped found Kyōritsu Joshi Shokugyō Gakkō (now Kyōritsu Women's University) and served as its principal from 1925 until her death in 1938. Shimoda Utako worked for the imperial court, and then ran a private school, Tokyo Jojuku, which was designed for women and girls from the nobility. She helped found Kazoku Jogakkō (Peeresses' School). She also founded Jissen Jogakkō (Jissen Girls' High School) and Joshi Kōgei Gakkō (Women's Crafts School).
[256] Hiratsuka, 'Tozashi', pp. 39–40.
[257] Hiratsuka, *Genshi*, vol. 2, p. 128.

who was then a self-supporting and poor art student, in Chigasaki
(Kanagawa Prefecture) in August 1912.[258] She was introduced to him
by the owner of the Tōundō Publishing Company, the publisher of
Seitō at that time. Okumura and Hiratsuka's friends, who disapproved
of their budding relationship, tried to separate them. This succeeded
for a time but their relationship developed nevertheless. Hiratsuka's
mother became wary of Okumura, and he was ejected from his lodging because his landlady disapproved of regular visits from the infamous 'new woman' Hiratsuka.[259] Up until then she had never seriously
thought about leaving her parents' house, but her affection for
Okumura made her realise that it was time to become independent
of her parents.[260] As stated in 'Yo no fujintachi e', Hiratsuka had no
aspiration to legal marriage.[261] She wanted to cohabit although this
would lay her and her partner open to public criticism. As she was
unsure whether he would contemplate this, she sent him eight questions to discover his views.[262] These were:

1. Whatever difficulty or trouble may happen to us in the future, will
   you be able to endure this with me? Whatever external pressure
   may be put upon us, will you never leave me?
2. Supposing that I demand marriage from you, what will you reply
   to this?
3. If I hate the relationship between man and woman under the existing marriage system, and do not wish to have a legal marriage,
   what attitude will you adopt to this?
4. If I wish to cohabit with you rather than marry you, what will you
   answer to this?
5. If I wish neither marriage nor cohabitation with you and wish to
   live separately and meet on odd afternoons and nights, what will
   you say to this?
6. What kind of view do you have of children? If I love you and have
   a sexual appetite but have no procreative desire, how will you
   respond?

---

[258] Hiratsuka, Watakushi, pp. 138–9. Okumura Hiroshi was born in 1891 in
Fujisawa City (Kanagawa Prefecture) as the eldest son of Okumura Ichitarō, a
retired businessman. His elderly and blind father disapproved of his becoming a
painter, but he left his parents' house at the age of nineteen, going to Tokyo to
study painting at Nihon Suisaiga Kenkyūjo (Institute of Japanese Water-Colour
Painting).
[259] Hiratsuka, Genshi, vol. 2, pp. 52–7, 149–54; Hiratsuka, Watakushi, pp. 147–8;
Kobayashi, Hito to Shisō, pp. 136–7.
[260] Hiratsuka, Genshi, vol. 2, p. 151.
[261] Hiratsuka, 'Yo no fujintachi e', p. 31.
[262] Hiratsuka, Genshi, vol. 2, pp. 160–1.

7. Do you really intend to move out of your lodging? I am wondering whether you are ready to move out at any time if you have enough money.
8. What hopes or expectations do you hold as to our success together in the future?[263]

Okumura, who received a letter containing these questions from Hiratsuka, later wrote in his autobiography *Meguriai* (*Encounter*) about how he felt about them:

> I was bombarded with these questions, and felt completely bewildered. Her questions were itemized, which I found most unpleasant. As she cited one supposition after another, I felt as if I was being tested. These questions were completely tasteless and hurt my sensitivity. I also wondered whether any other man had ever been thrown questions like these to answer.[264]

Although he felt humiliated by them, he taxed himself to answer them because he felt that they were delicate questions and required careful responses.[265] His answers to questions 1–4 and 7 were affirmative, but he felt that question 5 was impossible to answer. He also stated that he could not possibly give an honest answer to question 8, as he was only a novice artist and was not able to make any clear financial plans.[266] His answer to question 6 was as follows:

> I like all children and find them very adorable. I am pretty certain that I would find our children far more lovable. I wonder what kind of children will be born to us. I find sexual desire, which refuses to have children, deceitful. It will be understandable if you want to wait to have a child until the financial prospects for us look bright.[267]

He concluded his answers with the following statement:

> As you point out, I can see that various difficulties await us. I also know that we must overcome them to fulfil our love. Whatever may happen to us, I will endure them as long as we are together. I also wish to develop our love into a more genuine, nobler and more admirable one.[268]

---

[263] Cited in Okumura Hiroshi, *Meguriai* (1956), pp. 171–2.
[264] *Ibid.*, p. 178.
[265] *Ibid.*, p. 176.
[266] *Ibid.*, p. 179.
[267] *Ibid.*, pp. 178–9.
[268] *Ibid.*, pp. 179–80.

Okumura's answers demonstrated his willingness to cohabit with Hiratsuka. They also revealed his personality, sincerity and flexibility. He was willing to disregard conventional 'common sense', which suited her.[269] There cannot have been many Japanese men who would have responded in the patient way that he did. Hiratsuka was very pleased with his answers:

> His way of answering my questions was very natural and frank, which was typical of him. His answers also demonstrated that he was not shackled by old customs and conventional ideas. I was impressed with his flexible and adaptable answers. I discovered strength in his answers as well.[270]

Hiratsuka felt reassured, and her determination to leave her parents' house hardened. After they found a place to live, she needed to inform her parents about her decision to leave and cohabit with Okumura. She found it difficult to discuss such a delicate subject with them, so she wrote instead, describing Okumura's personality, expressing her feelings for him, saying how she had reached her decision, and what steps had been taken in preparation for their life together.[271] In the previous year she had criticised marriage in her article 'Yo no fujintachi e'.[272] She had now decided to put her views into practice. A few days after she handed the letter to her mother, she left her parents' home (on 13 January, 1914) and started a new life with Okumura in a rented house in Sugamo, Tokyo, which was largely inhabited by lower-middle class people.[273]

She published this seemingly private letter to her parents in *Seitō* under the title of 'Dokuritsu suru ni tsuite ryōshin e' ('Addressed to my parents with regard to my becoming independent').[274] In her autobiography she wrote:

---

[269] Horiba, *Seitō no Jidai*, pp. 192–4; Maruoka, 'Seitō kara Kokusai Fujin Nen e', p. 10; Ide, *Seitō no Onnatachi*, pp. 182–4.

[270] Hiratsuka, *Genshi*, vol. 2, p. 161.

[271] *Ibid.*, p. 182.

[272] Hiratsuka, 'Yo no fujintachi e', p. 31.

[273] Hiratsuka, *Watakushi*, pp. 148–9; Hiratsuka, *Genshi*, vol. 2, p. 159; Hiratsuka Raichō, 'Musume ni haha no isan o kataru', *Shin Nyoen* (March & April, 1937), reprinted in Hiratsuka, *Chosakushū*, vol. 6, pp. 228–9; Hiratsuka, 'Fujin undō 50-nen o kaerimite', pp. 398–9.

[274] Hiratsuka, *Watakushi*, p. 149.

I was opposed to the old 'feudal' marriage system, and I wanted to lay a foundation of new sexual morality based upon our free cohabitation, which I believed was the natural outcome of our love. I wanted to let other women know how significant it was for me to put my ideas into practice, to avoid legal marriage and to cohabit with Okumura. I was convinced that what I was doing then was closely related to many contemporary women's concerns, so I dared to publish my family letter in Seitō.[275]

In this letter she justified her decision, which was in those days considered unthinkable:

Yesterday you [Hiratsuka's mother] said that it would be immoral for me to live with a young man without marrying him. You also asked me what I would do if I became pregnant. As I am dissatisfied with the existing marriage system, I have no intention to enter a legal marriage ... It might be odd if a man and a woman, who do not love each other, live together. In this case their cohabitation may need to be approved by others. However, it is the most natural thing for a couple like us, who love each other, to live in the same house. As long as we agree to do this, it does not matter if we marry legally ... I also have good reason to decline legal marriage, since marriage law is full of provisions about women's obligations which are extremely disadvantageous to women. Moreover, convention and morality, as they exist in our society, impose unreasonable restrictions upon married women. For example, they have to respect their parents-in-law, are compelled to obey their husbands and parents-in-law, and are expected to fulfil forced duties and make all the sacrifices. There are too many burdens in married women's lives. I do not want to put myself into such a handicapped position. As Hiroshi [her partner, Okumura] understands my reasons and point of view, he does not expect me to marry him legally.[276]

This letter revealed the extent of Hiratsuka's criticism of the *ie* system and the Meiji Civil Code, and her refusal to acquiesce to it.[277] After the letter was published and their cohabitation became public, they were subject to the following criticisms: Okumura was Hiratsuka's junior by five years; their relationship was based on free love; their union was immoral; and they ignored marriage law and refused to

---

[275] Hiratsuka, *Genshi*, vol. 2, pp. 184–5.

[276] Hiratsuka Raichō, 'Dokuritsu suru ni tsuite ryōshin e', *Seitō*, 4:2 (February, 1914), reprinted in Kobayashi & Yoneda (eds), *Hiratsuka Raichō Hyōronshū*, p. 56.

[277] Horiba, *Seitō no Jidai*, pp. 194–8; Suzuki, *Joseishi o Hiraku*, vol. 1, pp. 28–9; Ide, *Seitō no Onnatachi*, pp. 184–8; Ide, 'Kaisetsu', p. 17.

register their relationship.[278] The house nameplate with both Hiratsuka and Okumura's names alongside each other was repeatedly stolen. She was convinced that this was done by people who disapproved of her relationship, and who regarded her conduct as outrageous.[279] According to Hiratsuka, the press suggested that she was pregnant even before she conceived her first child.[280] In spite of all this, she stayed remarkably calm. Her dignified manner, self-confidence, and determination to maintain her principles impressed her friends and associates.

From the February 1914 issue, Hiratsuka had to take on virtually all responsibility for *Seitō* herself, since the other founders had either left the Society or had little time for *Seitō* because of their family circumstances.[281] As she became independent from her parents at this time, one might have expected her to take more interest in running *Seitō*. However, this was not so, and her contributions to the magazine from 1914 showed signs of mental exhaustion.[282] She became profoundly fatigued and the quality of *Seitō* soon declined.

According to Ide Fumiko, Hiratsuka's poor financial situation was to blame—losing her parents' financial support was a blow to her.[283] Since Okumura did not have a steady income, she now had to earn her own living by writing articles. In addition, *Seitō* was in financial difficulties. Yasumochi Yoshiko, one of the founders, believed that *Seitō*'s publisher, the Tōundō Publishing Company, was making excessive profits.[284] As a result of *Seitō*'s increased circulation (it had increased to three thousand), disputes over profits led to the Tōundō Publishing Company refusing to publish the magazine.[285] *Seitō* was now transferred to the Shōbundō Company, which was less effective in marketing the magazine.[286] As a result, *Seitō*'s circulation fell, and it became

---

[278] Hiratsuka, *Watakushi*, p. 150.
[279] Hiratsuka, *Genshi*, vol. 2, p. 185.
[280] Hiratsuka, *Watakushi*, pp. 155–6.
[281] Hiratsuka, *Genshi*, vol. 2, p. 219.
[282] Ide, 'Kaisetsu', p. 18.
[283] *Ibid.*, pp. 18–9; Ide, *Seitō no Onnatachi*, pp. 195–6.
[284] Hiratsuka, *Genshi*, vol. 2, pp. 177–8. The sales agency of *Seitō* was changed to the Tōundō Publishing Company from September 1912, and the publisher took full responsibility for its management. The publisher had a good reputation for literature and literary criticism, being responsible for Kitahara Hakushū's *Kiri no Hana* (*Flowers of a Paulownia*) and Ishikawa Takuboku's *Kanashiki Gangu* (*Sad Toys*).
[285] Horiba, *Seitō no Jidai*, p. 188.
[286] Ide, *Seitō no Onnatachi*, p. 14.

financially insecure.[287] Hiratsuka began to receive many unsold copies from the publisher. As she was responsible for *Seitō*'s finances, she had to cover its losses. She could no longer ask her mother for help, and she tried unsuccessfully to find another publisher.[288]

Compounding these problems, Yasumochi Yoshiko withdrew from the forefront of *Seitō* in spring 1914, due to illness.[289] Yasumochi had been Hiratsuka's right-hand woman, and had taken charge of running *Seitō* on a day-to-day basis, sharing editorial work with Hiratsuka and Nakano Hatsuko. Yasumochi's withdrawal left Hiratsuka to run *Seitō* single-handedly. She felt unable to ask other key Seitō members to assist, because many of them had children and were preoccupied with child-rearing and domestic duties.[290] These were Hiratsuka's reasons for the decline of *Seitō*. Itō Noe commented that:

> The Seitō Society used to be lively and had many active leading members who were close to Hiratsuka. However, within a year after the Seitō Society's lecture meeting in February 1913, the Society began to decline and became inert. Many key members left it because of public and social pressure. The remaining key members began to withdraw into their own shells. As a result, the Society lacked a cooperative spirit and fluent communication, and accordingly *Seitō* began to decline as well.[291]

Many of these leading members came from upper-middle or middle class backgrounds, and they were sensitive to public criticism, preferring to avoid it. Itō Noe noted the growing uncooperative atmosphere in the Society, although Hiratsuka made no mention of this. Itō also thought that Hiratsuka and Yasumochi differed over how the Society and its magazine ought to be run. This is one reason why Yasumochi withdrew.[292] Moreover, Itō was convinced that *Seitō*'s financial crisis was caused by Hiratsuka and Yasumochi's lack of managerial skill and their failure to negotiate effectively with publishers.[293]

---

[287] Horiba, *Seitō no Jidai*, p. 188; Ide, 'Kaisetsu', p. 19.
[288] Hiratsuka, *Genshi*, vol. 2, p. 219.
[289] Hiratsuka Raichō, 'Henshūshitsu yori', *Seitō*, 4:5 (May, 1914), pp. 117–8. According to Hiratsuka, Yasumochi had a minor nervous breakdown, because of an affair with a married man.
[290] Hiratsuka, *Watakushi*, p. 154.
[291] Itō Noe, 'Zatsuon 13', *Osaka Mainichi Shinbun* (10 April, 1916).
[292] Horiba, *Seitō no Jidai*, p. 202.
[293] *Ibid.*, p. 203.

There were further reasons for the decline, which both Itō and Hiratsuka omitted from their explanations. Many members disapproved of Hiratsuka's extra-marital relationship with Okumura, and eyed him critically.[294] Iwano Kiyoko openly criticised him for his financial dependence on Hiratsuka.[295] Kobayashi Katsu, who disliked Okumura's personality and disapproved of his relationship with Hiratsuka, reduced her links with *Seitō* and joined a new women's literary magazine, *Safuran* (*Saffron*), which was launched by Otake Kōkichi in March 1914.[296] Hiratsuka's deepening relationship with Okumura weakened her ties with other Seitō members. She found it hard to edit and manage *Seitō* on her own, and in the May 1914 issue she wrote:

> The weight of running *Seitō* bears heavily on me every day, from early morning to late at night. I feel sorry for myself for having endured it without complaining.[297]

In spite of the declining state of *Seitō* and other difficulties, Hiratsuka managed to publish the April, May, June, July and August 1914 issues. There was a special issue in April, a collection of ten short stories.[298] Among them Nogami Yaeko's 'Atarashii seimei' ('A new life'), an account of her giving birth, and Saiga Koto's 'Yogisha' ('Night train') were outstanding works.

---

[294] Ide, *Seitō no Onnatachi*, pp. 194–5; Ide, 'Kaisetsu', p. 19.

[295] Iwano Kiyoko, 'Omotte iru koto', *Seitō*, 4:5 (May, 1914), pp. 105–9.

[296] Hiratsuka, *Genshi*, vol. 2, p. 198; Ide, 'Kaisetsu', p. 19; Ide, *Seitō no Onnatachi*, p. 195. Kobayashi Katsu (1894–1974) was a daughter of Kobayashi Kiyochika (a well-known painter, illustrator and Ukiyoe print designer). She joined Seitō from November 1911. In 1913 she was in charge of proof-reading and assisted with editorial work. On Kobayashi Katsu, see Hiratsuka Raichō o Yomu Kai (ed.), *Seitō no 50-nin*, pp. 50–1.

[297] Hiratsuka Raichō, 'Henshūshitsu yori', *Seitō*, 4:5 (May, 1914), pp. 117–8. From June 1914 *Seitō* was published and marketed by the Tōkyōdō Publishing Company. Hiratsuka moved the Seitō office to her rented house in Kami Komagome in Tokyo. She titled the June issue *kakushin kinengō* (improved commemorative issue) trying to restore public interest in *Seitō*. However, there was no sign of improved style and content.

[298] They are Yamada Waka, 'Tagusa tori', *Seitō*, 4:4 (April, 1914), pp. 1–8; Nogami Yaeko, 'Atarashii seimei', *Seitō*, 4:4, pp. 9–27; Kokubun Masao, 'Gassō', *Seitō*, 4:4, pp. 28–70; Kawada Yoshi, 'Akaki ki no me', *Seitō*, 4:4, pp. 71–84; Hamano Yuki, 'Komori', *Seitō*, 4:4, pp. 85–97; Matsui Shizuyo, 'Kyō ningyō', *Seitō*, 4:4, pp. 98–110; Saiga Koto, 'Yogisha', *Seitō*, 4:4, pp. 111–35; Yasuda Satsuki, 'Sado bushi', *Seitō*, 4:4, pp. 136–68; Katō Midori, 'Wakarete no nisan-nichi', *Seitō*, 4:4, pp. 169–91; Itō Noe, 'Madoi', *Seitō*, 4:4, pp. 192–203.

Saiga Koto's 'Night train' was also autobiographical.[299] It featured a young student heroine who refused to accept her family's orders to marry her brother-in-law after he became a widower. She left her family home and was travelling on a night train. In her real life, when Saiga was at the Japan Women's College, her elder sister (the heiress of her family) died and her family tried to force her to marry her late sister's husband, to maintain the family name.[300] Saiga ran away and stayed with her mentor's family. Her heroine's outburst against conventional family ties in favour of liberty appealed to many female readers.[301]

Seitō was also adversely affected by the outbreak of World War I.[302] Japan declared war against Germany on 23 August, 1914. Horiba Kiyoko argued that the war was responsible for the sharp decline in *Seitō*'s sales and its popularity, and for Hiratsuka's failure in negotiations with publishers.[303] The press was eager to report the most up-to-date news, like war reports, and it lost much of its interest in women's issues. This put an end to the so-called '*onna no jidai*' ('era of women'), which had started in 1910 when (for good or ill) newspapers had extensively reported women's issues.[304] Many magazines also now focused upon war issues. *Seitō* by comparison hardly discussed them. As a result, *Seitō*'s circulation decline seems natural. The only work to appear in *Seitō* which dealt with the First World War was Saiga Koto's article 'Senka' ('The devastations of war'), in which she expressed a pacifist view.[305] Seitō women, especially Hiratsuka, did not know much about the war, and did not show any interest in it.[306] Hiratsuka later admitted how little interest she took in some of the major international developments of the period. This indifference to many international and social issues was a trait that recurred at a number of points in her career.

---

[299] Saiga Koto (1892–1973) studied at the Japan Women's College, but left before graduation. In spring 1912 she joined Seitō, and began to contribute to it in 1914. In 1918 she married Harada Minoru (a scholar of education and later a professor of Waseda University). On Saiga Koto, see Hiratsuka Raichō o Yomu Kai (ed.), *Seitō no 50-nin*, pp. 52–3; Hiratsuka, *Genshi*, vol. 2, pp. 242–5.

[300] Horiba, *Seitō no Jidai*, p. 42; Hiratsuka Raichō o Yomu Kai (ed.), *Seitō no 50-nin*, p. 52; Hiratsuka, *Genshi*, vol. 2, p. 243.

[301] Ide, 'Kaisetsu', p. 20.

[302] Ide, *Seitō no Onnatachi*, p. 189.

[303] Horiba, *Seitō no Jidai*, p. 218.

[304] *Ibid.*, p. 219.

[305] Saiga Koto, 'Senka', *Seitō*, 5:10 (November, 1915), pp. 88–103.

[306] Hiratsuka, *Genshi*, vol. 2, p. 244.

In spite of her limitations as editor of *Seitō*, Hiratsuka successfully recruited new female authors, including Kanbara Fusae in 1914, who frequently contributed to *Seitō*.[307] Itō Noe made the biggest impact in *Seitō* in 1914. Itō had joined the Seitō Society in 1912, and had made rapid progress in written expression.[308] Later Hiratsuka wrote that Itō's article 'Dōyō' ('Unrest') in 1913 aroused much public interest.[309] Itō countered public criticism of the Seitō Society and *Seitō*, and wrote articles rebutting criticism from Nishikawa Fumiko (the editor of *Seitō*'s rival magazine, *Shin Shin Fujin*), Shimoda Jirō (a female educationalist) and Shimoda Utako (a leading figure in women's circles at that time).[310] In contrast to the vigour of Itō Noe, Hiratsuka apparently showed signs of considerable fatigue. In her autobiography she wrote:

> Because of my mental and physical exhaustion, I began to suffer from splitting headaches, which made me unable to work for many days. I had great difficulty in even sorting out mail to the Seitō Society.[311]

Due to her poor health, the September 1914 issue (planned as a special number to celebrate *Seitō*'s third anniversary) never appeared. The October issue was the last to be edited by Hiratsuka. Soon after its appearance, Hiratsuka left Tokyo with Okumura for the Onjuku Coast in Kazusa in Chiba Prefecture.[312] She was now exhausted,

[307] Ide, 'Kaisetsu', p. 20.

[308] Hiratsuka, *Genshi*, vol. 2, pp. 165–8. On Itō Noe, see Appendix 1; Hiratsuka Raichō o Yomu Kai (ed.), *Seitō no 50-nin*, pp. 14–5; Muramatsu & Watanabe, *Gendai Josei Bungaku Jiten*, pp. 47–9; Ikeda Michiko, 'Itō Noe', in Setouchi Harumi (ed.), *Hangyaku no Onna no Roman* (1989), pp. 98–127; Ken Miyamoto, 'Itō Noe and the Bluestockings', *Japan Interpreter*, 10:2 (Autumn 1975), pp. 190–204; Sievers, *Flowers in Salt*, pp. 171–5; Hane, *Reflections on the Way to the Gallows*, pp. 21–4; Hiratsuka Raichō, 'Seinen Tsuji Jun-shi', in Hiratsuka, *Chosakushū*, vol. 5, pp. 309–12; Hiratsuka Raichō, 'Shizenjo Itō Noe-san', *Fujin Kōron* (November & December, 1923), reprinted in Hiratsuka, *Chosakushū*, vol. 3, pp. 346–8; Hiratsuka Raichō, 'Itō Noe-san no arukareta michi', *Shin Nihon* (July & August, 1917), reprinted in Hiratsuka, *Chosakushū*, vol. 2, pp. 295–334; Hiratsuka Raichō, 'Iwayuru jiyū renai to sono seigen', *Osaka Mainichi Shinbun* (4 January, 1917), reprinted in Hiratsuka, *Chosakushū*, vol. 2, pp. 256–7.

[309] Hiratsuka, *Genshi*, vol. 2, p. 167. Itō Noe's article 'Dōyō' appeared in the August 1913 issue of *Seitō*.

[310] Itō Noe, 'Nishikawa Fumiko-shi no *Fujin Kaihōron* o yomu', *Seitō*, 4:5 (May, 1914), pp. 29–36; Itō Noe, 'Shimoda Jirō-shi ni: Nihon fujin no kakushin jidai ni tsuite', *Seitō*, 4:7 (July, 1914), pp. 91–106; Itō Noe, 'Shimoda Utako joshi e', *Seitō*, 4:9 (October, 1914), pp. 64–72.

[311] Hiratsuka, *Genshi*, vol. 2, p. 220.

[312] Kobayashi, *Hito to Shisō*, p. 147; Hiratsuka Raichō, 'Onjuku yori', *Seitō*, 4:10 (November, 1914), reprinted in Hiratsuka, *Chosakushū*, vol. 1, pp. 373–9.

and desperately needed to recuperate. She asked Itō Noe to run the Seitō Society during her absence and to edit the November and December issues. After editing these issues, Itō completely took over the editorship and other responsibilities in January 1915.[313]

Seitō *under Itō's Editorship*

According to Itō Noe, there were three rumours about this change.[314] One was speculation that Hiratsuka was pregnant. Another was that Hiratsuka had separated from Okumura. A third was that there was discord between Itō and Hiratsuka. Itō strongly denied all these, and it is important to consider the real reasons for the transition. Hiratsuka's account was given in her autobiography and in an article in *Seitō*.[315] According to her, she had received a long letter from Itō on 7 November 1914, refusing to edit the December issue unless Hiratsuka permanently handed over the entire work to Itō Noe:

> When I left Tokyo for Onjuku, I did not expect to give up *Seitō*. Moreover, I did not have the slightest intention of handing it over to Itō . . . I felt responsible to *Seitō* because I had started it. However, I must admit that taking all responsibility for *Seitō* lay like a heavy weight on my shoulders . . . In order to lead a more relaxed and enjoyable life with Okumura, I felt that I must end the publication of *Seitō*. On the other hand, I felt it very regrettable and heartbreaking to end my role with *Seitō*, as I had launched and put much effort into it, and it still had a promising future. I began to think that if Itō could really manage to sustain *Seitō*, it might be the best solution.[316]

Later Hiratsuka confessed that she had been pushed into the change by Itō's forcefulness and enthusiasm.[317]

Itō's version was given in her article '*Seitō* o hikitsugu ni tsuite' ('With regard to taking over *Seitō*') in *Seitō*. She slightly criticised Hiratsuka for having distanced herself from *Seitō* and for having given preference to her private life. Itō wrote:

---

[313] Hiratsuka, *Genshi*, vol. 2, pp. 227–8.

[314] Itō Noe, '*Seitō* o hikitsugu ni tsuite', *Seitō*, 5:1 (January, 1915), reprinted in Itō Noe, *Itō Noe Zenshū*, 2 vols (1970), vol. 2, pp. 102–16.

[315] Hiratsuka Raichō, '*Seitō* to watashi—*Seitō* o Noe-san ni oyuzurisuru ni tsuite', *Seitō*, 5:1 (January, 1915), pp. 110–34; Hiratsuka, *Genshi*, vol. 2, pp. 223–8.

[316] *Ibid.*, p. 225.

[317] *Ibid.*, p. 227.

> I am a person from the countryside, who used to be nothing but
> Hiratsuka's assistant, but please observe how I am going to improve
> *Seitō*. I will rely on my own ability . . . I will continue *Seitō* with my
> utmost strength.[318]

Some women's historians, including Yoneda Sayoko, believe that Itō
seized *Seitō* from Hiratsuka and Itō's strong-mindedness explains the
take-over.[319] However, *Seitō*'s hand-over to Itō was probably unavoidable, for she was better suited to running it than Hiratsuka. Itō sur-
passed Hiratsuka in enthusiasm, vitality, and in her social awareness.
From this time Hiratsuka concentrated on her private life. In contrast, Itō declared that she wanted to thrust herself into society by
means of *Seitō*.[320] Her attitude appealed to Ikuta Chōkō, who had
recently launched a review called *Hankyō* (*Echo*) with Morita Sōhei.[321]
Hankyō was a magazine of literary reviews, but it also published political criticism.[322] In it Ikuta stated that literature should not turn its
back on the world.[323] He urged literary men and women to take
more interest in social issues. Itō's attitude resembled Ikuta's, and
he wanted *Seitō* to emulate *Hankyō*. In her autobiography Hiratsuka
mentioned that Ikuta washed his hands of *Seitō* from early 1913.[324]
Nevertheless, Ikuta probably continued to help *Seitō* financially through
his role in the Nichigetsu Publishing Company, which issued his journal *Hankyō*. It was through him that *Seitō* was moved to the Nichigetsu
Publishing Company, to restore its financial difficulties.[325]

Hiratsuka and Itō never consulted other members of the Society
when they decided that Itō should control *Seitō*.[326] Both overlooked
the fact that *Seitō* was a magazine read by all members of the Society.
Both treated *Seitō* as if it was their private possession. Itō discussed
the changes she was planning to make:

---

[318] Itō, '*Seitō* o hikitsugu ni tsuite', pp. 111–2.
[319] Yoneda, '*Seitō* no ryakudatsu', pp. 106–7; Yoneda, '*Seitō* to shakai no setten', p. 76; Horiba, *Seitō no Jidai*, pp. 224–5.
[320] Itō, '*Seitō* o hikitsugu ni tsuite', p. 107.
[321] Yoneda, '*Seitō* no ryakudatsu', p. 107; Yoneda, '*Seitō* no shakai no setten',
p. 78.
[322] Uranishi Kazuhiko, 'Kaidai', in Fuji Shuppan (ed.), *Hankyō, Kaidai, Sōmokuji,
Sakuin* (1985), pp. 5–12.
[323] Yoneda, '*Seitō* to shakai no setten', pp. 74–9.
[324] Hiratsuka, *Genshi*, vol. 2, pp. 121–2.
[325] Yoneda, '*Seitō* to shakai no setten', p. 70; Hiratsuka, *Genshi*, vol. 2, p. 223.
[326] Ide, 'Kaisetsu', p. 22.

First of all, I will remove all existing regulations from the Seitō Society. From now on *Seitō* will have no regulations, no policies, no convictions and no principles. Anybody, who desperately needs to have principles, and cannot do without regulations, will be most welcome to make them up individually. I will provide a magazine with no principles, and with policies for all women, but I will decline male participation in principle. If a man writes a worthwhile article on women's causes, or one beneficial to women, I will seriously consider publishing it. However, I would like to continue to reserve it mainly for women. Anybody who would like to use *Seitō* as a stepping-stone to her social success is welcome to do so. Anybody who wants to express her views in *Seitō* will be free to do so . . . Please let me reject or accept contributions entirely at my own discretion.[327]

She immediately put this policy into practice, and the regulations of the Seitō Society were not printed from the February 1915 issue onwards.[328] *Seitō*'s editorial and publishing rights were transferred from Nakano Hatsuko (one of the founders who had these nominal rights) to Itō Noe.[329] The Seitō Society's office was moved to Itō's rented accommodation in Koishikawa, Tokyo, where it lost the refined and cultured atmosphere of a literary salon, and received fewer visitors.[330] *Seitō* began to take on the character of Itō's personal magazine, which Hiratsuka immediately resented.

Although Itō embarked on her new task with vigour and optimism, *Seitō*'s tight financial situation did not improve, and there was hardly any improvement in its literary quality and circulation after her take-over. Yet even though *Seitō* had new contributors during Itō's period, its contents and format remained almost unchanged. As before, *Seitō*'s contents were divided into two categories—literary pieces (comprising *tanka* poems, short stories and translations) and articles on women's issues. Frequent contributors during this period included Nogami Yaeko, Yamada Waka, Yasuda Satsuki, Saiga Koto, Ikuta Hanayo and Mikajima Yoshiko.[331]

---

[327] Itō, '*Seitō* o hikitsugu ni tsuite', pp. 114–5.

[328] Itō Noe, 'Henshūshitsu yori', *Seitō*, 5:2 (February, 1915), pp. 130–1.

[329] Horiba, *Seitō no Jidai*, p. 224. Nakano Hatsuko's name appeared as an editor from its inaugural issue to December 1914. She never published her literary work in *Seitō*.

[330] Ide, 'Kaisetsu', p. 23.

[331] Mikajima Yoshiko (1886–1927) was a teacher and contributed her *tanka* poems to *Subaru* (*The Pleiades*). She joined Seitō in 1912 and published 1039 *tanka* poems in *Seitō*. On Mikajima Yoshiko, see Hiratsuka Raichō o Yomu Kai (ed.), *Seitō no*

After Hiratsuka withdrew from the leading role, she began to write a full-length serialized novel called *Tōge* (*The Mountain Pass*), based on the Shiobara Incident, for the *Jiji Shinpō*, to increase her income.[332] However, she continued to contribute some articles to *Seitō*.

Among literary pieces published in *Seitō* during this period Nogami Yaeko's serial translation of the Russian mathematician Sonya Kova-levsky's biography, and Mikajima Yoshiko's many *tanka* poems are most outstanding in their literary qualities.[333] With regard to articles on women's issues published over this period, three key women's topics were discussed: *teisō* (chastity), *datai* (abortion) and *baishun* (prostitution).

The subject of chastity was first raised by Ikuta Hanayo. Ikuta wrote an article 'Taberu koto to teisō to' ('Supporting yourself and chastity'), which appeared in *Hankyō* (*Echo*).[334] In it Ikuta made the following remarks:

> It is inevitable and forgivable for a financially desperate woman, who can find no alternative, to sell her chastity (as the last resort) in order to support herself and her family. For me, supporting herself ought to be her primary concern, and her chastity ought to be her secondary concern. Losing her chastity is neither immoral nor sinful, but it is believed so by present conventional morals. This is mainly because being a virgin turns out to be an advantageous prerequisite for mar-riage. As long as she agrees to this loss, and is prepared for the dis-advantages she may face in the event of her marriage, she is free to lose her virginity to support herself before marriage.[335]

50-nin, pp. 86–7; Muramatsu & Watanabe, *Gendai Josei Bungaku Jiten*, pp. 322–3. Yasuda Satsuki (1887–1933) joined Seitō in March 1912. She supported her fam-ily by dressmaking, divorced her husband, had tuberculosis and in 1933 commit-ted suicide. On Yasuda Satsuki, see Hiratsuka Raichō o Yomu Kai (ed.), *Seitō no 50-nin*, pp. 96–7; Hiratsuka, 'Seitō jidai', pp. 203–7; Hiratsuka Raichō, 'Tomodachi no isho', in Hiratsuka, *Chosakushū*, vol. 5, pp. 352–5.

[332] Hiratsuka, *Genshi*, vol. 2, pp. 229–30. Against her will, Hiratsuka gave up this serialized novel halfway, partly because she became pregnant and suffered from bad morning sickness, and partly because she could not endure Okumura's jealousy of her previous love affairs.

[333] Ide, 'Kaisetsu', p. 23. Nogami Yaeko (1885–1985) published her maiden work 'Enishi' in *Hototogisu* (1907). She joined Seitō in September 1911, but left the follow-ing month. However, after Itō Noe took over, Nogami regularly published work in *Seitō*. On Nogami Yaeko, see Hiratsuka Raichō o Yomu Kai (ed.), *Seitō no 50-nin*, pp. 68–9; Muramatsu & Watanabe, *Gendai Josei Bungaku Jiten*, pp. 255–60; Lewell, *Modern Japanese Novelists*, pp. 310–5; Schierbeck, *Japanese Women Novelists in the 20th Century*, pp. 29–33; Tanaka, *To Live and to Write*, pp. 147–52; Katō, *A History of Japanese Literature*, p. 298.

[334] Ikuta Hanayo, 'Taberu koto to teisō to', *Hankyō*, 1:5 (September, 1914), pp. 33–8. This article was based on her rape by an employer when she was an office worker.

[335] *Ibid.*, pp. 35–6.

As Ikuta stated, women's virginity was highly valued at that time, and there was much prejudice against women who lost their virginity before marriage.[336] Ikuta's remarks were something of a bombshell, which challenged the social expectations for unmarried women, and provoked public outrage.[337]

Yasuda Satsuki responded to this article by criticising Ikuta's views about chastity, and expressed her own:

> To me, chastity should be the most precious thing for a woman. Supporting herself ought to come after her chastity.[338]

Yasuda, who valued chastity above all else, could not accept Ikuta's idea of exchanging it for food. She described Ikuta's view as a weak and deceitful opinion, one that was most insulting to women.[339] She was adamant that she would be prepared even for starvation to maintain her irreplaceable chastity, which was also her dignity.

Itō Noe participated in the debate with her article 'Teisō ni tsuite no zakkan' ('My impressions of chastity').[340] She argued that a woman's virginity was insignificant in a love marriage, though she did not approve of Ikuta's approach of treating female chastity like a commodity, and putting a commercial value on it.[341]

Hiratsuka also contributed with her article 'Shojo no shinka' ('The real value of a virgin').[342] She made the following comments:

> Chastity has to be valued. Virginity is precious. Women must not give up chastity without much thought. As these ideas regarding chastity have become pervasive, people are convinced that losing one's virginity is immoral. I cannot possibly agree with this. Why does an unmarried woman who has lost her virginity before marriage have to be criticised by the public? . . . In my view all women must cherish and preserve their chastity until the most suitable time for them to lose it.

---

[336] Men's virginity was not taken up as the subject for discussion at all. Unlike women, men, who had sexual freedom, were free to lose their virginity at any time.

[337] Horiba, *Seitō no Jidai*, p. 211; Ide, *Seitō no Onnatachi*, p. 191; Tanaka, *Josei Kaihō no Shisō*, p. 195.

[338] Yasuda Satsuki, 'Ikiru koto to teisō to: *Hankyō* kugatsugō "taberu koto to teisō to" o yonde' ('Life and chastity—after reading the article entitled "Supporting yourself and chastity"'), *Seitō*, 4:11 (December, 1914), reprinted in Horiba (ed.), *Seitō Josei Kaihō Ronshū*, p. 243.

[339] *Ibid.*, p. 245.

[340] Itō Noe, 'Teisō ni tsuite no zakkan', *Seitō*, 5:2 (February, 1915), reprinted in Horiba (ed.), *Seitō Josei Kaihō Ronshū*, pp. 250–9.

[341] *Ibid.*, pp. 252–3.

[342] Hiratsuka Raichō, 'Shojo no shinka', *Shin Kōron* (March, 1915), reprinted in Hiratsuka, *Chosakushū*, vol. 2, pp. 53–60.

It is improper for women to lose it at inappropriate times, but it is equally sinful for women not to lose their chastity at the most suitable time. When is the most suitable time for women to lose their virginity? In my view it is when women's sensual desire arises from their affection towards their lovers and they truly feel the need to be physically united with their lovers ... According to the public view, the most suitable time for women to abandon their chastity is upon their marriage. From my point of view, legal marriages—the great majority of which are loveless and arranged—are hideous, repulsive and wicked. I agree that even the conduct of the most unfortunate unmarried women who have to sell their chastity is an offence. However, to me their offence is definitely less than that of modest and faithful women who married their husbands without love, and who indifferently lost their virginity to such husbands. I look forward to the day when the formal, loveless, arranged marriages will be abolished and taken over by love marriages, and women will be able to lose their chastity at the most ideal time, without regret.[343]

The heated debate over chastity in *Seitō* was taken up by the *Yomiuri Shinbun* (*Yomiuri Newspaper*), which had launched a women's supplement. Special issues with articles on chastity were published there.[344]

The second main women's issue discussed in *Seitō* during Itō's editorship was abortion. In the Edo period abortion was overlooked by the Tokugawa Shōgunate.[345] However, after the Meiji Restoration, the Meiji government introduced the *Fukoku Kyōhei* policy (the plan for building 'a rich country with a strong army'), which remained in force during the Meiji and to some extent the Taishō periods.[346] Under this policy extra labourers, to work in factories for low wages, and soldiers were required by the government to augment Japan's national strength. As the state wanted to control childbirth and increase population, abortion was strictly forbidden and was made illegal by the *Keihō* (Criminal Law) promulgated in 1880, becoming effective in 1882.[347] Under this law any woman having an abortion and any medical doctor or midwife performing an abortion became

---

[343] *Ibid.*, pp. 57–60.

[344] Ide, 'Kaisetsu', p. 24. The *Yomiuri Shinbun* carried out questionnaires which were filled in by prominent figures. According to the results, all agreed that female chastity was vital, but none of them made any mention of male celibacy.

[345] Fujin Kyōdō Hōritsu Jimusho (ed.), *Ima Naze Yūsei Hogohō Kaiaku ka* (1983), p. 54.

[346] *Ibid.*, p. 54; Katō, *Ai wa Jidai o Koete*, p. 73; Jane Condon, *A Half Step Behind: Japanese Women Today* (1985, Tokyo, 1991), p. 86.

[347] Sōgō Joseishi Kenkyūkai (ed.), *Sei, Ai, Kazoku*, p. 178; Muriel Jolivet, *Japan: the Childless Society?* (1993, London, 1997), p. 121.

criminals, incurring imprisonment of up to five years.[348] Under this
law, once women became pregnant they had no choice but to have
the baby, no matter how poor they were or what their health was.
However, in reality large numbers of women, with many children,
in poor health or in financial difficulties, turned to illegal abortion,
although they were aware of the legal and health risks of this.[349] It
was quite natural for women, including Seitō women, to take an
increasing interest in abortion, especially the freedom of birth control
and women's right to have an abortion. Yasuda Satsuki, a member
of Seitō, was the first to speak of abortion in her article 'Gokuchū
no onna yori otoko ni' ('From a woman behind bars to a man') in
the June 1915 issue of Seitō.[350] She used the format of a letter addressed
from a heroine in jail, charged with having an illegal abortion by
her partner she had cohabited with. The heroine gave a detailed
account of how she responded to the judge's questions, and how she
tried to justify her abortion. Yasuda, who was married and pregnant with her first child, expressed a view in favour of abortion
through her heroine:

> When I conceived, I felt neither a baby's life nor personality. I felt
> that the baby I was carrying inside me was nothing but a small attach-
> ment to my own body. Therefore I did not have the slightest instinc-
> tive love towards the baby.[351]

Yasuda stated that a woman should not become a mother unless
she could provide her baby with a decent home and living.[352] She
felt that certain sacrifices like abortions were unavoidable in some
circumstances. Yasuda was adamant that her heroine had no choice
but to follow her convictions and have an abortion, even though
this was illegal. One sees how radical Yasuda's advocacy of the rights
of women over their own bodies was. As Yasuda's article contra-
vened state policy, public sale of this issue of Seitō was prohibited.[353]

---

[348] Ide, 'Kaisetsu', p. 24; Horiba, Seitō no Jidai, p. 231; Ide, Seitō no Onnatachi,
p. 227.

[349] Sōgō Joseishi Kenkyūkai (ed.), Sei, Ai, Kazoku, pp. 206–7.

[350] Yasuda Satsuki, 'Gokuchū no onna yori otoko ni', Seitō, 5:6 (June, 1915),
reprinted in Horiba (ed.), Seitō Josei Kaihō Ronshū, pp. 260–70.

[351] Ibid., pp. 262–3.

[352] Ibid., pp. 266–8.

[353] Hiratsuka, Genshi, vol. 2, p. 233. This was the third time the sale of Seitō was
banned.

Responding to Yasuda's article, Hiratsuka, Itō and Yamada expressed their own views on abortion. Itō, who was pregnant with her second child, wrote 'Shishin' ('My private note').[354] In it she spoke with disapproval of Yasuda's view:

> Yasuda thinks that her baby is a part of her own body as long as the baby stays inside her womb, but I cannot agree with her. I feel that the baby has its own life and develops its personality even when unborn. Having an abortion means killing the precious life of the baby.[355]

Yamada Waka, who supported Ellen Key's 'glorification of motherhood', wrote 'Datai ni tsuite' ('With regard to abortions').[356] In it she attacked abortion:

> I think that both abortions and birth control are equally sinful. They are immoral because they destroy women's personal happiness as well as the nation's prosperity.[357]

Yamada's conservative view was probably similar to that of most members of the public. Hiratsuka joined the debate with her 'Kojin to shite no seikatsu to sei to shite no seikatsu tono aida no sōtō ni tsuite' ('The struggle between a woman's personal life and her sexual life').[358] This was written in the form of a letter to Itō Noe, and discussed her life with Okumura and the problems she had when she discovered her pregnancy:

> When I first realised that I was pregnant, I began to develop anxieties and fears. Among these, my greatest concern was that having a child might prevent me from having a peaceful personal life and accomplishing my work. Just like you, I also worried about my tight financial situation, but the issue of how to harmonise my personal life with my sexual life and motherhood seemed more important to me than the financial problem . . . In the early days of my pregnancy I nursed delusions of having an abortion. Unlike you, I did not have a guilty conscience about having an abortion, but I was not sure that denying life to the child I was carrying in my body and aborting it would be wise

---

[354] Itō Noe, 'Shishin', *Seitō*, 5:6 (June, 1915), reprinted in Horiba (ed.), *Seitō Josei Kaihō Ronshū*, pp. 271–6.

[355] *Ibid.*, p. 273.

[356] Yamada Waka, 'Datai ni tsuite', *Seitō*, 5:8 (September, 1915), reprinted in Horiba (ed.), *Seitō Josei Kaihō Ronshū*, pp. 296–303.

[357] *Ibid.*, p. 300.

[358] Hiratsuka Raichō, 'Kojin to shite no seikatsu to sei to shite no seikatsu tono aida no sōtō ni tsuite', *Seitō*, 5:8 (September, 1915), reprinted in Horiba (ed.), *Seitō Josei Kaihō Ronshū*, pp. 277–95.

or beneficial to my present and future relationship with Okumura. As I did not want to do anything I would regret in the future, I decided not to abort my baby. However, if I meet a woman who has calmly had an abortion to improve herself (for the sake of her art, study or other undertaking), and to contribute by strong conviction to social progress and the development of civilization, I cannot possibly accuse her of having committed an inexcusable crime.[359]

This article described her struggle between expectant motherhood and her desire to retain an individual and independent life. Such a dilemma was common to women who tried to combine work with child-bearing and rearing. In this article Hiratsuka stated that giving birth to a small number of children would lead to low child mortality rates and to the bringing up of healthier and better-educated children. It would also give women more opportunity to find their way into wider society. She stressed the need for women to have freedom over birth control, which she claimed to be 'a civilized nation's privilege as well as duty'.[360] Her statement was extremely fearless considering that the government strongly discouraged the spread of information about birth control. The government was convinced that birth control was a dangerous idea to obstruct the growth of national power and to corrupt public morals, and it accordingly tried to prevent women from even talking about birth control and its methods in public.[361] Although Hiratsuka's statement was interpreted as treachery or disloyalty to the state, it was the first public advocacy of the freedom of birth control in Japan. It laid down a significant foundation for the later discussions on the subject.[362] Similarly, after the discussion on abortion among the Seitō women,

---

[359] Ibid., pp. 287, 291–2.

[360] Ibid., p. 286.

[361] Katō, Ai wa Jidai o Koete, p. 73; Yamashita, Nihon Josei Kaihō Shisō no Kigen, p. 111.

[362] A full-scale birth control campaign was later launched by Katō Shidzue, who believed that birth control was the prerequisite for success in the women's emancipation movement. Although the American birth control pioneer Margaret Sanger's visit to Japan in 1922 was greatly interrupted by the government, Katō was inspired by Sanger's visit and founded a birth control study group in 1922. In 1931 she also helped to found the Nihon Sanji Seigen Renmei (the Women's Birth Control League of Japan). She became its chairwoman and Hiratsuka became a member. The League launched a movement to educate Japanese women about birth control. Katō also opened the first birth control advice clinic in Tokyo in 1934. However, the government suppressed her birth control activities. She was sent to prison and her clinic was forced to close. See Katō, Ai wa Jidai o Koete, pp. 72–83; Ishimoto, Facing Two Ways, pp. 225–36; Hopper, A New Woman of Japan, pp. 56–7, 220–7.

other feminists such as Yamakawa Kikue began to proclaim openly that the government should allow women with financial difficulties, poor health or eugenic problems to have abortions.[363]

The third women's issue discussed in *Seitō* during Itō's editorship was prostitution. Itō wrote 'Gōman kyōryō ni shite futtei naru Nihon fujin no kōkyō jigyō ni tsuite' ('With regard to Japanese women's public undertakings which are self-important, narrow-minded and inconsistent').[364] In it she criticised the campaign to abolish licensed prostitution conducted by the Kyōfūkai (the Women's Christian Temperance Union), and stated that this campaign was merely a charitable one by bourgeois women living in comfort.[365] She expressed much sympathy for prostitutes, stating that they have good reasons for doing such work. She criticised the Kyōfūkai for being too optimistic and over-ambitious in aiming for the complete abolition of licensed prostitution within six years.[366]

Yamakawa Kikue argued against Itō's view of prostitution, and stated that licensed prostitution was a hangover from the feudal era, and that it should be abolished.[367] Yamakawa supported the Kyōfūkai's campaign, and many contemporary feminists felt that she got the better of Itō in their published debates.[368]

---

[363] During the war the militarist government, which needed to recruit more able-bodied young men as soldiers, tightened its ban on abortions, and spread the slogan 'Umeyo fuyaseyo' ('Bear more children and increase the population'). However, the Kokumin Yūsei Hō (the National Eugenic Law of 1940), which was modelled on the law in Nazi Germany, permitted some women to have an abortion if this would save the mother's life or eliminate specific genetic defects. This law was replaced by a more liberal law called the Yūsei Hogo Hō (the Eugenic Protection Law) in 1948. The new law allowed women with one of the following conditions to have an abortion: because of rape; leprosy, hereditary illness or mental defect; because her life would be endangered by pregnancy or birth; or desperate economic plight. Condon, *A Half Step Behind*, pp. 86, 90; Jolivet, *Japan: the Childless Society*, p. 99; Samuel Coleman, *Family Planning in Japanese Society: Traditional Birth Control in a Modern Urban Culture* (1983, Princeton, New Jersey, 1991), pp. 19–20; Fujin Kyōdō Hōritsu Jimusho (ed.), *Ima Naze Yūsei Hogo Hō Kaiaku ka*, pp. 54–7.

[364] Itō Noe, 'Gōman kyōryō ni shite futtei naru Nihon fujin no kōkyō jigyō ni tsuite', *Seitō*, 5:11 (December, 1915), reprinted in Horiba (ed.), *Seitō Josei Kaihō Ronshū*, pp. 312–26.

[365] *Ibid.*, pp. 319–24.

[366] *Ibid.*, p. 323.

[367] Yamakawa Kikue, 'Nihon fujin no shakai jigyō ni tsuite Itō Noe-shi ni kou', *Seitō*, 6:1 (January, 1916), reprinted in Horiba (ed.), *Seitō Josei Kaihō Ronshū*, pp. 327–37.

[368] Cited in Horiba, *Seitō no Jidai*, pp. 246–7; Ide, 'Kaisetsu', p. 24.

Hiratsuka made no comments on prostitution. She remained indifferent to the issue even after she visited the Yoshiwara.[369] Although her visit gave her an opportunity to investigate the issue, she never took it up seriously. Hiratsuka's upper-middle class upbringing was very different from that of prostitutes, and she made little effort to understand their motives and work.

A significant characteristic of *Seitō* during Itō's time as editor was its increasing expression of anarchist views.[370] Itō introduced news about Ōsugi Sakae (a leading anarchist to whom she became romantically attached in 1915) in the editor's postscript in *Seitō*, and commended his anarchist magazine *Kindai Shisō* (*Modern Thought*), which was under threat of prohibition.[371]

Although *Seitō* did not decline in quality under Itō's editorship, it became thinner and less attractively presented because of its worsening financial situation. Moreover, because Itō was absent from Tokyo for four months awaiting the birth of her child in her hometown in Fukuoka, Kyūshū, the Nichigetsu Publishing Company managed *Seitō* on her behalf, and Ikuta Hanayo acted as an editor.[372] No August 1915 issue was published, though *Seitō* survived 13 months after Itō had taken over the editorship. The publication came to an abrupt end in February 1916. Changes in Itō's personal and domestic circumstances were the immediate cause.[373] Itō, who was married to Tsuji Jun and had two children with him, was dissatisfied with her marriage. A strained financial situation, and constant quarrels with her mother-in-law and sister-in-law contributed to estrangement between her and her husband.[374] This rift widened through Itō's

---

[369] Hiratsuka, *Genshi*, vol. 2, p. 39.

[370] Ide, 'Kaisetsu', p. 25.

[371] Ōsugi Sakae (1885–1923) was a foremost anarchist in the Taishō period. He was influenced by Kōtoku Shūsui, and became involved with the Heiminsha. He was frequently sent to jail. In 1912 he launched an anarchist journal *Kindai Shisō* (*Modern Thought*). He was also notorious for his affairs with Kamichika Ichiko and Itō Noe. He survived being stabbed by Kamichika. In the aftermath of the Kantō Great Earthquake he was murdered by the military police, in an event known as the Amakasu Incident. On Ōsugi Sakae, see Ōsugi Sakae, *Jijoden: Nihon Dasshutsu Ki* (1991); Chiya Michio, 'Ōsugi Sakae to atarashii onnatachi', *Rekishi to Jinbutsu Tokushū: Kindai Renai Jiken Hiwa* (April, 1980), pp. 98–103.

[372] Hiratsuka, *Genshi*, vol. 2, p. 278.

[373] Ide, *Seitō no Onnatachi*, p. 239.

[374] *Ibid.*, pp. 242–3.

inclination to anarchism, following her reading of Emma Goldman.[375] Itō began to find Tsuji's selfish life style disturbing, and they were not able to compromise.[376] The final blow for Itō was that Tsuji had an affair with Itō's cousin (who was living in their household) while Itō was pregnant with her second child.[377] Itō was driven to despair and wrote about her very personal domestic problems in *Seitō*.[378] She vented her anger against her adulterous husband, and put her disconsolate feelings into writing. A meeting with Ōsugi Sakae changed her outlook, and she fell in love with him. He was a leading anarchist and they shared the same convictions.[379] She abandoned her husband and children to live with Ōsugi in April 1916.

When Itō published the February 1916 issue, she gave no indication that it would be the last.[380] Perhaps she wanted to suspend publication until she could resolve her domestic problems. However, she never revived *Seitō*, and seems to have become preoccupied with her new life with Ōsugi. It is surprising that Itō discontinued *Seitō* without consulting Hiratsuka and other *Seitō* members.[381] However, Hiratsuka was not offended and saw its termination as unavoidable. Hiratsuka herself was fully preoccupied with domestic life, looking after her baby daughter Akemi (who was born in December 1915), and nursing her partner Okumura, who had contracted tuberculosis.[382] She was worried about medical and other expenses, and the demise of *Seitō* seems to have been a matter of dwindling concern to her. Hiratsuka lost contact with Itō after moving to Chigasaki in Kanagawa

---

[375] Ide, 'Kaisetsu', p. 22; Hiratsuka, *Genshi*, vol. 2, p. 277; Tanaka (ed.), *Josei Kaihō no Shisō*, pp. 196–8. Emma Goldman (1869–1940) was known as 'the Queen of the Anarchists' and 'Red Emma'. She was born in Lithuania, and when her father tried to marry her off at 15 she emigrated to the United States with her sister. She was outspoken and campaigned for workers' rights, women's emancipation and birth control. Although she was frequently arrested, she continued writing and lecturing. She also edited the monthly anarchist magazine *Mother Earth* between 1906 and 1917. Her writings include *Anarchism and Other Essays* (1911). On Emma Goldman, see Spender, *Women of Ideas*, pp. 497–507; Alix Kates Shulman, 'Emma Goldman: Anarchist Queen', in Dale Spender (ed.), *Feminist Theories: Three Centuries of Women's Intellectual Traditions* (London, 1983), pp. 218–28.

[376] Ide, *Seitō no Onnatachi*, pp. 18–20.

[377] *Ibid.*, p. 253; Hiratsuka, *Genshi*, vol. 2, p. 278.

[378] Itō Noe, 'Gūkan nisan', *Seitō*, 5:7 (July, 1915), reprinted in Itō, *Itō Noe Zenshū*, vol. 2, pp. 157–63.

[379] Ide, 'Kaisetsu', p. 25; Ide, *Seitō no Onnatachi*, pp. 252–60; Hiratsuka, *Watakushi*, p. 163; Horiba, *Seitō no Jidai*, p. 248.

[380] Itō Noe, 'Henshūshitsu yori', *Seitō*, 6:2 (February, 1916), pp. 89–90.

[381] Hiratsuka, *Genshi*, vol. 2, p. 283.

[382] Hiratsuka, *Watakushi*, pp. 158–60.

Prefecture, where Okumura was in a T.B. sanatorium, although she heard that Itō had left her husband to live with Ōsugi.[383] Hiratsuka later expressed how she felt about the discontinuation of *Seitō*:

> I did not have any regret or guilt about the way in which *Seitō* was brought to an end. This was mainly because I felt that I had fulfilled my duty to *Seitō*, devoting myself to it for five years.[384]

The demise of *Seitō* marked a turning point in Hiratsuka's life, and in her autobiography she stated that the end of *Seitō*, when she was 30 years old, 'ended my youth'.[385]

Conclusion

It is indisputable that Hiratsuka helped raise the confidence of other women by creating and editing *Seitō*.[386] In this regard, she made an enduring contribution to raising the quality of women's writing. Hiratsuka's initial aims for *Seitō* had been to improve women's literature and recruit more talented female writers. She fulfilled those aims. A handful of its writers (such as Nogami Yaeko and Okamaoto Kanoko) later became quite eminent.[387] *Seitō* also promoted women's writing, and some of its short stories pioneered the expression of women's experience.[388] Moreover, in the Seitō Society Hiratsuka united women with literary interests, who had formerly been isolated in male-dominated literary circles, creating an ideal place for women to discuss literature, exchange views and ideas, and comment on each other's work. Members of the Seitō Society became a close and intellectually self-sufficient women's literary network. How conscious Hiratsuka was of the record of the English Bluestocking Society is unclear, but the achievements of the Seitō Society resembled those of its English namesake.

---

[383] Hiratsuka, *Genshi*, vol. 2, p. 274.

[384] Hiratsuka, *Genshi*, vol. 3, p. 30.

[385] Hiratsuka, *Genshi*, vol. 2, p. 288.

[386] Kobayashi, *Hito to Shisō*, p. 6; Ide, 'Kaisetsu', pp. 9–10; Ide, *Seitō no Onnatachi*, pp. 17–8; Horiba, *Seitō no Jidai*, p. 3; Yamashita, *Nihon Josei Kaihō Shisō no Kigen*, p. 94.

[387] Tanaka (ed.), *Josei Kaihō Shisō*, pp. 198–9; Katō, *A History of Japanese Literature*, p. 298; Tanaka (ed.), *To Live and to Write*, pp. 147–52, 199–203; Lewell, *Modern Japanese Novelists*, pp. 310–5, 336–9.

[388] Ide, *Seitō no Onnatachi*, pp. 63–6.

Seitō, in being edited and controlled by women, contrasted sharply with earlier women's magazines, almost all of which were edited by men.[389] Prior to *Seitō*, *Sekai Fujin* (*Women of the World*) and *Fujin no Tomo* (*Women's Companion*) were edited by women, but even for these men had acted as editorial advisors.[390] Although Fukuda Hideko edited *Sekai Fujin*, she was greatly assisted by her male socialist friends, such as Sakai Toshihiko and Ishikawa Sanshirō.[391] The view that women were incapable of running a magazine by themselves was widely accepted by male and female writers. Before the initial issue of *Seitō*, many writers did not take the venture seriously, and Mozume Kazuko's brother stated that if *Seitō* managed to publish three issues it would be a miracle.[392] In the face of such pessimism and low expectations, *Seitō* lasted more than five years, while most earlier women's magazines had usually been discontinued after the first couple of issues.

Even so, we have seen that the Seitō Society and *Seitō* had some literary limitations. At that time Hiratsuka was largely indifferent to general political matters, and this indifference was shared by the great majority of other members. As Murakami Nobuhiko stated, *Seitō* was commonly apolitical.[393] For example, it was inaugurated soon after the judicial sentence in connection with the High Treason Incident, but it had nothing to say about that.[394] Hiratsuka called the incident '*harukana yosogoto*' ('a matter of no concern to her').[395] Her indifference to the event contrasted strikingly with the views of many other writers, like Ishikawa Takuboku, who were very shocked and showed this in their writing.[396] Similarly, Hiratsuka and other

---

[389] Miki, 'Meiji fujin zasshi no kiseki', p. 3.

[390] *Ibid.*, pp. 90–7; Itoya, *Josei Kaihō no Senkusha*, pp. 175–6. *Fujin no Tomo* (*Women's Companion*) was initially called *Katei no Tomo* (*Friends of the Home*), and was launched in 1903. The name was changed to *Fujin no Tomo* in 1908. It was published by Hani Motoko, and aimed to improve women's lives, providing practical advice.

[391] Murata, *Fukuda Hideko*, pp. 141–51. Ishikawa Sanshirō was a socialist who worked for the newspaper *Yorozu Chōhō* as a reporter before joining the Heiminsha. He contributed to the *Heimin Shinbun* (*Commoners' Newspaper*), and helped launch a Christian-socialist magazine *Shin Kigen* (*New Era*).

[392] Hiratsuka, *Genshi*, vol. 1, p. 342.

[393] Murakami Nobuhiko, *Meiji Joseishi*, vol. 4 (1971), p. 422.

[394] Suzuki, *Joseishi o Hiraku*, vol. 1, p. 48.

[395] Cited in Yoneda Sayoko, 'Kaisetsu', in Hiratsuka Raichō (ed. by Kobayashi Tomie & Yoneda Sayoko), *Hiratsuka Raichō Hyōronshū* (1987), p. 334.

[396] Hiraide Hizuru, 'Takuboku to Osamu to Shūsui to', *Kokubungaku*, 9:15 (December, 1964), p. 134; Yoneda, 'Jidai o ikinuku', p. 62. Ishikawa Takuboku (1886–1912), a

Seitō women had little interest in World War I.[397] Only one anti-war essay appeared in *Seitō*.[398]

Almost all the works in *Seitō* have been forgotten now, and they have more historical than enduring literary value. Only two pieces achieve a mention in most critical studies of Japanese literature: Yosano's 'Sozorogoto' and Hiratsuka's 'Genshi josei wa taiyō de atta'. This was partly because works published in *Seitō* were usually very short due to limitations of space, and partly because they were socially constrained, and not always of high literary quality. Hiratsuka excused this by stating that *Seitō* came into the limelight quickly, and did not have time to develop its literary potential.[399]

It is important to compare the Seitō Society with its rival the Shin Shin Fujinkai (Real New Women's Association), so as to understand the diversity of contemporary women's movements. The Seitō Society's magazine changed direction in 1913, and began to deal more with women's social and political problems. This contrasted with the Real New Women's Association's magazine, the *Real New Women*, which dealt with women's social problems from the start.[400] Hiratsuka became keen to develop discussion about aspects of women's emancipation, and published some special issues on this theme. As she also wanted to introduce Ellen Key and other feminists like Olive Schreiner, she published translations of their work in *Seitō* and also created space in *Seitō* to develop discussion of their views.[401] However, most other members were more interested in women's literature than feminist theories and women's issues, and essays on such issues were always a minor concern.[402] By contrast *Real New Women*'s main subjects were always women's social issues.[403]

The women's issues which *Seitō* discussed were very circumscribed. They were personal family problems (separation, divorce, cohabitation and husband's adultery) common to middle and upper-middle class women, largely social rather than political matters. *Seitō* women

---

poet and novelist, was known for his *tanka* poems. He became a socialist after the High Treason Incident.

[397] Horiba, *Seitō no Jidai*, pp. 219–20.

[398] Saiga Koto, 'Senka', *Seitō*, 5:10 (November, 1915), pp. 88–103.

[399] Cited in Horiba Kiyoko, 'Kaisetsu', in Horiba (ed.), *Seitō Josei Kaihō Ronshū*, p. 366.

[400] Okano, 'Kaisetsu', p. 7; Nishikawa, *Heiminsha no Onna*, pp. 343–48.

[401] Tanaka (ed.), *Josei Kaihō no Shisō*, pp. 192–3.

[402] Ide, 'Kaisetsu', p. 11.

[403] Nishikawa, *Heiminsha no Onna*, pp. 368–71; Okano, 'Kaisetsu', p. 7.

took little interest in lower-status women. This differed from contributors to *Real New Women*, who wrote many stories involving working-class women's experience.[404] Unlike Hiratsuka, Nishikawa Fumiko, the editor of *Real New Women*, believed that women's emancipation must include such women and encouraged their participation in political activities. As Yamakawa Kikue pointed out:

> The women's movement which the Seitō Society promoted did not reflect the heart-rending cries of needy and destitute women for equal opportunities in education and employment, but reflected upper-middle class women's leisurely calls for equal opportunities to live a more pleasurable life.[405]

Yamakawa's views were shared by some women's historians like Inoue Kiyoshi and Yamazaki Tomoko.[406] Inoue, a Marxist historian, thought the Seitō Society 'bourgeois' and had a correspondingly low opinion of it. He evaluated the socialist Fukuda Hideko more highly than Hiratsuka.[407] Similarly, Yamazaki Tomoko argued that the Seitō Society formed part of elite women's history.[408] As these historians pointed out, the 'bourgeois' orientation of the Seitō Society was one of its weakest points.

The work which the Seitō Society engaged in was also much narrower than that of the Real New Women's Association. The latter laid down a wider range of goals to improve women's status: promotion of female job opportunities; abolition of the sexual division of labour; advocacy of women's self-awareness, independence and freedom; realization of equality of the sexes; refusal to accept male-centred principles; establishment of women's suffrage; the formation of a peaceful society in which men and women compensate for each other's weaknesses; and the establishment of women's clubs and the extension of women's activities.[409] By comparison, the Seitō Society

---

[404] Nishikawa, *Heiminsha no Onna*, pp. 369–71.

[405] Yamakawa Kikue, 'Shin Fujin Kyōkai to Sekirankai', *Taiyō* (July, 1921), reprinted in Yamakawa Kikue (ed. by Suzuki Yūko), *Yamakawa Kikue Josei Kaihō Ronshū*, vol. 2 (1984), p. 11.

[406] Inoue, *Nihon Joseishi*, p. 243; Yamazaki Tomoko, *Sandakan Hachiban Shōkan: Teihen Joseishi Joshō* (1972), pp. 9–10.

[407] Inoue, *Nihon Joseishi*, pp. 230–1, 243.

[408] Yamazaki, *Sandakan Hachiban Shōkan*, p. 9.

[409] Nishikawa, *Heiminsha no Onna*, pp. 378–84. The Real New Women's Association did not restrict its interest to women's issues, but extended to more general causes including charity and relief work. It organised meetings and raised funds for the

organised speech meetings with female speakers such as Iwano Kiyoko and Itō Noe, and founded a small study group to discuss women's issues in Japan.[410] In the Real New Women's Association such discussion developed into political action, like the suffrage campaign.[411] But the Seitō Society's feminist discussion went no further than theoretical dispute in print. It never developed into political action, such as presenting petitions to Parliament or organising demonstrations. It seems very quiescent compared to such organisations as the Pankhursts' Women's Social and Political Union, or the Real New Women's Association. Unlike the latter, the Seitō Society did not demand legal reform, and no reference to the franchise was made.[412]

The publication of *Seitō*, between 1911 and 1916, coincided with the activities of the women's movement in Britain, led by the Pankhursts, whose activities had a great impact on the development of women's movements in other countries.[413] The Japan-British Exhibition was held at Shepherds Bush in London in 1910, and many journalists in Japan were sent to Britain to report on the event.[414] They witnessed many women's demonstrations organised by the Pankhursts.[415] As male journalists were intrigued by the English women's agitation,

---

relief of famines in the Hokkaidō and Tōhoku areas, and when the Great Kantō Earthquake occurred in 1923, it immediately set up a women's action group to do relief work.

[410] Hiratsuka, *Genshi*, vol. 2, pp. 98–9.

[411] Okano, 'Kaisetsu', p. 13. Apart from its suffrage campaigns, the Real New Women's Association also founded an agency which provided information about job vacancies, family problems, and women's health, and a hostel for working women. It also ran courses on legal issues.

[412] Yamakawa, 'Shin Fujin Kyōkai to Sekirankai', p. 11.

[413] Christine Bolt, *The Women's Movements in the United States and Britain from the 1790s to the 1920s* (Hemel Hempstead, 1993), p. 202.

[414] Ayako Hotta-Lister, 'The Japan-British Exhibition of 1910: the Japanese organizers', in Ian Nish (ed.), *Britain & Japan: Biographical Portraits* (1994), pp. 146–57; 'Nichiei hakurankai, kyō Rondon ni kaijō', *Tokyo Asahi Shinbun* (14 May, 1910); 'Celebrated for the first time outside Japan: The festival of the rice harvest, at the Anglo-Japanese Exhibition', *The Illustrated London News* (27 August, 1910); 'Hairy Ainos [sic] before the King and the Queen: a unique presentation', *The Illustrated London News* (13 August, 1910); 'The Japan-British Exhibition', *The Times* (14 May, 1910); 'The Japan-British Exhibition, the Women's Congress', *The Times* (21 May, 1910); 'Eikōshitsu no mochū nimo kakawarazu kaikai sareru', *Jiji Shinpō* (14 May, 1910); 'Nyūjōsha roppyaku-man, yosō ijō no seikyō no uchi ni heikai', *Kokumin Shinbun* (30 October, 1910); 'Japan in London', *The Times* (19 July, 1910); 'Japanese journalists in London', *The Times* (13 May, 1910).

[415] Horiba, *Seitō no Jidai*, pp. 50–1; *Osaka Mainichi Shinbun* (4–5 July, 1910); *Tokyo Asahi Shinbun* (1–3 August, 1910).

which was alien to them, they interviewed some English feminists
and wrote detailed accounts. As a result, in 1910 a series of articles,
reporting on suffrage demonstrations led by the Pankhursts, appeared
in such Japanese newspapers as *Osaka Mainichi Shinbun* and *Tokyo
Asahi Shinbun*.[416] The *Real New Women* swam with this current, and
published such news, much like its predecessor, *Sekai Fujin* (*Women of
the World*).[417] By contrast *Seitō* never discussed or even mentioned the
British women's movement.

This contrast between *Seitō* and *Real New Women* seems to have
stemmed from differences in their editors' characters and views on
women's emancipation. Nishikawa, the editor of *Real New Women*,
was an activist rather than a theorist, and believed that the women's
movement ought to be realistic and practical.[418] She was open-minded
and keen to learn tactics and strategy from women's movements in
the west, being willing to adopt them herself. However, when Hiratsuka
later wrote of these years, she criticised the priorities of the western
women's movement:

> The women's movement in Europe and America demanded women's
> legal, political, economic and occupational rights and freedom from
> the very beginning, which I disapproved of. This was because I felt
> that these demands were external, partial and unessential. I intently
> advocated the need for women's spiritual freedom and independence
> through my activities in the Seitō Society. I felt that the first thing
> women ought to do was to appreciate themselves, to become aware
> of their dignity and emancipate themselves. They had to achieve free-
> dom and independence of spirit in their internal lives before demand-
> ing rights to freedom and independence in their external lives. In other
> words, my effort in my Seitō days was confined to the narrow limits
> of Japanese women's self-revolution and self-change. This was a kind
> of spiritual or religious movement, but it did not reach the stage of
> being a social movement.[419]

Similar comments had been made in Hiratsuka's *Seitō* manifesto,
'Genshi josei wa taiyō de atta'. She made it clear there that achiev-

---

[416] Kikuchi Yūhō, 'Katei shisō no fukkatsu', *Osaka Mainichi Shinbun* (4–5 July,
1910); Hasegawa Nyozekan, 'Rokugatsu jūhachinichi no ichiman yūyo no suffragettes
no daigyōretsu', *Tokyo Asahi Shinbun* (1–3 August, 1910).

[417] Okano, 'Kaisetsu', p. 10.

[418] Nishikawa, *Heiminsha no Onna*, p. 383. A short biographical sketch of Nishikawa
Fumiko is given in Appendix 1.

[419] Hiratsuka Raichō, 'Shakai kaizō ni taisuru fujin no shimei: *Josei Domei* sōkan
no ji ni kaete', *Josei Domei*, 1 (October, 1920), p. 3.

ing women's emancipation, including suffrage, was not the main matter to be settled:

> Women's freedom and emancipation! The voice of women's freedom
> and emancipation reached our ears quite a while ago . . . I wonder
> whether the meanings of freedom and emancipation have been greatly
> misunderstood. There are all kinds of women's issues involved in
> women's emancipation. Even if women escaped from external pres-
> sure and restrictions, were given so-called higher education, were given
> the opportunity to find employment, were given suffrage, and given
> the opportunity to become independent from their parents and hus-
> bands and to lead independent lives, they would still not be fully eman-
> cipated. These conditions may help to create better opportunities and
> circumstances for women to attain true emancipation. However, to me
> these are nothing but temporary expedients and measures. They are
> neither aims nor ideals. What then is women's emancipation in the
> real sense, which I wish to achieve? It is nothing less than to make
> women bring their ability into full play. In order to achieve this, we
> must first remove everything which will obstruct their development.[420]

Although a group of men tried to persuade Hiratsuka at the time of
Seitō to take up the cause of female suffrage,[421] she gave the following account of why she did not:

> I must admit that I was not at all interested in the women's suffrage
> issue during my Seitō period. This was because my immediate goal
> then was completely to remove 'feudalistic' ideas and feelings rooted
> in women's minds. In order to do this, I felt that it would be more
> logical to begin my work by altering women's internal lives. Therefore
> I had no intention of working for women's suffrage at that time.[422]

Hiratsuka held to this view throughout her involvement with Seitō.
She also gave another reason for not developing it into a wider
movement:

> The women's circles at that time did not have their eyes open to the
> possibility of a social movement. It was certain that Japanese women
> had not made the fundamental preparations required to launch such
> a movement. The fundamental and initial step required for women
> was the establishment of their identity. As Japanese women at that
> time hardly had their own identities, I felt that wakening them to their

---

[420] Hiratsuka, 'Genshi josei wa taiyō de atta', p. 47.
[421] Hiratsuka Raichō, 'Waga kuni ni okeru fujin mondai no sekaiteki ichi', in
Hiratsuka, Chosakushū, vol. 1, pp. 409–10.
[422] Hiratsuka, Genshi, vol. 3, pp. 47–8.

selfhood and establishing such identities ought to be achieved before
everything else for women.[423]

As Hiratsuka later wrote, in its emphasis upon creating female
confidence and personal expression, the Seitō Society had some characteristics in common with the very early stages of the women's
movements in western countries. It did not compare with the contemporary British women's movement led by the Pankhursts, but
despite modest aims it received much publicity, partly because of
alleged scandals involving its members. Hiratsuka later gave her own
assessment of the Seitō Society's position in the Japanese women's
movement:

> It need scarcely be said that my effort to improve women's status in
> my Seitō days was only made through my writing. This might be
> classed as pertaining to a very early stage of the women's movement,
> and could be described in a few words as saying that 'Women are
> also human beings'. It was no more than the first voice crying for
> women's awakening.[424]

In this respect the Seitō Society provided a voice for women, albeit
a literary one. Its magazine gave members and readers courage to
express their feelings and to believe that they might have literary
merit. It served as a vehicle to promote female talent and self-awareness, increased readers' awareness of some social issues, and created
an ideal opportunity to discuss women's causes.[425] It contributed
important ideas to later feminists, and under some definitions may
be viewed as a 'feminist' development which laid much groundwork
in the Japanese women's movement. Seitō's issues on 'new women'
also sparked the 'new women boom', which spread across other magazines and newspapers, making both male and female editors realise
the significance of women's social and political issues.[426] Extensive
discussions about many women's concerns such as marital problems,
divorce, birth control and abortion began to appear elsewhere, fol-

---

[423] Hiratsuka, 'Shakai kaizō ni taisuru fujin no shimei', p. 3.
[424] Ibid., p. 3.
[425] Hiratsuka Raichō, 'Fujin undō gojū-nen o kaerimite', Fujin Kōron (November,
1961), reprinted in Hiratsuka, Chosakushū, vol. 7, pp. 393–4; Hiratsuka Raichō,
'Seitōsha no koto', Taiyō (June, 1927), reprinted in Hiratsuka, Chosakushū, vol. 4,
pp. 303–4.
[426] Horiba, Seitō no Jidai, pp. 171–80; Tanaka (ed.), Josei Kaihō no Shisō, pp. 200–3;
Hiratsuka Raichō, 'Seitōsha wa donna yakume o shita deshō', in Hiratsuka, Chosakushū,
vol. 4, pp. 332–3.

lowing the lead of *Seitō*.[427] Some other women's magazines were inaugurated under the influence of *Seitō*, *Shin Shin Fujin* (*The Real New
Women*) being a good example.[428] It took another five years for
Hiratsuka to realise the necessity for a women's political reform
movement which encompassed suffrage, but Seitō was an important
stepping stone in the passage of both her and Japanese women to
that state of awareness.[429]

---

[427] Ide, 'Kaisetsu', p. 15; Ide, *Seitō no Onnatachi*, pp. 147–61; Horiba, *Seitō no Jidai*, pp. 171–4.
[428] *Ibid.*, pp. 160–1, 251; Matsuda, *Fujin Kōron no 50-nen*, pp. 7–10.
[429] Hiratsuka, *Genshi*, vol. 3, pp. 47–8.

CHAPTER FIVE

CONTROVERSY OVER MOTHERHOOD

Hiratsuka Raichō as a Mother

After *Seitō*, Hiratsuka devoted herself to her family for a while.[1] She gave birth to her daughter Akemi in December 1915 and to her son Atsubumi in September 1917. Most of her time was taken up with child-rearing, domestic work, and the nursing of Okumura, who was still suffering from tuberculosis.[2] In addition, she earned money by writing articles on women's issues for prestigious magazines such as *Chūō Kōron* to support her family. She had no time to become further involved with women's causes, and her career as a spokeswoman was suspended.

The only noticeable radical action she took over this period was to enter her two children in her family register rather than Okumura's. Hiratsuka had not married Okumura. She asked her parents to let her go through the official procedure of having her name removed from their family register, to establish a separate branch, creating her own register in which she was head of family.[3] She had her children entered in her own register. Hiratsuka's aim in establishing her own family register was to demonstrate her hostility to the *ie* system. Okumura did not interfere. Hiratsuka retained her position as an unmarried mother until August 1941, when she married Okumura.[4]

---

[1] Hiratsuka Raichō, 'Haha to narite', *Chūō Kōron* (February, 1916), reprinted in Hiratsuka, *Chosakushū*, vol. 2, pp. 143–4. This article was also reprinted in Hiratsuka, *Josei no Kotoba* (1926), and Hiratsuka, *Gendai no Danjo e* (1917).

[2] Hiratsuka Raichō, 'Haha to shite no ichinenkan', *Fujin Kōron* (May, 1917), reprinted in Hiratsuka, *Chosakushū*, vol. 2, pp. 266–7. This article was also reprinted in Hiratsuka, *Gendai no Danjo e* (1917).

[3] Hiratsuka, *Genshi*, vol. 2, pp. 260–1.

[4] Hiratsuka later found that her two children had been recorded as *shiseiji* (illegitimate), because she had had their names entered in her register rather than Okumura's. Okumura wrote in his autobiography that he would have preferred to marry Hiratsuka and have their children entered in his register. See Hiratsuka, *Genshi*, vol. 4, pp. 37–40; Kobayashi, *Hito to Shisō*, pp. 151, 207–8; Okumura, *Meguriai*, p. 178.

Hiratsuka's personal experiences as mother, nurse of a sick partner and breadwinner helped her to mature beyond her *Seitō* days. Her restricted financial circumstances, and the difficulty of combining motherhood and writing, altered the personal and sometimes self-absorbed feminist ideas of her *Seitō* days into a view that was more aware of women's problems, one that had a direct influence upon her later feminist activity.

Hiratsuka now rediscovered the importance of Ellen Key's teaching of *bosei hogo* (the protection of motherhood), which was manifested especially in her *Love and Marriage*.[5] In her *Seitō* days, Hiratsuka was fascinated by Key's works and translated some of them, such as *Love and Marriage* (which appeared in *Seitō*).[6] However, she later admitted that she did not fully appreciate Key's views until she became a mother.[7] In *Love and Marriage* Key advocated women's freedom of love and their rights as mothers. According to Key, the most important role for human beings was reproduction, and creating new life and child-rearing were women's main missions in life.[8] She also stated that a mother's place was at home and she disapproved of industrial capitalism and the ways in which women were driven from home as low-wage workers and made to compete with men. She advocated the improvement of working conditions for women and related social reforms. Key was particularly concerned about the conditions of working mothers with small children.[9] She argued that mothers' absence from home harmed children who would be the future of society. She was also convinced that most women could not combine domestic lives with other careers, and suggested that mothers should devote themselves to child-rearing. The state should appreciate these roles and provide mothers with financial assistance, since motherhood was the source of all social virtue.

Hiratsuka found it extremely hard to combine child-rearing with a writing career and admired Key's work.[10] She began to realise the

---

[5] Hiratsuka, *Genshi*, vol. 3, pp. 30–1.
[6] Maruoka Hideko, *Fujin Shisō Keiseishi Nōto*, vol. 1 (1975), p. 108.
[7] Hiratsuka, *Genshi*, vol. 3, pp. 30–1.
[8] Shimada Setsuko, 'Ellen Key no bosei shugi', in Ichibangase Yasuko (ed.), *Nyūmon Josei Kaihōron* (1975), pp. 123–5; Nagahata Michiko, 'Bosei to sei o mitsumete', in Yamakawa Kikue Seitan 100-nen o Kenensuru Kai (ed.), *Gendai Feminizumu to Yamakawa Kikue* (1990), pp. 197–9; Kobayashi, *Hito to Shisō*, p. 159.
[9] Ellen Key (trans. by Harada Minoru), *Renai to Kekkon*, 2 vols (1930–1), vol. 1, pp. 75–124; Nagahata, 'Bosei to sei o mitsumete', pp. 197–9.
[10] Suzuki Yūko, *Joseishi o Hiraku*, vol. 1 (1989), pp. 50–1; Nishikawa Yūko, 'Hitotsu

significance of the protection of motherhood and later made the following remarks:

> If women want to achieve real freedom and independence, then rights for mothers should first be firmly established. I don't really think women's freedom and independence can ever exist in society unless the rights of mothers are guaranteed.[11]

Okumura's recovery from tuberculosis in 1918 freed her from nursing him, and the employment of a housemaid provided more time for Hiratsuka to reflect upon these issues.[12] Hiratsuka and Yosano developed a heated debate over the rights and wrongs of the state protecting motherhood. Yamakawa Kikue and Yamada Waka also later participated in this debate.[13] The argument became later known as the *bosei hogo ronsō* (controversy over the protection of motherhood), and it intensified between 1918 and 1919.[14] The four women who participated were all different in age, social status, politics and social views. Their articles were published in leading magazines, such as *Taiyō* (*Sun*) and *Fujin Kōron* (*Women's Review*).[15]

Leading Japanese women's history books in the decade after the war, including Inoue Kiyoshi's *Nihon Joseishi*, made no mention of this debate, and ignored the significant part which it played in the Japanese women's movement.[16] According to the women's historian,

---

no keifu—Hiratsuka Raichō, Takamure Itsue, Ishimure Michiko', in Wakita Haruko (ed.), *Bosei o Tou: Rekishiteki Hensen*, vol. 2 (1985), p. 164.

[11] Hiratsuka, *Genshi*, vol. 3, p. 31.

[12] *Ibid.*, pp. 30–2.

[13] Kōuchi Nobuko, 'Kaidai', in Kōuchi Nobuko (ed.), *Shiryō: Bosei Hogo Ronsō* (1984), pp. 302–13.

[14] *Ibid.*, pp. 289–90.

[15] *Ibid.*, pp. 323–33; Yamashita, *Nihon Josei Kaihō Shisō no Kigen*, pp. 112–4; Matsuda Fumiko (ed.), *Fujin Kōron no 50-nen* (1965), pp. 27–8; Tanaka (ed.), *Josei Kaihō no Shisō*, pp. 202–3. Yosano, Hiratsuka, Yamakawa and Yamada were extremely productive, and between February 1918 and June 1919 they wrote about 120 articles on women's issues, 47 of which explicitly dealt with the protection of motherhood. See also Appendix 7.

[16] One of the first women's historians to pay special attention to the subject was Takamure Itsue. She gave a good account of Hiratsuka's *bosei shugi* in her *Josei no Rekishi* (*Women's History*). Takamure discussed Ellen Key's theories, and her advocacy of state payments to mothers. See Takamure, *Josei no Rekishi*, vol. 2, pp. 291–8. Another women's historian who took early notice of the debate was Tatewaki Sadayo. In her book *Nihon no Fujin* (*Japanese Women*) she outlined its role in the women's movement. See Tatewaki, *Nihon no Fujin*, pp. 33–6. Tatewaki's reference to it was taken up by Kōuchi Nobuko, who carried out extensive research on the subject. She published a compilation of the most significant articles by the four women. See Kōuchi (ed.), *Shiryō: Bosei Hogo Ronsō* (1984). See also Maruoka, *Fujin*

Kano Mikiyo, the term, '*bosei hogo*' first appeared in Japan in 1916.[17] The first person to use it is believed to have been Yamada Waka's husband, Yamada Kakichi.[18] He had close associations with Ichikawa and Hiratsuka, taught them English, and read Key's works with them.[19] He also introduced them to the ideas of the German association 'Bund für Mutterschutz' (The Motherhood Protection League, founded in 1905), which was directly influenced by Key.[20] He wrote an article on this German association for a magazine called *Joō* (*Queen*), which was published as 'Bosei Hogo Dōmei ni tsuite' ('On the Motherhood Protection League') in August 1916.[21] This article was the first to introduce the 'Bund für Mutterschutz' to Japanese readers.[22] Yamada discussed its main objectives, which were to protect

---

Shisō Keiseishi Nōto, vol. 1, pp. 105–27; Kōuchi Nobuko, 'Bosei hogo ronsō no rekishiteki igi: ronsō kara undō e no tsunagari', *Rekishi Hyōron*, 195 (November, 1966), pp. 28–41; Kōuchi, 'Kaidai', pp. 289–321; Sakurai Kinue, *Bosei Hogo Undōshi* (1987), pp. 48–51; Tsukamoto Shūko, 'Yosano Akiko, Hiratsuka Raichō, Yamakawa Kikue no bosei hogo ronsō', in Ichibangase Yasuko (ed.), *Nyūmon Josei Kaihōron* (1975), pp. 223–55; Nishikawa, 'Hitotsu no keifu', pp. 162–73; Suzuki, *Joseishi o Hiraku*, vol. 1, pp. 49–67; Murakami Yasuko, 'Bosei hogo ronsō to gendai', in Gurūpu Bosei Kaidoku Kōza (ed.), *Bosei o Kaidokusuru* (1991), pp. 209–25; Nagahata, 'Bosei to sei o mitsumete', pp. 199–205.

In English, see Barbara Molony, 'Equality versus difference: the Japanese debate over 'motherhood protection', 1915–50', in Janet Hunter (ed.), *Japanese Women Working* (London, 1993), pp. 122–48; Barbara Molony, 'State and women in modern Japan: feminist discourses in the Meiji and Taishō eras', in Janet Hunter (ed.), *Japan: State and People in the Twentieth Century* (London, 1999), pp. 38–9; Laurel Rasplica Rodd, 'Yosano Akiko and the Taishō debate over the 'New Women', in Gail Lee Bernstein (ed.), *Recreating Japanese Women, 1600–1945* (Berkeley, 1991), pp. 189–98; Mackie, *Creating Socialist Women in Japan*, pp. 86–94. Rodd's article only briefly mentioned that the debate was influenced by western feminists like Schreiner and Key, and did not place it within an international framework. By contrast, Molony focused on historical aspects, although she gave an excellent overview of changes in the term 'bosei hogo', and the legal reforms affecting motherhood in Japan between 1915 and 1950.

[17] Kano Mikiyo, 'Bosei no tanjō to Tennōsei', in Ehara Yumiko *et al.* (eds), *Bosei* (1995), pp. 56–7.

[18] Yamada Kakichi was educated in America, had an aptitude for languages, and was well acquainted with western feminist theories. Although he was less known than his wife, he had rescued Waka from prostitution in America, and had helped educate her. He also recommended that she join the Seitō Society.

[19] Hiratsuka, *Genshi*, vol. 2, pp. 169–74; Ichikawa, *Jiden: Senzen Hen*, pp. 37–8; Yamazaki Tomoko, *Ameyuki-san no Uta: Yamada Waka no Suki Naru Shogai* (1978, 1991 edn), pp. 31–2.

[20] Kano, 'Bosei no tanjō', p. 57.

[21] Yamada Kakichi, 'Bosei Hogo Dōmei ni tsuite', *Joō*, 8 (August, 1916), reprinted in Kōuchi (ed.), *Shiryō*, pp. 247–52.

[22] Kano, 'Bosei', p. 57; Ōhinata Masami, 'Bosei gainen o meguru genjō to sono mondaiten', in Ehara *et al.* (eds), *Bosei*, pp. 29–30.

mothers and children from financial crises and moral danger, to give both financial protection and general support, including mothers of illegitimate children, and to reform sexual morals.[23] Yamada also discussed the German League's activities.

In this article he first translated the German word 'Mutterschutz' (a German word for the Swedish 'moderskap', translated as 'motherhood' in English) into a new Japanese expression, '*bosei*'.[24] He translated the 'Bund für Mutterschutz' into '*Bosei Hogo Dōmei*' (the Motherhood Protection League).[25] The new term's usage was initially very limited in Japan. Yosano Akiko contributed most to its wider usage.[26] Yosano used *bosei* in the title of her article, 'Bosei henchō o haisu' ('I refuse to over-emphasise the significance of motherhood'), and in her text.[27] The term then came into wider use, and by early 1918 had become established, older expressions like '*botai*' having died out by late 1917.[28]

The Context of the Protection of Motherhood Debate

This controversy over motherhood was closely related to the growing problems of working women with children at that time. With the advance of large-scale industries and production during and after the Russo-Japanese War (1904–1905), the scope of women's work was much extended.[29] Besides the former occupations which women had been engaged in—factory and agricultural work, elementary school teaching, midwifery, nursing, journalism and so on—they now began to take up new occupations, like dentists, clerks in banks and insurance

---

[23] Yamada, 'Bosei Hogo Dōmei', pp. 248–52.

[24] Kano, 'Bosei no tanjō', p. 57; Ōhinata, 'Bosei gainen o meguru genjō to sono mondaiten', p. 29. Other Japanese expressions such as '*botai*' and '*boken*' were used by Yamada Waka, Hiratsuka and Yamakawa Kikue before 1916. Yamada's wife had frequently used '*botai*' in her Japanese translations from Ellen Key's *The Century of the Child* (translated as *Jidō no Seiki*), which appeared in *Seitō*. Both Hiratsuka and Yamakawa Kikue translated Ellen Key's *The Renaissance of Motherhood* as *Boken no Fukkatsu*.

[25] Yamada, 'Bosei Hogo Dōmei', pp. 247–52.

[26] Kano, 'Bosei no tanjō', pp. 57–8.

[27] Yosano Akiko, 'Bosei henchō o haisu', *Taiyō*, 22:2 (February, 1916), reprinted in Kōuchi (ed.), *Shiryō*, pp. 28–38.

[28] Ehara Yumiko, 'Ribu no shuchō to boseikan', in Gurūpu Bosei Kaidoku Kōza (ed.), *Bosei o Kaidokusuru* (1991, 1992 edn), pp. 197–9.

[29] Sakurai, *Bosei Hogo Undōshi*, p. 48; Hayashi *et al.* (eds), *Nihon Joseishi*, p. 232; Sōgō Joseishi Kenkyūkai (ed.), *Bunka to Shisō*, p. 217.

companies, employees in post offices and railway companies, shop
assistants, waitresses and typists.[30] The number of female workers,
many of them middle-class, increased dramatically.[31] There were a
number of reasons for this. The engagement of the main European
powers in World War I was in many ways Japan's economic opportunity, allowing it to begin the international supply of many goods
and services hitherto monopolised by the west.[32] The economy moved
increasingly from light industry to heavy manufacturing; the pre-war
depression lifted as the war started, and war also brought growth in
the textile industries.[33] Increased demand for money and state financing
associated with war, produced considerable inflation. At the same
time, rising taxation began to threaten the standard of living of many,
including members of the middle class.[34] As a result, many middle-
class women had to work to assist family budgets, although such
work was not usually in the factories associated with Japanese indus-
trialization. Subjects relating to women's work, in a growing number of occupations, became frequent topics in public discussion.

During World War I the term 'shokugyō fujin' (working women)
began to be widely used. The numbers of these who were married
with children also increased.[35] These changes brought many problems
with them. There was the difficulty of combining work and married
life, especially during pregnancy, childbirth and child-rearing. This
problem beset almost all young married women in employment
regardless of their social background and occupation. There was no
state maternity support for them.[36] Heavily pregnant women often
worked right through until childbirth, and had to return to work
without much convalescence. Very few private or public childcare
facilities existed to look after working women's children.[37] Mothers
had to make their own private arrangements, often relying on parents,
relatives and friends. Babies born to working mothers were reported
to have much higher mortality rates than those whose mothers stayed

---

[30] Murakami Nobuhiko, *Taishō-ki no Shokugyō Fujin* (1983), p. 11.
[31] Hayashi *et al.* (eds), *Nihon Joseishi*, pp. 232–3; Yoneda, *Kindai Nihon Joseishi*,
vol. 1, p. 146.
[32] Esashi Akiko & Ide Fumiko, *Taishō Demokurashii to Josei* (1977), pp. 56–7.
[33] Tatewaki, *Nihon no Fujin*, pp. 39–40.
[34] Hayashi *et al.* (eds), *Nihon Joseishi*, p. 232.
[35] *Ibid.*, p. 238.
[36] Sakurai, *Bosei Hogo Undōshi*, pp. 39–41.
[37] Yoneda, *Kindai Nihon Joseishi*, vol. 1, pp. 112–3.

at home.[38] As in many western countries, the Japanese public began to take an increasing interest in women's working conditions, and to discuss reasons for high levels of child mortality.[39] Integral to this debate was the appalling condition of some female workers, especially in the textile sector, who were forced to endure long hours of night and shift work, in unhygienic working conditions which adversely affected their health.[40] Their lack of childcare facilities aggravated infant and child mortality. Against this background, with Japanese wartime mobilization and production increasingly reliant on an expanded proletariat, but with concerns for the health of future soldiers being expressed, concern was focused upon the health of mothers, potential mothers and children. The need to build day nurseries was stressed, to enable mothers to go out to work without detrimental social effects.[41] Women's work was often accepted by the public, but steps were advocated to mitigate the likely consequences for working women.

Early Debate: Yosano versus Hiratsuka

In this context, the debate over the protection of motherhood developed between the four protagonists discussed here. They expressed different perspectives which became the main source of political discussion at the time. Ellen Key's writing had a great impact and her name often appeared in the debates.[42] Most women's history books state that this debate dated from 1918, with Yosano Akiko's 'Joshi no tetteishita dokuritsu' ('Women's complete independence'), in the March 1918 issue of *Fujin Kōron (Women's Review)*.[43] It is also often

---

[38] Hayashi *et al.* (eds), *Nihon Joseishi*, p. 238.

[39] Matsuda (ed.), *Fujin Kōron no 50-nen*, p. 27.

[40] Yamashita, *Nihon Josei Kaihō Shisō no Kigen*, p. 115; Sievers, *Flowers in Salt*, pp. 77–8; Tsurumi, *Factory Girls*, pp. 85–9; Janet Hunter, 'Textile factories, tuberculosis and the quality of life in industrializing Japan', in Hunter (ed.), *Japanese Women Working*, pp. 71–89; Mackie, *Creating Socialist Women in Japan*, pp. 75–6; Barbara Molony, 'Activism among women in the Taishō cotton textile industry', in Bernstein (ed.), *Recreating Japanese Women, 1600–1945*, pp. 231–3.

[41] Yoneda, *Kindai Nihon Joseishi*, vol. 1, pp. 112–3.

[42] The first English translation of Key's *Love and Marriage* appeared in America in 1911. Translations of some of Key's writings appeared in *Seitō*, and in 1917 *Love and Marriage* was translated by Harada Minoru. Nagahata, 'Bosei to sei o mitsumete', p. 199; Yamamoto, *Yama no Ugoku Hi Kitaru*, pp. 128–32.

[43] Hayashi *et al.* (eds), *Nihon Joseishi*, p. 237; Tanaka, *Josei Kaihō no Shisō*, pp. 203–4.

claimed that the debate was inaugurated in May 1918 by Hiratsuka's article 'Bosei hogo no shuchō was iraishugi ka' ('Is the request for the protection of motherhood a kind of parasitism?'), in response to Yosano.[44] However, some historians date the debate back to 1916, when Yosano wrote 'Bosei henchō o haisu' ('I refuse to over-emphasise the significance of motherhood').[45] This article appeared in the February 1916 issue of *Taiyō* (*Sun*).[46] It was severely attacked by Hiratsuka in her 'Bosei no shuchō ni tsuite Yosano Akiko-shi ni atau' ('I challenge Yosano Akiko's ideas on motherhood.'), in *Bunsho Sekai* (*The World of Writing*).[47]

Women's historians such as Suzuki Yūko and Kōuchi Nobuko suggest that after this article by Hiratsuka, the controversy lasted from 1916 to 1919, with the most heated argument taking place in 1918–19.[48] Suzuki and Kōuchi see two broad phases of argument. Suzuki compared the controversy to a boxing match, and called the first phase '*bosei hogo ronsō no daiichi raundo*' (the first round of the controversy) and the second, '*bosei hogo ronsō no daini raundo*' (the second round of the controversy).[49] Unlike many historians who have not acknowledged the first phase, both Kōuchi and Suzuki stress the significance of this initial period. Kōuchi wrote that

> The full-scale controversy over the protection of motherhood took place between 1918 and 1919. However, articles on women's causes written by the four women concerned between 1916 and 1918 strongly influenced the full-scale debate. It is no exaggeration to say that these preliminary articles embodied these women's original ideas on the protection of motherhood. These articles were the foundations of their later discussion of the pros and cons of the protection of motherhood, and therefore one cannot fully investigate this debate without giving full consideration to the articles written before 1918.[50]

---

[44] Tatewaki, *Nihon no Fujin*, p. 33; Yoneda, *Kindai Nihon Joseishi*, vol. 1, p. 143; Nishikawa, 'Hitotsu no keifu', p. 168.

[45] Suzuki, *Joseishi o Hiraku*, vol. 1, pp. 52–4; Kōuchi, 'Kaidai', pp. 289–90; Kano, 'Bosei', pp. 57–8; Murakami, 'Bosei hogo ronsō to gendai', pp. 209–11.

[46] Yosano Akiko, 'Bosei henchō o haisu', *Taiyō*, 22:2 (February, 1916), reprinted in Kōuchi (ed.), *Shiryō*, pp. 28–38.

[47] Hiratsuka Raichō, 'Bosei no shuchō ni tsuite Yosano Akiko-shi ni atau', *Bunsho Sekai*, 11:5 (May, 1916), reprinted in Kōuchi (ed.), *Shiryō*, pp. 38–45. This article was also reprinted in Hiratsuka's books, *Gendai no Danjo e* (1917), *Josei no Kotoba* (1926) and *Mushiro Josei no Sei o Reihai Seyo* (1977).

[48] Kōuchi, 'Kaidai', pp. 289–90.

[49] Suzuki, *Joseishi o Hiraku*, vol. 1, pp. 52–3.

[50] Kōuchi, 'Bosei hogo ronsō no rekishiteki igi', pp. 28–9.

In particular, two articles written before 1918 deserve special attention. They are Yosano's 'Bosei henchō o haisu' ('I refuse to over-emphasise the significance of motherhood'), and Hiratsuka's 'Bosei no shuchō ni tsuite Yosano Akiko-shi ni atau' ('I challenge Yosano Akiko's ideas on motherhood'). Yosano began her article with summaries of both Tolstoy and Ellen Key's teachings on women:

> Tolstoy taught us that women must devote themselves to their natural mission, which is to give birth to as many healthy, able-bodied children as possible, to bring them up and to educate them. Similarly, Ellen Key stated that an essential element in a woman's life is to become a mother.[51]

Yosano, who gave birth to eleven children, was content to accept the role of mother:

> I neither refuse to accept my role as a mother, nor do I regret it. I am quite satisfied with being a mother. I discovered a new side of myself after becoming a mother, which gave me a reasonable degree of satisfaction.[52]

However, Yosano, who was also known as a leading poet, essayist and women's commentator, could not wholly subscribe to Tolstoy and Ellen Key's views. She criticised their teachings and called them '*zettai bosei chūshinsetsu*' (the theory placing absolute trust in motherhood).[53] She questioned whether being a mother was the central element in a woman's life. Yosano's own answer to this was negative, and she challenged Tolstoy and Key on two grounds. She was convinced that there must be much else in life for women apart from motherhood.

> The fact that I became a mother has never been the most important factor in my life. Even after I became a mother, I continued to be somebody's wife, a friend to other people, a member of the Japanese nation, and a human being. I am a human being who is absorbed in my thoughts, composes *tanka* poems, writes articles, and is also engaged in many other different kinds of mental and physical work.[54]

Yosano applied her own example to other women, arguing that a person should take on as many roles as she or he can effectively

---

[51] Yosano, 'Bosei henchō o haisu', p. 28.
[52] *Ibid.*, p. 28.
[53] *Ibid.*, p. 33.
[54] *Ibid.*, p. 32.

carry out. She also criticised Ellen Key for assuming that mothers should take entire responsibility for their children, and for not acknowledging the crucial role played by fathers.[55] Yosano advocated significant paternal involvement in child-rearing:

> I have given birth to and brought up many children. Through my years of experience I sincerely feel that children grow up properly not only under the care of their mothers but also under the care of their fathers. I also feel that for parents to leave their children in the hands of wet nurses, maids, nursery teachers and foster parents is a sin. Tolstoy and Ellen Key only valued the important role mothers play in children's lives, and had no respect for fathers' roles towards children. Through my experience I realise that a father's love and his role in child-rearing and children's education is equally as important as a mother's.[56]

By introducing the concept of fatherhood as well as motherhood, Yosano sought to justify her view that it was erroneous to place absolute emphasis on motherhood.

Responding to Yosano, Hiratsuka wrote 'Bosei no shuchō ni tsuite Yosano Akiko-shi ni atau'.[57] Hiratsuka corrected Yosano's misunderstanding of Key's views. Hiratsuka objected to Yosano representing Key as thinking that being a mother was essential for women, and that women who failed to produce children were selfish.[58] Hiratsuka claimed that this summary of Key was entirely mistaken. She went on to justify Key's views, stating that Key's position was that whether women had children or not was entirely their own choice, although Key certainly did value motherhood and evaluated it positively.[59] Hiratsuka provided readers with a more accurate summary of Key's ideas. She also discussed why Key focused on motherhood rather than any other women's issue, and placed Key's contributions in the wider context of women's movements.

Yosano accepted Hiratsuka's criticism. In her article 'Hiratsuka Haruko-sama' ('Addressed to Hiratsuka Haruko'), she admitted that she had misunderstood Key's ideas.[60] The unprotesting attitude of

---

[55] *Ibid.*, p. 34.
[56] *Ibid.*, p. 36.
[57] Hiratsuka, 'Bosei no shuchō ni tsuite Yosano Akiko-shi ni atau', pp. 38–45.
[58] *Ibid.*, p. 39.
[59] *Ibid.*, p. 41.
[60] Yosano Akiko, 'Hiratsuka Haruko-sama', *Taiyō*, 22:7 (June, 1916), reprinted in Kōuchi (ed.), *Shiryō*, p. 50.

this article contrasts with the stubborn attitude seen in her later controversy with Hiratsuka, and her language lacked the vitality of her later writing. The strain of her life, the fatigue of combining child-rearing with being a writer, seems to have permeated this article. She even disclosed this weakness, and excused it by stating that her family circumstances made her unable to think reflectively or to read widely, resulting in her careless remarks about Key.[61] Such a humble response to Hiratsuka cut short this early debate.

It was not until early 1918 that a fuller controversy began, in the form of the heated debate between Hiratsuka and Yosano from March 1918 to April 1919. Yosano published 'Joshi no tetteishita dokuritsu' ('Women's complete independence'), which was part of her 'Shieiroku' ('Records of the Purple Shadows').[62] She opposed new western ideas advocating the protection of motherhood:

> I cannot possibly agree with the advocacy made by women's movements in America and western Europe, requesting the state to give special financial protection to women during the periods of their pregnancy, childbirth and the early stages of childcare.[63]

The western feminist movements to which Yosano was referring were those supporting Key's advocacy of state payments to mothers, particularly the 'Bund für Mutterschutz' in Germany.[64] Yosano objected strongly to these. She valued women's economic independence, and found it hard to accept the view that wives were dependent on their husbands in exchange for procreative services. Yosano called such dependency *'dorei dōtoku'* ('slave morality').[65] On the same principle she refused to accept western feminist demands that the state should provide mothers with financial assistance. She argued that wives' marital dependence was no better than women's dependence on the

---

[61] *Ibid.*, p. 50.

[62] Yosano Akiko, 'Joshi no tetteishita dokuritsu', *Fujin Kōron*, 3:3 (March, 1918), reprinted in Kōuchi (ed.), *Shiryō*, pp. 85–6.

[63] *Ibid.*, p. 85.

[64] On the Bund für Mutterschutz (the Motherhood Protection League), see Irene Stoehr, 'Housework and motherhood: debates and policies in the women's movement in Imperial Germany and the Weimar Republic', in Gisela Bock & Pat Thane (eds), *Maternity & Gender Policies: Women and the Rise of the European Welfare States, 1880s–1950s* (London, 1991), pp. 215–25; Seth Koven & Sonya Michel, 'Introduction: "Mother worlds"', in Seth Koven & Sonya Michel (eds), *Mothers of a New World: Maternalist Politics and the Origins of Welfare States* (London, 1993), pp. 14–6.

[65] Yosano, 'Joshi no tetteishita dokuritsu', p. 85.

state. In linguistic terms these two forms of dependency were easily confused and classified under the category of '*iraishugi*' (the principle of relying on others on all occasions). Yosano advised women not to rely on others—whether husband or state—under any circumstances, and to stand on their own feet.[66]

Yosano's remarks on traditional marriage practice resembled the South African writer Olive Schreiner's famous analysis of marriage as 'a form of legalised prostitution in which the economic and emotional dependence of women on men was institutionalised and justified in a sexual form.'[67] Moreover, Yosano's ideal of women—who have stopped being 'sex parasites' and who have taken up jobs and become independent of men—corresponds with Olive Schreiner's definition of 'new women'.[68] By this term Schreiner meant women who had already effected some change away from 'sex-parasitism' and who were working towards the possibility of a new life of equality.[69] Such resemblance between Schreiner's and Yosano's views was not coincidental. Yosano had certainly read Schreiner's book *Woman and Labour* and been influenced by it.[70]

In her article Yosano also made specific suggestions about the actions that ought to be taken by women to prevent their dependence on others:

> The general role which I am recommending both men and women to follow in the future is that neither should get married nor start a family until both have saved enough money or obtained sufficient earn-

---

[66] *Ibid.*, p. 85.

[67] Liz Stanley, 'Olive Schreiner: new women, free women, all women', in Dale Spender (ed.), *Feminist Theorists: Three Centuries of Women's Intellectual Traditions* (London, 1983), p. 236. Olive Schreiner (1855–1920) was a South African writer and political activist. After she came to England in 1881, she entered London intellectual circles and became acquainted with radical intellectuals such as Eleanor Marx, Havelock Ellis and Edward Carpenter. On her return to South Africa, she married a farmer and politician, Samuel Cronwright, with whom she campaigned for suffrage and racial justice. Later she went back to England and was closely involved with suffrage and peace movements. Her *Woman and Labour* manifested her main ideas about women's place in society. On Schreiner, see Stanley, 'Olive Schreiner', pp. 230–43; Dale Spender, *Women of Ideas and What Men Have Done to them, from Aphra Behn to Adrienne Rich* (1982, London, 1983 edn), pp. 646–56; Ruth Brandon, *The New Women and the Old Men* (1990, London, 1991 edn), pp. 44–94.

[68] Yosano, 'Joshi no tetteishita dokuritsu', p. 85. See also Olive Schreiner, *Woman and Labour* (1911, London, 1978 edn), pp. 33–150.

[69] Stanley, 'Olive Schreiner', p. 237.

[70] This is evident in Yosano Akiko, 'Joshi no shokugyōteki dokuritsu o gensoku to seyo' *Jogaku Sekai*, 18:1 (January, 1918), reprinted in Kōuchi (ed.), *Shiryō*, p. 84.

ing power to bring financial security, and to pay for the care and education required for their future children. Even in the case of a man with financial security who has a female partner without such security, the couple should avoid marriage and children until she also gains financial independence. To me women with no financial independence, who get married and have children in expectation of their husbands' finances are still adopting the '*iraishugi*' (principle of depending upon others). This will lead them to downgrade their status, becoming their male partners' slaves or encroaching on male labour, even if a genuine, intimate love relationship exists between them. To me, love marriage which does not take women's economic independence into consideration is still an unsatisfactory, incomplete marriage, and cannot possibly be regarded as an ideal marriage in the future.[71]

Yosano made it clear, moreover, that she disliked the idea of women who had no savings for their pregnancy and child-rearing, requesting the state to provide for them in return for their reproductive services. She stated that such requests to the state would have an extremely damaging effect on women's social status. Such requests would downgrade women's status to the level of disabled or old people, who cannot work and have to live in state nursing homes.[72]

Yosano concluded by emphasising that producing and bringing up children was not the state's responsibility but parents', and that parents were expected to fulfil their full responsibilities towards children.[73] In the case of either the father or mother's death, the remaining partner should be expected to take full responsibility. It was absolutely essential for husbands and wives to acquire economic independence in order to fulfil their duties towards their children. This was the form of Yosano's ideas, which were strongly opposed to Ellen Key's 'glorification of motherhood' and advocacy of state payment to mothers.

Hiratsuka was disappointed by these negative views on the protection of motherhood.[74] She expected Yosano, a working mother with eleven children, to be more sympathetic and understanding towards mothers. Hiratsuka was particularly disturbed by Yosano's strong rejection of state financial protection.[75] Hiratsuka protested by

---

[71] Yosano, 'Joshi no tetteishita dokuritsu', p. 85.
[72] *Ibid.*, pp. 85–6.
[73] *Ibid.*, p. 86.
[74] Hiratsuka, *Genshi*, vol. 3, p. 32.
[75] *Ibid.*, pp. 33–4.

writing 'Bosei hogo no shuchō wa iraishugi ka' ('Is the request for the protection of motherhood a kind of parasitism?').[76] In it she challenged Yosano and attempted to show how vital state provision was to mothers, especially working mothers.[77]

Hiratsuka claimed that Yosano had overlooked significant points. Yosano was an idealist, who tended to have a loose grasp of reality; moreover, her observations could be narrow and partial. She examined each incident, phenomenon or ideology individually, treating each as a disconnected entity, as if it had no association with any other. She rarely saw issues in their wider context, or attempted to analyse how far an incident or phenomenon was cross-related to other matters. This was especially apparent in her discussion of social issues. She was also prone to jump to hasty conclusions.

Hiratsuka criticised Yosano for failing to take account of her own rarity among women, as she had unusual natural gifts, talent and energy. She had very high expectations of ordinary women, and measured others by her own standards. As a result, according to Hiratsuka, Yosano's views ended up becoming *kūron* (empty theory), without more general applicability.[78] Hiratsuka went on to support state welfare provision for illegitimate children.

> Fundamentally mothers are the precious source of life. Before women produce children, they are regarded as nothing but mere individual beings, but through their worthwhile act of giving birth to children, their status as trivial individual beings is raised to the point where they are considered to be socially and nationally important beings. Protecting mothers is necessary not only for the sake of their own happiness but also for the happiness of society as a whole and the future of all human beings.[79]

Hiratsuka believed that children were not simply possessions of their mothers, who had the closest influence upon them, but also of society and the state. To her, children were the future destiny of Japan. Given their future contributions, Hiratsuka felt that the state should

---

[76] Hiratsuka Raichō, 'Bosei hogo no shuchō wa iraishugi ka', *Fujin Kōron*, 3:5 (May, 1918), reprinted in Kōuchi (ed.), *Shiryō*, pp. 86–91. This article was also reprinted in Hiratsuka's books, *Fujin to Kodomo no Kenri* (1919), *Josei no Kotoba* (1926) and *Mushiro Nyonin o Reihai Seyo* (1977).
[77] Hiratsuka, 'Bosei hogo no shuchō wa iraishugi ka', p. 87.
[78] *Ibid.*, p. 87.
[79] *Ibid.*, p. 89.

show deep interest in the number and quality of children and protect them.

> The state must not put children's entire affairs into their parents' hands. The state must protect children in all respects of its own accord, and ensure children's growth in mind and body. This is a natural obligation of the state. In order to achieve full protection of children, mothers ought to be protected as well.[80]

Hiratsuka regarded child-bearing and rearing as a social good, conducive to national well-being. She suggested that the National Treasury should subsidise all costs incurred by mothers. Hiratsuka's ideas on the protection of motherhood were almost identical to those of Ellen Key.

An elaboration of Yosano's views on women's absolute independence can be found in her article 'Joshi no shokugyōteki dokuritsu o gensoku to seyo' ('Women should make it a rule to obtain economic independence through paid work'), published in January 1918, two months prior to her article 'Joshi no tetteishita dokuritsu' ('Women's complete independence').[81] Yosano stated that Japanese women were far inferior to western women in mental and productive capacity at work. She argued that this was caused by two major factors—Japanese women's poor physical condition, and their utter ignorance and lack of education.[82] The former originated from their poor diet: women, who were dependent on men, felt uncomfortable about eating in men's presence, and as a result failed to obtain adequate nutrition. Women's ignorance was the result of their poor education. The first problem could easily be solved by improvement of their food intake, and the resolution of the second difficulty required better female education, equal to that for men. In order to fulfil these objectives women would first have to obtain financial independence. Yosano believed that women would gain freedom by working for wages.[83]

Yosano placed an absolute trust in women's independence, and she seems not to have considered how the state might facilitate this. Hiratsuka did not deny the value of women's independence. She even stated that economic independence was an essential condition

---

[80] *Ibid.*, p. 89.
[81] Yosano, 'Joshi no shokugyōteki dokuritsu o gensoku to seyo', pp. 81–4.
[82] *Ibid.*, p. 81.
[83] *Ibid.*, p. 82.

for all women to obtain—regardless of marital status—in order to maintain their dignity.[84] Hiratsuka's view was that economic independence would indeed be important for women to elevate their social status and to claim or assert their rights, but that it would be a mistake at this time to place the highest value on it. She questioned Yosano's views:

> I wonder whether women's economic independence deserves the highest value or not. I also wonder whether it is worth women's while to make great sacrifices to achieve economic independence. Even supposing that women's economic independence is indeed of such high value, I think that it will be absolutely impossible for mothers to achieve financial independence in a real sense.[85]

Hiratsuka drew attention to unmarried women and tried to show how difficult it was even for them to achieve economic autonomy:

> When you talk about women's work casually, without much thought, you must remember that the range of work women can do nowadays is still very limited. Moreover, women's salaries and wages are so low that they can only manage to live from hand to mouth, even though they work as hard as carthorses all day long . . . If one put Yosano's theory into practice (that women must not get married or start a family until they become financially fully independent), it would be very likely that the majority of Japanese women of marriageable age, who could produce children, would remain single. Needless to say, this is an impossible ideal, which cannot be put into practice today. Attempting to keep women of marriageable age, who are capable of producing healthy children, unmarried and in the labour market for a long period of time (or for the rest of their lives), would not only be unfortunate for women but would also bring a great loss to the state.[86]

Hiratsuka then turned her attention from the case of unmarried women to that of married women. She argued that if unmarried women, who did not have any family obligations and worked full-time, were struggling to survive financially, then it would be virtually impossible for married women, especially mothers with small children, to obtain economic independence, apart from an extremely limited number of extraordinary women with special skills, such as Yosano Akiko.[87]

---

[84] Hiratsuka, 'Bosei hogo no shuchō wa iraishugi ka', p. 90.
[85] *Ibid.*, p. 90.
[86] *Ibid.*, p. 90.
[87] *Ibid.*, pp. 90–1.

Using her own experience, Hiratsuka believed that the state should provide mothers with financial protection during pregnancy, child-birth and the early stages of child-rearing. These views clearly originated from Ellen Key. They had already been put into effect to varying degrees in some western countries, although not in the developed institutionalised manner that was later to emerge, for example in Britain under the Attlee government after 1945. It was still rare, even in western countries, to find such assistance for motherhood, and in an international context Hiratsuka's views were very progressive indeed. Liberal and Conservative governments in the west had long adopted policies that insisted on self-reliance, and in this they were probably closer to Yosano than Hiratsuka, although of course they could not be identified with Yosano's feminist motivations.

As stated earlier, Hiratsuka's ideas here stemmed from Ellen Key, but they were slightly different and more developed than Key's initial teaching.[88] Key disapproved of mothers' work being outside the home, while Hiratsuka disapproved of mother's work outside the home during the early stages of child-rearing. With regard to state financial protection, Hiratsuka's ideas took a more concrete form than Key's. Hiratsuka advocated family allowances to help protect motherhood, much like her British counterpart Eleanor Rathbone.[89]

---

[88] On Ellen Key's ideas of state protection of motherhood, see Rowbotham, *A Century of Women*, pp. 621–2; Koven & Michel, 'Introduction', pp. 15–7; Jane Lewis, *Women in England, 1870–1950* (Brighton, 1984), pp. 100, 128–9; Stoehr, 'Housework and motherhood', p. 217; Harada Minoru, 'Erisu-shi jobun', in Ellen Key (trans. by Harada Minoru), *Renai to Kekkon*, vol. 1 (1930), pp. 5–14; Hiratsuka Raichō, 'Sekai no josei, Ellen Key', *Fujin no Tomo* (December, 1927), reprinted in Hiratsuka, *Chosakushū*, vol. 4, pp. 320–4; Hiratsuka Raichō, 'Ellen Key joshi', *Shin Nihon* (September, 1914), reprinted in Hiratsuka, *Chosakushū*, vol. 1, pp. 398–406.

[89] Eleanor Rathbone (1872–1946) was a suffragist and social reformer in Britain. She was a leading speaker for the Women's Suffrage Society led by Mrs. Fawcett. After suffrage was granted to British women, she campaigned for women's social issues such as family allowances and widows' pensions. In 1918 she published a pamphlet *Equal Pay and the Family*, in which she outlined a policy for family endowment. In 1929 she was elected as Independent Member for the Combined English Universities, and in the 1930s she fought for family allowances in Parliament. On Eleanor Rathbone, see Mary McIntosh, 'Social anxieties about lone motherhood and ideologies of the family', in Elizabeth Bortolaia Silva (ed.), *Good Enough Mothering?* (London, 1996), p. 151; Jane Lewis, 'Models of equality for women: the case of state support for children in twentieth-century Britain', in Gisela Bock & Pat Thane (eds), *Maternity and Gender Policies: Women and the Rise of the European Welfare States, 1880s–1950s* (1991, London, 1994 edn), pp. 73–89; Pat Thane, *Foundations of the Welfare State* (London, 1982); June Hannam, 'Women and politics', in June Purvis (ed.), *Women's History: Britain, 1850–1945* (London, 1995), p. 235; Jane Lewis, *Women in England, 1870–1950* (Brighton, 1984), pp. 103–5; Johanna Alberti, *Eleanor Rathbone* (London, 1996).

Rathbone founded the small Family Endowment Society in 1917, through which she ran her energetic campaign for family allowances. She also established the Children's Minimum Council in 1934 to work for the same objective. There were many similarities between Rathbone and Hiratsuka's views of family allowances. Rathbone is best remembered for her analysis and justification of such allowances, and many of her points were also made by Hiratsuka. Rathbone first campaigned for them in 1917, which coincided with the protection of motherhood debate in Japan. Like Hiratsuka, Rathbone was particularly anxious that women's contributions as mothers should receive recognition and be rewarded. Rathbone believed that motherhood was largely incompatible with work external to the home, and when she proposed family allowances she argued that these would pay women a wage at home, and so give them a dignified and secure economic status.[90]

Rathbone's view of family allowances differed in some respects from Hiratsuka's. Rathbone had a long-standing concern for the condition of working-class mothers, and she mounted her campaign for family allowances for the sake of that group, rather than for middle or upper-middle class women.[91] On the other hand, Hiratsuka initially demonstrated most concern for middle-class working mothers, and overlooked the predicament of working-class employed women. It took some time for her to re-focus her efforts to encompass working-class women. Rathbone proposed that cash allowances should be paid to the mother in her own right as well as to her on behalf of each child.[92] The sum was proportional to the number of children. Hiratsuka proposed that a cash allowance be paid to the mother, in recognition of her domestic work, regardless of the number of children involved.[93] Rathbone also advocated widows' pensions. In this regard, Rathbone's conception of family allowances, which included graded widows' pensions and child allowances, was more complex

---

[90] Alberti, *Eleanor Rathbone*, pp. 76–8; Lewis, 'Models of equality for women', p. 74; Jane Lewis, 'Eleanor Rathbone, 1872–1946', in Paul Barker (ed.), *Founders of the Welfare State* (London, 1984), p. 84.

[91] *Ibid.*, p. 85.

[92] *Ibid.*, p. 86.

[93] Hiratsuka, 'Bosei hogo mondai ni tsuite futatabi Yosano Akiko-shi ni yosu', pp. 112–6. This article was also reprinted in Hiratsuka's books, *Fujin to Kodomo no Kenri* (1919) and *Josei no Kotoba* (1926).

than Hiratsuka's. Hiratsuka, who cohabited with her partner and gave birth to two illegitimate children, wanted allowances to go to unmarried mothers as well, but Rathbone did not support this.[94] It also seems clear that Rathbone was far more dedicated to the cause of family allowances than Hiratsuka. Rathbone fought for family allowances over a very long period indeed.[95] The cause became closely tied to her name. On the other hand, Hiratsuka never entered the political arena, partly because she had less opportunity (in Japan) to do so, and her campaign for family allowances was much more limited. As Hiratsuka never referred to Rathbone in writing, it is impossible to trace direct links between the two women, or even to find out whether Hiratsuka was familiar with Rathbone's ideas and whether they influenced her. These were ideas that were widely discussed in western women's circles at the time; but it is not usually appreciated that such discussion had direct counterparts in Japan, which may have been derivative, but which were certainly almost exactly contemporary.

Yosano Akiko appeared unable to remain silent in the face of Hiratsuka's views, and in response she wrote 'Hiratsuka-san to watashi no ronsō' ('The debate between Hiratsuka and myself'), in *Taiyō* (*Sun*).[96] Yosano said that Hiratsuka's criticism of her ideal of women becoming mentally and financially independent was most unexpected. Although Yosano acknowledged the significant roles mothers played, and agreed with Hiratsuka that mothers should be protected, she was offended by Hiratsuka's criticism.[97] She criticised Hiratsuka for having attached such absolute importance to motherhood, rather than to the independence of women which she felt should come first.[98] This discussion became more heated over time. Both of them stuck rigidly to their initial ideas.

It is interesting to observe the views that contemporary women had on the Hiratsuka—Yosano debate. The highly regarded women's newspaper *Fujo Shinbun* (*the Women's Newspaper*) was quick to take up

---

[94] Hiratsuka, 'Bosei hogo no shuchō wa iraishugi ka', pp. 88–91; Lewis, 'Eleanor Rathbone', pp. 87–8; Alberti, *Eleanor Rathbone*, p. 75.

[95] Lewis, 'Models of equality for women', p. 73; Anne Crawford *et al.* (eds), *The Europa Biographical Dictionary of British Women* (London, 1983), pp. 338–9.

[96] Yosano Akiko, 'Hiratsuka-san to watashi no ronsō', *Taiyō*, 24:7 (June, 1918), reprinted in Kōuchi (ed.), *Shiryō*, pp. 96–104.

[97] *Ibid.*, p. 96.

[98] *Ibid.*, pp. 97–8.

the issues.[99] A piece entitled 'Hiratsuka Raichō joshi ni' ('Addressed to Hiratsuka Raichō') appeared in May 1918.[100] It was a direct response to Hiratsuka's 'Bosei hogo no shuchō wa iraishugi ka'. Its female author, Haruura, commented on Hiratsuka's views:

> When I read Yosano's article, criticising advocacy of the protection of motherhood, I shared exactly the same disapproval of Yosano's opinion as yourself. Yosano tried to force her views on motherhood—which originated from her natural gifts, energy and learning—onto uneducated women. As a result, her idea ended up as empty theory, an impractical proposition, lacking any effect on real society.[101]

However, Haruura turned her criticism onto Hiratsuka as well:

> Although Yosano has been introducing idealistic thought in her writing, which bears no relation to the realities of life, her conduct as a wife and mother is down to earth and reliable. She set a good example to housewives. On the other hand, you [Hiratsuka] did not bother to have your marriage registered and continued to live in sin even after the birth of your daughter, Akemi. You unnecessarily made your daughter's life hell and made her suffer the humiliation of being an illegitimate child, someone considered to be a social outcast. You ignored the customary system in the real world. Taking your anti-social behaviour into consideration, Yosano is far more realistic than yourself.[102]

Haruura criticized Hiratsuka for not bringing her views about the protection of motherhood into line with her own daily practice. Haruura's comments also demonstrated a moralistic and conventional view of marriage and mothers' responsibilities towards children.

Another article on the debate appeared in *Fujo Shinbun*.[103] The author approved of Hiratsuka's views:

> The issue of the protection of motherhood used to be nothing but a private whisper among a handful of pioneers, people with advanced

---

[99] *Fujo Shinbun* (*Women's Newspaper*) was a progressive women's weekly newspaper edited by Fukushima Shiro, which aimed to improve women's status. It dealt with many women's issues including the promotion of women's education, women's suffrage and the protection of motherhood.

[100] Haruura, 'Hiratsuka Raichō joshi ni', *Fujo Shinbun*, 937 (3 May, 1918), reprinted in Kōuchi (ed.), *Shiryō*, pp. 258–9.

[101] *Ibid.*, p. 258.

[102] *Ibid.*, p. 259.

[103] Anon., 'Bosei yōgo to keizaiteki dokuritsu: Yosano fujin tai Hiratsuka joshi no ronsen' ('The protection of motherhood and women's economic independence: controversy over the protection of motherhood, Mrs Yosano versus Ms Hiratsuka'), *Fujo Shinbun*, 951 (9 August, 1918), reprinted in Kōuchi (ed.), *Shiryō*, pp. 262–5.

views. However, with Yosano and Hiratsuka's debate as a start, the subject and its related issues have promoted much public attention, which is a very good sign, an unexpected but most welcoming encouragement for those advocating protection of motherhood, like myself.[104]

This article expressed the hope that Hiratsuka's request for state financial provision for mothers would soon be accomplished.[105]

An article 'Ikuji jigyō wa shiji nari ya' ('Is child-rearing a personal matter?') in *Fujo Shinbun* also commented on Hiratsuka's views:

> Your newspaper [*Fujo Shinbun*] ardently advocated the protection of motherhood. Similarly, Hiratsuka enthusiastically preached the necessity for the protection of motherhood ... To me, such views are pure theory, lacking a sense of the realities of life. On the whole, this discussion of the subject does not deserve praise ... I think that the frequent news relating to mothers and children which appears in newspapers almost every day (such as mothers drowning themselves and their children, or killing their children and then committing suicide) reveal that the state protection of motherhood is a pressing business, and that these incidents convey this message more compellingly than Hiratsuka's and other agitators' theories on the subject.[106]

The author pointed to the weakness of Hiratsuka's discussion, introduced real examples to show why state protection was needed urgently, and clarified the classes of women who most needed a state allowance. Other articles like these appeared in *Fujo Shinbun*, and they indicate that the Yosano-Hiratsuka debate had stirred many other women to consider the issues, and indeed had persuaded many of the urgent need for state maternity protection.

Later Development of the Controversy over Motherhood

Their debate was also quietly observed by other feminists like Yamada Waka and Yamakawa Kikue. They broke their silence in September 1918.[107] Yamada wrote an article 'Bosei hogo mondai: Yosano-shi

---

[104] *Ibid.*, pp. 262–3.
[105] *Ibid.*, pp. 264–5.
[106] Anon., 'Ikuji jigyō wa shiji nari ya', *Fujo Shinbun* (30 August, 1918), reprinted in Kōuchi (ed.), *Shiryō*, pp. 265–6.
[107] Kōuchi, 'Kaidai', pp. 309–13; Yamakawa, *Onna Nidai no Ki*, p. 213; Esashi Akiko, 'Yamakawa Kikue', in Setouchi Harumi (ed.), *Meiji Josei no Chiteki Jōnetsu* (1989), pp. 288–9.

to Hiratsuka-shi no shoron ni tsuite' ('The subject of the protection
of motherhood with special reference to Yosano and Hiratsuka's
respective views') which appeared in *Taiyō* (*Sun*).[108] Yamakawa's article was entitled 'Bosei hogo to keizaiteki dokuritsu: Yosano, Hiratsuka
nishi no ronsō' ('The protection of motherhood and women's economic independence, focusing on the dispute between Yosano and
Hiratsuka').[109] Both Yamada and Yamakawa directly addressed the
debate between Hiratsuka and Yosano. Yamada had been active in
the third phase of the Seitō Society, and had then played an active
part in journalism.[110] She wrote numerous articles for newspapers
and magazines, which established her reputation as a women's commentator, and she even launched her own magazine *Fujin to Shinshakai*
(*Women and the New Society*) in March 1920.[111] As a women's writer,
it was natural for Yamada to engage in this controversy. Yamada
examined the discussion between Yosano and Hiratsuka. She gave
a brief outline of their debate, assessing strengths and weaknesses of
their arguments, and followed this with an attack on Yosano:

> Yosano persistently advocates the absolute necessity for women to lead
> economically and mentally independent lives . . . However, to be hon-
> est with you, I always have doubts about the implications of the term,
> '*joshi no dokuritsu*' ('women's independence').[112]

Yamada outlined the reasons for her lack of faith in the idea of
women's independence:

> I am quite sure that there must be some praiseworthy and remark-
> able women in this world, who can make a comfortable income and
> at the same time be capable of maintaining their mental independence.
> There must be some women with special skills or talents, which enable
> them to earn a relatively large income at home while looking after
> their children. If women have special skills and determine to use them,
> they will be quite capable, with some assistance, of handling all the

---

[108] Yamada Waka, 'Bosei hogo mondai: Yosano-shi to Hiratsuka-shi no shoron
ni tsuite', *Taiyō*, 24:11 (September, 1918), reprinted in Kōuchi (ed.), *Shiryō*, pp.
147–160.

[109] Yamakawa Kikue, 'Bosei hogo to keizaiteki dokuritsu: Yosano, Hiratsuka nishi
no ronsō', *Fujin Kōron*, 3:9 (September, 1918), reprinted in Kōuchi (ed.), *Shiryō*, pp.
132–46.

[110] Yamazaki, *Ameyuki-san no Uta*, pp. 184–207; Hiratsuka Raichō, 'Seitō jidai',
Asuka (January–July, 1937), reprinted in Hiratsuka, *Chosakushu*, vol. 6, pp. 182–6.

[111] *Ibid.*, pp. 208–13; Yasutaka Misako, 'Yamaka Waka', in Setouchi Harumi (ed.),
Jiritsushita Onna no Eikō (1989), pp. 84–5.

[112] Yamada, 'Bosei hogo mondai', p. 147.

household affairs, miscellaneous domestic duties and childcare. However, the number of such remarkable women is so small that one cannot possibly apply their special case to that of ordinary women, who comprise the majority.[113]

Yamada criticised Yosano's views on the absolute priority of women's independence for being too idealistic and for failing to face up to reality. She called Yosano's view '*amari ni sangyōteki shakaiteki jijitsu o mushishita kūsō*' ('a fantasy which completely ignored social and industrial elements').[114] Yamada went on to state that even men, who did not carry extra burdens such as pregnancy and childbirth, were confronting financial difficulties under current circumstances, and found it extremely hard to acquire financial independence. It would be virtually impossible for married women with children to achieve this. Yamada's argument was very reminiscent of Hiratsuka's, and Yamada, who also followed Ellen Key's 'glorification of motherhood', supported Hiratsuka's view on the need for mothers to receive financial protection. As Yamada's discussion overlapped with Hiratsuka's, her contribution to the controversy has been underestimated. However, Yamada's argument was not identical to Hiratsuka's, differing in a number of ways.

Hiratsuka criticised Yosano for placing absolute trust in female economic independence. She did not completely deny its value, only pointing out that it was impossible for women during pregnancy, childbirth and child-rearing. Hiratsuka never confronted the issue of what effects 'independence' might have on married women. Yamada however was more explicit:

> At one time married women, who were very much taken by attractive words such as 'independence', began to feel that pleasing their husbands to get housekeeping money from them was a very humiliating or shameful thing to do. Therefore they rushed into rather thoughtless and hasty decisions, taking up jobs in offices and factories. However, these women are now experiencing all kinds of problems.[115]

Yamada argued that such married women, with jobs outside their home and financial independence from their husbands, in fact gained nothing. Her view was that if women stayed at home they were

---

[113] *Ibid.*, pp. 148–9.
[114] *Ibid.*, p. 148.
[115] *Ibid.*, p. 149.

under the rule of their husbands, and if they went out to work, they fell under the rule of capitalist employers. In this respect, Yamada argued that married women's economic 'independence' did not improve women's status at all. It simply entailed the change from one form of subordination to another—from husbands to employers. She argued that if women had to endure subordination in either option, it would be far more sensible for them to stay at home and look after the children they loved, and this would also bring more security and stability to the family.[116]

Yamada tried further to justify her views against married women's economic independence by noting the harm working mothers would be likely to cause their children:

> If ordinary women decide to take up jobs, they will not have many options. They will have to leave the entire care of their children in the hands of others. As a result, their children will be more likely to be placed in vulnerable situations where they will be exposed to danger and will carry higher risks of becoming immoral.[117]

She also wrote that working mothers would be likely to neglect their husbands and home duties, and disturb domestic peace and stability. These negative statements against working mothers contrasted with Hiratsuka's view about married women's economic independence. Unlike Hiratsuka, Yamada placed absolute trust in home life. Yamada was happily married to her academic husband, Kakichi, and was clearly satisfied with her domesticity. She explained how precious and beneficial the home was to children and husbands, and what an important role mothers played at home:

> Home is the residence of the spirits and souls of husbands, wives and their children. Children grow up in good health at home where they can get their mothers' affection and their tender loving care. Similarly, husbands recoup their energy at home, where things are put in order and well looked after by their wives' loving care. One must not underestimate the real value of this significant work that wives do at home. Their work at home is incomparably more worthwhile than the work they do at the factory or in the office.[118]

---

[116] *Ibid.*, p. 149.
[117] *Ibid.*, p. 149.
[118] *Ibid.*, p. 150.

These views remind one of the teaching of '*ryōsai kenbo*'. Yamada, who was once a prostitute and like many other prostitutes had become unable to conceive children, was obsessed by children, and felt strongly and deeply about their protection.[119]

Although both Yamada and Hiratsuka thought about what action should be taken to protect motherhood, and reached a consensus that mothers would require state financial provision, there was a subtle difference between their views. Hiratsuka expected the state to provide mothers with financial assistance and to take full responsibility for them. However, she did not refer to the responsibilities which fathers ought to have towards their wives and children. On the other hand, Yamada proposed that a fundamental change was needed in both men's and the state's attitude towards mothers who were staying at home.[120] She pointed out that the Meiji Civil Code stipulated that husbands had a duty to support their children and wives, but in practice children and wives came under the rule of husbands.[121] In reality husbands had taken it for granted that their wives did domestic and childcare work without payment. Husbands had become so accustomed to this, and found it so convenient, that the idea that their wives should be paid for domestic work and child-rearing never occurred to them. Yamada felt that the time had come for women to stop providing free services to their husbands, and to require that their spouses pay them money for their domestic work and childcare at home:

> Women should no longer provide men with free service at home. Women have been doing this worthwhile, responsible work at home for the sake of husbands and children without getting paid for a long time, without getting any credit for it. It is time for women to force men to pay women in return for all the worthwhile, time-consuming work women do at home, which includes housekeeping and bringing up children. It is natural and very reasonable for wives to demand that their husbands start paying them money, in return for running their households and bringing up children. In the event of their husbands' death or when husbands became incapable of paying money to their wives, the state should provide women with children with financial assistance instead of their husbands.[122]

---

[119] Yamazaki, *Ameyuki-san no Uta*, pp. 227–8.
[120] Yamada, 'Bosei hogo mondai', p. 151.
[121] *Ibid.*, p. 149.
[122] *Ibid.*, pp. 149–50.

Yamakawa Kikue also made a major contribution to this controversy. She wrote 'Bosei hogo to keizaiteki dokuritsu' ('The protection of motherhood and economic independence').[123] Although Yamakawa was the youngest and least conspicuous female commentator among the four participants in the controversy, she skilfully evaluated Yosano and Hiratsuka's dispute. Yamakawa saw their debate as being over a fundamental difference as to whether it was possible for a child-rearing woman to take up paid work.[124] She found it difficult to support Yosano. She criticised her for assessing social issues (like the protection of motherhood) from a narrow middle-class perspective, and overlooking working-class women's views. Yamakawa described Yosano's approach towards social issues as 'a debate which begins with the bourgeoisie and ends with the bourgeoisie'.[125] She cited Yosano's opinion that:

> All problems in society can be solved entirely by an individual person's effort. An individual's poverty is caused by his/her lack of effort, and is the natural consequence of his/her own deeds.[126]

To Yamakawa this was simple-minded. However, she had some respect for Yosano's advocacy of women's economic independence, and claimed to appreciate Yosano's contributions, especially in their bearing upon middle-class women, making them more aware of their social situation. However, Yamakawa basically supported Hiratsuka's views, giving the following justification:

> Needless to say it is very difficult for women who are in the middle of child-rearing to take up or continue work outside the home, unless they leave the entire care of their children in the hands of others. Therefore I personally find it an absolutely normal and natural gesture for child-rearing women, which is one of the most significant social duties, to request the state to support them.[127]

Yamakawa drew the following conclusions about the debate:

> As far as Yosano and Hiratsuka's respective arguments about the protection of motherhood are concerned, I must admit that there is some truth in what both of them have said. The need for women's eco-

---

[123] Yamakawa, 'Bosei hogo to keizaiteki dokuritsu', pp. 132–46.
[124] *Ibid.*, pp. 132–3.
[125] *Ibid.*, pp. 136–7.
[126] *Ibid.*, p. 136.
[127] *Ibid.*, p. 140.

nomic independence advocated by Yosano and the need for the protection of motherhood put forward by Hiratsuka are both significant.
Although they claimed that these two agendas would be incompatible,
I believe that they may be compatible. I feel that if women can achieve
the two purposes together, women's status in this society will become
more secure.[128]

Although Yamakawa acknowledged the benefits of these two
approaches, she believed that their fulfilment would neither solve the
fundamental problems of women, nor rescue women from cruelty in
Japan. In this regard Yamakawa's perspective was quite different
from those of Yosano and Hiratsuka.

> To me the fundamental solution for existing women's problems would
> be nothing less than a change in economic relations themselves, which
> have brought about women's predicaments and aggravated them. Unlike
> Yosano, I would not consider women's suffrage as the basic solution.
> And unlike Hiratsuka, I would not consider the state's goodwill as the
> fundamental solution.[129]

For Yamakawa the solution was a socialist revolution in Japan, and
her view was more radical than Yosano's or Hiratsuka's.[130] Yamakawa,
who was married to the leading socialist Yamakawa Hitoshi, and
was much influenced by other socialists and by the Russian Revolution,
was convinced that the only way to improve the whole society as
well as to upgrade women's status was a transformation of capitalist society into a socialist state.[131] Her ideology was thus fundamentally left-wing and anti-capitalist, rather than being 'feminist' within
the framework of an accepted capitalist society.

Yamakawa's views were more abstract, and theoretically logical,
than Yosano's and Hiratsuka's, which by comparison can strike one
as more personal, emotional and subjective. Another characteristic
of Yamakawa's argument was her predilection for analysing the controversy over the protection of motherhood in an international context. Yamakawa was proficient in English, having studied at Joshi
Eigaku Juku and previously done some translation work; she was

---

[128] *Ibid.*, p. 142.
[129] *Ibid.*, pp. 142–3.
[130] *Ibid.*, p. 146.
[131] Nagahata, 'Bosei to sei o mitsumete', pp. 205–7; Yamakawa, *20-seiki o Ayumu*,
pp. 78–83; Esashi & Ide, *Taishō Demokurashii to Josei*, p. 88; Yamashita, *Nihon Josei
Kaihō Shisō no Kigen*, p. 118; Murakami, 'Bosei hogo ronsō to gendai', pp. 213–4;
Esashi, 'Yamakawa Kikue', p. 288.

widely read and well-informed about the history of women's movements in western countries and she had extensive knowledge of western feminists' work.[132] Yamakawa explained the fundamental differences
between *joken undō* (the women's rights movement), which began to
emerge in Europe towards the end of the eighteenth century, and to
become more accepted in the second half of the nineteenth century,
and *boken undō* (the maternal rights movement), which emerged in
Scandinavia in the early nineteenth century as an alternative to the
older *joken undō*.[133]

Yamakawa drew attention to the social context from which *joken
undō* emerged. She argued that it had been needed to accommodate
changes associated with the rapid rise of Japanese capitalism, that it
was grounded in the nature of capitalist society, and that its ultimate
function was to realize power for women within capitalist society.[134]
She explained the circumstances of its emergence:

> As capitalism was approaching completion, the harm that it caused
> started to become clear. On an individual level, various charitable and
> relief works came into fashion, and on a social level various policies
> were advocated as a palliative for the miserable conditions consequent
> upon capitalism. *Boken undō*, as advocated by Ellen Key, is one such
> social policy. *Boken undō* has emerged in opposition to *joken undō*.[135]

Yamakawa was at pains to compare *joken undō* to *boken undō*:

> *Joken undō* wholeheartedly emphasised the development of women's
> intellects, while *boken undō* valued women's feelings. The former advo-
> cated free and open competition, while the latter worried over the
> results of free competition. The latter objected to the capitalistic spirit
> and the exploitation of women and children as workers. It cried out
> for a ban on female and child labour, and for their protection.[136]

Yamakawa's assessment of *joken undō* and *boken undō* was followed by
a careful examination of their weaknesses. She criticised *joken undō*,
whose ultimate purpose was an accommodation to capitalist society,

---

[132] Yamakawa, *Onna Nidai no Kī*, pp. 131–9; Sakai Toshihiko, 'Fujinkai no san
shisōka: Yasano Akiko, Hiratsuka Haruko, Yamakawa Kikue', *Onna no Sekai* (October,
1918), reprinted in Sakai Toshihiko (ed. by Suzuki Yūko), *Sakai Toshihiko Josei Ronshū*
(1983), pp. 357–9; Sakai Toshihoko, 'Onna to iu katsuzō o yōsenu hyōronka, *Josei
Kaizō*' (August, 1924), reprinted in Sakai, *Sakai Toshihiko Josei Ronshū*, pp. 360–1.
[133] Yamakawa, 'Bosei hogo to keizaiteki dokuritsu', pp. 132–5.
[134] *Ibid.*, pp. 134–5.
[135] *Ibid.*, p. 134.
[136] *Ibid.*, pp. 132–3.

for acquiescing in capitalism unconditionally, and for ignoring its ills
and the damage it caused.[137] She stated that *boken undō* assessed capitalist society more critically, and examined its ruinous consequences.
In this regard, Yamakawa argued that *boken undō* was one step ahead
of *joken undō*. However, Yamakawa was not satisfied with *boken undō*
either, and she criticised it for submitting tamely to merely partial
relief measures. She regarded Ellen Key's ideas on the protection of
motherhood as worthwhile, if rather obvious. Yamakawa concluded
that the great disadvantage of *boken undō* was that it introduced halfway measures, and fell short of a complete solution to the problem.[138]

In addition to her analysis of western women's movements, Yamakawa went a step further and tried to place Yosano and Hiratsuka's
feminist ideas (as shown in this debate) into the framework of those
western movements. She compared them at an international level,
and drew the following conclusion:

> Yosano Akiko's discussion of the protection of motherhood begins with
> her emphasis on women as individuals, advocates the need for women's
> freedom of education, for the extension of the scope of women's occu-
> pations, and for women's economic independence, and ends with the
> demand for women's suffrage. Yosano's discussion carries forward the
> tradition of the so-called *joken undō* . . . On the other hand, Hiratsuka
> values and emphasises the gendered differences of women compared
> to men, explains the harmful effect which equal opportunities for both
> sexes would have on women, and advocates the right to be a mother
> and all the rights which will come with being a mother. Hiratsuka's
> ideas demonstrate that Hiratsuka is opposed to *joken undō*, and her
> emphasis on motherhood certainly belongs to the tradition of *boken
> undō*.[139]

Yamakawa also compared Yosano and Hiratsuka to western feminists and stated that if Yosano was to be classified as a Japanese
version of Mary Wollstonecraft, Hiratsuka (who was attempting to
make up for imperfections of *jokenron* and take women's emancipation forward in a much broader sense) could be classified as an Ellen
Key in Japan.[140] This discussion demonstrated Yamakawa's knowledge of western feminist movements, and her skill in evaluating
them, which helped her to gain public recognition. For example,

---

[137] *Ibid.*, p. 134.
[138] *Ibid.*, pp. 134–5.
[139] *Ibid.*, p. 137.
[140] *Ibid.*, p. 137.

Fujo Shinbun (*Women's Newspaper*) made the following favourable remarks
on Yamakawa:

> The author of the long, detailed, thorough and well-written article
> which appeared in the September issue of *Fujin Kōron* is Yamakawa
> Kikue. I was overwhelmed by the most welcome fact that such an
> outstanding article, demonstrating the author's principles and ideology,
> was written by a woman. I was also extremely pleased to find that
> the standard of her writing was as high as a man's. In many ways
> her article was extremely encouraging to other women, and marks a
> great step in the progress of Japanese women.[141]

Such complimentary views were shared by others, and helped Yamakawa to establish her feminist career.[142] Yamakawa wrote much more
on women's causes and played an active part in promoting women's
status through her literary career. The controversy over the protection
of motherhood launched her as one of the most prominent women's
commentators in Japan.

Following Yamakawa and Yamada's articles addressed to Yosano
and Hiratsuka, Yosano wrote 'Rōdō to fujin' ('Work and women'),
which appeared in *Yokohama Bōeki Shinpō* (*Yokohama Trade News*).[143]
Here Yosano criticised both Hiratsuka and Yamada for being conservative.[144] Yosano repeatedly insisted that women could work, that
they needed economic and mental independence, and that state
financial support for mothers was an irrelevance:

> I have learned through my own experience, from my girlhood until
> now, that women are quite capable of working. I learned the philos-
> ophy of labour from Tolstoy; and Olive Schreiner also taught me the
> modern significance of labour. My real and close observation of women's
> labour in Japan, as well as in Europe, has confirmed to me that women
> are able to work.[145]

In order to justify her views, Yosano adopted Schreiner's argument
from *Woman and Labour*. In it Schreiner advocated the urgent need
to create a society which would enable both men and women to
choose any job suited to their ability. She argued that women should

---

[141] Anon., 'Yamakawa joshi no ronpyō', *Fujo Shinbun*, 954 (30 August, 1918),
reprinted in Kōuchi (ed.), *Shiryō*, p. 268.
[142] Sakai, 'Fujinkai no san shisōka', pp. 351–60.
[143] Yosano Akiko, 'Rōdō to fujin', *Yokohama Bōeki Shinpō*, 6327 & 6334 (20 & 27
October, 1918), reprinted in Kōuchi (ed.), *Shiryō*, pp. 161–7.
[144] *Ibid.*, p. 161.
[145] *Ibid.*, p. 161.

be allowed to take up all possible jobs without making any distinction of sex, since women in ancient times had been just as valuable workers as men.[146] Yosano stated that this argument applied to Japanese women in earlier centuries. Japanese women had for centuries engaged in agriculture, which Yosano stressed.[147] She drew attention to women's contributions as workers during the First World War, and pointed out that women did a wide range of jobs which used to be considered men's work, in order to make up for shortages in the male workforce, and that as a reserve labour force they were successful in replacing absent men. Yosano stated that such contributions proved that women were capable of doing any job.

She justified the need for women's economic and financial independence from many different angles, using evidence to prove that women were capable of engaging in many occupations and performing them well, making effective use also of quotations from Schreiner's *Woman and Labour*. Yosano acknowledged Schreiner's contributions to the women's movement, arguing that Schreiner's feminist stress on female independence, and her views on women's independence, provided the key to women's emancipation.[148]

Yosano also criticised Hiratsuka and Yamada for claiming that much work was too heavy for women, and for having wrongly assumed that women's work equated largely with factory work, one of the more exploitative activities. Yosano argued that there were other kinds of work for women, and she pointed out that women's occupational choices were widening. She advocated giving women more education and occupational training, to enable them to choose the most appropriate job, one that matched each woman's strength, intellect, technical skills and family circumstances.[149] This would also widen female options in terms of choosing better jobs. Yosano subsequently wrote further on this, retaining her original view that women's independence would be the key to female emancipation.[150]

[146] Schreiner, *Women and Labour*, pp. 83–98.
[147] Yosano, 'Rōdō to fujin', pp. 162–3.
[148] *Ibid.*, p. 162.
[149] *Ibid.*, pp. 163–4.
[150] Yosano Akiko, 'Hiratsuka, Yamakawa, Yamada san joshi ni kotau', *Taiyō*, 24:13 (November, 1918), reprinted in Kōuchi (ed.), *Shiryō*, pp. 177–92; Yosano Akiko, 'Joshi Kaizō no kisoteki kōsatsu', *Kaizō*, 1 (April, 1919), reprinted in Kōuchi (ed.), *Shiryō*, pp. 239–41; Yosano Akiko, 'Haruyoi sengo', *Waseda Bungaku*, 161 (April, 1919), reprinted in Kōuchi (ed.), *Shiryō*, pp. 242–4.

Hiratsuka persisted with her own original views, as in two further articles, 'Shi to sono zengo o mite' ('Having seen "Before and after death"') and 'Gendai katei fujin no nayami' ('Troubles of contemporary housewives').[151] These illustrate much continuity in her views, still advocating state financial protection for women. For Hiratsuka protection of motherhood was the ideal. However, the debate had shown that this would be a difficult result to achieve, and would have to be a very long-term aim. She therefore narrowed down the scale of her demands and set out a compromise agenda. In 'Gendai katei fujin no nayami' ('Troubles of contemporary housewives'), she gave a vivid description of the problems she was having in her own life, in attempting to combine childcare and a career:

> When our maid left our house for good, I was pretty desperate. As I had been relying greatly on her assistance, I felt as if I were completely lost, and could not possibly settle down to do my writing, which kept us going financially. I have piles of domestic work to do. Looking after two small children, who are now two and four years old, I have to do the cooking, cleaning, laundry and sewing. My time is completely taken up with such domestic work. Sometimes there is more than I can manage. I hardly have time to sit down to put my feet up all day, apart from meal times. My elder child usually goes to bed between seven and eight o'clock at night, so she is much easier to deal with. On the other hand, if my younger one has taken a long midday nap he is unsettled and continues to be mischievous even after ten o'clock at night. After both of them go to sleep, I fold up the washing (most of which is baby's diapers) and tidy up toys which are scattered about the house. By the time I finish sorting out everything and eventually find peace and quiet, a list of things I should be doing or that I would like to do start to come into my head. I say the following to myself: I fancy reading today's newspaper. I must re-read letters I have received from all sorts of people and must finish writing replies to them. I must get on with the article which I am writing to get money. I like the idea of reading magazines. How shall I find money for tomorrow? I must finish the article I am writing now as soon as possible, and receive a fee for it, otherwise I will be in trouble financially and face starvation. While I am thinking of such incoherent things, time passes quickly and I find that it is already eleven or twelve o'clock at night before I can do anything productive. Around that time I start to feel sleepy, partly because the strain of

---

[151] Hiratsuka Raichō, 'Shi to sono zengo o mite', *Yūben*, 9:13 (December, 1918), reprinted in Kōuchi (ed.), *Shiryō*, pp. 204–6; Hiratsuka Raichō, 'Gendai katei fujin no nayami', *Fujin Kōron*, 4:1 (January, 1919), reprinted in Kōuchi, *Shiryō*, pp. 207–13.

my domestic work and childcare begins to tell on me, but partly because I cannot get a good night's sleep. I have to get up quite a few times, even in the middle of the night, for the children. What is worse, the children are anxious to get up early in the morning, so I, who have nobody to relieve me or take my place, have to get up early with the children whether I like it or not. I am always short of sleep. Although I have many things I must do or would like to do, I am always seized with such uncontrollable tiredness and sleepiness that I cannot stay awake and end up going to bed before I finish reading even one or two pages of the newspaper. This has become my routine.[152]

This statement is worth quoting at length, because her account of life as a working mother raised questions which all working mothers in Japan had to confront. Hiratsuka went on to argue that these housewives were often worn out, because of domestic work and childcare, which involved irregular hours day and night.[153] She asserted that if mothers with small children also had to take up work outside the home, in addition to such demanding household work, they would end up crippled for life, or in an early grave, before middle age.[154] The conclusion Hiratsuka drew was that it was absolutely impossible for women with small children to combine childcare with paid work, and so it was vital for the state to provide them with financial support while their children were small.[155]

Conclusion

What conclusions emerged? As Kōuchi stated, the controversy over the protection of motherhood presaged 'three of the paths the women's movement has taken in the twentieth century.'[156] Parallel positions were taken in many other countries, then and subsequently. The four Japanese participants' views over the issue of *bosei hogo* divided into three alternative options, represented by Yosano, Hiratsuka and Yamakawa (Yamada's views basically agreeing with Hiratsuka's). The four women stuck fast to their respective positions and showed no inclination to compromise.

---

[152] *Ibid.*, pp. 208–9.
[153] *Ibid.*, p. 209.
[154] *Ibid.*, p. 210.
[155] *Ibid.*, p. 213.
[156] Kōuchi, 'Kaidai', p. 319. Similar comment was also made by Yoneda Sayoko. See Yoneda, *Kindai Nihon Joseishi*, vol. 1, pp. 149–50.

Although the debate stimulated discussion of women's causes, it had obvious limitations. The controversy was merely an ideological or theoretical dispute in print, lacking a practical dimension. These feminist theories were not translated into action. Yamakawa, Yamada and Hiratsuka all advocated protection of motherhood, and requested state financial aid, but they had no plans to put their ideas into effect. Hiratsuka's demand for state financial provision for mothers did not enter into detail, and did not clarify specifically for whom such provision should be made. Was it intended only for mothers who gave birth to illegitimate children, or all mothers? Would state provision be limited only to the periods of pregnancy and childbirth, or would it be extended to child-rearing? How long would it last? Hiratsuka failed to answer any of these questions.

Yamada Waka was the only one to put forward a concrete proposal. She had studied the maternal protection policy adopted in Germany.[157] She suggested the implementation of a new social insurance system including motherhood insurance, as based upon the German example.[158] However, even she never stimulated any political campaign for improved rights for mothers.[159] A similar weakness can be seen in *Seitō*. Those taking part in the controversy never established any organisation to encourage women to work for the protection of motherhood, and achieved no new legislation.[160] Japan had to wait until 1925, when the Nihon Rōdō Kumiai Hyōgikai (Council of Japanese Trade Unions) was established, which put forward practical demands.[161]

Another limitation of the controversy was that it was a dispute within the female middle-class intelligentsia.[162] Although Yamada, Hiratsuka and Yosano referred to working-class women and especially to textile workers, they were mainly concerned with their own class.[163] By the time of this controversy the exploitation of female

---

[157] Kōuchi, 'Bosei hogo ronsō no rekishiteki igi', pp. 35–6; Kōuchi, 'Kaidai', p. 312; Stoehr, 'Housework and motherhood', pp. 215–25; Koven & Michel, 'Introduction', pp. 14–6.

[158] Yamada, 'Bosei hogo mondai', pp. 154–9.

[159] Maruoka, *Fujin Shisō Keiseishi Nōto*, vol. 1, pp. 129–30.

[160] Kōuchi, 'Bosei hogo ronsō no rekishiteki igi', p. 38.

[161] Sakurai, *Bosei Hogo Undōshi*, pp. 49–50.

[162] Kōuchi, 'Bosei hogo ronsō no rekishiteki igi', p. 38.

[163] Yamada Waka, 'Ko o motta haha no nayami: gendai no nayami to shite no fujin shokugyō mondai', *Fujin Kōron*, 4:1 (January, 1919), reprinted in Kōuchi (ed.), *Shiryō*, pp. 214–23; Yosano Akiko, 'Hiratsuka, Yamakawa, Yamada san joshi ni

factory and textile workers had become clearer to the public.[164] Even some men had started to question how to improve working-class women's conditions and motherhood. However, Yamada, Yosano and Hiratsuka never really appreciated that the protection of motherhood among working-class women was a far more serious priority than their own predicament. Their contacts with such women were very limited. Hiratsuka's horizons were very limited, and she criticised factory women for being uneducated. She even stated that they were incapable of launching a women's labour campaign.[165]

Yamakawa Kikue was genuinely concerned about the lower class, especially female textile workers, and had become devoted to their cause long before 1918. She visited the Fuji Gasu Spinning Mill in Tokyo with people from the Salvation Army around Christmas 1908, when she was still a student at Joshi Eigaku Juku, and was shocked to see the conditions there.[166] Her experiences became the starting point for her feminist activities. Compounding her outlook was her involvement with the socialist, Yamakawa Hitoshi, whom she married in 1916. Thus Yamakawa Kikue was already a socialist by the time of this debate, and her participation highlighted working-class women.

However, even Yamakawa Kikue never made any direct appeal to the public on the need to protect working-class mothers.[167] This was mainly because she had a wider perspective on women's problems, believing that their solution required a socialist society.

The controversy was therefore undeveloped, and did not voice more practical ideas, as espoused for example by Maruoka Hideko in 1936.[168] Maruoka stated that maternity provision ought to be an issue for ordinary working women, from farm workers to factory operatives, and that its main objectives should include specific problems of mothers and children, relevant to their respective social and employment contexts.

---

kotau', *Taiyō*, 24:13 (November, 1918), reprinted in Kōuchi (ed.), *Shiryō*, pp. 176–92; Hiratsuka, 'Gendai katei fujin no nayami', pp. 207–13.

[164] Sakurai, *Bosei Hogo Undōshi*, pp. 49–51.

[165] Hiratsuka, 'Gendai katei fujin no nayami', pp. 209–10.

[166] Yamakawa Kikue's memory of this visit was later vividly described in her autobiography. See Yamakawa, *Onna Nidai no Kī*, pp. 139–42.

[167] Kōuchi, 'Bosei hogo ronsō no rekishiteki igi', pp. 36–7.

[168] Maruoka Hideko made this statement in her article entitled 'Boshi hogo no ichi shikaku' which appeared in the February 1936 issue of *Fujin Bungei*. See Maruoka, *Fujin Shisō Keiseishi*, vol. 1, p. 126.

The controversy was still highly significant. Molony correctly stated that 'the motherhood protection debate left a significant legacy'.[169] She pointed out that the protagonists introduced to political and social discourse much of the terminology of motherhood protection, including the phrase itself, which would be frequently remoulded during the next six decades.[170] Women's issues after the controversy of course became more diverse and were couched in broader terms than simply the protection of motherhood.

Another feature of the debate, as Tsukamoto Shūko stated, was that it was 'onna ni yoru onna no tame no onna no ronsō' (a women's controversy developed solely by women for the benefit of women).[171] The four women involved argued from their own personal experiences. Their views about women's causes, formulated for the first time during the controversy, became the starting point for their ideas over long subsequent periods of feminist activity. The range of views encapsulates many of the later terms of reference for feminist thinking in Japan, and mirror also the theoretical alternatives taken up by feminists in other countries. Given the dismissive views sometimes taken of Japanese feminism, it is worth noting how early (in international terms) was the formulation of these theoretical positions by Japanese feminists.

The debate made the public more aware of issues relating to the protection of motherhood. Tatewaki Sadayo correctly indicated that the three points of view in the controversy (whether one should opt for socialism, women's economic independence, or the central value of motherhood), encompassed dominant options within the ideas of Japanese women at that time.[172] Although the controversy originally embraced the single subject of motherhood, in the course of its development it extended to many other women's issues, including employment, economic independence, and suffrage. Kōuchi Nobuko stated that the controversy in effect presented 'fujin kaihō no kihonteki mitorizu' (a rough sketch map of the agenda of women's liberation in Japan).[173]

---

[169] Molony, 'The Japanese debate over motherhood protection', p. 129.
[170] *Ibid.*, p. 129.
[171] Tsukamoto, 'Yosano Akiko, Hiratsuka Raichō, Yamakawa Kikue no bosei hogo ronsō', p. 248.
[172] Tatewaki, *Nihon no Fujin*, pp. 33–6.
[173] Kōuchi, 'Bosei hogo ronsō no rekishiteki igi', p. 29.

The controversy embraced the problems which the women's movement was likely to face in the future, and presented strategic options for the movement. The debate was also a stepping stone in these women's feminist careers. It led them in new political and legal directions.[174] As a preparatory period for the women's movement, it opened up a set of possibilities for the establishment of structured women's political associations, such as the Shin Fujin Kyōkai (the Association of New Women) founded by Hiratsuka, and the Sekirankai (the Red Wave Society), whose main objectives were to raise female status and extend women's socio-political rights.[175] The debate set the stage for a wider public discussion of women's roles and participation in society.[176]

Yosano Akiko continued to write articles on women's issues in leading magazines. She sought the realisation of complete democracy, and turned her energy towards female education and political reform.[177] She co-founded a private educational institution called Bunka Gakuin (the Cultural Academy) in Tokyo in 1921, with her husband Tekkan, Imura Isaku, Kawarazaki Natsu and others.[178] The academy became a suitable place to advance her theories of women's economic independence. Her close association with the Academy gave her opportunities to work for the realisation of a new society in which husbands and wives would take equal responsibility for their households.[179]

Yamakawa became more absorbed in left-wing politics. She was involved in launching socialist women's organisations such as the Sekirankai (the Red Wave Society) and Yōkakai (the Eighth Day

---

[174] Rodd, 'Yosano Akiko and the Taishō debate', p. 198.

[175] *Ibid.*, p. 198.

[176] Kōuchi, 'Kaidai', pp. 318–20.

[177] Yosano wrote a few articles on women's suffrage. As with her earlier stance on motherhood, she rarely participated in the practical aspects of women's campaigns. See Rodd, 'Yosano Akiko and the Taishō debate' p. 198; Ichikawa, *Jiden: Senzen Hen*, pp. 219–21; Yamamoto, *Yama no Ugoku Hi Kitaru*, pp. 212–3.

[178] This was a mixed higher educational institution, which comprised *daigakubu* (a university section) and *chūgakubu* (a middle school section). Its main objective was to provide both male and female students with an artistic education, which valued freedom and individuality. Yosano taught classical Japanese literature at this academy, and in other ways too she devoted herself to female education. See Sōgō Joseishi Kenkyūkai (ed.), *Bunka to Shisō*, p. 220; Tsukamoto, 'Yosano Akiko, Hiratsuka Raichō, Yamakawa Kikue no bosei hogo ronsō', p. 241; Irie Shunkō (ed.), *Yosano Akiko* (1985), pp. 77–8; Jō Natsuko, 'Yosano Akiko', in Setouchi Harumi (ed.), *Hi to Moeta Joryū Bungaku* (1989), pp. 41–6.

[179] Rodd, 'Yosano Akiko and the Taishō debate', p. 198.

Society).[180] She played a very active role in developing socialist theory in Japan from a female perspective. When the Nihon Rōdō Kumiaikai Hyōgikai (the Japan Trade Unions Council) was formed in 1925, Yamakawa was closely associated with its women's section.[181] The conference it organised between September and October 1925 was considered to be 'the first [women's] conference in Japan which raised working women's problems as a main topic for serious discussion'.[182] Yamakawa drew up plans for the women's section, which included a full investigation of the living and employment conditions of women in Japan.[183] If one compares Yamakawa's initial view of the protection of motherhood with the demands she made in this programme, one sees notable shifts in her position. She was now advocating concrete action and organisational change, and emphasised the need for campaigns to improve working conditions. Her seven-point programme laid a basis for the revival of the motherhood debate in the labour movement. The women's section of the Nihon Rōdō Kumiaikai Hyōgikai (the Japan Trade Unions Council) served as 'one vehicle for attempting to further both maternity benefits and equal employment for women'.[184]

Yamada Waka's views on motherhood were the most practical, and probably had the firmest connection to everyday life. After the controversy Yamada Waka worked further on this subject. She wrote articles in leading women's magazines, such as *Shufu no Tomo* (*Housewives' Companion*), and established herself as a leading female commentator.[185]

---

[180] Tsukamoto, 'Yosano Akiko, Hiratsuka Raichō, Yamakawa Kikue no bosei hogo ronsō', pp. 246–7; Sōgō Joseishi Kenkyūkai (ed.), *Bunka to Shisō*, p. 220; Suzuki, *Joseishi o Hiraku*, vol. 2, pp. 113–5; Esashi, 'Yamakawa Kikue', p. 290; Mackie, *Creating Socialist Women in Japan*, pp. 102–5, 160–1; Hane, *Reflections on the Way to the Gallows*, p. 163.

[181] Molony, 'The Japanese debate over motherhood protection', p. 129.

[182] Sakurai, *Bosei Hogo Undōshi*, pp. 50–2.

[183] Mackie, *Creating Socialist Women in Japan*, pp. 111–2. The plans Yamakawa drew up clarified the main objectives of the women's section of the Japan Trade Unions Council, and the Council's policy stated what action should be taken for the sake of female workers, and what methods should be used to develop such campaigns. See Sakurai, *Bosei Hogo Undōshi*, p. 53; Molony, 'The Japanese debate over motherhood protection', pp. 129–30.

[184] Yamakawa's concern for protecting motherhood was long-lasting. She was appointed as the first director of the *Fujin Shōnen Kyoku* (Women and Minors' Bureau) in the Ministry of Labour in 1947. This was an entirely appropriate role for her, one that made best use of her long-standing interest in these issues. See Sakurai, *Bosei Hogo Undōshi*, p. 50.

[185] Yamazaki, *Ameyuki-san no Uta*, pp. 217–8.

She advised women in her advice column of the *Asahi Shinbun*, and helped some of them in a private capacity.[186] Yamazaki Tomoko, who wrote a biography of Waka, interviewed several women who were looked after by her, and stressed her philanthropic work for women.[187] Yamazaki also stressed a characteristic common to all her interviewees' assessments of Waka, which was that her role as '*kagirinaki bosei no hito*' (a woman who had boundless maternal affection) had struck them much more than her written theories about motherhood.[188]

Compared to Yamakawa and Hiratsuka, who were voicing their ideas to safeguard motherhood in the early and mid 1920s, Yamada Waka did not start campaigning until the 1930s, when the subject was an even greater matter for public discussion.[189] The Fusen Kakutoku Dōmei (Women's Suffrage League) took the initiative in discussing concrete steps to protect mothers and children, most notably in the fifth Zen Nihon Fusen Taikai (National Convention of Women's Suffrage) on 18 February 1934.[190] In this convention the immediate enactment of the Boshi Hojo Hō (the Mothers and Children's Allowance Law) was advocated.[191] On 29 September 1934 the Bosei Hogo Hō Seitei Sokushin Fujin Renmei (Women's League for the Promotion of the Enactment of the Law to Protect Motherhood) was founded.[192] This League had many eminent feminists as its active members, and

---

[186] *Ibid.*, p. 208; Tomoko Yamazaki (trans. by Wakako Hironaka & Ann Kostant), *The Story of Yamada Waka: From Prostitute to Feminist Pioneer* (1985), p. 137.

[187] Yamazaki, *Ameyuki-san no Uta*, pp. 216–27.

[188] *Ibid.*, p. 228.

[189] *Ibid.*, p. 228. The economic crisis in c. 1929–34, consequent upon the Great Slump, relegated labourers and peasant farmers to a life of even more extreme poverty. *Boshi katei* (fatherless families or mother-and-child families) were particularly badly hit by the depression. The number of joint mother and child suicides increased sharply. Such incidents were reported in newspapers almost every day, which drew public attention, and as a consequence provision for motherhood began to be discussed frequently. A campaign demanding that the state protect mothers and children—the most vulnerable groups in society—was launched at this time.

[190] *Ibid.*, pp. 228–9; Ichikawa, *Jiden: Senzen Hen*, pp. 218–29. The first National Convention of Women's Suffrage was held in 1930, and after that the convention was held every year.

[191] Molony, 'The Japanese debate over motherhood protection', p. 131.

[192] Ichikawa, *Jiden: Senzen Hen*, pp. 356–8. According to the rules the League laid down, its main objective was to achieve the enactment of the *Bosei Hogo Hō* (the Motherhood Protection Law), which would provide mothers who had small children with financial support, and would thus reinforce their motherhood. The League's name was changed to *Bosei Hogo Dōmei* (The Protection of Motherhood League) the following year.

Yamada Waka was elected as its Chairwoman.[193] Yamada became
central to a significant *bosei hogo undō* (motherhood protection campaign). The League took immediate action, submitting the Boshi Fujo
Hō Seitei ni Kansuru Seigansho (a written petition concerning the
enactment of the Mothers and Children's Allowance Law) to the 67th
Diet.[194] The League also organised various events and social gatherings in order to draw public attention to its activities. Its persistent efforts at last bore fruit, and the bill passed the Diet under the
name of the Boshi Hogo Hō (The Mother-Child Protection Law),
on 13 March, 1937.[195] It granted financial assistance to mothers with
children under 13 years of age, and to grandmothers who had to
look after grandchildren under 13 years of age.[196]

The active role which Yamada Waka played as Chairwoman of
the Protection of Motherhood League, and in particular the League's
role in the enactment of this new Act to protect motherhood, raised
her status considerably. Yamada Waka's enduring dedication to these

---

[193] Yamazaki, *Ameyuki-san no Uta*, pp. 229–30. The League's active members comprised many prominent women who had been working for women's movements
over a long period, such as Kaneko Shigeri, Sakai Magara, Ichikawa Fusae and
others.

[194] Ichikawa, *Jiden: Senzen Hen*, pp. 363–4; Mackie, *Creating Socialist Women*, pp.
145–8; Molony, 'The Japanese debate over motherhood', p. 131; Yamazaki, *Ameyuki-
san*, p. 231; 'Boshi fujo hō seitei yōbō ni kansuru ken kengi' (26 October, 1935),
in Ichibangase Yasuko (ed.), *Nihon Fujin Mondai Shiryō Shūsei*, vol. 6 (1978), p. 294;
Kaneko Shigeri, 'Boshi fujo hō seitei sokushin undōshi', *Shakai Jigyō*, 20:10 (January,
1937), reprinted in Ichibangase (ed.), *Nihon Fujin Mondai Shiryō Shūsei*, vol. 6, pp.
294–302. The main objective of this petition was quite specific: to provide mothers of small children, who had lost their husbands and could not make a living,
with financial assistance, and so to deter them from committing mother-child suicide. The League also submitted the *Boshi Hōmu ni Kansuru Seigansho* (a written petition concerning the establishment of homes for mothers and children) to the Home
Office. This requested the construction of homes to accommodate mothers with
small children, who could not make a living, in order to reduce mother-child suicides. On 13 May, 1936, the League submitted the *Boshi Fujo Hōan* (a Mothers and
Children's Allowance bill) to the Diet. The main objective of this bill was to provide mothers with children in extreme poverty with financial assistance, to guarantee them a minimum standard of living, and so to enable them to bring up
healthy children. In the bill the League requested the state to provide mothers with
children under the age of fifteen years with an allowance of 30 *sen* per day to the
mother, and 20 *sen* per day to each child. The League also demanded that the
costs of these allowances should be met by the National Treasury.

[195] Molony, 'The Japanese debate over motherhood', p. 131; 'Dai 70-kai teikoku
gigai shūgiin gunji kyūgo hō chū kaisei hōritsu angai ikken iinkai giroku', 5 & 6 (6
& 8 March, 1937), reprinted in Ichibangase (ed.), *Nihon Fujin Mondai Shiryō Shūsei*,
vol. 6, pp. 302–11.

[196] Yamazaki, *Ameyuki-san no Uta*, p. 231.

causes placed her in the forefront of these feminists. Indeed, Yamazaki Tomoko, a biographer of Yamada Waka, gave Yamada the complementary title '*bosei no keshin no hito*' (a person who is the incarnation of motherhood).[197]

Hiratsuka was not as committed to the motherhood campaign as Yamada.[198] However, she did translate her views into practice, by founding the Shin Fujin Kyōkai (the Association of New Women) in 1919.[199] The need to improve rights for women with children was one of the main objectives of the Association.[200] Previously Hiratsuka had been mainly concerned with middle and upper-middle class women. She now drew attention to working-class women's occupational and educational conditions which affected their roles as mothers.[201]

---

[197] *Ibid.*, p. 230.

[198] Yasutaka, 'Yamada Waka', p. 90.

[199] Tanaka (ed.), *Josei Kaihō no Shisō*, pp. 205–6; Yoneda, *Kindai Nihon Joseishi*, vol. 1, pp. 149–50.

[200] Hiratsuka, *Genshi*, vol. 3, pp. 50–1.

[201] *Ibid.*, pp. 57–9.

CHAPTER SIX

HIRATSUKA RAICHŌ AND THE ASSOCIATION OF NEW WOMEN

Introduction

Eight years after the foundation of the Seitō Society and less than a year after the protection of motherhood controversy ended, Hiratsuka Raichō founded another women's organisation, the Shin Fujin Kyōkai (the Association of New Women), in autumn 1919. Like many of the activities Hiratsuka was involved in, this Association was not studied before 1945. However, from then most general books on Japanese women's history written in Japanese referred to the Association, and acknowledged its significant role in the history of women's organisations.[1] Even so, detailed research on the Association has been very limited.[2] Moreover, almost all existing works omit certain key questions. For example, they do not discuss how the social and political climate in 1919 coloured the Association, and how it differed

---

[1] See Inoue, *Nihon Joseishi*, p. 255; Tatewaki, *Nihon no Fujin*, pp. 49–54; Takamure, *Josei no Rekishi*, vol. 2, pp. 298–305; Tanaka, *Josei Kaihō no Shisō to Kōdō*, pp. 205–8; Hayashi *et al.* (eds), *Nihon Joseishi*, pp. 243–4; Suzuki, *Joseishi o Hiraku*, vol. 1, pp. 71–5; Yoneda, *Kindai Nihon Joseishi*, vol. 1, pp. 150–4; Esashi & Ide, *Taishō Demokurashii to Josei*, pp. 90–103; Nagoya Joseishi Kenkyūkai (ed.), *Haha no Jidai*, pp. 153–65. Some books in English briefly discuss the Association as well. See Mackie, *Creating Socialist Women*, pp. 104–5; Hane, *Reflections on the Way to the Gallows*, p. 163; Sievers, *Flowers in Salt*, p. 187; Rodd, 'Yosano Akiko and the Taishō debate over the "new women"', p. 198, in Gail Bernstein, *Recreating Japanese Women, 1600–1945* (1991).

[2] For works on the Association in Japanese, see Kodama Katsuko, '*Josei Dōmei fukkoku ni atatte*' in Domesu Shuppan (ed.), *Josei Dōmei Kaisetsu, Sōmokuji, Sakuin* (1985), pp. 9–19; Matsuo Takayoshi, '*Taishōki fujin no seijiteki jiyū kakutoku undō: Shin Fujin Kyōkai kara Fusen Kakutoku Dōmei e*', in Domesu Shuppan (ed.), *Josei Dōmei Kaisetsu* (1985), pp. 23–49; Yoshimi Kaneko, *Fujin Sanseiken* (1971), pp. 141–53; Ichikawa Fusae & Kodama Katsuko (eds), *Fujin Sanseiken Undō Shōshi* (1981), pp. 35–79. In English, see K. S. Molony, 'One woman who dared: Ichikawa Fusae and the Japanese women's suffrage movement' (unpublished Ph.D. thesis, University of Michigan, 1980), pp. 94–151; Barbara Molony, 'State and women in modern Japan: feminist discourses in the Meiji and Taishō eras', in Janet Hunter (ed.), *Japan: State and People in the Twentieth Century* (London, 1999), pp. 39–50; Robins-Mowry, *The Hidden Sun*, pp. 65–9; Akiko Tokuza, *The Rise of the Feminist Movement in Japan* (1999), pp. 107–91.

from other contemporary women's associations like the Sekirankai (the Red Wave Society). They also omit any account of how Hiratsuka's outlook on the Association differed from that of her two co-workers, Oku and Ichikawa.[3] There has been hardly any evaluation of the impact of the Association on the later development of women's political activities, apart from the partial amendment of the Peace Police Law.

The Foundation of the Association of New Women

It is significant that Hiratsuka's founding of the Association of New Women was completely different from her founding of the Seitō Society. She had founded the Seitō Society reluctantly and for a time did not take her involvement with it seriously.[4] By comparison, she established the Association with much determination. She later stated that her urge to launch a women's political and social campaign had become 'uncontrollable'.[5] She felt that it was vital to establish a women's organisation with features that the Seitō Society had lacked. This was to be an organised political movement. The aim grew out of her arguments about the protection of motherhood:

> Through my experience of having been closely involved with the controversy about the protection of motherhood, I realised at last that the time had come for me to launch social reforms from a woman's standpoint. If women have no political rights, they will achieve nothing. It is absolutely crucial for them to obtain political rights.[6]

This quotation is significant in two respects. Hiratsuka had finally decided to put her ideas into practice. The controversy between the four leading female commentators about motherhood went no further than a heated discussion in print, and did not develop into a

---

[3] For example, Akiko Tokuza gave a good survey of the Association's activities. She focused on Oku Mumeo's contributions. K. S. Molony also gave a detailed account of the activities of the Association from its foundation to when Ichikawa left it, but had little to say on its later stage, after Ichikawa's resignation. Since Molony's main concern was to examine Ichikawa's involvement, her work did not assess Oku and Hiratsuka's contributions. This omission is also very common in Japanese articles on the subject.

[4] Hiratsuka, *Genshi*, vol. 1, pp. 317–9; Hiratsuka, *Watakushi*, pp. 73–5.

[5] Hiratsuka, *Genshi*, vol. 3, pp. 49–52, 73; Hiratsuka, *Watakushi*, pp. 170–1.

[6] Hiratsuka, *Genshi*, vol. 3, p. 47.

campaign to petition the Diet for better protection for mothers. This was now to change with the creation of Hiratsuka's new women's organisation. The quotation also demonstrates that Hiratsuka had finally come to realise the key importance of women's political rights, if she was going to achieve legal changes concerning the protection of motherhood.

Hiratsuka gave the following explanation clarifying the reason why she decided to found the Association.

> At that time I felt that the time was ripe for women to start working for their own political rights. I was hoping that someone else was going to make the first move, so I patiently waited for a while. However, there was no sign of that, so I realised that I ought to take the first step, advocating the need for women's political and social reform, and founding a women's association. I was pretty convinced that if I took the first steps and provided other women with a lead, some women would follow me, take an active role, and greatly contribute.[7]

And so she founded the Association of New Women. The Association was founded after the First World War, at a time of sweeping social change. The Russian Revolution had created the first 'socialist' country in the world. The efforts of women's suffrage campaigns in advanced western countries were finally being rewarded. Canada (in 1918), Austria (in 1919), Germany (in 1919), Sweden (in 1919), Luxembourg (in 1919), the Netherlands (in 1919), and the U.S.A. (in 1920) were among the countries where the right to vote was gained by women after the war.[8] Such wider changes favourable to women exerted a strong influence on the Japanese women's movement, including the foundation of the Association of New Women.

Apart from such international influences, the foundation of the Association was also encouraged by the domestic social and political climate. Taishō 'Democracy' had a great impact on much of Japanese society. It increased workers' class consciousness and helped to raise both intellectuals' and labourers' interest in politics, resulting in a growing demand for universal suffrage.[9] During the 41st

---

[7] Hiratsuka, 'Shin Fujin Kyōkai no kaiko', *Fujin Kōron* (March-July 1923), reprinted in Hiratsuka, *Chosakushū*, vol. 3, pp. 277-8.

[8] Lisa Tuttle, *Encyclopedia of Feminism* (1986, London, 1987 edn), pp. 370-1. In Britain the Electoral Reform Bill became law in January 1918, and all women aged thirty and over obtained the vote.

[9] Imai Seiichi, *Taishō Demokurashii* (1984, 1991 edn), pp. 226-7.

Session of the Diet, the Kokumintō (the People's Party), the Kenseikai (the Kensei Party) and the Seiyūkai (the Seiyū Party, which was the party in power) submitted separate bills to extend the male electorate.[10] Yet none of these political parties at that time requested universal male suffrage. As a result, Hara's Cabinet extended the vote to men who paid more than three yen tax instead of ten yen. This increased the electorate from 1.5 million to 3.3 million.[11] It was in this context that women and male workers became more aware of their political potential and launched their campaigns for the right to vote.

Moreover, the economic situation in Japan after the First World War led to rice riots and strikes. Japan reaped much benefit from the war, and some people experienced unprecedented economic prosperity.[12] On the other hand, poor farmers, fishermen and labourers did not gain and suffered from high inflation, which was induced by the upturn of the economy. In particular, a sharp increase in the price of rice in the first half of 1918 was especially detrimental. Labourers' industrial actions and tenant farmers' disputes increased sharply.[13] On 3 August 1918 about three hundred women living in a fishing village in Toyama Prefecture protested against the soaring price of rice.[14] Following this protest in Toyama, a large number of so-called "rice riots" took place in many areas.[15] The government

---

[10] Shinobu Seizaburō, *Taishō Demokurashii-shi*, 2 vols (1958), vol. 2, pp. 489–504; Esashi & Ide, *Taishō Demokurashii to Josei*, pp. 80–5, 90. The Kenseikai (Constitutional Party) was a political party founded in October 1916. It was a relatively progressive party, and supported international cooperation and further domestic political reform. The Seiyūkai was one of the major political parties between 1900 and 1940. It was also called the Rikken Seiyūkai (Friends of Constitutional Government Party). It was founded in September 1900 by Itō Hirobumi, and came into power in October 1900. The Seiyūkai's popularity reached its peak under Hara Kei, who became the third party leader in 1914 and was appointed prime minister in September 1918. In 1940 the party was dissolved.

[11] Kano Masanao, *Taishō Demokurashii* (1976), p. 178; Imai, *Taishō Demokurashii*, pp. 227–8.

[12] Yoneda, *Kindai Nihon Joseishi*, vol. 1, pp. 128–9; Esashi & Ide, *Taishō Demokurashii to Josei*, pp. 56–60.

[13] Imai, *Taishō Demokurashii*, pp. 225–6.

[14] Yoneda, *Kindai Nihon Joseishi*, vol. 1, pp. 128–32; Esashi & Ide, *Taishō Demokurashii to Josei*, pp. 64–8; Kano, *Taishō Demokurashii*, pp. 161–6; Imai, *Taishō Demokurashii*, pp. 174–81; Shinobu, *Taishō Demokurashii*, vol. 2, pp. 476–82.

[15] Yoneda, *Kindai Nihon Joseishi*, vol. 1, pp. 131–2; Esashi & Ide, *Taishō Demokurashii to Josei*, pp. 64–6; Kano, *Taishō Demokurashii*, p. 166; Shinobu, *Taishō Demokurashii-shi*, p. 482; Imai, *Taishō Demokurashii*, pp. 179–80.

sent police and armed forces to suppress such actions. Labourers in factories, who were sympathetic to rice protests, were also influenced by the Russian Revolution, and they too started industrial action.[16] They demanded shorter working hours and a rise in wages. The incidence of such industrial action rose steadily after the war, and in this regard Japan shared the tendencies of many other industrial societies at that time.

Although Hiratsuka was aware of international trends in social and labour problems, she rarely referred to them in her writing until her visit to textile mills in Nagoya, in summer 1919. This visit contributed significantly to her decision to found the Association a few months later. The visit to Nagoya was initially made by invitation to give a lecture for a women's summer school there, sponsored by the Nagoya Newspaper Company and the Chūkyō Fujinkai (the Chūkyō Women's Society).[17] During this trip she visited textile mills and came to know Ichikawa Fusae, who acted as her guide. The relationship they formed led to their foundation of the Association.

At that time the conditions of female factory workers were frequently discussed in the press, with many articles appearing on this issue. Hiratsuka was asked to write some articles on the problems of working women by a left-wing newspaper called the *Kokumin Shinbun* (*the People's Newspaper*) long before she visited Nagoya, and she used her trip to do this.[18] She visited eleven factories including Aichi Orimono (Aichi Textile Factory), Kondō Bōseki (Kondō Spinning Mill) and Tōyō Bōseki (Tōyō Spinning Mill), seeing at first-hand conditions in them.[19] She left few details about the eleven factories which she visited, but in her article she gave an account of Aichi Textile Factory, one of the worst of its kind:

> What I saw there was a hellish sight. Immediately after I stepped into a work room of the factory, the first thing which came into view was the terrible sight of innumerable fragments of cotton dust floating all

[16] Yoneda, *Kindai Nihon Joseishi*, vol. 1, pp. 130–1; Esashi & Ide, *Taishō Demokurashii to Josei*, p. 70.

[17] Hiratsuka, *Genshi*, vol. 3, pp. 56–7; Ichikawa, *Jiden: Senzen Hen*, pp. 42–4; Hiratsuka, 'Shin Fujin Kyōkai no kaiko', pp. 273–4. An account of this summer school is given by Tokuza. Tokuza, *The Rise of the Feminist Movement in Japan*, pp. 115–7.

[18] Hiratsuka, *Genshi*, vol. 3, p. 57.

[19] Hiratsuka Raichō, 'Nagoya chihō no jokō seikatsu', *Kokumin Shinbun* (8–12 September, 1919), reprinted in Hiratsuka, *Chosakushū*, vol. 3, p. 91.

over the place. When I looked around the place, everywhere was entirely covered with this cotton dust ... Dust was gathered on the hair of female workers, which made them look as if they were wearing *watabōshi* [white veils worn by brides dressed in traditional wedding kimonos]. Dust covered their eyelashes and cheeks, and stuck on their sweaty foreheads and cheeks, just like downy hair ... What surprised me even more was the fact that the great majority of women working there were nothing but children, between thirteen and sixteen years old. I was told that the oldest female worker there was thirty-five, and about half of them were children. There were hardly any female workers older than twenty ... Children who were still at a playful age had entirely lost their childlike appearance, and had withered and shrivelled faces. At work they were surrounded by cotton dust which whirled around all the time. They had to put up with the heat of the place, which was above ninety degrees Fahrenheit, as well as the constant bustling noise coming from machinery, which disrupted any peace of mind. What was worse, they were forced to work twelve-hour shifts, and their bodies and minds were tied to the spinning machines. When I came in direct contact with such a wretched and cruel scene, my heart was filled with anger.[20]

One sees here the shock of an upper middle-class woman confronted for the first time with the harsh reality of modern industry in Japan's cotton mills. Hiratsuka called these female child workers '*fushigina chīsana obasan*' ('small strange women with children's figures but middle-aged women's worn-out faces').[21] She wrote of how their prematurely aged eyes and unhealthy looking faces became imprinted in her mind. She was convinced that their inflamed, bloodshot eyes, often blurred with mucus, their extremely pale faces, sallow complexions and wooden expressionless looks were all indicative of ill health, and especially of respiratory disorders.[22]

Their wretched working environment was not the only thing that came to her attention. Hiratsuka's heart also sank when she saw the most unhygienic conditions in their dormitories.[23] She recalled that their dormitories were poorly ventilated and got so little sunshine

---

[20] *Ibid.*, pp. 93–4.
[21] *Ibid.*, p. 94.
[22] *Ibid.*, pp. 94–5. Similar accounts of female textile factory workers' conditions are given in Sievers, *Flowers in Salt*, pp. 77–8; Tsurumi, *Factory Girls*, pp. 85–9; Molony, 'Activism among women', pp. 231–3.
[23] Hiratsuka, 'Nagoya chihō no jokō seikatsu', p. 100; Hiratsuka, *Genshi*, vol. 3, p. 61.

that they looked as if they were in basements.[24] Although the size of each room was 12 *jō* (a twelve mat room) and thus quite spacious, the rooms were packed with women. Bedding had to be shared between women working different shifts of twelve hours each.[25] She also recalled seeing in these empty and dreary rooms a small magazine entitled *Tsutome* (*Duties*), which was distributed by the textile company. It was aimed at female textile workers, and was clearly designed as a tool with which to indoctrinate them. In its pages one found articles preaching the sacredness of work, the virtue of saving, and the virtue of self-sacrifice and obedience to employers, all promoting the interests of the latter rather than of the female employees.

As Hiratsuka admitted, what she saw in Nagoya was far worse than the second-hand information obtained from newspaper and magazine reports.[26] She was particularly indignant at the ways in which women workers were being misused by factory owners. Her anger was expressed as follows:

> As I began to have a better understanding of the position female factory workers were placed in, I became no longer able to overlook the ways in which 'capitalists' were taking advantage of innocent female factory workers, who did nothing but endure and obey their employers. I could not possibly ignore such cruel and damaging forms of exploitation of women. I could not help protesting against capitalists' exploitation, not only from my humanitarian standpoint but from my viewpoint on the protection of motherhood.[27]

This made her determine to found a new women's association. After Hiratsuka returned home from Nagoya in summer 1919, her plan for an association quickly took shape.[28] The first thing she did was find co-workers to assist her. Unlike when she launched the Seitō Society, she was now more experienced and knew who she needed

---

[24] Hiratsuka's account of the dormitories is given in Hiratsuka, *Genshi*, vol. 3, pp. 62–3; Hiratsuka, 'Nagoya chihō no jokō seikatsu', pp. 100–4.

[25] For a similar account of female factory workers' unhygienic conditions in dormitories, see Tsurumi, *Factory Girls*, pp. 90–2.

[26] Hiratsuka, *Genshi*, vol. 3, p. 60; Hiratsuka, 'Jokōkoku Nihon', in Hiratsuka, *Chosakushū*, vol. 3, p. 58; Hiratsuka, 'Waga kuni ni okeru jokō mondai', *Fujin Kōron* (June, 1919), reprinted in Hiratsuka, *Chosakushū*, vol. 3, pp. 61–85.

[27] *Ibid.*, p. 59.

[28] Hiratsuka, *Watakushi*, pp. 170–1.

for this venture. She chose Ichikawa Fusae and Oku Mumeo.[29] Ichikawa worked with Hiratsuka from the beginning of the Association (autumn 1919) and Oku joined them from early January 1920.[30] Both were familiar with working women's problems, and interested in learning more about them, which suited one of the main objectives of her association. Oku had worked for Fuji Gasu Spinning Mill as a factory hand.[31] Ichikawa had worked for the women's section of the Yūaikai, an early trade union, as a secretary.[32] She had edited its journal, *Rōdō Fujin* (*Working Women*), and also organised a working women's conference for the Yūaikai.[33] Prior to this, Ichikawa had worked for the Nagoya Newspaper Company as its first female journalist.[34] She took charge of women's columns and wrote a serial on existing women's associations in Nagoya, which brought her into contact with their representatives. Similarly, Oku had worked for a political magazine called *Rōdō Sekai* (*World of Labour*) as a journalist.[35] She had written many articles on female factory workers, based on her own experience. Both Ichikawa and Oku had experience of work and a strong interest in improving women's working conditions. This contrasted sharply with Hiratsuka's co-workers in the earlier Seitō Society, almost all of whom were well-brought up

---

[29] Hiratsuka, *Genshi*, vol. 3, pp. 70–2.

[30] Ichikawa, *Jiden: Senzen Hen*, pp. 50–1; Oku, *Nobi*, p. 47.

[31] *Ibid.*, pp. 40–4; Tokuza, *The Rise of the Feminist Movement in Japan*, pp. 100–1; Hiratsuka, 'Oku Mumeo-san no koto', *Fujin Kōron* (December, 1925), reprinted in Hiratsuka, *Chosakushū*, vol. 4, pp. 148–50.

[32] Ichikawa, *Jiden: Senzen Hen*, pp. 45–8; Tokuza, *The Rise of the Feminist Movement in Japan*, pp. 114–15. *Yūaikai* (Workers' Friendly Society) was one of earliest workers' organisations in Japan, founded by Suzuki Bunji (a labour leader) in August 1912. It played a significant part in the development of a labour movement in Japan. In September 1919 it changed its name to *Dai Nihon Rōdō Sōdōmei Yūaikai* (Greater Japan Labour Federation Workers' Friendly Society) and then subsequently to *Nihon Rōdō Sōdōmei* (Japan General Federation of Labour). On the *Yūaikai*, see Imai, *Taishō Demokurashii*, pp. 90–5; Suzuki Yūko, *Josei to Rōdō Kumiai*, 2 vols (1990), vol. 1, pp. 25–91; Esashi & Ide, *Taishō Demokurashii to Josei*, pp. 70–1. The key work in English on the *Yūaikai* is Stephen Large, *The Yūaikai, 1912–1919* (1972).

[33] Mackie, *Creating Socialist Women in Japan*, pp. 77–80, 108–9; Ichikawa, *Jiden: Senzen Hen*, pp. 45–8; Suzuki, *Josei to Rōdō Kumiai*, vol. 1, pp. 46–64; Tokuza, *The Rise of the Feminist Movement in Japan*, p. 115. The Yūaikai Women's Division published *Yuai Fujin* (*Yuai Woman*) from 1916 to 1918. It later became *Rōdō Fujin* (*Labour Women*).

[34] Ichikawa, *Jiden: Senzen Hen*, pp. 34–6; Nagoya Joseishi Kenkyūkai, *Haha no Jidai*, pp. 313–5; Tokuza, *The Rise of the Feminist Movement in Japan*, p. 113.

[35] Oku, *Nobi*, pp. 39–44; Tokuza, *The Rise of the Feminist Movement in Japan*, . 118.

young women who had no real working background. Oku and Ichikawa were also well-educated, motivated and capable women. Although they had never been involved in women's movements before, they met Hiratsuka's requirements as members of the new women's association. During her trip to Nagoya, Hiratsuka became impressed by Ichikawa, who she later described as:

> a woman gifted with interests in social affairs, which was rare for a Japanese woman in those days. She had wide understanding of social problems and ideology. She is a model career woman in modern Japan. Ichikawa is 'a new woman' in all regards. She has common sense and a fine practical brain. She possesses business talent. She has a mind which responds cautiously but quickly. She has a body like a man's.[36]

Hiratsuka was struck by Ichikawa's vitality, enthusiasm, youth and organisational skill.[37] Ichikawa immediately accepted Hiratsuka's proposal that she become her closest colleague.[38] Ichikawa was enthusiastic to work for women's causes, and supported the launching of a women's movement to advocate women's emancipation and the improvement of their status. Ichikawa later wrote that she had faith in Hiratsuka as a leader. And so these two women launched the Association of New Women in early November 1919.[39] According to Hiratsuka's recollections in 1923, she initially planned to follow a policy similar to the Seitō Society, which was to inaugurate a high-class magazine for women dealing with political and social issues, to recruit like-minded people through the magazine, and then to launch various social campaigns.[40]

The first thing Hiratsuka and Ichikawa undertook was to draw up a concrete plan for the new association, which Hiratsuka provisionally called the Nihon Fujin Kyōkai (the Japanese Women's Association).[41] She formulated six objectives:

1. The Association will demand women's suffrage to reorganise society. The Association will also request the abolition of 'feudalistic'

---

[36] Hiratsuka Raichō, 'Shin Fujin Kyōkai no Kaiko', *Fujin Kōron* (March-July 1923), reprinted in Hiratsuka, *Chosakushū*, vol. 3, p. 274.
[37] Hiratsuka, *Genshi*, vol. 3, p. 50; Hiratsuka Raichō, 'Ichikawa Fusae-san no koto', *Fujin Kōron* (March, 1925), reprinted in Hiratsuka, *Chosakushū*, vol. 4, p. 108.
[38] Ichikawa, *Jiden: Senzen Hen*, pp. 50–1.
[39] Hiratsuka, *Watakushi*, pp. 169–72.
[40] Hiratsuka, 'Shin Fujin Kyōkai no kaiko', p. 272.
[41] Hiratsuka, *Genshi*, vol. 3, p. 50.

laws disadvantageous to women. It will aim to protect motherhood. It will launch campaigns to fulfil these objectives.

2. The Association will keep in touch with other women's groups in
   all parts of Japan, act in conjunction with them, and organise a
   large-scale nationwide women's union.
3. The Association will hold lectures dealing with the problems of
   women and labour, difficulties in everyday life and other social
   problems in Japan.
4. The Association will publish its own journal.
5. The Association will build a school, to serve as an educational
   institution designed for working women, and it will publish a working women's newspaper. The Association will use these as a base
   to establish strong women's trade unions.
6. The Association will build a women's hall, which will provide
   women with various further facilities.[42]

This initial plan for the Association shared only two similarities with
the main objectives of the Seitō Society, which were points 3 and
4—though as far as point 4 was concerned, the Association's lectures were intended to cover a much wider range of social and labour
problems than the Seitō Society's focus on women's problems.

Point 1 clarified the Association's intention of focusing on social
and political campaigns, such as women's suffrage and legal reform.
(The Seitō Society had never organised any social and political campaigns.) Point 2 showed that Hiratsuka's initial narrow ideas about
women's causes in her Seitō days had now much expanded. Although
the Seitō Society had very limited membership and did not cooperate with other women's societies, the Association's initial plan
demonstrated that Hiratsuka had finally begun to see the need to
act in conjunction with other women's organisations. While the Seitō
Society had been aimed at middle and upper-middle class educated
women with literary interests, point 5 showed that the Association
intended to attract working-class women as well as those from higher
social groups. It was quite ironic that the Association's manifesto
bore a striking resemblance to that of the Shin Shin Fujinkai (the
Real New Women's Association), the Seitō Society's rival society,
which Hiratsuka had criticised earlier.[43]

---

[42] Hiratsuka, *Watakushi*, pp. 171–2.
[43] Nishikawa, *Heiminsha no Onna*, pp. 346–8.

Points 5 and 6, which planned to set up schools and other facilities for working-class women, and also to establish a women's hall, demonstrated the broadened awareness of Hiratsuka's understanding of working-class women. In particular, point 6 (the building of a women's hall) was well ahead of her time. Although Hiratsuka did not clarify where this idea came from, Ichikawa assumed that Hiratsuka had taken it from the ideas behind Hull House in Chicago.[44] Later when Ichikawa visited Hull House, she became convinced that it had served as a model for the women's hall Hiratsuka planned in this initial manifesto.[45] However, the first women's hall (which Hiratsuka had hoped to found in 1919) was not finally established until 1977 in Japan.[46] Hiratsuka's idea in 1919 to establish a women's hall appears in retrospect to be both advanced and perhaps overly ambitious for its time.

That limitation aside, the initial plan for the Association was carefully conceived. Hiratsuka was keen to address a variety of problems facing women from various social backgrounds, and she hoped to enhance their opportunities and status. She also realised the necessity of educating and training them. The key to this enlarged perspective on her part lay in her visit to the textile mills in Nagoya. That visit made her realise that the only way to rescue such vulnerable female workers was to provide them with education, which would give them a new perspective on their lives. She wished to see them educated to the level of their western counterparts, who had come to see that they had rights and entitlements as workers, and

---

[44] Hull House was one of the first settlement establishments with an international reputation, and it was situated in the heart of Chicago where many immigrants lived. It provided them with a restaurant, a gymnasium, and additional educational and other facilities.

[45] Ichikawa, *Jiden: Senzen Hen*, pp. 106–7.

[46] The first women's hall in Japan was called the Kokuritsu Fujin Kyōiku Kaikan (National Women's Education Centre), which was founded in 1977 in Saitama Prefecture. With the foundation of this centre as a start, a great number of women's centres and halls, which aimed to promote women's status and provide women with occupational and educational training, were founded throughout Japan in the 1980s and 1990s. On the National Women's Education Centre, see Josei no Jōhō o Hirogeru Kai (ed.), *Onnatachi no Benrichō* (1991), p. 55; The Kokuritsu Fujin Kyōiku Kaikan, *Kokuritsu Fujin Kyōiku Kaikan Shōkai Video* (video, produced by the Kokuritsu Fujin Kyōiku Kaikan, Saitama, n.d.); personal interview with Nishibori Wakako (head librarian of the Kokuritsu Fujin Kyōiku Kaikan Library), 10 April, 1991, Ranzan, Saitama Prefecture.

had set up their own trade unions, organising campaigns advocating improvement in their working conditions.[47] Hiratsuka's proposal to build a school designed for working women, and her view of the necessity to found a women's trade union—seen in her plan for the Association—demonstrated her response to the conditions of these textile workers. She wanted to enhance their sense of personal worth, and give them the opportunity to fight for improvements in their working conditions.[48] Although her visit to the Nagoya mills caused her much shock and concern, it had as its result the enlargement of her women's programme. From then on she was no longer able to ignore working-class women's issues.

Hiratsuka's Participation in a Women's Conference in Osaka

While Hiratsuka was at an early stage of drafting the objectives of the Association, the Osaka Asahi Newspaper Company approached her and asked her to address a large women's conference in Osaka.[49] As this conference was sponsored by the newspaper company, she knew that it would receive much publicity and public attention. She saw this as an ideal opportunity to make an initial appeal for support for her new women's association.[50] Although she was not fully ready for a public announcement, she did not want to let such an opportunity slip. By the time Hiratsuka attended the conference on 24 November 1919, she had completed the manifesto of her new association which Ichikawa named the Shin Fujin Kyōkai (The Association of New Women).[51] The conference was designed to bring all middle-class women's organisations in the Kinki, Sanyō, Shikoku, Hokuriku and Kyūshū regions together.[52] It was held at a public hall in Nakanoshima in Osaka—a large flourishing city. It bore witness to women's recent progress, received much public attention, and

---

[47] Hiratsuka, *Genshi*, vol. 3, pp. 49–52.
[48] Hiratsuka, *Watakushi*, pp. 170–2.
[49] Hiratsuka, *Genshi*, vol. 3, pp. 52–3; Ichikawa, *Jiden: Senzen Hen*, p. 51.
[50] Hiratsuka, *Watakushi*, pp. 172–3.
[51] Ichikawa, *Jiden: Senzen Hen*, p. 51; Ichikawa Fusae, 'Sōritsu yori *Josei Dōmei* hakkan made, part 1', *Josei Dōmei*, 1 (October, 1920), p. 45.
[52] Tokuza, *The Rise of the Feminist Movement in Japan*, p. 122.
[53] Hayashi *et al.* (eds), *Nihon Joseishi*, p. 243. The number of participants was

was the largest women's conference held in Japan up to that time.[53]

This conference was the first occasion when women's associations and societies based in the Kansai region met together. It launched the Zen Kansai Fujin Rengōkai (All-Kansai Federation of Women's Organisations).[54] The main theme of the conference was 'to attempt to revive women's contemporary life, which has many faults, on the basis of women's joint forces'.[55] During the conference many women's associations demanded women's suffrage and the improvement of women's living conditions.

Hiratsuka gave a speech entitled 'Fujin no danketsu o nozomu' ('I really hope to see solidarity among women').[56] Her talk fitted well with the main theme of the conference. It began with a strong appeal to the representatives of women's associations:

> If you allow me to express my expectations about the future of the All-Kansai Federation of Women's Organisations, I hope that it will not end by being temporary, but will be long-sustained. I also hope that it will develop into an influential body, with an active social role, not only for the sake of women in the Kansai region, but for all women in Japan.[57]

This speech was an extended version of the manifesto of the Association of New Women.[58] The key issues raised in her speech were almost identical to those in her manifesto:

> The time has come for all women to unite in their interest to fulfil their obligations and pursue their rights. Now is the time when women should enrich themselves and broaden their education. Now is also the

about four thousand. All of them were women, divided into two categories. One comprised delegates and members of women's associations and societies, in the Kinki, Sanyō, Chūgoku, Hokuriku and Kyūshū regions, while the other comprised a female public from all parts of the Kansai region. The women's groups which participated comprised women's occupational, social, religious, and local societies or associations, mainly dominated by middle-class women. In addition, representatives of foreign women living in Japan also attended.

[54] Hiratsuka, Genshi, vol. 3, p. 53; Hiratsuka Raichō, 'Fujin no danketsu o nozomu: Kansai Fujinkai Rengōkai ni oite' (lecture delivered in Osaka, 24 November, 1919), reprinted in Hiratsuka, Chosakushū, vol. 3, pp. 125–7.

[55] Hiratsuka, Genshi, vol. 3, p. 53; Hiratsuka, Watakushi, p. 174; Hayashi et al. (eds), Nihon Joseishi, p. 243.

[56] The content of her talk was printed in the evening edition of the Osaka Asahi Shinbun (24 November, 1920).

[57] Hiratsuka, 'Fujin no danketsu o nozomu', p. 125.

[58] Shin Fujin Kyōkai, 'Sengen', Josei Dōmei, 1 (October, 1920), p. 1.

time when women should make efforts to elevate their social status by
their solidarity, and cooperate with men and participate in campaigns
to improve society in order to acquire rights as women and mothers.
If women do not rise to this opportunity now, there is no doubt that
our future society will continue to be a male-dominated one excluding women. We believe that the great majority of misfortunes afflicting
mankind and the world result from male-dominated societies. We do
not believe that Japanese women will remain ignorant and incapable
for ever. There are already quite a few learned and able 'new women'
in our women's circles. We do not doubt that in addition to these
recognised women, there are many more thoughtful and capable women
with opinions of their own, who are as yet unknown. Why haven't
these women's abilities been united and come into play as a social
influence? We wonder whether this is because each woman is in a
state of utter isolation, does not have any contact with any other
women, and does not make any effort to combine her ability with
other women's to work for a common aim. Moreover, there have not
been any women's organisations, which help to unite them. In view
of these circumstances, we have decided to unite our comrades and
found the Association of New Women as an organ for women's col-
lective ability, even though we are fully aware of our limitations. We
will dedicate ourselves to promoting women's solidarity, the protection
of women, the improvement of women's status in society, the advancement of women's interests, and the acquisition of women's rights. We
are determined to achieve all these aims.[59]

Both in her speech and the Association's manifesto Hiratsuka conveyed two significant messages. One was that although women had
been underestimated, the time had come for them to express their
views and display their abilities. She argued that Japan had produced a number of able and learned women such as Yajima Kajiko,
who could become leaders of a women's social movement.[60] Women
no longer needed to prove their ability, and were capable of launching a social movement for their rights. They should reconstruct their
place in society. The other message was a stress on female collaboration. Although there were many women's organisations, including
a nationwide one, Kyōfūkai (the Women's Christian Temperance
Union) and local middle-class women's groups such as Tōkakai (the
Tenth Day Group in Osaka), Chūkyō Fujinkai (the Chūkyō Women's

---

[59] *Ibid.*, p. 1. This is my translation, but I consulted Tokuza's version. See Tokuza,
The Rise of the Feminist Movement in Japan, pp. 123–4.
    [60] *Ibid.*, pp. 125–7.

Society in Nagoya) and the PL-Kai (comprising progressive wives of faculty members at Kyoto University), they tended to be isolated from each other.[61] She wanted them to combine for women's causes.

After Hiratsuka returned to Tokyo, she and Ichikawa had to change their initial plan and abandon the idea of a women's magazine to promote their campaign. This was mainly because an anonymous donor who had agreed to finance the magazine pulled out.[62] Their priorities now became to promote the Association nationally, recruit as many supporters as possible, and raise funds.[63] They sent out the manifesto, with letters inviting membership, to friends, acquaintances, ex-members of the Seitō Society and progressive-minded people from various circles who might support the Association.[64] Ichikawa and Hiratsuka visited or wrote to many influential people, such as Yoshioka Yayoi (a pioneering female medical doctor) and men such as Uchida Roan (a critic and novelist), Abe Isoo (a socialist and Christian educator), Kobayashi Kissen (the chief editor of the Nagoya Newspaper Company), Kagawa Toyohiko (a religious leader well-known for his work in the slum areas of Kobe) and Sawayanagi Masatarō (a progressive educator), trying to persuade them to become members or supporters.[65]

They also made a public announcement in Tokyo about the Association to attract public interest. They placed their announcement in the *Tokyo Asahi Shinbun*, one of the most prestigious and widely read daily newspapers.[66] Their recruitment activity went well, and the Association received enthusiastic responses from many who had been sent membership invitations.[67] The press response was more favourable than Hiratsuka had expected. She was interviewed by the *Tokyo Asahi Shinbun*, which reported her actions and words in a neutral and accurate fashion:

---

[61] *Ibid.*, p. 128.

[62] Hiratsuka, 'Shin Fujin Kyōkai no kaiko', pp. 275–6.

[63] Hiratsuka, *Genshi*, vol. 3, pp. 81–2.

[64] Hiratsuka, 'Shin Fujin Kyōkai no kaiko', p. 276; Ichikawa, 'Sōritsu yori *Josei Dōmei* hakkan made, part 1', pp. 45–6.

[65] Ichikawa, *Jiden: Senzen Hen*, p. 57; Hiratsuka, 'Shin Fujin Kyōkai no kaiko', p. 278; Tokuza, *The Rise of the Feminist Movement in Japan*, pp. 128–9.

[66] *Tokyo Asahi Shinbun* (19 December, 1919); Ichikawa, *Jiden: Senzen Hen*, pp. 51–2.

[67] Hiratsuka, *Genshi*, vol. 3, p. 81; Hiratsuka, *Watakushi*, p. 176; Ichikawa, *Jiden: Senzen Hen*, p. 64.

Hiratsuka Raichō has decided to submit two petitions to the forth-
coming Diet session . . . She spoke of them as follows: "The main
objective of the first petition regarding marriage law is to prevent venereal disease. The success of the petition will be vital to protect both
women and children, and also to improve human qualities. I think
that the second petition regarding the Peace Police Law will be attained
relatively easily. On the other hand, I can see that achieving the first
petition will be very hard and will take much time. Even so, the gesture of actually submitting it still helps to make people aware of the
harm of venereal disease.[68]

Such favourable articles contrasted with the many distorted pieces
previously written by journalists on the Seitō Society and its members. The Seitō Society had constantly been a target of media criticism, far more so than the Association, which was taken seriously
and supported more widely. Hiratsuka believed that this more welcoming response reflected a changed climate of opinion, one more
sympathetic to female causes.[69] The public reception of the Association
was also favourable. Yosano Akiko's reaction to it is worth quoting.
She had disagreed with Hiratsuka over the protection of motherhood, but she very much welcomed this new venture:

How delighted I am in my heart to hear that the Association of New
Women has been established by Hiratsuka. I think that this is the best
news I have heard recently. To unite all Japanese women is a very
significant and indispensable task, and it is also a most difficult thing
to achieve. However, Hiratsuka is a perfect leader as well as founder,
and I have every confidence in her. I cannot think of anybody more
suitable for this than Hiratsuka. I really admire her courage and enthusiasm, volunteering to shoulder this heavy responsibility of establishing
the Association and trying to unite Japanese women.[70]

In December 1919 Ichikawa and Hiratsuka decided to scale down
many of the initial objectives and focus on two issues which they
felt were the most important. These were the amendment of Article
5 of the Peace Police Law, and the enactment of a law restricting

---

[68] *Tokyo Asahi Shinbun* (22 December, 1919). A similar article also appeared in
the *Yomiuri Shinbun*. See *Yomiuri Shinbun* (20 December, 1919).
[69] Hiratsuka, *Genshi*, vol. 3, pp. 81–2.
[70] Yosano Akiko, 'Shin Fujin Kyōkai no seigan undō', *Taiyō* (February, 1920),
reprinted in Yosano Akiko (ed. by Kano Masanao & Kōuchi Nobuko), *Yosano Akiko
Hyōronshū* (1985), p. 314.

marriage by men with venereal disease.[71] The venereal disease issue was Hiratsuka's idea. Ichikawa was young and single, and she confessed that she did not even know what venereal disease was.[72] Her ignorance of sexual matters was not exceptional, for unmarried women in her generation were discouraged from talking about sex, and their innocence was considered to be a virtue. Ichikawa was not enthusiastic about this cause, but she followed Hiratsuka.[73]

Hiratsuka's interest in this issue came about through some recent tragic events caused by venereal disease affecting women in her immediate circle. One such case involved a friend from her Japan Women's College days. This friend, who had married a medical doctor in her home town, was threatened with divorce by her husband on the grounds that she had supposedly infected him with venereal disease.[74] To Hiratsuka it was obvious that her friend, a gentle, serious-minded and honest person, was wholly innocent of any such charge, being completely inexperienced sexually and faithful to her husband, who was clearly to blame for his own illness. Hiratsuka challenged him over this matter, proclaiming her friend's innocence, but the husband denied any guilt. Under the Meiji Civil Code husbands were given many grounds to divorce their wives, and even innocent spouses like her friend were victims—she was divorced and her reputation tarnished.

Several progressive male doctors supported the Association of New Women. Dr. Tashiro Yoshinori, a member of the Meiji Medical Association told Hiratsuka that there were many other wives like her friend.[75] Hiratsuka became aware also of the injurious medical consequences of such diseases, which badly affected these women, some of whom became crippled as a result. Others gave birth to deformed children. In addition to the physical ailments, they also suffered mental and social humiliation. Many of them were divorced on the pretext that they had given the disease to their husbands. As Molony

[71] Hiratsuka, *Watakushi*, p. 176; Ichikawa, *Jiden: Senzen Hen*, p. 52; Hiratsuka, 'Shin Fujin Kyōkai no kaiko', p. 276.

[72] Ichikawa, *Jiden: Senzen Hen*, p. 53.

[73] *Ibid.*, p. 53.

[74] The account of Hiratsuka's friend's tragedy is given in Hiratsuka, *Genshi*, vol. 3, pp. 99–100.

[75] On Dr. Tashiro, see Hiratsuka, 'Chian Keisatsu Hō daigojō no shūsei to karyūbyō danshi no kekkon seigen', in Hiratsuka, *Chosakushū*, vol. 3, p. 207.

has stated, legal inequalities created hardship for women victimized by their infected husbands.[76] Hiratsuka, who had shown herself much concerned with maternal and child health, did not pass over this question without transforming it into a major public issue. In fact, Hiratsuka may have been inspired by recent developments in domestic legislation in Europe and the United States.

The other matter was the amendment of Article 5. Both Ichikawa and Hiratsuka felt that it would be fairly easy to achieve this.[77] This was mainly because their predecessors, such as Imai Utako and Iwano Kiyoko, had attempted to amend Article 5 more than a decade earlier.[78] Ichikawa and Hiratsuka were reviving an earlier campaign and they felt that opinions were turning in their favour.

The Association was better structured and more clearly focused than the Seitō Society. It had a distinctive political agenda and used legal and political processes to achieve its goals. Hiratsuka was now keen to ask others for advice. To draft a petition on the amendment of the Peace Police Law, Hiratsuka and Ichikawa consulted constitutional experts and Iwano Kiyoko.[79] To draft the petition on venereal disease, Hiratsuka obtained information from Dr. Tashiro, who had already submitted a petition entitled 'Karyūbyō ni kakaresu danshi no torishimari' ('control over men who contract venereal disease') to the Diet.[80] His petition had been unsuccessful, and Hiratsuka recalled that he encouraged them to petition the Diet on this issue.[81] Hiratsuka examined the documentation collected by Ichikawa, including similar laws and regulations in other countries to prevent the spread of venereal disease, and she drafted two separate petitions by the end of December 1919.[82] She also recruited another founder of the Association, Oku Mumeo, in that month.[83]

---

[76] Molony, 'State and women in modern Japan', p. 40.

[77] Ichikawa, *Jiden: Senzen Hen*, pp. 52–3; Hiratsuka, *Genshi*, vol. 3, pp. 88–95.

[78] Ichikawa Fusae, 'Chian Keisatsu Hō daigojō shūsei no undō, part 1', *Josei Dōmei*, 1 (October, 1920), pp. 25–6; Oku, *Nobi*, p. 47; Hiratsuka Raichō, 'Meiji matsunen yori Taishō shotō no waga fujin mondai', *Shin Nihon* (November, 1915), reprinted in Hiratsuka, *Chosakushū*, vol. 2, p. 108.

[79] Ichikawa, *Jiden: Senzen Hen*, p. 53.

[80] Hiratsuka, *Genshi*, vol. 3, p. 89; Hiratsuka, 'Chian Kensatsu Hō daigojō no shūsei to karyūbyō danshi no kekkon sengen', p. 207.

[81] *Ibid.*, p. 99. The content of Dr. Tashiro's petition is unknown.

[82] Ichikawa, *Jiden: Senzen Hen*, p. 53; Ichikawa, 'Chian Keisatsu Hō daigojō shūsei no undō, part 2', *Josei Dōmei*, 2 (November, 1920), p. 23.

[83] Hiratsuka, *Genshi*, vol. 3, p. 82; Oku, *Nobi*, pp. 45–7.

The 42nd Session of the Diet

On 6 January 1920 the first meeting of the Association was held at Hiratsuka's house in Tabata, Tokyo.[84] Closely following their predecessors' aim to revise Article 5, three founders and ten main supporters decided that the Association should start a campaign petitioning the government on the amendment of Article 5 and the enactment of a law restricting marriage by men with venereal disease.[85] However, as Ichikawa recalled, nobody present had any idea how to do this.[86] An ex-Seitō member and journalist, Kamichika Ichiko suggested that Ichikawa and Hiratsuka should look to politicians for advice.[87] Through Kamichika's contacts Ichikawa and Hiratsuka were introduced to Tomita Kōjirō, a member of the House of Representatives for Kōchi Prefecture, belonging to the Kenseikai (Constitutional Party).[88] Tomita, who had been a journalist and once participated in the Freedom and People's Rights Movement, was sympathetic to women's causes. He initiated Ichikawa and Hiratsuka into the art of political campaigning, giving many practical political suggestions.[89] According to Tomita, there were two possible approaches. One was to submit a written petition to both the House of Representatives and the House of Peers. As the Meiji Constitution stipulated, anybody who was a Japanese national, regardless of sex or occupation, was eligible to submit written political requests to the Diet through the hands of a Diet member.[90] This involved drawing up a petition and finding a Diet member to submit it. This tactic was applicable to both causes the Association decided to work towards. The other method was to

---

[84] Hiratsuka, *Genshi*, vol. 3, pp. 83–4; Ichikawa, 'Chian Keisatsu Hō daigojō shūsei no undō, part 1', p. 26. After this meeting Hiratsuka's house was used as the Association's head office. A list of the attendants at this meeting is also given by Tokuza. See Tokuza, *The Rise of the Feminist Movement in Japan*, p. 132.

[85] Hiratsuka, *Genshi*, vol. 3, p. 84; Oku, *Nobi*, p. 47.

[86] Ichikawa, *Jiden: Senzen Hen*, p. 55.

[87] Hiratsuka, *Genshi*, vol. 3, p. 90.

[88] Ichikawa, *Jiden: Senzen Hen*, p. 90. Tomita Kōjirō (1872–1938) was born in Kōchi Prefecture, and became chief editor of the *Dōyō Shinbun* in Kōchi. He then launched the *Kōchi Shinbun*, and became its president as well as its chief editor. He served ten times as a member of the House of Representatives, from 1908. On Tomita Kōjirō, see Nichigai Asoshiētsu (ed.), *Seijika Jinmei Jiten* (1990), p. 361.

[89] Hiratsuka, *Genshi*, vol. 3, pp. 90–1; Ichikawa, 'Chian Keisatsu Hō daigojō shūsei no undō, part 2', p. 23.

[90] Ichikawa, 'Chian Keisatsu Hō daigojō shūsei no undō, part 1', pp. 24–5.

lobby Diet members, to persuade some of them to submit a *kaisei hōan* (a bill to revise an existing law) to the Diet.[91] This was appropriate only to the amendment of the Peace Police Law since a law to restrict marriage by men with venereal disease had never existed before.

As the opening of the 42nd Session of the Diet was approaching in February 1920, Ichikawa and Hiratsuka opted for petitioning to promote their causes.[92] This could immediately be put into practice, while the second method required more thought, strategy and organisational skill, and needed more time to lobby Diet members.[93] Since Hiratsuka had already drafted the two petitions, they only had to find one or two Diet members who would agree to submit the petitions. Tomita advised that if a petition was presented under the joint signatures of many supporters rather than under one individual's name, it would attract more attention from the Diet and achieve more.[94] Hiratsuka and Ichikawa embarked on a full-scale signature-collecting campaign, and sent out three thousand copies of the two petitions and attached forms for people to sign and seal.[95] These were sent to all members of the Association, and to groups and individuals which Ichikawa and Hiratsuka thought would support them, including many women's associations or societies, leading girls' high schools, the head office of the Japan Women's College alumni association and its branches, and acquaintances of the Association's main members.[96]

The response to the signature collecting was immediate and much more favourable than Hiratsuka and Ichikawa had expected. They collected over 2,000 signatures for each petition by early February.[97] However, compared to the petition requesting amendment of Article 17 of the Peace Police Law, as submitted to the 41st Session of the

[91] Ichikawa, 'Chian Keisatsu Hō daigojō shūsei no undō, part 2', p. 23.
[92] Ichikawa, 'Chian Keisatsu Hō daigojō shūsei no undō, part 1', p. 28.
[93] Hiratsuka, *Genshi*, vol. 3, pp. 90–2; Ichikawa, *Jiden: Senzen Hen*, p. 57.
[94] Ichikawa, 'Chian Keisatsu Hō daigojō no undō, part 1', p. 28.
[95] Hiratsuka, *Genshi*, vol. 3, p. 90.
[96] Ichikawa, *Jiden: Senzen Hen*, p. 56; Hiratsuka Raichō, 'Karyūbyō danshi kekkon seigen hō seitei ni kansuru seigan undō', *Josei Dōmei*, 1 (October, 1920), p. 31.
[97] Ichikawa, 'Chian Keisatsu Hō daigojō shūsei no undō, part 1', p. 28; Hiratsuka, *Genshi*, vol. 3, p. 90; Ichikawa, *Jiden: Senzen Hen*, p. 56. Signed and sealed forms in favour of the two written petitions were sent back to the Association's head office between late January and early February 1920.

Diet by the Yūaikai with 5,618 signatures, the number of signatures Ichikawa and Hiratsuka collected was relatively small.[98] Ichikawa recalled that the Kyōfūkai, which was active in anti-prostitution campaigns, was most co-operative on the petition regarding venereal disease.[99] Almost all the members belonging to the Kyōfūkai's head office as well as its many branches signed.[100] But the head office of the Japan Women's College alumni association and its branches failed to respond. This was mainly because the head office issued an official warning to all its branches stating that its members should not become involved with the Association, founded by Hiratsuka, who had disgraced the College by the Shiobara Incident and her subsequent 'immoral' behaviour.[101]

Hiratsuka and Ichikawa added further touches to the petitions to make them more persuasive to Diet members. This involved rewording and polishing them, as advised by Dr. Hozumi (a professor of law at Tokyo University) and Hirayama Rokunosuke (a male lawyer whom Ichikawa had met at the Unitarian church in Tokyo).[102] Hirayama and Hozumi also introduced Hiratsuka and Ichikawa to many Dietmen.[103] As a result, apart from Tomita, other Diet members also made useful suggestions. Unlike in the Seitō days, when men were excluded from the Society, Ichikawa and Hiratsuka now welcomed male support. They also sought financial assistance from men, and received donations from Ōba Kakō (an executive of the Yomiuri Newspaper Company), Arishima Takeo (an eminent novelist), Fukuzawa Momosuke (Fukuzawa Yukichi's adopted son and a very successful businessman), and Katō Tokijirō, a director of the Heimin Byōin (the Common People's Hospital), who later participated in the birth control movement.[104] Hiratsuka and Ichikawa

---

[98] Imai, *Taishō Demokurashii*, pp. 226–7. Article 17 of the Peace Police Law banned labour organisations and strike activity, which was a vital blow to the labour movement.

[99] Ichikawa, *Jiden: Senzen Hen*, p. 57; Hiratsuka, 'Karyūbyō danshi kekkon seigen hō seitei ni kansuru seigan undō', p. 31.

[100] Hiratsuka, 'Karyūbyō danshi kekkon sengen hō seitei ni kansuru seigan undō', p. 31.

[101] Hiratsuka, *Genshi*, vol. 3, p. 90; Ichikawa, 'Chian Keisatsu Hō daigojō shūsei no undō, part 1', p. 28.

[102] Hiratsuka, 'Karyūbyō danshi kekkon seigen hō seitei ni kansuru seigan undō', pp. 31–2; Ichikawa, *Jiden: Senzen Hen*, p. 55.

[103] Tokuza, *The Rise of the Feminist Movement in Japan*, pp. 142–3.

[104] *Ibid.*, p. 69. On Katō Tokijirō, see Hopper, *A New Woman of Japan*, p. 152.

largely depended upon donations from such men and wealthy female supporters to run the Association, especially at its early stage.[105] The majority of these eminent men were introduced to Hiratsuka and Ichikawa by Ichikawa's male friends, from her journalist days, and through her association with the Yūaikai.

For the 42nd Session, Hiratsuka and Ichikawa submitted two petitions. One concerning the amendment of Article 5 was presented to the House of Representatives three times.[106] The idea of submitting the same petition to the House of Representatives with different signatures on three occasions came from Tomita.[107] He was convinced that this approach would produce more effective results. The same petition was also submitted to the House of Peers by Kamada Eikichi.[108]

The contents of this petition comprised *seigan jikō* (a list of items petitioned for), and *seigan no riyū* (the reasons for the petition). The *seigan jikō* consisted of two requests:

1. To delete the word 'women' from Clause 1, Article 5 of the Peace Police Law [and so allow women to join political organisations].
2. To delete the word 'women' from Clause 2, Article 5 of the Peace Police Law [and so allow women to organise and attend political assemblies].[109]

The Association's requests were similar to those made in previous petitions by socialist women and by Iwano Kiyoko. The other peti-

---

[105] Tokuza, *The Rise of the Feminist Movement in Japan*, p. 69. According to Ichikawa, the Association's running costs—comprising printing costs, postage and campaign expenses—for the first five months were 1,200 yen. About 1,000 yen came from supporters' donations, and the remainder became debt.

[106] Ichikawa, 'Chian Keisatsu Hō daigojō shūsei no undō, part 1', p. 28. This petition was first submitted on 7 February 1920, together with 1,000 signatures, by Tomita Kōjirō, who belonged to the *Kenseikai* (Constitutional Party). The second time it was handed in by Nemoto Tadashi, who belonged to the *Seiyūkai* (Society of Political Friends), on 11 February 1920. The third time it was presented by Suzuki Umejirō, who belonged to *Kokumintō* (the People's Party).

[107] *Ibid.*, p. 28.

[108] Ichikawa, *Jiden: Senzen Hen*, p. 57. Kamada Eikichi (1857–1934) graduated from and taught at Keiō University. He was elected to the House of Representatives in 1894. In 1897 he toured Europe and America. After he returned to Japan in 1899, he became Vice-Chancellor of Keiō University. In 1906 he became a nominated member of the House of Peers. He was known as an educationalist and was also a Privy Councillor. On Kamada Eikichi, see Nichigai Asoshiētsu (ed.), *Seijika Jinmei Jiten*, p. 149.

[109] Ichikawa, 'Chian Keisatsu Hō daigojō shūsei no undō, part 1', p. 26.

tion asking for a new law imposing restrictions on marriage for men suffering from venereal disease was submitted to the House of Representatives twice.[110] It was entitled *karyūbyō danshi no kekkon seigen ni kansuru seigansho* (the petition imposing restrictions on marriage for men suffering from venereal disease), and made the following requests.[111]

1. A man who is currently suffering from venereal disease should be forbidden from marrying.
2. A man who wishes to get married must show a medical certificate, signed by his doctor, confirming that he is free from venereal disease, to the woman he wishes to marry.
3. This certificate must be submitted to the registrar (the official in charge of family registration) to accompany marriage registration.
4. If a wife discovers after marriage that her husband has been hiding from her the fact that he is a sufferer from venereal disease, she can end her marriage.
5. If a husband contracts venereal disease after marriage or if his wife becomes infected from him, she can demand divorce.
6. If a wife contracts venereal disease from her husband, even after divorce, she can claim from her ex-husband considerable compensation, living expenses and doctor's fees, until she has fully recovered from the venereal disease.[112]

These six requests were accompanied by four major reasons for the petition. The same petition was also submitted to the House of Peers by the distinguished medical doctor and Diet member Miyake Shū.[113] The requests manifested Hiratsuka's concern about venereal disease and determination to protect mothers and children's health. They also demonstrated that Hiratsuka had read widely on the subject and had studied legislation enacted in some western countries to

---

[110] Hiratsuka, 'Karyūbyō danshi kekkon seigen hō seitei ni kansuru seigan undō', p. 31.

[111] The format of this petition was identical to that of the petition regarding the Peace Police Law.

[112] Hiratsuka, 'Karyūbyō danshi kekkon seigen hō seitei ni kansuru seigan undō', pp. 30–1.

[113] Ichikawa, *Jiden: Senzen Hen*, p. 57. Miyake Shū (1848–1938) went to France towards the end of the Edo period. After he returned to Japan, he studied western medicine. In 1876 he became a dean of the medical school of Tokyo Imperial University. In 1891 he became a nominated member of the House of Peers. On Miyake Shū, see Nichigai Asoshiētsu (ed.), *Seijika Jinmei Jiten*, pp. 514–5.

protect mothers and their children from venereal disease. Her pre-
ventive measures were drastic and one-sided in their focus upon men.
This did not help them to succeed. State-regulated prostitution continued to survive, Japanese society had a very tolerant attitude towards
men's sexual behaviour, and it was tolerated for Japanese men to
go to brothels and to have mistresses.

The 42nd Diet Session was an opportune time for the Association
to submit these petitions. This was when campaigns for universal
male suffrage reached a climax.[114] Many mass meetings and public
demonstrations advocating universal male suffrage were held outside
the Diet building. Inside the Diet, the Kenseikai and the Kokumintō
finally submitted bills for universal male suffrage.[115] These parties
aimed to gain more electoral support through such policies and to
increase their political influence. The minority Kokumintō was quick
to submit a bill to abolish the property qualification for voting, and
to give the suffrage and eligibility for election to any man over 20
years.[116] The Kenseikai, which was the largest non-government party,
submitted a more conservative bill to give the suffrage and eligibility for election to any man over 25 years.[117] However, the Seiyūkai
(the party in power) resisted universal male suffrage, and argued that
this would threaten the social structure. Even so, an anticipation of
change produced an atmosphere which the feminists felt would favour
their own campaign.

Apart from petitioning, Ichikawa and Hiratsuka also organised the
Association's first speech meeting, pretending that it was a study
meeting, on 21 February, 1920 at the YMCA Hall in Kanda, Tokyo—
since women were banned from organising and attending political
meetings.[118] The meeting had six speakers: two female (Yamada Waka
and Iwano Kiyoko) and four male (Ōba Kakō, an executive of the
Yomiuri Newspaper Company, Ōyama Ikuo, a professor of Waseda
University, and two Diet members, Uehara Etsujirō and Kurosu
Ryūtarō). This meeting had some five hundred participants, and it
raised morale in the Association and engaged other members in the

---

[114] Yoneda, *Kindai Nihon Joseishi*, vol. 1, p. 150; Esashi & Ide, *Taishō Demokurashii to Josei*, p. 90.
[115] Imai, *Taishō Demokurashii*, p. 235.
[116] *Ibid.*, p. 237.
[117] *Ibid.*, p. 237.
[118] Ichikawa, *Jiden: Senzen Hen*, p. 58; Hiratsuka, *Genshi*, vol. 3, p. 92.

work.[119] However, it was restricted in many regards and did not give participants a chance to discuss political issues and the details of the Association's petitioning campaign. This was because a policeman attended and monitored the meeting. Even so, the lecture meeting received much media attention and was reported in major newspapers, creating good publicity for the Association.[120]

The petition on venereal disease was first considered in the Second subcommittee Meeting for Petitions in the House of Representatives, on 23 February 1920.[121] After Arakawa Gorō's summary of the petition, Saitō Kiichi commented on it:[122]

> We also are extremely concerned about syphilis. This is because its harm is not limited only to actual sufferers, but also extends to their descendants. The disorder and harm caused by the disease will be transmitted even to the patients' grandchildren. Their brains will be badly affected by the disease. As a result, some people become insane and others retarded. Various other symptoms will develop as well. I support the petition's idea of laying down regulations to control venereal disease to improve the Japanese nation's health. However, it would be difficult to put into practice the method of control suggested in this petition. A much more effective method of imposing restrictions on sufferers from venereal disease ought to be found to solve the problem. It will be better to leave the issue to the government authorities and let them investigate the subject.[123]

Mr Shio, a government representative who followed Saitō's speech, was equally reassuring and confirmed that the government had started to look into the matter and had founded a hygiene investigative committee a few years previously. He stated that this committee had been investigating the prevention of venereal disease and planned to

---

[119] An account of the Association's first speech meeting is given in Ichikawa, *Jiden: Senzen Hen*, p. 59.

[120] *Tokyo Nichi Nichi Shinbun* (22 February, 1920). See also Tokuza, *The Rise of the Feminist Movement in Japan*, p. 134.

[121] Hiratsuka, 'Karyūbyō danshi kekkon seigen hō seitei ni kansuru seigan undō', pp. 32–3.

[122] Arakawa Gorō (1865–1944) studied law at Nihon University. After he worked for the Ministry of Communications, he became chairman of the Association of Nationwide Private Schools. He joined the Kenseikai and became chairman of its Political Affairs Research Committee. He was first elected in 1904, and served ten terms as a member of the House of Representatives. See Nichigai Asoshiētsu (ed.), *Seijika Jinmei Jiten*, p. 24.

[123] Cited in Hiratsuka, 'Karyūbyō danshi kekkon seigen hō seitei ni kansuru seigan undō', p. 33.

send a doctor to Europe, where preventative measures against vene-real disease had been assessed, for further consideration.

Saitō's and Shio's speeches manifested a good understanding of the appalling nature of the disease, and an eagerness to find pre-ventive methods, even though they were unconvinced by the sug-gestions in the Association's petition. Due to their favourable responses, the vote taken by the subcommittee was *sankō sōken* (forwarding the petition to the government for reference).[124] This was a better result than Hiratsuka had expected. Because of the nature of her petition (imposing strict restrictions only on men), she had anticipated strong criticism of the petition. However, speeches in the committee were surprisingly positive and encouraging to the Association.

The petition requesting amendment of Article 5 was also discussed on 23 February 1920 in the *seigan daini bunkakai* (Second Subcommittee Meeting for Petitions).[125] Although Hiratsuka and Ichikawa placed high hopes on this petition, it failed and the vote was for forward-ing the petition to the government for reference, a poor result which was probably due to their neglect of lobbying.[126]

The two petitions to the House of Peers were shelved there. This was because the House of Representatives was suddenly dissolved on 26 February 1920, and the 42nd Session consequently ended.[127] The sudden closure of the Diet was due to a bill to grant all men over 25 years the vote, submitted by the opposition Kenseikai. Although this bill was discussed, Hara Kei (the Prime Minister and leader of the Seiyūkai), thought that universal male suffrage was 'dangerous' and so dissolved the Diet.[128]

---

[124] *Ibid.*, p. 34.

[125] Ichikawa, 'Chian Keisatsu Hō daigojō shūsei no undō, part 1', p. 28. The normal procedure of this Subcommittee meeting was to start with a brief outline of the petition, which would be given by the member of the House of Representatives who had presented the petition to the subcommittee members. This summary was usually followed by questions to the presenter, which led to discussion of the peti-tion. It always ended with the taking of a vote on the petition.

[126] *Ibid.*, pp. 28–30. This was one of three possible verdicts; *saitaku* (adopted or approved), *fusaitaku* (disapproved) and *sankō sōken*.

[127] Ichikawa, *Jiden: Senzen Hen*, p. 59; Hiratsuka, *Genshi*, vol. 3, p. 94.

[128] Oku, *Nobi*, p. 49. Hara Kei (1856–1921) was legally trained, became a news-paper reporter, and also worked for the Ministry of Foreign Affairs. He became chief editor of *Osaka Mainichi Shinbun*. He joined the Rikken Seiyūkai (Constitutional Society of Political Friends) in 1900, and in 1902 he was elected to the House of Representatives. In 1918 he became prime minister. He was known as the 'heimin saishō' (commoner prime minister). Hara, who had consolidated his power with an

After the closure of the 42nd Session, Hiratsuka and Ichikawa formally established the Association on 28 March, 1920.[129] About seventy people (about twenty men and fifty women), who were members or supporters of it, attended the inaugural meeting. Among male attendants were Yamazaki Kesaya (a lawyer), Kamada Eikichi (a member of the House of Peers as well as the vice-chancellor of Keiō University), Sakai Toshihiko (a leading socialist), Ōyama Ikuo (a professor of Waseda University), Ōba Kakō (an executive of the *Yomiuri Newspaper*), Akita Ujaku (a writer), Shimonaka Yūsaku (the chief editor of *Fujin Kōron*), Shimonaka Yasaburō (the president of Heibon Publishing Company), Katō Tokijirō (the director of Heimin Hospital), Fukushima Shirō (the president of the Fujo Newspaper Company), Hirayama Rokunosuke (a lawyer) and Takano Jūzō (a businessman and an active supporter of women's causes).[130] The male participants were well-known and influential figures with extensive contacts, who would be of much use to the Association, providing Ichikawa and Hiratsuka financial assistance and opportunities for them to develop much wider networks in different fields. The female participants were dominated by ex-Seitō members, some members of other women's organisations such as the Kyōfūkai, and journalists who had a large circle of acquaintants. School teachers, office workers and housewives were also among female participants.

---

absolute majority in the House of Representatives, blocked passage of the bill to realise universal male suffrage in the 42nd, 43rd and 44th Sessions. Hara, who had now provoked much public antipathy, was assassinated in Tokyo on 4 November 1921, stabbed by a man who shunted trains at Ōtsuka Station. Even after his death the Seiyūkai stayed in power for some time, but in the general election of 1924 it was defeated by the Kenseikai, which had supported universal male suffrage. Under the new government, on 29 March 1925 during the 50th Session of the Diet, universal male suffrage was finally realised. This increased the electorate from 3.3 million to 12.5 million. On Hara Kei, see Nichigai Asoshiētsu (ed.), *Seijika Jinmei Jiten*, p. 431.

[129] An account of the ceremony is given in Ichikawa, *Jiden: Senzen Hen*, pp. 63–70; Hiratsuka, *Genshi*, vol. 3, pp. 107–10; Oku, *Nobi*, pp. 50–1; Ichikawa, 'Sōritsu yori Josei Dōmei hakkan made, part 1', pp. 46–7.

[130] A list of participants is given in Ichikawa, *Jiden: Senzen Hen*, p. 64; Hiratsuka, *Genshi*, vol. 3, pp. 107–8; Oku, *Nobi*, pp. 50–1. On Takano Jūzō, see Hiratsuka Raichō, 'Raichō no jiku', *Fujin Minshu Shinbun* (10 January, 1949), reprinted in Hiratsuka, *Chosakushū*, vol. 7, pp. 50–1; Hiratsuka Raichō, 'Bisogen no Raichō', *Tokyo Nichi Nichi Shinbun* (28 & 29 June, 1940), reprinted in Hiratsuka, *Chosakushū*, vol. 6, pp. 319–22. On Ōyama Ikuo, see Hiratsuka Raichō, 'Ōyama sensei no omoide', in Hiratsuka, *Chosakushū*, vol. 7, pp. 348–9.

Three *riji* (directors)—Ichikawa, Oku and Hiratsuka—and ten *hyōgiin* (trustees) were officially appointed at this inaugural meeting.[131] A manifesto, general principles and regulations, drafted by Hiratsuka, were discussed and approved. This manifesto was identical to the initial manifesto Hiratsuka drew up in autumn 1919. The general plan outlined the Association's four fundamental principles. These were:

1. The Association will advocate equal opportunities for men and women in order to let women develop their ability freely.
2. Although the Association supports the view that women's value is the same as men's, it will acknowledge their differences between men and women, and advocate the need for their cooperation.
3. The Association will recognise the significant social value of the family.
4. The Association will defend the rights of women, mothers and children, attempt to improve their rights and protect them from all obstructions aimed to destroy their rights.[132]

These indicated the direction in which the Association was heading to improve women's status. Points 3 and 4, manifesting high regard for family values and mothers' and children's rights, were very similar to the priorities Hiratsuka had expressed during the controversy over the protection of motherhood.

The more detailed regulations of the Association, going beyond this manifesto, were more carefully conceived than those of the Seitō Society. They also demonstrated Hiratsuka's strong desire to develop the Association into a well structured and democratically run one. In the regulations Hiratsuka specified the possible future activities that the Association would undertake. There were very similar to the initial plan which she had drawn up in autumn 1919.

After the inaugural meeting, Hiratsuka and Ichikawa made more efforts to increase the Association's members through advertisements. As a result, membership rose to 331 within the next six months.[133] The Association's members were both men and women of all ages

---

[131] Hiratsuka, *Genshi*, vol. 3, pp. 108–10; Ichikawa, *Jiden: Senzen Hen*, pp. 64–8.

[132] Hiratsuka, *Genshi*, vol. 3, p. 108; Ichikawa, *Jiden: Senzen Hen*, pp. 66–7. I also consulted Molony's translation. See Molony, 'State and women in modern Japan', p. 44.

[133] Ichikawa, *Jiden: Senzen Hen*, p. 68.

from much wider class, political and educational backgrounds than those of the Seitō Society. They also came from diverse occupational fields, and the Association recruited some members from working-class backgrounds like female textile workers and male factory supervisors, although many members were from the upper-middle or middle classes. Unlike the Seitō Society, Hiratsuka and Ichikawa were keen to recruit male members who were sympathetic to female causes. Among these were writers, artists, government officials, businessmen, students, teachers, university professors, journalists, medical doctors and politicians. As far as female members were concerned, there were far more working women in the Association than in the Seitō Society, and many of them were school teachers.

The 43rd Session of the Diet

For the 43rd Session Ichikawa and Hiratsuka continued to petition, but in addition they decided upon a different tactic for the amendment of the Peace Police Law.[134] This involved lobbying Diet members and persuading them to present the revising bill. Ichikawa and Hiratsuka now gave high priority to this because they realised that petitioning was unlikely to produce any immediate effect, even if a petition was adopted in the Petition Committee at the House of Representatives.[135] If they could persuade Diet members to present a bill, and if it was passed by both Houses and sanctioned by the Emperor, it would immediately come into force.[136] They therefore gave priority to this method to promote their campaign on the Peace Police Law.

When the election to choose new members of the House of Representatives took place on 10 May, 1920, the Association supported the election of those who were sympathetic to the Association.[137]

---

[134] Oku, *Nobi*, p. 52.
[135] Ichikawa, *Jiden: Senzen Hen*, p. 71.
[136] Ichikawa, 'Chian Keisatsu Hō daigojō shūsei no undō, part 2', p. 23.
[137] Ichikawa, *Jiden: Senzen Hen*, pp. 70–1; Ichikawa, 'Sōritsu yori *Josei Dōmei* hakkan made, part 1', pp. 49–50. As women were banned from making campaigning speeches for candidates under the Peace Police Law, Hiratsuka and Ichikawa supported certain candidates in writing, recommending them to electors. They also asked local newspapers to publish their recommendations.

Immediately after the 43rd Session was convened, Hiratsuka and Ichikawa gave a dinner party for the newly elected members of the House of Representatives whom they had supported.[138] Further arrangements were made to submit a bill to amend the Peace Police Law. Ichikawa and Hiratsuka also approached the leaders of the Seiyūkai (which was in power) to persuade them to present a joint bill to revise the law, which Hiratsuka later recalled in her autobiography:

> Ichikawa and I made great efforts, visiting all the houses of the lead-ers of the Seiyūkai without appointments early in the morning before they left their homes. During the daytime we spent the whole day in the Diet. Although security guards reprimanded us, we ignored them, and thrust our visiting cards before the leaders of the Seiyūkai. At night we waited for their return home, which was always late, often eleven or midnight. When they eventually came home, we demanded interviews with them. In this way we continued to have many sleep-less days.[139]

As it was legal for women to sit in the public gallery to hear Diet sessions, Ichikawa and Hiratsuka frequently attended sittings of the Diet, and encouraged other members of the Association to do like-wise.[140] Their requests came to nothing however, mainly because the Seiyūkai refused to submit a bill.[141] In spite of this, Hiratsuka and Ichikawa's lobbying campaign was rewarding in other ways. Other Diet members promised to promote the amendment. Matsumoto Kunpei, an Independent member of the House of Representatives, who had once worked as a journalist and received a university edu-cation in America, was very sympathetic towards women's causes. He agreed to draft and present a bill which would completely meet Hiratsuka and Ichikawa's wishes to amend both Clauses 1 and 2 of Article 5.[142] Diet members apart from members of the Seiyūkai agreed

---

[138] Ichikawa, 'Chian Keisatsu Hō daigojō shūsei no undō, part 2', pp. 25–6.
[139] Hiratsuka, *Genshi*, vol. 3, pp. 136–7.
[140] Ichikawa, *Jiden: Senzen Hen*, pp. 75, 95.
[141] Ichikawa, 'Chian Keisatsu Hō daigojō shūsei no undō, part 3', *Josei Dōmei*, 3 (December, 1920), pp. 28–9.
[142] Ichikawa, 'Chian Keisatsu Hō daigojō shūsei no undō, part 2', p. 30. Matsumoto Kunpei (1871–1944) did his undergraduate degree at Philadelphia University, and then took a doctorate in literature at Brown University in America. He became a newspaper reporter of the *New York Tribune*, and then a journalist for the *Tokyo Nichi Nichi Shinbun*. He was a member of the House of Representatives, and was affiliated

to support the bill. This bill was called *Chian Keisatsu Hō Chū Kaisei Hōritsuan* (a bill to revise the Peace Police Law), and was submitted to the House of Representatives on 10 July 1920.[143] Apart from Matsumoto Kunpei, the names of three other Independent Diet members were listed as *teishutsusha* (presenters of the bill). Thirty other Diet members comprising Independent members and members belonging to the Kenseikai and the Kokumintō became supporters of the bill. The Kokumintō and Kenseikai, both of which had supported universal male suffrage since the 42nd Session, showed more sympathy for the Association's petitions than the Seiyūkai, which rejected universal male suffrage. The bill comprised *kaisei jikō* (the list of items to revise) which requested the deletion of the word 'women' from Clauses 1 and 2 of Article 5, and *riyūsho* (the reasons for the revision).[144] The following reasons were given:

> It is a requirement for the people of a constitutional country such as Japan to be politically well-informed. One cannot overlook the significant roles played by mothers and wives who understand politics. They contribute to spreading and broadening of political knowledge among the general public. It is a vital requirement for a *ryōsai kenbo* (a good wife and wise mother) to have an excellent political understanding, to fulfil her duty as her children's educator and bring them up to be good constitutional citizens ... Article 5 of the Peace Police Law prohibits women from joining political organisations, from attending public political meetings and from becoming organisers of political meetings. Continuing to refuse to give women freedom to obtain political knowledge and to engage in political activities is terribly anachronistic. These bans will not bring constitutional government to a successful conclusion in any true sense. Nowadays women are permitted to visit the Diet and listen to debates in sessions of both the House of Peers and the House of Representatives. They are also permitted to engage in political discussions in newspapers and magazines. The legal provisions of Clauses 1 and 2 of Article 5 considerably contradict the above mentioned political rights which women have been enjoying and practising for some time. These provisions should, therefore, be deleted from the law immediately.[145]

---

to the Chūritsutō (the Independent Party). On Matsumoto Kunpei, see Nichigai Asoshiētsu (ed.), *Seijika Jinmei Jiten*, p. 499.

[143] Ichikawa, *Jiden: Senzen Hen*, p. 72.

[144] Ichikawa, 'Chian Keisatsu Hō daigojō shūsei no undō, part 3', pp. 29–30.

[145] *Ibid.*, p. 30.

With the advancement of male suffrage, more politicians became sympathetic towards the Association's request to amend Article 5. Many politicians who had received higher education in western countries or had previous careers as journalists were most favourable to the campaign.

Apart from parliamentary campaigning and lobbying, Ichikawa and Hiratsuka employed a further method to promote their campaigns. They organised a second lecture meeting entitled 'Fujin dantai yūshi rengō kōenkai' ('The lecture meeting organised by united voluntary women's groups'), which was held at the Meiji Kaikan (Meiji Hall) in Kanda, Tokyo on 18 July, 1920.[146] It was the Association's first joint meeting with other women's organisations, and demonstrated Hiratsuka's eagerness to promote collaboration between the Association and other women's groups. The lecture meeting was successful and attracted more public attention—the hall was filled to capacity in spite of an entrance fee of 20 sen, and almost all the audience were women.[147] As Ichikawa and Hiratsuka had hoped, the speech meeting received some cooperation from a selected number of women's organisations and their representatives made speeches. It also received backing from some Diet members, and most significantly Matsumoto Kunpei and Nagai Ryūtarō, both of whom who had spent some time in America or Britain studying, made most encouraging speeches in support of women's political reform and female suffrage.[148] The newspaper coverage of the meeting was favourable and helped to legitimise and publicise the Association's activities. It attracted much public attention and contributed to recruit more supporters.[149]

---

[146] Ichikawa, *Jiden: Senzen Hen*, p. 73; Ichikawa, 'Chian Keisatsu Hō daigojō shūsei no undō, part 3', p. 30. An account of the lecture meeting is given in Tokuza, *The Rise of the Feminist Movement in Japan*, pp. 144–5.

[147] Ichikawa, 'Chian Keisatsu Hō daigojō shūsei no undō, part 3', p. 30.

[148] Ichikawa, *Jiden: Senzen Hen*, p. 74. Nagai Ryūtarō (1881–1944) studied at Waseda University and Manchester College, Oxford University from 1906 to 1909. After he returned to Japan, he taught colonial and social policy at Waseda University. He became editor of a liberal journal of the day called *Shin Nippon*. In 1920 he was first elected, and served eight terms, as a member of the House of Representatives, affiliated to the Kenseikai (Constitutional Party). He established himself as an eloquent politician with a progressive stance, and was particularly known in the 1920s as a 'champion of the masses'. He advocated universal suffrage and criticised the Hara Cabinet. See Nichigai Asoshiētsu (ed.), *Seijika Jinmei Jiten*, p. 366.

[149] *Asahi Shinbun* (19 July, 1920). See also Tokuza, *The Rise of the Feminist Movement in Japan*, pp. 145–6.

Ichikawa also organised a summer intensive course, which was held at the Ochanomizu Girls' High School for a week from 25 July 1920, and Hiratsuka assisted her.[150] This course featured many eminent lecturers including the novelist Arishima Takeo, Hozumi Shigetō (a law professor of Tokyo University), Ōyama Ikuo (a scholar, writer and politician) and Hasegawa Nyozekan (a journalist). Nearly a hundred members of the Association attended, many of them from provincial areas. It helped the participants gain understanding of political issues such as women's political rights and the significance of the two petitions the Association had been working for.

During the 43rd session Ichikawa and Hiratsuka worked even harder to promote their cause than in the previous diet session, as Hiratsuka later recollected:

> Perhaps in my entire life I have not overworked so much or driven myself so relentlessly as during July 1920. In the middle of the intense heat of summer, covered with dust and sweat, I carried out excessive parliamentary lobbying for this special and short session of the Diet . . . I worked from early in the morning to late at night (until the time of my last train). At times I missed even my last train. At such times I went to acquaintances' houses which were nearby, and asked them to put me up. I dashed around all day campaigning and doing various other jobs for the Association, and I was utterly exhausted. The fact that I had spent much time at home before this involvement with the Association did not help me either. It required an inconceivable amount of effort for such an unsociable person as myself to do this type of work. I constantly had to drive myself as hard as possible. Apart from physical exhaustion, worries about my children and my house followed me all the time. I grew very thin as a result.[151]

This quotation demonstrates how committed Hiratsuka was to the Association's campaigns. More significantly it illustrates the adjustments she had made as a leader, and erased the rather negative picture people had of Hiratsuka's suitability as a leader of women's political campaigns. Ichikawa later wrote about it and made the following comments:

> Hiratsuka had been considered to be a woman who spent a great deal of her time in her study, up until July 1920. However, her intense

---

[150] Accounts of this summer intensive course are given in Hiratsuka, *Genshi*, vol. 3, p. 123; Ichikawa, *Jiden: Senzen Hen*, p. 77; Tokuza, *The Rise of the Feminist Movement in Japan*, pp. 141–3; Hiratsuka, 'Ōyama sensei no omoide', p. 349.

[151] Hiratsuka, *Genshi*, vol. 3, p. 134. Hiratsuka was then living in Tabata, Tokyo.

parliamentary campaigns during the 43rd Session proved that this impression was wrong. She visited many Diet members to lobby them, and also made frequent visits to the Diet by herself, which surprised me.[152]

How far did the Association succeed in promoting the two petitions and bill during this Diet session? As far as the petition regarding venereal disease was concerned, it was discussed in the First Sub-committee of the Petition Committee at the House of Representatives on 16 July 1920.[153] Although this petition had hardly been criticised at all in the 42nd Session, it met much stronger objections from members of this subcommittee.[154] For example, Takada Kōhei, of the House of Representatives was strongly opposed, and gave the following reason:

> The petition states that it is perfectly acceptable for women with vene-real disease to marry freely, but that the same thing does not apply to men. If such a biased, one-sided petition is accepted, our country will end up becoming a *joson danhi* (a female-dominated society) rather than a *danson johi* (a male-dominated one). I think that imposing restric-tions on marriage because of venereal disease for men only is too one-sided and biased.[155]

Takada's opposing speech against the petition was followed by three more speeches, all of which strongly disapproved of the petition, and demonstrated male speakers' conservative views.[156] They were con-tent with existing marriage law, which favoured men and the *ie* sys-tem. They tried to maintain the status quo. They found the petition threatening. They took the view that Japan was fundamentally different from advanced western countries, and had no intention to follow the example of those countries, where more effective measures against venereal disease were being taken. There was a consensus among them that imposing restrictions on marriage for men only was unfair. The result of the vote was *fusaitaku* (against the petition), which was a more unsatisfactory result than before.[157] There were two main

---

[152] Ichikawa, *Jiden: Senzen Hen*, p. 95.
[153] Hiratsuka, 'Karyūbyō danshi kekkon seigen hō seitei ni kansuru seigan undō', p. 35.
[154] *Ibid.*, pp. 35–6.
[155] *Ibid.*, p. 36.
[156] *Ibid.*, p. 36. Three further speeches were made by Asaga Chōbei, Shimizu Ichitarō and Matsushita Teiji.
[157] *Ibid.*, p. 36.

reasons for this. Ichikawa later explained in her autobiography that she and Hiratsuka hardly had time to campaign for this cause during this diet session because they were preoccupied with other matters.[158] In addition the male public became opposed to the restrictions being only on men with venereal disease. Many Diet members shared this view.

On the other hand, the Association made good progress on the Peace Police Law. This was considered in the Petition Committee on 16 July, 1920, and was easily and unanimously adopted.[159] The bill to revise the Law also went before the House of Representatives, on 19 July 1920.[160] One of the presenters of the bill, Tabuchi Toyokichi, gave the following account of why Article 5 ought to be revised:

> What I am advocating is the need for universal male suffrage. I am not requesting you to consider female suffrage. However, I feel that we ought to give women freedom to hold political assemblies and form political organisations, since they are equal humans to men and faithful to the nation.[161]

Tabuchi, who was an Independent Diet member in the House of Representatives, had also been educated in Germany and valued women's role in society. He felt that endowing women with minimum political rights was absolutely vital.[162] After his speech the bill was discussed at committee stage by Mr Kawamura, the chief of police and public security, expressed the following view:

> Now that society has progressed, we admit that it is necessary to remove Clause 2, Article 5. In other words, continuing to ban women from attending political meetings is anachronistic. Its revision is appropriate. However, we feel that it is still premature for women to join political associations and then to take an active part in politics.[163]

---

[158] *Ibid.*, p. 35.

[159] Hiratsuka, *Genshi*, vol. 3, p. 133.

[160] Ichikawa, 'Chian Keisatsu Hō daigojō shūsei no undō, part 3', pp. 31–2.

[161] Cited in Shin Fujin Kyōkai, 'Fujin no seijiteki jiyū o shuchōseru Tabuchi-shi no enzetsu', *Josei Dōmei*, 3 (December, 1920), p. 16. See also 'Dai 43-kai Teikoku Gikai Shūgiin Giin Giji Sokkiroku', no. 14 (20 July, 1920), in *Teikoku Gikai Gijiroku (the Imperial Diet Proceedings)*, microfilm, pp. 265–8.

[162] Tabuchi Toyokichi (1882–1943) studied politics at Waseda University, before moving to Berlin, Leipzig and Munich Universities. He was first elected in 1920, and served five terms as an Independent member of the House of Representatives. See Nichigai Asoshiētsu (ed.), *Seijika Jinmei Jiten*, p. 332.

[163] Cited in Ichikawa, 'Chian Keisatsu Hō daigojō shūsei no undō, part 3', p. 32.

His view represented government opinion, but showed that the Association's lobbying had began to influence the government. However, no more committees to finalise the matter were held before the dissolution of the 43rd Session on 28 July, and the bill was shelved as a result.[164]

The Inauguration of the Women's League

After the dissolution of the 43rd Session, Ichikawa and Hiratsuka prepared for the publication of the Association's journal *Josei Dōmei* (the *Women's League*). Oku took on the editorship, Ichikawa took charge of its management, and Hiratsuka was responsible for fund raising.[165] With a donation of one thousand yen plus free printing paper, they produced an inaugural issue in October 1920. These were sent to members of the Association, and were sold at main bookshops.[166]

The front cover of the *Women's League* was designed by Hiratsuka's partner, Okumura Hiroshi, and the Association's general principles appeared on the front page.[167] The issue was sixty pages long, its contents dominated by articles by Ichikawa and Hiratsuka, which were progress reports on the Association's campaigns for the amendment of the Peace Police Law and restrictions on marriage for men with venereal disease.[168] The only non-political or non-social article was Mikajima Yoshiko's *tanka* entitled 'Yūzora' ('Evening Sky').[169]

---

[164] Ichikawa, *Jiden: Senzen Hen*, p. 76.

[165] *Ibid.*, p. 78; Hiratsuka, *Genshi*, vol. 3, p. 143; Oku, *Nobi*, p. 55.

[166] Hiratsuka, *Genshi*, vol. 3, p. 144. When the inaugural issue of the *Women's League* was published, the members of the Association numbered only 331.

[167] Shin Fujin Kyōkai, 'Kōryō', *Josei Dōmei*, 1 (October, 1920). See Appendix 8.

[168] Hiratsuka Raichō, 'Sengen', *Josei Dōmei*, 1 (October, 1920), p. 1; Shin Fujin Kyōkai, 'Shin Fujin Kyōkai kiyaku', *Josei Dōmei*, 1, p. 55; Hiratsuka Raichō, 'Shakai kaizō ni taisuru fujin no shimei', *Josei Dōmei*, 1, pp. 2–11; Kyōikubu Kenkyūkai, 'Zenkoku onna kyōinkai no soshiki ni tsuite', *Josei Dōmei*, 1, pp. 12–8; Ichikawa Fusae, 'Chian Keisatsu Hō daigojō shūsei no undō, part 1', *Josei Dōmei*, 1, pp. 23–30; Hiratsuka Raichō, 'Karyūbyō danshi no kekkon seigen hō seitei ni kansuru seigan undō', *Josei Dōmei*, 1, pp. 30–6; Ichikawa Fusae, 'Sōritsu yori *Josei Dōmei* hakkan made', *Josei Dōmei*, 1, pp. 44–51; Yamanouchi Mina, 'Ichi jokō no shuki', *Josei Dōmei*, 1, pp. 37–40; Hozumi Shigetō, 'Hikaku konin hōron', *Josei Dōmei*, 1, pp. 57–60. See Appendix 9.

[169] Mikajima Yoshiko, 'Yūzora', *Josei Dōmei*, 1 (October, 1920), p. 43.

Among the articles which appeared in the inaugural issue, Hiratsuka's essay 'Shakai kaizō ni taisuru josei no shimei' ('Women's mission for social reconstruction') was of great significance. In it she expressed her disappointment with the society in which she lived:

> Our society is built on men's selfishness and physical strength. It disregards women, motherhood and children. It is very unpleasant, inconvenient and disadvantageous to women ... Women have to expose themselves to much danger in this society. It is also virtually impossible for women to give full play to their ability and fulfil themselves.[170]

Hiratsuka pointed out many limitations affecting women, and then advocated the urgent need to destroy the male-dominated society, which was seen by her as one of the consequences of capitalism. She wanted to reconstruct society, to create one in which women, children and the family would be protected and women emancipated.[171] She urged that only women were capable of achieving these changes. She also stressed that joint efforts by many women with a firm sense of mission would be needed.[172] Her emphasis on female cooperation corresponded with the main objective of the Association. Her article was very appropriate as an opening statement for the *Women's League*.

Unlike *Seitō*, the *Women's League* had very strong political content from its inauguration. It published detailed progress reports on the Association's parliamentary campaigns, and gave a record of speeches and events inside and outside the Diet relating to the causes which the Association worked for. It also published international news, giving progress reports on western countries' women's movements, especially regarding the suffrage issue. The *Women's League* shared many similarities with early British and American female suffrage organisations' publications, such as *Votes for Women* and *Suffragette*.[173] However, unlike the latter (which achieved a large circulation), the *Women's League* did not sell well. According to Hiratsuka and Oku, the inaugural issue received a favourable response, and Hiratsuka later recalled

---

[170] Hiratsuka, 'Shakai kaizō ni taisuru fujin no shimei', pp. 7–8.
[171] *Ibid.*, p. 10.
[172] *Ibid.*, p. 11.
[173] *Votes for Women* was the official organ of the Women's Social and Political Union in Britain. Its inaugural issue was published in October 1907, with a circulation of 2,000. By 1910 its circulation had gone up to nearly 40,000. Tuttle, *Encyclopedia of Feminism*, p. 336.

that many enquiries about membership of the Association came to
the office of the *Women's League*.[174] But in spite of this initial success,
the *Women's League* failed to increase its circulation, and many copies
were returned unsold.[175] This appears to have been because, by comparison with *Seitō*, the *Women's League* had a strong political tone, and
only attracted readers who were interested in the Association's parliamentary campaigns. In addition, unlike the cover of *Seitō*, the
Women's League's was dull, monochrome in layout, far from eye-catch-
ing, and was printed on poor quality paper.[176]

The Hiroshima Incident

After the inauguration of the *Women's League*, Ichikawa and Hiratsuka
recruited more members in provincial areas and established more
local branches. They invited 260 people from all areas attending the
second *zenkoku shōgakkō onna kyōinkai* (national gathering for female
elementary school teachers), in October 1920, to a reception at the
Chūōtei Restaurant in Marunouchi, Tokyo, discussing with them
the possibility of founding a society for such teachers within the
Association.[177] Ichikawa recalled that there was much interest in form-
ing Association branches in their areas. In November Hiratsuka visited Nagoya, Nara, Osaka, Kashiwazaki, Kobe and Fukuyama, meeting
female school teachers, successfully appealing to them to establish
more branches.[178] Her discussions with female teachers in Hiroshima
Prefecture led to the creation of three new branches (Fukuyama,
Hiroshima and Mihara).[179] However, these three branches were fre-

---

[174] Oku, *Nobi*, p. 55; Hiratsuka, *Genshi*, vol. 3, p. 160.

[175] Ichikawa, *Jiden: Senzen Hen*, p. 79.

[176] See Appendix 8. The *Women's League* was published every month between
October 1920 and May 1921, just before Ichikawa left the Association, under the
name of Ichikawa as editor and publisher. After Ichikawa's resignation, the June,
July and August 1921 issues were published under Oku's name. There were no
issues between September and December 1921. Although the January 1922 issue
was published, only three more issues (April, June and December 1922) were published before it was discontinued. The December 1922 issue, published under
Sakamoto Makoto's name, was the last.

[177] Ichikawa, *Jiden: Senzen Hen*, pp. 80–1.

[178] Hiratsuka, *Genshi*, vol. 3, pp. 164–5; Oku, *Nobi*, p. 55; Hiratsuka Raichō,
'Hokuriku yori kansai e', *Josei Dōmei* (December, 1920), pp. 33–7.

[179] Ichikawa, *Jiden: Senzen Hen*, pp. 81–2.

quently harassed by the police, and the conservative prefectural and school authorities.[180] It was argued that the Association had strong political overtones, and that it was inexcusable for female school teachers to join it. Members of these branches were summoned to local government offices for investigation. An official notice to dissolve these branches was issued. As a result, many members left the Association and cancelled subscriptions to the *Women's League*. The Hiroshima and Mihara branches were dissolved, this being called the Hiroshima Incident by the Association's members.[181] Hiratsuka mounted a counter-attack, and wrote letters to the prefectural governor, the prefectural and school authorities, the Ministries of Justice and Education. She also wrote for major newspapers such as *Asahi Shinbun* and *Kokumin Shinbun*, appealing to public opinion.[182] She and Ichikawa published a special issue of the *Women's League* on this.[183] Hiratsuka's efforts were rewarded by the prefectural authorities in Hiroshima softening their manner: they issued a statement allowing female teachers to join the Association, as it now appeared not to be a political one.[184] They were allowed to establish branches and subscribe to the *Women's League*, but were banned from signing petitions on the Peace Police Law revision as this was considered 'political'.[185] The Hiroshima Incident attracted much attention. The wide newspaper publicity helped to recruit more new members. The Association also succeeded in founding more than 30 branches and grew into a nation-wide organisation. In such regards the Association was comparable (on a smaller scale) to the British Women's Social and Political Union (W.S.P.U.), which had about seventy branches in Britain (by August 1907).

The 44th Session of the Diet

For the 44th Session of the Diet, convened on 25 December 1920, the Association used the same tactics as before. However, it now

---

[180] An account of harassment is given in Ichikawa, *Jiden: Senzen Hen*, pp. 82–3; Hiratsuka, *Genshi*, vol. 3, pp. 167–70.
[181] Ichikawa, *Jiden: Senzen Hen*, pp. 83–5.
[182] Hiratsuka, *Genshi*, vol. 3, pp. 168–9, 171.
[183] This appeared as part of the January 1921 issue of *Josei Dōmei*.
[184] Ichikawa, *Jiden: Senzen Hen*, p. 83.
[185] *Ibid.*, p. 84.

submitted three petitions—the two old ones and a new petition
requesting women's suffrage, called the *Shūgiin Giin Senkyo Hō kaisei
ni kansuru seigansho* (petition concerning amendment of the electoral
law to choose members of the House of Representatives).[186] This
made two major requests to amend Article 8 of the Law. One was
to delete the word *'danshi'* (man) from Section 1, Article 8 of the
Electoral Law, and the other was to delete Section 3, Article 8 completely.[187] Fifteen reasons, provided by Hiratsuka, were given.

The reason why the Association decided to submit this new petition was closely related to the climate of the time. Strong demands
for universal male suffrage were continually being made. Responding
to them, the Association's members argued that suffrage should be
given not only to men but also to women. In November 1920, copies
of this petition were sent out, together with copies of the other two
petitions, to many women's organisations and to hundreds of individuals to collect signatures.[188] The new petition was submitted to
the House of Peers as well as the House of Representatives.[189]

Ichikawa and Hiratsuka amended the initial petition on venereal
disease submitted to the 42nd and 43rd Sessions because of the
strong criticism it had received.[190] They realised that the petition, as
it stood, had little chance of success. The title of the petition was
changed to *karyūbyōsha ni taisuru kekkon seigen narabini rikon seikyū ni*

---

[186] Shin Fujin Kyōkai, 'Shūgiin Giin Senkyo Hō kaisei ni kansuru seigansho',
Josei Dōmei, 3 (December, 1920), p. 2. See Appendices 10, 13 and 14.
[187] Section 1, Article 8 of the Electoral Law stipulated that any male subject over
twenty-five had the right to vote. Section 3, Article 8 laid down that anyone who
had been paying more than three yen national direct tax had the right to vote.
[188] Ichikawa, *Jiden: Senzen Hen*, p. 88.
[189] *Ibid.*, p. 88. On 29 January 1921 this petition containing 2,355 signatures in
favour (957 male signatures and 1,398 female signatures) was handed in to the
House of Representatives by Nagai Ryūtarō. The same petition containing 2,174
signatures was presented to the House of Peers by Yamawaki Gen. Yamawaki, a
former judge who was married to Yamawaki Fusako, the headmistress of *Yamawaki
Kōtō Jogakkō* (Yamawaki Girls' High School), was more progressive than his contemporary Diet members, and had been the first member to speak on the matter
of women's suffrage in the House of Peers, long before the Association of New
Women asked him to deal with this petition. On Yamawaki Gen, see Hiratsuka
Raichō, 'Waga kuni no fujin sanseiken mondai ni tsuite', *Chūgai* (April, 1919),
reprinted in Hiratsuka, *Chosakushū*, vol. 3, p. 53.
[190] Shin Fujin Kyōkai, 'Karyūbyōsha ni taisuru kekkon seigen narabi ni rikon
seikyū ni kansuru seigansho', *Josei Dōmei*, 3 (December, 1920), pp. 4–7; Hiratsuka
Raichō, 'Karyūbyō to zenshugakuteki kekkon seigen hō', *Josei Dōmei*, (November,
1920), pp. 35–40.

kansuru seigansho (a petition requesting restrictions on marriage and divorce for people suffering from venereal disease).[191] The revised petition was longer and different from the initial petition in a number of respects. Unlike the initial petition the revised version imposed restrictions on marriage for both men and women. The initial petition emphasised the need for a man to submit a medical certificate, but never asked a woman to submit a medical certificate to confirm that she was free from venereal disease. Article 9 of the revised petition stated that a woman could not refuse to submit a medical certificate at her potential husband's request. In addition to the submission of his certificate, a scheme requiring a man to apply for a licence to marry or cohabit with a partner was introduced in the revised petition. Moreover, the idea of imposing a fine on men and women who violated the regulations was newly introduced in the revised version. The revised petition clearly sought to impose much tighter control over people suffering from venereal disease. This petition was presented to both the House of Peers and the House of Representatives.[192]

The petition regarding amendment of Article 5 was also presented to both Houses.[193] Ichikawa and Hiratsuka conducted active lobbying

---

[191] The outline of the petition is given in Shin Fujin Kyōkai, 'Karyūbyōsha ni taisuru kekkon seigen narabini rikon seikyū ni kansuru seigansho', pp. 4–7.

[192] Shin Fujin Kyōkai, 'Daiyonjūyon gikai to Kyōkai no undō', *Josei Dōmei*, 5 (February, 1921), p. 1. The revised petition was handed in to the House of Representatives on 29 January 1921 by Arakawa Gorō (a member of the House of Representatives attached to the Kenseikai), Nemoto Tadashi (a member of the House of Representatives attached to the Seiyūkai) and Chūma Okimaru (a member of the House of Representatives attached to the Kenseikai), together with 2,440 signatures in favour of the petition (1,035 male signatures and 1,405 female signatures). The same petition was presented to the House of Peers by Miyake Shū. Nemoto Tadashi (1851–1933) went to America in 1877 to study at Vermont State University. After he returned to Japan in 1890, he established the *Nihon Kinshu Dōmei* (Japan Temperance League) with Andō Tarō. He joined the Jiyūtō (Liberal Party) and later became a member of the Seiyūkai (Society of Political Friends). He was first elected in 1898, and served eleven terms in the House of Representatives. On Nemoto Tadashi, see Nichigai Asoshiētsu (ed.), *Seijika Jinmei Jiten*, p. 401. Chūma Okimaru (1871–1936) studied medicine at Tokyo Imperial University, and became assistant director of the Hyōgo Prefectural Himeji Hospital. He then had his own medical practice in Amagasaki, and became president of the Medical Association in Amagasaki City. In 1925 he was first elected, and served three terms, as a member of the House of Representatives. On Chūma Okimaru, see Nichigai Asoshiētsu (ed.), *Seijika Jinmei Jiten*, p. 337.

[193] Shin Fujin Kyōkai, 'Daiyonjūyon gikai to Kyōkai no undō', p. 1. Hirooka Uichirō (attached to the Seiyūkai) presented the petition to the House of

campaigns as before.[194] They gave high priority to lobbying Diet members of the Seiyūkai, who had refused to submit a bill to revise Article 5 in the previous Diet. Ichikawa and Hiratsuka had little chance of success in the Diet unless they received support from the Seiyūkai, which was still in power. Hiratsuka, Ichikawa and ten other members of the Association had an informal meeting with Hirooka Uichirō, Secretary-General of the Seiyūkai, on 29 October 1920, to discuss the revision of Article 5.[195] This meeting was successful, and Hirooka agreed to submit a bill for the amendment of Clause 2, Article 5. He assured them that he would let this bill pass in the 44th Session. He kept his promise and submitted the Seiyūkai's bill on 28 January 1921.[196]

Although Ichikawa and Hiratsuka had made progress in talks with the Seiyūkai, they were not entirely satisfied with the Seiyūkai's bill, which failed to include the revision of Clause 1. They now asked Independent Diet members to submit a separate bill to revise both Clauses, as in the previous session.[197] On 1 February, 1921 Oshigawa Katayoshi, Tabuchi Toyokichi and Matsumoto Kunpei presented the bill requesting the removal of the word 'women' from Clauses 1 and 2.[198]

Before these two bills, the Kokumintō submitted a bill to revise Article 5, the contents of which were identical to the Independent Diet members' bill.[199] The Kenseikai also submitted a bill to revise Clause 2 of Article 5 and Article 17 of the Peace Police Law.[200] In

---

Representatives, with 2,440 signatures in favour of the petition (1,102 male and 1,338 female signatures), on 29 January 1921, and Kamada Eikichi submitted it to the House of Peers.

[194] Hiratsuka Raichō, 'Hiretsu naru danshi no taido', *Fujin Kōron* (April, 1920), reprinted in Hiratsuka, *Chosakushū*, vol. 3, p. 129.

[195] Ichikawa, *Jiden: Senzen Hen*, p. 90. Hirooka Uichirō (1867–1941) studied law at Nihon Hōritsu Gakkō (Japan Law School), and became a lawyer. From 1915 he served six terms as a member of the House of Representatives, being affiliated to the *Seiyūkai*. He became its whip (the Chairman of its Executive Council). On Hirooka Uichirō, see Nichigai Asoshiētsu (ed.), *Seijika Jinmei Jiten*, p. 445.

[196] Ichikawa, 'Chikei daigojō dainikō kaiseian Shūgiin tsūka', *Josei Dōmei*, 6 (March, 1921), p. 35.

[197] Ichikawa, *Jiden: Senzen Hen*, p. 91.

[198] Ichikawa, 'Chikei daigojō dainikō kaiseian Shūgiin tsūka', p. 35. See also 'Dai 44–kai Teikoku Gikai Shūgiin Giin Giji Sokkiroku', no. 11 (6 February, 1921), in *Teikoku Gikai Gijiroku*, microfilm, pp. 211–2; 'Dai 44–kai Teikoku Gikai Shūgiin Giin Giji Sokkiroku', no. 10 (4 February, 1921), in *Teikoku Gikai Gijiroku*, microfilm, p. 167.

[199] Ichikawa, 'Chikei daigojō dainikō kaiseian Shūgiin tsūka', p. 36.

[200] Ichikawa, *Jiden: Senzen Hen*, p. 91.

response to public pressure, four political parties now competed in submitting bills to revise the Peace Police Law, and four bills were all presented to the 44th Session. This was a very promising development.

How far did the Association succeed in promoting their three main causes during this Diet session? The petition regarding women's suffrage was first considered in the Petition Committee of the House of Representatives, but was defeated.[201] The great majority of the members felt that it was not yet time to give women the vote. The unsuccessful result of this petition could be easily predicted in advance, even by the Association's main members. Ichikawa stated that it was very hard to imagine that this petition would be accepted, when even the amendment of Article 5 had not yet been achieved. The same petition regarding women's suffrage submitted to the House of Peers was shelved.[202]

Although this petition was unsuccessful, it was the first in Japan submitted by a women's organisation. In this regard it was an event of major significance. Many early feminists in Britain and America felt that the vote would enable women to secure other rights, and a general amelioration of their living conditions. In Britain the Kensington Society produced the first petition for women's enfranchisement, and John Stuart Mill presented it to a predictably unresponsive Parliament in June 1866. By the early twentieth century, the suffrage issue had come to dominate the women's movement in America and Britain, and women in those countries struggled over an extended period to win the vote.

However, this was less the case in Japan. Japanese feminists including Hiratsuka thought that the first hurdle for them was the amendment of the Peace Police Law. These Japanese feminists knew that they would not be able to launch a women's suffrage movement unless and until that law was amended. As a result, campaigns to amend the Act dominated the women's movement in Japan, and the suffrage movement was seen as a secondary and dependent matter. When Hiratsuka founded the Association, she also took this view; but, to a greater extent than many other women's groups, the Association came to state more openly the significance of female

---

[201] *Ibid.*, p. 88.
[202] *Ibid.*, p. 88.

suffrage. It changed its direction, to advocate female suffrage in the 44th session of the Diet, thus carrying out the first organised women's suffrage campaign in Japan. This came about fifty-five years later than J.S. Mill's initiative in Britain, but in spite of this relative delay, the suffrage petition demonstrated that the Association had come to realise how important it was for women to obtain the vote. In its emphasis on this, the Association might be classified as the first women's movement in Japan in a western political sense.

The petition regarding venereal disease was submitted to the House of Representatives and discussed by the Petition Committee on 7–8 February. Although it had been much altered in response to public criticism, the modifications had no effect, and the petition was again defeated. The petition on the amendment of Article 5 was discussed in the Petition Committee in the House of Representatives on 14 February 1921, and it was passed.[203] The same petition submitted to the House of Peers by one of its members, Kamada Eikichi, was shelved.[204]

The four bills to revise Article 5 were first discussed at the Peace Police Law committee meetings of the House of Representatives in February 1921.[205] Of the four bills, the Seiyūkai's bill to revise only Clause 2 of Article 5 was passed unanimously in the House of Representatives.[206] The prospects for the revised bill improved. There was still, however, a major barrier to surmount, which was to have the bill passed in the House of Peers. The bill went before a plenary session of the House of Peers on 1 March 1921, and was referred to a committee.[207] On 25 March it was passed by the committee, and was then placed before the plenary session of the House of Peers, scheduled for the last day of the 44th Session.[208]

According to Ichikawa, the bill was discussed at about 6 o'clock in the evening, and the chairman, Nakagawa, gave a summary report explaining how the bill to revise the Peace Police Law had been

---

[203] *Ibid.*, p. 90.
[204] *Ibid.*, p. 90.
[205] Ichikawa Fusae, 'Chikei daigojō dainikō kaiseian Shūgiin tsūka, part 1', *Josei Dōmei*, 6 (March, 1921), p. 37.
[206] Ichikawa, *Jiden: Senzen Hen*, p. 91.
[207] Ichikawa, 'Chikei daigojō dainikō kaiseian Shūgiin tsūka, part 2', *Josei Dōmei*, 7 (April, 1921), p. 39.
[208] *Ibid.*, p. 41; Ichikawa, *Jiden: Senzen Hen*, p. 91.

passed in the previous committee.[209] His report was followed by Baron Shimizu's opposing speech. Baron Shimizu Motoji was a member of the House of Peers, and was notorious for being highly conservative and inflexible. Oku, Ichikawa and Hiratsuka who attended this session, vividly remembered his speech.

> Recently various people's ideas have come into fashion . . . I [Shimizu] believe that allowing women to attend political meetings will be contrary to their interests. If permitted to do this, they might end up with cooking ash on their faces, rather than face powder. They may even do worse, and put kettle ash on their faces.[210]

Shimizu was a traditionalist who disapproved of anything likely to change the status of women and to threaten the male-dominated family system, and he desperately wanted to stop the progress of the bill. Oku recalled that she was disgusted and offended by his argument against it.[211] Hiratsuka described his speech as absurd.[212]

Responding to Shimizu's remarks, Kamada Eikichi, who had spent some time in western Europe and wanted Japanese women to gain some political rights, was supportive towards the amendment.[213] His speech was followed by Mr Kobashi Kazuta, the Vice-Minister of the Interior Ministry. Even Kobashi endorsed Kamada's view, and stated that the government approved of the revised bill.[214] All members of the Association who were present at the House of Peers were therefore extremely hopeful, feeling that the bill was about to be approved. This optimism was short-lived, and was destroyed by Baron Fujimura Yoshirō's opposing speech:

> As the House of Peers is a model assembly, I do not have any objection to women sitting in the visitors' public gallery to hear that House of Peers in session. It is perfectly acceptable for women to do so. I do not think that this will cause any harm. However, I have strong reservations about women conducting political campaigns. Political

---

[209] Shin Fujin Kyōkai, 'Kizokuin ni okeru chikei kaisei hōritsuan no iinkai oyobi honkaigi giji sokki', *Josei Dōmei*, 8 (May, 1921), p. 57.

[210] Cited in *ibid.*, p. 57; 'Dai 44-kai Teikoku Gikai Kizokuin Giji Sokkiroku', no. 26 (27 March, 1921), in *Teikoku Giin Gijiroku*, microfilm, p. 497.

[211] Oku, *Nobi*, p. 57.

[212] Hiratsuka, *Genshi*, vol. 3, p. 179.

[213] Shin Fujin Kyōkai, 'Kizokuin ni okeru chikei kaisei hōritsuan no iinkai oyobi honkaigi giji sokki', pp. 57–8. See also 'Dai 44-kai Teikoku Gikai Kizokuin Giji Sokkiroku', no. 26 (27 March, 1921), in *Teikoku Giin Gijiroku*, microfilm, p. 497.

[214] *Ibid.*, p. 497.

action by women goes against the law of nature from the physiologi-
cal viewpoint as well as from the psychological viewpoint . . . It is not
women's duty to conduct political campaigns together with men. Women
must fulfil their own duty at home . . . I strongly believe that if women
go out into the world and begin to conduct political campaigns, there
will be bad results. There are many examples in history, from ancient
times, to prove this. Indeed, women who have had political power in
the past, such as Taira no Masako [sic, Hōjō no Masako, the wife of
Minamoto Yoritomo, the first shōgun in the Kamakura period], Empress
Soku Temmu Gō and Queen Elizabeth I, turned out to be disastrous
political leaders and produced bad political consequences. I think that
women's political activities go against our country's native traditions,
customs and history. Moreover, allowing women to carry out political
campaigns will go against our family system, which is the foundation
of social structure in our country.

Recently a strange women's organisation [i.e. Association of New
Women], whose members call themselves 'atarashii onna' (new women),
has been attempting various political activities. I personally find this
organisation's actions most unpleasant . . . I am emphatically opposed
to women's political campaigns.[215]

As with Shimizu's speech, Fujimura's words represented a view of
women shared by many Japanese men. However, unlike Shimizu's
speech, Fujimura's speech was more articulate, carefully structured
and forceful and it had a damaging effect. It undermined the favourable
atmosphere of the plenary session. Oku, Hiratsuka and Ichikawa all
agreed that before Fujimura's speech, a view in favour of passing
the bill was dominant in the House of Peers, but after Fujimura
spoke there was a marked change in the tone of the meeting.[216]
Hiratsuka commented:

When Baron Fujimura took his seat after his speech, not only women
in the visitors' gallery [mainly members of the Association] but also
Diet members were dumbstruck. The Diet members were worn out

---

[215] *Ibid.*, pp. 497–8; Fujimura Yoshirō, 'Chikei gojō kaikin ni danzen hantaisu',
Josei Dōmei, 8 (May, 1921), p. 5. Fujimura Yoshirō (1871–1933) graduated from St
John's College, Cambridge. Between 1906 and 1909 he worked for the London
branch of the Mitsui Bussan (Mitsui General Trading Company). After he returned
to Japan in 1909, he succeeded his father as family head and became a Baron. In
1918 he became a member of the House of Peers. He was nicknamed 'kamakiri
danshaku' ('praying mantis baron') because of his sharp criticism of successive cabinets. See Nichigai Asoshiētsu (ed.), *Seijika Jinmei Jiten*, p. 458.
[216] Hiratsuka, *Genshi*, vol. 3, p. 179; Oku, *Nobi*, p. 58; Ichikawa, *Jiden: Senzen Hen*,
p. 95.

by then because of long-sustained discussion of many bills. There was nobody to speak after Fujimura. The chairman felt that there was nothing further to discuss regarding the bill, and he closed the debate and took a vote on it. His expressionless voice announced that the bill was rejected as a minority opinion.[217]

Ichikawa, Hiratsuka and Oku had believed that Hirooka Uichirō would pass the Seiyūkai's bill in this diet session and were convinced that they would achieve revision of Clause 2, Article 5. It was natural that they were devastated. Hiratsuka described Fujimura's speech as most unexpected:

> Since the 42nd session, we [members of the Association] had continuously worked on parliamentary campaigns, lobbying, regardless of the weather, to achieve the amendment of Article 5. We had also endured countless hardships, anger, unpleasantness and nonsense to promote our parliamentary campaigns. However, our efforts were not rewarded. Instead, the bill to revise Article 5 was killed simply by Baron Fujimura's damaging criticism, which I found very exasperating. I felt at that time that this bill, which aimed to open political doors to women, who accounted for about 50 per cent of the entire population of Japan, was the most important among all the bills considered in this plenary session of the House of Peers.[218]

When the bill was rejected, Tajima Hide, the youngest member of the Association, who was disgusted by Fujimura's speech, broke into angry words, stating that she wanted to attack him.[219] She recommended other members to stop parliamentary campaigns as they were a waste of time. Ichikawa Fusae stated that if Japan had had British militant suffragettes, they would have taken physical action against Fujimura.[220] Ichikawa's comment demonstrated that the Association was aware of militant suffragists in Britain and the progress which they were making through aggressive direct action.

About ten years prior to the foundation of the Association, the Pankhursts in Britain had led the Women's Social and Political Union (W.S.P.U.) into a suffrage campaign of militancy in which thousands of women broke the law. These women organised mass demonstrations

---

[217] Hiratsuka, *Genshi*, vol. 3, p. 179.

[218] *Ibid.*, pp. 179–80.

[219] Ichikawa Fusae, 'Fujimura Danshaku wa honki dewa arumai' ('Baron Fujimura cannot be serious'), *Fujin Dōmei*, 8 (May, 1921), p. 6.

[220] *Ibid.*, p. 8.

and marches, trespassed in buildings, disrupted political speeches, damaged or destroyed property by window-breaking, by burning and bombing buildings, cutting telephone and telegraph lines, and destroying mail-boxes.[221] The Pankhursts hoped to make the electors and the Government so uncomfortable that they would give women the vote to put an end to the nuisance. The W.S.P.U.'s activities had a great impact not only on the British public but also on many suffragists abroad, who often adopted such tactics.[222] However, these tactics were not used by the members of the Association of New Women.

They could have translated anger into direct action and violence, but they desisted. Instead Ichikawa published the Association's criticism of Fujimura's speech in the May 1921 issue of the *Women's League*.[223] Ichikawa and Hiratsuka held a meeting to review the Association's activities, regretting that they had not lobbied the House of Peers sufficiently, and determined to improve their lobbying to achieve the amendment during the next diet session.[224] The Association's approaches were on the whole polite, socially respectable and law-abiding.

It is ironic to find that the reason why Baron Fujimura objected to the revised bill was closely related to his intimidating first-hand experience of militant British suffragettes while he was in London.[225] Although he did not mention this experience in his speech, he later confessed this when Oku confronted him and inquired about the real reason for his refusal to support the revised bill.[226] He gave the following account:

---

[221] As a consequence, many of them were arrested and imprisoned, and in prison some suffragettes went on hunger strikes, and were forcibly fed. In response, the Cat and Mouse Act was passed by Parliament in Britain on 25 April 1913.

[222] For example, Alice Paul, the American suffrage campaign leader, used militant tactics that she learned from the British suffragettes during her stay in England when she founded the Congressional Union for Woman Suffrage in April 1913, to re-vitalise the activities of American suffragists. She was herself arrested several times, and in 1917 was jailed for picketing the White House.

[223] Fujimura Yoshirō, 'Chikei gojō kaikin ni danzen hantaisu', *Josei Dōmei*, 8 (May, 1921), p. 5; Ichikawa Fusae, 'Fujimura Danshaku wa honki dewa arumai', *Josei Dōmei*, 8 (May, 1921), pp. 6–8; Yamada Waka, 'Kizokuin no taido o oshimu', *Josei Dōmei*, 8, pp. 8–11; Tanaka Takako, 'Fujimura Danshaku no mo o hiraku', *Josei Dōmei*, 8, pp. 11–5.

[224] Hiratsuka, *Genshi*, vol. 3, p. 180.

[225] Oku, *Nobi*, p. 67.

[226] *Ibid.*, p. 66.

I agree with the Association's fundamental view that the existing Peace Police Law, which treats women just like children, is very unfair. I also think that we must give wider and fairer recognition to women's status. On the other hand, I have mixed feelings about giving political power to Japanese women. This is mainly because of the appalling, shocking and outrageous scenes I once witnessed in London. During my stay in London, I had the opportunity to see many militant women's suffrage campaigns organised by the notorious British suffragettes. I saw many women with bobbed hair, whose appearance could hardly be distinguished from men. I saw these women walk arm in arm with others and march through the main streets of London. They sometimes shouted 'Votes for women'. I also saw them put up their suffrage posters at every street corner. In addition to this their actions went to extremes, and they began to throw fire into post-boxes, and to smash the windows of government offices. They became utterly out of control. This first-hand experience of militant British suffragettes made me realise that our country's family system would be destroyed if such militant, violent women as the British suffragettes began to appear in Japan. As a result, in order to prevent such an intolerable and unpleasant situation, I took precautions against it by taking action, with other members of the House of Peers who were concerned about the matter, to stop the revised bill passing through the House of Peers.[227]

Fujimura had determined to stop all Japanese women's political activities before they reached the campaigning stage of their British equivalents.[228] He over-estimated the ability of the Association to take matters to British extremes. In fact, the Association did not have the ability to develop their campaign to such a militant state, which would have required stronger leadership and closer collaboration among a larger membership.

Ichikawa's Resignation from the Association

Nevertheless the Association had made some progress, notably in the campaign to revise Article 5. It seemed to have strengthened its cooperative spirit, although this impression proved illusory. After the closing of the 44th Session, the Association faced two crises. The first was when Ichikawa, who had been its driving force, expressed her intention to resign. She announced this in the editorial of the

---

[227] Cited in *ibid.*, p. 67.
[228] *Ibid.*, p. 67.

May 1921 *Women's League*.[229] This was confirmed at the Association's
first general meeting on 12 June, 1921.[230] On 29 July 1921, Ichikawa
left for America.[231] She explained that the main reason for her leaving was to observe the American women's movement.[232] In America
the female suffrage amendment, which had been presented to every
Congressional session from 1878, had been finally ratified on 26
August, 1920. America seemed to be the best venue to observe the
ongoing momentum of the women's movement. Ichikawa listed two
other reasons for her resignation.[233] One was that she had over-
worked in the Association's foundation, and was completely worn
out. The second related to her financial circumstances. She explained
that she hardly ever received any pay from the Association, and had
to depend on her brother and sister, which embarrassed her. The
Yomiuri Newspaper Company had offered to send her to America
as its correspondent. This was a paid job, and she gladly accepted
the offer.

When Ichikawa left in June 1921, she gave only these ostensible
reasons. Her fellow workers, Yamanouchi Mina and Oku Mumeo,
later confirmed that there was truth in them, but they indicated a
much more serious reason.[234] This was the friction between Hiratsuka
and Ichikawa, which was apparent to them. Later in her autobiography Ichikawa recollected this time, trying to find the cause of the
tension between Hiratsuka and herself, and explained:

> Hiratsuka was very actively involved with the Association's campaigns,
> which surprised me. Together with me, she paid frequent visits to the
> Diet and its members' houses to gain their support. She normally hated
> doing such work, but she did it without complaining. However, from
> late 1921 she became less involved with the campaigns. I presumed
> that she was exhausted. I also formed the impression that Hiratsuka
> began to change her view of me. I felt that she started to be harsh
> and cold-hearted towards me.'[235]

[229] Ichikawa Fusae, 'Henshūshitsu yori', *Josei Dōmei*, 8 (May, 1921), p. 67.
[230] Ichikawa, *Jiden: Senzen Hen*, pp. 96–8.
[231] Yamada Mito, 'Ichikawa joshi no gaiyū o okuru, *Josei Dōmei*, 9 (June, 1921),
pp. 52–3.
[232] Ichikawa, *Jiden: Senzen Hen*, p. 96; Ichikawa Fusae, 'Goaisatsu', *Josei Dōmei*, 10
(July, 1921), p. 32.
[233] Ichikawa, *Jiden: Senzen Hen*, pp. 95–6.
[234] Oku, *Nobi*, pp. 61–2; Yamanouchi Mina, *Yamanouchi Mina Jiden: 12-sai no Bōseki
Jokō kara no Shōgai* (1975); pp. 85–7.
[235] Ichikawa, *Jiden: Senzen Hen*, p. 95.

Unlike Ichikawa, Yamanouchi Mina, who lived with Ichikawa and
for a time assisted her work for the Association, was very critical of
Hiratsuka. She gave a detailed explanation of how and why friction
between Ichikawa and Hiratsuka developed.[236] According to her,
Ichikawa admired Hiratsuka when the venture began, but came to
see Hiratsuka's weaknesses as a leader. Hiratsuka submitted her
articles to the *Women's League* late almost every month, and failed
to submit her riposte to Baron Fujimura's speech in the Diet.[237]
Yamanouchi also wrote of how the two women were incompatible
in their values and personalities. This conflict between them originated in their class differences. Yamanouchi herself came from a
poor farming background, had worked as a textile worker, and she
was also disillusioned by Hiratsuka's way of living.

> Hiratsuka's lifestyle was completely different from that of ordinary com-
> moners. For example, one day she was so hard up for money that she
> could not buy any side dishes [dishes to go with boiled rice]. However,
> when she obtained money the next day, she entirely forgot how pressed
> for money she had been the day before, and immediately spent it all.
> She even bought a melon [considered a luxury for commoners at that
> time] from a fruit shop called Senbikiya [a long-established and very
> expensive fruit store in Tokyo]. Moreover, her husband [sic., her
> partner] Okumura always seemed to be simply lazing around doing
> nothing. I found it very difficult to understand why Hiratsuka did not
> make him work to earn money . . .[238]

Yamanouchi wrote that Ichikawa, who also came from a poor farming
background and lived a frugal life, found it hard to accept Hiratsuka's
upper-middle class tastes. Yamanouchi recalled that Ichikawa, who
had a strong sense of morality, never understood the relationship
between Hiratsuka and her partner Okumura, and that she was
appalled by his 'irresponsible lifestyle'.[239]

Yamanouchi believed that Ichikawa and Hiratsuka's temperaments
were also incompatible.[240] Yamanouchi admired Ichikawa's qualities,
and described her as serious, punctual, well-organised, reliable and

---

[236] Yamanouchi, *Jiden*, pp. 83–7.
[237] Hiratsuka's article was scheduled to appear in the May 1921 issue of the
Women's League.
[238] Yamanouchi, *Jiden*, p. 84.
[239] *Ibid.*, p. 84.
[240] *Ibid.*, pp. 92–4.

dedicated.[241] But Yamanouchi portrayed Hiratsuka as a moody, unpredictable, disorganised and self-centred woman.[242] These characteristics were condemned by many other leading members of the Association, and their sentiments fuelled the rift which developed among them.

Oku's sense of the relationship between Ichikawa and Hiratsuka differed from Yamanouchi's. She admitted that a personal clash existed, but she gave different reasons for it:

> Among all the reasons, the worst reason for this internal conflict in the Association was a shortage of money. Moreover, both Ichikawa and Hiratsuka worked too hard, and their physical fatigue was followed by mental exhaustion. This was the source of irritation and conflict.[243]

Oku confirmed that members of the Association at its head office divided into two mutually critical groups, the supporters of Ichikawa or Hiratsuka. She described the tension in the head:

> I do not know from when the Association's main members began to be so irritable and to criticise each other. At the beginning the atmosphere at head office was cheerful and filled with great excitement and enthusiasm. However, this pleasant tone completely disappeared, the atmosphere became utterly intolerable, and the members did nothing but discover each other's faults. In particular, the criticism of Hiratsuka by Ichikawa and her close associates intensified.[244]

Oku, who was already married and had one child, felt sympathetic towards Hiratsuka, who was juggling her work for the Association with bringing up two small children and supporting her family through her writing. She felt that Ichikawa and her associates' criticism of Hiratsuka was unfair, but she did not defend Hiratsuka.[245]

Hiratsuka's Withdrawal from the Association

Hiratsuka responded with her article 'Daiikkai sōkai ni nozomi kako ichinen han o kaisō shitsutsu' ('My recollections of the Association

---

[241] *Ibid.*, pp. 67, 84–5.
[242] *Ibid.*, pp. 93, 84.
[243] Oku, *Nobi*, p. 61.
[244] *Ibid.*, p. 61.
[245] *Ibid.*, p. 62.

of New Women over the past eighteen months having attended its first general assembly').[246] Its publication coincided with Ichikawa's resignation, and revealed Hiratsuka's feelings about the Association.

> What a busy, hurried and impossibly overworked time I have had for the past one and a half years! This is the first honest thought that comes to me when I look back over my involvement with the Association since its foundation.'[247]

This was followed by many negative and sarcastic comments. Hiratsuka was unhappy about the way the Association had been run. She was particularly disappointed by the great majority of members, who were not actively involved with it. Almost all the work was done by three founding members. In a depressed state, Hiratsuka openly criticised Ichikawa. One might have expected her to estimate the achievements and limitations of the Association, and to discuss concrete measures to overcome weaknesses and to promote it further. However, Hiratsuka failed to do this and gave the impression that she did not take the future of the Association seriously. As Yamanouchi pointed out, Hiratsuka made no further effort to develop the Association.[248] Shortly after this Hiratsuka withdrew from the forefront of the Association because of illness. Hiratsuka described this:

> I was taken ill with serious autotoxemia which I had never experienced before. The illness was due to my physical and mental exhaustion caused by overworking on the endless work for the Association. I had frequent severe headaches, vomiting and diarrhoea, which forced me to abstain from food for many days. As a result, working for the Association was out of the question.[249]

According to Oku, Hiratsuka went to Mount Akagi in Tochigi Prefecture with her family for a change of climate to recuperate, without telling anybody in the Association.[250] Unlike Ichikawa, Hiratsuka did not resign, but withdrew and remained an executive in name only.[251] During her convalescence she was not directly involved, but the Association's members wrote to her regularly. The loss of these

---

[246] Hiratsuka Raichō, 'Daiikkai sōkai ni nozomi kako ichinen han o kaisō shitsutsu', *Josei Dōmei*, 7 (July, 1921), pp. 2–7.

[247] *Ibid.*, p. 2.

[248] Yamanouchi, *Jiden*, p. 92.

[249] Hiratsuka, *Genshi*, vol. 3, p. 181.

[250] Oku, *Nobi*, pp. 62–3.

[251] Hiratsuka, *Genshi*, vol. 3, pp. 230–3.

influential founders was a fatal blow to the Association. Oku was left alone to deal with the aftermath, and she wrote of her difficulties:

> I was very surprised at Ichikawa's decision to leave the Association, but I could guess why she had reached that conclusion. I respected it. Ichikawa also informed us of her departure beforehand, so we had time to prepare for it. As far as Hiratsuka's move to Mount Akagi was concerned, I also understood why she did that. But unlike Ichikawa, Hiratsuka did not give us any notice when she departed. This naturally left us completely at a loss.[252]

Oku called a meeting on the future of the Association with its remaining members.[253] The common view was that they should continue campaigning. The Association's campaigns were now receiving support from more people, newspapers and magazines. All political parties were taking up the issue of the Peace Police Law. So the members decided that they would reorganise and make a fresh start under the leadership of Oku.

The 45th Session of the Diet

For the 45th Session the Association began signature-collecting, submitted petitions, lobbied Diet members, and persuaded them to present bills to revise the Peace Police Law.[254] Due to Ichikawa's resignation and Hiratsuka's withdrawal from the Association this time lobbying had to be done by more inexperienced members of the Association. They put most effort into lobbying members of the House of Peers.[255] The Association's members persistently followed Diet members, called at their houses and demanded interviews.[256] They especially targeted Baron Fujimura. Oku described him as the most difficult barrier the Association had to surmount.[257] He finally agreed to an interview, and met Oku at his house one night.[258]

---

[252] Oku, *Nobi*, pp. 62–3.
[253] An account of the meeting is given in Oku, *Nobi*, pp. 62–4.
[254] Hiratsuka, *Genshi*, vol. 3, pp. 184–6.
[255] Sakamoto Makoto, 'Chikei daigojō shūsei undō no gairyaku', *Josei Dōmei* (June, 1912), pp. 5–6.
[256] *Ibid.*, p. 6; Oku, *Nobi*, p. 64.
[257] *Ibid.*, p. 65.
[258] An account of Oku's interview with Fujimura is given in Oku, *Nobi*, pp. 65–8.

According to Oku, Fujimura, who was terrified by militant British suffragettes, had become convinced that the Association of New Women was harmful and intending to emulate British suffragettes. He was very surprised to meet Oku carrying her baby on her back, and changing her baby's nappy in front of him and his wife. Fujimura, who had no children, was particularly impressed with Oku's way of changing her baby's nappy. Oku, who was a caring and devoted mother, was completely different from the stereotype he had about feminists. Behaving in this way, Oku won him over.[259] He became convinced that the Association's campaign would be safe as long as it was conducted by mothers like Oku. He withdrew his opposition to the revising bill, and promised to persuade other members of the House of Peers to let the bill through.

The Seiyūkai's bill to revise the Peace Police Law was submitted to the House of Representatives on 1 February, 1922.[260] By then three other bills to revise Article 5 had been submitted by the Kokumintō, Kenseikai and Independent Diet members. All bills were discussed in the House of Representatives. Leading members of the Association such as Sakamoto, Kodama and Moroki went to the House of Peers every day, and met many members.[261] They wrote letters requesting support to members whom they had not met. In March, 1922, the Seiyūkai's bill to revise the law was approved in the House of Representatives. It then went before the committee of the House of Peers. As promised Baron Fujimura used his influence in favour of the bill and it passed on 22 March. Finally, it was submitted to a plenary session of the House of Peers, and discussed on 25 March, 1922, the last day of the 45th Session.[262] Sakamoto Makoto, who attended this session, gave an account of how it finally passed:

> At eleven-forty the Vice-Chairman of the Committee, Hattori Kazumi, made a report on our bill. It was followed by a brief but most encouraging address in support of it. After this the Chairman took a vote. Our faces were flushed with excitement. Our bodies naturally leant forwards, and we listened with strained ears. "The bill has been passed

---

[259] As Robins-Mowry stated, Fujimura came to realise that Japanese women could both maintain feminine qualities and sustain an interest in public affairs. See Robins-Mowry, *The Hidden Sun*, pp. 67–8.

[260] Sakamoto, 'Chikei daigojō shūsei undō no gairyaku', p. 7.

[261] An account of the Association's campaigning and lobbying during the 45th session is in Sakamoto, 'Chikei daigojō shūsei undō no gairyaku', pp. 7–9.

[262] *Ibid.*, pp. 9–10.

by a majority." The voice of Mr Tokugawa, the Chairman, announcing the result of the vote, sounded like a pleasant gold bell in my
ears.[263]

Although the two petitions regarding venereal disease and women's
suffrage failed again, the Association had succeeded in amending
Clause 2, Article 5, as from 10 May, 1922. This had taken two
years. Japanese women finally could organise and attend political
assemblies, although they were still unable to be members of political parties. Hiratsuka viewed the amendment as the result of
Sakamoto's lobbying:

> We must give Sakamoto much credit for this achievement. Sakamoto,
> who is a practical woman and a realist, stuck to her principles and
> fought to the bitter end to achieve this target. She skilfully carried out
> the parliamentary campaigns. The Association's achievement means
> that we women have got over the first hurdle towards female suffrage.
> We ought to be very grateful.[264]

On 8 April 1922 a celebration was held at the Association's head
office.[265] The Association's Kobe branch organised a women's political speech meeting to celebrate, at Kobe Kirisutokyō Seinen Kaikan
(the Kobe Christian Youth Hall), co-sponsored by other progressive
women's groups in Hyōgo Prefecture.[266] The hall was packed with
more than 1,500 people, the great majority of them women.[267]

  This meeting was the first ever held under the auspices of women.
Of course, in the 1880s when the Freedom and People's Rights
Movement was at its height, some women such as Kishida Toshiko
and Fukuda Hideko made political speeches. But those meetings were
sponsored by men, and women played minor roles. The Association's
meeting was held twenty-two years after the enactment of the Peace
Police Law, over which period there had been no women's political speeches.

  The Association's head office also held a women's political speech
meeting to celebrate the event at the Chūō Bukkyō Kaikan (Central

---

[263] *Ibid.*, p. 11. See also 'Dai 45-kai Teikoku Gikai Kizokuin Giin Giji Sokkiroku',
no. 32 (25 March, 1922), in *Teikoku Gikai Gijiroku*, microfilm, p. 975.

[264] Hiratsuka, *Genshi*, vol. 3, p. 188.

[265] Sakamoto, 'Chikei daigojō shūsei undō no gairyaku', p. 12.

[266] Hiratsuka, *Genshi*, vol. 3, pp. 202–3; Oku, *Nobi*, p. 69.

[267] About ten women made speeches. The topics of these included 'Mothers and
women's suffrage', 'My ideal politics' and 'The discussion of defects in the current
laws of Japan'.

Buddhist Hall) in Kanda, Tokyo on 15 May 1922.[268] Hiratsuka, who was still convalescing in Sakuzan in Tochigi Prefecture, could not attend, and sent a message of congratulations which was read out on her behalf.[269] The Association's other branches and other women's groups began to hold similar meetings to celebrate. Oku remembered that she was treated as a celebrity and was constantly asked to give speeches.[270] The June 1922 issue of the *Women's League* reported the Association's members' reaction under the heading of 'Chikei shūsei [Chian Keisatsu Hō shūsei] no yorokobi' ('Delight at the amendment of the Peace Police Law').[271]

The Dissolution of the Association

The members were in high spirits and determined to amend Clause 1, Article 5 of the Peace Police Law, and to obtain women's suffrage. Many observers believed that the Association had a promising future, and it looked as though its political campaign might develop into a larger feminist movement. However, it never fulfilled these expectations, and members were soon discussing its possible dissolution. A special committee met at Kodama Shinko's house on 8 December, 1922, and discussed the Association's future.[272] After a heated discussion for and against dissolution, the committee decided to end the Association. With this meeting, the Association came to an end.

It is important to consider why this happened. There were ostensible reasons, and less apparent real reasons. One involved Oku, who gave birth to a premature baby in August 1922.[273] It lived for only a week. Oku was severely ill after childbirth, and confined to bed. Later she blamed herself for devoting herself to the Association, and for paying almost no attention to her health during her pregnancy,

---

[268] Hiratsuka, *Genshi*, vol. 3, p. 203.

[269] *Ibid.*, p. 203; Hiratsuka Raichō, 'Chikei gojō shūseian tsūka shukuga enzetsukai ni yosete', in Hiratsuka, *Chosakushū*, vol. 3, pp. 262–4.

[270] Oku, *Nobi*, p. 69.

[271] Shin Fujin Kyōkai, 'Chikei shūsei no yorokobi', *Josei Dōmei*, 14 (June, 1922), pp. 20–5.

[272] An account of this special committee is given in Oku, *Nobi*, p. 72.

[273] Shin Fujin Kyōkai, 'Kaiin dayori', *Josei Dōmei*, 3:10 (October, 1922), p. 11; Shin Fujin Kyōkai, 'Henshūshitsu nite', *Josei Dōmei*, 3:10 (October, 1922), p. 12.

which affected her baby.[274] In fact she wrote that the face of her
dead baby became imprinted on her mind, and she suffered from
depression.[275] She found it extremely difficult to come to terms with
her child's death, and could not put her heart into work for the
Association.

Another reason was Hiratsuka's request for the Association's dissolution.[276] Although she had retired from its forefront, she remained
a figurehead. Some time in early December 1922 she expressed a
desire to dissolve the Association. This forced other members to
reconsider its future, and some of them came to support her view.

These reasons contributed to the Association's dissolution, but they
were probably minor causes. There can be no doubt that Ichikawa's
resignation and Hiratsuka's withdrawal were important factors in its
dissolution. Their loss was so damaging that the Association never
recovered, even though Oku tried hard to reconstruct it. Under Oku,
the remaining members appeared to be reunited, but this stability
did not last long. Even during the 45th Diet Session, discord in the
Association came to the surface. In mid-February the Association's
head office received a note under the joint signatures of the four
members of the Association's Osaka Branch—which was one of the
most powerful branches.[277] The note informed the head office that:

> The Osaka branch will become independent from the head office, and
> continue its activities under the name of Osaka Shin Fujin Kyōkai
> (Osaka New Women's Association).[278]

In this note two reasons were given to explain the decision to become
independent. These were that Hiratsuka had withdrawn from the
forefront of the Association because of her illness, and that there
seemed to be a lack of understanding among the current organisers
at the head office, adversely affecting the Association's work.[279]

Hiratsuka found the Osaka branch's decision irrevocable and made
the following comments:

---

[274] Oku, *Nobi*, p. 70.
[275] *Ibid.*, pp. 70–1.
[276] *Ibid.*, p. 72.
[277] Hiratsuka, *Genshi*, vol. 3, p. 228; Shin Fujin Kyōkai, 'Shin Fujin Kyōkai Osaka
shibu no dokuritsu sengen ni taishite okuru kōkaijō', *Josei Dōmei*, 14 (June, 1922),
p. 27; Shin Fujin Kyōkai Osaka Shibu, 'Osaka shibu dokuritsu ni tsuite', *Josei Dōmei*,
13 (April, 1922), p. 14.
[278] *Ibid.*, p. 14.
[279] Hiratsuka, *Genshi*, vol. 3, p. 228.

The Osaka branch had been initially organised under the leadership of ex-Seitō members and my friends. Their trust in me and friendship with me formed the basis of the branch. Therefore it was easy to see why the branch quickly lost confidence in the head office after my withdrawal. Moreover, compared to my time, the head office failed to show careful consideration for its branches and to keep in close contact with them.[280]

These comments manifested Hiratsuka's possessiveness towards the Association. Hiratsuka, who still had contacts with members of the Osaka branch in a private capacity, could easily have persuaded them to compromise and cooperate with executive members in the head office. However, she did not do so, and simply criticised that office.

Even after the revision of the Peace Police Law, a difference of views over the course which the Association should take caused friction between Oku and Sakamoto, who were then running the Association. Sakamoto, who laid more stress upon parliamentary campaigning and lobbying, and was pleased by the outcome of such tactics, wanted to continue to use the same methods to promote women's suffrage and other women's causes. On the other hand, Oku had never been a strong supporter of parliamentary campaigns, and wanted to change their direction, so as to mobilise working women.[281]

Oku's and Sakamoto's differences became a source of friction between them. This conflict came into the open on 15 May 1922, when the women's political speech meeting to mark the enforcement of the revised Peace Police Law was held in Tokyo.[282] This meeting should have been a celebratory occasion, and its key organisers, Oku and Sakamoto, should have shared this feeling with other members. Instead, it ended as a disaster. They had a heated argument over whether Yamanouchi Mina should deliver a speech. Oku had invited Yamanouchi—who had helped the Association in Ichikawa's days—to speak as a representative of working women, as Oku wished

---

[280] *Ibid.*, p. 228.

[281] Oku, *Nobi*, pp. 71–2. Although Oku admitted that parliamentary campaigns and lobbying were effective, and was pleased with the revision of the law, she confessed to uncontrollable anger and frustration. She admitted that doubts over parliamentary campaigns, which had lingered in her mind for some time, began to take shape clearly.

[282] Hiratsuka, *Genshi*, vol. 3, pp. 203–4.

to include working women's issues.[283] However, Sakamoto had not been consulted, and she tried to stop Yamanouchi's speech on the grounds that the Association was not designed for the female workers who Yamanouchi represented. Hiratsuka could not attend the meeting, but in her autobiography she commented that:

> This first women's political speech meeting organised by women in Tokyo ended in failure partly because of a lack of communication between the Association's executive members, and partly because it was poorly prepared. Oku's and Sakamoto's quarrel sounded most undignified, and it exposed the Association's limitations, and a split within it. I felt that the fact that it was organised by inexperienced people also contributed very much to the poor result.[284]

After this, Hiratsuka, as a constant observer of the Association, felt that the conflict between Oku and Sakamoto intensified.[285] It divided into rival supporters of Oku and Sakamoto. There were other clashes between Sakamoto and other leading members. Hiratsuka confessed that she received many critical letters from executive members after this meeting. She found these letters quite intolerable, and became depressed because their criticism intensified.[286] Hiratsuka's wish to escape from this discord underlay her request to dissolve the Association.[287] The Association now only paid lip service to the ideal of women's co-operation, and a lack of mutual understanding became a major factor in its dissolution.

The Association's Limitations

Other limitations were pointed out by Yamakawa Kikue (who never joined the Association and became a member of its rival the Sekirankai, the Red Wave Society) and Yamanouchi Mina, who joined the Association and left it shortly after.[288] Yamakawa criticised the

---

[283] Yamanouchi, *Jiden*, pp. 95–6.
[284] Hiratsuka, *Genshi*, vol. 3, p. 205.
[285] *Ibid.*, p. 206.
[286] *Ibid.*, pp. 206–8.
[287] *Ibid.*, p. 229.
[288] The Sekirankai (the Red Wave Society) was the first socialist-feminist organisation founded by women in Japan, from April 1921. The Society's membership was open only to women, and it had very strong political affiliations. It had four

Association for being 'bourgeois', excluding women from other classes and overlooking working-class women. She depicted it as old-fashioned, aristocratic, self-righteous, opinionated and pleasure-seeking, and its activities as 'burujoa no yūgi' ('bourgeois women's amusement').[289] Yamakawa felt that this bourgeois character emanated from Hiratsuka, the founder.[290] Yamakawa's criticism was not entirely appropriate, for Hiratsuka did not now overlook working-class women. Through her visits to textile factories in Nagoya, she saw working-class female vulnerability within industrial capitalism.[291] Greatly disheartened by these factory scenes, she listed the improvement of working-class women's conditions among the initial objectives of the Association, as well as in its regulations. She also welcomed working-class participation in her Association.[292] The Association had recruited some working-class men and women as members, but they were a minority.[293] It was led by three women with many contacts among the upper-middle and middle classes. Its members were mainly well-to-do women, seeking admission into an elite male political culture. The Association thus had a genteel atmosphere, one that created

founders, some advisors such as Yamakawa Kikue and Itō Noe, and less than fifty members, the great majority of whom were related to male socialists. The Society took part in the Second May Day Procession, held in Japan on 1 May 1921. However, it was short-lived and dissolved in 1922 because its activities were suppressed by the government, and many of its central figures were sent to prison. On the Sekirankai, see Yamakawa, *Onna Nidai no Ki*, p. 228; Esashi, 'Yamakawa Kikue', p. 290; Yoneda, *Kindai Nihon Joseishi*, vol. 1, pp. 158–60; Esashi & Ide, *Taishō Demokurashii to Josei*, pp. 187–203; Esashi Akiko, *Sameyo Onnatachi: Sekirankai no Hitobito* (1980), pp. 129–35, 173–6; Kondō Magara, 'Taishō-ki no musan fujin undō to watashi: Sekirankai o chūshin ni', in Nagahata Michiko & Ogata Akiko (eds), *Feminizumu Ryōran: Fuyu no Jidai e no Hōka* (1990), pp. 21–7; Mackie, *Creating Socialist Women in Japan*, pp. 102–5; Hane, *Reflections on the Way to the Gallows*, pp. 125–75, p. 55. See also letter from Sakai Magara to Sakai Tameko and Sakai Toshihiko, entitled 'Sekirankai kessei aisatsu', April, 1921 (Archive of Hōsei Daigaku Ōhara Shakai Mondai Kenkyūjo, Tokyo).

[289] Yamakawa Kikue, 'Shin Fujin Kyōkai to Sekirankai', *Taiyō* (July, 1921), reprinted in Yamakawa Kikue (ed. by Suzuki Yūko), *Yamakawa Kikue Josei Kaihō Ronshū*, vol. 2 (1984), pp. 13–5.

[290] *Ibid.*, p. 15.

[291] Hiratsuka, 'Nagoya chihō no jokō seikatsu', pp. 86–107; Hiratsuka, *Genshi*, vol. 3, pp. 60–5.

[292] This contrasted with Emmeline and Christabel Pankhurst, the leaders of the British W.S.P.U., who openly proclaimed that they wanted only hand-picked middle-class women for their movement, and who disavowed working-class women.

[293] Ichikawa, *Jiden: Senzen Hen*, p. 64; Yoneda, *Kindai Nihon Joseishi*, vol. 1, pp. 151, 156.

uneasiness among working-class members. For example, Yamanouchi
Mina, who came from a working-class background, and had been a
textile worker and a female representative of a textile workers' union,
became alienated from the Association and left it.[294] She blamed
Hiratsuka for the Association's class bias.[295] Yamanouchi confirmed
that from a working-class woman's point of view, Hiratsuka never
understood the real situation of labourers.[296] Clearly the Association
failed to fulfil Hiratsuka's wish to improve female working and living conditions, in spite of her growing appreciation of this area as
one needing reform.

The second major criticism which both Yamakawa and Yamanouchi
made was that the Association was never responsive to others or
democratically run, being controlled by Hiratsuka. Yamanouchi stated
that it had many councillors, directors, secretaries, and others who
had joined it for reasons which had little to do with Hiratsuka's own
personal appeal.[297] Accordingly, Yamanouchi felt that it ought to be
a more democratic organisation, one that allowed the views of these
people greater expression. According to Yamanouchi, Hiratsuka
regarded it as her private property since she was the founder, and
treated other executive members and directors as though they were
her assistants.[298] Yamanouchi stated that Hiratsuka did not trust them,
and was so possessive that when she resigned she asked other members either to dissolve the Association, or to change its name and
found a new organisation. Yamanouchi believed that Hiratsuka could
never conduct social campaigns as long as she maintained such an
undemocratic and selfish outlook.

Similarly, Yamakawa criticised the Association as 'Hiratsuka no
omocha' ('Hiratsuka's toy'), as being dominated by Hiratsuka, even
after she withdrew from its leadership.[299] Many other members had
little say in it. Yamakawa felt that the Association could not be separated from Hiratsuka, and that the unique individual character of
Hiratsuka imparted a very distinctive colour to it.[300] Yamakawa, who

---

[294] Yamanouchi, *Yamanouchi Mina Jiden*, pp. 86–7.
[295] *Ibid.*, p. 84.
[296] *Ibid.*, pp. 91–2.
[297] *Ibid.*, pp. 92–3.
[298] *Ibid.*, p. 92.
[299] Yamakawa, 'Shin Fujin Kyōkai to Sekirankai', p. 15.
[300] *Ibid.*, p. 15.

regretted this situation, still placed her hopes in the other members. In an article in *Taiyō* she appealed to them to reform it:

> I imagine that women who have gone as far as joining the Association are very progressive and courageous in taking that step. Therefore I wish that some of those fine members would take a much more active role in the Association on their own initiative, release the Association from Hiratsuka's control, promote more practical and deep-rooted campaigns among working women, who are the real strength in women's world, and unite the campaigns with proletarian ones. If the Association fails to do these things, its existence will become meaningless.[301]

In spite of this plea, no changes were made, and members like Yamanouchi simply left. Similarly in Britain, it is noticeable that the W.S.P.U. was dominated by Emmeline and Christabel Pankhurst and never run democratically.[302] However, compared to western feminist leaders such as Mrs Fawcett or Christabel and Emmeline Pankhurst, Hiratsuka possessed less distinguished qualities as a leader. Hiratsuka, who had a problem with her voice, avoided making speeches, unlike the Pankhursts who were eloquent and often spellbinding speakers.[303] Hiratsuka lacked the charisma, strong leadership, and determination to bring the members together in a unified and enduring way.

As Ichikawa Fusae later wrote, she and Hiratsuka knew almost nothing about politics, and were at a loss as to how to promote parliamentary campaigns when they founded the Association.[304] Almost all key members had no experience of political campaigning. This was a major limitation, as pointed out by Yamakawa Kikue. Yamakawa described the Association's campaign as 'ignorant and unethical', one depending heavily on politicians—even though there were no women in the Diet and the Association had to rely on male Diet members as spokesmen.[305] This situation was very similar to the early stage of the British suffrage movement, which depended heavily on male MPs.[306]

---

[301] *Ibid.*, pp. 14–5.
[302] Emmeline and Christabel Pankhurst demanded almost unquestioning loyalty from their followers. As a result some members became disillusioned with their autocratic style and broke away. See Bolt, *The Women's Movements*, pp. 191–2.
[303] Ichikawa, *Jiden: Senzen Hen*, p. 63.
[304] *Ibid.*, p. 55.
[305] Yamakawa, 'Shin Fujin Kyōkai to Sekirankai', p. 14.
[306] Banks, *Becoming a Feminist*, pp. 110–1, 121.

The Association's Contributions to the Women's Movement

Given these limitations, what contribution did the Association make to raise women's status, and how far did it advance the women's movement? What credit can be taken by Hiratsuka? Like the Seitō Society, the Association addressed issues that were important to women, and spoke out for women's needs. Hiratsuka had a distinctive political agenda for the Association, and its political activities contrasted with the Seitō Society. Hiratsuka and Ichikawa received useful advice from male Diet members, and learnt to conduct successful parliamentary lobbying for their three major causes. Unlike in her Seitō days, Hiratsuka became more focused and knew what she wanted to achieve in the Association. It had a clearer sense of direction and a more consistent female ideology than anything before it in Japan. Hiratsuka made good use of her family, literary and political connections, and appealed to other women's organisations for collaboration. She also recruited many members in provincial areas, founding many branches, and transforming the Association into a nationwide organisation.[307]

Hiratsuka recruited Oku and Ichikawa, who became major leaders of the Japanese women's movement. In her autobiography Oku explained the impact on her of the Association:

> I ended up being constant in my devotion to the women's movement for nearly seventy years, commencing with my involvement in the Association of New Women. I must admit that I was very reluctant to become involved with the Association at the beginning, and I was talked into it by my husband and Hiratsuka. At times I wonder what kind of life I might have led if I had not taken up the opportunity to work for the Association ... Once one sets foot in such a social venture, one cannot easily pull out. The starting point for me was my joining the Association. I can say that Hiratsuka and my husband determined the course of my life.[308]

Similarly, Ichikawa's subsequent activities grew out of her work with Hiratsuka in the Association. Unlike Oku, Ichikawa had shown much interest in women's causes before she joined the Association, although

---

[307] Ichikawa, *Jiden: Senzen Hen*, pp. 81–2; Hiratsuka, *Genshi*, vol. 3, pp. 164–5. See Appendix 12. See also Appendix 11.
[308] Oku, *Nobi*, pp. 46–7.

it was not clear that she would commit herself to them as she did.[309] Ichikawa stayed with the Association for two years, and it undoubtedly provided her with a valuable footing for her future prominence.

The Association's other achievements were stated in *Saikin no Shakai Undō* (*Recent Social Movements*):

> The Association of New Women achieved no more than the partial amendment of Article 5 of the Peace Police Law. No matter how small this achievement was, the Association's existence and activities certainly had a great influence upon Japanese women.[310]

The Association's campaigns on venereal disease and women's suffrage achieved little. Its main achievement was the amendment of the Peace Police Law, enabling women to attend or organise political meetings. This was the first legal change achieved by the women's movement in Japan. It took two years to achieve, more than twenty years after the first petitioning campaign for the cause had been started by socialist women like Imai Utako.[311]

With regard to its other aims, the Association produced some positive effects. It made many women in Japan, more aware of their political ineffectiveness, and kindled their aspirations for political freedom and independent voting. The Association's campaign for marital restrictions on persons with venereal disease had a wider educational import. It educated unmarried women, most of whom had probably never heard of venereal disease. As far as the Association's campaign for women's suffrage was concerned, it was the first Japanese women's group to advocate this publicly, and it submitted the first petition on it to the Diet.[312]

The Association's campaigns had much impact on the development of other women's organisations, as was pointed out in *Saikin no Shakai Undō* (*Recent Social Movements*):

---

[309] Ichikawa, *Jiden: Senzen Hen*, pp. 50–1.

[310] Cited in Matsuo, 'Taishō-ki fujin no seijiteki jiyū kakutoku undō', p. 48. *Saikin no Shakai Undō* (*Recent Social Movements*) was written by the Kyōchōkai (the Harmonization Society, which was founded in December, 1919). The Society conducted extensive research on labour and social problems and published books and periodicals.

[311] Itoya, *Josei Kaihō no Senkusha*, pp. 169–71; Yoneda, *Kindai Nihon Joseishi*, vol. 1., pp. 79–81; Yoshimi, *Fujin Sanseiken*, pp. 144–5; Kodama, *Fujin Sanseiken Undō Shōshi*, pp. 21–2; Kodama, '*Josei Dōmei* fukkoku ni atatte', pp. 14–5; Ooki, 'Meiji shakai shugi undō to josei', p. 123.

[312] Yoshimi, *Fujin Sanseiken*, p. 149.

Even before the Association of New Women was founded, more than
a few women's groups, such as Aikoku Fujinkai (the Patriotic Women's
Association) and Shōkō Fujinkai (the Women's Association for Com-
missioned Officers), had existed. But the main objectives of these associations were to promote better social contacts among women and cultivate
their minds. These associations never thought about working for an
improvement in women's status or the acquisition of women's rights.
However, the activities of the Association of New Women triggered a
self-awakening among women, and as a result many existing women's
organisations changed direction along similar lines.[313]

Comments like these were made by Hiratsuka in her autobiography.[314] Even the very conservative and upper-class women's association Aikoku Fujinkai, whose main objective was to aid the war
effort and assist military widows, was stimulated by the Association
of New Women, changed its direction, and began to undertake social
work.[315] And a women's Christian organisation, Kyōfūkai, whose
main campaign had been anti-prostitution, now joined the women's
suffrage movement.[316]

In these regards the Association was extremely significant. Yosano
Akiko stated that it brought the Japanese women's movement to the
more advanced status of its counterparts in America and Britain,
and it marked a new impetus for that movement after the Seitō
Society.[317]

The Association nevertheless remained a small pressure group
involved in petitioning and parliamentary lobbying, and it never participated in, or organised, any open demonstrations. It failed to turn
its campaign into a mass movement. This contrasted sharply with
its western counterparts such as the W.S.P.U. Even so, the Association's

---

[313] Cited in Matsuo, 'Taishō-ki fujin no seijiteki jiyū kakutoku undō', p. 48. The
Aikoku Fujinkai was founded by Okumura Ioko in 1901. It provided Japanese soldiers and their families with relief and assistance, and soon grew to be a nationwide organisation. Its membership increased dramatically during the Russo-Japanese
War. In the 1930s it had over 3 million members. In 1942 it was incorporated
into the Dainippon Fujinkai (Great Japan Women's Society), which was a national
organisation designed to make all women support Japan's war effort.
[314] Hiratsuka, *Genshi*, vol. 3, pp. 235–6.
[315] Suzuki, *Joseishi o Hiraku*, vol. 1, pp. 71–2; Matsuo, 'Taishō-ki fujin no seijiteki
jiyū kakutoku undō', p. 49.
[316] *Ibid.*, p. 49.
[317] Yosano Akiko, 'Shin Fujin Kyōkai no seigan undō', *Taiyō* (February, 1920),
reprinted in Yosano Akiko (ed. by Kano Masanao & Kōuchi Nobuko), *Yosano Akiko
Hyōronshū* (1985), p. 313.

political activities provided a significant precedent for the women's political movement, notably for female suffrage. Hiratsuka later recalled that the women's movement was enlivened by the Association, and that many independent women's political organisations were founded on its coat-tails throughout Japan.[318] These included the Fujin Renmei (the Women's Federal Union) and the Fujin Sansei Dōmei (the League for Women's Political Rights)—which were founded under the leadership of ex-members of the Association of New Women.[319]

Oku, Hiratsuka and Ichikawa went different ways after the dissolution of the Association. Oku briefly joined the Fujin Renmei (Women's Federal Union) but, disillusioned with parliamentary campaigns, lobbying, and women's suffrage issues, she soon left it and steered away from women's political movements.[320] Disenchanted with the Association of New Women's upper-middle class emphases, Oku drew more attention to the condition of working women and redirected her energies into setting up the society for working women called the Shokugyō Fujinsha (the Working Women's Society) in April 1923. She also inaugurated its magazine *Shokugyō Fujin* (*Working Women*).[321] Through this Society she hoped to help resolve the problems many working women had, and to improve their family and working lives.

Ichikawa resigned from the Association and went to America in 1921, the year after suffrage was gained by American women. She visited the head offices of women's organisations which had worked for women's suffrage, such as the National Woman's Party and the National League of Women's Voters, and met feminist leaders.[322] Her stay in America for two and a half years broadened her horizons, widened her feminist intellectual capacity, and helped form her as an internationally minded women's campaigner in Japan. In particular, her meeting with Alice Paul, the women's suffrage leader, was crucial for her outlook on female suffrage.[323] From that time she

---

[318] Hiratsuka, *Genshi*, vol. 3, pp. 235–6.

[319] Kodama, *Fujin Sanseiken Undō Shōshi*, pp. 90–130; Oku, *Nobi*, p. 72; Tatewaki, *Nihon no Fujin*, p. 56; Esashi & Ide, *Taishō Demokurashi to Josei*, p. 103; Matsuo, 'Taishō-ki fujin no seijiteki jiyū kakutoku undō', pp. 50–5.

[320] Oku, *Nobi*, pp. 71–2.

[321] *Ibid.*, pp. 75–88.

[322] Ichikawa, *Jiden: Senzen Hen*, pp. 115–20; Ichikawa, *Daikon no Hana*, pp. 144–6.

[323] *Ibid.*, pp. 210–3; Ichikawa, *Nonaka no Ippon Sugi*, pp. 31–4; Ichikawa, *Jiden, Senzen Hen*, pp. 117–8.

concentrated on developing the women's suffrage campaign in Japan.[324] After she returned to Japan, she joined the Fujin Sanseiken Kakutoku Kisei Dōmei (the League for the Attainment of Women's Suffrage), which was founded in December 1924. She became its leader and played a significant role in developing an active suffrage movement before World War II.

Hiratsuka, who was disappointed with the outcome of the Association, especially with its members' lack of unity and cooperative spirit, seemed to have lost her interest in the women's movement. She suffered from ill health, probably caused by overwork for the Association of New Women, and she felt bitter about the experience. She also felt guilty towards her partner Okumura and her two children, believing that her campaigning had led her to neglect them. Although the women's suffrage movement escalated after the dissolution of the Association, Hiratsuka withdrew from the mainstream of it. In contrast to Ichikawa's striking contributions to the women's movement, which were especially notable at this time, Hiratsuka now became little more than a background observer of the events and campaigns under way.

[324] Suzuki, *Joseishi o Hiraku*, vol. 1, pp. 121–2.

CHAPTER SEVEN

HIRATSUKA RAICHŌ'S LATER LIFE

Hiratsuka after the Association of New Women

After the dissolution of the Association of New Women, Hiratsuka continued to recuperate. Between July 1921 (when she withdrew from the forefront of the Association) and March 1923, she and her family stayed away from Tokyo, moving from place to place in the country.[1] She devoted herself now to child-rearing and to family tasks that had been neglected during her period of feminist activity.[2] This period of her life came to an end when her daughter reached school age. Hiratsuka wanted to educate her children in Tokyo, and they returned there in April 1923, settling in a rented house in Sendagaya, Tokyo, where they experienced the Great Kantō Earthquake of September 1923.[3] In 1925 they moved to Karasuyama, Tokyo, and in 1927 to Kinuta Village (now a town called Seijō), Tokyo, where Hiratsuka lived until her death.[4] Yoneda Sayoko called these years in Hiratsuka's life '*Hiratsuka's insei jidai*' ('The time when Hiratsuka

[1] The places they stayed during this time included Takeoka Coast in Chiba Prefecture and Nasu Hot Spring, Saku Mountain and Izu Mountain in Tochigi Prefecture. Hiratsuka, *Genshi*, vol. 3, pp. 238–9; Kobayashi, *Hito to Shisō*, pp. 183–4; Hiratsuka Raichō, 'Shunsō zappitsu', in Hiratsuka Raichō, *Kumo, Kusa, Hito* (1933), reprinted in Hiratsuka, *Chosakushū*, vol. 4, pp. 73–5; Hiratsuka Raichō, 'Sakuzan ni sumite', in Hiratsuka Raichō, *Boshi Zuihitsu* (1948), reprinted in Hiratsuka, *Chosakushū*, vol. 4, pp. 76–80; Hiratsuka Raichō, 'Aru haha no tegami: Tomimoto Kazue-san ni', in Hiratsuka, *Boshi Zuihitsu*, reprinted in Hiratsuka, *Chosakushū*, vol. 4, pp. 59–72; Hiratsuka Raichō, 'Shinteitō no tame ni', in Hiratsuka, *Chosakushū*, vol. 3, pp. 349–54.

[2] Hiratsuka, *Genshi*, vol. 3, pp. 238, 262–3.

[3] *Ibid.*, pp. 238, 242–7; Hiratsuka, 'Shunsō zappitsu', pp. 73–4; Hiratsuka Raichō, 'Sendagaya ni sumite', in Hiratsuka, *Kumo, Kusa Hito*, reprinted in Hiratsuka, *Chosakushū*, vol. 4, pp. 162–4; Hiratsuka Raichō, 'Shinsai zakki: kora e', *Josei Kaizō* (October & November, 1923), reprinted in Hiratsuka, *Chosakushū*, vol. 3, pp. 326–40.

[4] Hiratsuka Raichō, 'Kinuta-mura ni tateta watashitachi no ie', *Fujin no Tomo* (January, 1927), reprinted in Hiratsuka, *Chosakushū*, vol. 4, pp. 264–71; Hiratsuka Raichō, 'Kinuta mura ni sumite', *Yomiuri Shinbun* (18 May, 1936), reprinted in Hiratsuka, *Chosakushū*, vol. 6, pp. 125–6; Yoneda Sayoko, 'Kaisetsu', in Hiratsuka, *Chosakushū*, vol. 4, p. 381.

led a very secluded life'), and she disappeared from the public scene altogether, not participating in any political, social or feminist activities.[5] In 1924 Hiratsuka explained herself as follows:

> Even before I became a mother, I fully anticipated that there would be difficulties in combining my family life as a mother and my public life as a working member of society. As I was not facing this reality at that time, I had an optimistic view that I would somehow combine the two in the future . . . After I had children, I made every effort to solve the difficulty of combining these in my life. However, I could not do so, and gradually realised that this problem would not be easily solved. I came to realise that the two are utterly incompatible, which made me feel hopeless. I realised that loving my children and bringing them up properly, which seemed to be a most delicate and responsible work, could not possibly be done in my spare time. It ought to be full-time work . . . In my days of the Association of New Women I tried very hard to combine the two, but I ended up experiencing desolation, dissatisfaction, pain and downheartedness, because I could not throw my whole soul into either of them. I felt as if my heart was torn to pieces and I became completely worn out physically and mentally. If there is even one woman who proudly and convincingly says that she has succeeded in combining the two, I will be most envious of her.[6]

Hiratsuka openly admitted her difficulties, and opted for home life. She was in a fragile state after her feminist campaigns, her children had complained about her activities, and Okumura was unhappy with Hiratsuka allowing the Association of New Women to use their house as an office, as the many visitors destroyed his privacy.[7] She was also disappointed with the outcome of the Association, especially with its members' lack of support for her.[8] She stated that her co-workers had no cooperative discipline and developed negative feelings towards each other.[9] She was also dissatisfied with the ways in which other women's organisations were operating then. They lacked unity, had many internal factions, and were mutually isolated from

---

[5] *Ibid.*, p. 380.

[6] Hiratsuka Raichō, 'Haha to shite no watakushi no seikatsu', in Hiratsuka, *Fujin no Tomo* (March, 1924), reprinted in Hiratsuka, *Chosakushū*, vol. 4, pp. 24–5. This article was also reprinted in Hiratsuka, *Kumo, Kusa, Hoto.*

[7] Hiratsuka, *Genshi*, vol. 3, pp. 194, 224; Hiratsuka Raichō, 'Shin Fujin Kyōkai no kaiko', *Fujin Kōron* (March-July, 1923), reprinted in Hiratsuka, *Chosakushū*, vol. 3, pp. 295–6.

[8] Kobayashi, *Hito to Shisō*, p. 182; Ide, *Kindai to Shinpi*, pp. 185–6.

[9] Hiratsuka, *Genshi*, vol. 3, p. 231.

each other.[10] In these circumstances she came to despair of women's political campaigns, became indifferent to them, and decided to concentrate upon her family life.[11] In 1925 she commented to one newspaper reporter that:

> Nowadays the mere thought of the so-called women's movement gives me the shivers. I have grown to dislike the women's movement so much that there is no way for me to return to it. Such a return would drive me to an early grave.[12]

She cut ties with her ex-associates and seemed to become entirely indifferent to women's issues for a while. The only non-domestic work she did between July 1921 and 1928 was occasional writing for magazines, which she did largely because Okumura's income was not sufficient to keep their family and she needed the money.[13] Unlike during her days in the Association of New Women, when she wrote on women's issues, the great majority of these articles between 1921 and 1927 were on nature, children, family life and child education. While she lived in Karasuyama she became very attached to nature, and wrote naturistic pieces on the area entitled 'Karasuyama yori' ('From Karasuyama') which appeared in the *Fujo Shinbun* (*Women's Newspaper*).[14] Many of these were later published in a book entitled *Kumo, Kusa, Hito* (*Clouds, Grass and People*).[15]

An issue which came into prominence during this time was her interest in children's education. She took this very seriously, sending

[10] *Ibid.*, pp. 235–6.

[11] Yoneda, 'Kaisetsu', in Hiratsuka, *Chosakushū*, vol. 4, pp. 379–80.

[12] Hiratsuka Raichō, 'Karasuyama yori', *Fujo Shinbun* (20 September, 1925), reprinted in Hiratsuka, *Chosakushū*, vol. 4, p. 132.

[13] Hiratsuka Raichō, 'Watakushitachi no binbō ni tsuite', *Fujin Kōron* (December, 1926), reprinted in Hiratsuka, *Chosakushū*, vol. 4, pp. 213–7; Hiratsuka, 'Katei no shigoto o shokugyō to misu', *Fujin no Tomo* (April, 1925), reprinted in Hiratsuka, *Chosakushū*, vol. 4, p. 114.

[14] Hiratsuka Raichō, 'Aru hi no kodomo', *Fujo Shinbun* (8 March, 1925), reprinted in Hiratsuka, *Chosakushū*, vol. 4, p. 112; Hiratsuka Raichō, 'Haru ga kita', *Fujo Shinbun* (12 April, 1925), reprinted in Hiratsuka, *Chosakushū*, vol. 4, pp. 116–7; Hiratsuka Raichō, 'Take bayashi', *Fujo Shinbun* (28 June, 1925), reprinted in Hiratsuka, *Chosakushū*, vol. 4, pp. 118–9; Hiratsuka Raichō, 'Kuri no hana', *Fujo Shinbun* (12 July, 1925), reprinted in Hiratsuka, *Chosakushū*, vol. 4, p. 120; Hiratsuka Raichō, 'No no hana', *Fujo Shinbun* (19 July, 1925), reprinted in Hiratsuka, *Chosakushū*, vol. 4, pp. 121–2; Hiratsuka Raichō, 'Dōshin', *Fujo Shinbun* (26 July, 1925), reprinted in Hiratsuka, *Chosakushū*, vol. 4, p. 123; Hiratsuka Raichō, 'Mugi no me', *Fujo Shinbun* (31 January, 1926), reprinted in Hiratsuka, *Chosakushū*, vol. 4, p. 181.

[15] Hiratsuka Raichō, *Kumo, Kusa, Hito* (1933).

her children to Seijō Shōgakkō (Seijō Elementary School), a unique private school founded by the educationalist Sawayanagi Masatarō in 1917.[16] This was an experimental school where methods to improve elementary education were explored and Sawayanagi's progressive educational theories were applied.[17] It had a distinctive atmosphere which made pupils feel free and relaxed. The main objectives of the school were to value children's personality, to help them develop it, and to encourage intellectual curiosity. It had an original curriculum, without *shūshin* (morals) classes or any examinations. As the school kept its pupil numbers low, teachers were able to teach intensively and indulgently.[18]

Hiratsuka hated her state schools, where the Ministry of Education's opinions were enforced and where pupils were provided with a standardised education.[19] She also disapproved of government-designated textbooks, as used in almost all schools at that time. She condemned these as insipid, their contents being the remnants of the old moral education emphasising obedience, militarist ideas and utilitarianism, none of which had any regard for children's feelings.[20] She stated that it was a sin to tie children's lively spirits to such textbooks. Seijō Elementary School was one of the rare schools where government-designated textbooks were not used, and its school policy matched her intention to bring up her children to be free-spirited and unique individuals with strong personalities.[21] It was logical for her to send her children there, even though its fees were notoriously expensive.[22]

---

[16] Hiratsuka Raichō, 'Kodomo o Seijō Shōgakkō ni ireta koto ni tsuite', *Fujin no Tomo* (March, 1926), reprinted in Hiratsuka, *Chosakushū*, vol. 4, pp. 186–8; Hiratsuka Raichō, 'Musume no kekkonshiki ni nozomite', *Fujin Kōron* (May, 1938), reprinted in Hiratsuka, *Chosakushū*, vol. 6, p. 260. Sawayanagi (1865–1927) served as vice-minister of education. He also worked as vice-chancellor of Tōhoku and Kyōto Universities, and was one of the leaders of progressive education in Japan. He later added a junior high school and a high school to his Seijō Elementary School. In 1950 Seijō University was founded. On Sawayanagi, see Seijō Gakuen Kyōiku Kenkyujo (ed.), *Sawayanagi Masatarō Kyōiku Ronshō* (1987); Karasawa Tomitarō (ed.), *Zusetsu Kyōiku Jinbutsu Jiten*, 3 vols (1984), vol. 3, pp. 91–4.

[17] An account of education in Seijō Elementary School is given in Shōji Kazuaki, *Sawayanagi Masatarō to Seijō Kyōiku* (1974); Karasawa (ed.), *Zusetsu Kyōiku Jinbutsu Jiten*, vol. 1, pp. 412–6.

[18] Hiratsuka, *Genshi*, vol. 3, p. 255.

[19] *Ibid.*, p. 255.

[20] Hiratsuka, 'Kodomo o Seijō Shōgakkō ni ireta koto ni tsuite', p. 187.

[21] *Ibid.*, p. 187.

[22] Hiratsuka, *Genshi*, vol. 3, pp. 254–5.

Her choice of school for children was not directly relevant to her feminist activity, and did not become a matter of public confrontation, but it demonstrated her radicalism and scepticism towards state education.

It is worth asking how the public interpreted Hiratsuka's seclusion. Contemporary feminists were very doubtful that such a woman could really be satisfied with an isolated family-orientated life.[23] Okamoto Kanoko and other women, who had known Hiratsuka well, lamented her inactive role:

> It is a great pity that such a capable woman as Hiratsuka is simply staying at home and doing nothing. It is a complete waste of her talent. If she had not had either a family or children, she would have done a great deal of work for other women.[24]

In spite of such concerns, Hiratsuka explained that she never regretted her decision to give up her feminist activity in this way.[25] She was very contented with her life as a full-time mother, and found great pleasure in watching children grow up.[26] This was of course all consistent with Ellen Key's views on motherhood. However, Hiratsuka had reached this state of mind after a hard struggle to combine feminist activity and child-rearing. She admitted that before and just after their births she had seen them as enemies sent to destroy her public life.[27] But her negative feeling towards children rapidly disappeared, and she described them as 'gifts from Heaven, who made me feel indescribably fruitful, ample and content'.[28] This period was an important part in her life as a woman, and her child-rearing experiences helped her to mature and accomplish herself, marking also a significant transition in her feminism. Women's historians have ignored this period because she had withdrawn from the mainstream of the women's movement and was inactive as a campaigner, and most of her writings at this time seem irrelevant to women's causes. Such neglect is not entirely justified at the level of autobiographical understanding. In addition, Hiratsuka became

---

[23] *Ibid.*, pp. 288–9.
[24] Cited in Hiratsuka Raichō, 'Haha no kansha', in Hiratsuka Raichō, *Haha no Kotoba* (1937), reprinted in Hiratsuka, *Chosakushū*, vol. 4, p. 241.
[25] Hiratsuka, *Genshi*, vol. 3, p. 289.
[26] *Ibid.*, p. 288.
[27] Hiratsuka, 'Haha no kansha', p. 241.
[28] *Ibid.*, p. 241.

more focused upon working-class issues which she had often ignored earlier. This was closely related to political changes. Universal male suffrage was achieved in 1925 for all males over twenty-five years.[29] Taking advantage of this, some proletarian political parties were formed, and working-class women's organisations were founded by women who could not join the male parties.[30] In this political climate Hiratsuka began to place high hopes in the working class, as manifested in her article 'Katei no shigoto o shokugyō to miru' ('One must regard women's domestic life as paid work').[31]

She had become more aware of the problems facing working mothers who had to earn their own livings, and in this article she suggested that women's domestic work (including child-rearing) should be accorded a status commensurate with paid occupations, and should be given a proper economic value.[32] Society should financially reward full-time mothers for their creditable services in this role. This argument developed the position that she had taken in the controversy over the protection of motherhood. When involved in that debate, she had suggested that the state should remunerate mothers to protect motherhood, a view that she held on to in the Association of New Women.[33] She had expected the state to create better circumstances for working mothers with children. However, by 1925 she had completely lost faith in the state.[34] She realised that she would never find an ideal society which would give women financial independence to fulfil their duties as mothers, at least not under conditions of capitalism. She now described 'capitalist' society as one dominated by capitalists' autocracy, male oppression, and the power of money, and began to regard it as her enemy.[35] She took an increasing interest in the new proletarian parties, and began to express

---

[29] Kano, *Taishō Demokurashii*, p. 360; Imai, *Taishō Demokurashii*, p. 435.

[30] Hiratsuka Raichō, 'Musan seitō to fusen undō', *Fujo Shinbun* (3 February, 1927), reprinted in Hiratsuka, *Chosakushū*, vol. 4, pp. 273–4; Hiratsuka Raichō, 'Musan seitō to musan fujin dantai', *Fujo Shinbun* (20 February, 1927), reprinted in Hiratsuka, *Chosakushū*, vol. 4, p. 275.

[31] Hiratsuka Raichō, 'Katei no shigoto o shokugyō to miru', *Fujin no Tomo* (April, 1925), reprinted in Hiratsuka, *Chosakushū*, vol. 4, pp. 113–5.

[32] *Ibid.*, p. 115.

[33] Hiratsuka, 'Bosei hogo no shuchō wa iraishugi ka', p. 89.

[34] Yoneda, 'Kaisetsu', in Hiratsuka, *Chosakushū*, vol. 4, p. 392.

[35] Hiratsuka Raichō, 'Shokugyō Fujin Renmei ni tsuite', in Hiratsuka, *Chosakushū*, vol. 4, p. 249.

a strong affinity with some proletarian women's organisations.[36] She became convinced that only they would be capable of destroying capitalist society, and that the destiny of Japan rested upon their shoulders.[37] She also began to believe that such working-class movements would promote a campaign for women's political reform, including women's suffrage, and would help to resolve other women's causes such as the protection of motherhood.[38] This line of thinking was quite a radical departure for a thinker who has hitherto sometimes been thought of as a bourgeois feminist.

Hiratsuka wanted as many members of proletarian political parties as possible voted into the Diet in the February 1928 general election.[39] She wrote articles supporting them between spring 1927 and 1928.[40] Her article 'Fusen undōsha e: zen fujin dantai yo, fusen o sono kōryō ni kakagetaru musan seitō o ōen seyo' ('Addressed to women's suffrage campaigners: all women's organisations, support proletarian political parties which include women's suffrage in their programme') was a good example. After the dissolution of the Association of New Women, the women's suffrage movement had made much progress. The Fujin Sanseiken Kakutoku Kisei Dōmei (the League for the Attainment of Women's Suffrage), founded in December 1924, greatly contributed to this.[41] It welcomed collaboration from

---

[36] Hiratsuka Raichō, 'Waga fujin sanseiken undō no shōrai', *Josei Kaizō* (January, 1924), reprinted in Hiratsuka, *Chosakushū*, vol. 4, pp. 20–1. This article was also reprinted in Hiratsuka, *Josei no Kotoba* (1926).

[37] Hiratsuka, *Genshi*, vol. 3, pp. 269–72.

[38] Hiratsuka Raichō, 'Tenkanki ni tateru Nihon no fujin sanseiken undō', *Fujin no Tomo* (April, 1927), reprinted in Hiratsuka, *Chosakushū*, vol. 4, pp. 280–1.

[39] Yoneda Sayoko, 'Bosei shugi no rekishiteki igi: *Fujin Sensen* jidai no Hiratsuka Raichō o chūshin ni', in Joseishi Sōgō Kenkyūkai (ed.), *Nihon Joseishi*, vol. 5 (1982, 1985 edn), pp. 131–2; Kobayashi, *Hito to Shisō*, p. 187.

[40] Hiratsuka, 'Tenkanki ni tateru Nihon no fujin sanseiken undō', pp. 276–81; Hiratsuka Raichō, 'Musan seitō to fujin undō', *Fujo Shinbun* (3 February, 1927), reprinted in Hiratsuka, *Chosakushū*, vol. 4, pp. 273–4; Hiratsuka Raichō, 'Musan seitō to musan fujin dantai', *Fujo Shinbun* (20 February, 1927), reprinted in Hiratsuka, *Chosakushū*, vol. 4, p. 275; Hiratsuka Raichō, 'Fusen undō o ika ni michibiku beki ka', *Fujin Kōron* (July, 1928), reprinted in Hiratsuka, *Chosakushū*, vol. 5, pp. 54–61; Hiratsuka Raichō, 'Fusen undōsha e: zen fujin dantai yo, fusen o sono kōryō ni kakagetaru musan seitō o ōen seyo', *Tokyo Nichi Nichi Shinbun* (6 February, 1928), reprinted in Hiratsuka, *Chosakushū*, vol. 5, pp. 20–7.

[41] The League for the Attainment of Women's Suffrage lasted sixteen years and was relatively long-lived compared with many other women's organisations which predated it. The name Fujin Sanseiken Kakutoku Kisei Dōmei was changed to the Fusen Kakutoku Dōmei in April 1925. Hiratsuka, *Genshi*, vol. 3, p. 236; Kodama,

all women's organisations, uniting them in a common aim.[42] It was more structured and larger-scale than Hiratsuka's Association of New Women, and shared more similarities with western suffrage organisations such as the W.S.P.U. in Britain. Hiratsuka had refrained from commenting on the women's suffrage movement since the dissolution of the Association of New Women, but she was dissatisfied with the tactics used by the women's suffrage organisations.[43] In 'Fusen undōsha e: zen fujin dantai yo, fusen o sono kōryō ni kakage taru musan seitō o ōen seyo' she criticised them for using the same methods as the Association of New Women to promote women's suffrage.[44] She argued that in her Association she had no option but to search for Dietmen willing to support women's suffrage, and then to persuade them to submit women's suffrage petitions and bills, since none of the political parties had included women's suffrage in their programmes.[45] Her argument now changed, for since working-class parties now included women's suffrage in their programmes, it was logical for women's suffrage organisations to stop relying on the established political parties (which still did not approve of votes for women), and instead to support the more sympathetic and newly founded proletarian parties.[46]

These parties had no MPs before the 1928 election, when they returned 8 MPs.[47] However, they held less than a fiftieth of the seats in the Diet, and hardly had any power.[48] They also suffered from internal divisions; and the proletarian women's organisations, in which Hiratsuka placed high hopes, failed to develop active suffrage campaigns.[49] Hiratsuka stopped writing articles supporting these groups

---

Fujin Sanseiken Undō Shōshi, pp. 131–292; Ichikawa, Jiden: Senzen Hen, pp. 144–6; Matsuo, 'Taishō-ki fujin no seijiteki jiyū kakutoku undō', pp. 62–8, 76; Morosawa, Onna no Rekishi, vol. 2, pp. 209–10; Esashi & Ide, Taishō Demokurashii to Josei, p. 264; Yoshimi, Fujin Sanseiken, p. 158.

[42] Matsuo, 'Taishō-ki fujin no seijiteki jiyū kakutoku undō', pp. 74–6.

[43] Hiratsuka, Genshi, vol. 3, p. 270.

[44] Hiratsuka, 'Fusen undōsha e: zen fujin dantai yo, fusen o sono kōryō ni kakage taru musan seitō o ōen seyo', pp. 21–2.

[45] Ibid., p. 22.

[46] Ibid., pp. 23–5.

[47] Kobayashi, Hito to Shisō, p. 186; Esashi & Ide, Taishō Demokurashii to Josei, p. 289. 219 members of the Seiyūkai and 217 members of the Minseitō were elected. These two parties accounted for more than 90 per cent of Diet members in the House of Representatives.

[48] Orii Miyako, 'Raichō to shōhi kumiai undō', in Hiratsuka Raichō o Yomu Kai (ed.), Raichō Soshite Watashi (1988), pp. 37–8.

[49] Yoneda, 'Kaisetsu', in Hiratsuka, Chosakushū, vol. 4, p. 394; Yoneda, 'Kaisetsu', in Hiratsuka, Chosakushū, vol. 5, p. 410.

from mid 1928. She no longer saw working-class parties as instru-
mental to her main purpose, which was to create a new society in
which women would be valued and emancipated, and their talents
and motherhood fully appreciated.[50]

Hiratsuka's Participation in the Consumers' Movement

Before long she sought means to this end in the consumers' cooperative movement. She became involved in this after reading the
works of the Russian anarchist Kropotkin, in particular his *Mutual
Aid* (which was translated as *Sōgō Fujo Ron* in Japanese).[51] In it he
stated that there were two entirely different features affecting living
creatures: the struggle for existence and mutual support.[52] He argued
that mutual support is the most significant characteristic to preserve
species as well as to develop them further. He also stated that even
in modern society, which appears to pursue only individual benefit,
various forms of mutual support organisations such as trade unions,
cooperative societies and educational and artistic organisations exist.
Kropotkin gave a detailed account of cooperative societies, and argued
that as self-governing social organisations they were the most moralistic form of social life ever discovered.

In her autobiography Hiratsuka wrote that she was highly inspired
by this book and was awakened to the cooperative spirit, which she
described as an instinct common to mankind.[53] She then took a
strong interest in cooperative societies. In 1929 the Tokyo Kyōdōsha
(Tokyo Co-Workers' Society), a cooperative society led by trade
unionists, founded a branch in Seijō, and she became an active member.[54] When the branch had troubles with its head office, she helped
to found an independent cooperative society called 'Warera no ie'

---

[50] *Ibid.*, p. 408.
[51] Orii, 'Raichō to shōhi kumiai undō', p. 38; Hiratsuka, *Genshi*, vol. 3, p. 290;
Kobayashi, *Hito to Shisō*, p. 189; Yoneda, 'Bosei shugi no rekishiteki igi', p. 132;
Yoneda 'Kaisetsu', in Hiratsuka, *Chosakushū*, vol. 5, p. 408.
[52] The outline of this book is given in Hiratsuka, *Genshi*, vol. 3, pp. 290–1;
Hiratsuka Raichō, 'Honnō to shite no kyōdōshin no hatten: shizenteki dōtoku ni
tsuite', in Hiratsuka, *Chosakushū*, vol. 5, pp. 227–35.
[53] Hiratsuka, *Genshi*, vol. 3, pp. 290–1.
[54] *Ibid.*, p. 290; Yoneda, 'Bosei shugi no rekishiteki igi', p. 133; Hiratsuka Raichō,
'Kinuta-mura zassō', *Fujo Shinbun* (22 June–21 September, 1930), reprinted in
Hiratsuka, *Chosakushū*, vol. 5, pp. 203–6; Takamure, *Josei no Rekishi*, vol. 2, p. 307.

('Our house') in 1930.[55] She became its chairwoman and devoted herself to it. Her family circumstances had made it easier for her to return to such a commitment. Her children had nearly completed their elementary school education by then and no longer needed her full-time care and attention.[56]

As she became more involved, she was more persuaded that the cooperative society movement might be able to destroy capitalist society and construct a new self-governing society.[57] She was most impressed with the ways in which the cooperative society movement was conducted:

> Although the cooperative society movement is based on class consciousness, it does not resort to force but employs peaceful and sensible measures. It aims to restore women's lives as consumers on the basis of mutual support and cooperative spirit. The movement is most suitable for women's lives and appeals to their feelings because women are the main consumers. Even very ordinary women can participate in the movement.[58]

She was also attracted by the fact that women could become involved in the consumer movement in the intervals between their child-rearing activities, without disrupting their child-rearing.[59]

The initial objective of the cooperative society that she chaired was to form an economically self-governing consumers' union which would be jointly administered by its members.[60] Their everyday goods would be purchased jointly to reduce the cost, and consumers could become producers and lead self-sufficient lives. The family economy of every household would be socialized and equalized and no profits need be made.

This cooperative society's activities included selling kimonos and haberdashery cheaply, exchanging or recycling unwanted items, organ-

---

[55] Kobayashi, *Hito to Shisō*, pp. 189–90; Hiratsuka, *Genshi*, vol. 3, p. 292; Hiratsuka, 'Kinuta-mura zassō', pp. 207–8; Hiratsuka, 'Honnō to shite no kyōdōshin no hatten', pp. 232–3; Yoneda, 'Bosei shugi no rekishiteki igi', p. 133; Takamure, *Josei no Rekishi*, vol. 2, pp. 307–8.

[56] Hiratsuka, *Genshi*, vol. 3, p. 295; Yoneda, 'Kaisetsu', in Hiratsuka, *Chosakushū*, vol. 5, p. 413.

[57] Hiratsuka, 'Honnō to shite no kyōdōshin no hatten', p. 235; Hiratsuka Raichō, '*Fujin Sensen* ni sanka shite', *Fujin Sensen*, 1:2 (April, 1930), pp. 37–8.

[58] *Ibid.*, p. 38.

[59] Yoneda, 'Kaisetsu', in Hiratsuka, *Chosakushū*, vol. 5, p. 414.

[60] Hiratsuka Raichō, 'Mōkenai shōbai: shōhi kumiai ni tsuite', *Josei Shinbun*, 74 (29 September, 1930), reprinted in Hiratsuka, *Chosakushū*, vol. 5, pp. 219–20.

ising cookery classes and food tasting gatherings, selling fresh milk, vegetables and fruit direct from the farms in Mishima in Shizuoka Prefecture, and selling dishes cooked by members of the society.[61] These activities were a natural extension of housewives' work. However, their husbands and children were also involved and assisted the work, for example by looking after the cooperative shop, and printing and distributing the society's leaflets.

Hiratsuka became very committed to this society. She was actively involved in its financial side and in administering and running it on a day-to-day basis.[62] As she was eager to expand it, she made impassioned appeals to women throughout Japan advocating the development of cooperative societies, especially in articles published in 1930–32.[63] The time was most appropriate for such an appeal. After the Great Slump in 1929, cities contained many unemployed people and in rural areas many poor farmers' daughters were sold into prostitution to survive.[64] Mother-and-child double suicides and cases of murdered children due to adverse living conditions increased and had become serious social problems.[65] Hiratsuka advocated the enactment of a law to protect mothers and children.[66] At the same time she urged the necessity to found cooperative societies throughout Japan, which would neither exploit their customers nor seek any profits.[67] She believed that cooperative societies would help to save people from financial difficulties.[68] She wanted to see hospitals and medical facilities founded and run by cooperatives.[69]

---

[61] Hiratsuka, *Genshi*, vol. 3, pp. 292–7; Hiratsuka Raichō, 'Kyōdō suiji wa ikaga', in Hiratsuka, *Chosakushū*, vol. 6, pp. 157–8.

[62] Kobayashi, *Hito to Shisō*, p. 190.

[63] Hiratsuka, 'Mōkenai shōbai', pp. 218–20; Hiratsuka Raichō, 'Shōhi kumuai to fujin no ichi', *Fujin no Tomo* (October, 1932), reprinted in Hiratsuka, *Chosakushū*, vol. 5, pp. 297–303; Hiratsuka Raichō, 'Haha yo te o tore, hitan no arashi no naka de: mura mura ni iryō kumiai o motō', *Miyako Shinbun* (19 & 20 August, 1932), reprinted in Hiratsuka, *Chosakushū*, vol. 5, pp. 291–6.

[64] Yoneda, 'Kaisetsu', in Hiratsuka, *Chosakushū*, vol. 5, pp. 412–3.

[65] Hiratsuka Raichō, 'Mushiro Boshi Hogo Hō o seitei seyo', *Fujin Kurabu* (August, 1930), reprinted in Hiratsuka, *Chosakushū*, vol. 5, p. 217.

[66] *Ibid.*, pp. 216–7; Hiratsuka Raichō, 'Boshi Hogo Hō ni yosu', *Josei Tenbō* (April, 1937), reprinted in Hiratsuka, *Chosakushū*, vol. 6, p. 244.

[67] Hiratsuka, 'Mōkenai shōbai', pp. 218–20.

[68] Hiratsuka Raichō, 'Chūsan katei fujin to shōhi kumiai undō', in Hiratsuka, *Chosakushū*, vol. 5, pp. 236–7.

[69] Hiratsuka, 'Haha yo te o tore, hitan no arashi no naka de', pp. 294–6; Hiratsuka Raichō, 'Kyōdō kumiai soshiki ni yoru byōin no setsuritsu: iryō seido no kaikaku', in Hiratsuka, *Chosakushū*, vol. 5, pp. 257–8.

Her society went well and recruited 'about 120 members', but after 1935 some of these withdrew because of family circumstances or illness, which led to financial problems.[70] After the outbreak of the Sino-Japanese War in 1937, the move towards a wartime control economy also began to threaten the activities of independent cooperative societies. The fatal blow was the Kokka Sōdōin Hō (General Mobilization Law) in 1938, which was intended to regulate and administer human and physical resources in preparation for war.[71] The law also gave the military government power to control all goods for sale, transport and communication. Hiratsuka had remained very active in her society for nearly ten years, but it could no longer operate in these circumstances.[72] It came to an end in 1938.[73]

Hiratsuka had high expectations for this cooperative society. She believed that capitalism would be undermined by an impoverishment of people and a growth of cooperation following the Depression.[74] Yet it achieved little. It was based in a small area, Seijō, and never developed into a larger movement. It was dominated by middle-class people who were relatively affluent and had little interest in broader social issues.[75]

Hiratsuka also joined the Nihon Sanji Chōsei Fujin Renmei (the Women's Birth Control League of Japan) and the Datai Hō Kaisei Kisei Dōmei (the Association for Promoting the Amendment of the Abortion Law), both of which were founded in 1932.[76] They were opposed to the government's strict control over abortion and birth control and its strong encouragement to produce more children. They believed that having children ought to be an individual woman's decision. They demanded that women should have freedom for

---

[70] Hiratsuka, *Genshi*, vol. 3, p. 297.

[71] Hunter, *Concise Dictionary of Modern Japanese History*, p. 140; Kobayashi, *Hito to Shisō*, p. 191; Hiratsuka, *Genshi*, vol. 3, p. 297; Orii, 'Raichō to shōhi kumiai undō', p. 40; Ichikawa, *Jiden: Senzen Hen*, p. 443; Nishikawa Yūko, 'Sensō e no keisha to yokusan no fujin', in Joseishi Sōgō Kenkyūkai (ed.), *Nihon Joseishi*, vol. 5 (1982, 1985 edn), p. 235; Suzuki, *Joseishi o Hiraku*, vol. 1, p. 173; Nagahara & Yoneda, *Onna no Shōwashi*, pp. 71–2.

[72] Yoneda, 'Bosei shugi no rekishiteki igi', p. 133.

[73] Hiratsuka, *Genshi*, vol. 3, p. 297.

[74] Hiratsuka, 'Mōkenai shōbai', pp. 219–20.

[75] Suzuki, *Joseishi o Hiraku*, vol. 1, p. 177; Yoneda, 'Kaisetsu', in Hiratsuka, *Chosakushū*, vol. 5, p. 415.

[76] Hopper, *A New Woman of Japan*, pp. 26–7, 42–3, 56; Ishizaki Nobuko, 'Senkanki Nihon no sanji seigen undō to Raichō', in Hiratsuka Raichō o Yomu Kai (ed.), *Raichō Soshite Watashi*, part 3 (1991), pp. 17, 31–3.

abortion and birth control, and developed active campaigns even though abortion was then illegal.[77] Hiratsuka was one of the first Japanese women advocating that women should have freedom of birth control and abortion, which she did even in her Seitō days.[78] She supported birth control campaigns conducted by the Women's Birth Control League of Japan and the Association for Promoting the Amendment of the Abortion Law.[79] However, she seems not to have become actively involved in them, and did not write about them.[80] She seems to have been preoccupied with the cooperative society. For the same reason her contribution to the Musan Fujin Geijutsu Renmei (the Proletarian Women's Arts League), which she joined in 1930, was also very limited.[81]

Hiratsuka's Participation in the Musan Fujin Geijutsu Renmei

This League was founded by Takamure Itsue in 1930.[82] Hiratsuka joined it for two major reasons. She was closely associated with Takamure Itsue, who recommended that Hiratsuka become a member.[83] Hiratsuka thought highly of Takamure's enthusiasm and originality of literary expression, and even stated that she admired Takamure more than any other contemporary women.[84] Apart from

[77] *Ibid.*, pp. 28–35. The Association entered into direct negotiations with the penal reform committee over this issue. However, it met strong opposition from the Home Office and the Association's campaign came to an end shortly after that.

[78] See Hiratsuka, 'Sanjisū seigen no mondai', in Hiratsuka, *Chosakushū*, vol. 2, pp. 238–42; Hiratsuka Raichō, 'Hinin no kahi o ronzu', *Nihon Hyōron* (September, 1917), reprinted in Hiratsuka, *Chosakushū*, vol. 2, pp. 335–40.

[79] Ishizaki, 'Senkanki Nihon no sanji seigen', pp. 17, 31–3; Hopper, *A New Woman of Japan*, p. 56.

[80] Hiratsuka's name appeared in the membership lists of both these organizations. However, in her autobiography and other writings she never discussed her participation, and it is impossible to find out much about this.

[81] Suzuki, *Joseishi o Hiraku*, vol. 1, p. 178.

[82] Hiratsuka, *Genshi*, vol. 3, p. 303; Takamure, *Josei no Rekishi*, vol. 2, pp. 305–6; Takamure Itsue, *Hi no Kuni no Onna no Nikki* (1965), pp. 233–4.

[83] Yoneda, 'Kaisetsu', in Hiratsuka, *Chosakushū*, vol. 5, p. 411; Hiratsuka, *Genshi*, vol. 3, p. 303.

[84] Kobayashi, *Hito to Shisō*, p. 190; Hiratsuka, *Genshi*, vol. 3, pp. 305–6; Hiratsuka Raichō, 'Takamure Itsue-san', in Hiratsuka, *Kumo, Kusa, Hito* (1926), reprinted in Hiratsuka, *Chosakushū*, vol. 4, pp. 221–2; Hiratsuka Raichō, 'Takamure Itsue-san no Renai Sōsei o yomu', in Hiratsuka, *Kumo, Kusa, Hito* (1926), reprinted in Hiratsuka, *Chosakushū*, vol. 4, p. 223.

Takamure, the League's motives also strongly appealed to Hiratsuka.[85] She was particularly impressed with the following principles:

1. We [the members of the League] determine to push aside state power and aim to create a self-governing society.
2. We will uncover everyday facts which represent male autocracy, and do this as a tactic to make ordinary women aware of male autocracy and realise their own strength in society.
3. We feel that it is our obligation to present new ideas and new subjects from women's standpoint, to construct a new culture and develop a new society.[86]

Its main objectives to destroy existing society and construct a new self-governing society through female solidarity were very similar to those of Hiratsuka's cooperative society. Takamure's League was highly influenced by anarchism, and wished to create a society where state power and politics would be dismissed and nature would be valued.

The League's activities included study meetings, including ones with the Zenkoku Nōmin Geijutsu Renmei (the National Farmers' Arts League), in which farmers from many areas participated.[87] The Proletarian Women's Arts League organised public lectures, and also published *Fujin Sensen* (*Women's Front*) from March 1930.[88]

Takamure was an admirer of Hiratsuka and called her *Women's Front* 'daini no *Seitō*' ('the second *Seitō*') in its opening manifesto. She acknowledged the role which *Seitō* had played, and clarified her own objectives as follows:

We women achieved individual self-awakening through *Seitō*, which was our first step. Now we women are awakening to our own worth and our own strength in society, and have decided to launch a paramount campaign to emancipate all human beings.[89]

---

[85] Kobayashi, *Hito to Shisō*, p. 191; Yoneda, 'Kaisetsu', in Hiratsuka, *Chosakushū*, vol. 5, p. 412.

[86] Takamure Itsue, 'Kōryō', *Fujin Sensen*, 1:1 (March, 1930), p. 4.

[87] Takamure, *Hi no Kuni no Onna no Nikki*, pp. 236–7; Yoneda, 'Bosei shugi no rekishiteki igi', p. 138.

[88] One of these lectures, held in May 1931, was terminated halfway through by the police who attended it. Five thousand copies of the inaugural issue of *Fujin Sensen* were published. It was sold for twenty sen. Kōno Nobuko, *Takamure Itsue* (1990), p. 122; Kōno Nobuko, *Kindai Josei Seishinshi* (1982), p. 173; Takamure, *Hi no Kuni no Onna no Nikki*, p. 236.

[89] Takamure Itsue, '*Fujin Sensen* ni tatsu', *Fujin Sensen*, 1:1 (March, 1930), p. 8.

Unlike *Seitō*, *Women's Front* was a magazine permeated with anarchist advocacy. Each issue had feature articles on topics like the women's movement, and against large cities and the family.[90] For example, in a special issue attacking the family, *Women's Front* criticised contemporary family life for its male control and for comprising a system which was approved by the state.[91] It urged the need to deny such family life entirely, to oust men from power and to displace male-orientated viewpoints.[92]

In spite of its themes, *Women's Front* had little influence in promoting women's status, and it is almost forgotten by women's historians now. It lasted only sixteen months, ending in June 1931.[93] Takamure was persuaded to run it by her husband, who had initially promised to assist in editorial work.[94] However, he quickly lost interest, and she ended up running it single-handedly. Its office was at her house and she had to deal with many visitors.[95] She also had to write four or five articles for each issue.[96] Her editorial role suffered from overwork. *Women's Front* began to weaken, its sales falling sharply from January 1931, and its publisher demanded that Takamure share the losses.[97] Takamure had planned to combine running *Women's Front* with her own research on women's history, but she failed in this, her time being monopolised by *Women's Front*.[98] Under these circumstances she chose to abandon the magazine for research on women's history, and the League was also dissolved.[99]

---

[90] The April 1930 issue of *Fujin Sensen* had a special section on 'katei hitei' ('the denial of family'). The special issue which appeared in October 1930 was on 'tokai hitei' ('the denial of cities'). The title of the January 1931 special issue was 'war-era no fujin undō' ('Our women's movement').

[91] Takamure Itsue, 'Katei hitei ron', *Fujin Sensen*, 1:2 (April, 1930), pp. 21–3; Matsumoto Masae, 'Josei no shakai shugi', *Fujin Sensen*, 1:2 (April, 1930), pp. 6–8; Mochizuki Yuriko, 'Jiyū to Katei', *Fujin Sensen*, 1:2 (April, 1930), pp. 4–5; Sumii Sueko, 'Jijidai no katei', *Fujin Sensen*, 1:2 (April, 1930), pp. 9–11; Kamiya Shizuko, 'Otoko o keru', *Fujin Sensen*, 1:2 (April, 1930), p. 17; Ifukuda Keiko, 'Teisōkan no tenkai', *Fujin Sensen*, 1:2 (April, 1930), pp. 12–5.

[92] Takamure Itsue, 'Katei hitei ron', pp. 21–3; Matsumoto Masae, 'Josei no shakai shugi', pp. 6–8.

[93] Yoneda, 'Kaisetsu', in Hiratsuka, *Chosakushū*, vol. 5, p. 412.

[94] Takamure, *Hi no Kuni no Onna no Nikki*, pp. 233–4.

[95] *Ibid.*, p. 237; Kōno, *Kindai Josei Seishinshi*, p. 173.

[96] Takamure, *Hi no Kuni no Onna no Nikki*, p. 237; Yoneda, 'Bosei shugi no rekishiteki igi', p. 134.

[97] Takamure, *Hi no Kuni no Onna no Nikki*, p. 237.

[98] *Ibid.*, p. 232; Kōno, *Takamure Itsue*, pp. 121–2.

[99] Takamure, *Hi no Kuni no Onna no Nikki*, pp. 244–7; Nishikawa Yūko, *Mori no*

Hiratsuka's contributions to the Proletarian Women's Arts League was limited to two articles in *Women's Front*.[100] In her article '*Fujin Sensen* ni Sankashite' ('Having participated in *Women's Front*') she recollected the Association of New Women and reviewed her contributions to it:

> When I was involved with the Association of New Women, I advocated the need for the reorganisation of society by women's efforts. However, my advocacy then was no more than a policy of trying to impose some restrictions on men and capitalists' oppression and greed, to protect women, children and motherhood.[101]

Compared to those days, her ideas became more radical, and she now advocated the necessity of destroying capitalist society to protect women and children. In this article she expressed the view that it would not be a socialist society, but self-government based on cooperatives, that would create a new ideal society.[102]

Hiratsuka did not value state socialism. One reason was explained in her article 'Shin seidōtoku no kaosu' ('The chaos of new sexual morality').[103] She stated that life in the Soviet Union was infested with prostitution, divorce and bigamous marriages, and that Soviet people's sex lives were in disorder under the pretext of freedom of love.[104] She blamed socialism for having caused such an apparent state of affairs. Another reason was given in her article 'Ikuji shakaika no shisō o saiginmi seyo' ('Re-examine the idea of socialization in child-rearing').[105] She expressed strong doubts about the ways in which the Soviet Union had provided child facilities such as day nurseries, kindergartens and play groups. She was adamant that the Soviet government had provided these not for the sake of the

---

Ie no Miko, Takamure Itsue (1982), p. 128; Yoneda, 'Kaisetsu', in Hiratsuka, *Chosakushū*, vol. 5, p. 412; Hiratsuka Raichō, 'Hi no onna hi no kuni ni kaeru: jomakushiki shukuji', *Nihon Dangi* (April, 1962), reprinted in Hiratsuka, *Chosakushū*, vol. 7, p. 404.

[100] Hiratsuka Raichō, '*Fujin Sensen* ni sanka shite', *Fujin Sensen*, 1:2 (April, 1930), pp. 34–9; Hiratsuka Raichō, 'Ichi ni no handō josei', *Fujin Sensen*, 1:4 (June, 1930), pp. 42–3.

[101] Hiratsuka, '*Fujin Sensen* ni sankashite', p. 37.

[102] *Ibid.*, pp, 38–9.

[103] Hiratsuka Raichō, 'Shin seidōtoku no kaosu', *Fujin Kōron* (August, 1929), reprinted in Hiratsuka, *Chosakushū*, vol. 5, pp. 119–31.

[104] *Ibid.*, pp. 125–6.

[105] Hiratsuka Raichō, 'Ikuji shakaika no shisō o saiginmi seyo', *Fujin no Tomo* (November, 1931), reprinted in Hiratsuka, *Chosakushū*, vol. 5, pp. 253–6.

children but to make effective use of their mothers' labour.[106] The
Soviet government, she felt, needed an unlimited workforce to construct a socialist nation, and wanted to use women's productive power
in the same ways as men's. It had provided childcare facilities to
separate mothers from their children, who would otherwise reduce
their production. Hiratsuka resented such a socialist approach. She
also criticised socialism for being male-orientated, prizing only productive labour, devaluing women's social role as creators of children
and disregarding motherhood.[107] She cast doubt on whether the
emancipation of women could be achieved by freeing women from
child-rearing and housework, and making them full-time workers.[108]
In the early 1930s the Japanese military government ruthlessly suppressed socialism, and it became extremely hard for anyone to obtain
accurate information about developments in the Soviet Union.[109]

From the Manchurian Incident in 1931, the influence of the army
in the Japanese government increased, and it is interesting to see
Hiratsuka's reaction. Although Hiratsuka never commented on the
Manchurian Incident, she wrote two articles criticising the military
government.[110] In 'Gunjinkan' she criticised such officers for having
had a strong sense of duty and responsibility, which led them not
to take a broad view of their actions.[111] In 'Me to chikara o uchi e'
('Directing one's attention and power to internal affairs of the country'), she referred to the state budget, 47 per cent of which comprised war expenditure.[112] She made sarcastic remarks stating that
since the Manchurian Incident Japan had done well internationally,
but had strained itself internally to its detriment.[113] She criticised
men for looking outside Japan, and praised women for paying more
attention to internal affairs. She stated that unlike men, women could

[106] *Ibid.*, p. 254.
[107] *Ibid.*, p. 256.
[108] *Ibid.*, p. 253.
[109] Yoneda, 'Kaisetsu', in Hiratsuka, *Chosakushū*, vol. 5, p. 417.
[110] One was 'Gunjinkan' ('My view of military officers') which she wrote in 1935,
and the other was 'Me to chikara o uchi e' ('Directing one's attention and power
to internal affairs of the country') which she wrote in 1936. Hiratsuka Raichō,
'Gunjinkan', *Miyako Shinbun* (12 October, 1935), reprinted in Hiratsuka, *Chosakushū*,
vol. 6, pp. 65–6; Hiratsuka, 'Me to chikara o uchi e: 36–nen no josei e no taibō',
in Hiratsuka, *Chosakushū*, vol. 6, pp. 87–8.
[111] Hiratsuka, 'Gunjinkan', p. 66.
[112] Hiratsuka, 'Me to chikara o uchi e', p. 87.
[113] *Ibid.*, p. 88.

see the country's limitations and mistakes, and they were attempting to correct them.[114] This article certainly demonstrated Hiratsuka's
challenge to the male military government and her hope that women
would bring the government to its senses and terminate such a military regime. Nevertheless, Japan entered the Sino-Japanese War in
1937, and further strengthened its armed forces.[115] After 1938 Hiratsuka
never criticised the military government. This was clearly related to
the developing political climate. After the introduction of the National
General Mobilization Law, freedom of speech was increasingly
eroded.[116] Anybody who spoke against the military government ran
the risk of being imprisoned.[117] Although she disapproved of the war,
she soon gave up criticising the government, realising that her critical writing would be censored. In her autobiography she claimed
that she had lost her will to write.[118]

Hiratsuka had objected to the family system of the Meiji Civil
Code, had refused to become Okumura's legal wife for twenty-seven
years, and had her children registered as illegitimate.[119] However, in
August 1941 she finally became Okumura's lawful wife, and her son
entered Okumura's family register with her.[120] His previous legal status was altered to that of Okumura's legal son.[121] One might think
that she had changed her view of the family system and no longer
resented it. In reality she still disapproved of it and held to her earlier beliefs. However, she reluctantly decided to put aside her convictions for the sake of her son, who was then a final-year student
at the department of science and technology at Waseda University.[122]
She foresaw that Japan would shortly enter a large-scale war and
that her son would probably soon be drafted, with a likelihood of
becoming an officer, given his technical knowledge acquired at university.[123] An illegitimate son had no chance of becoming a military

---

[114] *Ibid.*, p. 88.
[115] Yoneda, 'Kaisetsu', in Hiratsuka, *Chosakushū*, vol. 6, p. 416.
[116] *Ibid.*, p. 413.
[117] *Ibid.*, p. 427.
[118] Hiratsuka, *Genshi*, vol. 4, p. 18.
[119] Hiratsuka, *Genshi*, vol. 2, pp. 260–1; Hiratsuka, *Genshi*, vol. 4, p. 38; Kobayashi,
Hito to Shisō, p. 207.
[120] Hiratsuka, *Genshi*, vol. 4, pp. 37–8; Kobayashi, *Hito to Shisō*, p. 207.
[121] Hiratsuka, *Genshi*, vol. 4, p. 40. Her daughter Akemi had already married to
Tsukizoe Shōji as an illegitimate child.
[122] *Ibid.*, p. 17.
[123] *Ibid.*, p. 39.

officer.[124] She also knew that officers would have much higher survival chances. As a caring and devoted mother, Hiratsuka's main priority was the safety of her son, and she sacrificed her convictions to help her son's career and to minimise his risk.[125]

Hiratsuka During the Pacific War

Japan declared war against Britain and the United States on 8 December 1941. The military government was strengthened, and it invited well-known women to take up official posts.[126] In 1938 Yamada Waka and Yoshioka Yayoi became members of the central social work committee, which was a part of the Ministry of Welfare.[127] Hani Motoko was nominated as a member of the national savings encouragement committee, in the Ministry of Finance, which aimed to conduct a nationwide savings campaign to raise war funds.[128] When the state-sponsored Taisei Yokusankai (the Imperial Rule Assistance Association) was founded in October 1941, even women like Oku Mumeo and Ichikawa Fusae worked for the organisation and became its researchers.[129] In February 1942 three government-sponsored women's organisations were combined: the Aikoku Fujinkai (the Patriotic Women's Association), the Kokubō Fujinkai (the Greater Japan National Defense Women's Association) and the Rengō Fujinkai (the United Women's Association). They had conducted vigorous activities to assist the government. The Dainihon Fujinkai (the Greater

---

[124] Kobayashi, *Hito to Shisō*, p. 207.

[125] Hiratsuka, *Genshi*, vol. 4, p. 40. Her sacrifice was not wasted. As she expected, her son was drafted in February 1942, two months after he graduated from university. As he was no longer illegitimate, he became an engineering officer. He was stationed in Japan and never fought in the front line. See Yoneda, 'Kaisetsu', in Hiratsuka, *Chosakushū*, vol. 6, p. 433.

[126] Yoneda, 'Kaisetsu', in Hiratsuka, *Chosakushū*, vol. 6, p. 428; Ichikawa, *Jiden: Senzen Hen*, p. 443; Nishikawa Yūko, 'Sensō e no keisha to yokusan no fujin', in Joseishi Sōgō Kenkyūkai (ed.), *Nihon Joseishi*, vol. 5 (1982, 1985 edn), p. 238.

[127] *Ibid.*, p. 244,

[128] Yoneda, 'Kaisetsu', in Hiratsuka, *Chosakushū*, vol. 6, p. 428.

[129] The Imperial Rule Assistance Association's main objective was the concentration of national political power and the creation of a strong political structure. See Hunter, *Concise Dictionary of Modern Japanese History*, p. 67; Suzuki, *Joseishi o Hiraku*, vol. 1, pp. 173–4; Nishikawa, 'Sensō e no keisha to yokusan no fujin', p. 256; Oku, *Nobi*, p. 206; Ichikawa, *Jiden: Senzen Hen*, p. 529; Suzuki, *Joseishi o Hiraku*, vol. 2, p. 56; Nagahara & Yoneda, *Onna no Shōwashi*, pp. 95–6.

Japan Women's Association) was now founded from them.[130] Eminent
women such as Hatoyama Kaoruko, Yoshioka Yayoi and Hani
Setsuko were listed as founding members.[131] Ichikawa Fusae was later
nominated as its council member.[132] They joined the Dainihon Fujinkai
to raise the wartime reputation of women. However, they later
claimed that they were dragged into the war effort and were obliged
to cooperate with the government, often very much against their
will.[133] On the other hand, Hiratsuka had no intention of cooperating with the war in any way, and she remained silent. Her name
appeared in none of these government-sponsored women's organisations.[134] In her autobiography she stated that she was even annoyed
at attending meetings arranged by her local women's society and
neighbourhood association, which organised activities to assist the
war.[135] However, after her son was drafted, her resolution began to
weaken and she wondered whether she could continue not to participate in the war effort if she stayed in Tokyo. According to
Kobayashi, the only way for Hiratsuka to avoid government attention was to leave Tokyo and stay in a place where she was unknown.[136]
Her family circumstances made it easier to make this move, as her
children had left home.[137] After her cooperative society ended its
activities, she did not have any commitments in Tokyo. Her sister,
who had already evacuated Tokyo to live in Todai Village (now
Torite City) in Ibaraki Prefecture, strongly recommended the move.[138]
So Hiratsuka and Okumura left Tokyo for Todai Village, which was
then a remote rural area, in March 1942, even though the war had

[130] *Ibid.*, pp. 106–7; Hunter, *Concise Dictionary of Modern Japanese History*, p. 243;
Nishikawa, 'Sensō e no keisha to yokusan no fujin', p. 257; Ichikawa, *Jiden: Senzen
Hen*, pp. 544–9; Yoneda, 'Kaisetsu', in Kaisetsu, *Chosakushū*, vol. 6, p. 429.
    [131] Ichikawa, *Jiden: Senzen Hen*, p. 545; Nishikawa, 'Sensō e no keisha to yoku-
san no fujin', p. 257; Suzuki, *Joseishi o Hiraku*, vol. 2, p. 87.
    [132] Ichikawa, *Jiden: Senzen Hen*, p. 546; Nishikawa, 'Sensō e no keisha to yoku-
san no fujin', p. 257; Ichikawa, *Nonaka no Ippon Sugi*, pp. 136–7; Yoneda, 'Kaisetsu',
in Hiratsuka, *Chosakushū*, vol. 6, p. 429; Suzuki, *Joseishi o Hiraku*, vol. 1, pp. 144,
163–4.
    [133] Yoneda, 'Kaisetsu', in Hiratsuka, *Chosakushū*, vol. 6, p. 429; Ichikawa, *Nonaka
no Ippon Sugi*, p. 137; Suzuki, *Joseishi o Hiraku*, vol. 1, pp. 144, 163–4.
    [134] *Ibid.*, p. 178; Yoneda, 'Kaisetsu', in Hiratsuka, *Chosakushū*, vol. 6, p. 430.
    [135] Hiratsuka, *Genshi*, vol. 4, p. 18.
    [136] Kobayashi, *Hito to Shisō*, p. 191.
    [137] Hiratsuka, 'Ogaigawa tsūshin', *Shomotsu Tenbō* (May, 1944), reprinted in Hiratsuka,
Chosakushū, vol. 6, pp. 395–6; Hiratsuka, *Genshi*, vol. 4, p. 18.
    [138] Hiratsuka, *Genshi*, vol. 4, pp. 18–9.

started only a few months earlier and there were hardly any people leaving Tokyo yet.[139] They settled in a rented house, and she had to work in farming.[140] She kept a goat, made cheese, and grew her own vegetables.[141] She also caught river fish, fermented *miso* (soya bean paste) and preserved food, leading a self-sufficient life.[142] The vegetables and fruit she produced helped to feed her family who were living in Tokyo and suffering from serious food shortages. She regularly went to see her son, who had been drafted, taking various nutritious home-made dishes made out of vegetables and fruit.[143] Like many other mothers whose sons were drafted, Hiratsuka constantly worried about her son. She also took good care of her pregnant daughter and helped her in childbirth.[144] Her evacuation period was significant in two regards. Unlike the great majority of her contemporary feminists and other eminent women, Hiratsuka refused to lend any assistance to the government in spite of government pressure. She simply adopted a silent resistance to the war. She was in Todai at the end of the war, and lived there until 1947, when she returned to Tokyo.

Hiratsuka after the Pacific War

Under Allied Occupation, Japan experienced many legal changes. Japanese women's position also changed. On 17 December 1945 suffrage was granted to women.[145] The new Constitution of Japan, promulgated on 3 November 1946, coming into force on 3 May, 1947, and the new civil code which came into operation on 1 January, 1948, also gave women new legal rights.[146] It is interesting to see

---

[139] *Ibid.*, pp. 24–5.

[140] Hiratsuka Raichō, 'Ogaigawa tsūshin', *Shomotsu Tenbō* (May, 1944), reprinted in Hiratsuka, *Chosakushū*, vol. 6, p. 397; Hiratsuka Raichō, 'Haha musume no kaiwa', *Fujin Kōron* (September, 1942), reprinted in Hiratsuka, *Chosakushū*, vol. 6, pp. 370–1.

[141] *Ibid.*, pp. 371–2; Hiratsuka, 'Ogaigawa tsūshin', p. 397.

[142] *Ibid.*, pp. 398–9; Hiratsuka, *Genshi*, vol. 4, p. 27.

[143] *Ibid.*, pp. 34–6; Yoneda, 'Kaisetsu', in Hiratsuka, *Chosakushū*, vol. 6, p. 433.

[144] Hiratsuka, *Genshi*, vol. 4, p. 45.

[145] Inoue Kiyoshi, *Gendai Nihon Joseishi* (1962), pp. 48–50; Miyagi *et al.* (eds), *Shinkō Nihon Joseishi*, pp. 255–7; Nagahara & Yoneda, *Onna no Shōwashi*, p. 150.

[146] *Ibid.*, pp. 153–5; Vera Mackie, 'Feminist politics in Japan', *New Left Review*, 167 (January/February, 1988), p. 59; Ōe Shinoo, *Nihon no Rekishi: Sengo Henkaku* (1976), pp. 153–62.

how Hiratsuka reacted to these changes. She had submitted the first women's suffrage petition, and she discussed Japanese women's final acquisition of the vote in her article 'Watakushi no yume wa jitsugen shita ka' ('I wonder whether my dream has come true'):

> Women's suffrage suddenly fell into our hands. It was one of the first policies introduced by the Allied Forces. What an irony of fate this was. We Japanese women worked for the acquisition of women's suffrage for a long time, but we failed to achieve it. Now our long-sought suffrage was finally given to women by the Allied Forces. Part of me was pleased with the outcome, but another part of me could not openly rejoice in it. A thousand emotions crowded in upon my mind.[147]

This demonstrates her mixed feelings. She was grateful for women gaining the vote, but she regretted that it was not achieved by women themselves. Hiratsuka appreciated how the feminists had fought for women's political rights, and felt that their efforts would now be overlooked and regarded as fruitless.[148]

Hiratsuka reacted rather differently to the new constitution. She was delighted with it, making the following comments:

> My heart was completely brightened by the contents of the new constitution. Even if these are in line with the policy of the Allied Forces, there is no doubt that they reflected the general opinion of the Japanese people. What remarkable and drastic changes were made in the new constitution.[149]

She was particularly impressed by the legal changes of articles 14 and 24.[150] She thought that these articles largely ended legal discrimination against women, and opened the way to solving many

---

[147] Hiratsuka, 'Watashi no yume wa jitsugen shita ka', in Hiratsuka, *Chosakushū*, vol. 7, p. 32.

[148] Hiratsuka, *Genshi*, vol. 4, p. 54.

[149] Hiratsuka, 'Watakushi no yume wa jitsugen shita ka', p. 33.

[150] Hiratsuka, *Genshi*, vol. 4, pp. 56–7. Article 14 stipulates that all people in Japan are equal under the law and that there shall be no discrimination in political, economic or social relations because of race, creed, sex, social status or family origin. Article 24 stipulates that marriage shall be based only on the mutual consent of both sexes, and that it shall be maintained through mutual cooperation with the equal rights of husband and wife as its basis. With regard to choice of spouse, property rights, inheritance, choice of domicile, divorce and other matters pertaining to marriage and the family, laws shall be enacted from the standpoint of individual dignity and the essential equality of the sexes. Yoshida Yoshiaki (ed.), *Nihonkoku Kenpō* (1989), pp. 38–9, 58–9. The provisions of Article 24 of the new constitution removed the ideas of the *ie* system guaranteed under the old constitution.

female problems which pre-war Japanese feminists had been concerned with. She felt the same about the new civil code:

> The introduction of the new civil code, especially the family and inher-
> itance sections, brought in drastic and major changes affecting women.
> It completely overthrew the family system which used to tie them. This
> change was a kind of revolution to me, and I felt as if a burden had
> been lifted from my mind. My long-cherished dream since adolescence
> had finally come true.[151]

In her autobiography she expressed her gratitude to America for
having won the war and brought about these legal changes for
women, which she and the other feminists had themselves failed to
achieve.[152] She even said that if Japan had won the war, Japanese
women might have had to wait one hundred years for their emancipation.[153] Being content with these reforms for women, she did not
consider joining the *Shin Nihon Fujin Dōmei* (New Japan Women's
League), whose main objective was to further promote women's political rights, in spite of Ichikawa's attempt to persuade her.[154]

Hiratsuka's Participation in the Peace Movement

Instead, she began to show much interest in peace issues, and became
convinced that she should devote herself to these over the rest of
her life. When her son was called up for military service during the
war, Hiratsuka had constantly worried about his safety. She was also
grieved by the fact that the war killed children and soldiers who
were still teenagers. She had felt utterly hopeless, because she could
do nothing to stop the fighting and save these innocent people's lives.
This bitter experience fostered her pacifist ideas. Her wish to avoid

---

[151] Hiratsuka, *Genshi*, vol. 4, p. 60.
[152] *Ibid.*, p. 61. It is true that the feminist campaigns by Hiratsuka and her contemporary feminists hardly achieved anything. However, those pre-war campaigns
laid foundations for post-war legal changes affecting women, contributed to prepare
public opinion for change, and facilitated the post-war developments.
[153] Hiratsuka, 'Watakushi no yume wa jitsugen shita ka', p. 33.
[154] Hiratsuka, *Genshi*, vol. 4, pp. 53–4; Kobayashi, *Hito to Shisō*, p. 195; Kodama
Katsuko, *Oboegaki: Sengo no Ichikawa Fusae* (1985), pp. 18–23. The Shin Nihon Fujin
Dōmei was founded on 3 November 1945, by Ichikawa Fusae, other pre-war suffrage
leaders and ex-members of the pre-war Fusen Kakutoku Dōmei (Women's Suffrage
League). Its main objective was to give women more political education.

war again became stronger, and she was overjoyed at Article 9 of
the new constitution.

> Aspiring sincerely to an international peace based on justice and order,
> the Japanese people forever renounce war as a sovereign right of
> the nation and the threat or use of force as means of settling inter-
> national disputes. In order to accomplish the aim of the preceding
> paragraph, land, sea, and air forces, as well as other war potential,
> will never be maintained. The right of belligerency of the state will
> not be recognized'[155]

Hiratsuka set herself two major questions. One was how Japanese
women should maintain peace in Japan, and the other was how to
promote world peace.[156] She studied peace issues, and joined the
Sekai Renpō Kensetsu Dōmei (the League Aiming for the Foundation
of a World Federation), which was founded by Ozaki Yukio and
Kagawa Toyohiko in 1949.[157] The League campaigned for a common world constitution to bring international peace.

In 1950 MacArthur delivered his New Year's message, stating that
Japan would be allowed to possess self-defensive armed forces despite
Article 9.[158] He also revealed the U.S. intention to sign a new treaty
with Japan. Hiratsuka, who wanted to maintain the peace Japan had
recently obtained and was strongly opposed to Japanese rearmament,
could not overlook MacArthur's message.[159] She wrote a statement
entitled 'Hibusōkoku Nihon josei no kōwa mondai ni tsuite no kibō
yōkō' ('A list of requests regarding a peace treaty made by women
in Japan, an unarmed country').[160] On the day that the Korean War
started, it was sent to an advisor of the American State Department,
John Foster Dulles, who was in charge of the peace treaty negotia-
tion.[161] In the statement Hiratsuka proclaimed her strong opposition

---

[155] Yoshida, *Nihonkoku Kenpō*, p. 29.

[156] Hiratsuka, *Genshi*, vol. 4, p. 67.

[157] *Ibid.*, pp. 69–78; Nagahara & Yoneda, *Onna no Shōwashi*, pp. 173–4.

[158] Hiratsuka Raichō, 'Jinrui no heiwa e no ishi', *Fujin Kōron* (January, 1952),
reprinted in Hiratsuka, *Chosakushū*, vol. 7, pp. 197–9; Nagahara & Yoneda, *Onna
no Shōwashi*, p. 170.

[159] Hiratsuka, *Genshi*, vol. 4, pp. 95–100; Nagahara & Yoneda, *Onna no Shōwashi*,
pp. 173–5; Hiratsuka Raichō, 'Kenpō o mamorinukō', *Josei Shinbun* (11 September,
1950), reprinted in Hiratsuka, *Chosakushū*, vol. 7, pp. 116–7.

[160] Hiratsuka Raichō, 'Hibusōkoku Nihon josei no kōwa mondai ni tsuite no kibō
yōkō', in Hiratsuka, *Chosakushū*, vol. 7, pp. 101–2.

[161] *Ibid.*, p. 102; Nagahara & Yoneda, *Onna no Shōwashi*, pp. 174–5; Hiratsuka
Raichō, 'Hibusō no heiwa', *Fujin Minshu Shinbun* (29 July, 1950), reprinted in Hiratsuka,

to war and demanded the preservation of Article 9. She wanted the continuation of Japan's unarmed neutrality and the renunciation of war, as provided for by the Constitution. Japan should refuse to have U.S. military bases on its soil. It should establish friendly relations with China, and should sign an overall peace treaty with all the countries which it had fought in the war.[162]

This was followed by two further similar appeals.[163] However, the Yoshida Cabinet signed the San Francisco Peace Treaty with 48 countries (excluding the Soviet Union, China and India) on 8 September 1951.[164] Hiratsuka's wish to conclude an overall peace treaty with all the countries Japan had fought was thus not fulfilled. The Yoshida Cabinet also signed the U.S.-Japan Security Treaty, which stated America's right to continue to station troops and keep military bases in Japan.[165]

Hiratsuka was disappointed with this outcome. She saw an urgent need to form women's peace associations to launch peace campaigns. She consequently founded the Saigunbi Hantai Fujin Iinkai (Women's Committee against Rearmament) in December 1951, becoming its chairwoman.[166] In April 1953 she established the Nihon Fujin Dantai Rengōkai (Federation of Japanese Women's Groups), which is widely

---

Chosakushū, vol. 7, pp. 103–4; Hiratsuka Raichō, 'Nihon no haha no tachiba', *Sandei Mainichi* (13 August, 1950), reprinted in Hiratsuka, *Chosakushū*, vol. 7, p. 108; Hiratsuka Raichō, 'Chōsen no dōran to watashitachi josei no kakugo', *Shin Nyoen* (September, 1950), reprinted in Hiratsuka, *Chosakushū*, vol. 7, pp. 113–4. It was signed by five leading women: Jōdai Tano (the vice-chancellor of the Japan Women's University), Nogami Yaeko (a leading novelist), Uemura Tamaki (a Christian minister and active pacifist), Gauntlett Tsuneko (chairwoman of the Women's Christian Temperance Union) and Hiratsuka.

[162] Nagahara & Yoneda, *Onna no Shōwashi*, p. 175; Hiratsuka, *Genshi*, vol. 4, p. 98.

[163] On 8 February 1951 Hiratsuka submitted a second statement entitled 'Kōwa mondai ni kansuru Nihon josei no kibō yōkō' ('A list of requests for a peace treaty made by Japanese women'), which was a revised version of her first statement to Dulles in January 1951. This statement was followed by a third in August 1951: 'Mitabi hibusō koku Nihon josei no heiwa seimei' ('The third statement on peace made by women in Japan, which is an unarmed country'). See Hiratsuka, *Genshi*, vol. 4, pp. 109–17.

[164] When this treaty came into effect on 28 April, 1952, the Allied Forces' occupation in Japan came to an end. Nagahara & Yoneda, *Onna no Shōwashi*, pp. 178–9; Eguchi Hakuo, *Nihon no Rekishi: Gendai no Nihon* (1976), pp. 144–7; Ōe, *Sengo Henkaku*, pp. 296–304.

[165] It took effect from April 1952. Hunter, *Concise Dictionary of Modern Japanese History*, p. 239; Ōe, *Sengo Henkaku*, pp. 299–300; Nagahara & Yoneda, *Onna no Shōwashi*, pp. 178–9.

[166] Hiratsuka, *Genshi*, vol. 4, p. 121.

known by its abbreviation, Fudanren, and became its chairwoman.[167] Its main objectives were to hinder any revival of militarism and rearmament, to remove American military bases from Japan, oppose the manufacture and use of atom and hydrogen bombs and bacteriological weapons, and to collaborate with women internationally to pursue world peace.[168] After the Daigo Fukuryūmaru Jiken (the Fifth Lucky Dragon Incident) in March 1954,[169] Hiratsuka became more active in the anti-nuclear-bomb campaign and appealed to the Kokusai Minshu Fujin Renmei (International Democratic Women's Federation) to ban nuclear tests in any country, alongside the use of nuclear weapons, and to enter an international protest against them.[170] After the outbreak of the Vietnam War, Hiratsuka, who opposed the war, formed a society called the Betonamu Hanashiai no Kai (the Society to Discuss Vietnam) in May 1966, and organised campaigns against the war.[171] For example, she and members of the Nihon Fujin Dantai

---

[167] Kobayashi, *Hito to Shisō*, p. 202; 'Hito: Nihon Fujin Dantai Rengōkai no sanjū-go shūnen o sotsuju de mukaeta Kushida Fuki-san', *Asahi Shinbun* (23 November, 1988); Kushida Fuki, *Suteki ni Nagaiki* (1991), p. 156; 'Sōritsu sanjū-go shūnen o mukaeta Nihon Fujin Dantai Rengōkai kaichō, Kushida Fuki-san', *Yomiuri Shinbun* (29 November, 1988); 'Kyūjū go-sai de jiden shippitsu, ato nijū-nen bun', *Asahi Shinbun* (26 July, 1994); Hiratsuka Raichō, 'Hitotsu ni musubu chikara', *Sekai no Fujin to Nihon no Fujin*, 1 (December, 1953), reprinted in Hiratsuka, *Chosakushū*, vol. 7, pp. 242–4; Hiratsuka Raichō, '1954-nen no fujin undō no hōkō', *Jinrui Aizen Shinbun* (1 January, 1954), reprinted in Hiratsuka, *Chosakushū*, vol. 7, pp. 247–50.

[168] Kushida, 'Josei kaihō e no jōnetsu', pp. 39–40.

[169] While the U.S. was conducting a thermo-nuclear weapons test on Bikini Island, a Japanese fishing vessel called Daigo Fukuryū Maru (the Fifth Lucky Dragon) was travelling 125 miles from the site. As a result, the crew were showered by radioactive ash caused by the atomic bomb. One fisherman died and others suffered from radiation sickness. Their contaminated fish had to be disposed of. With this incident in mind, massive signature-collecting campaigns against nuclear tests and weapons were launched in Japan. Hunter, *Concise Dictionary of Modern Japanese History*, p. 15; Ōe, *Sengo Henkaku*, pp. 322–3; Eguchi, *Gendai no Rekishi*, pp. 217–9; Nagahara & Yoneda, *Onna no Shōwashi*, pp. 192–3; Hiratsuka, 'Sekai no fujin no inori', *Kita Nihon Shinbun* (3 January, 1963), reprinted in Hiratsuka, *Chosakushū*, vol. 7, pp. 416–7; Hiratsuka Raichō, 'Kotoshi koso kaku jikken teishi o', in Hiratsuka, *Chosakushū*, vol. 7, pp. 369–71; Hiratsuka, 'Kotoshi koso watashi no nengan no tasserareru toshi to shinakereba naranai: Kokusai Minshu Fujin Renmei e no messēji', in Hiratsuka, *Chosakushū*, vol. 7, pp. 362–4; Hiratsuka, 'Nihon fujin 10-nen no ayumi o kataru: Kokusai Minpuren 10-shūnen kinen ni yosete', *Fujin Gahō* (February, 1956), reprinted in Hiratsuka, *Chosakushū*, vol. 7. pp. 339–40.

[170] Hiratsuka, 'Kinjo zukiai', *Fujin no Tomo* (September, 1954), reprinted in Hiratsuka, *Chosakushū*, vol. 7, pp. 275–6; Hiratsuka, *Genshi*, vol. 4, pp. 181–5; Kushida, 'Josei kaihō e no jōnetsu', pp. 40–1; Ishii Ayako, 'Gensuibaku kinshi no uttae', in Maruoka Hideko *et al.*, *Hiratsuka Raichō to Nihon no Kindai* (1986), pp. 40–1.

[171] Hiratsuka Raichō, 'Hataraku hitobito to tomoni chikara zuyoi undō o: sekai ni takamaru Betonamu sensō hantai no kōdō', *Betonamu Hanashiai no Kai Nyūsu*, 11

Rengōkai sent many postcards, in which their strong anti-war feelings were expressed, to women in America, American soldiers in Japan and U.S. staff at the White House.[172]

It was through the peace movement that Hiratsuka overcame many of the limitations she had shown in her pre-war feminist activities. She gradually made international links with other women's organisations, notably as chairwoman of the Nihon Fujin Dantai Rengōkai.[173] This started with her first task, to send ten Japanese women delegates to the Sekai Fujin Taikai (World Women's Convention) in Copenhagen.[174] She regularly corresponded with chairwomen of other women's organisations, including Jolliot-Curie and Eugene Coton, and exchanged views about the women's peace movement.[175] She also invited some female peace activists to Japan to lecture. She met Marie Claude, who came to Japan to attend a World Rally Against Atomic and Hydrogen Bombs in Tokyo in August 1956, as a delegate from the Kokusai Minshu Fujin Renmei (the International Democratic Women's Federation).[176] Hiratsuka, who wanted to establish friendly relations with China, corresponded with Li Dequan, who was the deputy head of the Chinese National Democratic Women's Federation (Chūka Zenkoku Minshu Fujo Rengōkai). Hiratsuka met her in Tokyo in August 1956 when she came to Japan as a Chinese representative to attend a World Rally Against Atomic Weapons.[177] Although

---

(15 October, 1966), reprinted in Hiratsuka, *Chosakushū*, vol. 7, pp. 433–4; Hiratsuka Raichō, 'Betonamu Hanashiai no Kai ni yosete hitokoto', *Betonamu Hanashiai no Kai Nyūsu*, 1 (15 July, 1966), reprinted in Hiratsuka, *Chosakushū*, vol. 7, p. 432.

[172] Kobayashi, *Hito to Shisō*, p. 209.

[173] Hiratsuka, *Genshi*, vol. 4, pp. 134–40; Hiratsuka, 'Hitotsu ni musubu chikara', pp. 242–3; Hiratsuka, 'Ichi-nen no ayumi o kaerimite', *Sekai no Fujin to Nihon no Fujin*, 4 (25 July, 1954), reprinted in Hiratsuka, *Chosakushū*, vol. 7, pp. 269–70; Hiratsuka, 'Nihon fujin 10-nen no ayumi o kataru', pp. 337–9; Hiratsuka Raichō, 'Wuīn shūkai no seikō o inotte', in Hiratsuka, *Chosakushū*, vol. 7, pp. 366–8.

[174] Kobayashi, *Hito to Shisō*, p. 204; Kushida, 'Josei kaihō e no jōnetsu', p. 40; Hiratsuka, 'Hitotsu ni musubu chikara', p. 242; Hiratsuka Raichō, 'Ten no shita ni wa naranu mono nashi', in Hiratsuka, *Chosakushū*, vol. 7, pp. 240–1.

[175] Hiratsuka, *Genshi*, vol. 4, pp. 208–12; Hiratsuka Raichō, 'Kiyorakana tsuyosa: Enbashi Katsuko-san', *Asahi Jānaru* (24 September, 1961), reprinted in Hiratsuka, *Chosakushū*, vol. 7, pp. 390–1. See letters from Hiratsuka Raichō to Maruoka Hideko, 4 January, 1955, 10 January, 1955, 26 March, 1956 and 12 May, 1958, reprinted in Hiratsuka, *Chosakushū*, vol. 8, pp. 138–49. See also letter from Hiratsuka Raichō to Kobayashi Tomie, 4 April, 1955, reprinted in Hiratsuka, *Chosakushū*, vol. 8, pp. 33–4.

[176] Hiratsuka, *Genshi*, vol. 4, pp. 258–65.

[177] Hiratsuka Raichō, 'Li Dequan-san o omukaeshite', *Kaizō* (January, 1955), reprinted in Hiratsuka, *Chosakushū*, vol. 7, pp. 291–6.

Hiratsuka was also invited to many women's international peace conferences held abroad in the 1950s, she did not attend any of them
on account of her declining health and old age, sending other women
on her behalf.[178] It was also through the peace movement that she
overcame her reputation for having been a 'bourgeois feminist', for
she successfully brought together Japanese women from very different
social, educational and political backgrounds.[179]

In the peace movement the issues that she gave highest priority
to were a ban on atomic and hydrogen bombs and the abolition of
the U.S.-Japan Security Treaty, to remove American military bases
from Japan.[180] The U.S.-Japan Security Treaty had many defects.[181]
For example, it never specified the term of its validity. In the later
1950s the Kishi Cabinet had many negotiations with the United
States to revise this treaty. However, people in the peace movement
such as Hiratsuka felt that the revision would fortify the United
States-Japanese military alliance and might lead to Japan's rearmament. They organised massive protests throughout Japan to prevent
the Kishi Cabinet from signing the treaty revision, but in January
1960 Prime Minister Kishi signed the revised treaty called Nichibei
Shin Anzen Hoshō Jōyaku (the new U.S.-Japan Security Treaty).
That revised treaty clarified the United States' obligation of defence
in Japan and the need for the U.S. to consult with Japan regarding any military action taken by American troops based in Japan.
It also specified that its duration would be ten years. Many demonstrations were organised against the revised treaty in the 1960s, and
these activities escalated in 1969 in anticipation of Japan's right to
end the treaty in 1970. In the 1960s Hiratsuka made many speeches
and organised public campaigns against the revised treaty. Compared

[178] Maruoka, 'Seitō kara Kokusai Fujin Nen e', pp. 16–8; Hiratsuka Raichō, 'Shin
Chūgoku no Kokkeisetsu ni manekarete', Sekai no Fujin to Nihon no Fujin, 5 (25
September, 1954), reprinted in Hiratsuka, Chosakushū, vol. 7, pp. 277–82.
[179] Hiratsuka, 'Shūkaku o mezashite: 1954-nen fujin no kadai', Fujin Taimuzu (9
January, 1954), reprinted in Hiratsuka, Chosakushū, vol. 7, pp. 256–7; Hiratsuka,
'Ano hi no kangeki no naka de: Nihon Fujin Taikai o oete', Shin Josei (February,
1954), reprinted in Hiratsuka, Chosakushū, vol. 7, p. 259.
[180] Hiratsuka, Genshi, vol. 4, pp. 317–22; Kobayashi, 'Atarashii onna no negai',
p. 59; Yoneda, 'Jidai o ikinuku', pp. 62–3; Kobayashi, Hito to Shisō, pp. 204–5.
[181] On the U.S.-Japan Security Treaty, see Nagahara & Yoneda, Onna no Shōwashi,
pp. 209–13; Ōe, Sengo Henkaku, pp. 360–81; Eguchi, Gendai no Nihon, pp. 172–4;
Hunter, Concise Dictionary of Modern Japanese History, pp. 239–40.

with her pre-war feminist activities, she exhibited more perseverance in the peace movement. She was also a more effective leader. On 22 June 1970, one day before the expiration of the new U.S.-Japan Security Treaty (a revision of the 1951 U.S.-Japan Security Treaty), she gave a press conference appealing to women to join her campaign for the abrogation of the revised treaty.[182] The following day, which was the national united action day of campaigning for the abrogation of the Treaty, the eighty-four year old Hiratsuka held a demonstration with other members of the Nihon Fujin Dantai Rengōkai, who were carrying placards, near her house in Seijō, calling out 'Anpo o nakushite heiwana Nihon o' ('Abolish the security treaty and achieve peace in Japan').[183]

Even on her deathbed, Hiratsuka was concerned about the Vietnam war.[184] She died of cancer of the gall-bladder at the age of eighty-five on 24 May, 1971 at Yoyogi Hospital in Sendagaya, Tokyo. She was cremated at Shunjūen Cemetery in Ikuta, Kanagawa Prefecture. Obituaries lamenting her death appeared in many newspapers.[185]

---

[182] Kobayashi, *Hito to Shisō*, pp. 208-9; Nagahara & Yoneda, *Onna no Shōwashi*, pp. 249-50.

[183] In spite of Hiratsuka and other pacifists' efforts, the revised treaty was renewed. Yoneda, 'Jidai o ikinuku', pp. 62-3; Ikeda Emiko, 'Hibusō, hikōsen o mamorinuku', in Hiratsuka Raichō o Yomu Kai (ed.), *Raichō Soshite Watashi*, Part 3, p. 16; Kobayashi, *Hito to Shisō*, p. 209.

[184] Kushida, 'Josei kaihō e no jōnetsu', p. 39.

[185] These included 'Ribu no tōshi mo kenka: Sayonara Raichō-san', *Asahi Shinbun* (31 May, 1971); 'Hiratsuka Raichō-san ga shikyo', *Asahi Shinbun* (25 May, 1971); 'Hiratsuka Raichō-san okyō nashi mushūkyōsō', *Asahi Shinbun* (31 May, 1971); Ichikawa Fusae, 'Tsuyoi ishi de shinnen tsuranuku: Hiratsuka Raichō joshi o itamu', *Asahi Shinbun* (25 May, 1971); 'Wūman ribu no senkusha: Hiratsuka Raichō-san shikyo', *Mainichi Shinbun* (25 May, 1971); 'Nihon fujin undō no senkusha: Hiratsuka Raichō-san shikyo', *Akahata* (25 May, 1971); 'Kakukai no hitobito ga chōmon: Hiratsuka Raichō-san shikyo', *Akahata* (25 May, 1971).

CONCLUSION

Hiratsuka's life, as reconstructed from many sources, reveals a rare personality and identity, showing self-assurance and originality. Although she grew up at a time when many Japanese women faced severe discrimination and many constraints, she challenged the *ie* system and the conditions of women's subordination, and took many steps to destroy old customs and laws which restricted women. In her school days she opposed the *ryōsai kenbo* (good wives and wise mothers) education. Her opposition to the *ie* system and the morals expected of women contributed to the Shiobara Incident. Hiratsuka had gained more self-assurance by the time she launched *Seitō*, and had become more critical of the ways in which women were suppressed under the Meiji Civil Code. In her Seitō activities she appealed to women to regain positive female identities, and to fulfil their potential. It was also during her Seitō days that Hiratsuka declared herself to be 'a new woman', lived with her partner without marrying him, and registered their children as illegitimate, contrary to the Civil Code.

Through her own child-rearing experiences she realised the need to protect mothers and give them financial security. She became convinced that women's emancipation would never be fully achieved without the protection of motherhood, and this view was expressed in the debates she engaged in. Before long she realised that women's political rights, including suffrage, must have the highest priority. She founded the Association of New Women, launched petitioning and lobbying campaigns, and did much to heighten women's political awareness. After the Association she joined the women's consumer movement, which she believed to be an ideal campaign for women to reconstruct society. Hiratsuka avoided cooperating with the Pacific war effort. It was during the war that her pacifist views developed to lay the foundations of her post-1945 involvement in the peace movement. After the war she became a leader of the women's peace movement, taking steps to create a society in which women would be protected and educated. Her 85 years were atypical and dynamic: a series of fights against established views to improve women's status and achieve a peaceful world.

Hiratsuka's life had many trials and was by no means an unbroken series of triumphs. She was at times the focus of public criticism because of her progressive views, and in such circumstances her resolution was impressive. She had a strong desire to improve herself by constant self-education. She was also extremely sensitive to social changes, and was quick to respond to the times. In her book *Marumado Yori (From the Round Window)* she expressed a wish not only to be a supporter of new developments, but to be one herself.[1] As Yoneda Sayoko stated, Hiratsuka paid little heed to her past, discarding it as if it was an old kimono, and always advanced herself by pursuing something new.[2] In this, as in other regards, she was surprisingly forward-looking for a Japanese woman of her period.

Almost all existing work on Hiratsuka, both in Japanese and English, tends to see her forward-looking ideas and strong personality as the keys to the success of her feminist activities. They incline to overlook the social, political and historical context of her work. However, most of Hiratsuka's major initiatives were in the Taishō period. During that period democratic or pluralistic ideas proved increasingly influential in Japan. Such ideas were imported partly through western literature and drama, and exerted a powerful hold particularly on young people.[3] Many wished to escape from "feudalistic" ideas and emancipate themselves from convention, and movements dedicated to such ends began to emerge.[4] In 1916 the liberal thinker Yoshino Sakuzō advocated *minpon shugi* ('people as the basis'), teaching that the main concern of the state ought to be the welfare of its people, and that all political decisions ought to be based upon public opinion.[5] He also demanded the establishment of a party and cabinet system grounded on universal suffrage. His ideas gained popularity and inspired many intellectuals and students. As ideas of political pluralism developed, an increasingly aware general public took a growing interest in politics and reform.[6] The Rice Riots in 1918

---

[1] Hiratsuka Raichō, *Marumado yori* (1913), reprinted in Hiratsuka, *Chosakushū*, vol. 1, p. 8.

[2] Yoneda, 'Kaisetsu', in Hiratsuka, *Chosakushū*, vol. 4, p. 395.

[3] Matsuda, *Fujin Kōron no 50-nen*, pp. 6–7; Imai, *Taishō Demokurashii*, pp. 110–35; Esashi & Ide, *Taishō Demokurashii to Josei*, pp. 49–53.

[4] *Ibid.*, p. 4.

[5] *Ibid.*, pp. 45–6; Kano, *Taishō Demokurashii*, pp. 48–50; Imai, *Taishō Demokurashii*, pp. 165–6.

[6] Esashi & Ide, *Taishō Demokurashii to Josei*, p. 4.

underlined the extent to which popular political protest was developing.[7] Many among the working class became more aware of their exploited conditions, and were inspired by the foundation of the first trade union in Japan, the Yūaikai.[8] Other trade unions followed, starting to cohere into an active labour movement.[9] They organised strikes and demanded the improvement of working conditions, including higher wages and increased workers' rights.[10] After the Rice Riots universal suffrage campaigns became more frequent.[11] Even socialists, whose activities had been heavily suppressed since the High Treason Incident in 1910, began to revive their activities, in part influenced by the Russian Revolution.[12] Women also were influenced by the liberal or radical mood of the period.[13] Men continued to hold the dominant positions in society and women faced severe discrimination. However, many young unmarried women of good education became conscious of their own worth and wished to escape from restrictive lives and to reform existing conditions.[14] Discussion of a wide range of women's issues emerged. Women's cooperative action became more frequent, and they began to request participation in politics, and to agitate for a more democratic Civil Code.[15] These women's concerns also came to be voiced in new magazines such as *Fujin Kōron*, *Shufu no Tomo*, *Fujin Kurabu* and *Josei Kaizō*, which helped to raise female consciousness, and cultural and educational attainments among middle-class women.[16] Even general magazines with a large circulation, such as *Chūō Kōron* and *Taiyō*, began to direct their attention to women's questions and to devote special issues to women.[17]

Hiratsuka's feminist activities were inseparable from this climate in the Taishō period. Taishō Japan offered her opportunities which

---

[7] *Ibid.*, pp. 64–8; Kano, *Taishō Demokurashii*, pp. 161–8; Imai, *Taishō Demokurashii*, pp. 174–82; Yoneda, *Kindai Nihon Joseishi*, vol. 1, pp. 131–2.

[8] *Ibid.*, pp. 118–9.

[9] Imai, *Taishō Demokurashii*, p. 226; Esashi & Ide, *Taishō Demokurashii to Josei*, pp. 70–1.

[10] Yoneda, *Kindai Nihon Joseishi*, vol. 1, pp. 133–7; Esashi & Ide, *Taishō Demokurashii to Josei*, pp. 76–80.

[11] *Ibid.*, p. 90; Imai, *Taishō Demokurashii*, p. 226.

[12] *Ibid.*, pp. 167–71.

[13] Matsuda, *Fujin Kōron no 50-nen*, p. 7.

[14] *Ibid.*, pp. 6–8; Esashi & Ide, *Taishō Demokurashii to Josei*, pp. 5–6.

[15] Kano, *Taishō Demokurashii*, p. 237; Matsuda, *Fujin Kōron no 50-nen*, p. 32.

[16] Esashi & Ide, *Taishō Demokurashii to Josei*, pp. 87–8; Kano, *Taishō Demokurashii*, p. 238.

[17] Imai, *Taishō Demokurashii*, pp. 116–7.

were not so clearly open before. The petitioning and lobbying campaigns she conducted for the Association of New Women were supported by many male liberal thinkers and some socialists, who were
affected by Taishō pluralism. Hiratsuka received much advice from
men influencing the political process. Without their support, she and
her colleagues would have had no hope of achieving political change.
Because of the relative political tolerance of this period, her feminist activities were not much restricted by police and government
agencies, apart from occasional minor warnings by the police.[18] Her
feminist arguments published in magazines were hardly censored.
She also benefitted greatly from the growth of women's literature
and magazines. Although she was involved in minor scandals and
sometimes became the target of public criticism, the journalistic world
continued to give her many opportunities to express her views.[19] *Fujin
Kōron* was particularly sympathetic to her, and discussed subjects such
as female occupations, welfare, health, birth control, chastity, marriage and divorce.[20] Hiratsuka regularly contributed to *Fujin Kōron*,
being paid for doing so. It was in *Fujin Kōron* and *Taiyō* that Hiratsuka, Yosano, Yamakawa and Yamada developed their debate about
motherhood.[21] Such magazines were widely read, and played an
important role in spreading Hiratsuka's ideas and promoting her
campaigns.[22] In this and other ways, she took full advantage of the
auspicious climate of the Taishō period.

Hiratsuka commenced her feminist activity almost ten years before
any of her contemporary Japanese feminists, and the most distinguished role she rendered was as an initiator.[23] She inspired feminist debate, launched campaigns which became central to the Japanese
women's movement, and she brought Oku Mumeo and Ichikawa
Fusae into prominence.[24] Hiratsuka exerted a strong influence on

---

[18] Hiratsuka, *Genshi*, vol. 2, pp. 127–8; Imai, *Taishō Demokurashii*, pp. 116–7; Tokkō
Keisatsu Kokusho Henshū Iinkai (ed.) *Tokkō Keisatsu Kokusho* (1977), pp. 78–9.
[19] Imai, *Taishō Demokurashii*, p. 117.
[20] Esashi & Ide, *Taishō Demokurashii to Josei*, p. 87; Kano, *Taishō Demokurashii*, pp.
237–8.
[21] Matsuda, *Fujin Kōron no 50-nen*, pp. 27–8; Esashi & Ide, *Taishō Demokurashii to
Josei*, pp. 87–8.
[22] Matsuda, *Fujin Kōron no 50-nen*, p. 10.
[23] Kobayashi, *Hito to Shisō*, p. 4.
[24] Oku, *Nobi*, pp. 46–7; Ichikawa, *Jiden: Senzen Hen*, pp. 50–1; Ichikawa, *87-sai
no Seishun*; Ichikawa, *Nonaka no Ippon Sugi*, pp. 28–30.

many contemporary women.[25] Her unorthodox conduct and way of life gave many others an opportunity to compare themselves with her, to improve themselves educationally, and to gain self-confidence. She even affected people's vocabularies, producing linguistic changes.[26] 'Hiratsuka Raichō' became a synonym for *atarashii onna* (a new woman).[27]

Hiratsuka also had a considerable impact upon the writing of Japanese women's history. Her historical views about the earlier status of women in Japan were not grounded on general reading, but they influenced Takamure Itsue, who was probably the first female historian to challenge traditional male-centred history. She claimed that she had been inspired by Hiratsuka's manifesto 'Genshi josei wa taiyō de atta', which, from the early 1930s, stimulated her to write on the history of women.[28] She consulted family records, anthropological data, mythology and early literature, and argued in favour of Hiratsuka's statement historically. She called herself 'Hiratsuka's spiritual daughter'—a high regard that was reciprocated by Hiratsuka.[29] Without Hiratsuka, Takamure's well-researched and original works, including *Shōseikon no Kenkyū* (*Research on Matrilocal Marriage*), *Nihon Koninshi* (*The History of Japanese Marriage*) and *Josei no Rekishi* (*Women's History*), which made a great contribution to Japanese women's historiography, might never have been produced.

Because of Hiratsuka's remarkable achievements and influence, there has been a growing tendency among women's historians and the public to see her as an impeccable feminist and leader, superior to

---

[25] Yoneda, 'Jidai o ikinuku', p. 63.

[26] Momose Meiji *et al.*, *Meiserifu Nihonshi* (1987), pp. 214–6.

[27] Kobayashi Tomie, 'Atarashii onna no negai: Raichō no shōgai kara uketsugu', in Maruoka *et al.*, *Hiratsuka Raichō to Nihon no Kindai*, pp. 42–3; Horiba, *Seitō no Jidai*, pp. 148–50.

[28] Cited in Kōno Nobuko, *Takamure Itsue* (1990), pp. 130–2; Nishikawa, 'Hitotsu no keifu', p. 182.

[29] Cited in Hiratsuka, *Genshi*, vol. 3, pp. 305–10 and Kōno, *Takamure Itsue*, pp. 131–3. Hiratsuka's feelings towards Takamure are expressed in Hiratsuka Raichō, 'Takamure Itsue-shi no *Josei 2600-nen-shi*', *Tōkyōdō Geppō* (April, 1940), reprinted in Hiratsuka, *Chosakushū*, vol. 6, pp. 317–8; Hiratsuka Raichō, 'Takamure Itsue-san', in Hiratsuka, *Kumo, Kusa, Hito*, reprinted in Hiratsuka, *Chosakushū*, vol. 4, pp. 221–2; Hiratsuka Raichō, 'Takamure Itsue-san no *Renai Sōsei* o yomu', in Hiratsuka, *Kumo, Kusa, Hito*, reprinted in Hiratsuka, *Chosakushū*, vol. 4, pp. 223–5; Hiratsuka Raichō, 'Hi no onna hi no kuni ni kaeru: jomakushiki shukuji', *Nihon Dangi* (April, 1962), reprinted in Hiratsuka, *Chosakushū*, vol. 7, p. 404.

all other Japanese feminists.[30] This kind of praise needs to be handled with scepticism, and one needs to compare Hiratsuka with other contemporary feminists—like Ichikawa Fusae, Itō Noe, Kamichika Ichiko, Katō Shidzue, Oku Mumeo, Yamakawa Kikue, Yamanouchi Mina and Yamada Waka—to see how Hiratsuka compared with them.

All of these women expressed 'feminist' views from an early age, and showed considerable persistence in this over long periods, especially between 1910 and 1945. Some of them also set up women's associations and launched journals. In some cases their achievements may appear slight; yet what they accomplished was often beyond anything that they or other women would have conceived possible at an earlier stage of their lives. Their feminist campaigns brought them much public disapproval, especially if they leaned to socialism, and they faced much scrutiny and derision, with the agencies of government and public opinion against them.[31] In the face of this they showed remarkable fortitude and sense of mission, and their qualities and personalities had an enormous impact upon the development of the Japanese women's movement.[32]

Hiratsuka differed from many other feminists in that she had few international links. Ichikawa, Katō and Yamada had lived and studied in America in their youth, and Katō and Ichikawa in particular had visited America and other western countries to lecture or attend meetings.[33] After 1945 Yamakawa, Kamichika and Oku visited America

---

[30] Personal interview with Kobayashi Tomie, 30 May, 1991, Tokyo.

[31] Katō Shidzue, *Ai wa Jidai o Koete* (1988), pp. 108–11; Katō Shidzue, *Saiai no Hito Kanju e: Katō Shidzue Nikki* (1988), pp. 5–48; Yamanouchi, *Jiden*, pp. 133–42; Ichikawa, *Jiden: Senzen Hen*, pp. 576–84; Kodama Katsuko, *Shinanoji no Deai: Fusen Undō Oboegaki* (1985), pp. 104–6; Suzuki Yūko, 'Kurai tanima no jidai: senjika o ikiru', in Yamakawa Kikue Seitan 100-nen o Kinensuru Kai (ed.), *Gendai Feminizumu to Yamakawa Kikue*, pp. 245–76; Tokkō Kensatsu Kokusho Henshū Iinkai (ed.), *Tokkō Keisatsu Kokusho*, pp. 80–2.

[32] Suzuki, *Joseishi o Hiraku*, vol. 1, p. 8.

[33] Ichikawa, *Jiden: Senzen Hen*, pp. 104–23; Ichikawa Fusae, *Daikon no Hana: Ichikawa Fusae Zuisōshū* (1979), pp. 144–222; Katō, *Ai wa Jidai o Koete*, pp. 46–63, 92–7; Ishimoto, *Facing Two Ways*, pp. 174–85, 269; Hopper, *A New Woman of Japan*, pp. 11–2; Yamazaki, *Ameyuki-san no Uta*, pp. 64–171, 253–64; Yamazaki, *The Story of Yamada Waka*, pp. 69–104, 147–52; Tsunesaburō Kamesaka (ed.), *Who's Who in Japan* (1937), pp. 144–5, 178, 637; Susan J. Pharr, *Political Women in Japan: The Search for a Place in Political Life* (Berkeley, 1981), pp. 19–20. Katō visited many places in America including New York, California, Boston, Palm Beach, Dallas and towns in Texas, giving public lectures in English on Japanese women and culture and broadcasting interviews from the Feakins Lecture Bureau in 1932 and 1933. Her role overseas as an interpreter as well as a cultural 'go-between' was notable. After

and Europe to contact women's organisations and attend international women's conferences as Japanese delegates.[34] By comparison, Hiratsuka never went abroad, although she received countless invitations to international women's conferences or to meet leaders of women's organisations after 1945.[35]

Hiratsuka was also the least influenced by direct contact with western feminists. Ichikawa and Katō had close contacts with American feminists. During her two and a half year stay in America, Ichikawa met Alice Paul and others like her.[36] Ichikawa learned much about feminist campaigning from Paul. Similarly, Katō, who also spent time in America studying, became associated with a few American feminists and was greatly inspired by them.[37] Her encounter with the American birth control pioneer, Margaret Sanger, while Katō was studying in New York, transformed the direction of her life.[38] Katō developed an interest in birth control and studied this under Sanger's guidance, later opening a birth control clinic in Tokyo.[39]

By comparison with Katō and Ichikawa's close connections with American feminists, Hiratsuka did not really associate with any foreign female campaigners before the Pacific War. As we have seen, she read a wide range of books in English and translated some dealing with women's issues. These included *Love and Marriage* and *The Renaissance of Motherhood*, both by Ellen Key, and J.S. Mill's *The*

---

the Second World War, Ichikawa became head of the *Nihon Fujin Yūkensha Dōmei* (Japanese Women's Voters' Alliance) and toured America as a cultural representative under the sponsorship of the Rockefeller Foundation. Once she was elected as a Member of Parliament, she went to America to attend international women's conferences, and communicated in English with women from many other countries. She acted as a go-between on women's international affairs, and promoted contact between Japanese women and women from countries like Britain and America.

[34] Oku, *Nobi*, p. 207; Yamakawa, *Onna Nidai no Ki*, p. 374.

[35] Hiratsuka, *Genshi*, vol. 4, pp. 128–9; Letter from Hiratsuka Raichō to Maruoka Hideko, 4 January, 1955, reprinted in Hiratsuka, *Chosakushū*, vol. 8, pp. 138–9; Letter from Hiratsuka Raichō to Maruoka Hideko, 11 January, 1955, reprinted in Hiratsuka, *Chosakushū*, vol. 8, pp. 139–41; Letter from Hiratsuka Raichō to Nishikawa Kikuko, 11 May, 1958, reprinted in Hiratsuka, *Chosakushū*, vol. 8, pp. 129–30.

[36] Ichikawa, *Jiden: Senzen Hen*, pp. 117–9; Ichikawa, *Daikon no Hana*, pp. 210–3; Ichikawa, *Nonaka no Ippon Sugi*, pp. 31–4.

[37] Katō, *Ai wa Jidai o Koete*, pp. 57–60, 72–87, 97–101; Barbara Molony, 'Afterword', in Ishimoto, *Facing Two Ways*, pp. xvii–xxi; Hopper, *A New Woman of Japan*, pp. 33–4, 52–5.

[38] Ishimoto, *Facing Two Ways*, p. 183; Katō, *Ai wa Jidai o Koete*, pp. 42, 60.

[39] Katō, *Ai wa Jidai o Koete*, pp. 81–3. When Sanger visited Japan in 1922, following an invitation made by the *Kaizō Magazine*, Katō played an important role as her hostess and interpreter.

Subjection of Women, which was considered the Bible of the women's emancipation movement.[40] Although Hiratsuka was influenced by some European women like Ellen Key, her associations with such ideas were limited to reading and translation work. Hiratsuka did not make any attempt to meet or correspond with Key.[41] Indeed, Hiratsuka did not correspond with *any* foreign feminists before 1945, perhaps owing to a lack of confidence in her command of English. This was in striking contrast with the pre-1945 western affiliations established by Ichikawa and Katō, and with the close associations between American and British feminists.[42]

The third feature which distinguished Hiratsuka from other feminists of her time, including her western counterparts, was that she did not concentrate her energies upon one particular part of the women's movement. Generally speaking, many western as well as Japanese feminists were broadly active in women's campaigns, but each tended to have a particular speciality. Many of them believed that such specialisation was necessary to advance a cause fully. In the case of the British feminists, many of them had their own specific focus.[43] One can exaggerate such specialisms, and many historians

---

[40] Key's *Love and Marriage* was translated as *Renai to Kekkon*. Key's *Renaissance of Motherhood* was translated as *Bosei no Fukkō*. Mill's *The Subjection of Motherhood* was translated as *Fujin no Reizoku*. See Ellen Key (trans. by Hiratsuka Raichō), '*Renai to Kekkon*', *Seitō*, 3:1 (January, 1913), furoku, pp. 1–19 & 3:2 (February, 1913), furoku, pp. 23–7 & 3:3 (March, 1913), pp. 107–13 & 3:4 (April, 1913), pp. 112–23 & 3:6 (June, 1913), pp. 83–93 & 3:7 (July, 1913), pp. 125–35. See also Ellen Key (trans. by Hiratsuka Raichō), *Bosei no Fukkō* (1919); J.S. Mill (trans. by Hiratsuka Raichō), *Fujin no Reizoku*, in Heibonsha (comp.), *Shakai Shisō Zenshū*, vol. 36 (1929), pp. 201–301.

[41] Hiratsuka, *Genshi*, vol. 3, pp. 30–1; 266–8. Hiratsuka's regret at Ellen Key's death was expressed in Hiratsuka Raichō, 'Ellen Key joshi no shi', in Hiratsuka, *Kumo, Kusa, Hito*, reprinted in Hiratsuka, *Chosakushū*, vol. 4, pp. 218–20.

[42] Alice Paul and Lucy Burns established close ties with British feminists, being much influenced by the Pankhursts and adopting the latter's tactics on suffrage. Paul and Burns were keen to develop strong international links, and Paul became involved in the international women's movement after women gained the vote in America. See Bolt, *The Women's Movements in the United States and Britain*, pp. 202–3; Ryan, *Feminism and the Women's Movement*, p. 28.

[43] This feature was seen especially among the Victorian feminists. Many of them (whether involved in married women's property rights reform, educational and occupational reform, the campaign against the Contagious Diseases Acts or the franchise campaign) had their own particular focus. For example, Emily Davies withdrew from the suffrage campaign to concentrate her energies on women's educational reform, and she became a pioneer of women's higher education. Josephine Butler was best-known in connection with the agitation against the Contagious Diseases Acts, although she also showed interest in promoting higher education for women. Victorian feminists Lydia Becker, Millicent Garrett Fawcett, and Edwardian femi-

do this to simplify the historical record, associating particular issues with particular women in a way that obscures linking interests held in common. But in practical terms, there is some truth in pointing to how individual women concentrated upon certain issues.

Something similar may be said for the great majority of Japanese feminists. Ichikawa became involved with the Association of New Women and worked for a number of causes, but she concentrated her energies on the women's suffrage movement after she returned from America.[44] Oku, one of the leaders of the Association of New Women, later devoted herself to the welfare of working women, and to the consumer movement.[45] Yamanouchi focused on working-class women's protection, while Yamada committed herself to issues of motherhood.[46] Katō's major concern was birth control.[47] Yamakawa devoted herself in a more theoretical way to socialist feminism.[48] Many of these feminists were steadfast in such singular preoccupations until 1945, perhaps more so than their British or American counterparts.

---

nists Sylvia, Emmeline and Christabel Pankhurst all worked particularly for the suffrage movement, and it is that for which they are best known today. See Banks, *Becoming a Feminist*, pp. 46–72.

[44] Ichikawa, *Jiden: Senzen Hen*, pp. 126–413; Ichikawa, *Nonaka no Ippon Sugi*, pp. 50–105; Nuita Hanako (ed.), *Ichikawa Fusae Seitan 100-nen Kinen: Ichikawa Fusae to Fujin Sanseiken Undō* (1992), pp. 22–48; Ichikawa Fusae to Iu Hito Kankōkai (ed.), *Ichikawa Fusae to Iu Hito: 100-nen no Kaisō* (1982), pp. 11–27; Suzuki, *Joseishi o Hiraku*, vol. 1, pp. 121–39; Dee Ann Vavich, 'The Japanese woman's movement: Ichikawa Fusae—a pioneer in woman's suffrage', *Monumenta Nipponica*, 22 (1967), pp. 402–36; Kiyoko Takeda, 'Ichikawa Fusae: pioneer for women's rights in Japan', *Japan Quarterly*, 31:4 (October/December, 1984), pp. 410–5; Molony, 'One woman who dared', chapter 5.

[45] Oku, *Nobi*, pp. 75–196; 'Onna no tatakai nanajū-nen: Oku Mumeo-san ga jiden shuppan', *Yomiuri Shinbun* (7 October, 1988); '92-sai no shojo shuppan: Shufuren kaichō no Oku Mumeo-san jiden', *Asahi Shinbun* (7 October, 1988); 'Hyaku issai, Oku Mumeo-san shikyo: Shufuren sōsetsu, josei sanseiken ni jinryoku', *Asahi Shinbun* (7 July, 1997); 'Fujin sanseiken, saigo no rīdā: Oku Mumeo-san, oshamoji shinboru ni', *Asahi Shinbun* (7 July, 1997); 'Shufu no tame ni tatakai, Oku Mumeo-san o itamu', *Asahi Shinbun* (8 July, 1997); 'Sekibetsu, Shufuren, shodai kaichō, Oku Mumeo-san', *Asahi Shinbun* (15 July, 1997); Michiko Inukai, 'Japanese women raise the rice spoon of revolt', *UNESCO Courier*, 8 (August/September, 1975), pp. 12–5; Kamesaka, *Who's Who in Japan*, p. 425.

[46] Yamanouchi, *Jiden*, pp. 101–201; Yamazaki, *Ameyuki-san no Uta*, pp. 216–48, 265–80.

[47] Katō, *Ai wa Jidai o Koete*, pp. 79–83; Hopper, *A New Woman of Japan*, pp. 41–59.

[48] Suzuki Yūko, 'Kaisetsu', in Yamakawa, *Yamakawa Kikue Josei Kaihō Ronshū*, vol. 3, pp. 281–301; Suzuki Yūko, 'Kaisetsu', in Yamakawa Kikue (ed. by Suzuki Yūko), *Yamakawa Kikue Hyōronshū* (1990), p. 311; Tanaka, 'Gendai ni ikiru riron', p. 155; Hane, *Reflections on the Way to the Gallows*, pp. 163–4.

However, Hiratsuka was quite different. Although she continued
to retain her interest in the protection of motherhood after she had
children, she did not concentrate her energies upon one particular
cause. In her *Seitō* days her major concern was to raise female self-
awareness and self-confidence through writing. Then, in debating the
protection of motherhood, her main interest lay in that field. While
she was involved with the Association of New Women, she had three
main objectives—the amendment of Article 5 of the Peace Police
Law, the acquiring of female suffrage, and the protection of women
from men with venereal disease. She was also associated with the
women's consumer movement in Seijō in Tokyo where she lived
between 1930 and 1937.[49] She briefly joined the Musan Fujin Geijutsu
Renmei (The Proletarian Women's Arts League).[50] She showed some
interest in the birth control movement. After 1945 she devoted herself to the women's peace movement.[51] She moved through many
women's causes, and no commentator could describe her as single-
minded in her pursuit of any particular cause.

Moreover, Hiratsuka had versatile talent and was a person of
many varied literary and other interests. She was an active member
of the haiku society, composing many haiku poems.[52] She studied
Esperanto in her old age.[53] Her cultured literary activities contrasted
with the lives of other feminists, who devoted virtually all their lives
to their political and feminist careers. Hiratsuka embraced political
and non-political writing. Because of her wide literary interests, her
partner Okumura's career as a painter, and many other artistic and
theatrical pursuits, she was better-connected artistically and had wider
networks in many literary and artistic circles than any other con-

---

[49] Kobayashi, *Hito to Shisō*, pp. 189–90; Hiratsuka, *Genshi*, vol. 3, pp. 289–98;
Orii Miyako, 'Raichō to shōhisha kumiai undō', in Hiratsuka Raichō o Yomu Kai
(ed.), *Raichō Soshite Watashi* (1988), pp. 36–40.
[50] Kobayashi, *Hito to Shisō*, pp. 190–1; Hiratsuka, *Genshi*, vol. 3, pp. 303–10.
[51] Hiratsuka, *Genshi*, vol. 4, pp. 86–156; Ikeda Emiko, 'Raichō no heiwa shisō',
in Hiratsuka Raichō o Yomu Kai (ed.), *Raichō Soshite Watashi* (1988), pp. 41–46;
Ikeda Emiko, 'Hibusō, hikōsen o mamorinuku', in Hiratsuka Raichō o Yomu Kai
(ed.), *Raichō Soshite Watashi* (1991), pp. 7–15; Kobayashi, *Hito to Shisō*, pp. 198–209;
Kushida, 'Josei kaihō e no jōnetsu', pp. 39–41.
[52] Hiratsuka, *Genshi*, vol. 4, pp. 79–82.
[53] *Ibid.*, pp. 76–8; Ide, *Hiratsuka Raichō: Kindai to Shinpi*, pp. 244–5, 266; Hiratsuka
Raichō, 'Heiwa no tsubasa', *Fujin Taimuzu* (22 January, 1950), reprinted in Hiratsuka,
Chosakushū, vol. 7, p. 85; Hiratsuka Raichō, 'Jinrui ni hitotsu kotoba o', *Bungei Shunjū*
(March, 1951), reprinted in Hiratsuka, *Chosakushū*, vol. 7, pp. 143–4.

temporary feminist.[54] Her literary and artistic skill has been one of the main reasons for her enduring appeal.

Another feature which differentiated Hiratsuka from other Japanese feminists was that the others recruited and trained successors and family members for feminist activities. Some of them brought up their daughters to the cause. Katō sent her step-daughter to Margaret Sanger's birth control clinic to train her.[55] Ichikawa's adopted daughter, Misao, assisted her work, and followed in her footsteps.[56] Oku's daughter followed her mother into the women's consumer movement and became its leader.[57] However, Hiratsuka did not try to make her children adopt her feminism or interfere with their decisions, respecting their independent judgement.[58] They went their own ways, which were quite different from Hiratsuka's, and they did not assist her feminist activities. Her son became an engineer and after the war an academic at Waseda University.[59] Her daughter became a kindergarten teacher.[60] They had almost no public role.

The great majority of feminists who had played active parts in the women's movement before 1945 went into politics after suffrage was granted to Japanese women. In the first general election after the war, held on 10 April 1946, Katō and Yamanouchi stood as candidates.[61] Although Yamanouchi was defeated, Katō was successful and became active as a member of the House of Representatives, being attached to the Shakaitō (Socialist Party).[62] Oku, who stood as a candidate for the House of Councillors, was first elected in April 1947, and served three terms.[63] Yamakawa joined the Socialist Party

[54] Hiratsuka, *Genshi*, vol. 3, pp. 21–6, 260; Hiratsuka, *Genshi*, vol. 4, pp. 303–5; Ōoka Shōhei, 'Raichō sensei to watashi', in Maruoka *et al.*, *Hiratsuka Raichō to Nihon no Kindai* (1986), p. 27; personal interview with Usui Takeshi, 15 April, 1992, Tokyo; Letter from Hiratsuka Raichō to Nakanishi Ōdō, 14 August, 1964, reprinted in Hiratsuka, *Hiratsuka Raichō Chosakushū*, vol. 8, pp. 111–4.

[55] Katō, *Ai wa Jidai o Koete*, p. 142.

[56] Personal interview with Ichikawa Misao, 31 March, 1992, Tokyo; Ichikawa Misao, *Ichikawa Fusae Omoide Banashi* (1992), p. 11.

[57] Hoshi *et al.*, *Ōfū no 100-nin*, pp. 363–7; '92-sai no shojo shuppan', *Asahi Shinbun* (7 October, 1988).

[58] Personal interviews with Tsukizoe Akemi, 10 & 11 April, 1992, Tokyo.

[59] Hiratsuka, *Genshi*, vol. 4, p. 64.

[60] *Ibid.*, p. 64.

[61] Yamanouchi, *Jiden*, pp. 250–1; Katō, *Ai wa Jidai o Koete*, pp. 131–2.

[62] Yamanouchi, *Jiden*, p. 255; Katō, *Ai wa Jidai o Koete*, pp. 132–7; Ann Nakano, 'Shizue (Ishimoto) Katō: woman warrior', *PHP*, (February, 1984), pp. 68–72.

[63] Oku, *Nobi*, pp. 169–74.

in 1947, and during the coalition cabinet headed by Katayama Tetsu
was appointed as the first head of the Labour Ministry's Fujin Shōnen
Kyoku (Women's and Minors' Bureau).[64] Kamichika was elected in
1953, and then served four terms as a member of the House of Representatives until her retirement in 1969.[65] In 1953 Ichikawa was
elected to the House of Councillors as an Independent, and remained
there until her death in 1981 (except for a period between 1971 and
1974, as she was defeated in the 1971 election).[66] The same phenomenon can be seen among British feminists, once women over thirty
years of age received the vote in 1918.[67] The main reason why such
Japanese feminists and their western counterparts decided to go into
politics was their aspiration to be closer to sources of power, and
thus to have a greater chance of putting their ideas into effect. They
also knew that achieving political power was one of the best forms
of self-defence, and that it would enable them to promote ideas and
recruit sympathetic followers. The feminists who were successful in
winning elections used their political influence to promote women's
status. Hiratsuka was aware of such possibilities, but there is no evidence that she ever seriously considered entering political life. She
was largely satisfied with legal changes made to upgrade women's
status, and devoted herself instead to the peace movement after
the war.[68]

---

[64] Yano Setsu, 'Sōseiki no Rōdōshō Fujin Shōnen Kyokuchō jidai, I: sengo shoki
no josei rōdō mondai', in Yamakawa Kikue Seitan 100-nen o Kinensuru Kai (ed.),
Gendai Feminizumu to Yamakawa Kikue, pp. 34–62; Ikeno Hisa *et al.*, 'Sōseiki no Rōdōshō
Fujin Shōnen Kyokuchō jidai, II: Yamakawa Kyokuchō no fujin shōnen shitsu o
kataru', in Yamakawa Kikue Seitan 100-nen o Kinensuru Kai (ed.), *Gendai Feminizumu
to Yamakawa Kikue*, pp. 63–93.
[65] Tanaka Kazuko, 'Kaisetsu', in Kamichika Ichiko, *Josei Shisōshi* (1974), pp.
235–6; anon., 'Feminist Kamichika Ichiko', *East*, 25:2 (July/August, 1989), pp.
17–23.
[66] Ichikawa, *Nonaka no Ippon Sugi*, pp. 176–253; Kodama Katsuko, *Oboegaki: Sengo
no Ichikawa Fusae* (1985), pp. 92–201, 228–49, 286–8; Geoffrey Murray, 'Fusae
Ichikawa—choice of the young in Japan', *PHP*, 6:1 (January, 1975), pp. 35–41;
Patricia Murray, 'Ichikawa Fusae and the lonely red carpet', *Japan Interpreter*, 10:2
(Autumn, 1975), pp. 171–89; Eileen Carlberg, 'Women in the political system', in
Joyce Lebra *et al.* (eds), *Women in Changing Japan* (Stanford, 1976).
[67] Christabel Pankhurst stood for Parliament in 1918 for the Women's Party,
which she had founded with her mother in 1917. However, she failed to be elected
then or in subsequent attempts. Her mother, Emmeline, joined the Conservative
Party and in 1926 she became the candidate for Whitechapel and St. George. See
Mitchell, *The Fighting Pankhursts*, pp. 74–5, 168–9.
[68] Hiratsuka, *Genshi*, vol. 4, pp. 55–78; Kobayashi, *Hito to Shisō*, pp. 199–200.

Furthermore, Hiratsuka's political ideas lacked consistency, and in this they contrasted with many contemporary feminists. In the Association of New Women she disapproved of socialism. Socialist feminists such as Yamakawa Kikue described Hiratsuka as a bourgeois feminist. However, in the mid 1920s Hiratsuka supported proletarian political parties. When she was involved with the consumer movement, she was influenced by Kropotkin. In the 1930s when she became a member of the Musan Fujin Geijutsu Renmei (the Proletarian Women's Arts League) and was active in the consumer movement, she inclined to anarchism.[69] After 1945 she became a supporter of the Communist Party of Japan.[70] Nor were her religious leanings consistent. While at the Japan Women's College she attended church services, read the Bible and showed an interest in Christianity.[71] She later adopted Zen meditation and read Buddhist scriptures.[72] She retained much interest in Zen over a long period, but also developed an interest in Shintoism in her later life. Her sister believed in Ōmotokyō (the Ōmoto Religious Sect), which was a new form of Shintoism founded by Deguchi Nao in 1892.[73] Hiratsuka was also inclined to it after 1945, and especially sympathised with its views on peace issues and universal brotherhood.[74] However, she hardly discussed such religious views, and it is difficult to determine how committed she was to any of these various systems of belief.

These unpredictable qualities can be extended in another way. Hiratsuka was one of the few Japanese feminists who does not fit

---

[69] Hiratsuka, *Genshi*, vol. 3, pp. 303–7; Ide, *Hiratsuka Raichō: Kindai to Shinpi*, pp. 236–43.

[70] Indeed, a favourable obituary on Hiratsuka appeared in *Akahata* (*Red Flag*), the Communist Party newspaper, associating her with the movement to some extent. See 'Kakukai no hitobito ga chōmon', *Akahata* (25 May, 1971); 'Nihon fujin undō no senkusha, Hiratsuka Raichō-san shikyo', *Akahata* (25 May, 1971). See also letter from Hiratsuka Raichō to Toyota Sayaka, 15 July, 1968, reprinted in Hiratsuka, *Hiratsuka Raichō Chosakushū*, vol. 8, p. 105.

[71] Hiratsuka, *Genshi*, vol. 1, pp. 178–82.

[72] *Ibid.*, pp. 192–8, 207–13.

[73] Hiratsuka, *Genshi*, vol. 4, pp. 296–7. The Ōmoto Religious Sect (*Ōmotokyō*) teaches that mankind's aim is to help achieve the Kingdom of Heaven by perceiving that man and God are inter-dependent and one. Deguchi Nao's writings were called *Ofudesaki* and became the core teachings of the Ōmoto Religious Sect. On the Ōmoto Religious Sect, see Yasumaru Yoshio, *Deguchi Nao* (1987), pp. 3–11, 192–225; Murakami Shigeyoshi, 'Kaisetsu', in Deguchi Nao, *Ōmoto Shinyu: Ten no Maki* (1979), pp. 157–75.

[74] Ide, *Hiratsuka Raichō: Kindai to Shinpi*, pp. 244–51, 266; Tachi, 'Hiratsuka Raichō to *Ofudesaki*', pp. 109–11.

the classifications of British feminists which Olive Banks created.[75]
The first category was feminists who remained single, were not
influenced by men, and devoted their lives to feminist causes.[76] A
high proportion of Victorian and Edwardian feminists belonged here.[77]
Ichikawa, who decided to remain single in spite of a few marriage
proposals in her youth, and who committed herself to women's
suffrage, certainly fell into this category.[78]

A second category was the feminists married to men who gave
active support to the women's movement. This class could be further sub-divided into three categories: (a) those in which the wife
was initially an active feminist, and who had converted her husband
into a 'male feminist' or a keen supporter of the women's movement;
(b) those for whom the husband was initially an active 'male feminist', and had instigated feminist ideas in his wife; and (c) those for
whom a common sympathy for feminism had drawn husband and
wife together.[79] As Olive Banks stated, in Britain many couples (such
as Ethel and Philip Snowden) belonged to the first of these categories.[80] However, in Japan feminists belonging to that first category
were very rare.

In Britain Richard and Emmeline Pankhurst, Nora and Henry
Sidgwick, and Henry and Millicent Garrett Fawcett fell into the second category.[81] In the case of Hiratsuka's contemporary Japanese
feminists, many of them belonged to this category of women following a lead supplied by husbands. For example, Yamada Waka, who was
an uneducated prostitute in America, was rescued by her academic

---

[75] Banks, *Becoming a Feminist*, pp. 113–6.
[76] *Ibid.*, p. 113.
[77] For example, Mary Carpenter, Frances Power Cobbe and Emily Davies.
[78] Ichikawa, *Nonaka no Ippon Sugi*, pp. 43–52; Ichikawa, *Jiden: Senzen Hen*, pp. 33–4.
[79] Banks, *Becoming a Feminist*, pp. 113–4.
[80] *Ibid.*, p. 113.
[81] *Ibid.*, pp. 113–4. As Olive Banks pointed out, Richard Pankhurst (a legal scholar
and radical reformer and friend of John Stuart Mill) was already deeply committed
to the women's movement when he married Emmeline, and her first involvement
in the women's movement came largely through his encouragement. Similarly, Henry
Sidgwick had begun his work in Cambridge for women's higher education some
years before his marriage to Nora, and his prior eagerness for that cause gradually
involved his wife in the movement for women's higher education. Millicent Garrett
Fawcett was also encouraged by her husband, Henry Fawcett, a blind Cambridge
professor and Liberal M.P., who was senior to her by fourteen years. He gave her
'the benefit of his political experience' and provided her with an ideal opportunity
of mixing with his political friends, including John Stuart Mill.

husband Kakichi, and educated by him.[82] He introduced her to the ideas of western feminists and recommended that she join the Seitō Society.[83] He supported her feminist campaign for the protection of motherhood, and gave her much advice. Similarly, Katō's first husband, Ishimoto Keikichi, initially implanted ideas of women's emancipation in her, and sent her to America to receive further education to help her to become independent.[84] Katō's decision to work for the birth control movement was not taken upon her husband's recommendation but was her own choice.[85] Yet without her husband's radical ideas and his encouragement—which formed a pronounced contrast with most other contemporary Japanese husbands—the pioneer of the Japanese birth control movement would probably never have done any such work. Oku's husband did not exert a strong influence on her involvement in the women's movement, but he encouraged her to work for the Association of New Women, which took her into her first women's campaign.[86]

As far as the third category was concerned (of partners having a common sympathy for feminism), John Stuart Mill and Harriet Taylor, or Josephine and George Butler, were western examples of this.[87] Many British feminists chose husbands whose convictions appeared sympathetic to their own. In Japan, Yamakawa Kikue certainly belonged in this group. Her husband, Yamakawa Hitoshi, was a prominent figure in the socialist movement, and he deepened her emotional commitment to socialism as well as to the cause of working-class women.[88]

The last group was that of feminists whose activities were greatly inspired or encouraged by men who were not their husbands.[89] Sylvia Pankhurst was inspired by her friend Keir Hardie.[90] Her socialist

---

[82] Yamazaki, *Ameyuki-san no Uta*, pp. 153–4.

[83] *Ibid.*, pp. 184–207.

[84] Katō, *Ai wa Jidai o Koete*, pp. 44–57; Ishimoto, *Facing Two Ways*, p. 172; Hopper, *A New Woman of Japan*, p. 9.

[85] Katō, *Ai wa Jidai o Koete*, pp. 79–87.

[86] Oku, *Nobi*, p. 46.

[87] Banks, *Becoming a Feminist*, p. 114. George Butler provided Josephine with support and stability during her stormy time as leader of the movement against the Contagious Diseases Acts. She placed much reliance upon his judgement.

[88] Suzuki, 'Kaisetsu', in Yamakawa, *Yamakawa Kikue Hyōronshū*, pp. 312–3.

[89] Banks, *Becoming a Feminist*, p. 114.

[90] Mitchell, *The Fighting Pankhursts*, p. 185; Patricia W. Romero, *E. Sylvia Pankhurst: Portrait of a Radical* (1987, New Haven, 1990 edn), pp. 32–7, 109–10; Caroline Benn, *Keir Hardie* (London, 1992), pp. 215–26, 233–9.

ideas and her socialist-feminist activities were encouraged by him. Both Kamichika and Itō were greatly influenced by their shared lover, the already married Ōsugi Sakae, who was a well-known anarchist.[91] Under his influence Itō became absorbed in the writings of female anarchists such as Emma Goldman.

Compared to all these contemporary feminists, who can be fitted fairly easily into Banks' classification of western feminists, Hiratsuka was very unusual and less readily classifiable. She had a lifelong partner, Okumura Hiroshi, whom she eventually married twenty-seven years after she first cohabited with him.[92] Her feminism seems not to have been influenced by him. Nor did she make any recorded effort to convert him to her beliefs. Indeed, he could not by any stretch of the definition be said to be a 'male feminist'. The only link he had with her activities was via his work as a painter, for she sometimes asked him to design illustrations for front covers of her magazines, like *Seitō* and the *Women's League*.[93] He showed little interest in her involvement in the women's movement. Nor did he provide much income for them and their two children, leaving Hiratsuka to make ends meet when she was engaged in the Seitō Society and the Association of New Women.[94] To Ichikawa Fusae and Yamanouchi Mina, who were regular visitors at Hiratsuka's house while involved in the Association of New Women, he appeared to be a selfish and irresponsible man.[95] Hiratsuka however was always protective of him.[96] Okumura was not always passive and financially dependent on her. After the dissolution of the Association of New Women, he taught art at Seijō High School.[97] He also coached students in drama, and

---

[91] Yamakawa, *Onna Nidai no Ki*, pp. 173–5; Kamichika, *Jiden*, pp. 140–2.

[92] Hiratsuka, *Genshi*, vol. 4, pp. 37–40; Kobayashi, *Hito to Shisō*, pp. 207–8.

[93] Hiratsuka, *Genshi*, vol. 2, p. 49; Hiratsuka, *Genshi*, vol. 3, p. 144.

[94] *Ibid.*, pp. 192–3.

[95] Yamanouchi, *Jiden*, p. 84; Ichikawa, *Jiden: Senzen Hen*, pp. 69–70; Kobayashi, *Hito to Shisō*, p. 207.

[96] Hiratsuka, *Genshi*, vol. 3, pp. 193–4; Hiratsuka Raichō, 'Okumura Hiroshi no rafu sobyō ni tsuite', *Bungaku Sanpo*, 22 (1 September, 1964), reprinted in Hiratsuka, *Chosakushū*, vol. 7, p. 419.

[97] Hiratsuka discussed Okumura's teaching job in her autobiography. Prof. Usui and Ōoka Shōhei confirmed that both of them were taught by Okumura while they were students at Seijō High School. However, Okumura's name did not appear in the list of teaching staff there. See Hiratsuka, *Genshi*, vol. 3, p. 253; personal interview with Usui Takeshi, 15 April, 1992, Tokyo; Ōoka, 'Raichō sensei to watashi', pp. 12–3; Ōoka Shōhei, 'Ano jiyūna katei no funiki', in Ōtsuki Shoten (ed.), *Hiratsuka Raichō Chosakushū Geppō*, 1 (June, 1983), pp. 1–3; Seijō Kōtōgakkō (comp.), *Seijō*

was highly respected by them.[98] In the 1930s he established an artistic career as a jewellery designer, and became financially comfortable.[99] In some ways he helped Hiratsuka's work, being indifferent when many other partners at that time in Japan would have been downright hostile. He was not bound by the *ie* system and familial conventionalism; he was not authoritarian; nor did he try to impose any restrictions on her feminist activities—as a consequence she enjoyed much freedom in their relationship. In spite of the role Okumura played in Hiratsuka's life, he has been largely neglected by researchers on her. However, through my interviews with Prof. Usui and Hiratsuka's daughter, Okumura's contribution to Hiratsuka's feminist life became evident. Prof. Usui, an emeritus professor of Seijō University, who was taught by Okumura and frequently visited Hiratsuka's house with the novelist Ōoka Shōhei, recognised Okumura's qualities. He recalled that Okumura and Hiratsuka were a devoted couple and had great respect for each other.[100] Okumura treated her as his equal, and this left a strong impression on Usui. The free and relaxed atmosphere of Hiratsuka's family was completely different from his own household, in which his father exercised much authority over his mother.[101] Hiratsuka's daughter, Akemi, made the following comments on her parents' relationship:

> From my point of view, my father supported my mother in his own way. She worried deeply about failing to look after him, my brother and myself. One day she regretted this particularly, and let her feelings slip out, saying: 'I cannot even sew *yukata* [informal cotton kimonos for summer wear] for all of you, although summer is approaching.' At that time my father responded: 'You had better do things which nobody but you can do.' My father's statement became imprinted on my memory, although I was very young then. Unlike ordinary husbands those days, my father never demanded that my mother should fulfil the duties of an ordinary housewife. That may have been the best possible support my mother received from my father.[102]

Kōtōgakkō Shokuin Meibo (*A List of the Staff Working for Seijō High School*) (1925–35) (Seijō Gakuen Archive).

[98] Personal interview with Usui Takeshi, 15 April, 1992, Tokyo.
[99] *Ibid.*
[100] *Ibid.*
[101] Usui also remembered that Okumura and Hiratsuka were affectionate parents. Their young children were well looked after, very content and lively.
[102] Tsukizoe Akemi, 'Haha Hiratsuka Raichō no omoide', *Tosho*, 459 (October, 1987), p. 42.

Akemi's recollection indicates a flexible, open-minded and unpossessive husband, who treated his wife as an equal, and respected her commitment to women's causes: something indeed of a 'new man', at least in terms of Japanese males at that time.[103] Apart from Okumura, Hiratsuka was also fortunate to have extremely supportive parents and a sister who had faith in her. They never attempted to remould her personality, and gave her financial support throughout her life. This toleration and support from her family came despite the fact that Hiratsuka's personality tended towards moodiness. She was temperamental, and did not easily command loyal support from others.[104] She was inclined to monopolise and control the organisations which she joined. Her attitude towards her own children was different from this.[105] In her public life, there was little that was democratic about her running of women's organisations.[106]

It is instructive to assess Hiratsuka as a feminist leader in comparison with the other leading feminists. Although she had the foresight to launch the Seitō Society and the Association of New Women, she did not persevere with them, abandoning them to others while they were still in operation. This was partly because of her ill health and family circumstances. She did not have the self-sacrifice or staying power of some other Japanese and western feminist leaders. Japanese feminists usually stayed with their causes over long periods, but Hiratsuka did not remain at the forefront of the women's movement after the dissolution of the Association of New Women.[107]

Ichikawa and Katō were arrested for their activities regarding birth-control, women's suffrage and working women's reform.[108] Although Yamakawa and Yamanouchi escaped this, the police watched their movements closely. In spite of this, they were not discouraged and stuck to their socialist ideas. American suffragist leaders like Alice Paul and Lucy Burns were frequently jailed for militant activities.[109]

---

[103] *Ibid.*, pp. 41–4; personal interviews with Tsukizoe Akemi, 6–11 April, 1992, Tokyo; Tsukizoe Akemi, 'Waga haha', in Maruoka *et al.*, *Hiratsuka Raichō to Nihon no Kindai*, pp. 50–1; Tsukizoe, 'Haha, Hiratsuka Raichō no omoide', pp. 40–6.

[104] Yamanouchi, *Jiden*, pp. 84–6.

[105] Tsukizoe, 'Waga haha', pp. 50–1.

[106] Yamanouchi, *Jiden*, p. 93.

[107] Kobayashi, *Hito to Shisō*, p. 186.

[108] Ichikawa, *Jiden: Senzen Hen*, pp. 60–1; Katō, *Saiai no Hito Kanju e*, pp. 3–46.

[109] Tuttle, *Encyclopedia of Feminism*, pp. 52, 243–4; Bolt, *The Women's Movements*, p. 202.

British leaders such as Christabel, Emmeline and Sylvia Pankhurst were arrested and imprisoned more than a dozen times for conspiracy and incitement to violence.[110] One does not find such commitment from Hiratsuka.

In her pre-war feminist activities Hiratsuka lacked public charisma. She did not have great organisational ability or speech-making talent, and in these respects she differed from Ichikawa, or the Pankhursts, Millicent Fawcett and Josephine Butler in Britain.[111] Moreover, Hiratsuka's privileged upbringing, city-bred lifestyle, and refined manner and beauty, while helping her to lobby influential men, nevertheless worked against many of her activities as a feminist leader, arousing antipathy among some feminists from humbler backgrounds like Yamanouchi, or socialist feminists such as Yamakawa.[112] Such women described Hiratsuka as self-important and snobbish, a 'bourgeois feminist', who had little empathy with working-class women and their problems.[113]

There were thus defects in her leadership. Yamada Kakichi, who taught English to Hiratsuka and Ichikawa, was quick to notice this. He warned Ichikawa, and tried to dissuade Ichikawa from working with her when Hiratsuka established the Association of New Women: 'As Hiratsuka is a slipshod and capricious person, she is most unsuitable for organising women's political and social campaigns. It would be sensible to stay away from her.'[114] Ichikawa ignored the advice, but soon discovered its truth. It was to be one of the main reasons for her leaving the Association. Later, Ichikawa wrote that she had 'acted very wisely in quitting Hiratsuka's Association at that time',

---

[110] Emmeline and Sylvia went on hunger strike in prison and were forcibly fed. Their health suffered, but they continued to appear in public to give speeches even when physically debilitated and when re-arrest was threatened. See Mitchell, *The Fighting Pankhursts*, pp. 30–45, 96–101.

[111] Since her childhood, Hiratsuka suffered from a disorder of the vocal chords. She was notorious for having a very faint voice. This limited her speech-making. She frequently asked co-workers to read speeches on her behalf. See Kobayashi, *Hito to Shisō*, p. 212.

[112] Yamanouchi, *Jiden*, p. 84; Yamakawa Kikue, 'Hiratsuka Haruko-shi e: Shin Fujin Kyōkai ni kansuru shokan', *Fujin Kōron* (April, 1921), reprinted in Yamakawa Kikue (ed. by Suzuki Yūko), *Yamakawa Kikue Josei Kaihō Ronshū*, vol. 2 (1984), pp. 1–5.

[113] Yamanouchi, *Jiden*, pp. 88–93; Yamakawa, 'Shin Fujin Kyōkai to Sekirankai', pp. 10–7.

[114] Cited in Ichikawa, *Jiden: Senzen Hen*, p. 50.

and commented that if she had stayed it would have adversely affected her feminist development.[115]

Hiratsuka spotted promising young co-workers, like Oku and Ichikawa, but made little effort to encourage them as future leaders. She advocated collaboration among her fellow workers. However, she had difficulty in fulfilling this herself, tending to criticise or underestimate them, as in the Association of New Women.[116] This failing seems to have resulted from her strong and rather conceited personality. Her lack of collaborative skills stood in contrast to those of other feminist leaders.[117]

Although many women's historians who have written on Hiratsuka, especially Kobayashi Tomie, have tended to idolise her and describe her as an impeccable feminist leader, Hiratsuka was not in fact ideally suited as a leader of the pre-1945 women's movement. She could not rival Ichikawa, who was hardworking, patient, energetic, strong-willed, charismatic, and organisationally very adept. Ichikawa shared many qualities found in leading western feminists.[118] However, through

[115] *Ibid.*, p. 100.

[116] *Ibid.*, pp. 99–100; Hiratsuka Raichō, 'Shin Fujin Kyōkai no kaiko', *Fujin Kōron* (March–July, 1923), reprinted in Hiratsuka, *Hiratsuka Raichō Chosakushū*, vol. 3, pp. 270–323.

[117] For example, most of Susan Anthony's work for women's suffrage in America was achieved in cooperation with her friend, Elizabeth Cady Stanton. The achievements of the Congressional Union for Woman Suffrage owed much to the bond between Alice Paul and her friend Lucy Burns. Similarly, the success of the Women's Social and Political Union was a product of the working relationship between Emmeline Pankhurst and her daughter, Christabel. Nothing comparable to such unions characterized Hiratsuka's feminist activities. See Bolt, *The Women's Movements*, pp. 112–3, 202; Ryan, *Feminism and the Women's Movement*, pp. 20–8.

[118] Ichikawa believed that 'the women's movement would not be achieved in a day, and its good results will be brought by many years of assiduous effort and an accumulation of office work'. See Ichikawa, *87-sai no Seishun*. She was gifted with administrative ability, more so than other feminist leaders in Japan. For her, 'unity and a cooperative spirit will be the key to the success of the women's movement'. She showed much talent also in recruiting co-workers for suffrage campaigns, training them and making them work together. She had a strong sense of justice and responsibility, and was faithful to her associates, deriving much respect in return. In addition, Ichikawa possessed further traits not often found among feminist leaders. She had unique personal charm, and her background as a country-bred farmer's daughter, with a frugal lifestyle, seems to have rendered her approachable and trusted, even by working-class people, and gained her many supporters from diverse backgrounds. Her charitable help towards Yamanouchi Mina (accommodating and educating her when she lost her job) and for Yamataka Shigeri (when she became ill and faced a marital crisis) are two of many examples of this. Both in these personal and public regards, Ichikawa proved to be the most effective and striking

the post-1945 peace movement Hiratsuka overcame many limitations of her pre-war feminism, and formed international ties with many other women's organisations. She then showed more staying power, bringing together more effectively Japanese women from a wide range of backgrounds.

In spite of her limitations, one cannot overlook the role Hiratsuka played in the Japanese women's movement. She initiated many ideas and objectives, even though the woman who brought them to fruition was Ichikawa. Hiratsuka is rightly regarded as the main pioneer of the women's emancipation movement in Japan.[119] Without her inspiring literary ability, her vision and concerns, and her recognition of the possibilities in others, that movement would probably have developed more slowly. Hiratsuka's manifesto for *Seitō* made her the best known feminist in Japanese women's history. However, in broader Japanese history, her political activities through the Association of New Women had a far broader historical significance than her *Seitō* manifesto. The Association was the first nationwide women's organisation to conduct full-scale petitioning and lobbying campaigns in Japan, aiming to achieve women's political rights. It was also the first women's organisation to submit a women's suffrage petition to the Diet. It achieved the revision of Article 5, Clause 2 of the Peace Police Law, and gained women the right to organise and attend political assemblies. In part, its success was indebted to the more pluralistic atmosphere of so-called Taishō "democracy" and many changes in Japanese society at that time. Popular activism over this period included the rice riots in 1918 and many strikes by factory workers demanding better working conditions and higher wages. There were many campaigns for universal male suffrage from the 1890s. After the 1918 rice riots and the victory of the 'liberal' powers

---

feminist leader in Japan. Ichikawa Misao, *Ichikawa Fusae Omoide Banashi* (1992), pp. 185–203; Kodama, *Shinanoji no Deai*, pp. 202–5; Ichikawa Fusae to Iu Hito Kankōkai (ed.), *Ichikawa Fusae to Iu Hito*, pp. 11–5; 22–6; 182–5; 244–6; 'Fujin no teki to tatakai tsuzukete moetsukita Ichikawa-san', *Asahi Shinbun* (12 February, 1981); 'Ichikawa-san itami chikau', *Mainichi Shinbun* (12 February, 1981); 'Fujin undō ni ichi jidai kakusu', *Nihon Keizai Shinbun* (12 February, 1981); 'Seii to shinnen: onna no isshō', *Nihon Keizai Shinbun* (12 February, 1981); 'Reizen ni seiketsuna seiji o', *Mainichi Shinbun* (12 February, 1981); 'Sugasugashii toshi nokoshi: Ichikawa-san 87-sai hakkagetsu', *Yomiuri Shinbun* (12 February, 1981); 'Tachiba o koe sekibetsu no koe', *Asahi Shinbun* (12 February, 1981); personal interview with Nakamura Michiko, 20 May, 1992, Tokyo; personal interview with Nuita Hanako, 31 March, 1992, Tokyo.

[119] Kobayashi, *Hito to Shisō*, p. 4.

in the First World-War, public demonstrations demanding universal male suffrage, supported by the labour movement, were participated in by thousands of civilians. The political parties in the Diet, which were initially opposed to universal male suffrage, could no longer overlook it, and male suffrage for those over 25 years was finally achieved in 1925. The Association of New Women's political campaign for revision of Article 5 of the Peace Police Law took advantage of this political climate. The Association received much support from male Diet members, in particular those who had studied in western countries such as America and Britain, and who were impressed by well-educated western women with political knowledge. They came to accept the provision for Japanese women of basic political education and rights, so long as female rights were kept to a minimum so as not to threaten the family system. Police and government agencies, which were extremely ruthless towards socialists and suppressed their activities, were relatively tolerant towards middle or upper-middle class well-educated feminists, in particular towards Hiratsuka, who was well-connected and had access to influential men. There was hesitation to suppress her Association's lobbying and petitioning campaigns. The Association's magazine, the *Women's League*, was never banned, even though it was highly political and each issue gave accounts of the Association's political campaigns. Some sympathetic journalists were also supportive of the Association. In fact the changing policies of the Japanese state towards women remain an important and relatively neglected area of historical research.

The amendment of the Peace Police Law was the first legal change ever achieved by women for women in Japan—it had a significant impact on millions of women and gave them further self-confidence. Many took an increasing interest in politics and women's rights. Inspired by the Association of New Women, other women's organisations were founded. Women's issues became subjects of wide public interest and concern. Although the Association's suffrage campaigns were unsuccessful, they were taken over by the Fujin Sanseiken Kakutoku Kisei Dōmei (the League for the Attainment of Women's Suffrage), and laid a significant foundation for the women's suffrage movement. The Association also attracted Ichikawa and Oku, who became leading feminists, and were active as politicians after the Pacific War, working towards further improvement in women's status. Ichikawa was to play a key role in Japanese political history. In all this, one sees Hiratsuka's influence. Her literary style, Seitō, the

Association of New Women, and her choice of associates, were all to have a major impact, and they are her chief memorials.

Many of the women's questions Hiratsuka raised in the Taishō period continue to be of relevance today. Indeed they remain to be fully resolved. After 1945 legal reforms removed much social, political, educational and occupational discrimination against women, and many of the key causes feminists had campaigned for were partially or fully resolved. Women's status rose considerably in Japan. However, among the topics still to be solved is the protection of motherhood—how women can combine a job with child-rearing.[120] This issue has become the most significant and pressing for modern women, not least because the number of working mothers has greatly risen. The arguments Hiratsuka made on the protection of motherhood in the Taishō era have much relevance now. Many of her other views still raise controversial issues for women, in some cases proving relevant in very altered circumstances.

Later in her lifetime Hiratsuka's contributions were acknowledged publicly, and she received a commendation from Prime Minister Satō Eisaku for her service to women and for promoting their suffrage. This was made on 10 April, 1971, at a special ceremony to celebrate the 25th anniversary of women's acquisition of the vote, about a month before her death.[121] After Hiratsuka's death Japanese people gained deeper understanding of her importance in the women's movement, particularly through her four-volume autobiography and collected writings. She has since acquired considerable fame. The Japan Women's College alumni association, having erased Hiratsuka from its membership list immediately after the Shiobara Incident in 1908, restored her name to the list on 25 April 1992 in recognition of her distinguished service to the women's emancipation movement.[122] Today Hiratsuka is widely considered as the 'originator' of that movement in Japan, and she has a greater reputation than other contemporary feminists such as Ichikawa Fusae and Katō Shidzue, even though their feminist activities were longer-lived and perhaps

---

[120] Suzuki, *Joseishi o Hiraku*, vol. 1, pp. 45–6.

[121] She was critically ill and could not attend the ceremony. See 'Hiratsuka Raichō-san go shikyo', *Asahi Shinbun* (25 May, 1971).

[122] 'Hiratsuka Raichō, 'Fukken: Dōsōkai meibo ni hachijū yo-nen buri kisai', *Nihon Keizai Shinbun* (4 May, 1992); 'Hiratsuka Raichō no fujin undō minaosō: Hachijū yo-nen buri ni Fukken', *Mainichi Shinbun* (26 April, 1992).

more productive. She is also revered by some in Japan as a feminist icon. Yoneda Sayoko and Hiratsuka's daughter argue that this has been due to Kobayashi Tomie, whose writing did so much for Hiratsuka's reputation. This has certainly been important. But the key to her status has probably been her manifesto for *Seitō*, which became the virtual manifesto of the entire women's movement. At an opening conference to inaugurate the International Women's Decade, held in Mexico in June 1975, the chief Japanese delegate, the educationalist Fujita Taki, quoted Hiratsuka's words at the start of her speech:

> In ancient Japanese myth, the sun was the symbol of women. In the early twentieth century when Japan began to walk the way of a modern nation, the prominent activist of the women's emancipation movement, Hiratsuka Raichō, appealed to our Japanese women stating "In the beginning, woman was truly the sun. An authentic person. Now, woman is the moon. Living dependent on others, reflecting their brilliance . . . Now she must restore her concealed sun, reveal her hidden self and her own potential." Hiratsuka's phrase continues to inspire and encourage us even today.[123]

Making such a strong impression on Japanese women, her words thus survived time and space, having great appeal to young Japanese women now, giving them inspiration and reassurance.[124] In many people's eyes her manifesto has become inseparable from the history of the Japanese feminist movement, and is often seen as the spiritual source of Japanese feminism. Through her inspired writing, Hiratsuka Raichō's reputation has persisted well beyond her period. Taking on the quality of myth itself, her charismatic expression stands as a rare woman's voice from the past, a mark of her originality, her words having continued resonance.

---

[123] Cited in Kobayashi, *Hito to Shisō*, pp. 3–4.
[124] Maruoka, '*Seitō* kara Kokusai Fujin Nen e', pp. 5–6; Yoneda, 'Jidai o ikinuku', p. 63.

APPENDICES

BIOGRAPHICAL SKETCHES OF HIRATSUKA RAICHŌ'S CONTEMPORARY FEMINISTS AND FEMINIST WRITERS

1. *Fukuda (maiden name Kageyama) Hideko (1865–1927)*

Kageyama Hideko was born in Okayama as the second daughter of a low-ranking samurai of Bizen domain (in Okayama Prefecture). After the Meiji Restoration her father became a policeman, and her mother, who was well-educated, became a school teacher. At the age of fifteen, Hideko became an assistant teacher at a local elementary school, and at seventeen she founded a small private school for girls with her mother. Inspired by Kishida Toshiko's speech on women's rights in 1882, she participated in the Freedom and People's Rights Movement. After her school was closed down by the prefectural authorities, she went to Tokyo, and joined the Jiyūtō (Liberal Party).

In 1885 she was involved in the Osaka Incident (a military expedition to Korea plotted by liberal politicians who were active in the Freedom and People's Rights Movement), was arrested and sent to prison. Upon release in 1889, she lived with Ōi Kentarō (an active member of the Liberal Party who was also imprisoned for the Osaka Incident) and had an illegitimate son with him. She separated from Ōi, and ran a girls' vocational school in Tokyo in 1891, which she had to close down because of a series of deaths in the family. She then met Fukuda Yūsaku, who was a liberal thinker and had studied at the University of Michigan. She married Fukuda in 1892, and had two children with him. After her husband's death in 1900, she became acquainted with socialists such as Sakai Toshihiko and Kōtoku Shūsui, converted to socialism, and joined the Heiminsha (Commoners' Society). She helped launch the Christian socialist magazine, *Shin Kigen (New Era)*. She inaugurated the first socialist women's newspaper *Sekai Fujin (Women of the World)* in 1907 with the assistance of Ishikawa Sanshirō and Abe Isoo. In August 1909 *Sekai Fujin* was banned by the authorities. She also participated in the campaign for revision of Article Five of the Peace Police Law. She had lived with Ishikawa

Sanshirō between 1908 and 1913. In 1913 she published an article
'Fujin mondai no kaiketsu' ('The solution of women's issues') in *Seitō*.
In her later years she lived in poverty, and peddled kimono fabrics
to support herself and her children.

2. *Ichikawa Fusae (1893–1981)*

Ichikawa Fusae was born as the third daughter of Ichikawa Tōkurō
and Tatsu in Akechi Village, Onishi in Aichi Prefecture in 1893.
Although her father was an uneducated farmer, he valued education,
and encouraged his children to benefit even from higher education.
However, he was tyrannical towards his wife, who was illiterate, and
often beat her. Having regularly witnessed domestic violence at home,
Fusae determined to improve women's lot. At fourteen, she tried to
go to America, where her elder brother Tōkichi was studying, but
her application to travel there was rejected by the local police. After
she completed her elementary education, she went to Tokyo to study
at Joshi Gakuin (Women's Academy). She could not pay her tuition
fees there, and gave up her study after four months. She went home
and entered Aichi Girls' Higher School, which was a state-run training college for elementary school teachers. After her graduation she
became an elementary school teacher in her home town. She resigned
from her teaching job for reasons of ill health. She then went to
Nagoya and became the first female newspaper reporter for the
Nagoya Newspaper Company.

   In 1918 she returned to Tokyo, and worked as a stock broker's
office girl, a journalist and a private tutor. She also studied English
at a private school of Yamada Kakichi (husband of Yamada Waka)
who was a friend of her brother, Tōkichi. She first met Hiratsuka
Raichō there. In summer 1919 she went to Nagoya with Hiratsuka
to observe the harsh conditions of female factory textile workers.
Ichikawa was then appointed secretary of the women's division of
the Dainihon Rōdō Sōdōmei Yūaikai (Greater Japan Labour Federation Friendly Society). In October 1919 she left her job and founded
the Shin Fujin Kyōkai (Association of New Women) with Hiratsuka
in November 1919. In July 1921 she resigned from the Association
of New Women and went to America to study women's issues and
labour problems. She visited many women's groups and met Alice
Paul, the leader of the American women's suffrage movement. Paul

recommended Ichikawa to work for female suffrage. In January 1924 she returned to Japan, and began to work for the Tokyo branch of the International Labour Organisation. In December 1924 she also helped establish the Fujin Sanseiken Kakutoku Kisei Dōmei (League for the Attainment of Women's Suffrage) and launched its journal, *Fusen* (*Women's Suffrage*). She became the leader of the women's suffrage movement before the war, and campaigned for other women's political rights. Although Ichikawa was critical of the war, she co-operated with the military government and became a member of a few government-sponsored women's organisations, such as Dainihon Fujinkai (the Greater Japan Women's Association), Taisei Yokusankai (the Imperial Rule Assistance Association) and Dainihon Genron Hōkokukai (Great Japan Patriotic Speech Association).

In November 1945 she founded the Shin Nihon Fujin Dōmei (New Japan Women's League), whose main objectives were to improve women's political education and alter laws disadvantageous to women. In March 1947 she was purged from public office by a G.H.Q. directive on the grounds that she had been a member of the Dainihon Genron Hōkokukai (Great Japan Patriotic Speech Association) during the war. In October 1950 this ban was lifted, and she became the chairwoman of the Nihon Fujin Yūkensha Dōmei (League of Japanese Women Voters), which was earlier called the Shin Nihon Fujin Dōmei. In April 1953 she won her first election and became a member of the House of Councillors. She was elected five times. In 1971 she lost her bid for re-election, but with the strong support of women's groups she made a dramatic comeback in 1974 to regain a Diet seat. When re-elected in the general election of June 1980, she collected about 2.8 million votes, the highest among the 50 successful candidates in the national constituency. She remained single throughout her life, and adopted a daughter, Misao. She died of heart failure on 11 February 1981 at the age of 87.

3. Itō Noe (1895–1923)

Itō Noe was born in Fukuoka Prefecture as the eldest daughter of Itō Kamekichi and Ume. Her father failed in his business of processed farm products, and became a tile maker. After Noe finished her elementary school, she went to Tokyo, turning to her uncle for financial help to enable her to continue her education in Tokyo. She was admitted to the fourth year of Ueno Girls' High School in Tokyo in 1911. During her summer vacation in 1911, she was forced into an arranged marriage with Suematsu Fukutarō in her home town. Even after her marriage she was allowed to return to the same high school in Tokyo to complete her education. She was the most distinguished student in 1912. Just before her graduation she began an affair with an English teacher at her school, Tsuji Jun, and began to live with him. Noe asked her husband for a divorce, which was not given easily. Tsuji lost his job as a result.

In October 1912 she became a member of the Seitō Society, and regularly contributed to *Seitō*. Itō took over from Hiratsuka in January 1915 as its editor. She had strong socialist sympathies, but then developed an intimate relationship with Ōsugi Sakae, the anarchist leader. Under Ōsugi's influence she was converted to anarchism. She deserted her second husband, Tsuji Jun and her two children, and began to live with Ōsugi, who was married, and who also had a lover, Kamichika Ichiko. *Seitō* came to an end when she left Tsuji's house. Kamichika stabbed Ōsugi in February 1917, and this was termed the Hikage Teahouse Incident. He survived and Itō had five daughters with Ōsugi. When the first socialist women's organisation Sekirankai (Red Wave Society) was founded in 1922, she became a member. On 16 September 1923, in the aftermath of the Great Kantō Earthquake, Itō, Ōsugi and Ōsugi's nephew were arrested and killed by military police. This incident was known as the Amakasu Incident (after the police captain responsible).

4. *Kamichika Ichiko (1888–1981)*

Kamichika Ichiko was born as the third daughter of Kamichika Yōsai and Hana in Nagasaki Prefecture. Her father was a doctor of Chinese medicine. As both her father and her eldest brother died when she was three years old, her family became impoverished. Benefitting from her relatives' financial assistance, she went to Nagasaki Kassui Girls' High School, and then proceeded to the Joshi Eigaku Juku (Women's Institute of English Studies). While she was a student at Joshi Eigaku Juku, she became a member of the Seitō Society in August 1912, and wrote some articles for *Seitō* under her pen name, Sakaki Ō. However, the secret of her association with the Seitō Society emerged. As Joshi Eigaku Juku strongly disapproved of her membership of the Seitō Society, she was not allowed to graduate, and was sent to a girls' high school in Aomori Prefecture as a punishment. When that school discovered that she had been a member of the Seitō Society, she was dismissed from her teaching post.

She returned to Tokyo, and joined the Tokyo Nichi Nichi Newspaper Company (now the Mainichi Newspaper Company). She became a very successful female newspaper reporter. She also launched a women's literary magazine called *Safuran (Saffron)* with Otake Kōkichi. She began to develop her interest in socialism, and became acquainted with the anarchist leader, Ōsugi Sakae, with whom she became romantically involved. She gave financial assistance to him, and supported his anarchist movement.

In November 1917 she precipitated a scandal which was known as the Hikage Teahouse Incident. She stabbed Ōsugi at an inn called 'Hikage Teahouse' in Hayama in Kanagawa Prefecture, because he had begun to live with Itō Noe. Ōsugi was seriously injured, and she was sentenced to two years in prison. After her release, she made a living as a translator. In 1921 she married Suzuki Atsushi and had three children with him. She also continued her writing career, and contributed to a left-wing monthly literary magazine called *Tane Maku Hito (The Sowers)*, and participated in a proletarian literary movement. In 1928 she helped inaugurate Hasegawa Shigure's *Nyonin Geijutsu (Women's Arts)*. In 1929 she divorced her husband, and brought up her children on her own, supporting herself as a translator. After the war in 1947 she helped found the Minshu Fujin Kyōkai (Democratic Women's Association) and Jiyū Jinken Kyōkai (Association of Freedom and Human Rights). She became director of these two associations and was engaged in other issues of women's emancipation and the protection of fundamental human rights. In 1953 she was elected a member of the House of Representatives. She was elected four times, and served in the House of Representatives as a Japan Socialist Party member. She campaigned for human rights, women's rights and against prostitution. She retired from political life in 1969.

5. *Katō Shidzue (1897–2001) (her maiden name was Hirota and her first husband's surname was Ishimoto)*

Katō Shidzue was born as the eldest daughter of Hirota Ritarō (a former samurai who graduated from the Tokyo Imperial University and was a wealthy engineer) and Toshiko (who also came from a

noble and educated family). She was brought up in a privileged environment. After graduating from the Joshi Gakushūin (Peeresses'
School) in 1914, she married Baron Ishimoto Keikichi (who was a
graduate from the Tokyo Imperial University) by arranged marriage
at the age of seventeen. As her husband was the eldest son, she
experienced heavy pressure within the *ie* system. While living in Miike
in Kyūshū, where her husband worked for the Mitsui coal mines as
its engineer, she witnessed female coal miners working underground
in coal mines for twelve hours a day and saw the poverty, illness
and death that resulted from hard labour, harsh working conditions
and unwanted pregnancies. She greatly sympathised with such women.

Accompanying her husband to America in 1919, she studied English
and registered for a secretarial course at the Ballard School of the
Y.W.C.A. in New York. During her stay in America, she met Margaret
Sanger, the birth control pioneer. Shidzue was greatly inspired by
Sanger's saying 'No woman can call herself free who does not own
and control her body', and this became the driving force of her later
activities as a birth control campaigner in Japan. She returned to
Japan in 1920. When Sanger visited Japan in 1922, Shidzue acted
as her interpreter. In 1931 she established the Nihon Sanji Seigen
Renmei (Japan Birth Control League) and became its chairwoman.
After her husband left her to go to Manchuria, she supported herself and her two sons. In 1932 she toured and lectured in America
to earn money for her children's education. In 1934 she opened her
birth control guidance clinic in Shinagawa, Tokyo. She published
her English language autobiography *Facing Two Ways* in America in
1935, because of the strong recommendation of the American women's
historian, Mary Beard, whom Shidzue had met in 1922 when Mary
visited Japan with her husband, Austin Beard. Mary also recommended Shidzue to write a section on Japanese women's history for
the *Encyclopaedia of Women's History Throughout the World*, which was
the Austrian philosopher Mrs. Ashkenazy's international scheme.
Mary Beard had a considerable influence on the development of
Shidzue's feminism.

As her birth control activities were then considered dangerous, she
was arrested and imprisoned in 1937. Her clinic was closed down
in January 1938. In March 1944 she divorced her husband, and
married the labour leader, Katō Kanju, in 1944. In 1945 she gave
birth to a daughter at the age of forty-eight. In the first postwar

election in 1946 both Shidzue and Kanju were elected to the House of Representatives. In 1954 she founded the Nihon Kazoku Keikaku Renmei (Family Planning Federation of Japan). She was elected six times (twice to the House of Representatives and four times to the House of Councillors). She served as a Japan Socialist Party member, campaigning for women's rights and health. She retired from politics in 1974. She received the United Nations Population Award in 1988.

6. *Nishikawa Fumiko (1882–1960) (her maiden name was Shichi and her first husband's surname was Matsuoka)*

Nishikawa Fumiko was born as the second daughter of Shichi Izaemon and Ai in Gifu Prefecture. Her father was a village headman. After she finished elementary school in her home town, she went to Kyoto to study at Kyoto Prefectural Girls' High School, from which she graduated in 1902. She became acquainted with a poet, Matsuoka Kōson, and married him in November 1902. When he entered Tokyo Senmon Gakkō (now Waseda University), they moved to Tokyo. She became a member of the Shakai Shugi Kyōkai (Socialist Association), which was established in 1900 with Abe Isoo as its chairman. After her husband's death in 1904, she entered the Heiminsha (Commoners' Society) in her late husband's footsteps. She participated in the early campaign for revision of Article Five of the Chian Keisatsu Hō (Peace Police Law), which was organised by female members of the Commoners' Society. In 1905 she married Nishikawa Mitsujirō (1876–1940), who was also a member of the Commoners' Society. In 1908 he was sentenced to two years imprisonment. After he was released in 1910, he withdrew from the socialist movement altogether, and devoted the rest of his life to moral self-cultivation and study of the Chinese sages.

In 1913 Fumiko established the Shin Shin Fujinkai (Real New Women's Association), and launched its journal the *Shin Shin Fujin* (*Real New Women*), which came to an end in September 1923. She worked in the cause of a more realistic and popular women's emancipation movement, and for temperance. In 1924 she established the Fujin Sansei Dōmei (League for Women's Political Rights). After the war she turned to full-time writing.

7. *Oku (maiden name Wada) Mumeo (1895–1997)*

Oku Mumeo was born as the eldest daughter of Wada Jinzaburō and Hama in Fukui Prefecture. Her father was a blacksmith. As her mother endured poor health, she had to look after her four younger sisters and did all the housework. When she was fifteen her mother died, and her father remarried. After she graduated from Fukui Kenritsu Kōtō Jogakkō (Fukui Prefectural Girls' High School) in 1912, she entered the Japan Women's College.

After her graduation, she showed much interest in current social problems, and became a journalist for *Rōdō Sekai* (*Labour World*). She concealed her identity and began to work for a spinning factory to find out about the real working conditions of female textile workers. However, her identity was revealed, and she was dismissed. In 1919 she married Oku Eiichi. In January 1920 she joined the Association of New Women, and took charge after Ichikawa Fusae and Hiratsuka Raichō withdrew from it.

After the dissolution of the Association of New Women in December 1922, she established the Shokugyō Fujinsha (the Working Women's Society) in 1923 and launched its journal *Shokugyō Fujin* (*Working Women*), which later changed its name to *Fujin Undō* (*Women's Movement*). She also established settlements, child-care centres, and facilities designed for working women.

After the war she was elected to the House of Councillors in 1947. She was elected for three terms. In 1948 she founded the consumer group Shufu Rengōkai (Japan Housewives' Association) known by its abbreviation, Shufuren, which developed into a nationwide organisation.

8. *Tajima Hide (1901–1976)*

Tajima Hide was born in Aichi Prefecture as the daughter of a school teacher. After she graduated from Seiryū Girls' High School in Nagoya, she went to Tokyo. In 1920 she entered the Japan Women's College, but gave up her study there after the first term. In summer 1920 she became secretary of the Association of New Women under the recommendation of Ichikawa Fusae who was from the same province as Tajima. In 1921 she became acquainted with Yamakawa Kikue who was then a member of the Red Wave Society. From 1922 she attended the Suiyōkai (Wednesday Society) led by

Yamakawa Hitoshi. In 1924 she became secretary of the Fujin Sanseiken Kakutoku Kisei Dōmei (The League for the Attainment of Women's Suffrage). In 1926 she established the Fujin Rōdō Chōsajo (Working Women's Research Bureau) and also launched a journal, *Mirai (Future)*.

She became a chief secretary of the Kantō Fujin Dōmei (Kantō Women's League) in 1927 and was very active in the labour movement. She also became involved in Communist activities. The government ruthlessly suppressed communists, and in 1929 she was arrested and held in detention for two months. In 1934 she opened a home for orphans called 'Kodomo no ie' ('Children's house') in Tokyo. It was closed down because of pressure from the authorities.

Immediately after the war, she joined the Communist Party and was returned to the House of Representatives for a constituency in Aichi Prefecture in the first post-war election. She played an active part in the House of Representatives for about three years, before leaving the party and her job.

9. *Yamada (maiden name Asaba) Waka (1879–1957)*

Yamada Waka was the second daughter of a farming family, Asaba Yaheiji and Mie in Kurihama, Kanagawa Prefecture. After she finished her elementary school, she married Araki Hichijirō at the age of sixteen. Her family went bankrupt, and her husband, who was wealthy but mean, gave no financial help to them. Therefore she left him and sought work in Yokohama. In 1896 she decided to go to America seeking employment there and hoping to restore her family fortunes. However through deception she fell into the hands of a procuress, and was forced to work as a prostitute in Seattle, Washington from around 1897 to 1903. She was then known as Arabian Oyae. She escaped from the Seattle brothel with the help of a newspaper journalist, Tachii Nobusaburō, and took refuge in a Presbyterian mission house called Cameron House (a rehabilitation centre for former prostitutes) in San Francisco. She began to study at Yamada English School run by Yamada Kakichi, whom she married around in 1905.

In 1906 they returned to Japan and settled down in Yotsuya, Tokyo. Kakichi opened a small language school and taught foreign languages. His students included Ōsugi Sakae, Hiratsuka Raichō and

Ichikawa Fusae. He also educated his wife and encouraged her to contribute to *Seitō*. Her essays and translations appeared in *Seitō*. She also participated in the controversy over 'the protection of motherhood'. She launched her journal *Fujin to Shinshakai* (*Women and the New Society*) in 1920. She became a columnist of 'Advice to Women' for *Tokyo Asahi Shinbun* in 1931, and became widely known as an 'agony aunt' for troubled women.

After her husband's death in 1934, she was appointed as the first chairwoman of the Bosei Hogo Hō Seitei Sokushin Fujin Renmei (Alliance for the Promotion of a Mother and Child Protection Act), whose name was shortened to Bosei Hogo Renmei (Motherhood Protection Alliance) in 1935. The Diet agreed on a bill for financial support to poverty-stricken mothers with small children, and enacted the Boshi Hogo Hō (Motherhood Protection Law) in March 1937. In 1937 she toured and lectured in America. In 1939 she established a house for mothers and children and a nursery school in Shibuya, Tokyo. These were named the Hatagaya House for Mothers and Children and the Hatagaya Nursery School. In 1947 she established a retraining centre called Hatagaya Joshi Gakuen (Hatagaya Girls' School), and devoted her energies to the rehabilitation of former prostitutes.

10. *Yamakawa (maiden name Morita, but later took her mother's surname Aoyama) Kikue (1890–1980)*

Yamakawa Kikue was born as the second daughter of Morita Ryūnosuke and Chise. Her father studied French at Yokohama Foreign Language School, and was a government official. Her mother was a daughter of a Confucian scholar retained by the Mito Domain. Her mother was one of the first students who graduated from the Girls' Higher School in Tokyo. Kikue went to the Furitsu Daini Kōtō Jogakkō (Tokyo Prefectural Second Girls' High School). While she was a student there, she took her mother's maiden name, Aoyama. She attended the Keishū Literary Society, and first met Hiratsuka Raichō there. In 1908 she entered Joshi Eigaku Juku (Women's Institute of English Studies). Even from that early date she expressed her strong wishes to aid women's emancipation. She contributed some articles to *Seitō*.

After she graduated from the Women's Institute of English Studies in 1912, she attended lecture meetings organised by socialists, and began to show much interest in socialism. She came into contact with the members of the Heiminsha (Commoners' Society), and met the socialist Yamakawa Hitoshi at one of the Commoners' Society's meetings. In 1917 she married him, and began to study Marxism in earnest. In 1919 she participated in the controversy over 'the protection of motherhood', and first expressed her socialist feminist views in her writing. She established herself as a feminist theorist of socialism in a Japanese context. In 1922 she helped found the first women's socialist organisation, the Sekirankai (Red Wave Society) with Sakai Magara and Itō Noe. However, because of the government's suppression of socialist activities, the Red Wave Society was too short-lived to build a mass base among proletarian women or to launch a popular movement. Yamakawa Kikue also helped her husband edit the socialist journal *Rōnō* (*Labour-Farmer*).

The government's suppression of socialists intensified in the 1930s, and Hitoshi was arrested in 1937, and sent to prison for two years. Kikue went to the countryside in Kanagawa Prefecture, growing food to support herself and her son. After the war she and her husband joined the Japan Socialist Party. She was appointed as the first director of the Labour Ministry's Fujin Shōnen Kyoku (Women's and Minors' Bureau) in Katayama Tetsu's Cabinet in 1947. She left office in 1951.

11. *Yamanouchi Mina (1900–)*

Yamanouchi Mina was born in Miyagi Prefecture as a farmer's daughter. After she completed her elementary education in 1913, she went to Tokyo with her divorced aunt to work for Tokyo Mosurin Factory as a textile worker, at the age of twelve. She endured twelve-hour shifts, bad diet and poor living conditions. She participated in a trade union, and became a representative of the women's division of the Yūaikai Rōdō Sōdōmei (General Federation of Labour-Friendly Societies). In 1919 she was sacked by the Tokyo Mosurin Factory, and began to reside with Ichikawa Fusae. She started to go to school. She also became a member of the Association of New Women and assisted Ichikawa. While she worked for the Japan Tobacco and Salt Public Corporation in Shiba, Tokyo, during a school holiday, workers there went on strike. She wrote articles on this for the *Women's*

League, under the penname of Minato Hama. In early 1921 she left the Association of New Women and went back to the trade union movement.

She stayed with Yamakawa Hitoshi and Kikue for a while to study socialism, and became acquainted with many socialists. Following the recommendation of Shimonaka Yasaburō (the founder of the publishing house Heibonsha), she assisted the publication of *Rōdō Shūhō* (*Labour Weekly Paper*). In 1927 she helped establish the Kantō Fujin Dōmei (Kantō Women's League), which was aligned with the communist-influenced *Rōnōtō* (Labour-Farmer Party), and she campaigned for women's suffrage and an improvement in women's working conditions. She married Tachibana Shōichi and had two children with him. After her marriage, she withdrew from the forefront of trade union life. She learned dressmaking, and opened a dressmaking shop in Osaka.

Her shop was burnt down in an air raid in Osaka during World War II, and she and her family were evacuated to her home town in Miyagi Prefecture. In the first post-war election in April 1946 she stood unsuccessfully as a candidate for the House of Representatives, having the endorsement of the Communist Party. After she divorced her husband (who had an affair with her niece), she went to Tokyo to open a dressmaking shop in Ogikubo. In 1954 she started signature-collecting campaigns against atomic and hydrogen bombs, and was active in the peace movement.

12. *Yosano (maiden name was Hō) Akiko (1878–1942)*

Yosano Akiko was born as the third daughter of Hō Sōshichi and Tsune. Her house was a long-established confectionery shop in Sakai, Osaka Prefecture. She was brought up strictly, and had to help her family business. In 1891 she graduated from Sakai Girls' High School. At home she studied Japanese classics by herself, and joined a local poetry group. She began to contribute her *tanka* poems to *Myōjō* (*Morning Star*), which was an influential literary journal launched by Yosano Tekkan in 1900. In August 1900 she first met him when he gave a lecture in Osaka, and their relationship grew. In the following year she ran away from home, went to Tokyo and in spite of her family's strong opposition married Tekkan, who had earlier divorced his first wife. In the same year she published her first collection of poems, entitled *Midaregami* (*Tangled Hair*)—these were characterised by overflowing passion, vivid imagination, originality and sensuality. Her work was enthusiastically received, and she gained literary fame, being seen as the queen of *tanka* poets. During the Russo-Japanese War she published an anti-war poem entitled 'Kimi shinitamou koto nakare' ('My little brother, you must not die'). In 1907 she taught *tanka* poetry and *Genji Monogatari* (*The Tale of Genji*) in the Keishū Literary Society. She also began to translate *The Tale of Genji* into modern Japanese.

She managed to raise money for her husband, who became inactive in his writing after the discontinuance of *Myōjō*, and sent him to Europe in 1911. She became an advisory member of the Seitō Society and contributed to *Seitō* upon its inauguration in 1911. In 1912 she went to Paris to join her husband, and made a tour of Europe for four months. After she returned from Europe, she was active as a critic, and wrote on education and women's issues. In 1919 she participated in the controversy over 'the protection of motherhood'. She also published commentaries on classical and modern Japanese literature. In 1921 she co-founded the co-educational school Bunka Gakuin (Cultural Academy), which emphasised 'freedom or individualised education', and became its dean and lecturer. She bore and raised eleven children in spite of endless financial struggles, and earned her living through writing.

CHRONOLOGY OF SOCIAL AND WOMEN'S MOVEMENTS IN THE MEIJI AND TAISHŌ PERIODS
明治・大正期の婦人政策と社会の動き

1871: On 22 May the Household Registration Law was promulgated. On 29 August the Imperial Rescript Abolishing the Fiefs and Establishing Prefectures was issued.
On 23 December five girls including Tsuda Umeko left Japan for America to study there, together with the Iwakura Mission.
5月22日　戸籍法公布。
8月29日　廃藩置県。
12月23日　5名の少女（津田梅子他）岩倉特命全権大使一行と共に米国留学へ出発。

1872: The Fundamental Education Law was proclaimed on 5 September.
The State-owned Tomioka Silk Mill began to operate in November.
9月5日　学制発布。
11月　　官立模範工場富岡製糸場開業。

1873: In January the Meirokusha (the Meiji Six Society) was founded. On 15 May a wife became able to bring a suit for divorce for the first time.
1月　　明六社設立。
5月15日　妻からの離婚訴訟を許す。

1874: The Freedom and People's Rights Movement started.
1月　　自由民権運動始まる。

1875: On 6 February when he married, Mori Arinori signed a written agreement in which equality between husband and wife was mentioned.
2月6日　森有札、約定書交換の結婚を実践。

1876:   Doi Kōka published a book *Bunmeiron Onna Daigaku* (*Civilized
        Comments on the Greater Learning for Women*) in which he criticised
        Onna Daigaku (*The Greater Learning for Women*).
        土井光華『文明論女大学』刊行、『女大学』を批判。

1878:   On 16 September Kusunose Kita, who lived in Kōchi,
        demanded female household heads' right to vote for mem-
        bers of the ward assembly.
        9月16日　高知の楠瀬喜多、女戸主として区会議員の選挙権要求。

1882:   On 1 April Kishida Toshiko made a speech at a political
        meeting held in Osaka, organised by the Rikken Political
        Party.
        4月1日　岸田俊子、大阪の立憲政党演説会で演説。

1883:   On 28 November the Rokumeikan (Deer Cry Pavilion) was
        opened in Kōjimachi, Tokyo.
        11月28日　東京麹町に鹿鳴館開館。

1884:   In September Ogino Ginko became the first female medical
        doctor.
        9月　荻野吟子最初の女医となる。

1885:   On 20 July Iwamoto Zenji and others launched *Jogaku Zasshi*
        (*Women's Educational Magazine*).
        7月20日　巖本善治ら『女学雑誌』創刊。

1886:   On 12 June the first women's strike was carried out by female
        factory workers at Amemiya Silk Mill in Kōfu, Yamanashi
        Prefecture.
        On 6 December Yajima Kajiko and others established the
        Tokyo Fujin Kyōfūkai (Tokyo Women's Christian Temperance
        Union).
        6月12日　甲府雨宮製糸工場女工、日本最初のストライキ、これが甲
        府各地に波及。
        12月6日　矢島揖子ら、東京婦人矯風会設立。

1889:   On 11 February the Imperial Japanese Constitution (known
        as the Meiji Constitution) was promulgated.

On 28 September Ueki Emori published 'Tōyō no fujo' ('The oriental woman').

2月11日　大日本帝国憲法発布。

9月28日　植木枝盛「東洋之婦女」発表。

1890: On 1 July the first election to choose members of the House of Representatives took place.

On 25 July the Assembly and Political Organisation Law was promulgated. Women were banned from political activities as a result.

On 30 October The Imperial Rescript on Education was proclaimed.

The First Session of the Diet was convened.

7月1日　第一回衆議院議員選挙。

7月25日　集会及政社法公布、女子の政治活動禁止。

10月30日　教育勅語。

第1回帝国議会召集される。

1893: On 3 April the Japan Women's Christian Temperance Union was formed.

4月3日　日本基督教婦人矯風会結成。

1897: From 21 February onwards the members of the Japan Women's Christian Temperance Union including Yajima Kajiko submitted petitions to the Houses of Representatives and Peers requesting the enactment of a new law banning both male and female adultery.

2月21日から矯風会矢島揖子ら、男子姦通罪制定の請願を貴衆両院へ提出。

1898: On 21 June the two books of the Civil Code (the book of relatives and the book of inheritance) were promulgated. These books prescribed women's subordinate position.

6月21日　民法親族編、相続編公布（女子の隷属的位置を規定）。

1899: In April Fukuzawa Yukichi's articles on women's issues including 'Onna Daigaku hyōron' ('Criticism against The Greater Learning for Women'), and 'Shin Onna Daigaku', (The new Greater Learning for Women') appeared serially in Jiji Shinpō.

4月　福沢諭吉「女大学評論」「新女大学」を『時事新報』に連載。

1900: On 10 March the Peace Police Law was enacted, the provisions of which included a ban on political activity by women, and the right of the police to forbid, or disband political meetings.

3月10日　治安警察法により女子の集会結社禁止。

1901: Okumura Ioko formed the Aikoku Fujinkai (Patriotic Women's Association).

奥村五百子、愛国婦人会創立。

1903: On 2 April Sakai Toshihiko launched *Katei Zasshi* (*Family Magazine*).
On 15 November a socialist organisation called the *Heiminsha* (The Commoners' Society) was founded. The Society published *Heimin Shinbun* (*Commoners' Newspaper*).

4月2日　堺利彦『家庭雑誌』創刊。
11月15日　平民社設立、『平民新聞』刊。

1904: On 10 February the Russo-Japanese War began.
In September Yosano Akiko published 'Kimi shinitamou kotonakare' ('My brother, you must not die') in *Myōjō* (*Morning Star*).

2月10日　日露戦争起こる。
9月　　与謝野晶子「君死にたまふことなかれ」を『明星』に発表。

1905: On 17 October the Japan Young Women's Christian Association was founded.

10月17日　日本キリスト教女子青年会（日本ＹＷＣＡ）創設。

1907: On 1 January Fukuda Hideko launched *Sekai Fujin* (*Women of the World*).

1月1日　福田英子『世界婦人』創刊。

1908: On 20 January Hani Motoko inaugurated *Fujin no Tomo* (*Women's Companion*).

1月20日　羽仁もと子『婦人之友』発行。

1910: Kanno Suga and Kōtoku Shūsui were arrested in the 1910 High Treason Incident and executed in January 1911.

管野須賀、幸徳事件の嫌疑（11年死刑）。

1911:   On 29 March the Factory Law was promulgated.
        On 1 September *Seitō* was inaugurated.
        3月29日　　工場法公布。
        9月1日　　　『青鞜』創刊。

1912:   On 30 July the Emperor Meiji died and the name of the
        era was changed to Taishō.
        7月30日　　明治天皇死去、大正と改元。

1913:   Nishikawa Fumiko founded the Shin Shin Fujinkai (Real New
        Women's Association).
        西川文子ら新真婦人会結成。

1914:   On 1 April the *Yomiuri Shinbun* established a women's supple-
        ment. From May it also published a personal advice column.
        On 28 July the First World War began.
        4月1日　　　『読売新聞』婦人付録新設、5月から身上相談掲載。
        7月28日　　第一次世界大戦起こる。

1916:   On 1 January *Fujin Kōron* (*Women's Review*) was launched.
        In January Yoshino Sakuzō advocated *minpon shugi* (people
        as the base-ism).
        Taishō democracy commenced.
        In June the Yūaikai's women's division was formed.
        In August *Yūai Fujin* (*Yūai Woman*) was inaugurated.
        1月1日　　　『婦人公論』創刊。
        1月　　　　吉野作造、民本主義提唱、大正デモクラシー運動。
        6月　　　　友愛会婦人部新設。
        8月　　　　『友愛婦人』創刊。

1917:   In March *Shufu no Tomo* (*The Housewives' Companion*) was
        launched.
        3月　　　　『主婦之友』創刊。

1918:   On 3 August Rice Riots broke out among fishermen's wives
        in Toyama Prefecture.
        From September Yosano Akiko, Hiratsuka Raichō, Yamakawa
        Kikue and Yamada Waka were engaged in the controversy
        over 'the protection of motherhood'.
        8月3日　　　富山県漁民女房米騒動。

9月以降、 与謝野晶子、平塚らいてう、山川菊栄、山田わかの母性保
護論争。

1920: On 28 March the Association of New Women's foundation
       ceremony was held.
       Mass celebration of May Day first took place in Tokyo on
       2 May.
       3月28日   新婦人協会の発会式挙行。
       5月2日   最初のメーデー。

1921: The Sekirankai (Red Wave Society) was formed on 24 April.
       4月24日   赤瀾会結成。

1922: On 20 April the amended Peace Police Law was promulgated.
       4月20日   治警法五条改正公布。

1923: On 20 April Oku Mumeo set up the Working Women's
       Society.
       On 1 September the Great Kantō Earthquake occurred.
       4月20日   奥むめお、職業婦人社設立。
       9月1日   関東大震災。

1924: On 13 December the Fujin Sanseiken Kakutoku Kisei Dōmei
       (League for the Attainment of Women's Suffrage) was formed.
       (In April 1925 its name was changed to the Fusen Kakutoku
       Dōmei (Women's Suffrage League).
       12月13日   婦人参政権獲得期成同盟会結成（1925年4月、婦選獲得同
       盟と改称）。

1925: In March, universal suffrage for men was established.
       On 22 April the Peace Preservation Law was promulgated.
       普通選挙法成立。
       4月22日   治安維持法公布。

HIRATSUKA RAICHŌ'S FAMILY TREE

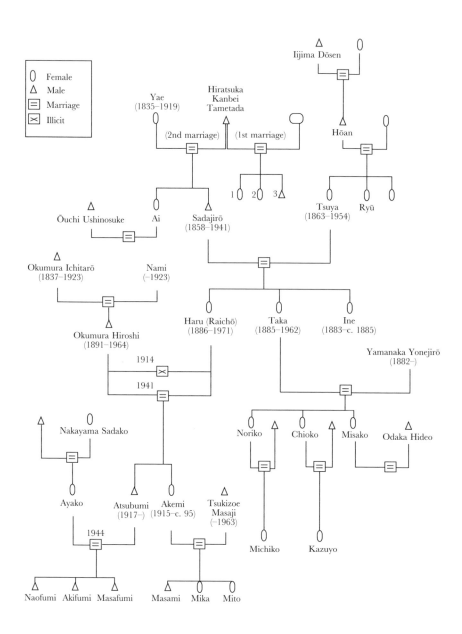

CHRONOLOGY OF HIRATSUKA RAICHŌ
平塚らいてう略年譜と関連事項

1886:   Hiratsuka Raichō (her real name was Haru) was born as the third daughter of Hiratsuka Sadajirō and his wife Tsuya, in Kōjimachi, Tokyo on 10 February.

明治 19 年：   2 月 10 日、東京麹町で、父定二郎、母光沢の三女として生まれる。本名は明。

1889:   The Imperial Japanese Constitution, known as the Meiji Constitution, was promulgated in February 1889 and became operative in November 1890.

明治 22 年：   大日本帝国憲法発布。

1890:   Raichō entered Fujimi Kindergarten.
The Assembly and Political Organisation Law was promulgated.
The Imperial Rescript on Education was proclaimed.

明治 23 年：   富士見幼稚園入学。
集会及政社法公布。
教育勅語発布。

1892:   Raichō entered Fujimi Elementary School.
明治 25 年：   富士見小学校入学。

1894:   Her family moved into a new house at 3, Akebono-chō. She changed her school to Seino Elementary School. The Sino-Japanese War broke out.

明治 27 年：   曙町 13 番地に移転。誠之小学校に転校。
日清戦争 (〜95)。

1898:   Raichō entered the Girls' High School attached to Tokyo Girls' Higher School, commonly known as Ochanomizu Girls' High School.

明治 31 年：   東京女子高等師範学校付属高等女学校（通称お茶の水高女）入学。

1900:   She rebelled against the educational system at Ochano-
               mizu Girls' High School, which focused on creating a
               good wife and wise mother, and then formed the 'Pirate
               Gang' with her classmates.
               The Peace Police Law was enacted.

明治 33 年 :   お茶の水高女の良妻賢母主義教育に反発し、級友と「海賊組」を創る。
               治安警察法公布。

1903:   Raichō graduated from the Girls' High School.
               She entered the Department of Domestic Science, Japan
               Women's College.

明治 36 年 :   東京女子高等師範学校付属高等女学校卒業。
               日本女子大学校家政科に入学。

1904:   She entered the College dormitory.
               The Russo-Japanese War began.

明治 37 年 :   大学寮生活に入る。
               日露戦争 (〜05)。

1906:   In March Raichō graduated from the College, and then
               took English courses at Tsuda Umeko's Women's Institute
               of English Studies. She also studied Chinese classics at
               Nishō Gakusha.

明治 39 年 :   3 月、日本女子大学校卒業。
               その後、女子英学塾、二松学舎に通い、英語、漢文を学ぶ。

1907:   In January she changed her English school to Seibi
               Women's English School. In May the Keishū Literary
               Society was formed through the good offices of Ikuta
               Chōkō. Hiratsuka Raichō contributed a short story, 'Ai
               no matsujitsu' ('The last day of love') to the magazine,
               for circulation among the Society's members.

明治 40 年 :   1 月、成美女子英語学校に転ずる。
               5 月、成美女子英語学校に生田長江のきもいりで、閨秀文学会が生まれ
               る。
               回覧雑誌に小説「愛の末日」を書く。

1908:   In January she received a letter commenting on 'The
               last day of love' from Morita Sōhei. She then devel-
               oped close relations with him.

In March she attempted a double suicide (the so-called Shiobara Incident) with Morita Sōhei.
In September she went to Shinshū (Nagano Prefecture).

明治 41 年： 1月、森田草平から「愛の末日」の批評の手紙をもらい、草平との交際深まる。
3月、森田草平と心中未遂事件（塩原事件）を起こす。
9月、信州に行く。

1909: She entered Seisoku English Language School.
明治 42 年： 正則英語学校入学。

1910: Hiratsuka Raichō attended Ikuta Chōkō's lectures on literature and ideas at his house.
The High Treason Incident occurred and twelve socialists including Kōtoku Shūsui were sentenced to death.
明治 43 年： 生田長江宅で、思想、文芸関係の講話を聴く。
大逆事件。

1911: In September the inaugural issue of *Seitō* was published.
明治 44 年： 9月、『青鞜』創刊。

1912: Hiratsuka Raichō was introduced to Okumura Hiroshi at Chigasaki (Kanagawa Prefecture) during the summer.
明治 45 年： 夏、茅ヶ崎で奥村博と出会う。

1914: She left her parents' house and started to live with her lover, Okumura Hiroshi.
The First World War began.
大正 3 年 ： 家を出て、奥村博と共同生活を始める。
第一次世界大戦 (〜18)。

1915: Raichō handed her editorship of *Seitō* over to Itō Noe.
In September Okumura Hiroshi became ill with tuberculosis and entered the Nankoin Hospital in Chigasaki (Kanagawa Prefecture).
On 9 December she gave birth to her daughter, Akemi.
大正 4 年 ： 『青鞜』の編集発行を伊藤野枝に委ねる。
9月、博、肺結核発病し、茅ヶ崎の南湖院に入院。
12月9日、長女曙生生まれる。

1916: Hiratsuka moved into a rented house near the hospital. In February the publication of *Seitō* was discontinued indefinitely, the last issue being vol. 6 no. 2.

大正 5 年 ： 南湖院の近くの借家に移転。

2 月、『青鞜』2 巻 2 号をもって無期休刊となる。

1917: In the summer she left Chigasaki and returned to Tokyo. On 24 September she gave birth to her son, Atsubumi. The Russian Revolution.

大正 6 年 ： 夏、茅ヶ崎を引き上げ、東京に戻る。

9 月 24 日、長男敦史生まれる。

ロシア革命。

1918: Raichō bought a house in Tabata, Tokyo. She began a controversy over 'the protection of motherhood' with Yosano Akiko.

Rice riots took place in Toyama Prefecture and then spread throughout the country.

大正 7 年 ： 田端に家を買う。与謝野晶子と母性保護論争を始める。

米騒動起こる。

1919: In the summer Raichō attended a women's summer school sponsored by the Nagoya Newspaper Company as a lecturer. She also visited textile factories in Aichi Prefecture.

In December she made public the objectives of the Association of New Women.

大正 8 年 ： 夏、「名古屋新聞」主催の婦人夏期講習会に講師として行き、愛知県下の繊維工場を視察。

12 月、新婦人協会の趣意書発表。

1920: In March the inaugural ceremony of the Association of New Women was held.

In October the Association's magazine, the *Women's League*, was launched.

大正 9 年 ： 3 月、新婦人協会発会式挙行。

10 月、新婦人協会の機関誌『女性同盟』発刊。

1921: Raichō became ill, and moved to Chiba Prefecture and then to the spa of Nasu in Tochigi Prefecture.

大正 10 年 ： 健康を損ね、静養のため千葉県、次いで栃木県那須温泉に移る。

1922: Article 5 of the Peace Police Law was partially amended.
The Association of New Women was dissolved.

大正 11 年： 治安警察法第 5 条 1 部改正。
新婦人協会解散。

1923: Raichō returned to Tokyo and began to live by writing.
The Great Kantō Earthquake.

大正 12 年： 帰京、以後、文筆生活に入る。
関東大震災。

1925: Okumura Hiroshi became a teacher at Seijō Gakuen.

大正 14 年： 博、成城学園の教師となる。

1929: The Wall Street Crash initiated the global economic
slump.

昭和 4 年 ： 世界大恐慌。

1930: Hiratsuka Raichō set up a consumers' association,
'Warera no ie' ('Our house') in Seijō, Tokyo and became
its leader.
She joined the *Musan Fujin Geijutsu Renmei* (the Prole-
tarian Women's Arts League) organised by Takamure
Itsue.

昭和 5 年 ： 成城に消費組合「我等の家」を設立、組合長となる。
高群逸枝らの無産婦人芸術連盟に参加。

1933: Japan withdrew from the League of Nations.

昭和 8 年 ： 日本、国際連盟脱退。

1941: Hiratsuka Raichō's father died.
She married Okumura Hiroshi mainly to legitimize her
son, who needed this to advance in the Japanese armed
forces.
7 December: Japan bombed Pearl Harbor and entered
World War II.

昭和 16 年： 父定二郎死去。博との婚姻届を出す。
12 月 7 日、日本真珠湾を攻撃し、第二次世界大戦に加わる。

1942: Raichō was evacuated to Ibaraki Prefecture and began
farming.

昭和 17 年： 茨城県に疎開、農耕生活に入る。

1945:   Japan accepted the Potsdam Declaration and surren-
                dered unconditionally.
昭和 20 年 :   8 月 15 日、敗戦。

1946:   The Constitution of Japan was promulgated.
昭和 21 年 :   日本国憲法公布。

1947:   Raichō returned to Tokyo in the spring and began to
                live with her son and daughter-in-law in Seijō, Tokyo.
昭和 22 年 :   春、疎開先から帰京し、成城の家で敦史夫妻と同居。

1951:   Japan signed the San Francisco Peace Treaty and U.S.-
                Japan Security Treaty.
昭和 26 年 :   サンフランシスコ講和条約調印。
                日米安全保障条約調印。

1953:   Raichō founded the *Nihon Fujin Dantai Rengōkai* (the
                Federation of Japanese Women's Groups) in April and
                became its chairwoman.
昭和 28 年 :   4 月、日本婦人団体連合会を結成、会長となる。

1954:   Her mother, Tsuya, died in December.
昭和 29 年 :   12 月、母光沢死去。

1955:   In April, Raichō published her autobiography *Watashi
                no Aruita Michi* (*The Road I Walked*).
                In December she resigned as chairwoman of the
                Federation of Japanese Women's Groups, and became
                its honorary president.
昭和 30 年 :   4 月、『わたしの歩いた道』刊行。
                12 月、日本婦人団体連合会の会長を辞任、名誉会長となる。

1962:   Her sister, Taka, died in April.
                In November she became a committee member of the
                Fusen Kaikan (Women's Suffrage Hall).
昭和 37 年 :   4 月、姉孝死去。
                11 月、婦選会館理事となる。

1964: Her husband Okumura Hiroshi died in February.

昭和 39 年： 2 月、奥村博死去。

1970: She was admitted to Yoyogi Hospital in Sendagaya, Tokyo, in August. She was discharged from hospital once and was admitted again in November.

昭和 45 年： 8 月、千駄ヶ谷の代々木病院に入院。

一旦退院後、11 月に再入院。

1971: She died of cancer on 24 May.

昭和 46 年： 5 月 24 日癌の為死亡。

CONTENTS OF THE INAUGURAL ISSUE OF *SEITŌ*,
1 SEPTEMBER, 1911
1911年（明治44年）9月1日発行の『青鞜』創刊号内容

Front—cover sketch by Naganuma Chieko
＜表紙絵＞　　長沼智恵子

Contents:
＜内容＞

1. Yosano Akiko's poetry entitled 'Sozorogoto' ('A rambling talk')
   そぞろごと（詩）　　与謝野晶子

2. Mori Shigeko's short story 'Shi no ie' ('The house of death')
   死の家（小説）　　森しげ子

3. Haiku poems entitled 'Sarusuberi' ('Indian lilacs') by Hakuu [Hakuu was Yasumochi Yoshiko's pen-name.]
   百日紅（俳句）　　白雨

4. Tamura Toshiko's short story entitled 'Namachi' ('Fresh blood')
   生血（小説）　　田村とし子

5. Hiratsuka Raichō's essay 'Genshi josei wa taiyō de atta' ('In the beginning woman was the sun')
   元始女性は太陽であった（感想）　　平塚らいてう

6. Kunikida Haruko's literary sketch 'Neko no nomi' ('Cats' fleas')
   猫の蚤（小品）　　国木田治子

7. A translation of Edgar Allan Poe's prose poem 'Shadow'
   影（散文詩、翻訳）　　ポオ

8. Araki Ikuko's comedy 'Yōshin no tawamure' ('Merry Gods' jest')
喜劇　陽神の戯れ（戯曲）　荒木郁子

9. Yoshiko's series of *tanka* (a Japanese poem of thirty-one syllables) entitled 'Iso no hiru' ('Leeches of the shore')
磯のひる（短歌）　　淑子

10. Mozume Kazuko's short story 'Tanabata no yoru' ('The night of the Festival of the Weaver')
七夕の夜（小説）　　物集和子

11. The translation of Merezhkovski's essay on Henrik Ibsen's *Hedda Gabler*
ヘッダガブラー論（翻訳）　メレジコウスキー

12. The general rules of the Seitō Society
青鞜社概則

13. Message from the editorial board
編集室より

THE FRONT COVER OF THE INAUGURAL
ISSUE OF *SEITŌ*

BIBLIOGRAPHICAL DEVELOPMENT OF THE 'CONTROVERSY OVER THE PROTECTION OF MOTHERHOOD'

In chronological order, the publications appeared as follows:

Yosano Akiko, 'Bosei henchō o haisu' ('I refuse to over-emphasise the significance of motherhood'), *Taiyō* (*Sun*), (February, 1916).
与謝野晶子「母性偏重を排す」『太陽』

Hiratsuka Raichō, 'Bosei no shuchō ni tsuite Yosano Akiko-shi ni atau' ('I challenge Yosano Akiko's ideas on motherhood.'), *Bunshō Sekai* (*The World of Writing*), (May, 1916).
平塚らいてう「母性の主張に就いて与謝野晶子氏に与ふ」『文章世界』

Yosano Akiko, 'Hiratsuka Haruko-sama' ('Addressed to Hiratsuka Haruko'), *Taiyō* (*Sun*), (June, 1916).
与謝野晶子「平塚明子様」『太陽』

Yamada Kakichi, 'Bosei Hogo Dōmei ni tsuite' ('On the Motherhood Protection League in Germany'), *Joō* (*Queen*), (August, 1916).
山田嘉吉「『母性保護同盟』に就いて」『女王』

Yosano Akiko, 'Joshi no shokugyōteki dokuritsu o gensoku to seyo' ('Women should make it a rule to obtain economic independence through paid work'), *Jogaku Sekai* (*The World of Women's Learning*), (January, 1918).
与謝野晶子「女子の職業的独立を原則とせよ」『女学世界』

Yosano Akiko, 'Joshi no tetteishita dokuritsu' ('Women's complete independence'), *Fujin Kōron* (*Women's Review*), (March, 1918).
与謝野晶子「女子の徹底した独立」『婦人公論』

Hiratsuka Raichō, 'Bosei hogo no shuchō wa iraishugi ka' ('Is the request for the protection of motherhood a kind of parasitism?'), *Fujin Kōron* (*Women's Review*), (May, 1918).
平塚らいてう「母性保護の主張は依頼主義か」『婦人公論』

Yosano Akiko, 'Hiratsuka-san to watashi no ronsō' ('The debate between Hiratsuka and myself'), *Taiyō* (*Sun*), (June, 1918).
与謝野晶子「平塚さんと私の論争」『太陽』

Hiratsuka Raichō, 'Bosei hogo mondai ni tsuite futatabi Yosano

Akiko-shi ni yosu' ('I write to Yosano Akiko again on the protection of motherhood'), *Fujin Kōron* (*Women's Review*), (July, 1918).
平塚らいてう「母性保護問題に就いて再び与謝野晶子氏に寄す」『婦人公論』

Yamakawa Kikue, 'Bosei hogo to keizaiteki dokuritsu—Yosano, Hiratsuka nishi no ronsō' ('The protection of motherhood and women's economic independence, focusing on the dispute between Yosano and Hiratsuka'), *Fujin Kōron* (*Women's Review*), (September, 1918).
山川菊栄「母性保護と経済的独立－与謝野、平塚二氏の論争」『婦人公論』

Yamada Waka, 'Bosei hogo mondai—Yosano-shi to Hiratsuka-shi no shoron ni tsuite' ('The subject of the protection of motherhood with special reference to Yosano and Hiratsuka's respective views'), *Taiyō* (*Sun*), (September, 1918).
山田わか「母性保護問題－与謝野氏と平塚氏の所論に就いて」『太陽』

Yosano Akiko, 'Rōdō to fujin' ('Work and women'), *Yokohama Bōeki Shinpō* (*Yokohama Trade News*), (October, 1918).
与謝野晶子「労働と婦人」『横浜貿易新報』

Yosano Akiko, 'Hiratsuka, Yamakawa, Yamada sanjoshi ni kotau' ('I reply to Hiratsuka, Yamakawa, and Yamada'), *Taiyō* (*Sun*), (November, 1918).
与謝野晶子「平塚、山川、山田三女史に答ふ」『太陽』

Yamakawa Kikue, 'Yosano Akiko-shi ni kotau' ('My response to Yosano Akiko'), *Fujin Kōron* (*Women's Review*), (December, 1918).
山川菊栄「与謝野氏に答ふ」『婦人公論』

Hiratsuka Raichō, 'Shi to sono zengo o mite' ('Having seen "Before and after death"'), *Yūben* (*Eloquence*), (December, 1918).
平塚らいてう「死と其前後を見て」『雄弁』

Hiratsuka Raichō, 'Gendai katei fujin no nayami' ('Troubles of contemporary housewives'), *Fujin Kōron* (*Women's Review*), (January, 1919).
平塚らいてう「現代家庭婦人の悩み」『婦人公論』

Yamada Waka, 'Ko o motta haha no nayami—gendai no nayami to shite no fujin shokugyō mondai' ('Troubles of mothers: women's occupational problems are current women's troubles'), *Fujin Kōron* (*Women's Review*), (January, 1919).
山田わか「子を持った母の悩み－現代の悩みとしての婦人職業問題」『婦人公論』

Yamada Waka, 'Haha no seikatsu o shite yoyū arashimeyo—saishōgendo rōginhō seitei no hitsuyō' ('Make mothers' lives free from financial pressure—the need to enact law to guarantee minimum wages'), *Fujin Kōron* (*Women's Review*), (March, 1919).

山田わか「母の生活をして余裕あらしめよ－最少限度労銀法制定の必要」『婦
　人公論』

Yosano Akiko, 'Joshi kaizō no kisoteki kōsatsu' ('Fundamental obser-
　vations on changing women'), *Kaizō* (*Reconstruction*), (April, 1919).
　与謝野晶子「女子改造の基礎的考察」『改造』

Yosano Akiko, 'Shunshō sengo' ('My shallow words in the early
　spring evening'), *Waseda Bungaku* (*Waseda Literature*), (April, 1919).
　与謝野晶子「春宵浅語」『早稲田文学』

THE FRONT COVER OF THE INAUGURAL ISSUE OF THE *WOMEN'S LEAGUE*

新婦人協會

機關雜誌

女性同盟

1

綱　領

一、婦人の能力を自由に發達せしめるため男女の機會均等を主張すること。

一、男女の價値同等觀の上に立ちて其の差別を認め協力を主張すること。

一、家庭の社會的意義を闡明すること。

一、婦人、母、子供の權利を擁護し、彼等の利益の增進を計ると共に之に反する一切を排除すること。

創　刊　號

宣言……社會改造に對する婦人の使命……らいてう………一

國際婦人參政權同盟會大會……………………………………二

全國女政員會の組織に就いて………………………教育部研究會…三

女子教育家は婦人參政權を何と見るか……………………………一三

'TEACHERS NEED THE VOTE!'

治安警察法第五條修正の運動（上）………………市 川 房 枝…一八

一女工の手記（女專賣局員養成の前後）……………………港………二五

花柳病男子の結婚制限法に關する請願運動……らいてう……まこ………三二

PLより……友愛婦人部の瓦解………三ヶ島淡子………四〇

短歌（最近婦人運動の傾向を速べ新婦人協會の發展を望む）……四三

創立より女性同盟發刊迄（上）……………市 川 房 枝………

恨告……會告…協會日誌……編輯室より

比較婚姻法論…………………………………………穗 積 重 遠…一

新婦人協會　東京　田端

大正九年十月一日（第三種郵便物認可）

大正九年十一月六日　印刷納本

大正九年十月九日發行（毎月一回一日發行）

THE CONTENTS OF THE INAUGURAL ISSUE OF
THE *WOMEN'S LEAGUE*
『女性同盟』第一号（創刊号）

The front cover presented the general principles of the Association of New Women and contents of the inaugural issue.
＜表紙＞　綱領

Contents:
＜内容＞

1. Declaration
   宣言

2. Hiratsuka Raichō's essay 'Shakai kaizō ni taisuru josei no shimei' ('Women's mission for social reconstruction')
   社会改造に対する婦人の使命　　　　　　　平塚らいてう

3. The conference report of the International Women's Suffrage League
   国際婦人参政権同盟会大会

4. Report on the formation of the National Women Teachers' Union
   全国女教員会の組織に就いて　　　　　　　　市川房枝

5. How do women educationalists see women's suffrage?
   女子教育家は婦人参政権を何と見るか

6. Teachers need the vote! A propaganda poster requesting suffrage for female teachers in America, created by the National American Woman Suffrage Alliance led by [Carrie Chapman] Catt
   TEACHERS NEED THE VOTE!（キャット婦人を会長とせる米国婦人参政権同盟会の女教師参政権要求宣伝ビラ）

7. 'The campaign for the amendment of Article 5 of the Peace Police Law', by Ichikawa Fusae
   治安警察法第五条修正の運動   市川房枝

8. 'The campaign requesting the enactment of a new law imposing restrictions on marriage for men with venereal disease', by Hiratsuka Raichō
   花柳病男子結婚制限法制定に関する請願運動   平塚らいてう

9. Report on the formation of societies for the study of women's issues
   研究会について

10. 'Memoirs of a factory girl', by Minato Hama [Minato Hama was Yamanouchi Mina's pen-name.]
    女工の手記   港はま＜山内みな＞

11. Report from a women's society called the P.L. Society
    ＰＬ会より

12. Five *tanka*s (Japanese poems of thirty-one syllables) entitled 'Yūzora' ('Evening Sky') by Mikajima Yoshiko
    夕空 ＜短歌五首＞   三ヶ島葭子

13. 'The development of the Association of New Women: from its foundation to the inauguration of its magazine, the *Women's League*', by Ichikawa Fusae
    創立より『女性同盟』発刊まで   市川房枝

14. The proceedings of the Association
    会報

15. Announcements from the Association
    会告

16. The history of the Association
    協会日誌抄

THE NUMBER OF SIGNATURES WHICH THE ASSOCIATION OF NEW WOMEN COLLECTED FOR THREE PETITIONS SUBMITTED TO THE 44TH SESSION OF THE DIET
（第４４議会に新婦人協会が提出した三種の請願の調印者数）

(A)　The petition requesting the revision of the Electoral Law to choose members of the House of Representatives.
（衆議院議員選挙法改正の請願書）
- ①　To the House of Representatives: 2,355
（衆議院）
- ②　To the House of Peers: 2,174
（貴族院）

(B)　The petition requesting the amendment of Article 5 of the Peace Police Law.
（治安警察法第５条修正の請願書）
- ①　To the House of Representatives: 2,440
（衆議院）
- ②　To the House of Peers: 2,200
（貴族院）

(C)　The petition requesting restrictions on marriage and divorce for people suffering from venereal disease.
（花柳病者の結婚制限並びに離婚請求に関する請願書）
- ①　To the House of Representatives: 2,440
（衆議院）
- ②　To the House of Peers: 1,905
（貴族院）

Source: Shin Fujin Kyōkai (ed.), *Josei Dōmei (Women's League)*, vol. 5, 1921, p. 41.

THE NUMBER OF MEMBERS OF THE ASSOCIATION OF NEW WOMEN (AS OF 25 FEBRUARY, 1921)
（大正１０年２月２５日現在の新婦人協会の会員数）

Type of membership （会員種類）	Number of members resident in Tokyo （在京人数）	Number of members from provincial areas （地方人数）	Total （合計）
Regular members （正会員）	65	156	221
First-class supporting members （第一種賛助員）	62	31	93
Second-class supporting members （第二種賛助員）	56	26	82
Sustaining members （維持会員）	11	5	16
Total （合計）	194	218	412

Source: Shin Fujin Kyōkai (ed.), *Josei Dōmei* (*Women's League*), vol. 6, 1921, p. 71.

APPENDIX TWELVE

NUMBERS OF PEOPLE BY PREFECTURE, WHO SIGNED EACH PETITION SUBMITTED TO THE HOUSE OF REPRESENTATIVES, DURING THE 44TH SESSION OF THE DIET
（第４４議会に提出した三種の請願の府県別調印者数）

A. The petition requesting the revision of the Electoral Law to choose members of the House of Representatives
（選挙法改正）

B. The petition requesting the amendment of Article 5 of the Peace Police Law
（治警５条修正）

C. The petition requesting restrictions on marriage and divorce for people suffering from venereal disease
（花柳病者結婚制限並びに離婚請求）

Name of prefecture （府県）	A	B	C
1. Tokyo （東京）	683	743	684
2. Hyōgo （兵庫）	468	505	505
3. Aichi （愛知）	203	242	219
4. Kyoto （京都）	113	104	117
5. Osaka （大阪）	112	95	118
6. Kanagawa （神奈川）	48	74	55

(*cont.*)

Name of prefecture (府県)	A	B	C
7. Hiroshima (広島)	51	64	58
8. Yamagata (山形)	44	45	50
9. Kagawa (香川)	36	45	42
10. Fukushima (福島)	32	44	44
11. Niigata (新潟)	39	37	41
12. Okayama (岡山)	39	35	41
13. Fukuoka (福岡)	39	40	35
14. Wakayama (和歌山)	36	37	35
15. Nara (奈良)	33	33	31
16. Miyagi (宮城)	32	31	18
17. Yamanashi (山梨)	27	20	22
18. Aomori (青森)	20	15	30
19. Ehime (愛媛)	21	11	32
20. Mie (三重)	21	15	25
21. Chiba (千葉)	22	20	17
22. Tokushima (徳島)	16	10	25

(*cont.*)

Name of prefecture (府県)	A	B	C
23. Hokkaidō (北海道)	18	15	14
24. Gifu (岐阜)	21	8	17
25. Shimane (島根)	15	13	17
26. Kōchi (高知)	15	12	14
27. Tochigi (栃木)	17	13	6
28. Iwate (岩手)	15	6	15
29. Gunma (群馬)	10	10	10
30. Miyazaki (宮崎)	10	10	10
31. Shiga (滋賀)	10	10	10
32. Nagano (長野)	13	8	8
33. Nagasaki (長崎)	8	10	10
34. Kagoshima (鹿児島)	10	10	5
35. Ishikawa (石川)	7	7	9
36. Kumamoto (熊本)	8	8	8
37. Fukui (福井)	7	7	7
38. Yamaguchi (山口)	7	6	7
39. Saitama (埼玉)	5	4	5

(cont.)

Name of prefecture (府県)	A	B	C
40. Ibaraki (茨城)	4	3	6
41. Akita (秋田)	3	5	4
42. Korea (朝鮮)	4	4	4
43. Ōita (大分)	3	3	4
44. Saga (佐賀)	3	0	4
45. Toyama (富山)	4	0	0
46. Shizuoka (静岡)	2	2	0
47. Tottori (鳥取)	0	0	1
48. America (米国)	1	1	1
Total (合計)	2,355	2,440	2,440

Source: Shin Fujin Kyōkai (ed.), *Josei Dōmei* (*Women's League*), vol. 5, 1921, pp. 41–2.

APPENDIX THIRTEEN

NUMBERS OF PEOPLE BY OCCUPATION, WHO SIGNED EACH PETITION, SUBMITTED TO THE HOUSE OF REPRESENTATIVES, DURING THE 44TH SESSION OF THE DIET
（第４４議会に提出した三種の請願の職業別調印者数）

A. The petition requesting the revision of the Electoral Law to choose members of the House of Representatives
（選挙法改正）

B. The petition requesting the amendment of Article 5 of the Peace Police Law
（治警５条修正）

C. The petition requesting restrictions on marriage and divorce for people suffering from venereal disease
（花柳病者結婚制限並びに離婚請求）

Occupation （種別）	A	B	C
1. Teacher （教員）	667	754	735
2. Housewife （家庭婦人）	558	571	568
3. Salaried worker （会社員）	353	352	364
4. Student （学生）	135	140	135
5. Merchant （商業）	140	130	127
6. Unemployed （無職）	89	73	89

(cont.)

Occupation (種別)	A	B	C
7. Government official (官吏)	76	86	86
8. Midwife or nurse (産婆看護婦)	73	70	76
9. Farmer (農業)	50	54	46
10. Priest (宗教家)	34	32	36
11. Medical doctor (医者)	32	32	34
12. Artist (芸術家)	30	28	28
13. Social or welfare worker (社会事業)	26	26	26
14. Writer (著述業)	24	25	20
15. Journalist (記者)	22	24	23
16. Sailor (船員)	23	21	24
17. Industrial worker (工業)	21	20	21
18. Lawyer (弁護士)	2	2	2
Total (合計)	2,355	2,440	2,440

Source: Shin Fujin Kyōkai (ed.), *Josei Dōmei* (*Women's League*), vol. 5, 1921, p. 43.

NUMBERS OF PEOPLE BY SEX, WHO SIGNED EACH PETITION, SUBMITTED TO THE HOUSE OF REPRESENTATIVES, DURING THE 44TH SESSION OF THE DIET
（第４４議会に提出した三種の請願の男女別調印者数）

A. The petition requesting the revision of the Electoral Law to choose members of the House of Representatives
（選挙法改正）

B. The petition requesting the amendment of Article 5 of the Peace Police Law
（治警５条修正）

C. The petition requesting restrictions on marriage and divorce for people suffering from venereal disease
（花柳病者結婚制限並びに離婚請求）

Sex （性別）	A	B	C
Male （男）	957	1,102	1,035
Female （女）	1,398	1,338	1,405
Total （合計）	2,355	2,440	2,440

Source: Shin Fujin Kyōkai (ed.), *Josei Dōmei* (*Women's League*), vol. 5, 1921, p. 43.

GLOSSARY

Aikoku Fujinkai	愛国婦人会	Patriotic Women's Association
Arakawa Gorō	荒川五郎	(1865–1944), politician
Araki Ikuko	荒木郁子	(1890–1943), member of the Seitō Society
Arishima Takeo	有島武郎	(1878–1923), novelist and literary critic
Atarashii onna	新しい女	new woman
Baba Kochō	馬場孤蝶	(1869–1940), translator and essayist
Baien	『煤煙』	*Smoke*
Bosei hogo	母性保護	the protection of motherhood
Bosei hogo ronsō	母性保護論争	the controversy over 'the protection of motherhood'
Bungei Kyōkai	文芸協会	the Literary Association founded by Tsubouchi Shōyō
Bunshō Sekai	『文章世界』	*The World of Writing*
Chian Iji Hō	治安維持法	the Peace Preservation Law
Chian Keisatsu Hō	治安警察法	the Peace Police Law
Chūma Okimaru	中馬興丸	(1871–1936), politician
Chūō Kōron	『中央公論』	*Central Review*
Dai Nihon Teikoku Kenpō	大日本帝国憲法	the Imperial Japanese Constitution
Fujimi Shōgakkō	富士見小学校	Fujimi Elementary School
Fujimi Yōchien	富士見幼稚園	Fujimi Kindergarten
Fujimura Yoshirō	藤村義朗	(1871–1933), politician
Fujin Kōron	『婦人公論』	*Women's Review*
Fujin Sansei Dōmei	婦人参政同盟	the League for Women's Political Rights
Fujin Sanseiken Kakutoku Kisei Dōmei	婦人参政権獲得期成同盟	the League for the Attainment of Women's Suffrage
Fujin Sensen	『婦人戦線』	*The Women's Front*
Fujin to Shinshakai	『婦人と新社会』	*Women and the New Society*
Fujo Shinbun	『婦女新聞』	*Women's Newspaper*
Fukuda (Kageyama) Hideko	福田（景山）英子	(1865–1927), participant in the Freedom and People's Rights Movement, socialist, feminist and editor of *Sekai Fujin*
Fukuzawa Yukichi	福沢諭吉	(1835–1901), liberal thinker, member of the Meiji Six Society and founder of Keiō University
Fusen Kakutoku Dōmei	婦選獲得同盟	the Women's Suffrage League
Gakusei	学制	the Fundamental Education Law

Goshiki no sake jiken	五色の酒事件	the five-coloured liquor incident
Hara Kei	原 敬	(1856–1921), politician, leader of the Seiyūkai and the prime minister (1918–1921)
Hasegawa Nyozekan	長谷川如是閑	(1875–1969), journalist and literary critic
Hasegawa Shigure	長谷川時雨	(1979–1941), member of the Seitō Society, playwright and founder of *Nyonin Geijutsu*
Heiminsha	平民社	the Commoners' Society
Heimin Shinbun	『平民新聞』	*Commoners' Newspaper*
Higuchi Ichiyō	樋口一葉	(1872–1896), novelist and poet
Hirata Tokuboku	平田禿木	(1873–1943), scholar of English literature and essayist
Hiratsuka (Okumura) Haru(ko)	平塚（奥村）明（子）	(1886–1971), the real name of Hiratsuka Raichō, feminist, founding member of the Seitō Society and of the Association of New Women, and participant in the controversy over 'the protection of motherhood'
Hiratsuka Raichō	平塚らいてう	(1886–1971), Hiratsuka Haru's pen-name
Hiratsuka Taka	平塚孝	(1885–1962), Hiratsuka Raichō's elder sister
Hiratsuka Sadajirō	平塚定二郎	(1858–1941), Hiratsuka Raichō's father
Hiratsuka Tsuya	平塚光沢	(1863–1954), Hiratsuka Raichō's mother
Hirooka Uichirō	広岡宇一郎	(1867–1941), politician
Hiroshima Jiken	広島事件	the Hiroshima Incident
Hori Yasuko	堀保子	contributor to *Seitō*, wife of Ōsugi Sakae and sister of Sakai Toshihiko's first wife
Hoshijima Nirō	星島二郎	(1887–1980), politician
Hozumi Shigetō	穂積重遠	(1883–1951), legal scholar and professor of Tokyo University
Ichikawa Fusae	市川房枝	(1893–1981), founding member of the Association of New Women, feminist, suffragette and politician
Ichinomiya Fusajirō	一宮房治郎	(1887–1948), politician
Ikuta Chōkō	生田長江	(1882–1936), translator, novelist, playwright and literary critic
Ikuta (Nishizaki) Hanayo	生田（西崎）花世	(1888–1970), member of the Seitō Society and contributor to *Nyonin Geijutsu*
Ishikawa Sanshirō	石川三四郎	Christian socialist, member of

		the Commoner's Society and contributor to *Sekai Fujin*
Itō Noe	伊藤野枝	(1895–1923), member of the Seitō Society, editor of *Seitō*, partner of Ōsugi Sakae and anarchist
Iwamoto Zenji	岩本善治	(1863–1943), principal of Meiji Girls' Academy and founder of the women's education journal *Jogaku Zasshi*
Iwano Hōmei	岩野泡鳴	(1873–1920), writer
Iwano (Endō) Kiyo(ko)	岩野（遠藤）清(子)	(1882–1920), member of the Seitō Society and wife of Iwano Hōmei
Jiyū Minken Undō	自由民権運動	the Freedom and People's Rights Movement
Jogaku Zasshi	『女学雑誌』	*Women's Educational Magazine*
Josei Dōmei	『女性同盟』	*Women's League*
Joshi Eigaku Juku	女子英学塾	Women's Institute of English Studies
Kaibara Ekken	貝原益軒	(1630–1714), Confucian scholar in the Edo period
Kaizoku gumi	海賊組	the Pirate Gang
Kaizō	『改造』	*Reconstruction*
Kamada Eikichi	鎌田栄吉	(1857–1934), politician and Vice-Chancellor of Keiō University
Kamichika Ichiko	神近市子	(1888–1981), writer, member of the Seitō Society, partner of Ōsugi Sakae, journalist, feminist and politician
Kanno Suga	管野須賀	(1881–1911), socialist and partner of Kōtoku Shūsui
karyūbyō	花柳病	venereal disease
Katō Kazuko	加藤籌子	(1883–1956), member of the Seitō Society, and wife of Oguri Fuyō
Katō Midori	加藤みどり	(1888–1922), member of the Seitō Society
Katō (Ishimoto) Shidzue	加藤（石本）シヅエ	(1897–2001), birth control campaigner, feminist and politician
Keishū Bungakukai	閨秀文学会	the Keishū Literary Society
Kinoshita Shigetarō	木下成太郎	(1865–1942), politician
Kishida (Nakajima) Toshiko	岸田（中島）俊子	(1861–1901), early feminist and participant in the Freedom and People's Rights Movement
Kiuchi Tei(ko)	木内 錠(子)	(1887–1919), founding member of the Seitō Society
Kobayashi Katsu	小林哥津	(1894–1974), member of the

		Seitō Society and contributor to *Safuran*
Kodama Shinko	児玉真子	member of the Association of New Women
Koganei Kimiko	小金井喜美子	(1870–1956), member of the Seitō Society, translator and younger sister of Mori Ōgai
Kokumin Shinbun	『国民新聞』	*People's Newspaper*
Kōtoku Shūsui	幸徳秋水	(1871–1911), founding member of the Commoner's Society and partner of Kanno Suga
Kunikida Haru(ko)	国木田治(子)	(1879–1962), writer, member of the Seitō Society and wife of Kunikida Doppo
Kusunose Kita	楠瀬喜多	(1833–1920), participant in the Freedom and People's Rights Movement
Kyōiku Chokugo	教育勅語	the Imperial Rescript on Education
Matsui Sumako	松井須磨子	(1886–1919), actress and partner of Shimamura Hōgetsu
Matsumoto Kunpei	松本君平	(1871–1944), politician
Meiji Minpō	明治民法	Meiji Civil Code
Meirokusha	明六社	the Meiji Six Society
Meiroku Zasshi	『明六雑誌』	the *Meiji Six Journal*
Mikajima Yoshiko	三ヶ島葭子	(1886–1927), poet and member of the Seitō Society
Miyake Shū	三宅 秀	(1848–1938), politician
Mori Arinori	森 有札	(1847–89), founding member of the Meiji Six Society, who became Education Minister in 1885
Mori Ōgai	森 鷗外	(1862–1922), novelist
Mori Shige(ko)	森 しげ(子)	(1880–1936), writer, member of the Seitō Society and wife of Mori Ōgai
Morita Sōhei	森田草平	(1881–1949), novelist and translator
Mozume Kazuko	物集和子	(1888–1979), founding member of the Seitō Society and daughter of Mozume Takami
Musan Fujin Geijutsu Renmei	無産婦人芸術連盟	The Proletarian Women's Arts League
Myōjō	『明星』	*Morning Star*
Nagai Ryūtarō	永井柳太郎	(1881–1944), politician
Naganuma (Takamura) Chieko	長沼（高村）智恵子	(1886–1938), artist and wife of Takamura Kōtarō
Nagoya Shinbunsha	名古屋新聞社	the Nagoya Newspaper Company

Nakamura Masanao	中村正直	(1832–1891), contributor to the *Meiji Six Journal* and translator
Nakano Hatsu(ko)	中野 初(子)	(1886–1983), founding member of the Seitō Society
Nakano Seigo	中野正剛	(1886–1943), politician
Nankoin	南湖院	the Nankoin Hospital
Naruse Jinzō	成瀬仁蔵	educationalist and founder of the Japan Women's College
Natsume Sōseki	夏目漱石	(1867–1916), novelist
Nemoto Tadashi	根本 正	(1851–1933), politician
Nihon Fujin Dantai Rengōkai	日本婦人団体連合会	the Federation of Japanese Women's Groups
Nihon Joshi Daigakkō	日本女子大学校	Japan Women's College
Nihon Joshi Daigaku	日本女子大学	Japan Women's University
Nihon Kirisutokyō Fujin Kyōfūkai	日本基督教婦人矯風会	Japan Women's Christian Temperance Union
Nishikawa (Matsuoka) Fumiko	西川（松岡）文子	(1882–1960), member of the Commoner's Society, founder of the Real New Women's Association and editor of *Shin Shin Fujin*
Nishō Gakusha	二松学舎	private school where Hiratsuka Raichō studied Chinese classics
Nogami Yaeko	野上弥生子	(1885–1985), novelist and contributor to *Seitō*
Ochanomizu Kōjo	お茶の水高女	Ochanomizu Girls' High School
Okada Yachiyo	岡田八千代	(1883–1962), member of the Seitō Society, sister of Osanai Kaoru and playwright
Okamoto Kanoko	岡本かの子	(1889–1939), member of the Seitō Society, poet and mother of Okamoto Tarō
Oku (Wada) Mumeo	奥（和田）むめお	(1895–1997), founding member of the Association of New Women, feminist, founder of journal *Shokugyō Fujin* and co-operative movement campaigner
Okumura Atsubumi	奥村敦史	(1917–), Hiratsuka Raichō's son
Okumura Hiroshi	奥村博（史）	(1891–1964), painter and Hiratsuka Raichō's husband
Okumura Ioko	奥村五百子	(1845–1907), founder of Patriotic Women's Association
Onna Daigaku	『女大学』	*The Greater Learning for Women*
Ōsugi Sakae	大杉 栄	(1885–1923), anarchist, editor of *Kindai Shisō*, husband of Hori Yasuko and partner of Kamichika Ichiko and Itō Noe

Otake Kōkichi (Tomimoto Kazue)	尾竹紅吉 (富本一枝)	(1893–1966), member of the Seitō Society, founder of *Safuran* and wife of Tomimoto Kenkichi
Ōyama Ikuo	大山郁夫	(1880–1955), professor at Waseda University and politician
Ryōsai kenbo	良妻賢母	'a good wife and wise mother'
Safuran	『番紅花』	*Saffron*
Saiga (Harada) Koto	斎賀（原田）琴	(1892–1973), member of the Seitō Society
Sakai Toshihiko	堺利彦	(1871–1933), socialist and writer
Sakamoto (Takada) Makoto	坂本（高田）真琴	(1899–1954), member of the Seitō Society and of the Association of New Women
Seibi Joshi Eigo Gakkō	成美女子英語学校	Seibi Women's English School
Seino Shōgakkō	誠之小学校	Seino Elementary School
Seisoku Eigo Gakkō	正則英語学校	Seisoku English Language School
Seitō	『青鞜』	*Seitō (Bluestocking)*
Seitōsha	青鞜社	the Seitō (Bluestocking) Society
Sekai Fujin	『世界婦人』	*Women of the World*
Sekirankai	赤瀾会	the Red Wave Society
Senuma Kayō	瀬沼夏葉	(1875–1915), member of the Seitō Society and translator
Shimamura Hōgetsu	島村抱月	(1871–1918), literary critic and playwright
Shimazaki Tōson	島崎藤村	(1872–1943), novelist and poet
Shimoda Utako	下田歌子	(1854–1936), educationalist
Shin Fujin Kyōkai	新婦人協会	the Association of New Women
Shin Shin Fujin	『新真婦人』	*The Real New Women*
Shin Shin Fujinkai	新真婦人会	the Real New Women's Association
Shiobara Jiken	塩原事件	the Shiobara Incident
Shirakaba	『白樺』	*White Birch*
Shokugyō Fujinsha	職業婦人社	the Working Women's Society
Shufu no Tomo	『主婦之友』	*The Housewives' Companion*
Shūgiin Giin Senkyo Hō	衆議院議員選挙法	the Electoral Law to choose members of the House of Representatives
Shūkai oyobi Seisha Hō	集会及政社法	Assembly and Political Organisation Law
Sōma Gyofū	相馬御風	(1883–1950), poet and literary critic
Subaru	『スバル』	the *Pleiades*
Suzuki Umeshirō	鈴木梅四郎	(1862–1940), politician
Tabuchi Toyokichi	田渕豊吉	(1882–1943), politician
Taigyaku Jiken	大逆事件	the High Treason Incident

Taishō demokurashii	大正デモクラシー	Taishō democracy
Taiyō	『太陽』	*Sun*
Tajima Hide	田島ひで	(1901–1976), member of the Association of New Women
Takami Yukimichi	高見之通	(1880–1962), politician
Takamure Itsue	高群逸枝	(1894–1964), writer, anarchist, editor of *Fujin Sensen* and feminist historian
Tamura Toshiko	田村俊子	(1884–1945), writer and member of the Seitō Society
Togawa Shūkotsu	戸川秋骨	(1870–1939), scholar of English literature and essayist
Tokyo Joshi Kōtō Shihan Gakkō	東京女子高等師範学校	Tokyo Girl's Higher School
Tokyo Kirisutokyō Fujin Kyōfūkai	東京基督教婦人矯風会	Tokyo Women's Christian Temperance Union
Tomita Kōjirō	富田幸次郎	(1872–1938), politician
Tōundō	東雲堂	Tōundō Publishing Company
Tsubouchi Shōyō	坪内逍遙	(1859–1935), novelist, playwright, critic, translator, professor of Waseda University, writer and founder of the literary association known as the Bungei Kyōkai
Tsuda Umeko	津田梅子	(1864–1929), educationalist and founder of the Women's Institute of English Studies (now Tsuda Juku Daigaku)
Tsukizoe (Okumura) Akemi	築添（奥村）曙生	(1915–c. 1995), Hiratsuka Raichō's daughter
Uehara Etsujirō	植原悦二郎	(1877–1962), politician
Ueki Emori	植木枝盛	(1857–1892), commentator on women's issues and active campaigner of the Freedom and People's Rights Movement
Ueno Yōko	上野葉子	(1886–1928), member of the Seitō Society
Warera no Ie	我等の家	Our house
Waseda Bungaku	『早稲田文学』	*Waseda Literature*
Yajima Kajiko	矢島揖子	(1833–1925), founder of the Japan Women's Christian Temperance Union
Yamada Kakichi	山田嘉吉	(1865–1934), husband of Yamada Waka
Yamada Waka	山田わか	(1879–1957), contributor to *Seitō*, feminist, participant in the controversy over 'the protection of motherhood', founder of *Fujin to Shakai* and

		an active member of the Motherhood Protection League
Yamakawa Hitoshi	山川 均	(1880–1958), socialist and husband of Yamakawa Kikue
Yamakawa (Aoyama) Kikue	山川（青山）菊栄	(1890–1980), socialist writer, translator, left-wing feminist and participant in the controversy over 'the protection of motherhood'
Yamane Masatsugu	山根正次	(1857–1925), politician
Yamanouchi Mina	山内みな	(1900–), member of the Association of New Women and labour historian
Yasuda (Harada) Satsuki	安田（原田）皐月	(1887–1933), member of the Seitō Society
Yasumochi Yoshiko	保持研子	(1885–1947), founding member of the Seitō Society
Yokohama Bōeki Shinpō	『横浜貿易新報』	*Yokohama Trade News*
Yosano Akiko	与謝野晶子	(1878–1942), poet, writer, critic, member of the Seitō Society, participant in the controversy over 'the protection of motherhood' and wife of Yosano Tekkan
Yoshioka Yayoi	吉岡弥生	(1871–1959), medical doctor and founder of Tokyo Women's Medical College
Yoshiwara torō jiken	吉原登楼事件	the visit to Yoshiwara incident
Yūai Fujin	『友愛婦人』	*Yūai Woman*
Yūben	『雄弁』	*Eloquence*

BIBLIOGRAPHY

Bibliographical note on sources

Inevitably, a far wider range of items were read for this book, but unfortunately there is not space to include all of them in the bibliography. Equally, given the enormous number of Japanese articles by Hiratsuka and her contemporary feminists, many of them footnoted here, it is impracticable to give a complete list of them in my bibliography. Therefore the bibliography is only a select one, which contains key publications. It is divided into four sections: Japanese primary sources, Japanese secondary sources, English primary sources and English secondary sources. The first two are given in both English and Japanese. Names of individual Japanese authors for Japanese sources appear with the family name preceding given name, in accordance with Japanese usage. However, in English sources produced by Japanese authors, the normal English practice has been followed (that is, their names appear with the given name proceeding the family name). Place of publication is Tokyo unless otherwise stated.

The Bibliography is arranged as follows

I. *Japanese Primary Sources*

(A) *Unpublished Material*

1. *Archival Sources*

(a)
Hiratsuka Raichō o Kinensuru Kai
平塚らいてうを記念する会
Seitōsha Jimu Nisshi.
『青鞜社事務日誌』

(b)
Hōsei Daigaku Ōhara Shakai Mondai Kenkyūjo
法政大学大原社会問題研究所

Letter from Sakai Magara to Sakai Tameko and Sakai Toshihiko, entitled 'Sekirankai
    kessei aisatsu', April 1921.
堺真柄から堺ためこ、堺利彦宛、赤瀾会結成挨拶状　1921年4月。

(c)
Kokuritsu Kokkai Toshokan
国立国会図書館
Kōno Hironaka Monjo
河野広中文書

Letter from Kusunose Kita to Kōno Hironaka, 6 December, 1903.
河野広中宛、楠瀬喜多書状、1903年12月6日。

(d)
Seijō Gakuen
成城学園

Seijō Kōtōgakkō (comp.), *Seijō Kōtōgakkō Shokuin Meibo* (1925–35).
成城高等学校編　『成城高等学校職員名簿』1925‐35年。

(e)
Tsuda Juku Daigaku
津田塾大学

Imperial message from Empress Meiji to Tsuda Umeko entitled 'Osata gaki'
    (November, 1872).
明治皇后から津田梅子宛お沙汰書、1872年11月。

Letter from Kaitakushi to Tsuda Umeko entitled 'Monjo Kaitakushi reisho' (November,
    1872).
開拓使から津田梅子宛、文書開拓使令書、1872年11月。

2. *Interviews*

Personal interview with Ichikawa Misao, 31 March, 1992, Tokyo.
市川ミサオ　聞き取り。

Personal interview with Kinpara Fuyuko, 19 January, 1996, Hamamatsu, Shizuoka
    Prefecture.
金原冬子　聞き取り。

Personal interview with Kobayashi Tomie, 30 May, 1991, Tokyo.
小林登美枝　聞き取り。

Personal interview with Nakamura Michiko, 20 May, 1992, Tokyo.
中村道子　聞き取り。

Personal interview with Nishibori Wakako, 10 April, 1991, Ranzan, Saitama Prefecture.
西堀わか子　聞き取り。
Personal interview with Nuita Hanako, 31 March, 1992, Tokyo.
縫田曄子　聞き取り。
Personal interview with Shutō Kunio, 1 April, 1992, Tokyo.
首藤邦夫　聞き取り。
Personal interviews with Tsukizoe Akemi, 6–11 April, 1992, Tokyo.
築添曙生　聞き取り。
Personal interview with Usui Takeshi, 15 April, 1992, Tokyo.
臼井毅　聞き取り。
Personal interview with Yamauchi Akino, 25 April, 1994, Tokyo.
山内昭野　聞き取り。
Personal interviews with Yoneda Sayoko, 10 April, 1993 & 23 December, 1993 &
    28 April, 1994 & 15 April, 1995, Tokyo.
米田佐代子　聞き取り。

(B) *Published Material*

1. *Writing by Hiratsuka Raichō*

(a) *Books*

Hiratsuka Raichō, *Boshi Zuihitsu* (1948).
平塚らいてう『母子随筆』１９４８年。
Hiratsuka Raichō, *Fujin to Kodomo no Kenri* (1919).
平塚らいてう『婦人と子供の権利』１９１９年。
Hiratsuka Raichō, *Gendai no Danjo e* (1917).
平塚らいてう『現代の男女へ』１９１７年。
Hiratsuka Raichō, *Gendai to Fujin no Seikatsu* (1914).
平塚らいてう『現代と婦人の生活』１９１４年。
Hiratsuka Raichō, *Genshi Josei wa Taiyō de Atta: Hiratsuka Raichō Jiden*, 4 vols (1971–3,
    1992 edn).
平塚らいてう『元始女性は太陽であった－平塚らいてう自伝』全４巻、１９９２年、
１９７１‐１９７３年（初版）。
Hiratsuka Raichō, *Haha no Kotoba* (1937).
平塚らいてう『母の言葉』１９３７年。
Hiratsuka Raichō (ed. by Hiratsuka Raichō Chosakushū Henshū Iinkai), *Hiratsuka
    Raichō Chosakushū*, 8 vols (1983–1984).
平塚らいてう著、平塚らいてう著作集編集委員会編『平塚らいてう著作集』全８巻、
１９８３－１９８４年。
Hiratsuka Raichō (ed. by Kobayashi Tomie & Yoneda Sayoko), *Hiratsuka Raichō
    Hyōronshū* (1987, 1991 edn).
平塚らいてう著、小林登美枝・米田佐代子編『平塚らいてう評論集』１９９１年、
１９８７年（初版）。
Hiratsuka Raichō, *Josei no Kotoba* (1926).
平塚らいてう『女性の言葉』１９２６年。
Hiratsuka Raichō, *Kumo, Kusa, Hito* (1933).
平塚らいてう『雲・草・人』１９３３年。
Hiratsuka Raichō, *Marumado yori* (1913).
平塚らいてう『円窓より』１９１３年。
Hiratsuka Raichō, *Mushiro Nyonin no Sei o Reihai Seyo* (1977).
平塚らいてう『むしろ女人の性を礼拝せよ』１９７７年。
Hiratsuka Raichō, *Tozahi aru Mado nite* (1913).
平塚らいてう『とざしある窓にて』１９１３年。

Hiratsuka Raichō, *Watakushi no Aruita Michi* (1955, 1994 edn).
平塚らいてう『わたくしの歩いた道』１９９４年、１９５５年（初版）。

(b) *Articles*

All these are also reprinted in Hiratsuka Raichō (ed. by Hiratsuka Raichō Chosakushū Henshū Iinkai), *Hiratsuka Raichō Chosakushū*, 8 vols (1983–84).

Hiratsuka Raichō, 'Akiko sensei to watakushi', *Tanka Kenkyū* (May, 1951).
平塚らいてう「晶子先生とわたくし」『短歌研究』１９５１年５月。
Hiratsuka Raichō, 'Ano jibun no Yamakawa-san', *Fujin Kōron* (November, 1925).
平塚らいてう「あの時分の山川さん」『婦人公論』１９２５年１１月。
Hiratsuka Raichō, 'Atarashii onna', *Chūō Kōron* (January, 1913).
平塚らいてう「新しい女」『中央公論』１９１３年１月。
Hiratsuka Raichō, 'Beikoku jōin giin ni okutta saigunbi hantai no apīru ni tsuite', *Sekai Kokka* (March, 1952).
平塚らいてう「米国上院議員に送った再ぐんび反対のアピールについて」『世界国家』１９５２年３月。
Hiratsuka Raichō, 'Betonamu Hanashiai no Kai ni yosete hitokoto', *Betonamu Hanashiai no Kai Nyūsu*, 1 (15 July, 1966).
平塚らいてう「ベトナム話し合いの会によせてひとこと」『ベトナム話し合いの会ニュース』
１号、１９６６年７月１５日。
Hiratsuka Raichō, 'Bosei hogo mondai ni tsuite futatabi Yosano Akiko-shi ni yosu', *Fujin Kōron*, (July, 1918).
平塚らいてう「母性保護問題に就いて再び与謝野晶子氏に寄す」『婦人公論』１９１８年７月。
Hiratsuka Raichō, 'Bosei hogo no shuchō wa iraishugi ka: Yosano Akiko-shi e', *Fujin Kōron* (May, 1918).
平塚らいてう「母性保護の主張は依頼主義か―与謝野晶子氏へ」『婦人公論』1918年５月。
Hiratsuka Raichō, 'Bosei no shuchō ni tsuite Yosano Akiko-shi ni atau', *Bunshō Sekai* (May, 1916).
平塚らいてう「母性の主張に就いて与謝野晶子氏に与う」『文学世界』1916年５月。
Hiratsuka Raichō, 'Chōsen no dōran to watashitachi josei no kakugo', *Shin Nyoen* (September, 1950).
平塚らいてう「朝鮮の動乱と私たち女性の覚悟」『新女苑』１９５０年９月。
Hiratsuka Raichō, 'Dai ikkai sōkai ni nozomi kako ichi-nen han o kaisō shitsutsu', *Josei Dōmei*, 10 (July, 1921).
平塚らいてう「第一回議会に臨み過去一年半を回想しつつ」『女性同盟』10号、1921年７月。
Hiratsuka Raichō, 'Dokuritsu suru ni tsuite ryōshin ni', *Seitō*, 4:2 (February, 1914).
平塚らいてう「独立するについて両親に」『青鞜』第４巻２号、1914年２月。
Hiratsuka Raichō, 'Ellen Key-joshi: shin fujin kan, shin renai kan', *Shin Nihon* (September, 1914).
平塚らいてう「エレン・ケイ女史―新婦人観・新恋愛観」『新日本』１９１４年９月。
Hiratsuka Raichō, 'Fujin no hi o mukaete', *Ie no Hikari* (April, 1950).
平塚らいてう「婦人の日を迎えて」『家の光』１９５０年４月。
Hiratsuka Raichō, 'Fujin no sekai taikai no yobikake ni kotaeru', *Heiwa Fujin Shinbun* (10 March, 1953).
平塚らいてう「婦人の世界大会のよびかけに答える」『平和ふじん新聞』1953年３月10日。
Hiratsuka Raichō, '*Fujin Sensen* ni sanka shite', *Fujin Sensen*, 1:2 (April, 1930).
平塚らいてう「『婦人戦線』に参加して」『婦人戦線』第１巻２号、1930年４月。
Hiratsuka Raichō, 'Fujin undō gojū-nen o kaerimite', *Fujin Kōron* (November, 1961).
平塚らいてう「婦人運動５０年をかえりみて」『婦人公論』１９６１年１１月。
Hiratsuka Raichō, 'Fukuda Hideko-san no omoide', *Tosho* (May, 1959).
平塚らいてう「福田英子さんのおもいで」『図書』１９５９年５月。

Hiratsuka Raichō, 'Fusae-san no koto', *Fujin Kōron* (March, 1925).
平塚らいてう「房枝さんのこと」『婦人公論』1925年3月。

Hiratsuka Raichō, 'Fusen undō o ikani michibiku beki ka', *Fujin Kōron* (July, 1928).
平塚らいてう「婦選運動をいかに導くべきか」『婦人公論』1928年7月。

Hiratsuka Raichō, 'Fusen undōsha e: zen fujin dantai yo, fusen o sono kōryō ni kakagetaru musan seitō o ōen seyo', *Fujin Undō* (March, 1928).
平塚らいてう「婦選運動者へ—全婦人団体よ、婦選をその綱領に掲げたる無産政党を応援せよ」
『婦人運動』1928年3月。

Hiratsuka Raichō, 'Gakkō o deta koro no watakushi', *Joseisen* (March, 1948).
平塚らいてう「学校を出たころのわたくし」『女性線』1948年3月。

Hiratsuka Raichō, 'Gendai katei fujin no nayami', *Fujin Kōron* (January, 1919).
平塚らいてう「現代家庭婦人の悩み」『婦人公論』1919年1月。

Hiratsuka Raichō, 'Genmaishoku no taiken o kataru', *Fujin Kōron* (December, 1942).
平塚らいてう「玄米食の体験を語る」『婦人公論』1942年12月。

Hiratsuka Raichō, 'Genshi josei wa taiyō de atta: Seitō hakkan ni saishite', *Seitō*, 1:1 (September, 1911).
平塚らいてう「元始女性は太陽であった—『青鞜』発刊に際して」『青鞜』第1巻1号、1911年9月。

Hiratsuka Raichō, 'Haha de aru yorokobi', *Shiro Bato* (February, 1937).
平塚らいてう「母である歓び」『白鳩』1937年2月。

Hiratsuka Raichō, 'Haha koso heiwa no chikara', *Sekai Seifu* (11 March, 1952).
平塚らいてう「母こそ平和の力」『世界政府』1952年3月11日。

Hiratsuka Raichō, 'Haha musume no kaiwa', *Fujin Kōron* (September, 1942).
平塚らいてう「母娘の会話」『婦人公論』1942年9月。

Hiratsuka Raichō, 'Haha to narite', *Chūō Kōron* (February, 1916).
平塚らいてう「母となりて」『中央公論』1916年2月。

Hiratsuka Raichō, 'Haha to shite no ichi-nen kan', *Fujin Kōron* (May, 1917).
平塚らいてう「母としての1年間」『婦人公論』1917年5月。

Hiratsuka Raichō, 'Haha yo te o tore, hitan no arashi no naka de: mura mura ni iryō kumiai o motou', *Miyako Shinbun* (19–20 August, 1932).
平塚らいてう「母よ手をとれ、悲嘆の嵐の中で—村々に医療組合を持とう」『都新聞』1932年8月
19日—20日。

Hiratsuka Raichō, 'Hamon: kansō', *Josei Dōmei*, 9 (June, 1921).
平塚らいてう「波紋（感想）」『女性同盟』9号、1921年6月。

Hiratsuka Raichō, 'Hamon: zakkan', *Josei Dōmei*, 5 (February, 1921).
平塚らいてう「波紋（雑感）」『女性同盟』5号、1921年2月。

Hiratsuka Raichō, 'Hataraku hitobito to tomoni chikara zuyoi undō o: sekai ni takamaru Betonamu Sensō hantai no kōdō', *Betonamu Hanashiai no Kai Nyūsu*, 11 (15 October, 1966).
平塚らいてう「働く人びととともに力づよい運動を—世界に高まるベトナム戦争反対の行動」『ベトナム
話し合いの会ニュース』11号、1966年10月15日。

Hiratsuka Raichō, 'Heiwa daishūkai e no yobikake', *Sekai no Fujin to Nihon no Fujin*, 3 (May, 1954).
平塚らいてう「平和大集会へのよびかけ」『世界の婦人と日本の婦人』3号、1954年5月。

Hiratsuka Raichō, 'Heiwa no tsubasa', *Fujin Taimuzu* (22 January, 1950).
平塚らいてう「平和のつばさ」『婦人タイムズ』1950年1月22日。

Hiratsuka Raichō, 'Heiwa o nozomu zenjosei ni uttaeru', *Minami Nihon Shinbun* (1 October, 1952).
平塚らいてう「平和を望む全女性に訴える」『南日本新聞』1952年10月1日。

Hiratsuka Raichō, 'Hibusōkoku Nihon josei yori Beikoku jōin giin shoshi ni uttaeru', *Fujin Kōron* (March, 1952).
平塚らいてう「非武装国日本女性より米国上院議員諸氏に訴える」『婦人公論』1952年3月。

Hiratsuka Raichō, 'Hibusō no heiwa', *Fujin Minshu Shinbun* (29 July, 1950).
平塚らいてう「非武装の平和」『婦人民主新聞』１９５０年７月２９日。

Hiratsuka Raichō, 'Hi no onna hi no kuni ni kaeru: jomakushiki shukuji', *Nihon Dangi* (April, 1962).
平塚らいてう「火の女火の国に帰る－除幕式祝辞」『日本談義』１９６２年４月。

Hiratsuka Raichō, 'Hinin no kahi o ronzu', *Nihon Hyōron* (September, 1917).
平塚らいてう「避妊の可否を論ず」『日本評論』１９１７年９月。

Hiratsuka Raichō, 'Hitotsu ni musubu chikara', *Sekai no Fujin to Nihon no Fujin*, 1 (December, 1953).
平塚らいてう「一つに結ぶ力」『世界の婦人と日本の婦人』１号、１９５３年１２月。

Hiratsuka Raichō, 'Hokuriku yori Kansai e', *Josei Dōmei*, 3 (December, 1920).
平塚らいてう「北陸より関西へ」『女性同盟』３号、１９２０年１２月。

Hiratsuka Raichō, 'Ichi, ni no handō josei', *Fujin Sensen*, 1:4 (June, 1930).
平塚らいてう「一、二の反動女性」『婦人戦線』第１巻４号、１９３０年６月。

Hiratsuka Raichō, 'Ikuji shakaika no shisō o saiginmi seyo', *Fujin no Tomo* (November, 1931).
平塚らいてう「育児社会化の思想を再吟味せよ」『婦人之友』１９３１年１１月。

Hiratsuka Raichō, 'Ito Noe-san no arukareta michi', *Shin Nihon* (July & August, 1917).
平塚らいてう「伊藤野枝さんの歩かれた道」『新日本』１９１７年７月及び８月。

Hiratsuka Raichō, 'Iwayuru jiyū renai to sono seigen', *Osaka Mainichi Shinbun* (4 Janurary, 1917).
平塚らいてう「いわゆる自由恋愛とその制限」『大阪毎日新聞』１９１７年１月４日。

Hiratsuka Raichō, 'Jiga no kakuritsu e no tatakai', *Fujin Kōron* (November, 1965).
平塚らいてう「自我の確立へのたたかい」『婦人公論』１９６５年１１月。

Hiratsuka Raichō, 'Jinrui ni hitotsu kotoba o', *Bungei Shunjū* (March, 1951).
平塚らいてう「人類に１つ言葉を」『文藝春秋』１９５１年３月。

Hiratsuka Raichō, 'Jinrui no heiwa e no ishi', *Fujin Kōron* (January, 1952).
平塚らいてう「人類の平和への意志」『婦人公論』１９５２年１月。

Hiratsuka Raichō, 'Joryū sakka ga yo ni deru made', *Bunshō Kurabu* (April, 1950).
平塚らいてう「女流作家が世にでるまで」『文章倶楽部』１９５０年４月。

Hiratsuka Raichō, '*Josei Dōmei* sōkangō sengen', *Josei Dōmei*, 1 (October, 1920).
平塚らいてう「『女性同盟』創刊号宣言」『女性同盟』１号、１９２０年１０月。

Hiratsuka Raichō, 'Karasuyama yori', *Fujo Shinbun* (28 June, 1925 – 6 July, 1926).
平塚らいてう「烏山より」『婦女新聞』１９２５年６月２８日－１９２６年７月６日。

Hiratsuka Raichō, 'Karyūbyō danshi kekkon seigenhō seitei ni kansuru seigan undō', *Josei Dōmei*, 1 (October, 1920).
平塚らいてう「花柳病男子結婚制限法制定に関する請願運動」『女性同盟』１号、１９２０年１０月。

Hiratsuka Raichō, 'Katei no shigoto o shokugyō to miru', *Fujin no Tomo* (April, 1925).
平塚らいてう「家庭の仕事を職業とみる」『婦人之友』１９２５年４月。

Hiratsuka Raichō, 'Kenpō o mamori nukō', *Josei Shinbun* (11 September, 1950).
平塚らいてう「憲法を守りぬこう」『女性新聞』１９５０年９月１１日。

Hiratsuka Raichō, 'Kinuta Mura ni sumite', *Yomiuri Shinbun* (18 May, 1936).
平塚らいてう「砧村に住みて」『読売新聞』１９３６年５月１８日。

Hiratsuka Raichō, 'Kinuta Mura ni tateta watashitachi no ie', *Fujin no Tomo* (January, 1927).
平塚らいてう「砧村に建てた私たちの家」『婦人之友』１９２７年１月。

Hiratsuka Raichō, 'Kinuta Mura yori', *Fujin Undō* (October, 1928).
平塚らいてう「砧村より」『婦人運動』１９２８年１０月。

Hiratsuka Raichō, 'Kinuta Mura zassō', *Fujo Shinbun* (22 June – 21 September, 1930).
平塚らいてう「砧村雑草」『婦女新聞』１９３０年６月２２日－９月２１日。

Hiratsuka Raichō, 'Kodomo ni misetai eiga', *Fujin no Tomo* (September, 1926).
平塚らいてう「子供に見せたい映画」『婦人之友』１９２６年９月。

Hiratsuka Raichō, 'Kodomo no kyōiku no koto nado: Kazue-san ni', *Fujin no Tomo* (October, 1924).

平塚らいてう「子供の教育のことなど（一枝さんに）」『婦人之友』１９２４年１０月。

Hiratsuka Raichō, 'Kodomo o Seijō Shōgakkō ni ireta koto ni tsuite', *Fujin no Tomo* (March, 1926).

平塚らいてう「子供を成城小学校に入れたことについて」『婦人之友』１９２６年3月。

Hiratsuka Raichō, 'Kōgen no aki', *Seitō*, 1:3 (November, 1911) & 1:4 (December, 1911).

平塚らいてう「高原の秋」『青鞜』第１巻3号及び4号、１９１１年１１月及び１２月。

Hiratsuka Raichō, 'Kojin toshite no seikatsu to sei toshite no seikatsu tono aida no sōtō ni tsuite', *Seitō*, 5:8 (September, 1915).

平塚らいてう「個人としての生活と性としての生活との間の争闘について」『青鞜』　第5巻8号、１９１5年9月。

Hiratsuka Raichō, 'Kokoro kara no shiji to kyōryoku o: Betonamu Sensō o owaraseru tame no futatsu no kokusai kaigi', *Betonamu Hanashiai no Kai Nyūsu*, 14 (30 March, 1968).

平塚らいてう「心からの支持と協力を－ベトナム戦争を終わらせるための二つの国際会議」『ベトナム話し合いの会ニュース』１４号、１９6８年3月30日。

Hiratsuka Raichō, 'Kokoro no heiwa undō', *Nihon Fujin Shinbun* (9 August, 1948).

平塚らいてう「心の平和運動」『日本婦人新聞』１９4８年8月9日。

Hiratsuka Raichō, 'Marumado yori: onna to shite no Higuchi Ichiyō', *Seitō*, 2:10 (October, 1912).

平塚らいてう「円窓より－女としての樋口一葉」『青鞜』第２巻１０号、１９１２年１０月。

Hiratsuka Raichō, 'Mejiro no omoide', *Tokyo Asahi Shinbun* (1–3 December, 1939).

平塚らいてう「目白の思い出」『東京朝日新聞』１９3９年１２月１日－１２月3日。

Hiratsuka Raichō, 'Mukashi no jogakusei to ima no jogakusei', *Josei Kaizō* (January, 1950).

平塚らいてう「昔の女学生と今の女学生」『女性改造』１９50年１月。

Hiratsuka Raichō, 'Mōkenai shōbai: shōhi kumiai ni tsuite', *Josei Shinbun* (20 September, 1930).

平塚らいてう「儲けない商売－消費組合について」『女性新聞』１９30年9月２０日。

Hiratsuka Raichō, 'Musan seitō to fusen undō', *Fujo Shinbun* (3 December, 1927).

平塚らいてう「無産政党と婦選運動」『婦女新聞』１９２７年１２月3日。

Hiratsuka Raichō, 'Musan seitō to musan fujin dantai', *Fujo Shinbun* (20 February, 1927).

平塚らいてう「無産政党と無産婦人団体」『婦女新聞』１９２７年２月２０日。

Hiratsuka Raichō, 'Mushiro Boshi Hogo Hō o seitei seyo', *Fujin Kurabu* (August, 1930).

平塚らいてう「むしろ母子保護法を制定せよ」『婦人倶楽部』１９30年8月。

Hiratsuka Raichō, 'Musume ni haha no isan o kataru', *Shin Nyoen* (March & April, 1937).

平塚らいてう「娘に母の遺産を語る」『新女苑』１９3７年3月及び4月。

Hiratsuka Raichō, 'Nagoya chihō no jokō seikatsu', *Kokumin Shinbun* (8–12 September, 1919).

平塚らいてう「名古屋地方の女工生活」『国民新聞』１９１9年9月8日－9月１２日。

Hiratsuka Raichō, 'Naki chichi o shinobite', *Fujin Kōron* (May, 1941).

平塚らいてう「亡き父を偲びて」『婦人公論』１９4１年5月。

Hiratsuka Raichō, 'Nihon ni okeru jokō mondai', *Fujin Kōron* (June, 1919).

平塚らいてう「日本における女工問題」『婦人公論』１９１9年6月。

Hiratsuka Raichō, 'Nihon no haha no tachiba', *Sandē Mainichi* (13 August, 1950).

平塚らいてう「日本の母の立場」『サンデー毎日』１９50年8月１3日。

Hiratsuka Raichō, '25–nen mae no watakushi', *Fujin no Tomo* (April, 1928).

平塚らいてう「２5年前のわたくし」『婦人之友』１９２8年4月。

Hiratsuka Raichō, 'Nishikawa Fumiko-shi no *Fujin Kaihōron* o hyōsu', *Seitō*, 4:5 (May, 1914).
平塚らいてう「西川文子氏の『婦人解放論』を評す」『青鞜』第4巻5号、1914年5月。

Hiratsuka Raichō, 'Nora-san ni', *Seitō*, 2:1 (January, 1912).
平塚らいてう「ノラさんに」『青鞜』第2巻1号、1912年1月。

Hiratsuka Raichō, 'Ōgai fusai to *Seitō*', *Bungei* (August, 1962).
平塚らいてう「鷗外夫妻と『青鞜』」『文芸』1962年8月。

Hiratsuka Raichō, 'Ogaigawa tsūshin', *Shomotsu Tenbō* (May, 1944).
平塚らいてう「小貝川通信」『書物展望』1944年5月。

Hiratsuka Raichō, 'Ōgai sensei ni tsuite', *Bungaku Sanpo* (October, 1962).
平塚らいてう「鷗外先生について」『文学散歩』1962年10月。

Hiratsuka Raichō, 'Oku Mumeo-san no koto', *Fujin Kōron* (December, 1925).
平塚らいてう「奥むめおさんのこと」『婦人公論』1925年12月。

Hiratsuka Raichō, 'Okumura Hiroshi no rafu sobyō ni tsuite', *Bungaku Sanpo* (September, 1964).
平塚らいてう「奥村博史の裸婦素描について」『文学散歩』1964年9月。

Hiratsuka Raichō, 'Onore to kataru', *Fujo Shinbun* (8 March, 1925).
平塚らいてう「おのれと語る」『婦女新聞』1925年3月8日。

Hiratsuka Raichō, 'Raichō no jiku', *Fujin Minshu Shinbun* (10 January, 1949).
平塚らいてう「雷鳥の軸」『婦人民主新聞』1949年1月10日。

Hiratsuka Raichō, '*Renai to kekkon*: honyaku oyobi shōkai', *Seitō*, 3:1 (January, 1913).
平塚らいてう「『恋愛と結婚』―翻訳及び紹介」『青鞜』第3巻1号、1913年1月。

Hiratsuka Raichō, '30-nen mae no watashi', *Fujo Shinbun* (10 May, 1930).
平塚らいてう「三十年前の私」『婦女新聞』1930年5月10日。

Hiratsuka Raichō, 'Seitō jidai', *Asuka* (January – July, 1937).
平塚らいてう「青鞜時代」『明日香』1937年1月―7月。

Hiratsuka Raichō, 'Seitōsha no koto', *Taiyō* (June, 1927).
平塚らいてう「青鞜社のこと」『太陽』1927年6月。

Hiratsuka Raichō, '*Seitō* to watashi: *Seitō* o Noe-san ni oyuzurisuru ni tsuite', *Seitō*, 5:1 (January, 1915).
平塚らいてう「『青鞜』と私―『青鞜』を野枝さんにお譲りするについて」『青鞜』第5巻1号、1915年1月。

Hiratsuka Raichō, 'Seitō undō no haikei', *Zuihitsu* (January, 1957).
平塚らいてう「青鞜運動の背景」『随筆』1957年1月。

Hiratsuka Raichō, 'Sekai heiwa e no michi', *Nihon Joshidai Shinbun* (20 September, 1950).
平塚らいてう「世界平和への道」『日本女子大新聞』1950年9月20日。

Hiratsuka Raichō, 'Sekai no josei: Ellen Key', *Fujin no Tomo* (December, 1927).
平塚らいてう「世界の女性―エレン・ケイ」『婦人之友』1927年12月。

Hiratsuka Raichō, 'Shakai kaizō ni taisuru fujin no shimei: *Josei Dōmei* sōkan no ji ni kaete', *Josei Dōmei*, 1 (October, 1920).
平塚らいてう「社会改造に対する婦人の使命―『女性同盟』創刊の辞に代えて」『女性同盟』1号、1920年10月。

Hiratsuka Raichō, 'Shi to sono zengo o mite', *Yūben* (December, 1918).
平塚らいてう「死とその前後を見て」『雄弁』1918年12月。

Hiratsuka Raichō, 'Shin Fujin Kyōkai no kaiko', *Fujin Kōron*, (March – July, 1923).
平塚らいてう「新婦人協会の回顧」『婦人公論』1923年3月―7月。

Hiratsuka Raichō, 'Shin Fujin Kyōkai no seigan undō ni tsuite Yosano Akiko-shi ni okotaeshimasu', *Chūō Kōron* (April, 1920).
平塚らいてう「新婦人協会の請願運動について与謝野晶子氏にお答えします」『中央公論』1920年4月。

Hiratsuka Raichō, 'Shinsai zakki: kora e', *Josei Kaizō* (October & November, 1923).
平塚らいてう「震災雑記―子らへ」『女性改造』1923年10月及び11月。

Hiratsuka Raichō, 'Shōhi kumiai to fujin no ichi', *Fujin no Tomo* (October, 1932).
平塚らいてう「消費組合と婦人の位置」『婦人之友』１９３２年１０月。

Hiratsuka Raichō, 'Shōhisha: chūō shijō no funsō to shōhi kumiai mondai', *Miyako Shinbun* (25 September, 1935).
平塚らいてう「消費者－中央市場の紛争と消費組合問題」『都新聞』１９３５年９月２５日。

Hiratsuka Raichō, 'Shojo no shinkachi', *Shin Kōron* (March, 1915).
平塚らいてう「処女の真価値」『新公論』１９１５年３月。

Hiratsuka Raichō, 'Shotaimen no inshō', *Subaru* (March, 1950).
平塚らいてう「初対面の印象」『スバル』１９５０年３月。

Hiratsuka Raichō, 'Shōwa fujin kaihō undōshi: Taiheiyō Sensō ni totsunyū suru made', *Josei Kaizō* (May-June, 1951).
平塚らいてう「昭和婦人解放運動史－太平洋戦争に突入するまで」『女性改造』１９５１年５月－８月。

Hiratsuka Raichō, 'Takamura Kōtarō to Chieko fusai', *Fujin Kōron* (August, 1951).
平塚らいてう「高村光太郎と智恵子夫妻」『婦人公論』１９５１年８月。

Hiratsuka Raichō, 'Tamura Toshiko-san', *Chūō Kōron* (August, 1914).
平塚らいてう「田村俊子さん」『中央公論』１９１４年８月。

Hiratsuka Raichō, 'Tasukaranu shōhisha', *Yomiuri Shinbun* (28 May, 1936).
平塚らいてう「助からぬ消費者」『読売新聞』１９３６年５月２８日。

Hiratsuka Raichō, 'Tenkanki ni tateru Nihon no fujin sanseiken undō', *Fujin no Tomo* (April, 1927).
平塚らいてう「転換期に立てる日本の婦人参政権運動」『婦人之友』１９２７年４月。

Hiratsuka Raichō, *Tōge* in *Jiji Shinpō* (1–21 April, 1915).
平塚らいてう「峠」『時事新報』１９１５年４月１日－２１日。

Hiratsuka Raichō, 'Tozashi aru mado nite', *Seitō*, 3:6 (June, 1913).
平塚らいてう「とざしある窓にて」『青鞜』第３巻６号、１９１３年６月。

Hiratsuka Raichō, 'Waga kuni no fujin sanseiken mondai ni tsuite', *Chūgai* (April, 1919).
平塚らいてう「我が国の婦人参政権問題について」『中外』１９１９年４月。

Hiratsuka Raichō, 'Waga shōjo no hi', in Ikuta Hanayo *et al.*, *Waga Shōjo no Hi* (Kyoto, 1942).
平塚らいてう「わが少女の日」生田花世他著『わが少女の日』１９４２年（京都）。

Hiratsuka Raichō, 'Watashi no mita Noe-san to iu hito', *Fujin Kōron* (November/December, 1923).
平塚らいてう「私の見た野枝さんという人」『婦人公論』１９２３年１１月・１２月合併号。

Hiratsuka Raichō, 'Watashi no shitteiru Kamichika Ichiko-san', *Onna no Sekai* (January, 1917).
平塚らいてう「私の知っている神近市子さん」『女の世界』１９１７年１月。

Hiratsuka Raichō, 'Yahina kōgeki o mikanete', *Chūō Kōron* (October, 1962).
平塚らいてう「野卑な攻撃をみかねて」『中央公論』１９６２年１０月。

Hiratsuka Raichō, 'Yonda *Magda*', *Seitō*, 2:6 (June, 1912).
平塚らいてう「読んだ『マグダ』」『青鞜』第２巻６号、１９１２年６月。

Hiratsuka Raichō, 'Yo no fujin tachi e', *Seitō*, 3:4 (April, 1913).
平塚らいてう「世の婦人たちへ」『青鞜』第３巻４号、１９１３年４月。

Hiratsuka Raichō, 'Yūshū', *Myōjō* (November, 1908).
平塚らいてう「幽愁」『明星』１９０８年１１月。

(c) *Translations*

Hiratsuka Raichō, *Bosei no Fukkō* (1919), a translation of Ellen Key, *Renaissance of Motherhood* (1910).
エレン・ケイ著、平塚らいてう訳『母性の復興』１９１９年。

Hiratsuka Raichō, *Fujin no Reizoku* in Heibonsha (ed.), *Shakai Shisō Zenshū*, vol. 36 (1929), a translation of J.S. Mill, *The Subjection of Women* (1869).
Ｊ・Ｓ・ミル著、平塚らいてう訳『婦人の隷属』平凡社編『社会思想全集』第３６巻、１９２９年。

2. *Autobiographies, Memoirs, Collected Works, Monographs by Hiratsuka Raichō's Contemporaries and Relatives*

Fukuda Hideko, *Warawa no Hanseigai* (1904, 1970 edn).
福田英子『妾の半生涯』１９７０年、１９０４年初版。

Ichikawa Fusae, *Daikon no Hana* (1979).
市川房枝『だいこんの花』１９７９年。

Ichikawa Fusae, *Ichikawa Fusae Jiden: Senzen Hen* (1974).
市川房枝『市川房枝自伝－戦前編』１９７４年。

Ichikawa Fusae, *Nonaka no Ippon Sugi* (1981).
市川房枝『野中の一本杉』１９８１年。

Ikuta Hanayo *et al.*, *Waga Shōjo no Hi* (Kyoto, 1941).
生田花世他著『わが少女の日』１９４１年（京都）。

Itō Noe, *Itō Noe Zenshū*, 2 vols (1970).
伊藤野枝『伊藤野枝全集』上・下巻、１９７０年。

Kamichika Ichiko, *Kamichika Ichiko Jiden: Waga Ai Waga Tatakai* (1972).
神近市子『神近市子自伝－わが愛わが闘い』１９７２年。

Katō Shidzue, *Ai wa Jidai o Koete* (1988).
加藤シヅエ『愛は時代を越えて』１９８８年。

Katō Shidzue, *Saiai no Hito Kanju e: Katō Shidzue Nikki* (1988).
加藤シヅエ『最愛のひと勘十へ－加藤シヅエ日記』１９８８年。

Kushida Fuki, 'Josei kaihō e no jōnetsu', in Maruoka Hideko *et al.*, *Hiratsuka Raichō to Nihon no Kindai* (1986).
櫛田ふき「女性解放への情熱」丸岡秀子他著『平塚らいてうと日本の近代』１９８６年。

Kushida Fuki, *Suteki ni Nagaiki* (1991).
櫛田ふき『素敵に長生き』１９９１年。

Maruoka Hideko, 'Seitō kara Kokusai Fujin Nen e', in Maruoka Hideko *et al.*, *Hiratsuka Raichō to Nihon no Kindai* (1986).
丸岡秀子「『青鞜』から国際婦人年へ」丸岡秀子他著『平塚らいてうと日本の近代』1986年。

Morita Sōhei, *Baien* (1909), in Chikuma Shobō (ed.), *Gendai Nihon Bungaku Taikei*, vol. 29 (1971 edn).
森田草平『煤煙』筑摩書房編、『現代日本文学大系29』1971年、1909年初版。

Nishikawa Fumiko (ed. by Amano Shigeru), *Heiminsha no Onna: Nishikawa Fumiko Jiden* (1984).
西川文子著、天野茂編『平民社の女・西川文子自伝』１９８４年。

Nishikawa Fumiko (ed. by Amano Shigeru), *Fujin Kaihōron* (1914, 1986 edn).
西川文子著、天野茂編『婦人解放論』１９８６年、１９１４年初版。

Okamoto Kanoko, *Okamoto Kanoko Zenshū*, 12 vols (1994).
岡本かのこ『岡本かのこ全集』全12巻、１９９４年。

Oku Mumeo, *Nobi Akaaka to: Oku Mumeo Jiden* (1988).
奥むめお『野火あかあかと－奥むめお自伝』１９８８年。

Okumura Hiroshi, *Meguriai* (1956).
奥村博史『めぐりあい』１９５６年。

Ōoka Shōhei, 'Raichō sensei to watashi', in Maruoka Hideko *et al.*, *Hiratsuka Raichō to Nihon no Kindai* (1986).
大岡昇平「らいてう先生とわたし」丸岡秀子他著『平塚らいてうと日本の近代』１９８６年。

Ōsugi Sakae, *Jijoden: Nihon Dasshutsu Ki* (1991).
大杉栄『自叙伝・日本脱出記』１９９１年。

Sakai Toshihiko (ed. by Suzuki Yūko), *Sakai Toshihiko Josei Ronshū* (1983).
堺利彦著、鈴木裕子編『堺利彦女性論集』１９８３年。

Takamure Itsue, *Hi no Kuni no Onna no Nikki* (1965).
高群逸枝『火の国の女の日記』１９６５年。

Tsukizoe Akemi, 'Haha, Hiratsuka Raichō no omoide', *Tosho* (October, 1987).
築添曙生「母、平塚らいてうの思い出」『図書』１９８７年１０月。

Tsukizoe Akemi, 'Haha ni yosu', Ōtsuki Shoten (ed.), *Hiratsuka Raichō Chosakushū Geppō*, 2 (August, 1983).
築添曙生「母に寄す」大月書店編『平塚らいてう著作集月報』2、１９８３年8月。

Tsukizoe Akemi, 'Waga haha', in Maruoka Hideko *et al.*, *Hiratsuka Raichō to Nihon no Kindai* (1986).
築添曙生「わが母」丸岡秀子他著『平塚らいてうと日本の近代』１９８６年。

Yamakawa Kikue, *20-seiki o Ayumu: Aru Onna no Ashiato* (1978).
山川菊栄『20世紀を歩む－ある女の足あと』１９７８年。

Yamakawa Kikue, *Onna Nidai no Ki* (1972, 1987 edn).
山川菊栄『おんな二代の記』１９８７、１９７２年初版。

Yamakawa Kikue, (ed. by Suzuki Yūko), *Yamakawa Kikue Hyōronshū* (1990).
山川菊栄著、鈴木裕子編『山川菊栄評論集』１９９０年。

Yamakawa Kikue, (ed. by Suzuki Yūko), *Yamakawa Kikue Josei Kaihō Ronshū* 3 vols (1984).
山川菊栄著、鈴木裕子編『山川菊栄女性解放論集』全3巻、１９８４年。

Yamanouchi Mina, *Yamanouchi Mina Jiden: 12-sai no Bōseki Jokō kara no Shōgai* (1975).
山内みな『山内みな自伝－12歳の紡績女工からの生涯』１９７５年。

Yosano Akiko (ed. by Kano Masanao & Kōuchi Nobuko), *Yosano Akiko Hyōronshū* (1985).
与謝野晶子著、鹿野政直・香内信子編『与謝野晶子評論集』１９８５年。

3. *Magazines*

Asuka
『明日香』
Bungaku Sanpo
『文学散歩』
Bungei
『文芸』
Bungei Shunjū
『文藝春秋』
Bunshō Kurabu
『文章倶楽部』
Bunshō Sekai
『文章世界』
Chūgai
『中外』
Chūō Kōron
『中央公論』
Fujin Gahō
『婦人画報』
Fujin Kōron
『婦人公論』
Fujin Kurabu
『婦人倶楽部』
Fujin no Tomo
『婦人之友』
Fujin Sekai
『婦人世界』
Fujin Sensen
『婦人戦線』
Fujin Undō
『婦人運動』

Hankyō
『反響』

Ie no Hikari
『家の光』

Jogaku Sekai
『女学世界』

Joō
『女王』

Josei Dōmei
『女性同盟』

Josei Kaizō
『女性改造』

Joseisen
『女性線』

Kaizō
『改造』

Kyōiku Jiron
『教育時論』

Meiroku Zasshi
『明六雑誌』

Myōjō
『明星』

Nihon Dangi
『日本談義』

Nihon Hyōron
『日本評論』

Onna no Sekai
『女の世界』

Sandē Mainichi
『サンデー毎日』

Seitō
『青鞜』

Sekai Fujin
『世界婦人』

Sekai Kokka
『世界国家』

Sekai no Fujin to Nihon no Fujin
『世界の婦人と日本の婦人』

Sekai Seifu
『世界政府』

Shin Kōron
『新公論』

Shin Nihon
『新日本』

Shin Nyoen
『新女苑』

Shin Shin Fujin
『新真婦人』

Shiro Bato
『白鳩』

Shomotsu Tenbō
『書物展望』

Subaru
『スバル』

Taiyō
『太陽』
Tanka Kenkyū
『短歌研究』
Tosho
『図書』
Waseda Bungaku
『早稲田文学』
Yokohama Bōeki Shinpō
『横浜貿易新報』
Yūben
『雄弁』
Zuihitsu
『随筆』

4. *Newspapers*

Akahata
『赤旗』
Akita Sakigake Shinpō
『秋田魁新報』
Asahi Shinbun
『朝日新聞』
Betonamu Hanashiai no Kai Nyūsu
『ベトナム話し合いの会ニュース』
Fujin Minshu Shinbun
『婦人民主新聞』
Fujin Taimuzu
『婦人タイムズ』
Fujo Shinbun
『婦女新聞』
Heiwa Fujin Shinbun
『平和ふじん新聞』
Jiji Shinpō
『時事新報』
Josei Shinbun
『女性新聞』
Kokumin Shinbun
『国民新聞』
Mainichi Shinbun
『毎日新聞』
Minami Nihon Shinbun
『南日本新聞』
Miyako Shinbun
『都新聞』
Nihon Fujin Shinbun
『日本婦人新聞』
Nihon Joshidai Shinbun
『日本女子大新聞』
Nihon Keizai Shinbun
『日本経済新聞』
Niroku Shinpō
『二六新報』
Osaka Asahi Shinbun
『大阪朝日新聞』

Osaka Mainichi Shinbun
『大阪朝日新聞』
Sanyō Shinpō
『山陽新報』
Tokyo Asashi Shinbun
『東京朝日新聞』
Tokyo Nichi Nichi Shinbun
『東京日日新聞』
Tokyo Niroku Shinbun
『東京二六新聞』
Yomiuri Shinbun
『読売新聞』
Yorozuhō
『万朝報』

5. *Parliamentary Records*

Teikoku Gikai Gijiroku (1890–1947).
『帝国議会議事録』１８９０年－１９４７年。

6. *Published Documents*

Ezashi Akiko (ed.), *Ai to Sei no Jiyū: Ie kara no Kaihō* (1989).
江刺昭子編『愛と性の自由、家からの解放』１９８９年。
Horiba Kiyoko (ed.), *Seitō Josei Kaihō Ronshū* (1991).
堀場清子編『青鞜女性解放論集』１９９１年。
Ichikawa Fusae *et al.* (eds), *Nihon Fujin Mondai Shiryō Shūsei*, 10 vols (1976–81).
市川房江他編『日本婦人問題資料集成』全１０巻、１９７６－１９８１年。
Kano Mikiyo (ed.), *Jiga no Kanata e: Kindai o Koeru Feminizumu* (1990).
加納実紀代編『自我の彼方へ、近代を超えるフェミニズム』１９９０年。
Kishida Toshiko (ed. by Suzuki Yūko), *Kishida Toshiko Hyōronshū* (1985).
岸田俊子著、鈴木裕子編『岸田俊子評論集』１９８５年。
Kōuchi Nobuko (ed.), *Shiryō: Bosei Hogo Ronsō* (1984).
香内信子編『資料・母性保護論争』１９８４年。
Koshō Yukiko (ed.), *Shiryō: Joseishi Ronsō* (1987).
古庄ゆき子編『資料・女性史論争』１９８７年。
Monbushō (comp.), *Gakusei 80-nen-shi* (1954).
文部省編『学制八十年史』１９５４年。
Monbushō (comp.), *Gakusei 120-nen-shi* (1992).
文部省編『学制百二十年史』１９９２年。
Nagahara Michiko & Ogata Akiko (eds), *Feminizumu Ryōran: Fuyu no Jidai e no Hōka* (1990).
尾形明子・永畑道子編『フェミニズム繚乱－冬の時代への放火』１９９０年。
Suzuki Yūko (ed.), *Josei: Hangyaku to Kakumei to Teikō to* (1990).
鈴木裕子編『女性・反逆と革命と抵抗と』１９９０年。
Suzuki Yūko (ed.), *Shiryō: Heiminsha no Onnatachi* (1986).
鈴木裕子編『資料・平民社の女たち』１９８６年。
Tokkō Keisatsu Kokusho Henshū Iinkai (ed.), *Tokkō Keisatsu Kokusho* (1977).
特高警察黒書編集委員会編『特高警察黒書』１９７７年。

7. *Videos*

Sakura Eigasha (producer), *87–sai no Seishun: Ichikawa Fusae Shōgai o Kataru* (1981).
桜映画社編『８７歳の青春－市川房枝生涯を語る』１９８１年。
Kokuritsu Fujin Kyōiku Kaikan (producer), *Kokuritsu Fujin Kyōiku Kaikan Shōkai Video* (n.d.).
国立婦人教育会館編『国立婦人教育会館紹介ビデオ』刊年不明。

8. *Privately Published Material*

(a) *Ferris Jogakuin Daigaku*

Ferris Jogakuin (ed.) *Kidder Shokanshū: Nihon Saisho no Joshi Kyōikusha no Kiroku* (Yokohama, 1970).
フェリス女学院編『キダー書簡集－日本最初の女子教育者の記録』１９７０年(横浜)。

Ferris Jogakuin 100-nen-shi Henshū Iinkai (ed.) *Ferris Jogakuin 100-nen-shi* (Yokohama, 1970).
フェリス女学院１００年史編集委員会編『フェリス女学院１００年史』１９７０年(横浜)。

Suzuki Minako *et al.* (eds), *Ferris Jogakuin 110-nen Shōshi* (Yokohama, 1982).
鈴木美南子他編『フェリス女学院１１０年小史』１９８２年(横浜)。

(b) *Nihon Joshi Daigaku*

Nakamura Masao (ed.), *Nihon Joshi Daigakkō 40-nen-shi* (1942).
中村政雄編『日本女子大学校四十年史』１９４２年。

Nihon Joshi Daigakkō (ed.), *Joshi Daigaku Kōgiroku, Jissen Rinri* (n.d.).
日本女子大学校編『女子大学講義録、実践倫理』刊年不明。

Nihon Joshi Daigakkō (comp.), *Nihon Joshi Daigakkō Sotsugyōsei Meibo* (1906–16).
日本女子大学校編『日本女子大学校卒業生名簿』１９０６年－１９１６年。

Nihon Joshi Daigaku (ed.), *Nihon Joshi Daigaku no 80-nen* (1981).
日本女子大学編『日本女子大学の八十年』１９８１年。

Nihon Joshi Daigaku Joshi Kyōiku Kenkyūjo (ed.), *Kongo no Joshi Kyōiku: Naruse Jinzō Joshi Daigaku Ronsenshū* (1984).
日本女子大学女子教育研究所編『今後の女子教育－成瀬仁蔵・女子大学論選集』１９８４年。

Nihon Joshi Daigaku Joshi Kyōiku Kenkyūjo Naruse Kinenkan (ed.), *Naruse Jinzō Kenkyū Bunken Mokuroku* (1984).
日本女子大学女子教育研究所成瀬記念館編『成瀬仁蔵研究文献目録』１９８４年。

Nihon Joshi Daigaku Joshi Kyōiku Kenkyūjo Naruse Kinen Kan (ed.), *Naruse Jinzō Sono Shōgai* (1990).
日本女子大学女子教育研究所成瀬記念館編『成瀬仁蔵その生涯』１９９０年。

Nihon Joshi Daigaku Toshokan (ed.), *Nihon Joshi Daigaku Naruse Bunko Mokuroku* (1979).
日本女子大学図書館編『日本女子大学成瀬文庫目録』１９７９年。

Nishina Setsu (ed.), *Naruse Sensei Den* (1928).
仁科節編『成瀬先生伝』１９２８年。

Nishina Setsu (ed.), *Naruse Sensei Kinenchō* (1936).
仁科節編『成瀬先生記念帖』１９３６年。

Nishina Setsu & Ōhashi Hiro (eds), *Naruse Sensei no Oshie* (1951).
仁科節・大橋広『成瀬先生のおしえ』１９５１年。

Ōfūkai (comp.), *Ōfūkai Kaiin Meibo.*
桜楓会編『桜楓会会員名簿』

Watanabe Eiichi (ed.), *Nihon Joshi Daigaku Sōritsusha Naruse Sensei* (1928).
渡辺英一編『日本女子大学創立者成瀬先生』１９２８年。

(c) *Seijō Gakuen*

Seijō Gakuen (comp.), *Seijō Gakuen Dōsōkai Meibo.*
成城学園編『成城学園同窓会名簿』。

Seijō Gakuen (comp.), *Seijō Gakuen Sotsugyōsei Meibo.*
成城学園編『成城学園卒業生名簿』。

Seijō Gakuen Kyōiku Kenkyūjo (ed.), *Sawayanagi Masatarō Kyōiku Ronshō* (1987).
成城学園教育研究所編『澤柳政太郎教育論抄』１９８７年。

(d) *Tsuda Juku Daigaku*

Yamazaki Takako (ed.), *Tsuda Juku 60-nen-shi* (1960).
山崎孝子編『津田塾六十年史』１９６０年。
Yamazaki Takako (ed.), *Tsuda Umeko Monjo* (1980, 1984 edn).
山崎孝子編『津田梅子文書』１９８４年、１９８０年（初版）。
Yoshikawa Toshikazu (ed.), *Tsuda Umeko Den* (1956).
吉川利一編『津田梅子伝』１９５６年。

II. *Japanese Secondary Sources*

(A) *Books and Articles*

Aida Kurakichi, *Fukuzawa Yukichi* (1974).
会田倉吉『福沢諭吉』１９７４年。
Amano Shigeru, 'Nishikawa Fumiko *Fujin Kaihōron* kaisetsu', in Nishikawa Fumiko, *Fujin Kaihōron* (1914, 1986 edn).
天野茂「西川文子『婦人解放論』解説」西川文子『婦人解放論』１９８６年、１９１４年（初版）。
Aoki Takako, *Kindaishi o Hiraita Joseitachi: Nihon Joshi Daigaku ni Mananda Hitotachi* (1990).
青木生子『近代史を拓いた女性たち－日本女子大学に学んだ人たち』１９９０年。
Bacon, Alice (trans. by Kuno Akiko), *Kazoku Jogakkō Kyōshi no Mita Meiji Nihon no Uchigawa* (1994).
アリス・ベーコン著・久野明子訳『華族女学校教師の見た明治日本の内側』１９９４年。
Chiya Michio, 'Ōsugi Sakae to atarashii onnatachi', *Rekishi to Jinbutsu Tokushū: Kindai Renai Jiken Hiwa* (April, 1980).
千谷道雄「大杉栄と新しい女たち」『歴史と人物特集、近代恋愛事件秘話』１９８０年４月。
Deguchi Nao, *Ōmoto Shinyu: Ten no Maki* (1979).
出口ナオ『大本神諭－天の巻』１９７９年。
Eguchi Hakuo, *Nihon no Rekishi: Gendai no Nihon* (1976).
江口朴郎『日本の歴史－現代の日本』１９７６年。
Emura Eiichi, *Meiji no Kenpō* (1992).
江村栄一『明治の憲法』１９９２年。
Esashi Akiko, *Sameyo Onnatachi: Sekirankai no Hitobito* (1980).
江刺昭子『覚めよ女たち、赤瀾会の人びと』１９８０年。
Esashi Akiko & Itoya Sumio, *Sengoshi to Josei no Kaihō* (1977).
江刺昭子・絲屋寿雄『戦後史と女性の解放』１９７７年。
Esashi Akiko & Ide Fumiko, *Taishō Demokurashii to Josei* (1977).
江刺昭子・井手文子『大正デモクラシーと女性』１９７７年。
Esashi Akiko, 'Yamakawa Kikue', in Setouchi Harumi (ed.), *Meiji Josei no Chiteki Jōnetsu* (1989).
江刺昭子「山川菊栄」瀬戸内晴美編『明治女性の知的情熱』１９８９年。
Fujii Chie & Kanamori Toshie, *Onna no Kyōiku 100-nen* (1977).
藤井治枝・金森トシエ『女の教育１００年』１９７７年。
Fujin Kyōdō Hōritsu Jimusho (ed.), *Ima Naze Yūsei Hogohō Kaiaku ka* (1983).
婦人協同法律事務所編『いまなぜ優生保護法改悪か』１９８３年。
Fukuchi Shigetaka, *Kindai Nihon Joseishi* (1977).
福地重孝『近代日本女性史』１９７７年。
Fukuo Takeichirō, *Nihon Kazoku Seidoshi Gaisetsu* (1972).
福尾猛市郎『日本家族制度史概説』１９７２年。
Fukuzawa Yukichi, *Gakumon no Susume* (1872–76, 1998 edn).
福沢諭吉『学問のすすめ』１９９８年、１８７２－７６年（初版）。
Fukuzawa Yukichi, *Onna Daigaku Hyōron, Shin Onna Daigaku* (1899).
福沢諭吉『女大学評論、新女大学』１８９９年。

Fukuzawa Yukichi, *Shintei Fukuō Jiden* (1899, 1990 edn).
福沢諭吉『新訂、福翁自伝』１９９０年、１８９９年（初版）。

Furuki Yoshiko, *Tsuda Umeko* (1992).
古木宜志子『津田梅子』１９９２年。

Fuse Akiko, *Kekkon to Kazoku* (1993).
布施晶子『結婚と家族』１９９３年。

Gotō Yasuko & Ōkubo Kazunori, *Josei to Hō* (1990).
後藤安子・大久保一徳『女性と法』１９９０年。

Grūpu Bosei Kaidoku Kōza (ed.), *Bosei o Kaidokusuru* (1991).
グループ「母性」解読講座編『母性を解読する』１９９１年。

Haga Noboru, *Ryōsai Kenboron* (1990).
芳賀登『良妻賢母論』１９９０年。

Hasegawa Hitoshi & Kōno Toshirō (eds), *Hasegawa Shigure: Hito to Shōgai* (1982).
長谷川仁・紅野敏郎編『長谷川時雨－人と生涯』１９８２年。

Hayashi Reiko *et al.* (eds), *Nihon Joseishi* (1987).
林玲子 他編『日本女性史』１９８７年。

Higuchi Kiyoyuki, *Nippon Joseishi Hakkutsu* (1979).
樋口清之『にっぽん女性史発掘』１９７９年。

Hino Takako, *Josei ga Kagayaku Jidai o Hiraku Hiratsuka Raichō* (1989).
日野多香子『女性が輝く時代を拓く平塚らいてう』１９８９年。

Hiraoka Toshio *et al.* (eds), *Meiji no Bungaku* (1972, 1985 edn).
平岡敏夫 他編『明治の文学』１９８５年、１９７２年（初版）。

Hiratsuka Raichō o Yomu Kai (ed.), *Raichō Soshite Watashi*, 3 vols (1987–91).
平塚らいてうを読む会編『らいてうそして私』全３巻、１９８７－９１年。

Hiratsuka Raichō o Yomu Kai (ed.), *Seitō no 50-nin* (1996, 1997 edn).
平塚らいてうを読む会編『「青鞜」の５０人』１９９７年、１９９６年（初版）。

Horiba Kiyoko, *Seitō no Jidai* (1988).
堀場清子『青鞜の時代』１９８８年。

Hoshi Ruriko *et al.* (eds), *Ōfū no 100-nin: Nihon Joshidai Monogatari* (1996).
星瑠璃子 他編『桜楓の百人、日本女子大物語』１９９６年。

Hosoi Wakizō, *Jokō Aishi* (1925, 1988 edn).
細井和喜蔵『女工哀史』１９８８年、１９２５年（初版）。

Hozumi Shigetō, *Rienjō to Enkiri Dera* (1942).
穂積重遠『離縁状と縁切寺』１９４２年。

Ichikawa Fusae to Iu Hito Kankōkai (ed.), *Ichikawa Fusae to Iu Hito: 100-nin no Kaisō* (1982).
『市川房枝というひと』刊行会編『市川房枝というひと－１００人の回想』１９８２年。

Ichikawa Misao, *Ichikawa Fusae Omoide Banashi* (1992).
市川ミサオ『市川房枝おもいで話』１９９２年。

Ide Fumiko, *Hiratsuko Raichō: Kindai to Shinpi* (1987).
井手文子『平塚らいてう－近代と神秘』１９８７年。

Ide Fumiko, 'Kaisetsu', in Fuji Shuppan (ed.), *Seitō Kaisetsu, Sōmokuji, Sakuin* (1983).
井手文子「解説」不二出版編『「青鞜」解説・総目次・索引』１９８３年。

Ide Fumiko, *Seitō no Onnatachi* (1975).
井手文子『「青鞜」の女たち』１９７５年。

Igarashi Tomio, *Enkiri Dera* (1972).
五十嵐富夫『縁切寺』１９７２年。

Ikeda Michiko, 'Itō Noe', in Setouchi Harumi (ed.), *Hangyaku no Onna no Roman* (1989).
池田みち子「伊藤野枝」瀬戸内晴美編『反逆の女のロマン』１９８９年。

Imai Seiichi, *Taishō Demokurashii* (1984, 1991 edn).
今井清一『大正デモクラシー』１９９１年、１９８４年（初版）。

Inoue Kiyoshi, *Gendai Nihon Joseishi* (1962).
井上清『現代日本女性史』１９６２年。

Inoue Kiyoshi, *Nihon Joseishi* (1948, 1954 edn).
井上清『日本女性史』１９５４年。１９４８年（初版）。

Inoue Teruko, *Joseigaku e no Shōtai* (1992).
井上輝子『女性学への招待』１９９２年。

Inoue Zenjō, *Kakekomi Dera Tōkeijishi* (1980).
井上禅定『駆込寺 東慶寺史』１９８０年。

Irie Shunkō (ed.), *Yosano Akiko* (1985).
入江春行編『与謝野晶子』１９８５年。

Ishii Ayako, 'Gensuibaku kinshi no uttae', in Maruoka Hideko *et al.*, *Hiratsuka Raichō to Nihon no Kindai* (1986).
石井あやこ「原水爆禁止の訴え」丸岡秀子他『平塚らいてうと日本の近代』１９８６年。

Ishii Ryōsuke, *Edo no Rikon: Mikudari Han to Enkiri Dera* (1965).
石井良助『江戸の離婚－三行り半と縁切寺』１９６５年。

Isomura Haruko, *Ima no Onna: Shiryō Meiji Joseishi* (1913, 1986 edn).
磯村春子『今の女－資料明治女性誌』１９８６年、１９１３年（初版）。

Itō Yasuko, *Joseishi Nyūmon* (1992).
伊藤康子『女性史入門』１９９２年。

Itoya Toshio, *Josei Kaihō no Senkusha: Nakajima Toshiko to Fukuda Hideko* (1984).
絲家寿雄『女性解放の先駆者、中島俊子と福田英子』１９８４年。

Itoya Toshio, *Kōtoku Shūsui* (1973).
絲家寿雄『幸徳秋水』１９７３年。

Itoya Toshio, *Meiji Ishin to Josei no Yoake* (1976).
絲家寿雄『明治維新と女性の夜明け』１９７６年。

Jō Natsuko, 'Hasegawa Shigure', in Setouchi Harumi (ed.), *Koi to Geijutsu e no Jōnetsu* (1989).
城夏子「長谷川時雨」瀬戸内晴美編『恋と芸術への情念』１９８９年。

Jō Natsuko, 'Yosano Akiko', in Setouchi Harumi (ed.), *Hi to Moeta Joryū Bungaku* (1989).
城夏子「与謝野晶子」瀬戸内晴美編『火と燃えた女流文学』１９８９年。

Joseishi Sōgō Kenkyūkai (ed.), *Nihon Joseishi*, 5 vols (1982, 1985 edn).
女性史総合研究会編『日本女性史』全５巻、１９８５年、１９８２年（初版）。

Kaibara Ekken, *Wazoku Dōshi Kun* (1710), in Matsuda Michio (ed.), *Kaibara Ekken* (1969).
貝原益軒「和俗童子訓」松田道雄編『貝原益軒』１９６９年。

Kamichika Ichiko, *Josei Shisōshi* (1974).
神近市子『女性思想史』１９７４年。

Kano Masanao, *Fujin, Josei, Onna* (1989).
鹿野政直『婦人・女性・おんな』１９８９年。

Kano Masanao, *Taishō Demokurashii* (1976).
鹿野政直『大正デモクラシー』１９７６年。

Kano Mikiyo, 'Bosei no tanjō to Tennōsei', in Ehara Yumiko *et al.* (eds), *Bosei* (1995).
加納実紀代「母性の誕生と天皇制」江原由美子他編『母性』１９９５年。

Karasawa Tomitarō, *Joshi Gakusei no Rekishi* (1979).
唐澤富太郎『女子学生の歴史』１９７９年。

Kasahara Kazuo, 'Nyonin shōki', in Tokyo Daigaku (ed.), *Tokyo Daigaku Kōkai Kōza: Otoko to Onna*, vol. 18 (1974).
笠原一男「女人正機」『東京大学公開講座１８ 男と女』１９７４年。

Katano Masako, 'Ryōsai kenbo shugi no genryū', in Kindai Joseishi Kenkyūkai (ed.), *Onnatachi no Kindai*, (1978).
片野真佐子「良妻賢母主義の源流」近代女性史研究会編『女たちの近代』１９７８年。

Kataoka Ryōichi, 'Morita Sōhei no ichi to sakufū', in Chikuma Shobō (ed.), *Gendai Nihon Bungaku Zenshū*, vol. 22 (1955).
片岡良一「森田草平の位置と作風」筑摩書房編『現代日本文学全集 ２２』１９５５年。

Katayama Kiyoichi, *Kindai Nihon no Joshi Kyōiku* (1984).
片山清一『近代日本の女子教育』１９８４年。

Katō Shūichi, *Nihon Bungakushi Josetsu*, 2 vols (1980).
加藤俊一『日本文学史序説』全2巻、1980年。

Key, Ellen (trans. by Harada Minoru), *Renai to Kekkon*, 2 vols (1930–1).
エレン・ケイ著、原田実訳『恋愛と結婚』上・下巻、1930‐31年。

Kinjō Kiyoko, *Hō Joseigaku no Susume* (1983, 1989 edn).
金城清子『法女性学のすすめ』1989年、1983年（初版）。

Kobayashi Shigeyoshi, *Meiji no Tokyo Seikatsu: Josei no Kaita Meiji no Nikki* (1991).
小林重喜『明治の東京生活－女性の書いた明治の日記』1991年。

Kobayashi Tomie, *Hiratsuka Raichō: Hito to Shisō* (1983, 1988 edn).
小林登美枝『平塚らいてう－人と思想』1988年、1983年（初版）。

Kobayashi Tomie, *Hiratsuka Raichō: Ai to Hangyaku no Seishun* (1977, 1986 edn).
小林登美枝『平塚らいてう、愛と反逆の青春』1986年、1977年（初版）。

Kobayashi Tomie & Kozai Yoshishige, *Ai to Jiritsu: Shikon, Raichō, Yuriko o Kataru* (1983).
小林登美枝・古在由重『愛と自立－紫琴・らいてう・百合子を語る』1983年。

Kobori Annu, 'Chichi e no tegami' in Mori Ōgai (ed. by Kobori Annu), *Tsuma e no Tegami* (1938, 1996 edn).
小堀杏奴「父への手紙」森鷗外著、小堀杏奴編『妻への手紙』1996年、1938年（初版）。

Kodama Katsuko, *Fujin Sanseiken Undō Shōshi* (1981).
児玉勝子『婦人参政権運動小史』1981年。

Kodama Katsuko, 'Josei Dōmei fukkoku ni atatte', in Domesu Shuppan (ed.), *Josei Dōmei Kaisetsu, Sōmokuji, Sakuin*, (1985).
児玉勝子「『女性同盟』復刻にあたって」ドメス出版編『「女性同盟」解説・総目次・索引』1985年。

Kodama Katsuko, *Oboegaki, Sengo no Ichikawa Fusae* (1985).
児玉勝子『覚書、戦後の市川房枝』1985年。

Kodama Katsuko, *Shinanoji no Deai* (1985).
児玉勝子『信濃路の出会い』1985年。

Kondō Tomie, 'Kanno Suga', in Setouchi Harumi (ed.), *Hangyaku no Onna no Roman*, (1989).
近藤富枝「菅野すが」瀬戸内晴美編『反逆の女のロマン』1989年。

Kōno Nobuko, *Kindai Josei Seishinshi* (1982).
河野信子『近代女性精神史』1982年。

Kōno Nobuko, *Takamure Itsue* (1990).
河野信子『高群逸枝』1990年。

Kōno Taeko, 'Matsui Sumako', in Setouchi Harumi (ed.), *Koi to Geijutsu e no Jōnen* (1989).
河野多恵子「松井須磨子」瀬戸内晴美編『恋と芸術への情念』1989年。

Kōuchi Nobuko, 'Bosei hogo ronsō no rekishiteki igi: ronsō kara undō e no tsunagari', *Rekishi Hyōron*, 195 (November, 1966).
香内信子「母性保護論争の歴史的意義－論争から運動へのつながり」『歴史評論』第195号、1966年11月。

Kōuchi Nobuko, 'Kaidai', in Kōuchi Nobuko (ed.), *Shiryō: Bosei Hogo Ronsō* (1984).
香内信子「解題」香内信子編『資料母性保護論争』1984年。

Kumasaka Atsuko, 'Morita Sōhei *Baien* no Tomoko', *Kokubungaku*, 25:4 (March, 1980).
熊坂敦子「森田草平『煤煙』の朋子」『国文学』第25巻4号、1980年3月。

Kurumi Akiko, 'Takamura Chieko', in Setouchi Harumi (ed.), *Koi to Geijutsu e no Jōnen* (1989).
来水明子「高村智恵子」瀬戸内晴美編『恋と芸術への情念』1989年。

Marukawa Kayoko, 'Fukuda Hideko', in Setouchi Harumi (ed.), *Hangyaku no Onna no Roman* (1989).
丸川賀世子「福田英子」瀬戸内晴美編『反逆の女のロマン』1989年。

Maruoka Hideko, *Fujin Shisō Keiseishi Nōto*, 2 vols (1975).
丸岡秀子『婦人思想形成史ノート』上・下巻、1975年。

Maruoka Hideko, *Tamura Toshiko to Watashi* (1977).
丸岡秀子『田村俊子とわたし』1977年。

Matsuda Fumiko, *Fujin Kōron no 50-nen* (1965).
松田ふみ子『婦人公論の５０年』１９６５年。

Matsuda Michio, 'Kaibara Ekken no jugaku', in Kaibara Ekken (ed. by Matsuda Michio), *Kaibara Ekken* (1969).
松田道雄「貝原益軒の儒学」貝原益軒著　松田道雄編『貝原益軒』１９６９年。

Matsumoto Seichō (ed.), *Meiji Hyakunen Hyaku Daijiken*, vol. 2 (1968, 1984 edn).
松本清張監修『明治百年　１００大事件』下巻、１９８４年、１９６８年（初版）。

Matsuo Takayoshi, 'Taishō fujin no seijiteki jiyū kakutoku undō: Shin Fujin Kyōkai kara Fusen Kakutoku Dōmei e', in Domesu Shuppan (ed.), *Josei Dōmei Kaisetsu, Sōmokuji, Sakuin* (1985).
松尾尊兊「大正期婦人の政治的自由獲得運動－新婦人協会から婦選獲得同盟へ」ドメス出版編『「女性同盟」解説・総目次・索引』１９８５年。

Mitsui Reiko (ed.), *Gendai Fujin Undōshi Nenpyō* (1974).
三井礼子編『現代婦人運動史年表』１９７４年。

Miyagi Eishō *et al.*, (eds), *Shinkō Nihon Joseishi* (1974).
宮城栄昌　他編『新稿日本女性史』１９７４年。

Miyoshi Yukio, 'Ichiyō to Nihon kindai no teihen', *Kokubungaku*, 25:15 (December, 1980).
三好行雄「一葉と日本近代の底辺」『国文学』第２５巻１５号、１９８０年１２月。

Momose Meiji *et al.*, *Mei Serifu Nihonshi* (1987).
百瀬明治　他『名セリフ日本史』１９８７年。

Morishita Misako, *Edo no Hanayome* (1992).
森下みさ子『江戸の花嫁』１９９２年。

Morita Sōhei, *Natsume Sōseki* (1967).
森田草平『夏目漱石』１９６７年。

Morosawa Yōko, *Onna no Rekishi*, 2 vols (1970).
もろさわようこ『おんなの歴史』上・下巻、１９７０年。

Motobayashi Katsuo, 'Onna no roman to jojō: Yosano Akiko to Yamakawa Tomiko', *Kokubungaku*, 25:15 (December, 1980).
本林勝夫「女のロマンと抒情－与謝野晶子と山川登美子」『国文学』第２５巻１５号、１９８０年１２月。

Murakami Nobuhiko, *Meiji Joseishi*, 4 vols (1969–72).
村上信彦『明治女性史』全４巻、１９６９‐７２年。

Murakami Nobuhiko, *Taishō-ki no Shokugyō Fujin* (1983).
村上信彦『大正期の職業婦人』１９８３年。

Murakami Yasuko, 'Bosei hogo ronsō to gendai', in Grūpu Bosei Kaidoku Kōza (ed.), *Bosei o Kaidoku Suru* (1991).
村上やすこ「母性保護論争と現代」グループ「母性」解読講座編『母性を解読する』１９９１年。

Murata Shizuko, *Fukuda Hideko: Fujin Kaihō Undō no Senkusha* (1959).
村田静子『福田英子－婦人解放運動の先駆者』１９５９年。

Nagahara Kazuko & Yoneda Sayoko, *Onna no Shōwashi* (1986).
永原和子・米田佐代子『おんなの昭和史』１９８６年。

Nagoya Joseishi Kenkyūkai (ed.), *Hana no Jidai* (Nagoya, 1969).
名古屋女性史研究会編『母の時代』１９６９年（名古屋）。

Nakamura Hidekatsu, 'Ochnomizu Joshi Daigaku no seiritsu', *Ochanomizu Joshi Daigaku Josei Bunka Shiryō Kanpō*, 2 (1980).
中村英勝「お茶の水女子大学の成立」『お茶の水女子大学女性文化資料館報』第２号、１９８０年。

Nakayama Kazuko, 'Onna de aru koto no imi: Seitō-ha o megutte', *Kokubungaku*, 25:15 (December, 1980).
中山和子「女であることの意味－青鞜派をめぐって」『国文学』第２５巻１５号、１９８０年１２月号。

Natsume Shinroku, 'Chichi no tegami to Morita-san', in Chikuma Shobō (ed.), *Gendai Nihon Bugaku Taikei*, vol. 29 (1971).
夏目伸六「父の手紙と森田さん」筑摩書房編『現代日本文学大系　２９』１９７１年。

Nishikawa Yūko, *Mori no Ie no Miko: Takamure Itsue* (1982).
西川祐子『森の家の巫女、高群逸枝』１９８２年。

Nozaki Kinue, 'Mori Arinori, Fukuzawa Yukichi, Ueki Emori no joseiron', in Ichibangase Yasuko (ed.), *Nyūmon Josei Kaihōshi* (1975).
野崎衣枝「森有礼、福沢諭吉、植木枝盛の女性論」一番ヶ瀬康子編『入門女性解放史』１９７５年。

Nuita Hanako (ed.), *Ichikawa Fusae Seitan 100–nen Kinen: Ichikawa Fusae to Fujin Sanseiken Undō* (1992).
縫田曄子編『市川房枝生誕１００年記念、市川房枝と婦人参政権運動』１９９２年。

Ochanomizu Daigaku Bunkyōiku Gakubu Fuzoku Yōchien (ed.), *Nenpyō Yōchien 100-nen-shi* (1976).
お茶の水大学文教育学部附属幼稚園編『年表幼稚園百年史』１９７６年。

Odagiri Hideo (ed.), *Kōza, Nihon Kindai Bungakushi*, 5 vols (1956).
小田切秀雄『講座　日本近代文学史』全5巻、１９５６年。

Ogata Akiko, *Nyonin Geijutsu no Sekai: Hasegawa Shigure to Sono Shūhen* (1980).
尾形明子『女人芸術の世界－長谷川時雨とその周辺』１９８０年。

Okano Yukie, 'Kaisetsu', in Fuji Shuppan (ed.), *Shin Shin Fujin Kaisetsu, Sōmokuji, Sakuin* (1994).
岡野幸江「解説」不二出版編『「新真婦人」解説・総目次・索引』１９９４年。

Ōba Minako, *Tsuda Umeko* (1990).
大庭みな子『津田梅子』１９９０年。

Ōe Shinoo, *Nihon no Rekishi: Sengo Henkaku* (1976).
大江志乃夫『日本の歴史－戦後変革』１９７６年。

Ōkubo Toshiaki (ed.), *Mori Arinori Zenshū*, 3 vols (1971).
大久保利謙編『森有礼全集』全3巻、１９７１年。

Ōmura Hiroyoshi, *Tsubouchi Shōyō* (1958).
大村弘毅『坪内逍遥』１９５８年。

Orii Miyako & Takai Yō, *Azami no Hana: Tomimoto Kazue Shōden* (1985).
折井美耶子・高井陽『薊の花－富本一枝小伝』１９８５年。

Rekishi Kagaku Kyōgikai (ed.), *Joseishi Kenkyū Nyūmon* (1991).
歴史科学協議会編『女性史研究入門』１９９１年。

Sakamoto Masanori, 'Myōjō no joryū sakka', *Kokubungaku*, 9:15 (December, 1964).
坂本政親「『明星』の女流作家」『国文学』第9巻15号、１９６４年12月。

Sakamoto Taketo, *Kōtoku Shūsui: Meiji Shakai Shugi no Ittōsei* (1984).
坂本武人『幸徳秋水・明治社会主義の一等星』１９８４年。

Sakurai Kinue, *Bosei Hogo Undōshi* (1987).
桜井絹江『母性保護運動史』１９８７年。

Sasabuchi Tomoichi, 'Myōjō ha no bungaku undō', *Kokubungaku*, 9:15 (December, 1964).
笹淵友一「『明星』派の文学運動」『国文学』第9巻15号、１９６４年12月。

Sasaki Hideaki, *Atarashii Onna no Tōrai* (Nagoya, 1994).
佐々木英昭『新しい女の到来』１９９４年。

Sawano Hisao, 'Arishima Takeo, Karuizawa jōshi jiken', *Rekishi to Jinbutsu* (April, 1980).
澤野久雄「有島武郎、軽井沢情死事件」『歴史と人物』１９８０年4月。

Seki Misao, 'Yosano Akiko to *Genji Monogatari*', *Kokubungaku*, 9:15 (December, 1964).
関みさを「与謝野晶子と『源氏物語』」『国文学』第9巻15号、１９６４年12月。

Setouchi Harumi, *Seitō* (1984, 1987 edn).
瀬戸内晴美『青鞜』１９８７年、１９８４年（初版）。

Setouchi Harumi, *Tamura Toshiko* (1964, 1976 edn).
瀬戸内晴美『田村俊子』１９７６年、１９６４年（初版）。

Setouchi Harumi, 'Tamura Toshiko', in Setouchi Harumi (ed.), *Hi to Moeta Joryū Bungaku* (1989).
瀬戸内晴美「田村俊子」瀬戸内晴美編『火と燃えた女流文学』１９８９年。

Shibukawa Hisako, *Kindai Nihon Joseishi: Kyōiku* (1970).
渋川久子『近代日本女性史・教育』１９７０年。

Shiga Tadashi, *Nihon Joshi Kyōikushi* (1977).
志賀匡『日本女子教育史』１９７７年。

Shigematsu Yasuo, 'Shokugyō toshite no joryū sakka: Meiji 28-nen to 29-nen no
    Ichiyō no shūshi ni furete', *Kokubungaku*, 25:15, (December, 1980).
重松泰雄「職業としての女流作家－明治２８、２９年の一葉の収支に触れて」『国文学』第２５巻１５号、
１９８０年１２月。
Shimada Setsuko, 'Ellen Key no bosei shugi', in Ichibangase Yasuko (ed.), *Nyūmon
    Josei Kaihōron* (1975).
島田節子「エレン・ケイの母性主義」一番ヶ瀬康子編『入門女性解放論』１９７５年。
Shioda Ryōhei, '*Myōjō*-ha no bungakushiteki igi', *Kokubungaku*, 9:15 (December, 1964).
塩田良平「『明星』派の文学史的意義」『国文学』第９巻１５号、１９６４年１２月。
Shōji Kazuaki, *Sawayanagi Masatarō to Seijō Kyōiku* (1974).
庄司和晃『沢柳政太郎と成城教育』１９７４年。
Sōgō Joseishi Kenkyūkai (ed.), *Nihon Josei no Rekishi: Bunka to Shisō* (1993).
総合女性史研究会編『日本女性の歴史・文化と思想』１９９３年。
Sōgō Joseishi Kenkyūkai (ed.), *Nihon Josei no Rekishi: Sei, Ai, Kazoku* (1992).
総合女性史研究会編『日本女性の歴史－性・愛・家族』１９９２年。
Sotozaki Mitsuhiro, *Kōchiken Fujin Kaihō Undōshi* (1975).
外崎光広『高知県婦人解放運動史』１９７５年。
Sotozaki Mitsuhiro, *Meiji Zenki Fujin Kaihōronshi* (Kōchi, 1963).
外崎光広『明治前期婦人解放論史』１９６３年。
Sotozaki Mitsuhiro, *Nihon Fujin Ronshi: Joseiron Hen*, vol. 1 (1986).
外崎光広『日本婦人論史－女性論篇』上巻、１９８６年。
Suzuki Yūko, *Joseishi o Hiraku*, 2 vols (1989).
鈴木裕子『女性史を拓く』上・下巻、１９８９年。
Tachi Kaoru, 'Hiratsuka Raichō to Ofudesaki', *Ochanomizu Joshi Daigaku Josei Bunka
    Shiryō Kanpō*, 7 (1986).
館かおる「平塚らいてうとお筆書」『お茶の水女子大学女性文化資料館報』第７号、１９８６年。
Tada Michitarō (ed.), *Ōsugi Sakae* (1984).
多田道太郎編『大杉栄』１９８４年。
Takagi Tadashi, *Mikudari Han: Edo no Rikon to Joseitachi* (1987).
高木侃『三くだり半－江戸の離婚と女性達』１９８７年。
Takagi Tadashi, *Mikudari Han to Enkiri Dera* (1992).
高木侃『三くだり半と縁切寺』１９９２年。
Takamura Kōtarō, *Chiekoshō Sonogo* (1950).
高村光太郎『智恵子抄その後』１９５０年。
Takamure Itsue, *Bokeisei no Kenkyū* (1938).
高群逸枝『母系制の研究』１９３８年。
Takamure Itsue, *Josei no Rekishi*, 2 vols (1954–8, 1972 edn).
高群逸枝『女性の歴史』上・下巻、１９７２年、１９５４‐８年（初版）。
Takamure Itsue, *Nihon Koninshi* (1963).
高群逸枝『日本婚姻史』１９６３年。
Takamure Itsue, *Shōseikon no Kenkyū* (1953).
高群逸枝『招婿婚の研究』１９５３年。
Takashima Nobuyoshi, *Kyōiku Chokugo to Gakkō Kyōiku* (1990).
高嶋伸欣『教育勅語と学校教育』１９９０年。
Tanaka Ariko, 'Kishida Toshiko', in Setouchi Harumi (ed.), *Shin Jidai no Paionia*
    (1989).
田中阿里子「岸田俊子」瀬戸内晴美編『新時代のパイオニア』１９８９年。
Tanaka Sumiko (ed.), *Josei Kaihō no Shisō to Kōdō: Senzen Hen* (1975).
田中寿美子編『女性解放の思想と行動－戦前編』１９７５年。
Tatewaki Sadayo, *Nihon no Fujin* (1957, 1976 edn).
帯刀貞代『日本の婦人』１９７６年、１９５７年（初版）。
Tonegawa Yutaka, 'Hōgetsu ni junjita joyū, Sumako', *Rekishi to Jinbutsu Tokushū:
    Kindai Renai Jiken Hiwa* (April, 1980).
利根川裕「抱月に殉じた女優 須磨子」『歴史と人物特集 近代恋愛事件秘話』１９８０年４月。

Tsubouchi Shōyō, *Iwayuru Atarashii Onna* (1912).
坪内逍遥『いわゆる新しい女』1912年。

Tsukamoto Shūko, 'Yosano Akiko, Hiratsuka Raichō, Yamakawa Kikue no bosei hogo ronsō', in Ichibangase Yasuko (ed.), *Nyūmon Josei Kaihō Ron* (1975).
塚本しう子「与謝野晶子、平塚らいてう、山川菊栄の母性保護論争」一番ヶ瀬康子編『入門女性解放論』1975年。

Uranishi Kazuhiko, 'Kaidai', in Fuji Shuppan (ed.), *Hankyō Kaidai, Sōmokuji, Sakuin* (1985).
浦西和彦「解題」不二出版編『「反響」解題・総目次・索引』1985年。

Usui Yoshimi, *Taishō Bungakushi* (1963).
臼井吉見『大正文学史』1963年。

Wada Yoshie, *Higuchi Ichiyō* (1972).
和田芳恵『樋口一葉』1972年。

Wakita Haruko (ed.), *Bosei o Tou: Rekishiteki Hensen*, 2 vols (1985).
脇田晴子編『母性を問う‐歴史的変遷』上・下巻、1985年。

Watanabe Tokusaburō, *Fukuzawa Yukichi: Katei Kyōiku no Susume* (1985).
渡辺徳三郎『福沢諭吉、家庭教育のすすめ』1985年。

Yamakawa Kikue Seitan 100-nen o Kinensuru Kai (ed.), *Gendai Feminizumu to Yamakawa Kikue* (1990).
山川菊栄生誕百年を記念する会編『現代フェミニズムと山川菊栄』1990年。

Yamamoto Chie, *Yama no Ugoku Hi Kitaru: Hyōden, Yosano Akiko* (1986).
山本千恵『山の動く日きたる・評伝与謝野晶子』1986年。

Yamamoto Shigemi, *Aa Nomugi Tōge* (1968, 1994 edn).
山本茂美『ああ野麦峠』1994年、1968年（初版）。

Yamashita Etsuko, *Nihon Josei Kaihō Shisō no Kigen* (1988).
山下悦子『日本女性解放思想の起源』1988年。

Yamazaki Takako, *Tsuda Umeko* (1962, 1988 edn).
山崎孝子『津田梅子』1988年、1962年（初版）。

Yamazaki Tomoko, *Ajia Josei Kōryūshi: Meiji, Taishō-ki Hen* (1995).
山崎朋子『アジア女性交流史‐明治・大正期篇』1995年。

Yamazaki Tomoko, *Ameyuki San no Uta: Yamada Waka no Sūki Naru Shōgai* (1978, 1991 edn).
山崎朋子『あめゆきさんの歌‐山田わかの数奇なる生涯』1991年、1978年（初版）。

Yamazaki Tomoko, *Sandakan Hachiban Shōkan: Teihen Joseishi Joshō* (1972).
山崎朋子『サンダカン八番娼館‐底辺女性史序章』1972年。

Yasumaru Yoshio, *Deguchi Nao* (1987).
安丸良夫『出口なお』1987年。

Yasutaka Misako, 'Yamada Waka', in Setouchi Harumi (ed.), *Jiritsushita Onna no Eikō* (1989).
保高みさ子「山田わか」瀬戸内晴美編『自立した女の栄光』1989年。

Yatayama Seiko, *Hi no Onna Raichō: Hiratsuka Raichō no Shōgai* (1991).
矢田山聖子『陽の女らいてう‐平塚らいてうの生涯』1991年。

Yoneda Sayoko, 'Bosei shugi no rekishiteki igi: *Fujin Sensen* jidai no Hiratsuka Raichō o chūshin ni', in Joseishi Sōgō Kenkyūkai (ed.), *Nihon Joseishi*, vol. 5 (1982, 1985 edn).
米田佐代子「母性主義の歴史的意義‐『婦人戦線』時代の平塚らいてうを中心に」女性史総合研究会編『日本女性史』第5巻、1985年、1982年（初版）。

Yoneda Sayoko, *Fujinron Nōto* (1986).
米田佐代子『婦人論ノート』1986年。

Yoneda Sayoko, 'Hasen no suifu: Hiratsuka Raichō no kindai', in Hiratsuka Raichō o Yomu Kai (ed.), *Raichō Soshite Watashi* (1988).
米田佐代子「破船の水夫‐平塚らいてうの近代」平塚らいてうを読む会編『らいてう、そして わたし』1988年。

Yoneda Sayoko, 'Hiratsuka Raichō ni okeru shizen to shakai', *Sōgō Joseishi Kenkyūkai Kaihō*, 4 (August, 1987).
米田佐代子「平塚らいてうにおける自然と社会」『総合女性史研究会会報』4号、1987年 8月。

Yoneda Sayoko, 'Hiratsuka Raichō o Yomu Kai no ayumi', in Hiratsuka Raichō o Yomu Kai (ed.), *Raichō Shoshite Watashi, Part III* (1991).
米田佐代子「平塚らいてうを読む会の歩み」平塚らいてうを読む会編『らいてうそしてわたし - Part III』1991年。

Yoneda Sayoko, 'Jidai o ikinuku', in Maruoka Hideko *et al.*, *Hiratsuka Raichō to Nihon no Kindai* (1986).
米田佐代子「時代を生きぬく」丸岡秀子他著『平塚らいてうと日本の近代』1986年。

Yoneda Sayoko, *Kindai Nihon Joseishi*, 2 vols (1972, 1990 edn).
米田佐代子『近代日本女性史』上・下巻、1990年、1972年（初版）。

Yoneda Sayoko, '*Seitō* no ryakudatsu', in Hiratsuka Raichō o Yomu Kai (ed.), *Raichō Soshite Watashi: Part III*, (1991).
米田佐代子「『青鞜』の略奪」平塚らいてうを読む会編『らいてうそしてわたし - Part III』1991年。

Yoneda Sayoko, '*Seitō* to shakai no setten: Raichō to Chōkō o chūshin ni', *Yamanashi Kenritsu Joshi Tandai Kiyō*, 24 (March, 1991).
米田佐代子「『青鞜』と社会の接点―らいてうと長江を中心に」『山梨県立女子短大紀要』24号、1991年3月。

Yoshida Yoshiaki (ed.), *Nihonkoku Kenpō* (1989).
吉田善明編『日本国憲法』1989年。

Yoshimi Kaneko, *Fujin Sanseiken* (1971).
吉見周子『婦人参政権』1971年。

Yoshimi Kaneko, 'Jiyū Minken Undō to josei: Fukuda Hideko o chūshin ni', in Morosawa Yōko & Setouchi Harumi (eds), *Kindai Nihonshi no Naka no Josei* (1980).
吉見周子「自由民権運動と女性―福田英子を中心に」もろさわようこ・瀬戸内晴美編『近代日本史の中の女性』1980年。

(B) *Reference Books*

Furubayashi Kamejirō (ed.), *Gendai Jinmei Jiten*, 2 vols (1912).
古林亀治郎編『現代人名辞典』上下巻、1912年。

Hisamatsu Senichi *et al.* (eds), *Gendai Nihon Bungaku Daijiten* (1965).
久松潜一他編『現代日本文学大事典』1965年。

Ichibangase Yasuko *et al.* (eds), *Nihon Josei Jinmei Jiten* (1993).
一番ヶ瀬康子他監修『日本女性人名辞典』1993年。

Josei no Jōhō o Hirogeru Kai (ed.), *Onnatachi no Benrichō* (1991).
女性の情報をひろげる会編『女たちの便利帳』1991年。

Karasawa Tomitarō (ed.), *Zusetsu Kyōiku Jinbutsu Jiten*, 3 vols (1984).
唐澤富太郎『図説教育人物事典』全3巻、1984年。

Kokushi Daijiten Henshū Iinkai (ed.), *Kokushi Daijiten*, 15 vols (1993).
国史大辞典編集委員会編『国史大辞典』全15巻、1993年。

Muramatsu Sadataka & Watanabe Sumiko (eds), *Gendai Josei Bungaku Jiten* (1990).
村松定孝・渡辺澄子編『現代女性文学辞典』1990年。

Nichigai Asoshiētsu (ed.), *Seijika Jinmei Jiten* (1990).
日外アソシエーツ編『政治家人名事典』1990年。

Nihon Daijiten Kankōkai (ed.), *Nihon Kokugo Daijiten*, 20 vols (1972–6).
日本大辞典刊行会編『日本国語大辞典』全20巻、1972‐76年。

Odagiri Susumu (ed.), *Nihon Kindai Bungaku Daijiten* (1984).
小田切進『日本近代文学大辞典』1984年。

Yokohama Josei Fōramu (ed.), *Onna no Netto Wākingu* (1987).
横浜女性フォーラム編『女のネットワーキング』1987年。

III. *English Primary Sources*

(A) *Published Material*

1. *Books*

Ishimoto, Shidzue, *Facing Two Ways: The Story of My Life* (1935, Stanford, 1984 edn).

2. *Newspapers*

The Illustrated London News.
The Times.

IV. *English Secondary Sources*

(A) *Books and Articles*

Alberti, Johanna, *Eleanor Rathbone* (London, 1996).
Andrew, Nancy, 'The Seitōsha: an early Japanese women's organisation, 1911–1916', *Harvard University East Asian Research Centre Papers on Japan*, 6 (1972).
Anon., 'Feminist Kamichika Ichiko', *East*, 25:2 (July/August, 1989).
Backus, Robert L., 'Matsudaira Sadanobu and samurai education', in Andrew Gerstle (ed.), *18th Century Japan: Culture and Society* (North Sydney, 1989).
Banks, Olive, *Becoming a Feminist: The Social Origins of 'First Wave' Feminism* (Brighton, 1986).
——, *Faces of Feminism* (Oxford, 1981).
Beasley, W.G., *The Rise of Modern Japan* (1990, London, 1995 edn).
Benn, Caroline, *Keir Hardie* (London, 1992).
Bernstein, Gail Lee (ed.), *Recreating Japanese Women, 1600–1945* (Berkeley, 1991).
Blacker, Carmen, *The Japanese Enlightenment: A Study of the Writings of Fukuzawa Yukichi* (1964, Cambridge, 1969 edn).
Bolt, Christine, *The Women's Movements in the United States and Britain from the 1790s to the 1920s* (Hemel Hempstead, 1993).
Braisted, William Reynolds, *Meiroku Zasshi: Journal of the Japanese Enlightenment* (Cambridge, Mass., 1976).
Brandon, Ruth, *The New Women and the Old Men* (1990, London, 1991 edn).
Carlberg, Eileen, 'Women in the political system', in Joyce Lebra *et al.* (eds), *Women in Changing Japan* (Stanford, 1976).
Chabot, Jeanette, 'Takamure Itsue: the first historian of Japanese women', *Women's Studies International Forum*, 8:4 (1985).
Cherry, Kittredge, *Womansword: What Japanese Words Say about Women* (1987, New York, 1991 edn).
Coleman, Samuel, *Family Planning in Japanese Society: Traditional Birth Control in a Modern Urban Culture* (1983, Princeton, 1991).
Condon, Jane, *A Half Step Behind: Japanese Women Today* (1985, Tokyo, 1991).
Cummings, William K., *Education and Equality in Japan* (Princeton, 1980).
Cunningham, Gail, *The New Woman and the Victorian Novel* (London, 1978).
Dalby, Lisa, *Geisha* (Berkeley, 1983).
D'Annunzio, Gabriele (trans. by Georgina Harding), *The Triumph of Death* (1894, New York, 1975 edn).
Davis, Jill, 'The New Woman and the new life', in Viv Gardner & Susan Rutherford (eds), *The New Woman and Her Sisters* (Hemel Hempstead, 1992).
Dore, R.P., *Education in Tokugawa Japan* (1965, London, 1992 edn).

Dunn, Charles J., *Everyday Life in Traditional Japan* (1969, London, 1989 edn).

Dyhouse, Carol, *No Distinction of Sex? Women in British Universities, 1870–1939* (London, 1995).

Ferris, Lesley, 'The golden girl', in Viv Gardner & Susan Rutherford (eds), *The New Woman and Her Sisters* (Hemel Hempstead, 1992).

Firth, C.D. Constance, *Constance Louisa Maynard* (London, 1969).

Fukuzawa, Yukichi (trans. by D.A. Dilworth), *An Encouragement of Learning* (1969).

—— (trans. and ed. by Eiichi Kiyooka), *Fukuzawa Yukichi on Japanese Women* (1988).

—— (trans. by Eiichi Kiyooka), *The Autobiography of Fukuzawa Yukuchi* (1960, 1981 edn).

Furuki, Yoshiko, 'Introduction', in Yoshiko Furuki *et al.* (eds), *The Attic Letters: Ume Tsuda's Correspondence to her American Mother* (New York, 1991).

Furuki, Yoshiko, *et al.* (eds), *The Attic Letters: Ume Tsuda's Correspondence to her American Mother* (New York, 1991).

Furuki, Yoshiko, *The White Plum: A Biography of Ume Tsuda* (New York, 1991).

Gardner, Viv, 'Introduction', in Viv Gardner & Susan Rutherford (eds), *The New Woman and Her Sisters* (Hemel Hempstead, 1992).

Gissing, George, *The Odd Women* (1893, London, 1984 edn).

Goode, John, *George Gissing: Ideology and Fiction* (London, 1978).

Hall, Ivan Parker, *Mori Arinori* (Cambridge, Mass., 1973).

Hane, Mikiso, *Reflections on the Way to the Gallows: Rebel Women in Prewar Japan* (Berkeley, 1988).

Hannam, June, 'Women and politics', in June Purvis (ed.), *Women's History: Britain, 1850–1945* (London, 1995).

Hayakawa, Noriyo, 'The development of women's history in Japan', in Karen Offen *et al.* (eds), *Writing Women's History: International Perspectives* (London, 1991).

Herstein, Sheila R., *Mid-Victorian Feminist, Barbara Leigh Smith Bodichon* (New Haven, 1985).

Hopper, Helen M., *A New Woman of Japan: A Political Biography of Katō Shidzue* (Boulder, Colorado, 1996).

Hotta-Lister, Ayako, 'The Japan-British Exhibition of 1910: the Japanese organizers', in Ian Nish (ed.), *Britain & Japan: Biographical Portraits* (1994).

Hunter, Janet (ed.), *Japanese Women Working* (London, 1993).

——, 'Labour in the Japanese silk industry in the 1870s: *The Tomioka Nikki* of Wada Ei', in Gordon Daniels (ed.), *Europe Interprets Japan* (Tenterden, Kent, 1984).

——, 'Textile factories, tuberculosis and the quality of life in industrializing Japan', in Janet Hunter (ed.), *Japanese Women Working* (London, 1993).

Hunter, Janet E., *The Emergence of Modern Japan: An Introductory History since 1853* (London, 1989).

Ibsen, Henrik, *A Doll's House* (1879, London, 1985).

Ikegami, Eiko, *The Taming of the Samurai: Honorific Individualism and the Making of Modern Japan* (Cambridge, Mass., 1995).

Inukai, Michiko, 'Japanese women raise the rice spoon of revolt', *UNESCO Courier*, 8 (August/September, 1975).

Jolivet, Muriel, *Japan: the Childless Society?* (1993, London, 1997).

Kaigo, Tokiomi, *Japanese Education: Its Past and Present* (1965).

Kaji, Etsuko & Inglis, Jean, 'Sisters against slavery: a look at anti-prostitution movements in Japan', *Ampo: Japan-Asia Quarterly Review*, 6:2 (Spring 1974).

Kamiyama, Tamie, 'Ideology and patterns in women's education in Japan' (unpublished Ph.D. thesis, Saint Louis University, 1977).

Kano, Masanao, 'Takamure Itsue: pioneer in the study of women's history', *Feminist International*, 2 (1980).

Katō, Shūichi (trans. & ed. by Don Sanderson), *A History of Japanese Literature from the Manyōshū to Modern Times* (Richmond, 1997).

Keene, Donald, *World Within Walls: Japanese Literature of the Pre-Modern Era, 1600–1867* (London, 1976).

Kikuchi, Dairoku, *Japanese Education: Lectures Delivered in the University of London* (London, 1909).

Knapp, Bettina L., *Images of Japanese Women: A Westerner's View* (New York, 1992).

Kobayashi, Tetsuya, *Society, Schools and Progress in Japan* (Oxford, 1976).

Kōsaka, Masaaki (ed.), *Japanese Thought in the Meiji Era* (1958).

Koven, Seth & Michel, Sonya, 'Introduction: "Mother worlds"', in Seth Koven & Sonya Michel (eds), *Mothers of a New World: Maternalist Politics and the Origins of Welfare States* (London, 1993).

Large, Stephen, *The Yūaikai, 1912–1919* (1972).

Ledger, Sally, *The New Woman: Fiction and Feminism at the Fin de Siecle* (London, 1997).

Lewis, Jane, 'Eleanor Rathbone, 1872–1946', in Paul Barker (ed.), *Founders of the Welfare State* (London, 1984).

Lewis, Jane, 'Models of equality for women: the case of state support for children in twentieth-century Britain', in Gisela Bock & Pat Thane (eds), *Maternity and Gender Policies: Women and the Rise of the European Welfare States, 1880s–1950s* (1991, London, 1994 edn).

——, *Women in England, 1870–1950* (Brighton, 1984).

Lucie-Smith, Edward, *Eroticism in Western Art* (London, 1972).

Mackie, Vera, *Creating Socialist Women in Japan: Gender, Labour and Activism, 1900–1937* (Cambridge, 1997).

Mackie, Vera, 'Feminist politics in Japan', *New Left Review*, 167 (January/February, 1988).

Manton, Jo, *Mary Carpenter and the Children of the Streets* (London, 1976).

Mason, R.H.P. & Caiger, J.G., *A History of Japan* (1973, 1997 edn).

McIntosh, Mary, 'Social anxieties about lone motherhood and ideologies of the family', in Elizabeth Bortolaia Silva (ed.), *Good Enough Mothering?* (London, 1996).

Meyer, Michael, *Ibsen on File* (London, 1985).

Mitchell, David, *The Fighting Pankhursts* (London, 1967).

Miyake, Yoshiko, 'Doubling expectations: motherhood and women's factory work under state management in Japan in the 1930s and 1940s', in Gail Lee Bernstein (ed.), *Recreating Japanese Women, 1600–1945* (Berkeley, 1991).

Miyamoto, Ken, 'Itō Noe and the Bluestockings', *Japan Interpreter*, 10:2 (Autumn 1975).

Molony, Barbara, 'Activism among women in the Taishō cotton textile industry', in Gail Lee Bernstein (ed.), *Recreating Japanese Women, 1600–1945* (Berkeley, 1991).

——, 'Afterword', in Shidzue Ishimoto, *Facing Two Ways: The Story of My Life* (1935, Stanford, 1984 edn).

——, 'Equality versus difference: the Japanese debate over 'motherhood protection', 1915–50', in Janet Hunter (ed.), *Japanese Women Working* (London, 1993).

——, 'State and women in modern Japan: feminist discourses in the Meiji and Taishō eras', in Janet Hunter (ed.), *Japan: State and People in the Twentieth Century* (London, 1999).

Molony, K.S., 'One woman who dared: Ichikawa Fusae and the Japanese women's suffrage movement' (unpublished Ph.D. thesis, University of Michigan, 1980).

Monnet, Livia, '"In the beginning woman was the sun": autobiographies of modern Japanese women writers, 1', *Japan Forum*, 1:1 (April, 1989).

Murray, Geoffrey, 'Fusae Ichikawa—choice of the young in Japan', *PHP*, 6:1 (January, 1975).

Murray, Patricia, 'Ichikawa Fusae and the lonely red carpet', *Japan Interpreter*, 10:2 (Autumn 1975).

Nakano, Ann, 'Shizue (Ishimoto) Katō: woman warrior', *PHP* (February, 1984).

Naruse, Jinzō, 'The education of Japanese women', in Ōkuma Shigenobu (ed.), *Fifty Years of New Japan*, vol. 2, (London, 1910).

Nolte, Sharon H. & Hastings, Sally Ann, 'The Meiji state's policy toward women, 1890–1910', in Gail Lee Bernstein (ed.), *Recreating Japanese Women, 1600–1945* (Berkeley, 1991).

Nosco, Peter, 'Introduction: Neo-Confucianism and Tokugawa discourse', in Peter Nosco (ed.), *Confucianism and Tokugawa Culture* (1984, Princeton, 1989 edn).

Okazaki-Ward, L.I., 'Women and their education in the Tokugawa period of Japan' (unpublished M.Phil. thesis, University of Sheffield, 1993).

Ooms, Herman, 'Neo-Confucianism and the formation of early Tokugawa ideology: contours of a problem', in Peter Nosco (ed.), *Confucianism and Tokugawa Culture* (1984, Princeton, 1989 edn).

Passin, Herbert, *Society and Education in Japan* (New York, 1965).

Pharr, Susan J., *Political Women in Japan: The Search for a Place in Political Life* (Berkeley, 1981).

Raddeker, Helene Bowen, *Treacherous Women of Imperial Japan: Patriarchal Fictions, Patricidal Fantasies* (London, 1997).

Reader, Ian, *et al.*, *Japanese Religions: Past and Present* (Folkestone, 1993).

Reich, Pauline, 'Japan's literary feminists: the Seitō group', *Signs*, 2:1 (Autumn 1976).

Robertson, Jennifer, 'The Shingaku woman: straight from the heart', in Gail Lee Bernstein (ed.), *Recreating Japanese Women, 1600–1945* (Berkeley, 1991).

Robins-Mowry, Dorothy, *The Hidden Sun: Women of Modern Japan* (Boulder, Colorado, 1983).

Rodd, Laurel Rasplica, 'Yosano Akiko and the Taishō debate over the "New Woman"', in Gail Lee Bernstein (ed.), *Recreating Japanese Women, 1600–1945* (Berkeley, 1991).

Romero, Patricia W., *E. Sylvia Pankhurst: Portrait of a Radical* (1987, New Haven, 1990 edn).

Rose, Barbara, *Tsuda Umeko and Women's Education in Japan* (New Haven, 1992).

Rowbotham, Sheila, *A Century of Women: The History of Women in Britain and the United States* (1997, London, 1999 edn).

Ryan, Barbara, *Feminism and the Women's Movement* (New York, 1992).

Satō, Toshihiko, 'Ibsen's drama and the Japanese Bluestockings', *Edda: Scandinavian Journal of Literary Research*, 5 (1981).

Schierbeck, Sachiko, *Japanese Women Novelists in the 20th Century* (Copenhagen, 1994).

Schreiner, Olive, *Woman and Labour* (1911, London, 1978 edn).

Seigle, Cecilia Segawa, *Yoshiwara: The Glittering World of the Japanese Courtesan* (Honolulu, 1993).

Setouchi, Harumi (trans. by Sanford Goldstein & Kazuji Ninomiya), *Beauty in Disarray* (1993).

Shimahara, Nobuo K., *Adaptation and Education in Japan* (New York, 1979).

Shively, Donald H., *The Love Suicide at Amijima* (1953, Ann Arbor, Michigan, 1991 edn).

Shulman, Alix Kates, 'Emma Goldman: Anarchist Queen', in Dale Spender (ed.), *Feminist Theories: Three Centuries of Women's Intellectual Traditions* (London, 1983).

Sievers, Sharon L., 'Feminist criticism in Japanese politics in the 1880s: the experience of Kishida Toshiko', *Signs*, 6:4 (Summer 1981).

——, *Flowers in Salt: The Beginnings of Feminist Consciousness in Modern Japan* (Stanford, 1983).

Simmons, Cyril, *Growing up and Going to School in Japan: Tradition and Trends* (Buckingham, 1990).

Smith, Robert J., 'The Japanese (Confucian) family: the tradition from the bottom up', in Tu Wei-Ming (ed.), *Confucian Traditions in East Asian Modernity: Moral Education and Economic Culture in Japan and the Four Mini-Dragons* (Cambridge, Mass., 1996).

Spender, Dale, *Women of Ideas and What Men Have Done to them, from Aphra Behn to Adrienne Rich* (1982, London, 1983 edn).

Stanley, Liz, 'Olive Schreiner: new women, free women, all women', in Dale Spender (ed.), *Feminist Theorists: Three Centuries of Women's Intellectual Traditions* (London, 1983).

Stephens, Michael D., *Education and the Future of Japan* (Folkestone, 1991).
——, *Japan and Education* (Basingstoke, 1991).
Stoehr, Irene, 'Housework and motherhood: debates and policies in the women's movement in Imperial Germany and the Weimar Republic', in Gisela Bock & Pat Thane (eds), *Maternity & Gender Policies: Women and the Rise of the European Welfare States, 1880s–1950s* (London, 1991).
Styan, J.L., *Modern Drama in Theory and Practice*, vol. 1 (1981, Cambridge, 1991 edn).
Takaishi, Shingorō, *Women and Widsom of Japan* (London, 1905).
Takeda, Kiyoko, 'Ichikawa Fusae: pioneer for women's rights in Japan', *Japan Quarterly*, 31:4 (October/December, 1984).
Tanaka, Yukiko, *To Live and to Write: Selections by Japanese Women Writers 1913–1938* (Seattle, 1987).
Teruoka, Yasutaka, 'The pleasure quarters and Tokugawa culture', in Andrew Gerstle (ed.), *18th Century Japan: Culture and Society* (North Sydney, 1989).
Thane, Pat, *Foundations of the Welfare State* (London, 1982).
Tokuza, Akiko, *The Rise of the Feminist Movement in Japan* (1999).
Tomida, Hiroko, *Japanese Writing on Women's History* (Nissan Occasional Paper Series, 26, Oxford, 1996).
——, 'The evolution of Japanese women's historiography', *Japan Forum*, 8:2 (1996).
——, *Women's History in Japan: Its Origins and Development* (Sheffield University East Asia Research Centre Papers, Sheffield, 1996).
Totman, Conrad, *Japan before Perry: A Short History* (Berkeley, 1981).
Tsurumi, Patricia, *Factory Girls* (Princeton, 1990).
Uno, Kathleen S., 'The death of "good wife, wise mother"?', in Andrew Gordon (ed.), *Postwar Japan as History* (Berkeley, 1993).
——, 'Women and changes in the household division of labor', in Gail Lee Bernstein (ed.), *Recreating Japanese Women, 1600–1945* (Berkeley, 1991).
Vavich, Dee Ann, 'The Japanese women's movement: Ichikawa Fusae—a pioneer in woman's suffrage', *Monumenta Nipponica*, 22 (1967).
Walthall, Anne, 'The life cycle of farm, women in Tokugawa Japan', in Gail Lee Bernstein (ed.), *Recreating Japanese Women, 1600–1945* (Berkeley, 1991).
Williams, Perry, 'Pioneer women students at Cambridge, 1869–81', in Felicity Hunt (ed.), *Lessons for Life: The Schoolings of Girls and Women, 1850–1950* (Oxford, 1987).
Yamashita, Samuel Hideo, 'Confucianism and the Japanese state, 1904–1945', in Tu Wei-Mung (ed.), *Confucian Traditions in East Asian Modernity* (Cambridge, Mass., 1996).
Yamazaki, Tomoko (trans. by Wakako Hironaka & Ann Kostant), *The Story of Yamada Waka: From Prostitute to Feminist Pioneer* (1985).
Yosano, Akiko (trans. by Sanford Goldstein & Shinoda Seishi), *Tangled Hair: Selected Tanka from Midaregami* (1987).

(B) *Reference Books*

Crawford, Anne, *et al.* (eds), *The Europa Biographical Dictionary of British Women* (London, 1983).
Hisamatsu, Senichi, *Biographical Dictionary of Japanese Literature* (New York, 1976).
Hunter, Janet E., *Concise Dictionary of Modern Japanese History* (Berkeley, 1984).
Kamesaka, Tsunesaburō (ed.), *Who's Who in Japan* (1937).
Kōdansha (comp.), *Japan: An Illustrated Encyclopedia* (1993, 1996 edn).
Lewell, John, *Modern Japanese Novelists: A Biographical Dictionary* (New York, 1993).
Onions, C.T. (ed.), *The Shorter Oxford English Dictionary*, 2 vols (London, 1983).
Penguin Biographical Dictionary of Women (London, 1998).
Tuttle, Lisa, *Encyclopedia of Feminism* (1986, London, 1987 edn).

INDEX